ILLUSTRATED SERIES™

MICROSOFT® OFFICE 365™

OFFICE 2016

for MEDICAL PROFESSIONALS

MICROSOFT® OFFICE 365™

OFFICE 2016

for MEDICAL PROFESSIONALS

For Microsoft® Office updates, go to sam.cengage.com

BESKEEN + DUFFY
FRIEDRICHSEN + REDING

CENGAGE
Learning®

Australia • Brazil • Mexico • Singapore • United Kingdom • United States

**Illustrated Microsoft Office 365 &
Office 2016 for Medical Professionals**
David Beskeen/Jennifer Duffy/Lisa Friedrichsen/Elizabeth
Eisner Reding

Senior Product Director: Kathleen McMahon

Senior Product Team Manager: Lauren Murphy

Product Team Manager: Andrea Topping

Associate Product Manager: Melissa Stehler

Content Development Manager: Leigh Hefferon

Senior Content Developer: Alyssa Pratt

Developmental Editor: Lisa Ruffolo

Product Assistant: Erica Chapman

Marketing Director: Michele McTighe

Marketing Manager: Jeffrey Tousignant

Marketing Coordinator: Cassie Cloutier

Senior Production Director: Wendy Troeger

Production Director: Patty Stephan

Content Project Manager: GEX Publishing Services

Designer: Diana Graham

Art Director: Diana Graham

Text Designer: Joseph Lee, Black Fish Design

Cover Template Designer: Lisa Kuhn, Curio Press, LLC
www.curiopress.com

Composition: GEX Publishing Services

For product information and technology assistance, contact us at
Cengage Learning Customer & Sales Support, 1-800-354-9706

For permission to use material from this text or product, submit all
requests online at **www.cengage.com/permissions**
Further permissions questions can be emailed to
permissionrequest@cengage.com

Mac users: If you're working through this product using a Mac, some of the
steps may vary. Additional information for Mac users is included with the
Data Files for this product.

Some of the product names and company names used in this book have
been used for identification purposes only and may be trademarks or
registered trademarks of their respective manufacturers and sellers.

Windows® is a registered trademark of Microsoft Corporation. © 2012
Microsoft. Microsoft and the Office logo are either registered trademarks
or trademarks of Microsoft Corporation in the United States and/or other
countries. Cengage Learning is an independent entity from Microsoft
Corporation and not affiliated with Microsoft in any manner. Microsoft
product screenshots used with permission from Microsoft Corporation.
Unless otherwise noted, all clip art is courtesy of openclipart.org.

Disclaimer: Any fictional data related to persons or companies or URLs used
throughout this text is intended for instructional purposes only. At the time
this text was published, any such data was fictional and not belonging to
any real persons or companies.

Disclaimer: The material in this text was written using Microsoft Windows
10 Professional and Office 365 Professional Plus and was Quality Assurance
tested before the publication date. As Microsoft continually updates the
Windows 10 operating system and Office 365, your software experience
may vary slightly from what is presented in the printed text.

Library of Congress Control Number: 2016943100
ISBN: 978-1-305-87857-0

Cengage Learning
20 Channel Center Street
Boston, MA 02210
USA

Cengage Learning is a leading provider of customized learning solutions
with employees residing in nearly 40 different countries and sales in more
than 125 countries around the world. Find your local representative at
www.cengage.com

Cengage Learning products are represented in Canada by
Nelson Education, Ltd.

For your course and learning solutions, visit **www.cengage.com**

Purchase any of our products at your local college store or at our
preferred online store **www.cengagebrain.com**

Printed in the United States of America
Print Number: 02   Print Year: 2017

Brief Contents

Contents

Office 2016

Excel 2016

Productivity Apps for School and Work

Corinne Hoisington

OneNote
Sway
Office Mix
Edge

Lochlan keeps track of his class notes, football plays, and internship meetings with OneNote.

Zoe is using the annotation features of Microsoft Edge to take and save web notes for her research paper.

Nori is creating a Sway site to highlight this year's activities for the Student Government Association.

Hunter is adding interactive videos and screen recordings to his PowerPoint resume.

© Rawpixel/Shutterstock.com

Being computer literate no longer means mastery of only Word, Excel, PowerPoint, Outlook, and Access. To become technology power users, Hunter, Nori, Zoe, and Lochlan are exploring Microsoft OneNote, Sway, Mix, and Edge in Office 2016 and Windows 10.

Learn to use productivity apps!
Links to companion **Sways**, featuring **videos** with hands-on instructions, are located on www.cengagebrain.com.

Introduction to OneNote 2016

notebook | section tab | To Do tag | screen clipping | note | template | Microsoft OneNote Mobile app | sync | drawing canvas | inked handwriting | Ink to Text

Bottom Line
- OneNote is a note-taking app for your academic and professional life.
- Use OneNote to get organized by gathering your ideas, sketches, webpages, photos, videos, and notes in one place.

As you glance around any classroom, you invariably see paper notebooks and notepads on each desk. Because deciphering and sharing handwritten notes can be a challenge, Microsoft OneNote 2016 replaces physical notebooks, binders, and paper notes with a searchable, digital notebook. OneNote captures your ideas and schoolwork on any device so you can stay organized, share notes, and work with others on projects. Whether you are a student taking class notes as shown in **Figure 1** or an employee taking notes in company meetings, OneNote is the one place to keep notes for all of your projects.

Figure 1: OneNote 2016 notebook

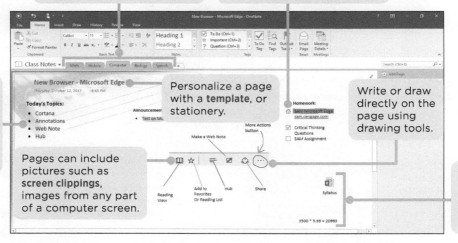

Each **notebook** is divided into sections, also called **section tabs**, by subject or topic.

Use **To Do tags**, icons that help you keep track of your assignments and other tasks.

Type on a page to add a **note**, a small window that contains text or other types of information.

Personalize a page with a **template**, or stationery.

Write or draw directly on the page using drawing tools.

Pages can include pictures such as **screen clippings**, images from any part of a computer screen.

Attach files and enter equations so you have everything you need in one place.

Creating a OneNote Notebook

OneNote is divided into sections similar to those in a spiral-bound notebook. Each OneNote notebook contains sections, pages, and other notebooks. You can use One-Note for school, business, and personal projects. Store information for each type of project in different notebooks to keep your tasks separate, or use any other organization that suits you. OneNote is flexible enough to adapt to the way you want to work.

When you create a notebook, it contains a blank page with a plain white background by default, though you can use templates, or stationery, to apply designs in categories such as Academic, Business, Decorative, and Planners. Start typing or use the buttons on the Insert tab to insert notes, which are small resizable windows that can contain text, equations, tables, on-screen writing, images, audio and video recordings, to-do lists, file attachments, and file printouts. Add as many notes as you need to each page.

Syncing a Notebook to the Cloud

OneNote saves your notes every time you make a change in a notebook. To make sure you can access your notebooks with a laptop, tablet, or smartphone wherever you are, OneNote uses cloud-based storage, such as OneDrive or SharePoint. **Microsoft OneNote Mobile app**, a lightweight version of OneNote 2016 shown in **Figure 2**, is available for free in the Windows Store, Google Play for Android devices, and the AppStore for iOS devices.

If you have a Microsoft account, OneNote saves your notes on OneDrive automatically for all your mobile devices and computers, which is called **syncing**. For example, you can use OneNote to take notes on your laptop during class, and then

Learn to use OneNote!
Links to companion **Sways**, featuring **videos** with hands-on instructions, are located on www.cengagebrain.com.

open OneNote on your phone to study later. To use a notebook stored on your computer with your OneNote Mobile app, move the notebook to OneDrive. You can quickly share notebook content with other people using OneDrive.

Figure 2: Microsoft OneNote Mobile app

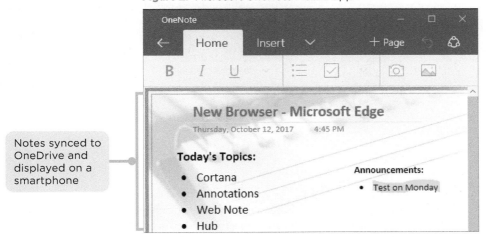

Notes synced to OneDrive and displayed on a smartphone

Taking Notes

Use OneNote pages to organize your notes by class and topic or lecture. Beyond simple typed notes, OneNote stores drawings, converts handwriting to searchable text and mathematical sketches to equations, and records audio and video.

OneNote includes drawing tools that let you sketch freehand drawings such as biological cell diagrams and financial supply-and-demand charts. As shown in **Figure 3**, the Draw tab on the ribbon provides these drawing tools along with shapes so you can insert diagrams and other illustrations to represent your ideas. When you draw on a page, OneNote creates a **drawing canvas**, which is a container for shapes and lines.

On the Job Now

OneNote is ideal for taking notes during meetings, whether you are recording minutes, documenting a discussion, sketching product diagrams, or listing follow-up items. Use a meeting template to add pages with content appropriate for meetings.

Figure 3: Tools on the Draw tab

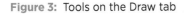
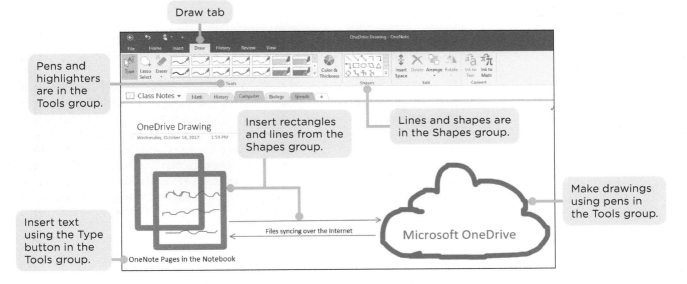

Draw tab

Pens and highlighters are in the Tools group.

Insert rectangles and lines from the Shapes group.

Lines and shapes are in the Shapes group.

Make drawings using pens in the Tools group.

Insert text using the Type button in the Tools group.

Files syncing over the Internet

Microsoft OneDrive

OneNote Pages in the Notebook

Converting Handwriting to Text

When you use a pen tool to write on a notebook page, the text you enter is called **inked handwriting**. OneNote can convert inked handwriting to typed text when you use the **Ink to Text** button in the Convert group on the Draw tab, as shown in **Figure 4**. After OneNote converts the handwriting to text, you can use the Search box to find terms in the converted text or any other note in your notebooks.

Figure 4: Converting handwriting to text

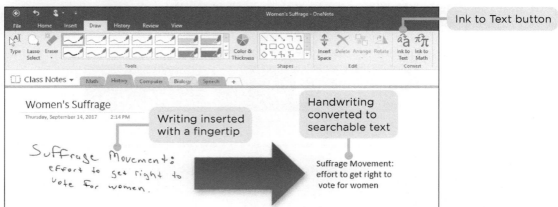

Use OneNote as a place to brainstorm ongoing work projects. If a notebook contains sensitive material, you can password-protect some or all of the notebook so that only certain people can open it.

Recording a Lecture

If your computer or mobile device has a microphone or camera, OneNote can record the audio or video from a lecture or business meeting as shown in **Figure 5**. When you record a lecture (with your instructor's permission), you can follow along, take regular notes at your own pace, and review the video recording later. You can control the start, pause, and stop motions of the recording when you play back the recording of your notes.

Figure 5: Video inserted in a notebook

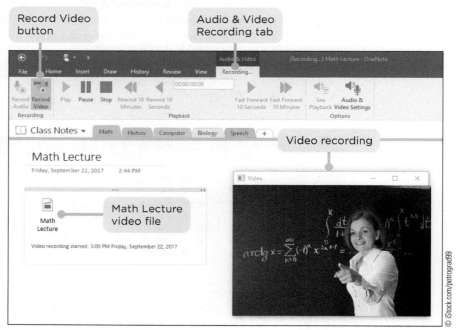

Try This Now

1: Taking Notes for a Week

As a student, you can get organized by using OneNote to take detailed notes in your classes. Perform the following tasks:

    a. Create a new OneNote notebook on your Microsoft OneDrive account (the default location for new notebooks). Name the notebook with your first name followed by "Notes," as in **Caleb Notes**.

    b. Create four section tabs, each with a different class name.

    c. Take detailed notes in those classes for one week. Be sure to include notes, drawings, and other types of content.

    d. Sync your notes with your OneDrive. Submit your assignment in the format specified by your instructor.

2: Using OneNote to Organize a Research Paper

You have a research paper due on the topic of three habits of successful students. Use OneNote to organize your research. Perform the following tasks:

    a. Create a new OneNote notebook on your Microsoft OneDrive account. Name the notebook **Success Research**.

    b. Create three section tabs with the following names:

- **Take Detailed Notes**
- **Be Respectful in Class**
- **Come to Class Prepared**

    c. On the web, research the topics and find three sources for each section. Copy a sentence from each source and paste the sentence into the appropriate section. When you paste the sentence, OneNote inserts it in a note with a link to the source.

    d. Sync your notes with your OneDrive. Submit your assignment in the format specified by your instructor.

3: Planning Your Career

Note: This activity requires a webcam or built-in video camera on any type of device.

Consider an occupation that interests you. Using OneNote, examine the responsibilities, education requirements, potential salary, and employment outlook of a specific career. Perform the following tasks:

    a. Create a new OneNote notebook on your Microsoft OneDrive account. Name the notebook with your first name followed by a career title, such as **Kara - App Developer**.

    b. Create four section tabs with the names **Responsibilities, Education Requirements, Median Salary**, and **Employment Outlook**.

    c. Research the responsibilities of your career path. Using OneNote, record a short video (approximately 30 seconds) of yourself explaining the responsibilities of your career path. Place the video in the Responsibilities section.

    d. On the web, research the educational requirements for your career path and find two appropriate sources. Copy a paragraph from each source and paste them into the appropriate section. When you paste a paragraph, OneNote inserts it in a note with a link to the source.

    e. Research the median salary for a single year for this career. Create a mathematical equation in the Median Salary section that multiplies the amount of the median salary times 20 years to calculate how much you will possibly earn.

    f. For the Employment Outlook section, research the outlook for your career path. Take at least four notes about what you find when researching the topic.

    g. Sync your notes with your OneDrive. Submit your assignment in the format specified by your instructor.

Introduction to Sway

Sway site | responsive design | Storyline | card | Creative Commons license | animation emphasis effects | Docs.com

Expressing your ideas in a presentation typically means creating PowerPoint slides or a Word document. Microsoft Sway gives you another way to engage an audience. Sway is a free Microsoft tool available at Sway.com or as an app in Office 365. Using Sway, you can combine text, images, videos, and social media in a website called a **Sway site** that you can share and display on any device. To get started, you create a digital story on a web-based canvas without borders, slides, cells, or page breaks. A Sway site organizes the text, images, and video into a **responsive design**, which means your content adapts perfectly to any screen size as shown in **Figure 6**. You store a Sway site in the cloud on OneDrive using a free Microsoft account.

Figure 6: Sway site with responsive design

You can display a Sway presentation in a web browser.

Sway uses responsive design to make sure pages fit perfectly on any device.

© iStock.com/marinello, © iStock.com/marekuliasz

Creating a Sway Presentation

You can use Sway to build a digital flyer, a club newsletter, a vacation blog, an informational site, a digital art portfolio, or a new product rollout. After you select your topic and sign into Sway with your Microsoft account, a **Storyline** opens, providing tools and a work area for composing your digital story. See **Figure 7**. Each story can include text, images, and videos. You create a Sway by adding text and media content into a Storyline section, or **card**. To add pictures, videos, or documents, select a card in the left pane and then select the Insert Content button. The first card in a Sway presentation contains a title and background image.

Figure 7: Creating a Sway site

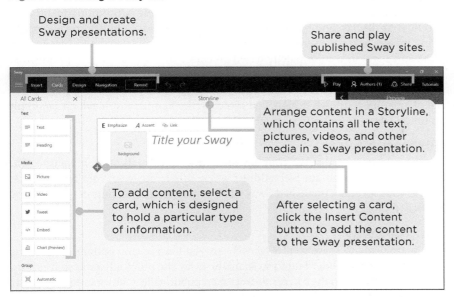

Design and create Sway presentations.

Share and play published Sway sites.

Arrange content in a Storyline, which contains all the text, pictures, videos, and other media in a Sway presentation.

To add content, select a card, which is designed to hold a particular type of information.

After selecting a card, click the Insert Content button to add the content to the Sway presentation.

Adding Content to Build a Story

As you work, Sway searches the Internet to help you find relevant images, videos, tweets, and other content from online sources such as Bing, YouTube, Twitter, and Facebook. You can drag content from the search results right into the Storyline. In addition, you can upload your own images and videos directly in the presentation. For example, if you are creating a Sway presentation about the market for commercial drones, Sway suggests content to incorporate into the presentation by displaying it in the left pane as search results. The search results include drone images tagged with a **Creative Commons license** at online sources as shown in **Figure 8**. A Creative Commons license is a public copyright license that allows the free distribution of an otherwise copyrighted work. In addition, you can specify the source of the media. For example, you can add your own Facebook or OneNote pictures and videos in Sway without leaving the app.

On the Job Now

If you have a Microsoft Word document containing an outline of your business content, drag the outline into Sway to create a card for each topic.

Figure 8: Images in Sway search results

Select the source of media objects

Information about Creative Commons licenses

Storyline title

The Market for Commercial Drones

Drag an image to the picture placeholder box

Suggested images in the search results

Designing a Sway

Sway professionally designs your Storyline content by resizing background images and fonts to fit your display, and by floating text, animating media, embedding video, and removing images as a page scrolls out of view. Sway also evaluates the images in your Storyline and suggests a color palette based on colors that appear in your photos. Use the Design button to display tools including color palettes, font choices, **animation emphasis effects**, and style templates to provide a personality for a Sway presentation. Instead of creating your own design, you can click the Remix button, which randomly selects unique designs for your Sway site.

Publishing a Sway

Use the Play button to display your finished Sway presentation as a website. The Address bar includes a unique web address where others can view your Sway site. As the author, you can edit a published Sway site by clicking the Edit button (pencil icon) on the Sway toolbar.

Sharing a Sway

When you are ready to share your Sway website, you have several options as shown in **Figure 9**. Use the Share slider button to share the Sway site publically or keep it private. If you add the Sway site to the Microsoft **Docs.com** public gallery, anyone worldwide can use Bing, Google, or other search engines to find, view, and share your Sway site. You can also share your Sway site using Facebook, Twitter, Google+, Yammer, and other social media sites. Link your presentation to any webpage or email the link to your audience. Sway can also generate a code for embedding the link within another webpage.

Figure 9: Sharing a Sway site

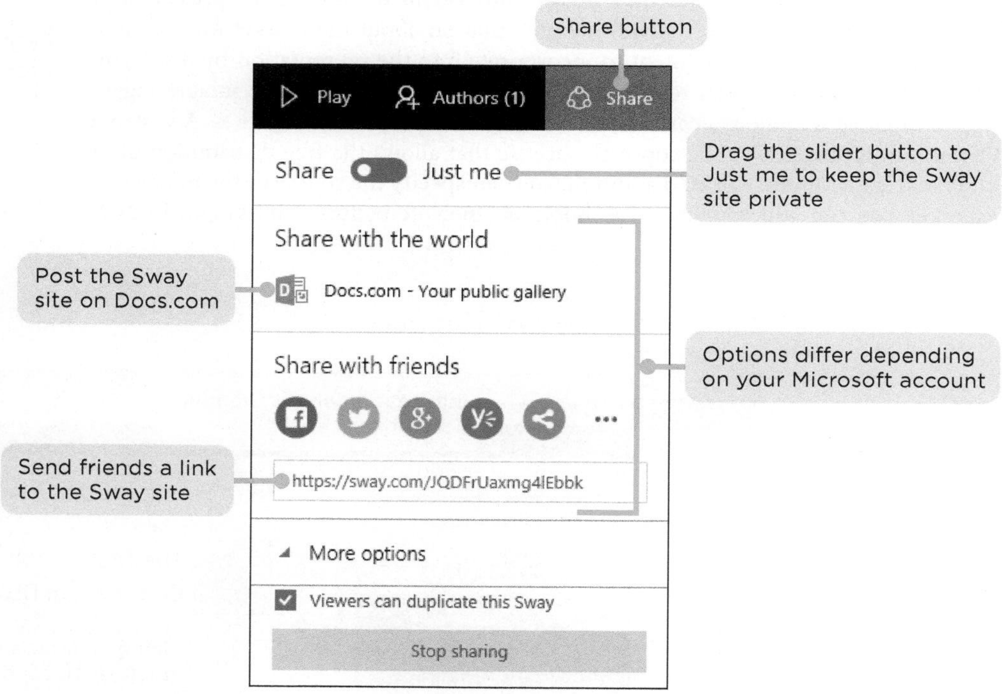

Share button

▷ Play	♀ Authors (1)	☁ Share

Share ⬤ Just me — Drag the slider button to Just me to keep the Sway site private

Share with the world

Post the Sway site on Docs.com — Docs.com - Your public gallery

Share with friends

Options differ depending on your Microsoft account

🄵 🐦 🄶 🅈 ⬦ ...

Send friends a link to the Sway site — https://sway.com/JQDFrUaxmg4lEbbk

◢ More options

☑ Viewers can duplicate this Sway

Stop sharing

Try This Now

1: Creating a Sway Resume

Sway is a digital storytelling app. Create a Sway resume to share the skills, job experiences, and achievements you have that match the requirements of a future job interest. Perform the following tasks:

> **Learn to use Sway!**
> Links to companion **Sways**, featuring **videos** with hands-on instructions, are located on www.cengagebrain.com.

a. Create a new presentation in Sway to use as a digital resume. Title the Sway Storyline with your full name and then select a background image.

b. Create three separate sections titled **Academic Background, Work Experience**, and **Skills**, and insert text, a picture, and a paragraph or bulleted points in each section. Be sure to include your own picture.

c. Add a fourth section that includes a video about your school that you find online.

d. Customize the design of your presentation.

e. Submit your assignment link in the format specified by your instructor.

2: Creating an Online Sway Newsletter

Newsletters are designed to capture the attention of their target audience. Using Sway, create a newsletter for a club, organization, or your favorite music group. Perform the following tasks:

a. Create a new presentation in Sway to use as a digital newsletter for a club, organization, or your favorite music group. Provide a title for the Sway Storyline and select an appropriate background image.

b. Select three separate sections with appropriate titles, such as Upcoming Events. In each section, insert text, a picture, and a paragraph or bulleted points.

c. Add a fourth section that includes a video about your selected topic.

d. Customize the design of your presentation.

e. Submit your assignment link in the format specified by your instructor.

3: Creating and Sharing a Technology Presentation

To place a Sway presentation in the hands of your entire audience, you can share a link to the Sway presentation. Create a Sway presentation on a new technology and share it with your class. Perform the following tasks:

a. Create a new presentation in Sway about a cutting-edge technology topic. Provide a title for the Sway Storyline and select a background image.

b. Create four separate sections about your topic, and include text, a picture, and a paragraph in each section.

c. Add a fifth section that includes a video about your topic.

d. Customize the design of your presentation.

e. Share the link to your Sway with your classmates and submit your assignment link in the format specified by your instructor.

Introduction to Office Mix

add-in | clip | slide recording | Slide Notes | screen recording | free-response quiz

To enliven business meetings and lectures, Microsoft adds a new dimension to presentations with a powerful toolset called Office Mix, a free add-in for PowerPoint. (An **add-in** is software that works with an installed app to extend its features.) Using Office Mix, you can record yourself on video, capture still and moving images on your desktop, and insert interactive elements such as quizzes and live webpages directly into PowerPoint slides. When you post the finished presentation to OneDrive, Office Mix provides a link you can share with friends and colleagues. Anyone with an Internet connection and a web browser can watch a published Office Mix presentation, such as the one in **Figure 10**, on a computer or mobile device.

Figure 10: Office Mix presentation

Adding Office Mix to PowerPoint

To get started, you create an Office Mix account at the website mix.office.com using an email address or a Facebook or Google account. Next, you download and install the Office Mix add-in (see **Figure 11**). Office Mix appears as a new tab named Mix on the PowerPoint ribbon in versions of Office 2013 and Office 2016 running on personal computers (PCs).

Figure 11: Getting started with Office Mix

Capturing Video Clips

A **clip** is a short segment of audio, such as music, or video. After finishing the content on a PowerPoint slide, you can use Office Mix to add a video clip to animate or illustrate the content. Office Mix creates video clips in two ways: by recording live action on a webcam and by capturing screen images and movements. If your computer has a webcam, you can record yourself and annotate the slide to create a **slide recording** as shown in **Figure 12**.

On the Job Now

Companies are using Office Mix to train employees about new products, to explain benefit packages to new workers, and to educate interns about office procedures.

Figure 12: Making a slide recording

Record your voice; also record video if your computer has a camera.

Use the Slide Notes button to display notes for your narration.

For best results, look directly at your webcam while recording video.

Use inking tools to write and draw on the slide as you record.

Choose a video and audio device to record images and sound.

When you are making a slide recording, you can record your spoken narration at the same time. The **Slide Notes** feature works like a teleprompter to help you focus on your presentation content instead of memorizing your narration. Use the Inking tools to make annotations or add highlighting using different pen types and colors. After finishing a recording, edit the video in PowerPoint to trim the length or set playback options.

The second way to create a video is to capture on-screen images and actions with or without a voiceover. This method is ideal if you want to show how to use your favorite website or demonstrate an app such as OneNote. To share your screen with an audience, select the part of the screen you want to show in the video. Office Mix captures everything that happens in that area to create a **screen recording**, as shown in **Figure 13**. Office Mix inserts the screen recording as a video in the slide.

On the Job Now

To make your video recordings accessible to people with hearing impairments, use the Office Mix closed-captioning tools. You can also use closed captions to supplement audio that is difficult to understand and to provide an aid for those learning to read.

Figure 13: Making a screen recording

Record the action on the screen within the red dashed outline.

Record audio while capturing your on-screen actions.

Select Area button

Inserting Quizzes, Live Webpages, and Apps

To enhance and assess audience understanding, make your slides interactive by adding quizzes, live webpages, and apps. Quizzes give immediate feedback to the user as shown in Figure 14. Office Mix supports several quiz formats, including a **free-response quiz** similar to a short answer quiz, and true/false, multiple-choice, and multiple-response formats.

Figure 14: Creating an interactive quiz

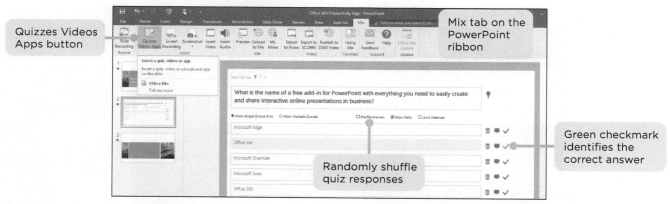

Sharing an Office Mix Presentation

When you complete your work with Office Mix, upload the presentation to your personal Office Mix dashboard as shown in Figure 15. Users of PCs, Macs, iOS devices, and Android devices can access and play Office Mix presentations. The Office Mix dashboard displays built-in analytics that include the quiz results and how much time viewers spent on each slide. You can play completed Office Mix presentations online or download them as movies.

Figure 15: Sharing an Office Mix presentation

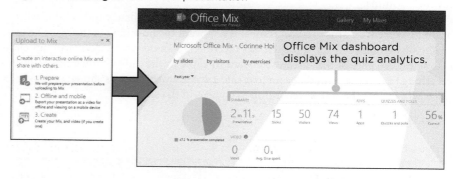

Try This Now

Learn to use Office Mix!
Links to companion **Sways**, featuring **videos** with hands-on instructions, are located on www.cengagebrain.com.

1: Creating an Office Mix Tutorial for OneNote

Note: This activity requires a microphone on your computer.

Office Mix makes it easy to record screens and their contents. Create PowerPoint slides with an Office Mix screen recording to show OneNote 2016 features. Perform the following tasks:

a. Create a PowerPoint presentation with the Ion Boardroom template. Create an opening slide with the title **My Favorite OneNote Features** and enter your name in the subtitle.

b. Create three additional slides, each titled with a new feature of OneNote. Open OneNote and use the Mix tab in PowerPoint to capture three separate screen recordings that teach your favorite features.

c. Add a fifth slide that quizzes the user with a multiple-choice question about OneNote and includes four responses. Be sure to insert a checkmark indicating the correct response.

d. Upload the completed presentation to your Office Mix dashboard and share the link with your instructor.

e. Submit your assignment link in the format specified by your instructor.

2: Teaching Augmented Reality with Office Mix

Note: This activity requires a webcam or built-in video camera on your computer.

A local elementary school has asked you to teach augmented reality to its students using Office Mix. Perform the following tasks:

a. Research augmented reality using your favorite online search tools.

b. Create a PowerPoint presentation with the Frame template. Create an opening slide with the title **Augmented Reality** and enter your name in the subtitle.

c. Create a slide with four bullets summarizing your research of augmented reality. Create a 20-second slide recording of yourself providing a quick overview of augmented reality.

d. Create another slide with a 30-second screen recording of a video about augmented reality from a site such as YouTube or another video-sharing site.

e. Add a final slide that quizzes the user with a true/false question about augmented reality. Be sure to insert a checkmark indicating the correct response.

f. Upload the completed presentation to your Office Mix dashboard and share the link with your instructor.

g. Submit your assignment link in the format specified by your instructor.

3: Marketing a Travel Destination with Office Mix

Note: This activity requires a webcam or built-in video camera on your computer.

To convince your audience to travel to a particular city, create a slide presentation marketing any city in the world using a slide recording, screen recording, and a quiz. Perform the following tasks:

a. Create a PowerPoint presentation with any template. Create an opening slide with the title of the city you are marketing as a travel destination and your name in the subtitle.

b. Create a slide with four bullets about the featured city. Create a 30-second slide recording of yourself explaining why this city is the perfect vacation destination.

c. Create another slide with a 20-second screen recording of a travel video about the city from a site such as YouTube or another video-sharing site.

d. Add a final slide that quizzes the user with a multiple-choice question about the featured city with five responses. Be sure to include a checkmark indicating the correct response.

e. Upload the completed presentation to your Office Mix dashboard and share your link with your instructor.

f. Submit your assignment link in the format specified by your instructor.

Introduction to Microsoft Edge

Reading view | Hub | Cortana | Web Note | Inking | sandbox

Bottom Line
- Microsoft Edge is the name of the new web browser built into Windows 10.
- Microsoft Edge allows you to search the web faster, take web notes, read webpages without distractions, and get instant assistance from Cortana.

Microsoft Edge is the default web browser developed for the Windows 10 operating system as a replacement for Internet Explorer. Unlike its predecessor, Edge lets you write on webpages, read webpages without advertisements and other distractions, and search for information using a virtual personal assistant. The Edge interface is clean and basic, as shown in **Figure 16**, meaning you can pay more attention to the webpage content.

Figure 16: Microsoft Edge tools

Forward button · New tab button · Web address in the Address bar · Add to favorites or reading list button · Reading view button · More button · Back button · Refresh (F5) button · Hub (Favorites, reading list, history, and downloads) button · Share Web Note button · Make a Web Note button

Learn to use Edge!
Links to companion **Sways**, featuring **videos** with hands-on instructions, are located on www.cengagebrain.com.

On the Job Now

Businesses started adopting Internet Explorer more than 20 years ago simply to view webpages. Today, Microsoft Edge has a different purpose: to promote interaction with the web and share its contents with colleagues.

Browsing the Web with Microsoft Edge

One of the fastest browsers available, Edge allows you to type search text directly in the Address bar. As you view the resulting webpage, you can switch to **Reading view**, which is available for most news and research sites, to eliminate distracting advertisements. For example, if you are catching up on technology news online, the webpage might be difficult to read due to a busy layout cluttered with ads. Switch to Reading view to refresh the page and remove the original page formatting, ads, and menu sidebars to read the article distraction-free.

Consider the **Hub** in Microsoft Edge as providing one-stop access to all the things you collect on the web, such as your favorite websites, reading list, surfing history, and downloaded files.

Locating Information with Cortana

Cortana, the Windows 10 virtual assistant, plays an important role in Microsoft Edge. After you turn on Cortana, it appears as an animated circle in the Address bar when you might need assistance, as shown in the restaurant website in **Figure 17**. When you click the Cortana icon, a pane slides in from the right of the browser window to display detailed information about the restaurant, including maps and reviews. Cortana can also assist you in defining words, finding the weather, suggesting coupons for shopping, updating stock market information, and calculating math.

Figure 17: Cortana providing restaurant information

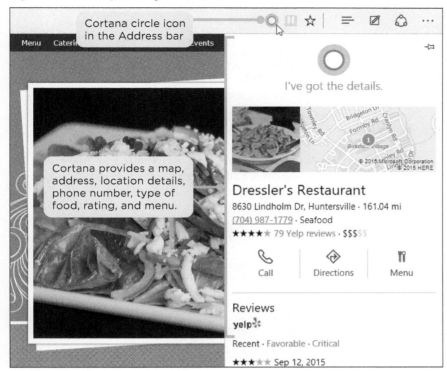

Cortana circle icon in the Address bar

Cortana provides a map, address, location details, phone number, type of food, rating, and menu.

Annotating Webpages

One of the most impressive Microsoft Edge features are the **Web Note** tools, which you use to write on a webpage or to highlight text. When you click the Make a Web Note button, an **Inking** toolbar appears, as shown in **Figure 18**, that provides writing and drawing tools. These tools include an eraser, a pen, and a highlighter with different colors. You can also insert a typed note and copy a screen image (called a screen clipping). You can draw with a pointing device, fingertip, or stylus using different pen colors. Whether you add notes to a recipe, annotate sources for a research paper, or select a product while shopping online, the Web Note tools can enhance your productivity. After you complete your notes, click the Save button to save the annotations to OneNote, your Favorites list, or your Reading list. You can share the inked page with others using the Share Web Note button.

On the Job Now

To enhance security, Microsoft Edge runs in a partial sandbox, an arrangement that prevents attackers from gaining control of your computer. Browsing within the **sandbox** protects computer resources and information from hackers.

Figure 18: Web Note tools in Microsoft Edge

Inking toolbar with Web Note tools for making annotations

Writing and drawing created with the Pen tool

Highlighted text

Save a copy of the webpage with annotations

Typed note

Try This Now

1: Using Cortana in Microsoft Edge

Note: This activity requires using Microsoft Edge on a Windows 10 computer.

Cortana can assist you in finding information on a webpage in Microsoft Edge. Perform the following tasks:

a. Create a Word document using the Word Screen Clipping tool to capture the following screenshots.

- Screenshot A—Using Microsoft Edge, open a webpage with a technology news article. Right-click a term in the article and ask Cortana to define it.
- Screenshot B—Using Microsoft Edge, open the website of a fancy restaurant in a city near you. Make sure the Cortana circle icon is displayed in the Address bar. (If it's not displayed, find a different restaurant website.) Click the Cortana circle icon to display a pane with information about the restaurant.
- Screenshot C—Using Microsoft Edge, type **10 USD to Euros** in the Address bar without pressing the Enter key. Cortana converts the U.S. dollars to Euros.
- Screenshot D—Using Microsoft Edge, type **Apple stock** in the Address bar without pressing the Enter key. Cortana displays the current stock quote.

b. Submit your assignment in the format specified by your instructor.

2: Viewing Online News with Reading View

Note: This activity requires using Microsoft Edge on a Windows 10 computer.

Reading view in Microsoft Edge can make a webpage less cluttered with ads and other distractions. Perform the following tasks:

a. Create a Word document using the Word Screen Clipping tool to capture the following screenshots.

- Screenshot A—Using Microsoft Edge, open the website **mashable.com**. Open a technology article. Click the Reading view button to display an ad-free page that uses only basic text formatting.
- Screenshot B—Using Microsoft Edge, open the website **bbc.com**. Open any news article. Click the Reading view button to display an ad-free page that uses only basic text formatting.
- Screenshot C—Make three types of annotations (Pen, Highlighter, and Add a typed note) on the BBC article page displayed in Reading view.

b. Submit your assignment in the format specified by your instructor.

3: Inking with Microsoft Edge

Note: This activity requires using Microsoft Edge on a Windows 10 computer.

Microsoft Edge provides many annotation options to record your ideas. Perform the following tasks:

a. Open the website **wolframalpha.com** in the Microsoft Edge browser. Wolfram Alpha is a well-respected academic search engine. Type **US$100 1965 dollars in 2015** in the Wolfram Alpha search text box and press the Enter key.

b. Click the Make a Web Note button to display the Web Note tools. Using the Pen tool, draw a circle around the result on the webpage. Save the page to OneNote.

c. In the Wolfram Alpha search text box, type the name of the city closest to where you live and press the Enter key. Using the Highlighter tool, highlight at least three interesting results. Add a note and then type a sentence about what you learned about this city. Save the page to OneNote. Share your OneNote notebook with your instructor.

d. Submit your assignment link in the format specified by your instructor.

Getting Started with Windows 10

CASE ▶ You are about to start a new job, and your employer has asked you to get familiar with Windows 10 to help boost your productivity. You'll need to start Windows 10 and Windows apps, work with on-screen windows and commands, get help, and exit Windows. *Note: With the release of Windows 10, Microsoft now provides ongoing updates to Windows instead of releasing new versions periodically. This means that Windows features might change over time, including how they look and how you interact with them. The information provided in this text was accurate at the time this book was published.*

Module Objectives

After completing this module, you will be able to:

- Start Windows 10
- Navigate the desktop and Start menu
- Point, click, and drag
- Start an app
- Work with a window
- Manage multiple windows
- Use buttons, menus, and dialog boxes
- Get help
- Exit Windows 10

Files You Will Need

No files needed.

Start Windows 10

Learning
Outcomes
• Power on a
  computer
• Log into
  Windows 10

Windows 10 is an **operating system**, a type of program that runs your computer and lets you interact with it. A **program** is a set of instructions written for a computer. If your computer did not have an operating system, you wouldn't see anything on the screen after you turned it on. Windows 10 reserves a special area called a **Microsoft account** where each user can keep his or her files. In addition, a Microsoft account lets you use various devices and services such as a Windows Phone or Outlook.com. You may have more than one Microsoft account. When the computer and Windows 10 start, you need to **sign in**, or select your Microsoft account name and enter a password, also called **logging in**. If your computer has only one Microsoft account, you won't need to select an account name. But all users need to enter a **password**, a special sequence of numbers and letters. Users cannot see each other's account areas or services without the other person's password, so passwords help keep your computer information secure. After you sign in, you see the Windows 10 desktop, which you learn about in the next lesson. **CASE** ▸ *You're about to start a new job, so you decide to learn more about Windows 10, the operating system used at your new company.*

STEPS

1. **Press your computer's** power button, **which might look like ⊙ or ▭⏻▭, then if the monitor is not turned on, press its** power button

   On a desktop computer, the power button is probably on the front panel. On a laptop computer it's likely at the top of the keys on your keyboard. After a few moments, a **lock screen**, showing the date, time, and an image, appears. See FIGURE 1-1. The lock screen appears when you first start your computer and also if you leave it unattended for a period of time.

   QUICK TIP
   To temporarily see the password characters, move the pointer ▹ over the eye icon ◉ next to the password box, then press and hold down the mouse button (or press and hold on a touch screen).

2. **Press [Spacebar], or click once to display the sign-in screen**

   The **sign-in screen** shows your Windows account picture, name, and e-mail address, as well as a space to enter your Microsoft account password. The account may have your name assigned to it, or it might have a general name like "Student" or "Lab User."

3. **Type your** password, **as shown in** FIGURE 1-2, **using uppercase and lowercase letters as necessary**

   If necessary, ask your instructor or technical support person what password you should use. Passwords are **case sensitive**, which means that if you type any letter using capital letters when lowercase letters are needed, or vice versa, Windows will not let you use your account. For example, if your password is "booklet43+", typing "Booklet43+" or "BOOKLET43+" will not let you enter your account. For security, Windows substitutes bullets for the password characters you type.

   TROUBLE
   If you see a message saying your password is incorrect, click OK to redisplay the password entry box. Type your password carefully, then click or tap →.

4. **Click or tap the** Submit button →

   The Windows 10 desktop appears. See FIGURE 1-3.

Using a touch screen with Windows

Windows 10 was developed to work with touch-screen computers, including tablets and smartphones. See FIGURE 1-4. So if you have a touch-screen device, you'll find that you can accomplish many tasks with gestures instead of a mouse. A **gesture** is an action you take with your fingertip directly on the screen, such as tapping or swiping. For example, when you sign into Windows 10, you can tap the Submit button on the screen, instead of clicking it.

FIGURE 1-4: **Touch-screen device**

FIGURE 1-1: **Lock screen with time and date**

Your lock screen contents may differ →

10:49
Friday, July 31

FIGURE 1-2: **Typing your password**

Your_Name@outlook.com
Your_Name@outlook.com

Your_Name@outlook.com
Your_Name@outlook.com

FIGURE 1-3: **Windows 10 desktop**

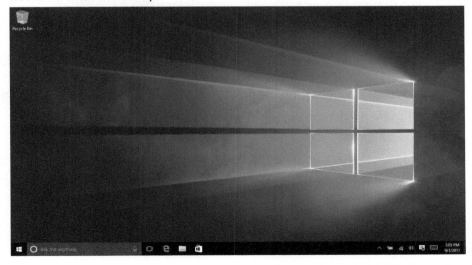

Recycle Bin

Ask me anything

3:03 PM
9/1/2017

Navigate the Desktop and Start Menu

Learning Outcomes
- Examine the desktop
- Open the Start menu
- View Start menu apps
- Close the Start menu

Every time you start your computer and sign in, the Windows 10 desktop appears. The **Windows 10 desktop** is an electronic work area that lets you organize and manage your information, much like your own physical desktop. The desktop contains controls that let you interact with the Windows 10 operating system. These controls are called its **user interface (UI)**. The Windows 10 user interface is called the **Windows 10 UI**. **CASE** *To become better acquainted with Windows 10, you decide to explore the desktop and Start menu.*

STEPS

1. **Examine the Windows 10 desktop**

   As shown in FIGURE 1-5, the desktop currently contains one item, an icon representing the **Recycle Bin**, an electronic wastepaper basket. You might see other icons, files, and folders placed there by previous users or by your school lab. The desktop lets you manage the files and folders on your computer. A **file** is a collection of stored information, such as a letter, video, or program. A **folder** is a container that helps you organize your files. A file, folder, or program opens in a window. You can open multiple windows on the desktop at once, and you can move them around so you can easily go back and forth between them. You work with windows later in this module. At the bottom of the screen is a bar called the **taskbar**, with buttons representing commonly used programs and tools. In a default Windows installation, the taskbar contains four buttons, described in TABLE 1-1. Also on the taskbar is the search box, which you can use to find an item on your computer or the Internet. On the right side of the status bar you see the **Notification area**, containing the time and date as well as icons that tell you the status of your computer. At the left side of the taskbar, you see the Start button. You click the **Start button** to display the **Start menu**, which lets you start the programs on your computer.

2. **Move the pointer to the left side of the taskbar, then click or tap the** Start button ⊞

   The Start menu appears, as shown in FIGURE 1-6. Your user account name and an optional picture appear at the top. The menu shows a list of often-used programs and other controls on the left, and variously-sized shaded rectangles called **tiles** on the right. Each tile represents an **app**, short for **application program**. Some tiles show updated content using a feature called **live tile**; for example, the Weather app can show the current weather for any city you choose. (Your screen color and tiles may differ from the figures shown here. Note that the screens in this book do not show live tiles.)

3. **Move the pointer near the bottom of the Start menu, then click or tap the** All apps **button**

   You see an alphabetical listing of all the apps on your computer. Only some of the apps are visible.

4. **Move the pointer into the list, until the gray scroll bar appears on the right side of the list, place the pointer over the** scroll box, **press and hold down the** mouse button, **then drag to display the remaining programs; on a touch screen, swipe the list to scroll**

5. **Click or tap the** Back button **at the bottom of the Start menu**

   The previous listing reappears.

6. **Move the pointer back up over the desktop, then click or tap once to close the Start menu**

FIGURE 1-5: **Windows 10 desktop**

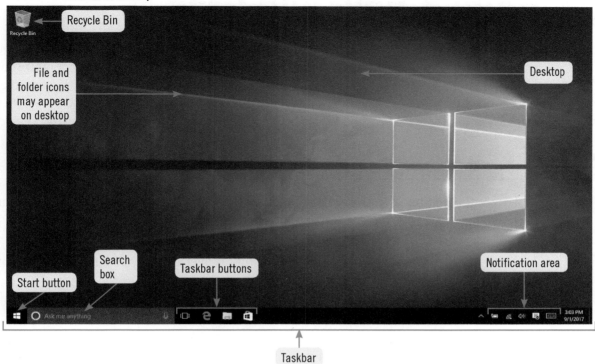

FIGURE 1-6: **Start menu**

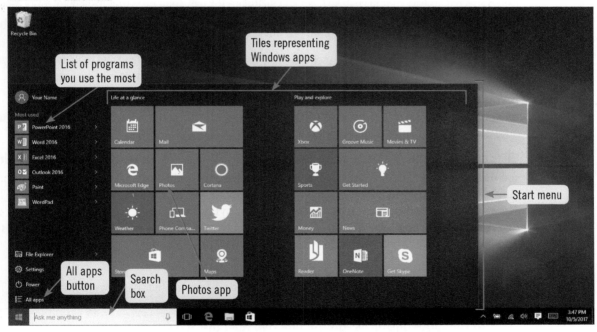

TABLE 1-1: **Windows taskbar buttons**

button	looks like	what it does
Task View		Shows miniatures of all open windows and lets you create multiple desktops, so you can switch from one to another
Microsoft Edge		Opens the Microsoft Edge web browser
File Explorer		Lets you explore the files in your storage locations
Store		Opens the Windows Store featuring downloadable apps, games, music, movies, and TV

Point, Click, and Drag

You communicate with Windows 10 using a variety of pointing devices (or, with a touch-screen device, your finger). A **pointing device** controls the movement of the **pointer**, a small arrow or other symbol that moves on the screen. Your pointing device could be a mouse, trackball, graphics tablet, or touchpad. There are five basic **pointing device actions** you use to communicate with your computer; see TABLE 1-2. Touch-screen users can tap, press, and tap and hold. **CASE** *You practice the basic pointing device actions.*

STEPS

1. **Locate the pointer ⬚ on the desktop, then move your pointing device left, right, up, and down (or move your finger across a touch pad or screen)**
   The pointer shape ⬚ is the **Select pointer**. The pointer moves in the same direction as your device.

2. **Move your pointing device so the Select pointer is over the Recycle Bin (if you are using a touch screen, skip this step)**
   You are **pointing to** the Recycle Bin icon. The icon becomes **highlighted**, looking as though it is framed in a box with a lighter color background. (Note that touch-screen users cannot point to items.)

3. **While pointing to the Recycle Bin icon, press and quickly release the left mouse button once (or tap the icon once), then move the pointer away from the Recycle Bin icon**
   You click or tap a desktop icon once to **select** it, which signals that you intend to perform an action. When an icon is selected, its background changes color and maintains the new color even when you point away from it.

4. **With a pointing device, point to (don't click) the Microsoft Edge button ⬚ on the taskbar**
   The button becomes highlighted and an informational message called a **ScreenTip** identifies the program the button represents. ScreenTips are useful because they help you to learn about the tools available to you. **Microsoft Edge** is the new Microsoft web browser that lets you display and interact with webpages.

5. **If you are using a pointing device, move the pointer over the time and date in the notification area on the right side of the taskbar, read the ScreenTip, then click or tap once**
   A pop-up window appears, containing the current time and date and a calendar.

6. **Click or tap on the desktop, point to the Recycle Bin icon, then quickly click or tap twice**
   You **double-clicked** (or double-tapped) the icon. You need to double-click or double-tap quickly, without moving the pointer. A window opens, showing the contents of the Recycle Bin, as shown in FIGURE 1-7. The area at the top of the window is the title bar, which displays the name of the window. The area below the title bar is the **Ribbon**, which contains tabs, commands, and the Address bar. **Tabs** are groupings of **buttons** and other controls you use to interact with an object or a program.

7. **Click or tap the View tab**
   The buttons on that tab appear. Buttons act as **commands**, which instruct Windows to perform tasks. The **Address bar** shows the name and location of the item you have opened.

8. **Point to the Close button ⬚ on the title bar, read the ScreenTip, then click or tap once**

9. **Point to the Recycle Bin icon, hold down the left mouse button, or press and hold the Recycle Bin image with your finger, move the mouse or drag so the object moves right as shown in FIGURE 1-8, release the mouse button or lift your finger, then drag the Recycle Bin back to its original location**

FIGURE 1-7: **Recycle Bin window**

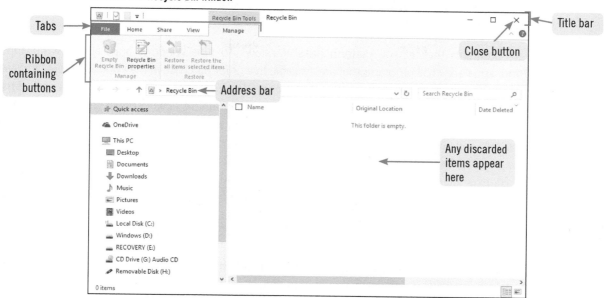

FIGURE 1-8: **Dragging the Recycle Bin icon**

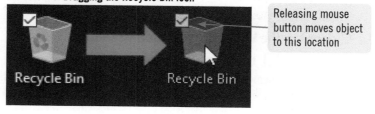

Releasing mouse button moves object to this location

TABLE 1-2: **Basic pointing device actions**

action	with a mouse	with a touch pad	use to
Point	Move mouse to position tip of pointer over an item	Move your finger over touch pad to position tip of pointer over an item	Highlight items or display small informational boxes called ScreenTips
Click	Press and release left mouse button once	Tap touch pad once	Select objects or commands, open menus or items on the taskbar
Double-click	Quickly press and release left mouse button twice	Tap touch pad twice in quick succession	Open programs, folders, or files represented by desktop icons
Drag	Point to an object, press and hold down left mouse button, move object to a new location, then release mouse button	Slide finger across touch pad to point to an object, press and hold left touch pad button, drag across touch pad to move object to new location, then release button	Move objects, such as icons, on the desktop
Right-click	Point to an object, then press and release right mouse button	Point to an object, then press and release right touchpad button	Display a shortcut menu containing options specific to the object

Selecting and moving items using touch-screen devices

If you use a touch-screen computer, a tablet, or a smartphone, you click desktop items by tapping them once on the screen. Tap an icon twice quickly to double-click and open its window. Press and hold an icon, then drag to move it. A touch-screen device does not let you point to an object without selecting it, however, as mice and touchpads do.

Start an App

Learning Outcomes
- Open the Start menu
- Start a Windows app
- Start a desktop app
- Close an app

Apps are programs that let you perform tasks. Windows 10 runs Windows apps and desktop apps. **Windows apps** are small programs that are available free or for purchase in the Windows Store, and can run on Windows desktops, laptops, tablets, and phones. Windows apps are also called **universal apps**. They are specially designed so they can stay open as you work without slowing down your computer, and often have a single purpose. Examples include the Photos app, which lets you view your photographs, and the OneDrive app, which lets you connect to files and programs you have stored on the Microsoft OneDrive website. **Desktop apps** are fully-featured programs; they may be available at an online store or on disk. For example, Microsoft Word allows you to create and edit letters, reports, and other text-based documents. Some smaller desktop apps called **Windows accessories**, such as Paint and Notepad, come already installed in Windows 10. **CASE** ▶ *To prepare for your new job, you start three apps.*

STEPS

1. **Click or tap the Start button ⊞, then click or tap the Weather tile, shown in FIGURE 1-9**
   The Weather app opens, letting you find the current weather in various locations.

2. **If you are asked to choose a location, begin typing your city or town, then click the full name if it appears in the drop-down list**
   The current weather for your selected city appears in Summary view. FIGURE 1-10 shows a forecast for Boston, MA.

QUICK TIP
If you have Microsoft Office installed on your computer, you might also see the OneNote 2016 desktop app, as shown in the figure.

3. **Click or tap the Weather app window's Close button ☒**

4. **Click or tap ⊞, then type onenote**
   Typing an app name is another way to locate an app. At the top of the Start menu, you see the OneNote Trusted Windows Store app listed, as shown in FIGURE 1-11. OneNote is a popular app that lets you create tabbed notebooks where you can store text, images, files, and media such as audio and video.

QUICK TIP
Some programs have both full-featured desktop apps and reduced, often free, Windows apps.

5. **Click or tap the OneNote Trusted Windows Store app name**
   The OneNote app opens, showing a blank notebook (or a notebook you have previously created).

6. **Click or tap the Close button ☒ in the upper right corner of the OneNote app window**
   You have opened two Windows apps, Weather and OneNote.

7. **Click or tap ⊞, then type paint**
   The top of the Start menu lists the Paint Desktop app, shown in FIGURE 1-12. Paint is a simple accessory that comes installed with Windows and lets you create simple illustrations.

QUICK TIP
You can also start a desktop app by clicking or tapping All apps, then clicking or tapping the app name in the scrollable list on the left side of the Start menu.

8. **Click or tap the Paint Desktop app name at the top of the Start menu**
   Other accessories besides Paint and Notepad include the Snipping Tool, which lets you capture an image of any screen area, and Sticky Notes, that let you create short notes.

Using the Windows Store

The Windows Store is an app that lets you find all kinds of apps for use on Windows personal computers, tablets, and phones. You can open it by clicking or tapping its tile on the Start menu or by clicking or tapping the Store button on the taskbar. To use the Windows Store, you need to be signed in to your Microsoft account. You can browse lists of popular apps, games, music, movies, and TV including new releases; you can browse the top paid or free apps. Browse app categories to find a specific type of app, such as Business or Entertainment. To locate a specific app, type its name in the Search box. If an app is free, you can go to its page and click the Free button to install it on your computer. If it's a paid app, you can click or tap the Free trial button to try it out, or click or tap its price button to purchase it. Any apps you've added recently appear in the Recently added category of the Start menu.

FIGURE 1-9: Weather tile on the Start menu

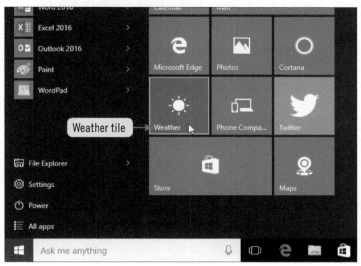

FIGURE 1-10: Weather app

FIGURE 1-11: OneNote Windows app name on Start menu

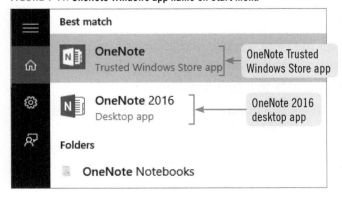

FIGURE 1-12: Paint Desktop app name on Start menu

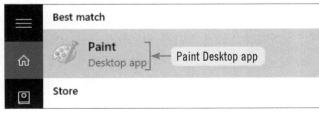

Work with a Window

Learning Outcomes
- Minimize, restore, and maximize a window
- Scroll a window
- Move a window

When you start an app, its **window**, a frame displaying the app's tools, opens. In many apps, a blank file also opens so you can start creating a new document. For example, in Paint, a blank document opens so you can start drawing right away. All windows in the Windows 10 operating system have similar window elements. Once you can use a window in one app, you will know how to work with windows in many other apps. **CASE** ▷ *To become more familiar with the Windows 10 user interface, you explore elements in the Paint window.*

DETAILS

Many windows have the following common elements. Refer to FIGURE 1-13:

- At the top of the window, you see a **title bar**, a strip that contains the name of the document and app. This document has not been saved, so it has the temporary name "Untitled" and the app name is "Paint."

- On the right side of the title bar, the **Window control buttons** let you control the app window. The **Minimize button** $\boxed{-}$ temporarily hides the window, making it a button on the taskbar. The app is still running, but its window is temporarily hidden until you click its taskbar button or its miniature window in Task view to reopen it. The **Maximize button** $\boxed{\square}$ enlarges the window to fill the entire screen. If a window is already maximized, the Maximize button changes to the **Restore Down button** $\boxed{\square}$, which reduces it to the last non-maximized size. Clicking or tapping the **Close button** $\boxed{\times}$ closes the app.

- Many windows have a **scroll bar** on the right side and/or the bottom of the window. You click (or press) and drag scroll bar elements to show additional parts of your document. See TABLE 1-3.

- Just below the title bar is the Ribbon, a bar containing tabs as well as a Help icon. The Paint window has three tabs: File, Home, and View. Tabs are divided into **groups** of buttons and tool palettes. The Home tab has five groups: Clipboard, Image, Tools, Shapes, and Colors. Many apps also include **menus** you click to show lists of commands, as well as **toolbars** containing buttons.

- The **Quick Access toolbar** lets you quickly perform common actions such as saving a file.

STEPS

1. **Click or tap the Paint window Minimize button** $\boxed{-}$
   The app is reduced to a taskbar button, as shown in FIGURE 1-14. The contrasting line indicates the app is still open.

2. **Click or tap the taskbar button representing the Paint app** 🎨 **to redisplay the app**

3. **Drag the gray scroll box down, notice the lower edge of the work area that appears, then click or tap the Up scroll arrow** 🔼 **until you see the top edge of the work area**

4. **Point to the View tab, then click or tap the View tab once**
   Clicking or tapping the View tab moved it in front of the Home tab. This tab has three groups containing buttons that let you change your view of the document window.

5. **Click the Home tab, then click or tap the Paint window Maximize button** $\boxed{\square}$
   The window fills the screen, and the Maximize button becomes the Restore Down button $\boxed{\square}$.

6. **Click the window's Restore Down button** $\boxed{\square}$ **to return it to its previous size**

7. **Point to the Paint window title bar (if you are using a pointing device), then drag about an inch to the right to move it so it's centered on the screen**

FIGURE 1-13: Typical app window elements

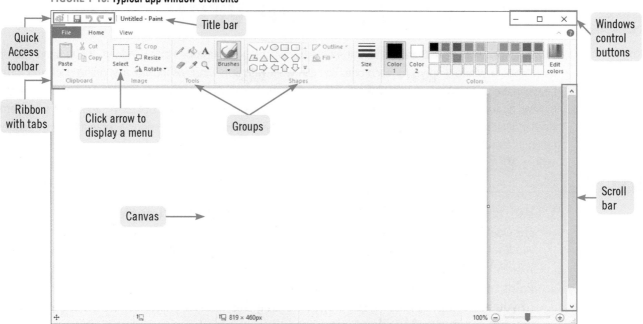

Quick Access toolbar

Title bar

Windows control buttons

Ribbon with tabs

Click arrow to display a menu

Groups

Canvas

Scroll bar

Windows 10

FIGURE 1-14: Taskbar with minimized Paint program button

Buttons without contrasting lines represent programs that are not open

Paint program button with contrasting line indicating program is open

Your buttons may differ

TABLE 1-3: Parts of a scroll bar

name	looks like	to use
Scroll box	(Size may vary)	Drag to scroll quickly through a long document
Scroll arrows		Click or tap to scroll up, down, left, or right in small amounts
Shaded area	(Above, below, or to either side of scroll box)	Click or tap to move up or down by one screen

Using the Quick Access toolbar

On the left side of the title bar, the Quick Access toolbar lets you perform common tasks with just one click. The Save button saves the changes you have made to a document. The Undo button lets you reverse (undo) the last action you performed.

The Redo button reinstates the change you just undid. Use the Customize Quick Access Toolbar button to add other frequently used buttons to the toolbar, move the toolbar below the Ribbon, or minimize the Ribbon to show only tabs.

Manage Multiple Windows

**Learning
Outcomes**
• Open a second
  app
• Activate a window
• Resize, snap, and
  close a window

You can work with more than one app at a time by switching among open app windows. If you open two or more apps, a window opens for each one. You can work with app windows individually, going back and forth between them. The window in front is called the **active window**. Any open window behind the active window is called an **inactive window**. For ease in working with multiple windows, you can move, arrange, make them smaller or larger, minimize, or restore them so they're not in the way. To resize a window, drag a window's edge, called its **border**. You can use the taskbar to switch between windows. See TABLE 1-4 for a summary of taskbar actions. **CASE** *Keeping the Paint app open, you open the OneNote app and then work with both app windows.*

STEPS

1. **With Paint open, click or tap the Start button ⊞, then the OneNote tile**

   The OneNote window appears as a second window on the desktop, as shown in FIGURE 1-15. The OneNote window is in front, indicating that it is the active window. The Paint window is the inactive window. On the taskbar, the contrasting line under the OneNote and Paint app buttons tell you both apps are open.

2. **Point to a blank part of the OneNote window title bar on either side of the app name (if you are using a pointing device), then drag the OneNote window down slightly so you can see more of the Paint window**

3. **Click or tap once on the Paint window's title bar**

   The Paint window is now the active window and appears in front of the OneNote window. You can make any window active by clicking or tapping it, or by clicking or tapping an app's icon in the taskbar.

4. **Point to the taskbar if you are using a pointing device, then click or tap the OneNote window button**

   The OneNote window becomes active. When you open multiple windows on the desktop, you may need to resize windows so they don't get in the way of other open windows.

5. **Point to the lower-right corner of the OneNote window until the pointer changes to ⬌, if you are using a pointing device, or tap and press the corner, then drag down and to the right about an inch to make the window larger**

   You can also point to any edge of a window until you see the ⬌ or ⬍ pointer, or tap and press any edge, then drag to make it larger or smaller in one direction only.

6. **Click or tap the Task View button ▣ on the taskbar, click or tap the Paint window, click or tap ▣ again, then click or tap the OneNote window**

   The **Task View button** is another convenient way to switch among open windows.

7. **Point to the OneNote window title bar if you are using a pointing device, drag the window to the left side of the screen until the pointer or your finger reaches the screen edge and you see a vertical line down the middle of the screen, then release the mouse button or lift your finger from the screen**

   The OneNote window instantly fills the left side of the screen, and any inactive windows appear on the right side of the screen. This is called the **Snap Assist** feature. You can also drag to any screen corner to snap open app windows to quarter-screen windows.

8. **Click or tap anywhere on the reduced-size version of the Paint window**

   The Paint window fills the right side of the screen. Snapping makes it easy to view the contents of two windows at the same time. See FIGURE 1-16.

9. **Click or tap the OneNote window Close button ✖, then click or tap the Maximize button ▢ in the Paint window's title bar**

   The OneNote app closes. The Paint app window remains open.

FIGURE 1-15: Working with multiple windows

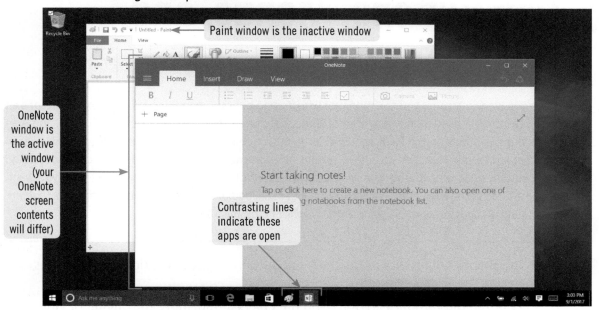

FIGURE 1-16: OneNote and Paint windows snapped to each side of the screen

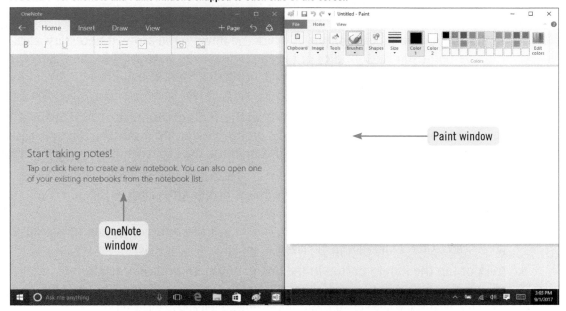

TABLE 1-4: Using the taskbar

to	do this
Add buttons to taskbar	Open an app, right-click or press its icon on the taskbar, then click or tap Pin this program to taskbar
Change order of taskbar buttons	Drag any icon to a new taskbar location
See a list of recent documents opened	Right-click or press taskbar app button
Close a document using the taskbar	Point to taskbar button, point to document image, then click its Close button
Minimize/Redisplay all open windows	Click or press Show desktop button (the thin bar) to the right of taskbar date and time
See preview of documents in taskbar	With a pointing device, point to taskbar button for open app
Bring a minimized window to the front	Click or press the Task View button, then click or tap the window or desktop you want in front
Rearrange windows on the desktop	Right-click taskbar, click Cascade Windows, Show windows stacked, or Show windows side by side

Learning
Outcomes
• Use a button and
  a menu
• Work in a dialog
  box

Use Buttons, Menus, and Dialog Boxes

When you work in an app, you communicate with it using buttons, menus, and dialog boxes. **Buttons** let you issue instructions to modify app objects. Buttons are often organized on a Ribbon into tabs, and then into groups like those in the Paint window. Some buttons have text on them, and others show only an icon that represents what they do. Other buttons reveal **menus**, lists of commands you can choose. And some buttons open up a **dialog box**, a window with controls that lets you tell Windows what you want. TABLE 1-5 lists the common types of controls you find in dialog boxes. **CASE** *You practice using buttons, menus, and dialog boxes to create some simple graphics in the Paint app.*

STEPS

QUICK TIP
You might see a
Shapes button
instead of a gallery.
If so, click the button,
then click or tap △.

1. **In the Shapes group, click or tap the** More button ⊽ **just to the right of the shapes, then click the** Triangle button △

2. **Click or tap the** Turquoise button ■ **in the Colors group, move the pointer or your finger over the white drawing area, then drag down and to the right, to draw a** triangle **similar to the one in** FIGURE 1-17
   The white drawing area is called the **canvas**.

QUICK TIP
If you need to move
the selected object,
use the keyboard
arrow keys to move it
left, right, up, or
down while it is still
selected.

3. **In the Shapes group, click or tap** ⊽**, click the** down scroll arrow **if necessary, click or tap the** Five-point star button, **click or tap the** Indigo color button ■ **in the Colors group, then drag a star shape near the triangle, using** FIGURE 1-17 **as a guide**
   Don't be concerned if your object isn't exactly like the one in the figure, or in exactly the same place.

4. **Click or tap the** Fill with color button ◈ **in the Tools group, click or tap the** Light turquoise color button ■ **in the Colors group, click or tap inside the** triangle, **click or tap the** Purple color button ■, **click or tap inside the** star, **then compare your drawing to** FIGURE 1-17

QUICK TIP
Windows apps
generally do not have
a menu bar; all the
tools you need are
included on the tabs.

5. **Click or tap the** Select list arrow **in the Image group, then click or tap** Select all, **as shown in** FIGURE 1-18
   The Select all command selects the entire drawing, as indicated by the dotted line surrounding the white drawing area. Other commands on this menu let you select individual elements or change your selection.

6. **Click or tap the** Rotate button **in the Image group, then click or tap** Rotate 180°
   You often need to use multiple commands to perform an action—in this case, you used one command to select the items you wanted to work with, and another command to rotate them.

7. **Click or tap the** File tab, **then click or tap** Print
   The Print dialog box opens, as shown in FIGURE 1-19. This dialog box lets you choose a printer, specify which part of your document or drawing you want to print, and choose how many copies you want to print. The **default**, or automatically selected, number of copies is 1, which is what you want.

8. **Click or tap** Print, **or if you prefer not to print, click or tap** Cancel
   The drawing prints on your printer. You decide to close the app without saving your drawing.

9. **Click or tap the** File tab, **click or tap** Exit, **then click or tap** Don't Save
   You closed the file without saving your changes, then exited the app. Most apps include a command for closing a document without exiting the program. However, Paint allows you to open only one document at a time, so it does not include a Close command.

FIGURE 1-17: Triangle and star shapes filled with color

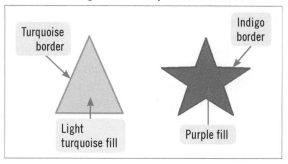

FIGURE 1-18: Select menu options

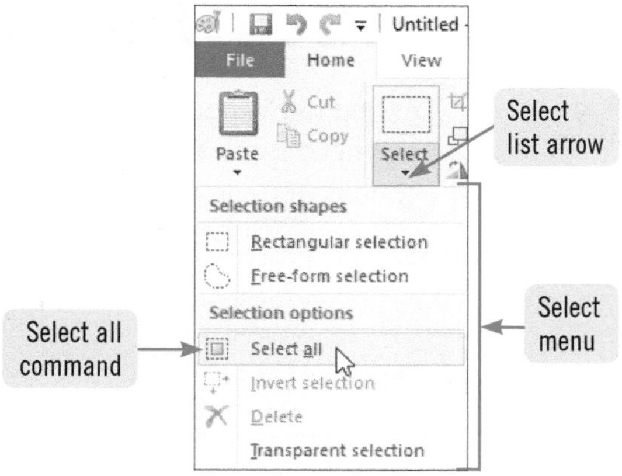

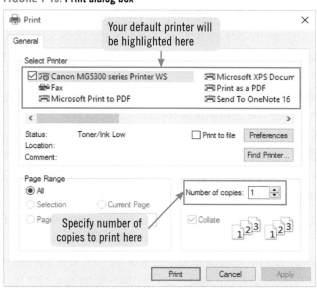

FIGURE 1-19: Print dialog box

TABLE 1-5: Common dialog box controls

element	example	description
Text box	1 - 27	A box in which you type text or numbers
Spin box	 1	A box with up and down arrows; you can click or tap arrows or type to increase or decrease value
Option button	●	A small circle you click or tap to select the option; only one in a set can be selected at once
Check box	☑	A small box that turns an option on when checked or off when unchecked; more than one in a set can be selected at once
List box		A box that lets you select from a list of options
Button	 Save	A button you click or tap to issue a command

Getting Started with Windows 10

Get Help

Learning Outcomes
- Explore the Getting Started app
- Search for Windows help using Cortana

As you use Windows 10, you might feel ready to learn more about it, or you might have a problem and need some advice. You can use the Windows 10 Getting Started app to learn more about help options. You can also search for help using Cortana, which you activate by using the search box on the taskbar. **CASE** ➤ *You explore Windows 10 help using the Get Started app and Cortana.*

STEPS

Note: Because Help in an online resource, topics and information are liable to change over time. If your screen choices do not match the steps below exactly, be flexible by exploring the options that are available to you and searching for the information you need.

1. **Click or tap the** Start button ⊞, **then in the Explore Windows section click or tap the** Get Started tile; **if the Explore Windows section does not appear on your Start menu, begin typing** Get Started, **then click or tap** Get Started Trusted Windows Store app **in the list**

   The Get Started app window opens. The window contains a menu expand button ☰ in the upper left and a bar containing buttons on the left side.

2. **Click or tap the** Menu Expand button ☰, **move the pointer over the list of topics, then scroll down to see the remaining topics**

3. **Click or tap the** Search and help topic, **click the** Search for anything, anywhere tile, **then read the information, as shown in** FIGURE 1-20, **scrolling as necessary**

4. **Click or tap the** Back button ← **in the top-left corner of the window, click the** Search for help tile, **then read the Search for help topic and watch any available videos**

5. **Click or tap** ☰, **click or tap a topic that interests you, then read the information or click or tap one of the tiles representing a subtopic if one is available**

6. **After you have read the information, click or tap the Get started window's** Close button ☒

   As the Help topic explained, you can also search the web for help with Windows using Cortana.

7. **Click in the** search box **on the taskbar, then type** windows help

   As you type, Cortana begins a search, and shows results on the Start menu. See FIGURE 1-21. Your results may also include topics from the Microsoft Store, the web, Store apps, and OneDrive, your online storage location.

8. **Click any web option that interests you**

9. **When you are finished, click or tap the window's** Close button ☒ **to return to the desktop**

FIGURE 1-20: **Get Started Search and Help topic**

Menu Expand button

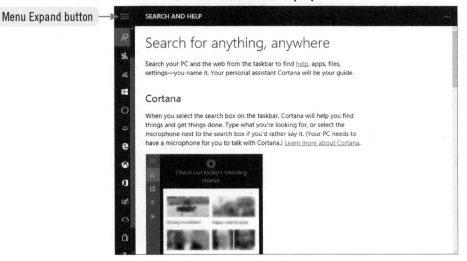

FIGURE 1-21: **Search results information**

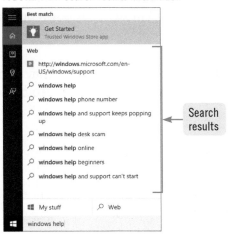

Search results

Using Cortana

Cortana is the digital personal assistant that comes with Windows 10 and Windows phones. You can interact with Cortana typing or using your voice. Use Cortana to search the web, remind you of events or appointments, set alarms, change computer settings, get directions, get current news and weather, track airline flights, play, and even identify music. FIGURE 1-22 shows Cortana's response to "What's the weather in New York?" which may also give a voice response. You call Cortana by saying, "Hey Cortana," or by clicking or tapping the microphone icon on the right side of the taskbar search box, and then asking a question or saying a command. Depending on your request, Cortana may reply out loud, display results in the Start menu, or display results in a Microsoft Edge web browser window. You may need to set up Cortana on your computer and answer security questions before you use it. The first time you use Cortana, you may be asked to answer questions to help the assistant recognize your voice or solve issues with your computer's microphone.

FIGURE 1-22: **Using Cortana to check the weather**

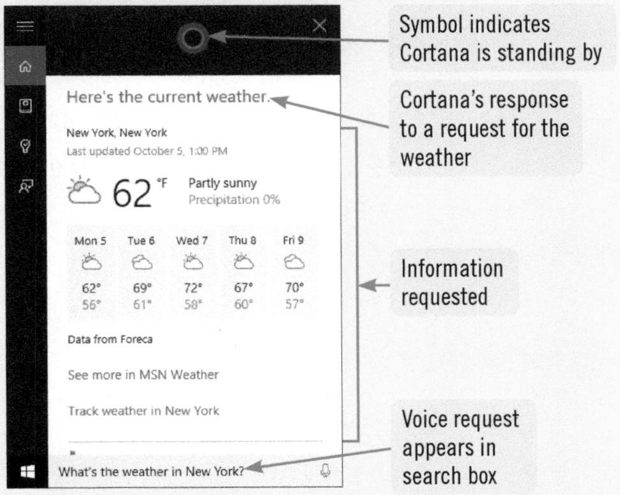

Symbol indicates Cortana is standing by

Cortana's response to a request for the weather

Information requested

Voice request appears in search box

Exit Windows 10

When you finish working on your computer, you should close any open files, exit any open apps, close any open windows, and exit (or **shut down**) Windows 10. TABLE 1-6 shows options for ending your Windows 10 sessions. Whichever option you choose, it's important to shut down your computer in an orderly way. If you turn off or unplug the computer while Windows 10 is running, you could lose data or damage Windows 10 and your computer. If you are working in a computer lab, follow your instructor's directions and your lab's policies for ending your Windows 10 session. **CASE** *You have examined the basic ways you can use Windows 10, so you are ready to end your Windows 10 session.*

STEPS

1. **Click or tap the** Start button ⊞**, then click or tap** Power

    The Power button menu lists shut down options, as shown in FIGURE 1-23.

2. **If you are working in a computer lab, follow the instructions provided by your instructor or technical support person for ending your Windows 10 session; if you are working on your own computer, click or tap** Shut down **or the option you prefer for ending your Windows 10 session**

3. **After you shut down your computer, you may also need to turn off your monitor and other hardware devices, such as a printer, to conserve energy**

FIGURE 1-23: **Shutting down your computer**

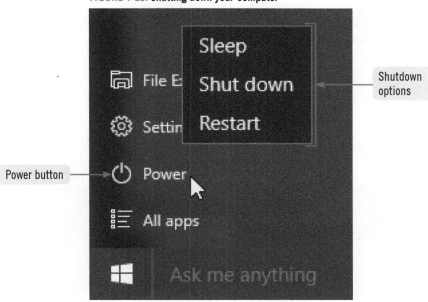

Power button →

Shutdown options

TABLE 1-6: **Power options**

option	description
Sleep	Puts computer in a low-power state while keeping any open apps open so you can return immediately to where you left off
Shut down	Closes any open apps and completely turns off the computer
Restart	Closes any open apps, shuts down the computer, then restarts it

Installing updates when you exit Windows

Sometimes, after you shut down your machine, you might find that your machine does not shut down immediately. Instead, Windows might install software updates. If you see an option on your Power menu that lets you update, you can click or tap it to update your software. If you see a window indicating that updates are being installed, do not unplug or press the power switch to turn off your machine. Let the updates install completely. After the updates are installed, your computer will shut down, as you originally requested.

Practice

Concepts Review

Label the elements of the Windows 10 window shown in FIGURE 1-24.

FIGURE 1-24

[handwritten: Recycle Bin] *[handwritten: Start menu]*

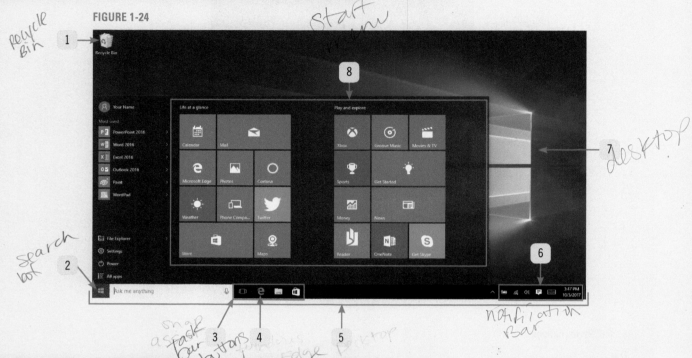

[handwritten: desktop] (7)

[handwritten: search box] (2)

[handwritten: snap assist] *[handwritten: task bar buttons]* (3) (4) *[handwritten: wireless Edge Desktop]* (5)

[handwritten: notification Bar] (6)

Match each term with the statement that best describes it.

9. Cortana *C*
10. Snap Assist *e*
11. Desktop app *F*
12. Microsoft account
13. User interface
14. Operating system
15. Windows app

a. A special area of the operating system where your files and settings are stored
b. Controls that let you interact with an operating system
c. The personal digital assistant in Windows 10
d. Full-featured program that is installed on a personal computer
e. Feature that displays windows at full height next to each other on the screen
f. Available from the Windows store, it runs on Windows laptops, tablets, and phones
g. A program necessary to run your computer

Select the best answer from the list of choices.

16. The bar containing buttons and other elements at the bottom of the Windows 10 desktop is called the _____.
    a. title bar
    b. address bar
    c. scroll bar
    d. taskbar

17. Paint is an example of a(n) _____.
    a. group
    b. accessory
    c. active window
    d. operating system

18. Which of the following is in the upper-left corner of a program window, and lets you perform common actions?

a. Application program **c.** Operating system

b. Quick Access toolbar **d.** Accessory program

19. The new Microsoft web browser is called Microsoft _____.

a. Paint **c.** Edge

b. WordPad **d.** File Explorer

Skills Review

1. Start Windows 10.

a. If your computer and monitor are not running, press your computer's and (if necessary) your monitor's power buttons.

b. If necessary, select the user name that represents your user account.

c. Enter your password, using correct uppercase and lowercase letters.

2. Navigate the desktop and Start menu.

a. Examine the Windows 10 desktop.

b. Open the Start menu.

c. Display all the apps using a command on the Start menu, and scroll the list.

d. Return to the Start menu.

e. Close the Start menu.

3. Point, click, and drag.

a. On the Windows 10 desktop, click or tap to select the Recycle Bin.

b. Point to display the ScreenTip for Microsoft Edge in the taskbar, and then display the ScreenTip for each of the other icons on the taskbar.

c. Double-click or double-tap to open the Recycle Bin window, then close it.

d. Drag the Recycle Bin to a different corner of the screen, then drag it back to its original location.

e. Click or tap the Date and Time area to display the calendar and clock, then click or tap it again to close it.

4. Start an app.

a. Open the Start menu, then start the Maps app. (If asked to allow Windows to access your location, do so if you like.)

b. Click or tap the icons on the left side of the Maps app window and observe the effect of each one.

c. Close the Maps app.

d. Reopen the Start menu, then type and click or tap to locate and open the Sticky Notes accessory.

e. Click or tap the Sticky Notes Close button, clicking or tapping Yes to delete the note.

f. Open the Weather Windows app.

5. Work with a window.

a. Minimize the Weather window, then use its taskbar button to redisplay the window.

b. Use the Weather app window's scroll bar or swiping to view the information in the lower part of the window, and then scroll or swipe up to display the top of it. (*Hint*: You need to move the pointer over the Weather app window, or swipe it, in order to display the scroll bar.)

c. Click or tap the menu expand button, then click Historical Weather.

d. Read the contents of the window, then click or tap two other menu buttons and read the contents.

e. Maximize the Weather window, then restore it down.

6. Manage multiple windows.

a. Leaving the Weather app open, go to the Start menu and type to locate the Paint app, open Paint, then restore down the Paint window if necessary.

b. Click or tap to make the Weather app window the active window.

c. Click or tap to make the Paint window the active window.

d. Minimize the Paint window.

Skills Review (continued)

e. Drag the Weather app window so it's in the middle of the screen.

f. Redisplay the Paint window.

g. Drag the Paint window so it automatically fills the right side of the screen.

FIGURE 1-25

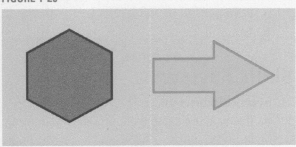

h. Click or tap the Weather app window image so it snaps to the left side of the screen.

i. Close the Weather app window, maximize the Paint window, then restore down the Paint window.

7. Use buttons, menus, and dialog boxes.

a. In the Paint window, draw a Dark red Hexagon shape, similar to the one shown in FIGURE 1-25.

b. Use the Fill with color button to fill the hexagon with a brown color.

c. Draw an Orange right arrow to the right of the hexagon shape, using the figure as a guide.

d. Use the Fill with color button to fill the orange arrow with a lime color.

e. Fill the drawing background with Light turquoise color, as shown in the figure.

f. Use the Select list arrow and menu to select the entire drawing, then use the Rotate command to rotate the drawing 180°.

g. Open the Print dialog box, print a copy of the picture if you wish, then close the Paint app without saving the drawing.

8. Get help.

a. Open the Get Started app, then use the menu expand button to display the available help topics.

b. Use the Menu button to display help for Cortana.

c. Click or tap a tile representing a Cortana help topic that interests you, read the help text, scrolling or swiping as necessary.

d. Display the Search and Help topic, then close the Get Started window.

e. In the search box on the taskbar, type Help Microsoft Account, then click the help Microsoft account result to search the web.

f. In the Microsoft Edge browser window, select a help topic that interests you, read the information (ignore any commercial offers), then click or tap the Microsoft Edge window's Close button.

9. Exit Windows 10.

a. Sign out of your account, or shut down your computer using the Shut down command in the Start menu's Power command or the preferred command for your work or school setting.

b. Turn off your monitor if necessary.

Independent Challenge 1

You work for Chicago Instruments, a manufacturer of brass instruments. The company ships instruments and supplies to music stores and musicians in the United States and Canada. The owner, Emerson, wants to know an easy way for his employees to learn about the new features of Windows 10, and he has asked you to help.

a. Start your computer if necessary, sign in to Windows 10, then use the search text box to search for **what's new in Windows 10**.

b. Click or tap the Search the web link in the Best match section at the top of the Help menu, then in the Microsoft Edge browser window, click or tap a search result that interests you.

c. Open the Getting Started app and review the new features listed there.

d. Using pencil and paper, or the Notepad accessory if you wish, write a short memo to Emerson summarizing, in your own words, three important new features in Windows 10. If you use Notepad to write the memo, use the Print button to print the document, then use the Exit command on the File tab to close Notepad without saving your changes to the document.

Independent Challenge 1 (continued)

e. Close the browser window, then sign out of your account, or shut down your computer using the preferred command for your work or school setting. Turn off your monitor if necessary.

Independent Challenge 2

You are the new manager of Katharine Anne's Garden Supplies, a business that supplies garden tools to San Diego businesses. Some of their tools are from Europe and show metric sizes. For her American customers, Katharine Anne wants to do a simple calculation and then convert the result to inches.

a. Start your computer and log on to Windows 10 if necessary, then type to locate the Windows app called Calculator, and start it.

b. Click or tap to enter the number 96 on the Calculator.

c. Click or tap the division sign (÷) button.

d. Click or tap the number 4.

e. Click or tap the equals sign button (=), and write down the result shown in the Calculator window. (*Hint*: The result should be 24.)

f. Select the menu expand button in the Calculator window, then under CONVERTER, select Length.

g. Enter 24 centimeters, and observe the equivalent length in inches.

h. Start Notepad, write a short memo about how Calculator can help you convert metric measurements to inches and feet, print the document using the Print command on the File tab, then exit Notepad without saving.

i. Close the Calculator, then sign out of your account, or shut down your computer using the preferred command for your work or school setting. Turn off your monitor if necessary.

Independent Challenge 3

You are the office manager for Erica's Pet Shipping, a service business in Dallas, Texas, that specializes in air shipping of cats and dogs across the United States and Canada. It's important to know the temperature in the destination city, so the animals won't be in danger from extreme temperatures when they are unloaded from the aircraft. Erica has asked you to find a way to easily monitor temperatures in destination cities. You decide to use a Windows app so you can see current temperatures in Celsius on your desktop. (Note: To complete the steps below, your computer must be connected to the Internet.)

a. Start your computer and sign in to Windows 10 if necessary, then on the Start menu, click or tap the Weather tile.

b. Click or tap the Search icon in the location text box, then type **Toronto**.

c. Select Toronto, Ontario, Canada, in the drop-down list to view the weather for Toronto.

d. Search on and select another location that interests you.

e. Close the app.

f. Open Notepad, write Erica a memo outlining how you can use the Windows Weather app to help keep pets safe, print the memo if you wish, close Notepad, then sign out, or shut down your computer.

Independent Challenge 4: Explore

Cortana, the Windows 10 personal digital assistant, can help you with everyday tasks. In this Independent Challenge, you explore one of the ways you can use Cortana.

a. Click or tap the microphone icon, to the right of the search box in the Windows 10 taskbar, to activate Cortana and display its menu. (*Note*: If you have not used Cortana before, you will not see the microphone icon until you answer some preliminary questions and verify your user account; you may also need to first help Cortana to understand your speaking voice.) Cortana displays a pulsating circle, indicating that she is listening for speech, and then shows you a greeting and some general information.

Independent Challenge 4: Explore (continued)

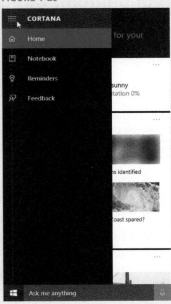

FIGURE 1-26

b. In the list of icons on the left side of the menu, click the menu expand button to show the names of each one, as shown in FIGURE 1-26.

c. Click or tap the Reminders button, then click the plus sign at the bottom of the menu. Click or tap Remember to…, then enter information for a to-do item, such as "Walk the dog." Click or tap the time box and use the spin boxes to set the time for one or two minutes from now. Click or tap the check mark, then click Remind to set the reminder. Click or tap the Reminders icon again to see your reminder listed, then click the desktop. When the reminder appears, click Complete.

d. Click or tap the microphone icon again, and when you see the pulsating circle, speak into your computer microphone and tell Cortana to remind you to do something in one minute. Click or tap Remind, then close the Cortana window. When the reminder appears, click or tap Complete.

e. Click or tap the Close button on the Cortana menu, then sign out of your account, or shut down your computer.

Visual Workshop

Using the skills you've learned in this module, open and arrange elements on your screen so it looks similar to FIGURE 1-27. Note the position of the Recycle Bin, and the size and location of the Notepad and Weather app windows, as well as the city shown. In Notepad, write a paragraph summarizing how you used pointing, clicking (or tapping), and dragging to make your screen look like the figure. Print your work if you wish, close Notepad and the Weather app without saving changes, then sign out or shut down your computer.

FIGURE 1-27

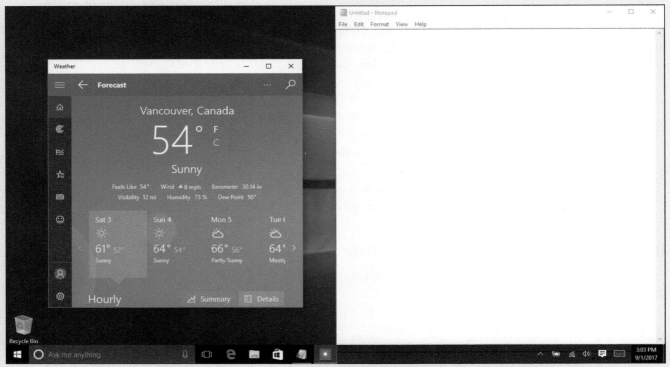

Understanding File Management

CASE ▶ Now that you are familiar with the Windows 10 operating system, your new employer has asked you to become familiar with **file management**, or how to create, save, locate and delete the files you create with Windows apps. You begin by reviewing how files are organized on your computer, and then begin working with files you create in the WordPad app. *Note: With the release of Windows 10, Microsoft now provides ongoing updates to Windows instead of releasing new versions periodically. This means that Windows features might change over time, including how they look and how you interact with them. The information provided in this text was accurate at the time this book was published.*

Module Objectives

After completing this module, you will be able to:

- Understand files and folders
- Create and save a file
- Explore the files and folders on your computer
- Change file and folder views

- Open, edit, and save files
- Copy files
- Move and rename files
- Search for files and folders
- Delete and restore files

Files You Will Need

No files needed.

Understand Files and Folders

As you work with apps, you create and save files, such as letters, drawings, or budgets. When you save files, you usually save them inside folders to help keep them organized. The files and folders on your computer are organized in a **file hierarchy**, a system that arranges files and folders in different levels, like the branches of a tree. FIGURE 2-1 shows a sample file hierarchy. **CASE** ▸ *You decide to use folders and files to organize the information on your computer.*

DETAILS

Use the following guidelines as you organize files using your computer's file hierarchy:

- **Use folders and subfolders to organize files**

  As you work with your computer, you can add folders to your hierarchy and name them to help you organize your work. As you've learned, folders are storage areas in which you can group related files. You should give folders unique names that help you easily identify them. You can also create **subfolders**, which are folders that are inside other folders. Windows 10 comes with several existing folders, such as Documents, Music, Pictures, and Videos, that you can use as a starting point.

- **View and manage files in File Explorer**

  You can view and manage your computer contents using a built-in program called **File Explorer**, shown in FIGURE 2-2. A File Explorer window is divided into **panes**, or sections. The **Navigation pane** on the left side of the window shows the folder structure on your computer. When you click a folder in the Navigation pane, you see its contents in the **File list** on the right side of the window. To open File Explorer from the desktop, click the File Explorer button 📁 on the taskbar. To open it from the Start menu, click the File Explorer shortcut.

- **Understand file addresses**

  A window also contains an **Address bar**, an area just below the Ribbon that shows the address, or location, of the files that appear in the File list. An **address** is a sequence of folder names, separated by the ⟩ symbol, which describes a file's location in the file hierarchy. An address shows the folder with the highest hierarchy level on the left and steps through each hierarchy level toward the right; this is sometimes called a **path**. For example, the Documents folder might contain subfolders named Work and Personal. If you clicked the Personal folder in the File list, the Address bar would show Documents ⟩ Personal. Each location between the ⟩ symbols represents a level in the file hierarchy. If you see a file path written out, you'll most likely see it with backslashes. For example, in FIGURE 2-1, if you wanted to write the path to the Brochure file, you would write "Documents\Reason2Go\Marketing\Brochure.xlsx. File addresses might look complicated if they may have many levels, but they are helpful because they always describe the exact location of a file or folder in a file hierarchy.

- **Navigate up and down using the Address bar and File list**

  You can use the Address bar and the File list to move up or down in the hierarchy one or more levels at a time. To **navigate up** in your computer's hierarchy, you can click a folder or subfolder name to the left of the current folder name in the Address bar. For example, in FIGURE 2-2, you can move up in the hierarchy three levels by clicking once on This PC in the Address bar. Then the File list would show the subfolders and files inside the This PC folder. To **navigate down** in the hierarchy, double-click a subfolder in the File list. The path in the Address bar then shows the path to that subfolder.

- **Navigate up and down using the Navigation pane**

  You can also use the Navigation pane to navigate among folders. Move the mouse pointer over the Navigation pane, then click the small arrows to the left of a folder name to show ⟩ or hide ﹀ the folder's contents under the folder name. Subfolders appear indented under the folders that contain them, showing that they are inside that folder.

FIGURE 2-1: Sample folder and file hierarchy

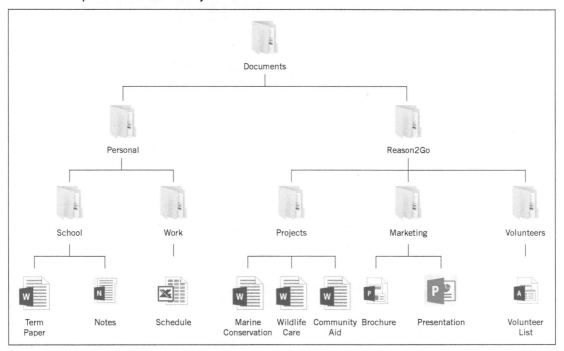

FIGURE 2-2: File Explorer window

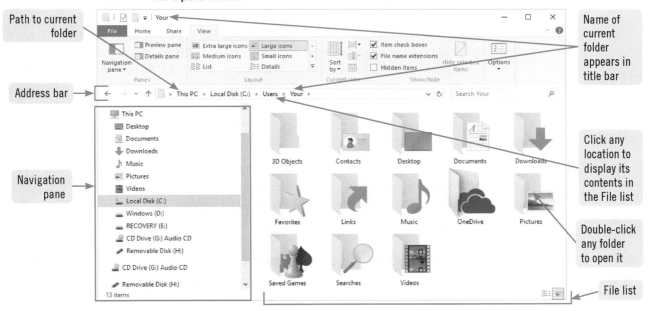

Plan your file organization

As you manage your files, you should plan how you want to organize them. First, identify the types of files you work with, such as images, music, and documents. Think about the content, such as personal, business, clients, or projects. Then think of a folder organization that will help you find them later. For example, you can use subfolders in the Pictures folder to separate family photos from business photos or to group them by location or by month. In the Documents folder, you might group personal files in one subfolder and business files in another subfolder. Then create additional subfolders to further separate sets of files. You can always move files among folders and rename folders. You should periodically reevaluate your folder structure to make sure it continues to meet your needs.

Create and Save a File

**Learning
Outcomes**
• Start WordPad
• Create a file
• Save a file

After you start a program and create a new file, the file exists only in your computer's **random access memory (RAM)**, a temporary storage location. RAM contains information only when your computer is on. When you turn off your computer, it automatically clears the contents of RAM. So you need to save a new file onto a storage device that permanently stores the file so you can open, change, and use it later. One important storage device is your computer's hard drive built into your computer. You might want to store your files online in an online storage location like Microsoft OneDrive. Or you might use a **USB flash drive**, a small, portable storage device that you plug into a USB port on your computer. **CASE** ▸ *You create a document, then save it.*

STEPS

1. **Click or tap the Start button, then type** word
   Available apps with "word" in their names are listed. See FIGURE 2-3.

2. **Click the** WordPad Desktop app listing**, then maximize the WordPad window if necessary**
   Near the top of the WordPad window you see the Ribbon containing buttons, similar to those you used in Paint in Module 1. The Home tab appears in front. A new, blank document appears in the document window. The blinking insertion point shows you where the next character you type will appear.

3. **Type** Company Overview**, then press [Enter] twice, type** Conservation**, press [Enter], type** Community Work**, press [Enter], type** Research**, press [Enter] twice, then type your name**
   See FIGURE 2-4.

4. **Click the** File tab**, then click** Save
   The first time you save a file using the Save button, the Save As dialog box opens. You use this dialog box to name the file and choose a storage location for it. The Save As dialog box has many of the same elements as a File Explorer window, including an Address bar, a Navigation pane, and a File list. Below the Address bar, the **toolbar** contains buttons you can click to perform actions. In the Address bar, you can see the Documents folder, which is the **default**, or automatically selected, storage location. But you can easily change it.

QUICK TIP
On a laptop computer, the USB port is on the left or right side of your computer.

5. **If you are saving to a USB flash drive, plug the drive into a USB port on your computer, if necessary**

TROUBLE
If you don't have a USB flash drive, you can save the document in the Documents folder on OneDrive, or you can ask your instructor which storage location is best.

6. **In the Navigation pane scroll bar, click the** down scroll arrow ⌄ **as needed to see This PC and any storage devices listed under it**
   Under This PC, you see the storage locations available on your computer, such as Local Disk (C:) (your hard drive) and Removable Disk (H:) (your USB drive name and letter might differ). Above This PC, you might see your OneDrive listed. These storage locations are like folders in that you can open them and store files in them.

7. **Click the name of your USB flash drive, or the folder where you store your Data Files**
   The files and folders in the location you chose, if any, appear in the File list. The Address bar shows the location where the file will be saved, which is now Removable Disk (H:) or the name of the location you clicked. You need to give your document a meaningful name so you can find it later.

TROUBLE
If your Save As dialog box does not show the .rtf file extension, click Cancel, open File Explorer, click the View tab, then in the Show/hide group, click the File name extensions check box to select it.

8. **Click in the** File name text box **to select the default name** Document.rtf**, type** Company Overview**, compare your screen to** FIGURE 2-5**, then click** Save
   The document is saved as a file on your USB flash drive. The filename Company Overview.rtf appears in the title bar. The ".rtf" at the end of the filename is the file extension that Windows added automatically. A **file extension** is a three- or four-letter sequence, preceded by a period, which identifies a file to your computer, in this case **Rich Text Format**. The WordPad program creates files in RTF format.

9. **Click the** Close button ✕ **on the WordPad window**
   The WordPad program closes. Your Company Overview document is now saved in the location you specified.

FIGURE 2-3: Results at top of Start menu

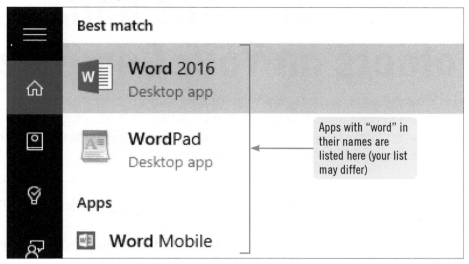

Best match

Word 2016
Desktop app

WordPad
Desktop app

Apps

Word Mobile

Apps with "word" in their names are listed here (your list may differ)

FIGURE 2-4: WordPad document

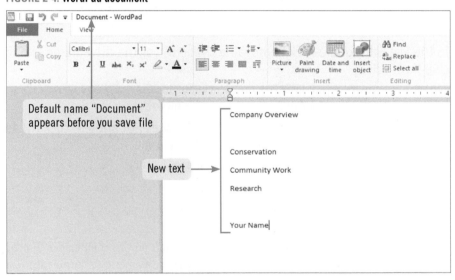

Default name "Document" appears before you save file

New text

Company Overview

Conservation

Community Work

Research

Your Name

FIGURE 2-5: Save As dialog box

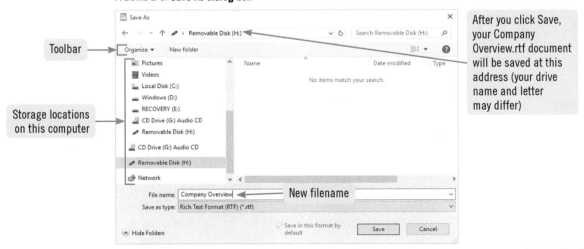

Toolbar

Storage locations on this computer

New filename

After you click Save, your Company Overview.rtf document will be saved at this address (your drive name and letter may differ)

Explore the Files and Folders on Your Computer

In a File Explorer window, you can navigate through your computer contents using the File list, the Address bar, and the Navigation pane. Examining your computer and its existing folder and file structure helps you decide where to save files as you work with Windows 10 apps. **CASE** ▶ *In preparation for organizing documents at your new job, you look at the files and folders on your computer.*

STEPS

1. **At the Windows desktop, click the** File Explorer button 🖿 **on the taskbar, then in the File Explorer Navigation pane, click** This PC

2. **If you do not see a band of buttons near the top of the window, double-click the** View tab

   The band containing buttons is called the **Ribbon**. Your computer's storage devices appear in a window, as shown in FIGURE 2-6. These include hard drives; devices with removable storage, such as CD and DVD drives or USB flash drives; portable devices such as smartphones or tablets; and any network storage locations. Colored bars shows you how much space has been taken up on your drives. You decide to move down a level in your computer's hierarchy and see what is on your USB flash drive.

3. **In the File list, double-click** Removable Disk (H:) **(or the drive name and letter for your USB flash drive)**

   You see the contents of your USB flash drive, including the Company Overview.rtf file you saved in the last lesson. You decide to navigate one level up in the file hierarchy.

4. **In the Address bar, click** This PC, **or if This PC does not appear, click the far-left** address bar arrow ▶ **in the Address bar, then click** This PC

   You return to the This PC window showing your storage locations.

5. **In the File list, double-click** Local Disk (C:)

   The contents of your hard drive appear in the File list.

6. **In the File list, double-click the** Users folder

   The Users folder contains a subfolder for each user account on this computer. You might see a folder with your user account name on it. Each user's folder contains that person's documents. User folder names are the names that were used to log in when your computer was set up. When a user logs in, the computer allows that user access to the folder with the same user name. If you are using a computer with more than one user, you might not have permission to view other users' folders. There is also a Public folder that any user can open.

7. **Double-click the folder with your user name on it**

   Depending on how your computer is set up, this folder might be labeled with your name; however, if you are using a computer in a lab or a public location, your folder might be called Student or Computer User or something similar. You see a list of folders, such as Documents, Music, and OneDrive. See FIGURE 2-7.

8. **Double-click** Documents **in the File list**

   In the Address bar, the path to the Documents folder is This PC ▶ Local Disk (C:) ▶ Users ▶ *Your User Name* ▶ Documents.

9. **In the Navigation pane, click** This PC

   You once again see your computer's storage locations. You can also move up one level at a time in your file hierarchy by clicking the Up arrow ↑ on the toolbar, or by pressing [Backspace] on your keyboard. See TABLE 2-1 for a summary of techniques for navigating through your computer's file hierarchy.

Understanding File Management

FIGURE 2-6: File Explorer window showing storage locations

Click this arrow if necessary to navigate to a different location

Storage locations on this PC

Colored bars show how full drives are

FIGURE 2-7: Your user name folder

Path to your user name folder contents

OneDrive

Your user name folder contents and view may differ

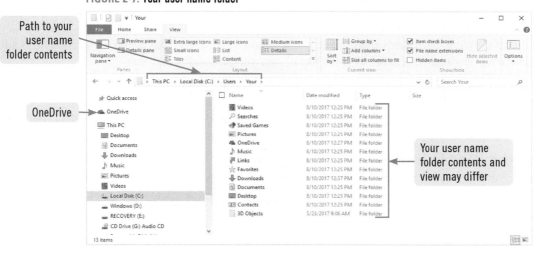

TABLE 2-1: Navigating your computer's file hierarchy

to do this	Navigation pane	Address bar	File list	keyboard
Move up in hierarchy	Click a drive or folder name	Click an item to the left of ➤ or Click the **Up to** button ↑		Press [**Backspace**]
Move down in hierarchy	Click a drive or folder name that is indented from the left	Click an item to the right of ➤	Double-click a folder	Press ↑ or ↓ to select a folder, then press [**Enter**] to open the selected folder
Return to previously viewed location		Click the **Back to** button ← or **Forward** button →		

Using and disabling Quick Access view

When you first open File Explorer, you see a list of frequently-used folders and recently used files, called Quick access view. Quick Access view can save you time by giving you one-click access to files and folders you use a lot. If you want File Explorer to open instead to This PC, you can disable Quick Access View. To do this, open a File Explorer window, click the View tab, click the Options button on the right side of the Ribbon, then click Change folder and search options. On the General tab of the Folder Options dialog box, click the Open File Explorer to list arrow, click This PC, then click OK.

Change File and Folder Views

Learning Outcomes
• View files as large icons
• Sort files
• Preview files

As you view your folders and files, you can customize your **view**, which is a set of appearance choices for files and folders. Changing your view does not affect the content of your files or folders, only the way they appear. You can choose from eight different **layouts** to display your folders and files as different sized icons, or as a list. You can change the order in which the folders and files appear, and you can also show a preview of a file in the window. **CASE** ▸ *You experiment with different views of your folders and files.*

STEPS

QUICK TIP
To expand your view of a location in the Navigation pane, click the Expand button ▸ next to that location.

1. **In the File Explorer window's Navigation pane, click** Local Disk (C:); **in the File list double-click** Users, **then double-click the** folder **with your user name**

   You opened your user name folder, which is inside the Users folder.

2. **Click the** View tab **on the Ribbon if necessary, then if you don't see eight icons in the Layout list, click the** More button ▼ **in the Layout group**

   The list of available layouts appears, as shown in FIGURE 2-8.

3. **Click** Extra large icons **in the Layout list**

   In this view, the folder items appear as very large icons in the File list. This layout is especially helpful for image files, because you can see what the pictures are without opening each one.

QUICK TIP
You can scroll up and down in the Layout group to see views that are not currently visible.

4. **On the View tab, in the Layout list, point to the other layouts while watching the appearance of the File list, then click** Details

   In Details view, shown in FIGURE 2-9, you can see each item's name, the date it was modified, and its file type. It shows the size of any files in the current folder, but it does not show sizes for folders.

5. **Click the** Sort by button **in the Current view group**

   The Sort by menu lets you **sort**, or reorder, your files and folders according to several criteria.

6. **Click** Descending **if it is not already selected with a check mark**

   Now the folders are sorted in reverse alphabetical order.

QUICK TIP
Clicking Quick Access in the Navigation pane displays folders you use frequently; to add a folder or location to Quick Access, display it in the File list, then drag it to the Quick Access list.

7. **Click** Removable Disk (H:) **(or the location where you store your Data Files) in the Navigation pane, then click** Company Overview.rtf **in the File list**

8. **Click the** Preview pane button **in the Panes group on the View tab if necessary**

   A preview of the selected Company Overview.rtf file you created earlier appears in the Preview pane on the right side of the screen. The WordPad file is not open, but you can still see the file's contents. See FIGURE 2-10.

9. **Click the** Preview pane button **again to close the pane, then click the window's Close button** ☒

Using the Windows Action Center

The Windows Action Center lets you quickly view system notifications and selected computer settings. To open the Action Center, click the Notifications button on the right side of the taskbar. The Action Center pane opens on the right side of the screen. Any new notifications appear in the upper part of the pane, including messages about apps, Windows tips, and any reminders you may have set. In the lower part of the pane, you see Quick Action buttons, shown in FIGURE 2-11, for some commonly-used Windows settings. For example, click Note to open the OneNote app; click the Brightness button repeatedly to cycle though four brightness settings; click the Airplane mode button to place your computer in airplane mode,

which turns off your computer's wireless transmission; click Quiet hours to silence your computer's notification sounds. Clicking the All settings button opens the Settings windows, where you can access all Windows settings categories. Note that the buttons available will vary depending on your hardware and software configuration.

FIGURE 2-11: Quick Action buttons

FIGURE 2-8: Layout options for viewing folders and files

FIGURE 2-9: Your user name folder contents in Details view

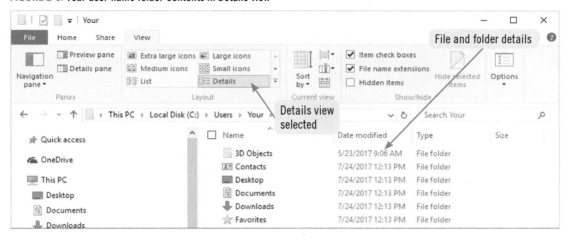

FIGURE 2-10: Preview of selected Company Overview.rtf file

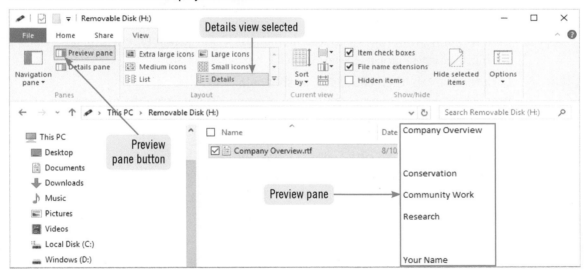

Customizing Details view

When you use File Explorer to view your computer contents in Details view, you see a list of the files and folders in that location. At the top of the list you see each item's Name, Size, Type, and Date Modified. If the list of file and folder details doesn't show what you need, you can customize it. To change a column's location, drag a column heading to move it quickly to a new position. To change the order of, or **sort**, your files and folders, click any column header to sort the list by that detail; click it a second time

to reverse the order. To show only a selected group of, or **filter**, files, click the ☑ icon to the right of the Name, Size, Type, or Date Modified, column headers, and select the check boxes for the type of items you want to include. To change the kind of details you see, right-click or tap-hold a column heading in Details view, then click or tap the detail you want to show or hide. To see more details or to change the list order, right-click or tap-hold a column title, then click or tap More.

Open, Edit, and Save Files

Learning
Outcomes
• Open a file
• Edit a file
• Save a file

Once you have created a file and saved it with a name to a storage location, you can easily open it and **edit** (make changes to) it. For example, you might want to add or delete text or add a picture. Then you save the file again so the file contains your latest changes. Usually you save a file with the same filename and in the same location as the original, which replaces the existing file with the most up-to-date version. To save a file you have changed, you use the Save command. **CASE** *You need to complete the company overview list, so you need to open the new Company Overview file you created earlier.*

STEPS

QUICK TIP

When you double-click a file in a File Explorer window, the program currently associated with that file type opens the file; to change the program, right-click a file, click Open with, click Choose another app, click the program name, select the Always use this app to open [file type] files check box, then click OK.

1. **Click the Start button, begin typing wordpad, then click the WordPad program if it is not selected or, if it is, simply press [Enter]**
   The WordPad program opens on the desktop.

2. **Click the File tab, then click Open**
   The Open dialog box opens. It contains a Navigation pane and a File list like the Save As dialog box and the File Explorer window.

3. **Scroll down in the Navigation pane if necessary until you see This PC and the list of computer locations, then click Removable Disk (H:) (or the location where you store your Data Files)**
   The contents of your USB flash drive (or the file storage location you chose) appear in the File list, as shown in **FIGURE 2-12**.

QUICK TIP

You can also double-click a file in the File list to open it.

4. **Click Company Overview.rtf in the File list, then click Open**
   The document you created earlier opens.

5. **Click to the right of the "h" in Research, press [Enter], then type Outreach**
   The edited document includes the text you just typed. See **FIGURE 2-13**.

QUICK TIP

To save changes to a file, you can also click the Save button 🖫 on the Quick Access toolbar (on the left side of the title bar).

6. **Click the File tab, then click Save, as shown in FIGURE 2-14**
   WordPad saves the document with your most recent changes, using the filename and location you specified when you previously saved it. When you save changes to an existing file, the Save As dialog box does not open.

7. **Click the File tab, then click Exit**
   The Company Overview document and the WordPad program close.

Comparing Save and Save As

Many apps, including Wordpad, include two save command options—Save and Save As. The first time you save a file, the Save As dialog box opens (whether you choose Save or Save As). Here you can select the drive and folder where you want to save the file and enter its filename. If you edit a previously saved file, you can save the file to the same location with the same filename using the Save command. The Save command updates the stored file using the same location and filename without opening the Save As dialog box. In some situations, you might want to save a copy of the existing document using a different filename or in a different storage location. To do this, open the document, click the Save As command on the File tab, navigate to the location where you want to save the copy if necessary, and/or edit the name of the file.

FIGURE 2-12: **Navigating in the Open dialog box**

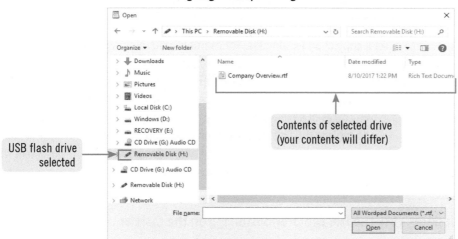

USB flash drive selected

Contents of selected drive (your contents will differ)

FIGURE 2-13: **Edited document**

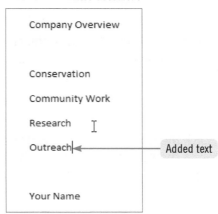

Added text

FIGURE 2-14: **Saving the updated document**

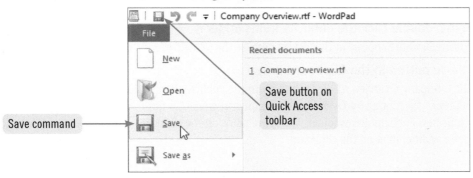

Save command

Save button on Quick Access toolbar

Using Microsoft OneDrive

Microsoft OneDrive is a location on the World Wide Web where you can store your files. Because OneDrive is an online location instead of a disk or USB device, it's often called a **cloud storage location**. When you store your files on OneDrive, you can access them from different devices, including laptops, tablets, and smartphones. Any changes you make to a file stored "in the cloud" are automatically made on OneDrive; this is known as **file syncing**. For example, if you make changes to a file from your laptop, and then open it on your tablet, you will see the changes. You can share OneDrive folders with others so they can view or edit files using a web browser such as Microsoft Edge or Internet Explorer. You can even have multiple users edit a document simultaneously. In Windows 10, OneDrive appears as a storage location in the navigation bar in File Explorer, and in the Open and Save As dialog boxes in Windows apps, so you can easily open, modify, and save files stored there. You can also download the free OneDrive Windows app from the Windows Store to help manage your OneDrive files from all your devices.

Copy Files

Learning Outcomes
• Create a new folder
• Copy and paste a file

Sometimes you need to make a copy of an existing file. For example, you might want to put a copy on a USB flash drive so you can open the file on another machine or share it with a friend or colleague. Or you might want to create a copy as a **backup**, or replacement, in case something happens to your original file. You can copy files and folders using the Copy command and then place the copy in another location using the Paste command. You cannot have two copies of a file with the same name in the same folder. If you try to do this, Windows asks you if you want to replace the first one, and then gives you a chance to give the second copy a different name. **CASE** *You want to create a backup copy of the Company Overview document that you can store in a folder for company publicity items. First you need to create the folder, then you can copy the file.*

STEPS

1. **On the desktop, click the** File Explorer button 📁 **on the taskbar**

2. **In the Navigation pane, click** Removable Disk (H:) **(or the location where you store your Data Files)**
   First you create the new folder you plan to use for storing publicity-related files.

QUICK TIP
You can also create a new folder by clicking the New folder button on the Quick Access toolbar (on the left side of the title bar).

3. **In the New group on the Home tab, click the** New folder button
   A new folder appears in the File list, with its default name, New folder, selected.

4. **Type** Publicity Items, **then press** [Enter]
   Because the folder name was selected, the text you typed, Publicity Items, replaced it. Pressing [Enter] confirmed your entry, and the folder is now named Publicity Items.

QUICK TIP
You can also copy a file by right-clicking the file in the File list and then clicking Copy, or you can use the keyboard by pressing and holding [Ctrl], pressing [C], then releasing both keys.

5. **In the File list, click the** Company Overview.rtf **document you saved earlier, then click the** Copy button **in the Clipboard group, as shown in** FIGURE 2-15
   After you select the file, its check box becomes selected (the check box appears only if the Item check boxes option in the Show/Hide group on the View tab is selected). When you use the Copy command, Windows places a duplicate copy of the file in an area of your computer's random access memory called the **clipboard**, ready to paste, or place, in a new location. Copying and pasting a file leaves the file in its original location.

6. **In the File list, double-click the** Publicity Items folder
   The folder opens. Nothing appears in the File list because the folder currently is empty.

QUICK TIP
To paste using the keyboard, press and hold [Ctrl] and press [V], then release both keys.

7. **Click the** Paste button **in the Clipboard group**
   A copy of the Company Overview.rtf file is pasted into the Publicity Items folder. See FIGURE 2-16. You now have two copies of the Company Overview.rtf file: one on your USB flash drive in the main folder, and another in your new Publicity Items folder. The file remains on the clipboard until you end your Windows session or place another item on the clipboard.

Copying files using Send to

You can also copy and paste a file using the Send to command. In File Explorer, right-click the file you want to copy, point to Send to, then in the shortcut menu, click the name of the device you want to send a copy of the file to. This leaves the original file on your hard drive and creates a copy in that location. You can send a file to a compressed file, the desktop, your Documents folder, a mail recipient, or a drive on your computer. See TABLE 2-2.

FIGURE 2-15: Copying a file

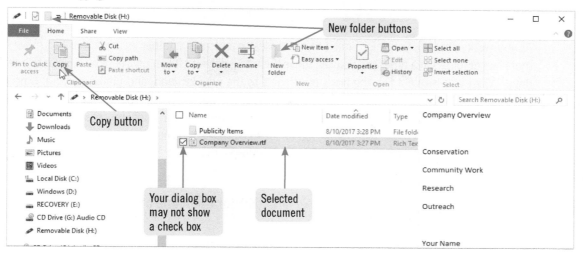

FIGURE 2-16: Duplicate file pasted into Publicity items folder

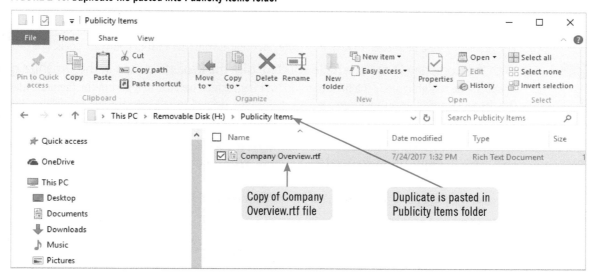

TABLE 2-2: Selected Send to menu commands

menu option	use to
Compressed (zipped) folder	Create a new, compressed (smaller) file with a .zip file extension
Desktop (create shortcut)	Create a shortcut (link) for the file on the desktop
Documents	Copy the file to the Documents library
Fax recipient	Send a file to a fax recipient
Mail recipient	Create an e-mail with the file attached to it (only if you have an e-mail program on your computer)
DVD RW Drive (D:)	Copy the file to your computer's DVD drive (your drive letter may differ)
CD Drive (G:) audio CD	Copy the file to your computer's CD drive (your drive letter may differ)
Removable Disk (H:)	Copy the file to a removable disk drive (your drive letter may differ)

Move and Rename Files

Learning Outcomes
• Cut and paste a file
• Rename a file

As you work with files, you might need to move files or folders to another location. You can move one or more files or folders at a time, and you can move them to a different folder on the same drive or to a different drive. When you **move** a file, the file is transferred to the new location, and unlike copying, it no longer exists in its original location. You can move a file using the Cut and Paste commands. Before or after you move a file, you might find that you want to change its name. You can easily rename it to make the name more descriptive or accurate. **CASE** *You decide to move your original Company Overview.rtf document to your Documents folder. After you move it, you edit the filename so it better describes the file contents.*

STEPS

1. **In the Address bar, click** Removable Disk (H:) **(or the name of the location where you store your Data Files) if necessary**

2. **Click the** Company Overview.rtf **document to select it**

3. **Click the** Cut button **in the Clipboard group on the Ribbon, as shown in** FIGURE 2-17

4. **In the Navigation Pane, under This PC, click** Documents
   You navigated to your Documents folder.

5. **Click the** Paste button **in the Clipboard group**
   The Company Overview.rtf document appears in your Documents folder and remains selected. See FIGURE 2-18. The filename could be clearer, to help you remember that it contains a list of company goals.

6. **With the Company Overview.rtf file selected, click the** Rename button **in the Organize group**
   The filename is highlighted. The file extension isn't highlighted because that part of the filename identifies the file to WordPad and should not be changed. If you deleted or changed the file extension, WordPad would be unable to open the file. You decide to change the word "Overview" to "Goals."

7. **Move the** I **pointer after the "w" in "Overview", click to place the insertion point, press** [Backspace] **eight times to delete** Overview, **type** Goals **as shown in** FIGURE 2-19, **then press** [Enter]
   You changed the name of the pasted file in the Documents folder. The filename now reads Company Goals.rtf.

8. **Close the File Explorer window**

Using Task View to create multiple desktops

As you have learned in Module 1, you can have multiple app windows open on your desktop, such as WordPad, Paint, and OneNote. But you might need to have a different set of apps available for a different project. Instead of closing all the apps and opening different ones, you can use Task View to work with multiple desktops, each containing its own set of apps. Then, when you need to work on another project, you can switch to another desktop to quickly access those apps. To open Task View, click the **Task View** button ⬓ on the taskbar. The current desktop becomes smaller and a New desktop button appears in the lower-right corner of the screen. Click the New desktop button. A new desktop appears in a bar at the bottom of the screen, which you can click to activate and work with its

apps. See FIGURE 2-20. To switch to another desktop, click the Task View button and click its icon.

FIGURE 2-20: **Working with multiple desktops in Task view**

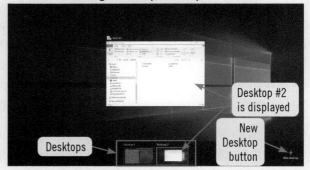

Desktops

Desktop #2 is displayed

New Desktop button

FIGURE 2-17: Cutting a file

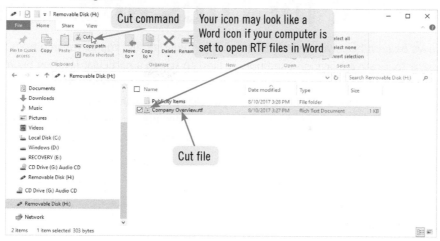

FIGURE 2-18: Pasted file in Documents folder

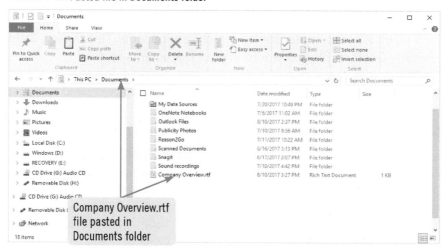

FIGURE 2-19: Renaming a file

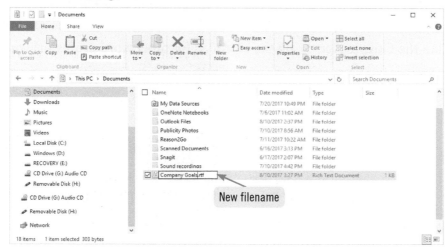

Search for Files and Folders

Learning
Outcomes
• Search for a file
• Open a found file

Windows Search helps you quickly find any app, folder, or file. You can search from the Search box on the taskbar to locate applications, settings, or files. To search a particular location on your computer, you can use the Search box in File Explorer. You enter search text by typing one or more letter sequences or words that help Windows identify the item you want. The search text you type is called your **search criteria**. Your search criteria can be a folder name, a filename, or part of a filename. **CASE** *You want to locate the Company Overview.rtf document so you can print it for a colleague.*

STEPS

1. **Click in the search box on the taskbar**
   The Cortana menu opens.

2. **Type company**
   The Search menu opens with a possible match for your search at the top, and some other possible matches below it. You may see results from The Windows Store, the Internet, or your computer settings.

3. **Click My stuff, near the bottom of the menu**
   This limits your search to the files and folders in your storage locations on this device. It includes documents with the text "company" in the title or in the document text.

QUICK TIP
If you navigate to a specific folder in your file hierarchy, Windows searches that folder and any subfolders below it.

4. **Scroll down if necessary to display search results under This Device, including the Company Goals.rtf file you stored in your Documents folder**
   See FIGURE 2-21. It does not find the Company Overview.rtf file stored on your Flash drive because it's searching only the items on this device. To open the found file, you could click its listing. You can also search using File Explorer.

5. **Click the File Explorer button 📁 on the taskbar, then click This PC in the Navigation pane**

QUICK TIP
Windows search is not case-sensitive, so you can type upper- or lowercase letters, and obtain the same results.

6. **Click in the Search This PC box to the right of the Address bar, type company, then press [Enter]**
   Windows searches your computer for files that contain the word "company" in their title. A green bar in the Address bar indicates the progress of your search. After a few moments, the search results, shown in FIGURE 2-22, appear. Windows found the renamed file, Company Goals.rtf, in your Documents folder, and the original Company Overview.rtf document on your removable drive, in the Publicity Items folder. It may also locate shortcuts to the file in your Recent folder. It's good to verify the location of the found files, so you can select the right one.

7. **Click the View tab, click Details in the Layout group then look in the Folder column to view the path to each file, dragging the edge of the Folder column header with the ↔ pointer to widen it if necessary**

TROUBLE
If you see a message asking how you want to open the file, click WordPad.

8. **Double-click the Company Overview.rtf document in your file storage location**
   The file opens in WordPad or in another word-processing program on your computer that reads RTF files.

9. **Click the Close button ✕ on the WordPad (or other word-processor) window**

Using the Search Tools tab in File Explorer

The **Search Tools tab** appears in the Ribbon as soon as you click the Search text box, and it lets you narrow your search criteria. Use the commands in the Location group to specify a particular search location. The Refine group lets you limit the search to files modified after a certain date, or to files of a particular kind, size, type, or other property. The Options group lets you repeat previous searches, save searches, and open the folder containing a found file.

FIGURE 2-21: Found file

FIGURE 2-22: Apps screen and Search pane

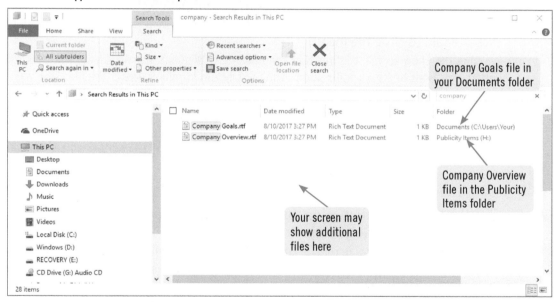

Using Microsoft Edge

When you search for files using the search box on the Windows taskbar and click Web, the new web browser called **Microsoft Edge** opens. You can also open Edge by clicking its icon  on the taskbar. Created to replace the older Internet Explorer browser, Edge is a Windows app that runs on personal computers, tablets, and smartphones. Edge features a reading mode that lets you read a webpage without ads. It also lets you annotate pages with markup tools such as a pen or highlighter, and add typed notes, as shown in **FIGURE 2-23**. You can also add pages to a Reading list or share them with OneNote or a social networking site.

FIGURE 2-23: Web page annotated in Microsoft Edge

Delete and Restore Files

Learning Outcomes
- Delete a file
- Restore a file
- Empty the Recycle Bin

If you no longer need a folder or file, you can delete (or remove) it from the storage device. By regularly deleting files and folders you no longer need and emptying the Recycle Bin, you free up valuable storage space on your computer. Windows places folders and files you delete from your hard drive in the Recycle Bin. If you delete a folder, Windows removes the folder as well as all files and subfolders stored in it. If you later discover that you need a deleted file or folder, you can restore it to its original location, as long as you have not yet emptied the Recycle Bin. Emptying the Recycle Bin permanently removes deleted folders and files from your computer. However, files and folders you delete from a removable drive, such as a USB flash drive, do not go to the Recycle Bin. They are immediately and permanently deleted and cannot be restored. **CASE** *You decide to delete the Company Goals document that you stored in your Documents folder.*

STEPS

1. **Click the Documents folder in the File Explorer Navigation pane**
   Your Documents folder opens.

2. **Click Company Goals.rtf to select it, click the Home tab, then click the Delete list arrow ⊠ in the Organize group; if the Show recycle confirmation command does not have a check mark next to it, click Show recycle confirmation (or if it does have a check mark, click ⊠ again to close the menu)**
   Selecting the Show recycle confirmation command tells Windows that whenever you click the Delete button, you want to see a confirmation dialog box before Windows deletes the file. That way you can change your mind if you want, before deleting the file.

3. **Click the Delete button ⊠ in the Organize group**
   The Delete File dialog box opens so you can confirm the deletion, as shown in FIGURE 2-24.

4. **Click Yes**
   You deleted the file. Because the file was stored on your computer and not on a removable drive, it was moved to the Recycle Bin.

5. **Click the Minimize button ⎯ on the window's title bar, examine the Recycle Bin icon, then double-click the Recycle Bin icon on the desktop**
   The Recycle Bin icon appears to contain crumpled paper, indicating that it contains deleted folders and/or files. The Recycle Bin window displays any previously deleted folders and files, including the Company Goals.rtf file.

6. **Click the Company Goals.rtf file to select it, then click the Restore the selected items button in the Restore group on the Recycle Bin Tools Manage tab, as shown in FIGURE 2-25**
   The file returns to its original location and no longer appears in the Recycle Bin window.

7. **In the Navigation pane, click the Documents folder**
   The Documents folder window contains the restored file. You decide to permanently delete this file after all.

8. **Click the file Company Goals.rtf, click ⊠ in the Organize group on the Home tab, click Permanently delete, then click Yes in the Delete File dialog box**

9. **Minimize the window, double-click the Recycle Bin, notice that the Company Goals.rtf file is no longer there, then close all open windows**

FIGURE 2-24: **Delete File dialog box**

FIGURE 2-25: **Restoring a file from the Recycle Bin**

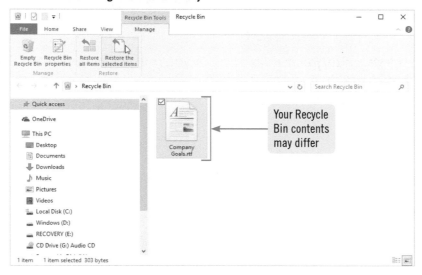

More techniques for selecting and moving files

To select a group of items that are next to each other in a window, click the first item in the group, press and hold [Shift], then click the last item in the group. Both items you click and all the items between them become selected. To select files that are not next to each other, click the first file, press and hold [Ctrl], then click the other items you want to select as a group. Then you can copy, cut, or delete the group of files or folders you selected. **Drag and drop** is a technique in which you use your pointing device to drag a file or folder into a different folder and then drop it, or let go of the mouse button, to place it in that folder. Using drag and drop does not copy your file to the clipboard. If you drag and drop a file to a folder on a different drive, Windows *copies* the file. However, if you drag and drop a file to a folder on the same drive, Windows *moves* the file into that folder

instead. See FIGURE 2-26. If you want to move a file to another drive, hold down [Shift] while you drag and drop. If you want to copy a file to another folder on the same drive, hold down [Ctrl] while you drag and drop.

FIGURE 2-26: **Moving a file using drag and drop**

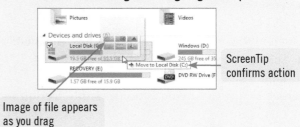

ScreenTip confirms action

Image of file appears as you drag

Practice

Concepts Review

Label the elements of the Windows 10 window shown in FIGURE 2-27.

FIGURE 2-27

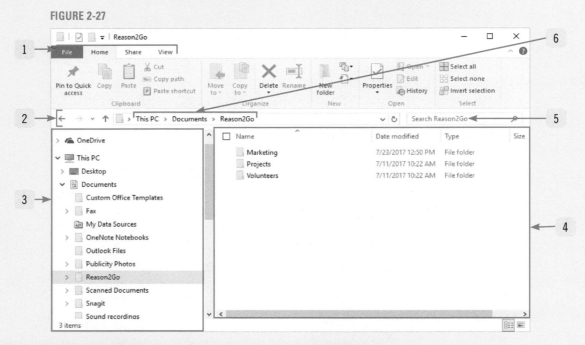

Match each term with the statement that best describes it.

7. View e
8. File extension d
9. Address bar c
10. Path a
11. Clipboard f
12. Snap Assist b

a. A series of locations separated by small triangles or backslashes that describes a file's location in the file hierarchy
b. A feature that helps you arrange windows on the screen
c. An area above the Files list that contains a path
d. A three- or four-letter sequence, preceded by a period, that identifies the type of file
e. A set of appearance choices for files and folders
f. An area of a computer's RAM used for temporary storage

Select the best answer from the list of choices.

13. Which part of a window lets you see a file's contents without opening the file?
   a. File list
   b. Address bar
   c. Navigation pane
   d. Preview pane

14. The new Microsoft web browser is called Microsoft _____.
   a. View
   b. Task
   c. Edge
   d. Desktop

15. The text you type in a Search text box is called:
   a. Sorting.
   b. RAM.
   c. Search criteria.
   d. Clipboard.

16. Which of the following is not a visible section in a File Explorer window?
   a. Clipboard
   b. Navigation pane
   c. File list
   d. Address bar

Skills Review

1. Understand files and folders.

a. Create a file hierarchy for an ice cream manufacturing business, using a name that you create. The business has departments for Product Development, Manufacturing, and Personnel. Product development activities include research and testing; manufacturing has facilities for ice cream and frozen yogurt; and Personnel handles hiring and payroll. How would you organize your folders and files using a file hierarchy of three levels? How would you use folders and subfolders to keep the documents related to these activities distinct and easy to navigate? Draw a diagram and write a short paragraph explaining your answer.

b. Use tools in the File Explorer window to create the folder hierarchy in the Documents folder on your computer.

c. Open NotePad and write the path of the Hiring folder, using backslashes to indicate levels in the hierarchy. Do the same for the Testing folder.

2. Create and save a file.

a. Connect your USB flash drive to a USB port on your computer, then open WordPad from the Start menu.

b. Type **Advertising Campaign** as the title, then start a new line.

c. Type your name, press [Enter] twice, then create the following list:

Menu ads

Email customers

Web page specials

Local TV spots

d. Save the WordPad file with the filename **Advertising Campaign.rtf** in the location where you store your Data Files, view the filename in the WordPad title bar, then close WordPad.

3. Explore the files and folders on your computer.

a. Open a File Explorer window.

b. Use the Navigation pane to navigate to your USB flash drive or the location where you store your Data Files.

c. Use the Address bar to navigate to This PC.

d. Use the File list to navigate to your local hard drive (C:).

e. Use the File list to open the Users folder, and then open the folder that represents your user name.

f. Open the Documents folder. (*Hint*: The path is This PC\Local Disk (C:) \Users\Your User Name\Documents.)

g. Use the Navigation pane to navigate back to This PC.

4. Change file and folder views.

a. Navigate to your Documents folder or the location of your Data Files using the method of your choice.

b. Use the View tab to view its contents as large icons.

c. View the folder's contents in the seven other views.

d. Sort the items in this location by date modified in ascending order.

e. Open the Preview pane, view a selected item's preview, then close the Preview pane.

5. Open, edit, and save files.

a. Start WordPad, then use the Open dialog box to open the Advertising Campaign.rtf document you created.

b. After the text "Local TV spots," add a line with the text **Social media**.

c. Save the document and close WordPad.

6. Copy files.

a. In the File Explorer window, navigate to the location where you store your Data Files if necessary.

b. Copy the Advertising Campaign.rtf document.

c. Create a new folder named **Advertising** on your USB flash drive or the location where you store your Data Files (*Hint*: Use the Home tab), then open the folder.

d. Paste the document copy in the new folder.

7. Move and rename files.

a. Navigate to your USB flash drive or the location where you store your Data Files.

b. Select the Advertising Campaign.rtf document located there, then cut it.

Skills Review (continued)

    c. Navigate to your Documents folder, then paste the file there.

    d. Rename the file **Advertising Campaign - Backup.rtf**.

8. Search for files and folders.

    a. Use the search box on the taskbar to search for a file using the search text **backup**. (*Hint*: Remember to select My stuff.)

    b. If necessary, scroll to the found file, and notice its path.

    c. Open the Advertising Campaign - Backup document from the search results, then close WordPad. (*Hint*: Closing the program automatically closes any open documents.)

    d. Open a File Explorer window, click in the search box, search your USB flash drive using the search text **overview**.

    e. Open the found document from the File list, then close WordPad.

9. Delete and restore files.

    a. Navigate to your Documents folder.

    b. Verify that your Delete preference is Show recycle confirmation, then delete the Advertising Campaign - Backup.rtf file.

    c. Open the Recycle Bin, and restore the document to its original location.

    d. Navigate to your Documents folder, then move the Advertising Campaign - Backup.rtf file to the Advertising folder on your USB flash drive (or the location where you store your Data Files).

Independent Challenge 1

To meet the needs of gardeners in your town, you have opened a vacation garden care business named GreenerInc. Customers hire you to care for their gardens when they go on vacation. To promote your new business, your website designer asks you to give her selling points to include in a web ad.

    a. Connect your USB flash drive to your computer, if necessary.

    b. Create a new folder named **GreenerInc** on your USB flash drive or the location where you store your Data Files.

    c. In the GreenerInc folder, create two subfolders named **Handouts** and **Website**.

    d. Use WordPad to create a short paragraph or list that describes three advantages of your business. Use **GreenerInc Selling Points** as the first line, followed by the paragraph or list. Include your name and email address after the text.

    e. Save the WordPad document with the filename **Selling Points.rtf** in the Website folder, then close the document and exit WordPad.

    f. Open a File Explorer window, then navigate to the Website folder.

    g. View the contents in at least three different views, then choose the view option that you prefer.

    h. Copy the Selling Points.rtf file, then paste a copy in the Documents folder.

    i. Rename the copied file **Selling Points Backup.rtf**.

    j. Cut the Selling Points Backup.rtf file from the Documents folder, and paste it in the GreenerInc\Website folder in the location where you store your Data Files, then close the File Explorer window.

Independent Challenge 2

As a freelance webpage designer for nonprofit businesses, you depend on your computer to meet critical deadlines. Whenever you encounter a computer problem, you contact a computer consultant who helps you resolve the problem. This consultant has asked you to document, or keep records of, your computer's available drives.

    a. Connect your USB flash drive to your computer, if necessary.

    b. Open File Explorer and go to This PC so you can view information on your drives and other installed hardware.

    c. View the window contents using three different views, then choose the one you prefer.

    d. Open WordPad and create a document with the text **My Drives** and your name on separate lines. Save the document as **My Drives.rtf**.

Independent Challenge 2 (continued)

e. Use Snap Assist to view the WordPad and File Explorer windows next to each other on the screen. (*Hint*: Drag the title bar of one of the windows to the left side of the screen.)

f. In WordPad, list the names of the hard drive (or drives), devices with removable storage, and any other hardware devices installed on the computer as shown in the Devices and Drives section of the window.

g. Switch to a view that displays the total size and amount of free space on your hard drive(s) and removable storage drive(s), and edit each WordPad list item to include the amount of free space for each one (for example, 22.1 GB free of 95.5 GB).

h. Save the WordPad document with the filename **My Drives** on your USB flash drive or the location where you store your Data Files.

i. Close WordPad, then maximize the File Explorer window. Navigate to your file storage location, then preview your document in the Preview pane, and close the window.

Independent Challenge 3

You are an attorney at Garcia and Chu, a large accounting firm. You participate in the company's community outreach program by speaking at career days in area schools. You teach students about career opportunities available in the field of accounting. You want to create a folder structure to store the files for each session.

a. Connect your USB flash drive to your computer (if necessary), then open the window for your USB flash drive or the location where you store your Data Files.

b. Create a folder named **Career Days**.

c. In the Career Days folder, create a subfolder named **Valley Intermediate**. Open this folder, then close it.

d. Use WordPad to create a document with the title **Accounting Jobs** at the top of the page and your name on separate lines, and the following list of items:
Current Opportunities:
Bookkeeper
Accounting Clerk
Accountant
Certified Public Accountant (CPA)

e. Save the WordPad document with the filename **Accounting Jobs.rtf** in the Valley Intermediate folder. (*Hint*: After you switch to your USB flash drive in the Save As dialog box, open the Career Days folder, then open the Valley Intermediate folder before saving the file.) Close WordPad.

f. Open WordPad and the Accounting Jobs document again, add **Senior Accountant** after Accountant, then save the file and close WordPad.

g. Store a copy of the file using the Save As command to your Documents folder, renaming it **Accounting Jobs - Copy.rtf**, then close WordPad.

h. In File Explorer, delete the document copy in your Documents folder so it is placed in the Recycle Bin, then restore it.

i. Open the Recycle Bin window, snap the File Explorer to the left side of the screen and the Recycle in to the right side, then verify that the file has been restored to the correct location.

j. Cut the file from the Documents folder and paste it in the Career Days\Valley Intermediate folder in your Data File storage location, then close all windows.

Independent Challenge 4: Explore

Think of a hobby or volunteer activity that you do now, or one that you would like to start. You will use your computer to help you manage your plans or ideas for this activity.

a. Using paper and pencil, sketch a folder structure with at least two subfolders to contain your documents for this activity.

b. Connect your USB flash drive to your computer, then open the window for your USB flash drive.

Independent Challenge 4: Explore (continued)

c. In File Explorer, create the folder structure for your activity, using your sketch as a reference.

d. Think of at least three tasks that you can do to further your work in your chosen activity.

e. Start a new WordPad document. Add the title **Next Steps** at the top of the page and your name on the next line.

f. Below your name, list the three tasks. Save the file in one of the folders created on your USB flash drive, with the title **To Do.rtf**.

g. Close WordPad, then open a File Explorer window and navigate to the folder where you stored the document.

h. Create a copy of the file, place the copied file in your Documents folder, then rename this file with a name you choose.

i. Delete the copied file from your Documents folder, restore it, then cut and paste the file into the folder that contains your To Do.rtf file, ensuring that the filename of the copy is different so it doesn't overwirte the To Do.rtf file.

j. Open Microsoft Edge using its button on the taskbar, click in the search text box, then search for information about others doing your desired hobby or volunteer activity.

k. Click the Make a Web Note button at the top of the window, click the Highlighter tool, then highlight an item that interests you.

l. Click the Share button, click Mail, choose your desired email account, then send the annotated page to yourself. You will receive an email with an attachment showing the annotated page.

m. Close Edge, your email program, and any open windows.

Visual Workshop

Create the folder structure shown in FIGURE 2-28 on your USB flash drive (or in the location where you store your Data Files). Create a WordPad document containing your name and today's date, type the path to the Midsize folder, and save it with the filename **Midsize.rtf** in a Midsize folder on your USB Flash drive or the location where you store your Data Files.

FIGURE 2-28

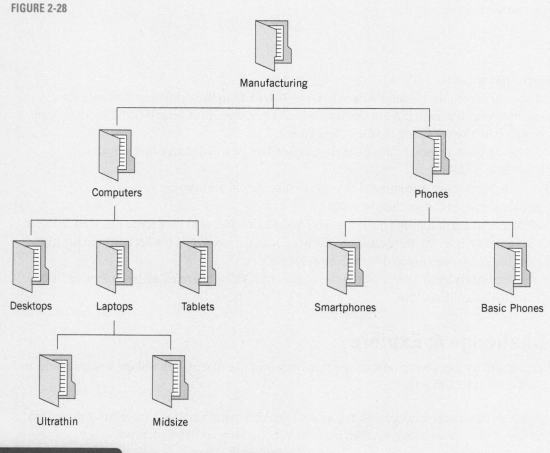

Understanding File Management

Getting Started with Microsoft Office 2016

CASE This module introduces you to the most frequently used programs in Office, as well as common features they all share.

Module Objectives

After completing this module, you will be able to:

- Understand the Office 2016 suite
- Start an Office app
- Identify Office 2016 screen elements
- Create and save a file

- Open a file and save it with a new name
- View and print your work
- Get Help, close a file, and exit an app

Files You Will Need

OF 1-1.xlsx

Understand the Office 2016 Suite

Learning Outcomes
- Identify Office suite components
- Describe the features of each app

Microsoft Office 2016 is a group of programs—which are also called applications or apps—designed to help you create documents, collaborate with coworkers, and track and analyze information. You use different Office programs to accomplish specific tasks, such as writing a letter or producing a presentation, yet all the programs have a similar look and feel. Microsoft Office 2016 apps feature a common, context-sensitive user interface, so you can get up to speed faster and use advanced features with greater ease. The Office apps are bundled together in a group called a **suite**. The Office suite is available in several configurations, but all include Word, Excel, PowerPoint, and OneNote. Some configurations include Access, Outlook, Publisher, Skype, and OneDrive. **CASE** *As part of your job, you need to understand how each Office app is best used to complete specific tasks.*

DETAILS

The Office apps covered in this book include:

- **Microsoft Word 2016**

  When you need to create any kind of text-based document, such as a memo, newsletter, or multipage report, Word is the program to use. You can easily make your documents look great by using formatting tools and inserting eye-catching graphics. The Word document shown in FIGURE 1-1 contains a company logo and simple formatting.

- **Microsoft Excel 2016**

  Excel is the perfect solution when you need to work with numeric values and make calculations. It puts the power of formulas, functions, charts, and other analytical tools into the hands of every user, so you can analyze sales projections, calculate loan payments, and present your findings in a professional manner. The Excel worksheet shown in FIGURE 1-1 tracks checkbook transactions. Because Excel automatically recalculates results whenever a value changes, the information is always up to date. A chart illustrates how the monthly expenses are broken down.

- **Microsoft PowerPoint 2016**

  Using PowerPoint, it's easy to create powerful presentations complete with graphics, transitions, and even a soundtrack. Using professionally designed themes and clip art, you can quickly and easily create dynamic slide shows such as the one shown in FIGURE 1-1.

- **Microsoft Access 2016**

  Access is a relational database program that helps you keep track of large amounts of quantitative data, such as product inventories or employee records. The form shown in FIGURE 1-1 can be used to generate reports on customer invoices and tours.

Microsoft Office has benefits beyond the power of each program, including:

- **Note-taking made simple; available on all devices**

  Use OneNote to take notes (organized in tabbed pages) on information that can be accessed on your computer, tablet, or phone. Share the editable results with others. Contents can include text, web page clips (using OneNote Clipper), email contents (directly inserted into a default section), photos (using Office Lens), and web pages.

- **Common user interface: Improving business processes**

  Because the Office suite apps have a similar **interface**, your experience using one app's tools makes it easy to learn those in the other apps. Office documents are **compatible** with one another, so you can easily **integrate**, or combine, elements—for example, you can add an Excel chart to a PowerPoint slide, or an Access table to a Word document.

  Most Office programs include the capability to incorporate feedback—called **online collaboration**—across the Internet or a company network.

FIGURE 1-1: Microsoft Office 2016 documents

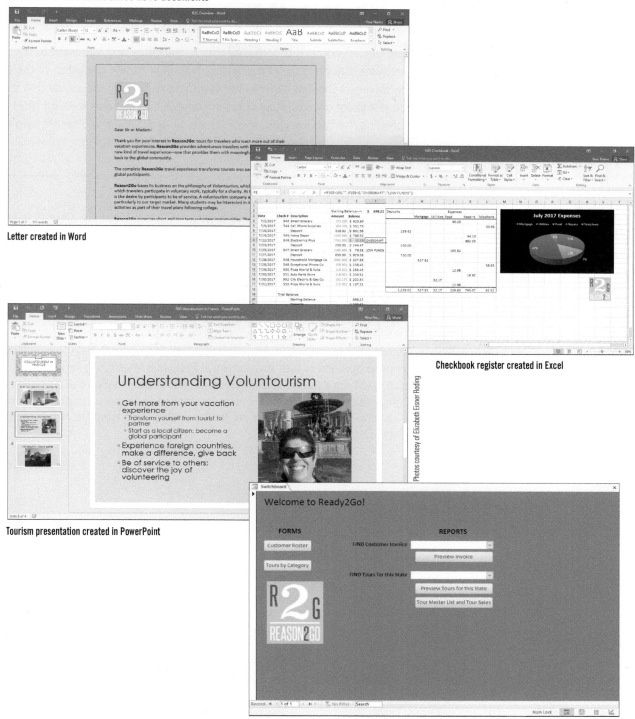

Letter created in Word

Checkbook register created in Excel

Tourism presentation created in PowerPoint

Form created in Access

Photos courtesy of Elizabeth Eisner Reding

What is Office 365?

Until recently, most consumers purchased Microsoft Office in a traditional way: by buying a retail package from a store or downloading it from Microsoft.com. You can still purchase Microsoft Office 2016 in this traditional way—but you can also now purchase it as a subscription service called Microsoft Office 365, which is available in a wide variety of configurations.

Depending on which configuration you purchase, you will always have access to the most up-to-date versions of the apps in your package and, in many cases, can install these apps on multiple computers, tablets, and phones. And if you change computers or devices, you can easily uninstall the apps from an old device and install them on a new one.

Start an Office App

Learning
Outcomes
• Start an Office app
• Explain the purpose
of a template
• Start a new blank
document

To get started using Microsoft Office, you need to start, or **launch**, the Office app you want to use. An easy way to start the app you want is to press the Windows key, type the first few characters of the app name you want to search for, then click the app name In the Best match list. You will discover that there are many ways to accomplish just about any Windows task; for example, you can also see a list of all the apps on your computer by pressing the Windows key, then clicking All Apps. When you see the app you want, click its name. **CASE** ▶ *You decide to familiarize yourself with Office by starting Microsoft Word.*

STEPS

1. **Click the Start button ⊞ on the Windows taskbar**

   The Start menu opens, listing the most used apps on your computer. You can locate the app you want to open by clicking the app name if you see it, or you can type the app name to search for it.

2. **Type word**

   Your screen now displays "Word 2016" under "Best match", along with any other app that has "word" as part of its name (such as WordPad). See FIGURE 1-2.

3. **Click Word 2016**

   Word 2016 launches, and the Word **start screen** appears, as shown in FIGURE 1-3. The start screen is a landing page that appears when you first start an Office app. The left side of this screen displays recent files you have opened. (If you have never opened any files, then there will be no files listed under Recent.) The right side displays images depicting different templates you can use to create different types of documents. A **template** is a file containing professionally designed content and formatting that you can easily customize for your own needs. You can also start from scratch using the Blank Document template, which contains only minimal formatting settings.

Enabling touch mode

If you are using a touch screen with any of the Office 2016 apps, you can enable the touch mode to give the user interface a more spacious look, making it easier to navigate with your fingertips. Enable touch mode by clicking the Quick Access toolbar list arrow, then clicking Touch/Mouse Mode to select it. Then you'll see the Touch Mode button 👆 in the Quick Access toolbar. Click 👆, and you'll see the interface spread out.

Using shortcut keys to move between Office programs

You can switch between open apps using a keyboard shortcut. The [Alt][Tab] keyboard combination lets you either switch quickly to the next open program or file or choose one from a gallery. To switch immediately to the next open program or file, press [Alt][Tab]. To choose from all open programs and files, press and hold [Alt], then press and release [Tab] without releasing [Alt]. A gallery opens on screen, displaying the filename and a thumbnail image of each open program and file, as well as of the desktop. Each time you press [Tab] while holding [Alt], the selection cycles to the next open file or location. Release [Alt] when the program, file, or location you want to activate is selected.

FIGURE 1-2: Searching for the Word app

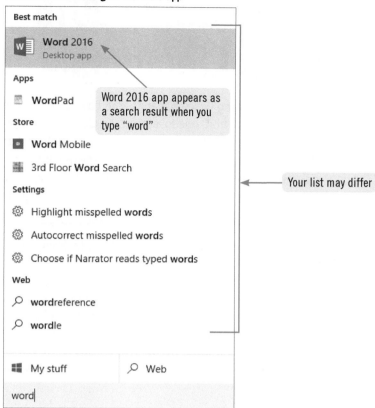

Word 2016 app appears as a search result when you type "word"

Your list may differ

FIGURE 1-3: Word start screen

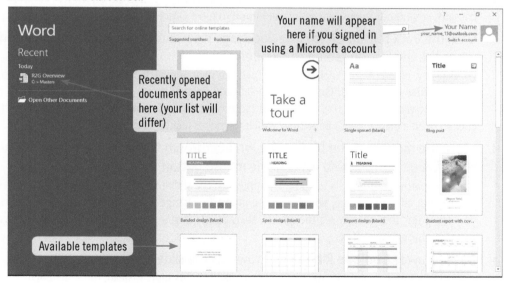

Your name will appear here if you signed in using a Microsoft account

Recently opened documents appear here (your list will differ)

Available templates

Using the Office Clipboard

You can use the Office Clipboard to cut and copy items from one Office program and paste them into others. The Office Clipboard can store a maximum of 24 items. To access it, open the Office Clipboard task pane by clicking the dialog box launcher 🔲 in the Clipboard group on the Home tab. Each time you copy a selection, it is saved in the Office Clipboard. Each entry in the Office Clipboard includes an icon that tells you the program it was created in. To paste an entry, click in the document where you want it to appear, then click the item in the Office Clipboard. To delete an item from the Office Clipboard, right-click the item, then click Delete.

Learning
Outcomes
• Identify basic
  components of
  the user interface
• Display and use
  Backstage view
• Adjust the zoom
  level

Identify Office 2016 Screen Elements

One of the benefits of using Office is that its apps have much in common, making them easy to learn and making it simple to move from one to another. All Office 2016 apps share a similar user interface, so you can use your knowledge of one to get up to speed in another. A **user interface** is a collective term for all the ways you interact with a software program. The user interface in Office 2016 provides intuitive ways to choose commands, work with files, and navigate in the program window. **CASE** ▶ *Familiarize yourself with some of the common interface elements in Office by examining the PowerPoint program window.*

STEPS

1. **Click the Start button ⊞ on the Windows taskbar, type** pow, **click** PowerPoint 2016, **then click** Blank Presentation

   PowerPoint starts and opens a new file, which contains a blank slide. Refer to FIGURE 1-4 to identify common elements of the Office user interface. The **document window** occupies most of the screen. At the top of every Office program window is a **title bar** that displays the document name and program name. Below the title bar is the **Ribbon**, which displays commands you're likely to need for the current task. Commands are organized onto **tabs**. The tab names appear at the top of the Ribbon, and the active tab appears in front. The **Share button** in the upper-right corner lets you invite other users to view your cloud-stored Word, Excel, or Powerpoint file.

QUICK TIP

The Ribbon in every
Office program
includes tabs specific
to the program, but
all Office programs
include a File tab and
Home tab on the left
end of the Ribbon.
Just above the File
tab is the **Quick
Access toolbar**,
which also includes
buttons for common
Office commands.

2. **Click the** File tab

   The File tab opens, displaying **Backstage view**. It is called Backstage view because the commands available here are for working with the files "behind the scenes." The navigation bar on the left side of Backstage view contains commands to perform actions common to most Office programs.

3. **Click the** Back button ⊙ **to close Backstage view and return to the document window, then click the** Design tab **on the Ribbon**

   To display a different tab, click its name. Each tab contains related commands arranged into **groups** to make features easy to find. On the Design tab, the Themes group displays available design themes in a **gallery**, or visual collection of choices you can browse. Many groups contain a **launcher**, which you can click to open a dialog box or pane from which to choose related commands.

4. **Move the mouse pointer ▷ over the** Ion Boardroom theme **in the Themes group as shown in** FIGURE 1-5, **but** *do not click* **the mouse button**

   The Ion Boardroom theme is temporarily applied to the slide in the document window. However, because you did not click the theme, you did not permanently change the slide. With the **Live Preview** feature, you can point to a choice, see the results, then decide if you want to make the change. Live Preview is available throughout Office.

TROUBLE

If you accidentally
click a theme, click
the Undo button on
the Quick Access
toolbar.

5. **Move ▷ away from the Ribbon and towards the slide**

   If you had clicked the Ion theme, it would be applied to this slide. Instead, the slide remains unchanged.

QUICK TIP

You can also use
the Zoom button
in the Zoom group
on the View tab to
enlarge or reduce
a document's
appearance.

6. **Point to the** Zoom slider ─────┃────── + 100% **on the status bar, then drag to the right until the Zoom level reads** 166%

   The slide display is enlarged. Zoom tools are located on the status bar. You can drag the slider or click the Zoom In or Zoom Out buttons to zoom in or out on an area of interest. **Zooming in** (a higher percentage), makes a document appear bigger on screen but less of it fits on the screen at once; **zooming out** (a lower percentage) lets you see more of the document at a reduced size.

7. **Click the** Zoom Out button ⊟ **on the status bar to the left of the Zoom slider until the Zoom level reads** 120%

FIGURE 1-4: PowerPoint program window

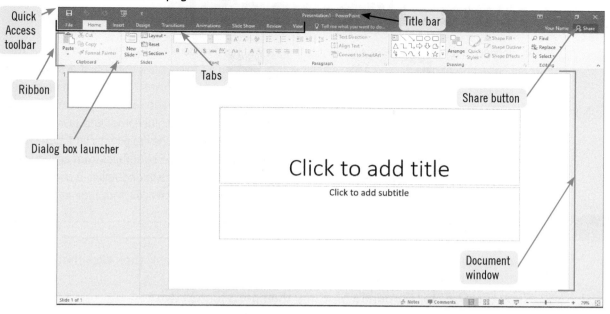

FIGURE 1-5: Viewing a theme with Live Preview

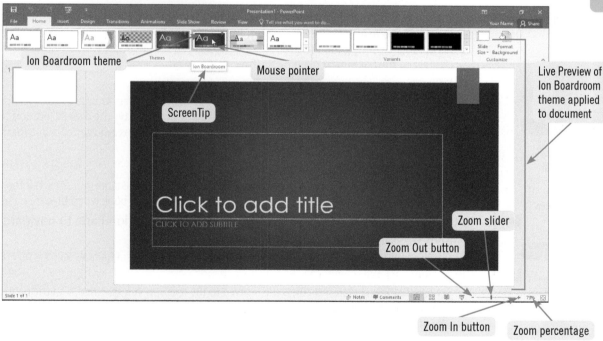

Using Backstage view

Backstage view in each Microsoft Office app offers "one stop shopping" for many commonly performed tasks, such as opening and saving a file, printing and previewing a document, defining document properties, sharing information, and exiting a program. Backstage view opens when you click the File tab in any Office app, and while features such as the Ribbon, Mini toolbar, and Live Preview all help you work *in* your documents, the File tab and Backstage view help you work *with* your documents. You can click commands in the navigation pane to open different places for working with your documents, such as the Open place, the Save place, and so on. You can return to your active document by clicking the Back button.

Office 2016

Create and Save a File

Learning Outcomes
• Create a file
• Save a file
• Explain OneDrive

When working in an Office app, one of the first things you need to do is to create and save a file. A **file** is a stored collection of data. Saving a file enables you to work on a project now, then put it away and work on it again later. In some Office programs, including Word, Excel, and PowerPoint, you can open a new file when you start the app, then all you have to do is enter some data and save it. In Access, you must create a file before you enter any data. You should give your files meaningful names and save them in an appropriate location, such as a folder on your hard drive or OneDrive so they're easy to find. **OneDrive** is a Microsoft cloud storage system that lets you easily save, share, and access your files from anywhere you have Internet access. **CASE** *Use Word to familiarize yourself with creating and saving a document. First you'll type some notes about a possible location for a corporate meeting, then you'll save the information for later use.*

STEPS

1. **Click the** Word button 📄 **on the taskbar, click** Blank document, **then click the** Zoom In button ➕ **until the level is** 120%, **if necessary**

2. **Type** Locations for Corporate Meeting, **then press [Enter] twice**

   The text appears in the document window, and the **insertion point** blinks on a new blank line. The insertion point indicates where the next typed text will appear.

QUICK TIP
A filename can be up to 255 characters, including a file extension, and can include upper- or lowercase characters and spaces, but not ?, ", /, \, <, >, *, |, or :.

3. **Type** Las Vegas, NV, **press [Enter], type** Chicago, IL, **press [Enter], type** Seattle, WA, **press [Enter] twice, then type your name**

4. **Click the** Save button 💾 **on the Quick Access toolbar**

   Because this is the first time you are saving this new file, the Save place in Backstage view opens, showing various options for saving the file. See FIGURE 1-6. Once you save a file for the first time, clicking 💾 saves any changes to the file *without* opening the Save As dialog box.

5. **Click** Browse

   The Save As dialog box opens, as shown in FIGURE 1-7, where you can browse to the location where you want to save the file. The Address bar in the Save As dialog box displays the default location for saving the file, but you can change it to any location. The File name field contains a suggested name for the document based on text in the file, but you can enter a different name.

QUICK TIP
Saving a file to the Desktop creates a desktop icon that you can double-click to both launch a program and open a document.

6. **Type** OF 1-Possible Corporate Meeting Locations

   The text you type replaces the highlighted text. (The "OF 1-" in the filename indicates that the file is created in Office Module 1. You will see similar designations throughout this book when files are named.)

7. **In the Save As dialog box, use the Address bar or Navigation Pane to navigate to the location where you store your Data Files**

   You can store files on your computer, a network drive, your OneDrive, or any acceptable storage device.

QUICK TIP
To create a new blank file when a file is open, click the File tab, click New on the navigation bar, then choose a template.

8. **Click** Save

   The Save As dialog box closes, the new file is saved to the location you specified, and the name of the document appears in the title bar, as shown in FIGURE 1-8. (You may or may not see the file extension ".docx" after the filename.) See TABLE 1-1 for a description of the different types of files you create in Office, and the file extensions associated with each.

TABLE 1-1: Common filenames and default file extensions

file created in	is called a	and has the default extension
Word	document	.docx
Excel	workbook	.xlsx
PowerPoint	presentation	.pptx
Access	database	.accdb

FIGURE 1-6: Save place in Backstage view

Saves to your OneDrive account

Click to display a list of recently accessed locations on this PC

Click to open the Save As dialog box

FIGURE 1-7: Save As dialog box

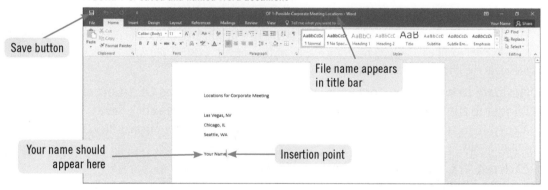

Navigation pane; your links and folders may differ

Address bar; your location may differ

File name field; your computer may not display file extensions

Save as type list

FIGURE 1-8: Saved and named Word document

Save button

File name appears in title bar

Your name should appear here

Insertion point

Saving files to OneDrive

All Office programs include the capability to incorporate feedback—called **online collaboration**—across the Internet or a company network. Using **cloud computing** (work done in a virtual environment), you can store your work in the cloud. Using OneDrive, a file storage service from Microsoft, you and your colleagues can create and store documents in the cloud and make the documents available anywhere there is Internet access to whomever you choose. To use OneDrive, you need a Microsoft Account, which you obtain at onedrive.live.com. Pricing and storage plans vary based on the type of Microsoft account you have. When you are logged into your Microsoft account and you

save a file in any of the Office apps, the first option in the Save As screen is your OneDrive. Double-click your OneDrive option, and the Save As dialog box opens displaying a location in the address bar unique to your OneDrive account. Type a name in the File name text box, then click Save and your file is saved to your OneDrive. To sync your files with OneDrive, you'll need to download and install the OneDrive for Windows app. Then, when you open Explorer, you'll notice a new folder called OneDrive has been added to your folder. In this folder is a sub-folder called Documents. This means if your Internet connection fails, you can work on your files offline.

Open a File and Save It with a New Name

Learning
Outcomes
• Open an existing
  file
• Save a file with a
  new name

In many cases as you work in Office, you need to use an existing file. It might be a file you or a coworker created earlier as a work in progress, or it could be a complete document that you want to use as the basis for another. For example, you might want to create a budget for this year using the budget you created last year; instead of typing in all the categories and information from scratch, you could open last year's budget, save it with a new name, and just make changes to update it for the current year. By opening the existing file and saving it with the Save As command, you create a duplicate that you can modify to suit your needs, while the original file remains intact. **CASE** ▶ *Use Excel to open an existing workbook file, and save it with a new name so the original remains unchanged.*

STEPS

1. **Click the** Start button ⊞ **on the Windows taskbar, type** exc, **click** Excel 2016, **click** Open Other Workbooks, This PC, **then click** Browse

    The Open dialog box opens, where you can navigate to any drive or folder accessible to your computer to locate a file.

2. **In the Open dialog box, navigate to the location where you store your Data Files**

    The files available in the current folder are listed, as shown in FIGURE 1-9. This folder displays one file.

3. **Click** OF 1-1.xlsx, **then click** Open

    The dialog box closes, and the file opens in Excel. An Excel file is an electronic spreadsheet, so the new file displays a grid of rows and columns you can use to enter and organize data.

4. **Click the** File tab, **click** Save As **on the navigation bar, then click** Browse

    The Save As dialog box opens, and the current filename is highlighted in the File name text box. Using the Save As command enables you to create a copy of the current, existing file with a new name. This action preserves the original file and creates a new file that you can modify.

5. **Navigate to where you store your Data Files if necessary, type** OF 1-Corporate Meeting Budget **in the File name text box, as shown in** FIGURE 1-10, **then click** Save

    A copy of the existing workbook is created with the new name. The original file, OF 1-1.xlsx, closes automatically.

6. **Click cell** A18, **type your name, then press [Enter], as shown in** FIGURE 1-11

    In Excel, you enter data in cells, which are formed by the intersection of a row and a column. Cell A18 is at the intersection of column A and row 18. When you press [Enter], the cell pointer moves to cell A19.

7. **Click the** Save button 🖫 **on the Quick Access toolbar**

    Your name appears in the workbook, and your changes to the file are saved.

Exploring File Open options

You might have noticed that the Open button in the Open dialog box includes a list arrow to the right of the button. In a dialog box, if a button includes a list arrow you can click the button to invoke the command, or you can click the list arrow to see a list of related commands that you can apply to the currently selected file. The Open list arrow includes several related commands, including Open Read-Only and Open as Copy.

Clicking Open Read-Only opens a file that you can only save with a new name; you cannot make changes to the original file. Clicking Open as Copy creates and opens a copy of the selected file and inserts the word "Copy" in the file's title. Like the Save As command, these commands provide additional ways to use copies of existing files while ensuring that original files do not get changed by mistake.

FIGURE 1-9: **Open dialog box**

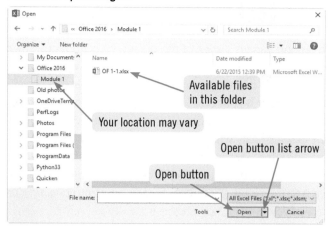

FIGURE 1-10: **Save As dialog box**

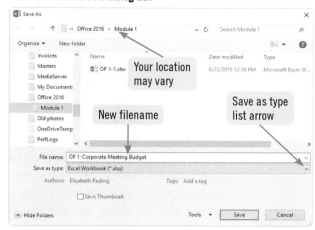

FIGURE 1-11: **Your name added to the workbook**

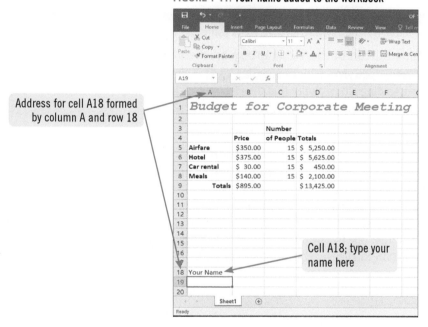

Working in Compatibility Mode

Not everyone upgrades to the newest version of Office. As a general rule, new software versions are **backward compatible**, meaning that documents saved by an older version can be read by newer software. To open documents created in older Office versions, Office 2016 includes a feature called Compatibility Mode. When you use Office 2016 to open a file created in an earlier version of Office, "Compatibility Mode" appears in the title bar, letting you know the file was created in an earlier but usable version of the program. If you are working with someone who may not be using the newest version of the software, you can avoid possible incompatibility problems by saving your file in another, earlier format. To do this in an Office program, click the File tab, click Save As on the navigation bar, then click Browse. In the Save As dialog box, click the Save as type list arrow in the Save As dialog box, then click an option in the list. For example, if you're working in Excel, click Excel 97-2003 Workbook format in the Save as type list to save an Excel file so it can be opened in Excel 97 or Excel 2003.

View and Print Your Work

Learning
Outcomes
• Describe and
  change views in
  an app
• Print a document

Each Microsoft Office program lets you switch among various **views** of the document window to show more or fewer details or a different combination of elements that make it easier to complete certain tasks, such as formatting or reading text. Changing your view of a document does not affect the file in any way, it affects only the way it looks on screen. If your computer is connected to a printer or a print server, you can easily print any Office document using the Print button in the Print place in Backstage view. Printing can be as simple as **previewing** the document to see exactly what the printed version will look like and then clicking the Print button. Or, you can customize the print job by printing only selected pages. You can also use the Share place in Backstage view or the Share button on the Ribbon (if available) to share a document, export to a different format, or save it to the cloud. **CASE** ▶ *Experiment with changing your view of a Word document, and then preview and print your work.*

STEPS

1. **Click the** Word program button ⬚ **on the taskbar**

   Word becomes active, and the program window fills the screen.

2. **Click the** View tab **on the Ribbon**

   In most Office programs, the View tab on the Ribbon includes groups and commands for changing your view of the current document. You can also change views using the View buttons on the status bar.

3. **Click the** Read Mode button **in the Views group on the View tab**

   The view changes to Read Mode view, as shown in FIGURE 1-12. This view shows the document in an easy-to-read, distraction-free reading mode. Notice that the Ribbon is no longer visible on screen.

4. **Click the** Print Layout button ⬚ **on the Status bar**

   You return to Print Layout view, the default view in Word.

5. **Click the** File tab, **then click** Print **on the navigation bar**

   The Print place opens. The preview pane on the right displays a preview of how your document will look when printed. Compare your screen to FIGURE 1-13. Options in the Settings section enable you to change margins, orientation, and related options before printing. To change a setting, click it, and then click a new setting. For instance, to change from Letter paper size to Legal, click Letter in the Settings section, then click Legal on the menu that opens. The document preview updates as you change the settings. You also can use the Settings section to change which pages to print. If your computer is connected to multiple printers, you can click the current printer in the Printer section, then click the one you want to use. The Print section contains the Print button and also enables you to select the number of copies of the document to print.

6. **If your school allows printing, click the** Print button **in the Print place (otherwise, click the** Back button ⬅ **)**

   If you chose to print, a copy of the document prints, and Backstage view closes.

QUICK TIP
To minimize the display of the buttons and commands on tabs, click the Collapse the Ribbon button ⌃ on the lower-right end of the Ribbon.

QUICK TIP
Office 2016 apps default to print to OneDrive.

QUICK TIP
You can add the Quick Print button ⬚ to the Quick Access toolbar by clicking the Customize Quick Access Toolbar button, then clicking Quick Print. The Quick Print button prints one copy of your document using the default settings.

Customizing the Quick Access toolbar

You can customize the Quick Access toolbar to display your favorite commands. To do so, click the Customize Quick Access Toolbar button ⬚ in the title bar, then click the command you want to add. If you don't see the command in the list, click More Commands to open the Quick Access Toolbar tab of the current program's Options dialog box. In the Options dialog box, use the Choose commands from list to choose a category, click the desired command in the list on the left, click Add to add it to the Quick Access toolbar, then click OK. To remove a button from the toolbar, click the name in the list on the right in the Options dialog box, then click Remove. To add a command to the Quick Access toolbar as you work, simply right-click the button on the Ribbon, then click Add to Quick Access Toolbar on the shortcut menu. To move the Quick Access toolbar below the Ribbon, click the Customize Quick Access Toolbar button, and then click Show Below the Ribbon.

FIGURE 1-12: Read Mode view

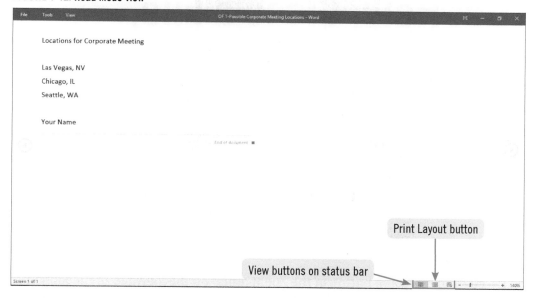

FIGURE 1-13: Print settings on the File tab

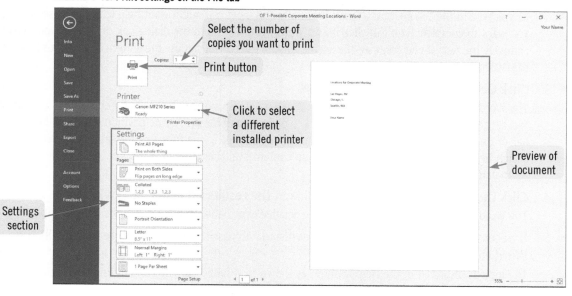

Creating a screen capture

A **screen capture** is a digital image of your screen, as if you took a picture of it with a camera. For instance, you might want to take a screen capture if an error message occurs and you want a Technical Support person to see exactly what's on the screen. You can create a screen capture using the Snipping Tool, an accessory designed to capture whole screens or portions of screens. To open the Snipping Tool, click the Start button on the Windows taskbar, type "sni", then click the Snipping Tool when it appears in the left panel. On the Snipping Tool toolbar, click New, then drag the pointer on the screen to select the area of the screen you want to capture. When you release the mouse button, the screen capture opens in the Snipping Tool window, and you can save, copy, or send it in an email. In Word, Excel, and PowerPoint 2016, you can capture screens or portions of screens and insert them in the current document using the Screenshot button in the Illustrations group on the Insert tab. Alternatively, you can create a screen capture by pressing [PrtScn]. (Keyboards differ, but you may find the [PrtScn] button in or near your keyboard's function keys.) Pressing this key places a digital image of your screen in the Windows temporary storage area known as the **Clipboard**. Open the document where you want the screen capture to appear, click the Home tab on the Ribbon (if necessary), then click the Paste button in the Clipboard group on the Home tab. The screen capture is pasted into the document.

Learning
Outcomes
• Display a
  ScreenTip
• Use Help
• Close a file
• Exit an app

Get Help, Close a File, and Exit an App

You can get comprehensive help at any time by pressing [F1] in an Office app or clicking the Help button on the title bar. You can also get help in the form of a ScreenTip by pointing to almost any icon in the program window. When you're finished working in an Office document, you have a few choices for ending your work session. You close a file by clicking the File tab, then clicking Close; you exit a program by clicking the Close button on the title bar. Closing a file leaves a program running, while exiting a program closes all the open files in that program as well as the program itself. In all cases, Office reminds you if you try to close a file or exit a program and your document contains unsaved changes. **CASE** ▶ *Explore the Help system in Microsoft Office, and then close your documents and exit any open programs.*

STEPS

1. **Point to the Zoom button in the Zoom group on the View tab of the Ribbon**

   A ScreenTip appears that describes how the Zoom button works and explains where to find other zoom controls.

   QUICK TIP
   You can also open Help (in any of the Office apps) by pressing [F1].

2. **Click the Tell me box above the Ribbon, then type Choose a template**

   As you type in the Tell me box, a Smart list anticipates what you might want help with. If you see the task you want to complete, you can click it and Word will take you to the dialog box or options you need to complete the task. If you don't see the answer to your query, you can use the bottom two options to search the database.

   QUICK TIP
   If you are not connected to the Internet, the Help window displays on the Help content available on your computer.

3. **Click Get Help on "choose a template"**

   The Word Help window opens, as shown in **FIGURE 1-14**, displaying help results for choosing a template in Word. Each entry is a hyperlink you can click to open a list of topics. The Help window also includes a toolbar of useful Help commands such as printing and increasing the font size for easier readability, and a Search field. Office.com supplements the help content available on your computer with a wide variety of up-to-date topics, templates, and training.

4. **Click the Where do I find templates link in the results list Word Help window**

   The Word Help window changes, and a more detailed explanation appears below the topic.

   QUICK TIP
   You can print the entire current topic by clicking the Print button 🖶 on the Help toolbar, then clicking Print in the Print dialog box.

5. **If necessary, scroll down until the Download Microsoft Office templates topic fills the Word Help window**

   The topic is displayed in the Help window, as shown in **FIGURE 1-15**. The content in the window explains that you can create a wide variety of documents using a template (a pre-formatted document) and that you can get many templates free of charge.

6. **Click the Keep Help on Top button 📌 in the lower-right corner of the window**

   The Pin Help button rotates so the pin point is pointed towards the bottom of the screen: this allows you to read the Help window while you work on your document.

7. **Click the Word document window, notice the Help window remains visible**

8. **Click a blank area of the Help window, click 📌 to Unpin Help, click the Close button ☒ in the Help window, then click the Close button ☒ in the Word program window**

   Word closes, and the Excel program window is active.

9. **Click the Close button ☒ in the Excel program window, click the PowerPoint app button 📱 on the taskbar if necessary, then click the Close button ☒ to exit PowerPoint**

   Excel and PowerPoint both close.

FIGURE 1-14: **Word Help window**

FIGURE 1-14: **Word Help window**

FIGURE 1-15: **Create a document Help topic**

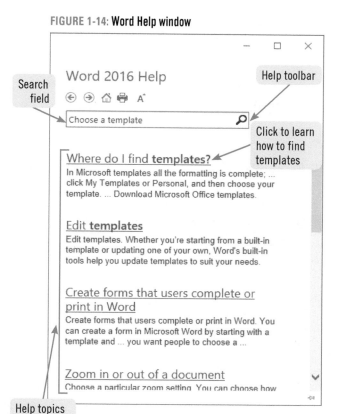

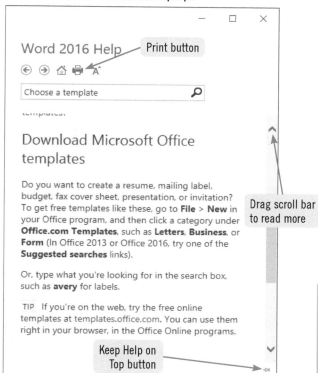

Using sharing features and co-authoring capabilities

If you are using Word, Excel, or PowerPoint, you can take advantage of the Share feature, which makes it easy to share your files that have been saved to OneDrive. When you click the Share button, you will be asked to invite others to share the file. To do this, type in the name or email addresses in the Invite people text box. When you invite others, you have the opportunity to give them different levels of permission. You might want some people to have read-only privileges; you might want others to be able to make edits. Also available in Word, Excel, and PowerPoint is real-time co-authoring capabilities for files stored on OneDrive. Once a file on OneDrive is opened and all the users have been given editing privileges, all the users can make edits simultaneously. On first use, each user will be prompted to automatically share their changes.

Recovering a document

Each Office program has a built-in recovery feature that allows you to open and save files that were open at the time of an interruption such as a power failure. When you restart the program(s) after an interruption, the Document Recovery task pane opens on the left side of your screen displaying both original and recovered versions of the files that were open. If you're not sure which file to open (original or recovered), it's usually better to open the recovered file because it will contain the latest information. You can, however, open and review all versions of the file that were recovered and save the best one. Each file listed in the Document Recovery task pane displays a list arrow with options that allow you to open the file, save it as is, delete it, or show repairs made to it during recovery.

Office 2016

Practice

Concepts Review

Label the elements of the program window shown in FIGURE 1-16.

FIGURE 1-16

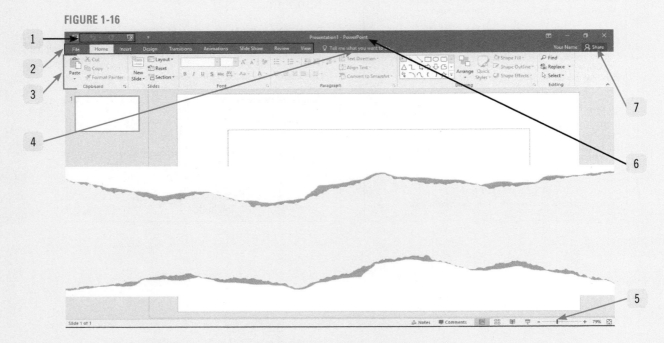

Match each project with the program for which it is best suited.

8. Microsoft PowerPoint
9. Microsoft Word
10. Microsoft Excel
11. Microsoft Access

a. Corporate convention budget with expense projections
b. Presentation for city council meeting
c. Business cover letter for a job application
d. Department store inventory

Independent Challenge 1

You just accepted an administrative position with a local independently owned insurance agent who has recently invested in computers and is now considering purchasing a subscription to Office 365. You have been asked to think of uses for the apps and you put your ideas in a Word document.

    a. Start Word, create a new Blank document, then save the document as **OF 1-Microsoft Office Apps Uses** in the location where you store your Data Files.

    b. Change the zoom factor to 120%, type **Microsoft Access**, press [Enter] twice, type **Microsoft Excel**, press [Enter] twice, type **Microsoft PowerPoint**, press [Enter] twice, type **Microsoft Word**, press [Enter] twice, then type your name.

    c. Click the line beneath each program name, type at least two tasks you can perform using that program (each separated by a comma), then press [Enter].

    d. Save the document, then submit your work to your instructor as directed.

    e. Exit Word.

Creating Documents with Word 2016

CASE ▷ You have been hired to work at the Riverwalk Medical Clinic, a large outpatient medical facility staffed by family physicians, specialists, nurses, and other allied health professionals. Shortly after reporting to your new position, the office manager, Tony Sanchez, R.N., asks you to use Word to create a memo to the clinic staff and a letter to the director of the clinic.

Module Objectives

After completing this module, you will be able to:

- Understand word processing software
- Explore the Word window
- Start a document
- Save a document
- Select text
- Format text using the Mini toolbar and the Ribbon
- Use a document template
- Navigate a document

Files You Will Need

WMP 1-1.docx

Word 2016
Module 1

Learning Outcomes
• Identify the features of Word
• State the benefits of using a word processing program

Understand Word Processing Software

A **word processing program** is a software program that includes tools for entering, editing, and formatting text and graphics. Microsoft Word is a powerful word processing program that allows you to create and enhance a wide range of documents quickly and easily. FIGURE 1-1 shows the first page of a report created using Word and illustrates some of the Word features you can use to enhance your documents. The electronic files you create using Word are called **documents**. One of the benefits of using Word is that document files can be stored on a hard disk, flash drive, or other physical storage device, or to OneDrive or another Cloud storage place, making them easy to transport, share, and revise. **CASE** *Before beginning your memo to the clinic staff, you explore the editing and formatting features available in Word.*

You can use Word to accomplish the following tasks:

*   **Type and edit text**
    The Word editing tools make it simple to insert and delete text in a document. You can add text to the middle of an existing paragraph, replace text with other text, undo an editing change, and correct typing, spelling, and grammatical errors with ease.

*   **Copy and move text from one location to another**
    Using the more advanced editing features of Word, you can copy or move text from one location and insert it in a different location in a document. You also can copy and move text between documents. This means you don't have to retype text that is already entered in a document.

*   **Format text and paragraphs with fonts, colors, and other elements**
    The sophisticated formatting tools in Word allow you to make the text in your documents come alive. You can change the size, style, and color of text, add lines and shading to paragraphs, and enhance lists with bullets and numbers. Creatively formatting text helps to highlight important ideas in your documents.

*   **Format and design pages**
    The page-formatting features in Word give you power to design attractive newsletters, create powerful résumés, and produce documents such as research papers, business cards, brochures, and reports. You can change paper size, organize text in columns, and control the layout of text and graphics on each page of a document. For quick results, Word includes preformatted cover pages, pull quotes, and headers and footers, as well as galleries of coordinated text, table, and graphic styles. If you are writing a research paper, Word makes it easy to manage reference sources and create footnotes, endnotes, and bibliographies.

*   **Enhance documents with tables, charts, graphics, screenshots, and videos**
    Using the powerful graphics tools in Word, you can spice up your documents with pictures, videos, photographs, screenshots, lines, preset quick shapes, and diagrams. You also can illustrate your documents with tables and charts to help convey your message in a visually interesting way.

*   **Use Mail Merge to create form letters and mailing labels**
    The Word Mail Merge feature allows you to send personalized form letters to many different people. You can also use Mail Merge to create mailing labels, directories, e-mail messages, and other types of documents.

*   **Share documents securely**
    The security features in Word make it quick and easy to remove comments, tracked changes, and unwanted personal information from your files before you share them with others. You can also add a password or a digital signature to a document and convert a file to a format suitable for publishing on the web.

FIGURE 1-1: A report created using Word

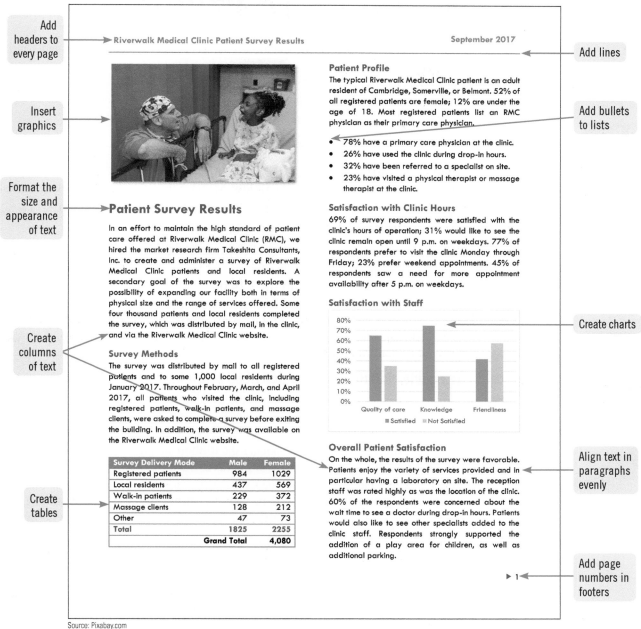

Add headers to every page

Insert graphics

Format the size and appearance of text

Create columns of text

Create tables

Add lines

Add bullets to lists

Create charts

Align text in paragraphs evenly

Add page numbers in footers

Source: Pixabay.com

The content of the report reads as follows:

Riverwalk Medical Clinic Patient Survey Results   September 2017

Patient Profile

The typical Riverwalk Medical Clinic patient is an adult resident of Cambridge, Somerville, or Belmont. 52% of all registered patients are female; 12% are under the age of 18. Most registered patients list an RMC physician as their primary care physician.

- 78% have a primary care physician at the clinic.
- 26% have used the clinic during drop-in hours.
- 32% have been referred to a specialist on site.
- 23% have visited a physical therapist or massage therapist at the clinic.

Satisfaction with Clinic Hours

69% of survey respondents were satisfied with the clinic's hours of operation; 31% would like to see the clinic remain open until 9 p.m. on weekdays. 77% of respondents prefer to visit the clinic Monday through Friday; 23% prefer weekend appointments. 45% of respondents saw a need for more appointment availability after 5 p.m. on weekdays.

Satisfaction with Staff

Overall Patient Satisfaction

On the whole, the results of the survey were favorable. Patients enjoy the variety of services provided and in particular having a laboratory on site. The reception staff was rated highly as was the location of the clinic. 60% of the respondents were concerned about the wait time to see a doctor during drop-in hours. Patients would also like to see other specialists added to the clinic staff. Respondents strongly supported the addition of a play area for children, as well as additional parking.

Patient Survey Results

In an effort to maintain the high standard of patient care offered at Riverwalk Medical Clinic (RMC), we hired the market research firm Takeshita Consultants, Inc. to create and administer a survey of Riverwalk Medical Clinic patients and local residents. A secondary goal of the survey was to explore the possibility of expanding our facility both in terms of physical size and the range of services offered. Some four thousand patients and local residents completed the survey, which was distributed by mail, in the clinic, and via the Riverwalk Medical Clinic website.

Survey Methods

The survey was distributed by mail to all registered patients and to some 1,000 local residents during January 2017. Throughout February, March, and April 2017, all patients who visited the clinic, including registered patients, walk-in patients, and massage clients, were asked to complete a survey before exiting the building. In addition, the survey was available on the Riverwalk Medical Clinic website.

Survey Delivery Mode	Male	Female
Registered patients	984	1029
Local residents	437	569
Walk-in patients	229	372
Massage clients	128	212
Other	47	73
Total	1825	2255
	Grand Total	4,080

► 1

Word 2016

Planning a document

Before you create a new document, it's a good idea to spend time planning it. Identify the message you want to convey, the audience for your document, and the elements, such as tables or charts, you want to include. You should also think about the tone and look of your document—are you writing a business letter, which should be written in a pleasant, but serious, tone and have a formal appearance, or are you creating a flyer that must be colorful, eye-catching, and fun to read? The purpose and audience for your document determine the appropriate design. Planning the layout and design of a document involves deciding how to organize the text, selecting the fonts to use, identifying the graphics to include, and selecting the formatting elements that will enhance the message and appeal of the document. For longer documents, such as newsletters, it can be useful to sketch the layout and design of each page before you begin.

Explore the Word Window

When you start Word, the Word start screen opens. It includes a list of recently opened documents and a gallery of templates for creating a new document. **CASE** ▶ *You open a blank document and examine the elements of the Word program window.*

STEPS

1. **Start** Word, **then click** Blank document

   A blank document opens in the **Word program window**, as shown in FIGURE 1-2. The blinking vertical line in the document window is the **insertion point**. It indicates where text appears as you type.

2. **Move the mouse pointer around the Word program window**

   The mouse pointer changes shape depending on where it is in the Word program window. You use pointers to move the insertion point or to select text to edit. TABLE 1-1 describes common pointers in Word.

3. **Place the mouse pointer over a button on the Ribbon**

   When you place the mouse pointer over a button or some other elements of the Word program window, a ScreenTip appears. A **ScreenTip** is a label that identifies the name of the button or feature, briefly describes its function, conveys any keyboard shortcut for the command, and includes a link to associated help topics, if any.

DETAILS

Using FIGURE 1-2 as a guide, find the elements described below in your program window:

• The **title bar** displays the name of the document and the name of the program. Until you give a new document a different name, its temporary name is Document1. The left side of the title bar contains the **Quick Access toolbar**, which includes buttons for saving a document and for undoing, redoing, and repeating a change. The right side of the title bar contains the **Ribbon Display Options button**, which you use to hide or show the Ribbon and tabs, the resizing buttons, and the program Close button.

• The **File tab** provides access to **Backstage view** where you manage files and the information about them. Backstage view includes commands related to working with documents, such as opening, printing, and saving a document. The File tab also provides access to your account and to the Word Options dialog box, which is used to customize the way you use Word.

• The **Ribbon** contains the Word tabs. Each **tab** on the Ribbon includes buttons for commands related to editing and formatting documents. The commands are organized in **groups**. For example, the Home tab includes the Clipboard, Font, Paragraph, Styles, and Editing groups. The Ribbon also includes the **Tell Me box**, which you can use to find a command or access the Word Help system, and the **Share button**, which you can use to save a document to the Cloud.

• The **document window** displays the current document. You enter text and format your document in the document window.

• The rulers appear in the document window in Print Layout view. The **horizontal ruler** displays left and right document margins as well as the tab settings and paragraph indents, if any, for the paragraph in which the insertion point is located. The **vertical ruler** displays the top and bottom document margins.

• The **vertical** and **horizontal scroll bars** are used to display different parts of the document in the document window. The scroll bars include **scroll boxes** and **scroll arrows**, which you use to scroll.

• The **status bar** displays the page number of the current page, the total number of pages and words in the document, and the status of spelling and grammar checking. It also includes the view buttons, the Zoom slider, and the Zoom level button. You can customize the status bar to display other information.

• The **view buttons** on the status bar allow you to display the document in Read Mode, Print Layout, or Web Layout view. The **Zoom slider** and the **Zoom level button** provide quick ways to enlarge and decrease the size of the document in the document window, making it easy to zoom in on a detail of a document or to view the layout of the document as a whole.

FIGURE 1-2: **Elements of the Word program window**

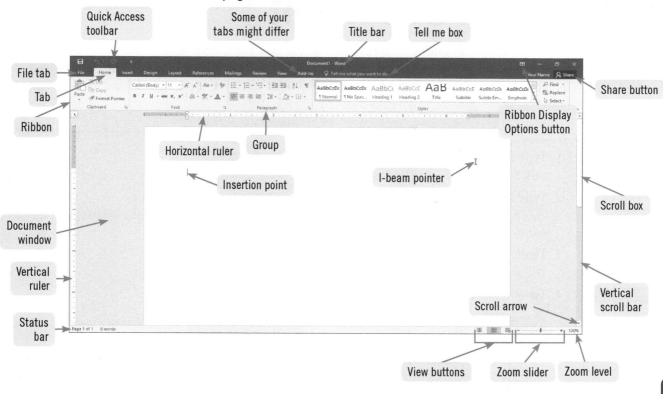

TABLE 1-1: **Common mouse pointers in Word**

name	pointer	use to
I-beam pointer	I	Move the insertion point in a document or to select text
Click and Type pointers, including left-align and center-align	$\mathrm{I}^{\equiv}\underline{\mathrm{I}}$	Move the insertion point to a blank area of a document in Print Layout or Web Layout view; double-clicking with a Click and Type pointer automatically applies the paragraph formatting (alignment and indentation) required to position text or a graphic at that location in the document
Selection pointer	⌖	Click a button or other element of the Word program window; appears when you point to elements of the Word program window
Right-pointing arrow pointer	⇗	Select a line or lines of text; appears when you point to the left edge of a line of text in the document window
Hand pointer	👆	Open a hyperlink; appears when you point to a hyperlink in a task pane or when you press [Ctrl] and point to a hyperlink in a document
Hide white space pointer	⊟	Hide the white space in the top and bottom margins of a document in Print Layout view
Show white space pointer	⊤	Show the white space in the top and bottom margins of a document in Print Layout view

Word 2016

Start a Document

You begin a new document by simply typing text in a blank document in the document window. Word uses **word wrap**, a feature that automatically moves the insertion point to the next line of the document as you type. You only press [Enter] when you want to start a new paragraph or insert a blank line. **CASE** ▶ *You type a quick memo to the clinic staff.*

STEPS

1. **Type** Riverwalk Medical Clinic, **then press** [Enter] **twice**
   Each time you press [Enter] the insertion point moves to the start of the next line.

2. **Type** TO:, **then press** [Tab] **twice**
   Pressing [Tab] moves the insertion point several spaces to the right. You can use the [Tab] key to align the text in a memo header or to indent the first line of a paragraph.

3. **Type** All employees, **then press** [Enter]
   The insertion point moves to the start of the next line.

4. **Type:** FROM: [Tab] [Tab] Tony Sanchez [Enter]
   DATE: [Tab] [Tab] March 13, 2017 [Enter]
   RE: [Tab] [Tab] Staff Meeting [Enter] [Enter]
   Red or blue wavy lines may appear under the words you typed, indicating a possible spelling or grammar error. Spelling and grammar checking is one of the many automatic features you will encounter as you type. TABLE 1-2 describes several of these automatic features. You can correct any typing errors you make later.

5. **Type** The next clinic staff meeting will be held on the 17th of March at 2 p.m. in the conference room on the ground floor., **then press** [Spacebar]
   As you type, notice that the insertion point moves automatically to the next line of the document. You also might notice that Word automatically changed "17th" to "17th" in the memo. This feature is called **AutoCorrect**. AutoCorrect automatically makes typographical adjustments and detects and adjusts typing errors, certain misspelled words (such as "taht" for "that"), and incorrect capitalization as you type.

6. **Type** Heading the agenda will be discussion of our annual Cambridgeport community health fair, the Clinic's biggest health and wellness outreach event. The fair is scheduled for September 2017.
   When you type the first few characters of "September," the Word AutoComplete feature displays the complete word in a ScreenTip. **AutoComplete** suggests text to insert quickly into your documents. You can ignore AutoComplete for now. Your memo should resemble FIGURE 1-3.

7. **Press** [Enter], **then type** The event will include free screenings and adult immunizations. A preliminary draft of the program for the health fair is attached. Bring your creative ideas to the meeting.
   When you press [Enter] and type the new paragraph, notice that Word adds more space between the paragraphs than it does between the lines in each paragraph. This is part of the default style for paragraphs in Word, called the **Normal style**.

8. **Position the** I **pointer after** biggest (but before the space) in the second sentence of the first paragraph, then click to move the insertion point after "biggest"

9. **Press** [Backspace] **seven times, then type** most well-attended
   Pressing [Backspace] removes the character before the insertion point.

10. **Move the insertion point before** clinic **in the first sentence, then press** [Delete] **seven times to remove the word "clinic" and the space after it**
    Pressing [Delete] removes the character after the insertion point. FIGURE 1-4 shows the revised memo.

FIGURE 1-3: **Memo text in the document window**

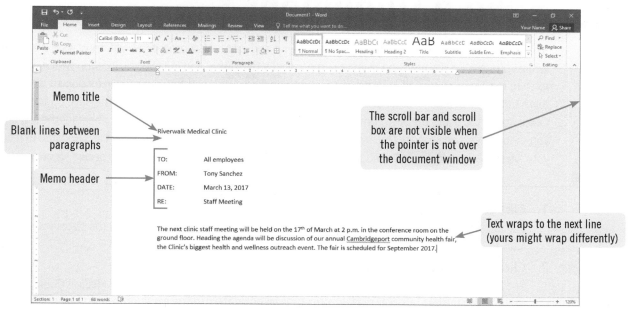

Memo title

Blank lines between paragraphs

Memo header

The scroll bar and scroll box are not visible when the pointer is not over the document window

Text wraps to the next line (yours might wrap differently)

FIGURE 1-4: **Edited memo text**

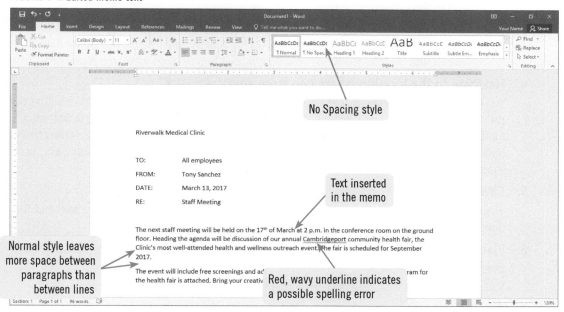

No Spacing style

Text inserted in the memo

Normal style leaves more space between paragraphs than between lines

Red, wavy underline indicates a possible spelling error

TABLE 1-2: **Automatic features that appear as you type in Word**

feature	what appears	to use
AutoComplete	A ScreenTip suggesting text to insert appears as you type	Press [Enter] to insert the text suggested by the ScreenTip; continue typing to reject the suggestion
AutoCorrect	A small blue box appears when you place the pointer over text corrected by AutoCorrect; an AutoCorrect Options button appears when you point to the blue box	Word automatically corrects typos, minor spelling errors, and capitalization, and adds typographical symbols (such as © and ™) as you type; to reverse an AutoCorrect adjustment, click the AutoCorrect Options list arrow, then click the option that will undo the action
Spelling and Grammar	A red wavy line under a word indicates a possible misspelling or a repeated word; a blue wavy line under text indicates a possible grammar error	Right-click red- or blue-underlined text to display a shortcut menu of correction options; click a correction option to accept it and remove the wavy underline

Word 2016

Save a Document

Learning
Outcomes
• Save a file using
a descriptive
filename
• Use the Save As
dialog box

To store a document permanently so you can open it and edit it at another time, you must save it as a **file**. When you **save** a document you give it a name, called a **filename**, and indicate the location where you want to store the file. Files created in Word 2016 are automatically assigned the .docx file extension to distinguish them from files created in other software programs. You can save a document using the Save button on the Quick Access toolbar or the Save command on the File tab. Once you have saved a document for the first time, you should save it again every few minutes and always before printing so that the saved file is updated to reflect your latest changes. **CASE** *You save your memo using a descriptive filename and the default file extension.*

STEPS

1. **Click the** Save button 🖫 **on the Quick Access toolbar**

   The first time you save a document, the Save As screen opens. The screen displays all the places you can save a file to, including OneDrive, your PC, or a different location.

TROUBLE
If you don't see the
extension .docx as
part of the filename,
the setting in
Windows to display
file extensions is
not active.

2. **Click** Browse **in the Save As screen**

   The Save As dialog box opens, similar to FIGURE 1-5. The default filename, Riverwalk Medical Clinic, appears in the File name text box. The default filename is based on the first few words of the document. The default file type, Word Document, appears in the Save as type list box. TABLE 1-3 describes the functions of some of the buttons in the Save As dialog box.

3. **Type** WMP 1-Staff Memo **in the File name text box**

   The new filename replaces the default filename. Giving your documents brief descriptive filenames makes it easier to locate and organize them later. You do not need to type .docx when you type a new filename.

4. **Navigate to the location where you store your Data Files**

   You can navigate to a different drive or folder in several ways. For example, you can click a drive or folder in the Address bar or the navigation pane to go directly to that location. You can also double-click a drive or folder in the folder window to change the active location. When you are finished navigating to the drive or folder where you store your Data Files, that location appears in the Address bar. Your Save As dialog box should resemble FIGURE 1-6.

5. **Click** Save

   The document is saved to the drive and folder you specified in the Save As dialog box, and the title bar displays the new filename, WMP 1-Staff Memo.docx.

6. **Place the insertion point before** September **in the first paragraph, type** early, **then press** [Spacebar]

   You can continue to work on a document after you have saved it with a new filename.

7. **Click** 🖫

   Your change to the memo is saved. After you save a document for the first time, you must continue to save the changes you make to the document. You also can press [Ctrl][S] to save a document.

Creating Documents with Word 2016

FIGURE 1-5: **Save As dialog box**

Active folder or
drive (yours might
differ)

Folders and files
in the active folder
or drive (yours
might differ)

Default filename and file
extension are selected

Click to change
the file type

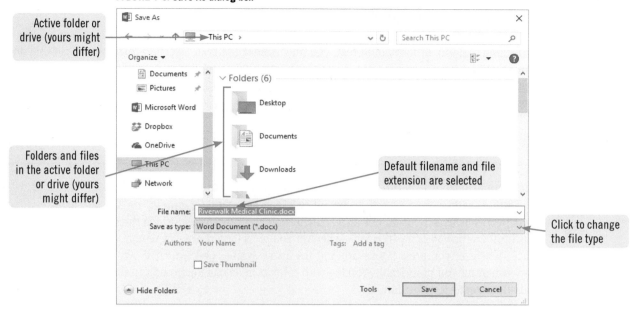

FIGURE 1-6: **File to be saved to the Mod 1 folder**

Click to create a new
folder in the active
folder or drive

Save location
(yours might differ)

Your dialog box might list
the files and folders in the
active drive or folder here

New filename

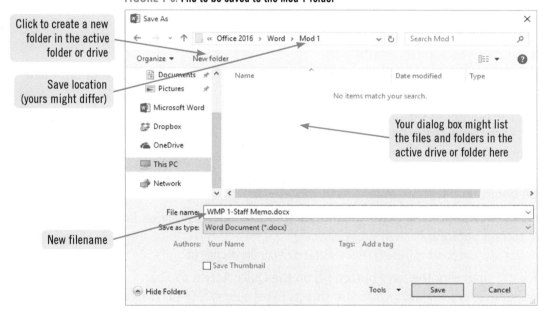

TABLE 1-3: **Save As dialog box buttons**

button	use to
Back	Navigate back to the last location shown in the Address bar
Forward	Navigate to the location that was previously shown in the Address bar
Up to	Navigate to the location above the current location in the folder hierarchy
Organize	Open a menu of commands related to organizing the selected file or folder, including Cut, Copy, Delete, Rename, and Properties
New folder	Create a new folder in the current folder or drive
Change your view	Change the way folder and file information is shown in the folder window in the Save As dialog box; click the Change your view button to toggle between views, or click the list arrow to open a menu of view options

Select Text

Learning Outcomes
• Select text using the mouse
• Use formatting marks

Before deleting, editing, or formatting text, you must **select** the text. Selecting text involves clicking and dragging the I-beam pointer across the text to highlight it. You also can click in the margin to the left of text with the ⤹ pointer to select whole lines or paragraphs. TABLE 1-4 describes the many ways to select text. **CASE** ▶ *You revise the memo by selecting text and replacing it with new text.*

STEPS

1. **Click the** Show/Hide ¶ **button** ¶ **in the Paragraph group**

   Formatting marks appear in the document window. **Formatting marks** are special characters that appear on your screen but do not print. Common formatting marks include the paragraph symbol (¶), which shows the end of a paragraph—wherever you press [Enter]; the dot symbol (·), which represents a space—wherever you press [Spacebar]; and the arrow symbol (→), which shows the location of a tab stop—wherever you press [Tab]. Working with formatting marks turned on can help you to select, edit, and format text with precision.

QUICK TIP
You deselect text by clicking anywhere in the document window.

2. **Click before** All employees, **then drag the** I **pointer over the text to select it**

   The words are selected, as shown in FIGURE 1-7. For now, you can ignore the floating toolbar that appears over text when you first select it.

3. **Type** Medical Staff

   The text you type replaces the selected text.

4. **Double-click** Tony, **type your first name, double-click** Sanchez, **then type your last name**

   Double-clicking a word selects the entire word.

TROUBLE
If you delete text by mistake, immediately click the Undo button on the Quick Access toolbar to restore the deleted text to the document.

5. **Place the pointer in the margin to the left of the RE: line so that the pointer changes to** ⤹, **click to select the line, then type** RE: [Tab] [Tab] Community Health Fair

   Clicking to the left of a line of text with the ⤹ pointer selects the entire line.

6. **Select** draft **in the first line of the second paragraph, type** list, **select** program for, **then type** booths and free screenings to be included in

7. **Select the sentence** The event will include free screenings and adult immunizations. **in the second paragraph, then press** [Delete]

   Selecting text and pressing [Delete] removes the text from the document.

QUICK TIP
Always save before and after editing text.

8. **Click** ¶, **then click the** Save button 💾 **on the Quick Access toolbar**

   Formatting marks are turned off, and your changes to the memo are saved. The Show/Hide ¶ button is a **toggle button**, which means you can use it to turn formatting marks on and off. The edited memo is shown in FIGURE 1-8.

FIGURE 1-7: Text selected in the memo

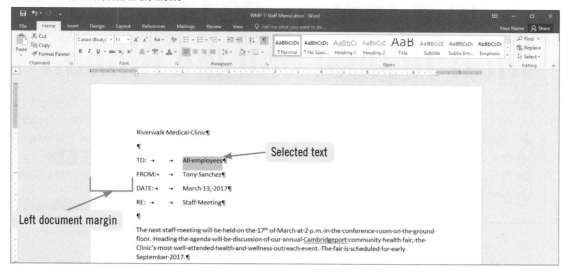

FIGURE 1-8: Edited memo with replacement text

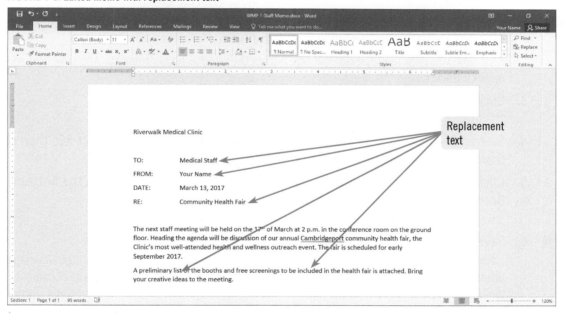

TABLE 1-4: Methods for selecting text

to select	use the pointer to
Any amount of text	Drag over the text
A word	Double-click the word
A line of text	Move the pointer to the left of the line, then click
A sentence	Press and hold [Ctrl], then click the sentence
A paragraph	Triple-click the paragraph or double-click with the pointer to the left of the paragraph
A large block of text	Click at the beginning of the selection, press and hold [Shift], then click at the end of the selection
Multiple nonconsecutive selections	Select the first selection, then press and hold [Ctrl] as you select each additional selection
An entire document	Triple-click with the pointer to the left of any text; press [Ctrl][A]; or click the Select button in the Editing group on the Home tab, and then click Select All

Format Text Using the Mini Toolbar and the Ribbon

Formatting text is a fast and fun way to spruce up the appearance of a document and highlight important information. You can easily change the font, color, size, style, and other attributes of text by selecting the text and clicking a command on the Home tab. The **Mini toolbar**, which appears above text when you first select it, also includes commonly used text and paragraph formatting commands. **CASE** *You enhance the appearance of the memo by formatting the text using the Mini toolbar. When you are finished, you preview the memo for errors and then print it.*

STEPS

1. **Select Riverwalk Medical Clinic**

   The Mini toolbar appears over the selected text, as shown in FIGURE 1-9. You click a formatting option on the Mini toolbar to apply it to the selected text. TABLE 1-5 describes the function of the buttons on the Mini toolbar. The buttons on the Mini toolbar are also available on the Ribbon.

2. **Click the Increase Font Size button A⃯ on the Mini toolbar six times, then click the Bold button B on the Mini toolbar**

   Each time you click the Increase Font Size button the selected text is enlarged. Applying bold to the text makes it thicker.

3. **Click the Center button ≡ in the Paragraph group on the Home tab**

   The selected text is centered between the left and right margins.

4. **Select TO:, click B , select FROM:, click B , select DATE:, click B , select RE:, then click B**

   Bold is applied to the memo header labels.

5. **Click the blank line between the RE: line and the body text, then click the Bottom Border button ⊞ in the Paragraph group**

   A single-line border is added between the heading and the body text in the memo.

6. **Save the document, click the File tab, then click Print**

   Information related to printing the document appears on the Print screen in Backstage view. Options for printing the document appear on the left side of the Print screen and a preview of the document as it will look when printed appears on the right side, as shown in FIGURE 1-10. Before you print a document, it's considered good practice to examine the document closely so you can identify and correct any problems.

7. **Click the Zoom In button ➕ on the status bar five times, then proofread your document carefully for errors**

   The document is enlarged in print preview. If you notice errors in your document, you need to correct them before you print. To do this, press [Esc] or click the Back button in Backstage view, correct any mistakes, save your changes, click the File tab, and then click the Print command again to be ready to print the document.

8. **Click the Print button on the Print screen**

   A copy of the memo prints using the default print settings. To change the current printer, change the number of copies to print, select what pages of a document to print, or modify another print setting, you simply change the appropriate setting on the Print screen before clicking the Print button.

9. **Click the File tab, then click Close**

   The document closes, but the Word program window remains open.

FIGURE 1-9: Mini toolbar

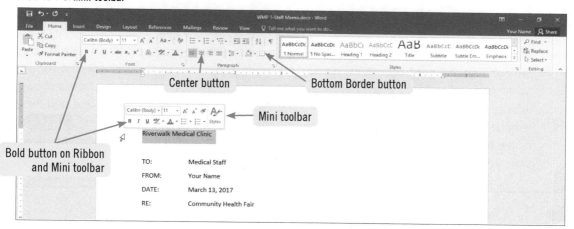

Center button

Bottom Border button

Mini toolbar

Bold button on Ribbon and Mini toolbar

FIGURE 1-10: Preview of the completed memo

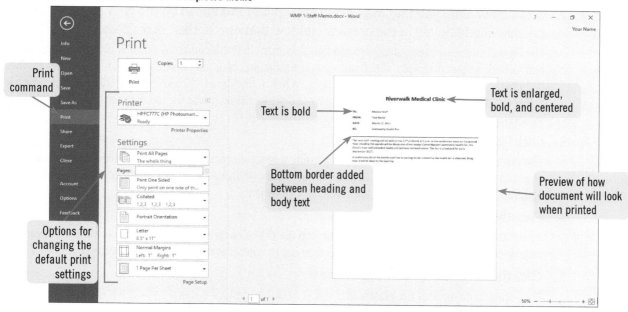

Print command

Text is bold

Text is enlarged, bold, and centered

Bottom border added between heading and body text

Preview of how document will look when printed

Options for changing the default print settings

TABLE 1-5: Buttons on the Mini toolbar

button	use to	button	use to
Calibri (Body)	Change the font of text	B	Apply bold to text
11	Change the font size of text	I	Apply italic to text
A	Make text larger	U	Apply an underline to text
A	Make text smaller	aby	Apply colored highlighting to text
(Format Painter)	Copy the formats applied to selected text to other text	A	Change the color of text
Styles	Apply a style to text	(bullets)	Apply bullets to paragraphs
		(numbering)	Apply numbering to paragraphs

Use a Document Template

Word includes many templates that you can use to create letters, reports, brochures, calendars, and other professionally designed documents quickly. A **template** is a formatted document that contains placeholder text and graphics, which you replace with your own text and graphics. To create a document that is based on a template, you use the New command on the File tab in Backstage view, and then select a template to use. You can then customize the document and save it with a new filename. **CASE** ▶ *You use a template to create a cover letter for a set of documents you will send to Dr. Carla Zimmerman, director of the clinic, who is attending a conference in Costa Rica.*

STEPS

1. **Click the File tab, then click New**

   The New screen opens in Backstage view, as shown in FIGURE 1-11. You can select a template from the gallery shown in this window, or use the search box and links in the Suggested Searches section to find other templates.

2. **Scroll down until you find the Cover Letter (blue) thumbnail on the New screen, click it, preview the template in the preview window that opens, then click Create**

   The Cover Letter (blue) template opens as a new document in the document window. It contains placeholder text, which you can replace with your own information. Your name might appear at the top of the document. Don't be concerned if it does not. When a document is created using this template, Word automatically enters the username from the Word Options dialog box at the top of the document and in the signature block.

3. **Click [Date] in the document**

   The placeholder text is selected and appears inside a content control. A **content control** is an interactive object that you use to customize a document with your own information. A content control might include placeholder text, a drop-down list of choices, or a calendar.

4. **Click the [Date] list arrow**

   A calendar opens below the content control. You use the calendar to select the date you want to appear on your document—simply click a date on the calendar to enter that date in the document.

5. **Click the Today button on the calendar**

   The current date replaces the placeholder text.

6. **Click [Recipient Name], type Dr. Carla Zimmerman, press [Enter], type Director, Riverwalk Medical Clinic, press [Enter], type c/o Rainforest Lodge, press [Enter], type P.O. Box 4397, press [Enter], then type Tamarindo 50309, COSTA RICA**

   You do not need to drag to select the placeholder text in a content control, you can simply click it. The text you type replaces the placeholder text.

7. **Click [Recipient], then type Dr. Zimmerman**

   The text you type replaces the placeholder text in the greeting line.

8. **Click the File tab, click Save As, then save the document as WMP 1-Zimmerman Letter to the location where you store your Data Files**

   The document is saved with the filename WMP 1-Zimmerman Letter, as shown in FIGURE 1-12.

FIGURE 1-11: New screen in Backstage view

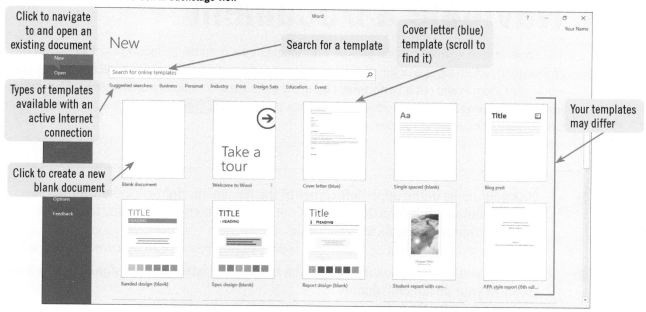

Click to navigate to and open an existing document

Search for a template

Cover letter (blue) template (scroll to find it)

Types of templates available with an active Internet connection

Your templates may differ

Click to create a new blank document

FIGURE 1-12: Document created using the Cover letter (blue) template

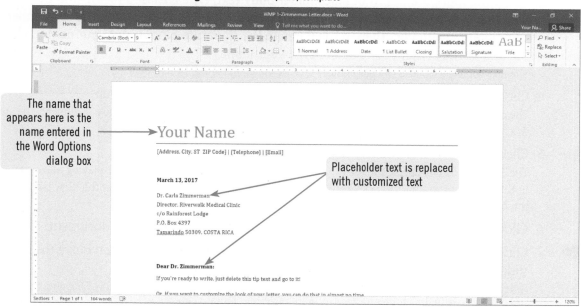

The name that appears here is the name entered in the Word Options dialog box

Placeholder text is replaced with customized text

Word 2016

Using the Undo, Redo, and Repeat commands

Word remembers the editing and formatting changes you make so that you can easily reverse or repeat them. You can reverse the last action you took by clicking the Undo button on the Quick Access toolbar, or you can undo a series of actions by clicking the Undo list arrow and selecting the action you want to reverse. When you undo an action using the Undo list arrow, you also undo all the actions above it in the list—that is, all actions that were performed after the action you selected. Similarly, you can keep the change you just reversed by using the Redo button

on the Quick Access toolbar. The Redo button appears only immediately after clicking the Undo button to undo a change.

If you want to repeat an action you just completed, you can use the Repeat button on the Quick Access toolbar. For example, if you just typed "thank you," clicking inserts "thank you" at the location of the insertion point. If you just applied bold, clicking applies bold to the currently selected text. You also can repeat the last action you took by pressing [F4].

Navigate a Document

Learning Outcomes
• Remove a content control
• Zoom, scroll, and use Word views

The Zoom feature in Word lets you enlarge a document in the document window to get a close-up view of a detail or reduce the size of the document in the document window for an overview of the layout as a whole. You zoom in and out on a document using the tools in the Zoom group on the View tab or you can use the Zoom level buttons and Zoom slider on the status bar. **CASE** ▸ *You find it is helpful to zoom in and out on the document as you finalize the letter.*

STEPS

TROUBLE
If your name does not appear in the content control, replace the text that does.

1. **Click your name in the upper-left corner of the document, right-click the** Your Name **content control, click** Remove Content Control **on the menu that opens, select your name, then type** Riverwalk Medical Clinic

   Removing the content control changes the text to static text that you can then replace with other text.

TROUBLE
If you do not see the vertical scroll box, move the pointer to the right side of the document window to display it.

2. **Drag the** vertical scroll box down **until the body of the letter and the signature block are visible in your document window**

   You **scroll** to display different parts of the document in the document window. You can also scroll by clicking the scroll arrows above and below the scroll bar, or by clicking the scroll bar.

3. **Select the** four paragraphs **of placeholder body text, type** Enclosed please find the documents you requested. I have also enclosed a draft list of events for the September community health fair.**, then, if the name in the signature block is not your name, select the text in the content control and type your name**

   The text you type replaces the placeholder text, as shown in **FIGURE 1-13**.

4. **Click the** View tab, **then click the** Page Width button **in the Zoom group**

   The document is enlarged to the width of the document window. When you enlarge a document, the area where the insertion point is located appears in the document window.

TROUBLE
The percentage number in your Zoom Level button might differ.

5. **Click the** Zoom level button `154%` **on the status bar**

   The Zoom dialog box opens. You use the Zoom dialog box to select a zoom level for displaying the document in the document window. You can also click the Zoom button in the Zoom group on the View tab to open the Zoom dialog box.

6. **Click the** Whole page option button, **then click** OK **to view the entire document**

QUICK TIP
You can also move the Zoom slider by clicking a point on the Zoom slide, or by clicking the Zoom Out and Zoom In buttons.

7. **Click** Riverwalk **to move the insertion point to the top of the page, then move the Zoom slider to the right until the Zoom percentage is approximately 230%**

   Dragging the Zoom slider to the right enlarges the document in the document window. Dragging the zoom slider to the left allows you to see more of the page at a reduced size.

8. **Click the** [Address...] content control, **type** Health, **click** [Telephone], **type** Wellness, **click** [Email], **type** rwmed.org, **then press** [Tab]

   You can replace placeholder text with information that is different from what is suggested in the content control.

9. **Click the** Read Mode button ▣ **on the status bar**

   The document appears in the document window in Read Mode view. Read Mode view hides the tabs and ribbon to make it easier to read documents on screen. Read Mode view is useful for reading long documents.

QUICK TIP
You can also click View on the menu bar, then click Edit Document to return to Print Layout view.

10. **Click the** Print Layout view button ▣ **on the status bar, click the** Zoom Out button ▬ **on the status bar until the zoom level is 100%, then save the document**

    The completed cover letter is displayed at 100% zoom level in Print Layout view, as shown in **FIGURE 1-14**.

11. **Submit the document to your instructor, close the file, then exit Word**

FIGURE 1-13: Replacement text and Zoom slider

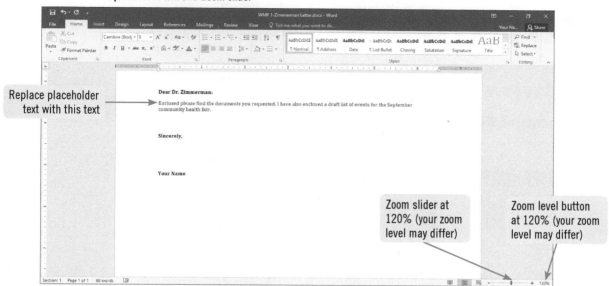

Replace placeholder text with this text

Zoom slider at 120% (your zoom level may differ)

Zoom level button at 120% (your zoom level may differ)

FIGURE 1-14: Completed letter

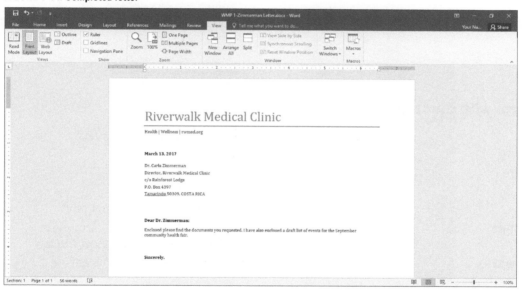

Using Word document views

Document **views** are different ways of displaying a document in the document window. Each Word view provides features that are useful for working on different types of documents. The default view, **Print Layout view**, displays a document as it will look on a printed page. Print Layout view is helpful for formatting text and pages, including adjusting document margins, creating columns of text, inserting graphics, and formatting headers and footers. Also useful is **Read Mode view**, which displays document text so that it is easy to read on screen. Other Word views are helpful for performing specialized tasks. **Web Layout view** allows you to format webpages or documents that will be viewed on a computer screen. In Web Layout view, a document appears just as it will when viewed with a web browser. **Outline view** is useful for editing and formatting longer documents that include multiple headings. Outline view allows you to reorganize text by moving the headings. Finally, **Draft view** shows a simplified layout of a document, without margins, headers and footers, or graphics. When you want to quickly type and edit text, it's often easiest to work in Draft View. You switch between views by clicking the view buttons on the status bar or by using the commands on the View tab. Changing views does not affect how the printed document will appear. It simply changes the way you view the document in the document window.

Practice

Concepts Review

Label the elements of the Word program window shown in FIGURE 1-15.

FIGURE 1-15

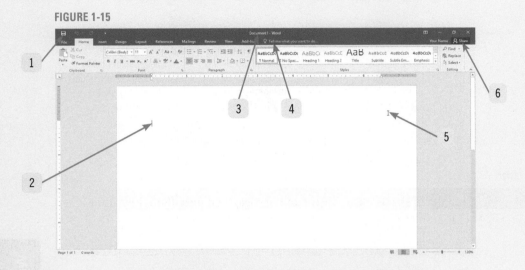

Match each term with the statement that best describes it.

7. **Ribbon**
8. **AutoCorrect**
9. **AutoComplete**
10. **Zoom slider**
11. **Status bar**
12. **Horizontal ruler**
13. **Template**
14. **Formatting marks**

a. A formatted document that contains placeholder text
b. Suggests text to insert into a document
c. Fixes certain errors as you type
d. Provides access to Word commands
e. Special characters that appear on screen but do not print
f. Displays tab settings and paragraph indents
g. Enlarges and reduces the document in the document window
h. Displays the number of pages in the current document

Select the best answer from the list of choices.

15. **Which of the following shows the number of words in the document?**
    a. The title bar
    b. The Ribbon
    c. The status bar
    d. The Mini toolbar

16. **Which tab includes buttons for formatting text?**
    a. View
    b. Page Layout
    c. Insert
    d. Home

17. **Which element of the Word window shows the top and bottom document margins settings?**
    a. Status bar
    b. View tab
    c. Vertical ruler
    d. Vertical scroll bar

18. **What is the default file extension for a document created in Word 2016?**
    a. .doc
    b. .dot
    c. .dotx
    d. .docx

19. **Which of the following is not included in a ScreenTip for a command?**

a. Link to a help topic on the command

c. Keyboard shortcut for the command

b. Alternative location of the command

d. Description of the function of the command

20. **Which view is best for reading text onscreen?**

a. Print Layout view

c. Read Mode view

b. Outline view

d. Draft view

Skills Review

1. **Explore the Word program window.**
   a. Start Word and open a new, blank document.
   b. Identify as many elements of the Word program window as you can without referring to the module material.
   c. Click the File tab, then click the Info, New, Save, Open, Save As, Print, Share, and Export commands.
   d. Click the Back button in Backstage view to return to the document window.
   e. Click each tab on the Ribbon, review the groups and buttons on each tab, then return to the Home tab.
   f. Point to each button on the Home tab and read its ScreenTip.
   g. Click the view buttons to view the blank document in each view, then return to Print Layout view.
   h. Use the Zoom slider to zoom all the way in and all the way out on the document, then return to 120%.

2. **Start a document.**
   a. In a new blank document, type **Clinton Labs FAX** at the top of the page, then press [Enter] two times.
   b. Type the following, pressing [Tab] as indicated and pressing [Enter] at the end of each line:
      To: [Tab] [Tab] **Seacoast Family Health**
      From: [Tab] [Tab] **Your Name**
      Date: [Tab] [Tab] **Today's date**
      Re: [Tab] [Tab] **Schedule change**
      Pages: [Tab] [Tab] **2**
      Fax: [Tab] [Tab] **(603) 555-5478**
   c. Press [Enter] again, then type **Effective September 15th, Clinton Labs will pick up laboratory specimens at 10 a.m. and 4:15 p.m. daily. We trust the addition of the afternoon pick-up time will improve the efficiency of our service. All abnormal results will continue to be reported to your office by telephone.**
   d. Press [Enter], then type **As always, we welcome your comments and suggestions on how we can better serve you. Our clients are important to us.**
   e. Insert this sentence at the beginning of the second paragraph: **The lab will continue to be open until 7:00 p.m. for drop-in service.**
   f. Using the [Backspace] key, delete **2** in the Pages: line, then type **1**.
   g. Using the [Delete] key, delete **4:15** in the first paragraph, then type **3:30**.

3. **Save a document.**
   a. Click the Save button on the Quick Access toolbar.
   b. Save the document as **WMP 1-Seacoast Family Health** with the default file extension to the location where you store your Data Files.
   c. After your name, type a comma, press [Spacebar], then type **Office Manager**.
   d. Save the document.

4. **Select text.**
   a. Turn on formatting marks.
   b. Select the **Re:** line, then type **Re:** [Tab] [Tab] **New morning pick-up time**

Skills Review (continued)

c. Select **September** in the first sentence, then type **October**.

d. Select **afternoon** in the second sentence of the first paragraph, then type **morning**.

e. Delete the sentence **Our clients are important to us**.

f. Turn off the display of formatting marks, then save the document.

5. **Format text using the Mini toolbar.**

a. Select **Clinton Labs FAX**, click the Increase Font Size button on the Mini toolbar six times, then apply bold.

b. Center **Clinton Labs FAX** on the page.

c. Apply a bottom border under **Clinton Labs FAX**.

d. Apply bold to the following words in the fax heading: **To:**, **From:**, **Date:**, **Re:**, **Pages:**, and **Fax:**.

e. Read the document using the Read Mode view.

f. Return to Print Layout view, zoom in on the document, then proofread the fax.

g. Correct any typing errors in your document, then save the document. Compare your document to FIGURE 1-16.

h. Submit the fax to your instructor, then close the document.

6. **Use a template.**

a. Click the File tab, click New, then scroll the gallery of templates.

b. Create a new document using the Fax cover sheet (Professional design) template.

c. At the top of the document, click the [Company Name] placeholder text, type **Clinton Labs**, delete the [Street Address] and [City...] content controls, click the [phone] placeholder text, type **Tel: 617-555-7482**, click the [fax] placeholder text, type **Fax: 617-555-1176**, click the [website] placeholder text, then type **www.clintonlabs.com**.

d. Type **Valley OB/GYN** to replace the "To:" placeholder text; type **555-2119** to replace the "Fax:" placeholder text; click the "Phone:" placeholder text, then press [Delete]; then type **New Clinton Labs pick-up time** to replace the "Re:" placeholder text.

e. If your name is not on the From line, select the text in the From content control, then type your name.

f. Insert today's date using the date content control.

g. Delete the "Pages:" and "cc:" placeholder text.

h. Save the document with the filename **WMP 1-Valley Fax** to the location where you store your Data Files, clicking OK if a warning box opens.

7. **Navigate a document.**

a. Scroll down until Comments is near the top of your document window.

b. Replace the Comments placeholder text with the following text: **Clinton Labs has added a morning pick-up time for laboratory specimens. Effective October 15th, Clinton Labs will pick up specimens at 10:00 a.m. and 3:30 p.m.**

c. Use the Zoom dialog box to view the Whole Page.

FIGURE 1-16

Clinton Labs FAX

To:	Seacoast Family Health
From:	Your Name, Office Manager
Date:	October 1, 2017
Re:	New morning pick-up time
Pages:	1
Fax:	(802) 555-5478

Effective October 15th, Clinton Labs will pick up laboratory specimens at 10:00 a.m. and 3:30 p.m. daily. We trust the addition of the morning pick-up time will improve the efficiency of our service. All abnormal results will continue to be reported to your office by telephone.

The lab will continue to be open until 7:00 p.m. for drop-in service. As always, we welcome your comments and suggestions on how we can better serve you.

Creating Documents with Word 2016

Skills Review (continued)

FIGURE 1-17

d. Use the Zoom slider to set the Zoom percentage at approximately 100%.

e. Read the document using the Read Mode view.

f. Return to Print Layout view, zoom in on the document, then proofread the fax.

g. Preview the document, then correct any errors, saving changes if necessary. Compare your document to FIGURE 1-17. Submit the document to your instructor, close the file, then exit Word.

FIGURE 1-17

Independent Challenge 1

Yesterday you interviewed for a job as medical office manager at Rose Medical Associates. You spoke with several people at the practice, including Yukiko Posey, director of human resources, whose business card is shown in FIGURE 1-18. You need to write a follow-up letter to Ms. Posey, thanking her for the interview and expressing your interest in the practice and the position. She also asked you to send her some documents you have created, which you will enclose with the letter.

a. Start Word and save a new blank document as **WMP 1-Posey Letter** to the location where you store your Data Files.

b. Begin the letter by clicking the No Spacing button in the Styles group. You use this button to apply the No Spacing style to the document so that your document does not include extra space between paragraphs.

c. Type a personal letterhead for the letter that includes your name, address, telephone number, and e-mail address. If Word formats your e-mail address as a hyperlink, right-click your e-mail address, then click Remove Hyperlink. (*Note: Format the letterhead after you finish typing the letter.*)

d. Three lines below the bottom of the letterhead, type today's date.

e. Four lines below the date, type the inside address, referring to FIGURE 1-18 for the information. Include the recipient's title, practice name, and full mailing address.

f. Two lines below the inside address, type **Dear Ms. Posey:** for the salutation.

g. Two lines below the salutation, type the body of the letter according to the following guidelines:

- In the first paragraph, thank her for the interview. Then restate your interest in the position and express your desire to work for the practice. Add any specific details you think will enhance the power of your letter.

- In the second paragraph, note that you are enclosing three samples of your work, and explain something about the samples you are enclosing.

- Type a short final paragraph.

h. Two lines below the last body paragraph, type a closing, then four lines below the closing, type the signature block. Be sure to include your name in the signature block.

i. Two lines below the signature block, type an enclosure notation. (*Hint*: An enclosure notation usually includes the word "Enclosures" or the abbreviation "Enc." followed by the number of enclosures in parentheses.)

j. Format the letterhead with bold, centering, and a bottom border.

k. Save your changes, preview the letter, submit it to your instructor, then close the document and exit Word.

FIGURE 1-18

Rose Medical Associates
www.rosemedical.com

Yukiko Posey
Director of Human Resources

438 W. 23rd Street, Suite 76
New York, NY 10011

p. 212.555.7028

yposey@rosemedical.com

Independent Challenge 2

Your company has recently installed Word 2016 on its company network. As the training manager, it's your responsibility to teach employees how to use the new software productively. Now that they have begun working with Word 2016, several employees have asked you about sharing documents with colleagues using OneDrive. In response, you wrote a memo to all employees explaining the Share feature. You now need to format the memo before distributing it.

a. Start Word, open the file **WMP 1-1.docx** from the location where you store your Data Files, clicking the Enable Editing button if prompted to do so, then read the memo to get a feel for its contents. Switch to Print Layout view if the document is not already displayed in Print Layout view.

b. Save the file as **WMP 1-Share Memo** to the location where you store your Data Files.

c. Replace the information in the memo header with the information shown in FIGURE 1-19. Make sure to include your name in the From line and the current date in the Date line.

d. Apply bold to **To:**, **From:**, **Date:**, and **Re:**.

e. Increase the size of **WORD TRAINING MEMORANDUM** to match FIGURE 1-19, center the text on the page, add a border below it, then save your changes.

f. Preview the memo, submit it to your instructor, then close the document and exit Word.

FIGURE 1-19

WORD TRAINING MEMORANDUM

To:	All employees
From:	Your Name, Training Manager
Date:	Today's date
Re:	Sharing documents

Independent Challenge 3

You are a pulmonologist and research investigator for numerous trials pertaining to the study of lung disease. The president of the Allied Lung Association, Lisa Branscombe, has asked you to be the keynote speaker at an upcoming conference on advances in the treatment and prevention of lung disease, to be held in Grand Teton National Park. You use one of the Word letter templates to write a letter to Dr. Branscombe accepting the invitation and confirming the details. Your letter to Dr. Branscombe should reference the following information:

- The conference will be held September 17–19, 2017, at the Jackson Lake Lodge in the park.
- You have been asked to speak for an hour on September 18, followed by one-half hour for questions.
- Dr. Branscombe suggested the lecture topic "Interventional Pulmonology: Advancements in Diagnosis and Treatment."
- Your talk will include a 45-minute slide presentation.
- The Allied Lung Association will make your travel arrangements.
- Your preference is to arrive at Jackson Hole Airport on the morning of September 17, and to depart on September 20. You would like to rent a car at the airport for the drive to the Jackson Lake Lodge.
- You want to fly in and out of the airport closest to your home.

a. Start Word, click the File tab, click New, and then search for and select an appropriate letter template. Save the document as **WMP 1-Branscombe Letter** to the location where you store your Data Files.

b. Replace the placeholders in the letterhead with your personal information. Include your name, address, phone number, and e-mail address. Delete any placeholders that do not apply. (*Hints*: Depending on the template you choose, the letterhead might be located at the top or on the side of the document. You can press [Enter] when typing in a placeholder to add an additional line of text. You can also change the format of text typed in a placeholder. If your e-mail address appears as a hyperlink, right-click the e-mail address and click Remove Hyperlink.)

Creating Documents with Word 2016

Independent Challenge 3 (continued)

   c. Use the [Date] content control to select the current date.

   d. Replace the placeholders in the inside address. Be sure to include Dr. Branscombe's title and the name of the organization. Make up a street address, city, and zip code.

   e. Type **Dear Dr. Branscombe:** for the salutation.

   f. Using the information listed previously, type the body of the letter:

- In the first paragraph, accept the invitation to speak.
- In the second paragraph, confirm the important conference details, confirm your lecture topic, and provide any relevant details.
- In the third paragraph, state your travel preferences.
- Type a short final paragraph.

   g. Type **Sincerely,** for the closing, then include your name in the signature block.

   h. Adjust the formatting of the letter as necessary. For example, remove bold formatting or change the font color of text to a more appropriate color.

   i. Proofread your letter, make corrections as needed, then save your changes.

   j. Submit the letter to your instructor, close the document, then exit Word.

Independent Challenge 4: Explore

Word includes a wide variety of templates that can help you create professional-looking documents quickly, including business letters, business cards, résumés, calendars, faxes, memos, labels, reports, blog posts, posters, invitations, certificates, newsletters, and holiday and party cards. In this independent challenge, you will explore the variety of Word templates available to you, and use a template to make a document that is helpful to you in your business or personal life. You might create business cards for yourself, a poster for an event, a letter for a job search, a new résumé, or an invitation to a party. Choose a template that allows you to personalize the text.

   a. Start Word, click the File tab, click New, then click each link after Suggested searches: (Business, Personal, Industry, Print, Design Sets, Education, Event) to explore the templates available to you.

   b. Preview all the templates for the type of document you want to create, and then select one to create a new document.

   c. Save the document as **WMP 1-Template Document** to the location where you store your Data Files.

   d. Replace the placeholders in the document with your personal information. Delete any placeholders that do not apply. (*Hints*: You can press [Enter] when typing in a placeholder to add an additional line of text. If an e-mail or web address appears as a hyperlink in your document, right-click the e-mail or web address and then click Remove Hyperlink.)

   e. Use the [Pick the date] content control to select a date if your document includes a date placeholder.

   f. Experiment with changing the font of the text in your document by using the Font list arrow on the Mini toolbar or in the Font group on the Home tab. (*Note*: Remember to use the Undo button immediately after you make the change if you do not like the change and want to remove it.)

   g. Experiment with changing the font size of the text in your document by using the Font Size list arrow on the Mini toolbar or in the Font group on the Home tab.

   h. Experiment with changing the color of text in your document using the Font Color button on the Mini toolbar or in the Font group on the Home tab.

   i. Make other adjustments to the document as necessary, using the Undo button to remove a change you decide you do not want to keep.

   j. Save your changes to the document, preview it, submit it to your instructor, then close the document and exit Word.

Visual Workshop

Create the cover letter shown in FIGURE 1-20. Before beginning to type, click the No Spacing button in the Styles group on the Home tab. Add the bottom border to the letterhead after typing the letter. Save the document as **WMP 1-Insurance Letter** to the location where you store your Data Files, submit the letter to your instructor, then close the document and exit Word.

FIGURE 1-20

Great Lakes Memorial Health Care

678 Ontario Street, Madison, WI 53701
Tel: 608-555-7283; www.greatlakesmemorialhealth.com

March 17, 2017

Ms. Ruth Thomas
827 Jefferson Street
Madison, WI 53704

Dear Ms. Thomas:

Thank you for choosing Great Lakes Memorial Health Care as your health care provider.

As a result of your recent visit to our emergency facility, our records show your primary care insurance as Midwest Indemnity (#60024 0226), policy #331 27 7625, and group #836225-33-049. At this time, our records show you do not have a secondary care insurance provider.

If the insurance information in this letter is correct, no action is required on your part.

If the insurance information is incomplete or incorrect, please contact us with more accurate billing information by calling a Financial Counselor at (608) 555-3600.

Once we have billed your insurance, we will send you a statement identifying any patient responsibility.

Sincerely,

Your Name
Patient Business Services
Great Lakes Memorial Health Care

Editing Documents

CASE You have been asked to edit and finalize a press release for a lecture series sponsored by the Riverwalk Medical Clinic. The press release should provide information about the series so that newspapers, radio stations, and other media outlets can announce it to the public. Press releases from the Riverwalk Medical Clinic are disseminated via the website and by e-mail. Before distributing the file electronically to your lists of press contacts, you add several hyperlinks and then strip the file of private information.

Module Objectives

After completing this module, you will be able to:

- Cut and paste text
- Copy and paste text
- Use the Office Clipboard
- Find and replace text
- Check spelling and grammar
- Research information
- Add hyperlinks
- Work with document properties

Files You Will Need

WMP 2-1.docx	WMP 2-5.docx
WMP 2-2.docx	WMP 2-6.docx
WMP 2-3.docx	WMP 2-7.docx
WMP 2-4.docx	

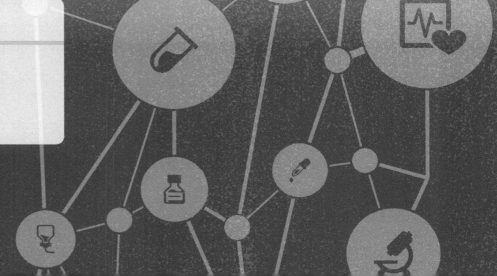

Cut and Paste Text

Learning Outcomes
- Open a document and save it with a new filename
- Edit text using formatting marks
- Cut and paste text

The editing features in Word allow you to move text from one location to another in a document. Moving text is often called **cut and paste**. When you **cut** text, it is removed from the document and placed on the **Clipboard**, a temporary storage area for text and graphics that you cut or copy from a document. You can then **paste**, or insert, text that is stored on the Clipboard in the document at the location of the insertion point. You cut and paste text using the Cut and Paste buttons in the Clipboard group on the Home tab. You also can move selected text by dragging it to a new location using the mouse. This operation is called **drag and drop**. **CASE** *You open the press release, save it with a new filename, and then reorganize the information in the press release using the cut-and-paste and drag-and-drop methods.*

STEPS

QUICK TIP
You can also click Open Other Documents at the bottom of the Recent list on the Word start screen to open the Open dialog box.

1. **Start Word, click Blank document, click the File tab, click This PC on the Open screen, click Browse to open the Open dialog box, navigate to the location where you store your Data Files, click WMP 2-1.docx, then click Open**

   The document opens in Print Layout view. Once you have opened a file, you can edit it and use the Save or the Save As command to save your changes. You use the **Save** command when you want to save the changes you make to a file, overwriting the stored file. You use the **Save As** command when you want to leave the original file intact and create a duplicate file with a different filename, file extension, or location.

TROUBLE
Click the Enable Editing button if necessary.

2. **Click the File tab, click Save As, click This PC, click Browse to open the Save As dialog box, type WMP 2-Lecture PR in the File name text box, then click Save**

   You can now make changes to the press release file without affecting the original file.

TROUBLE
If the headline and all six paragraphs of body text do not display in your document window, use the Zoom slider to change the zoom level.

3. **Replace Sienna Foss with your name, scroll down until the headline "Dr. Victoria Soares to Speak..." is at the top of your document window, then click the Show/Hide ¶ button ¶ in the Paragraph group on the Home tab to display formatting marks**

4. **Select lead and other heavy metals, (including the comma and the space after it) in the fourth body paragraph, then click the Cut button in the Clipboard group**

   The text is removed from the document and placed on the Clipboard. Word uses two different clipboards: the **system clipboard**, which holds just one item, and the **Office Clipboard** (the Clipboard), which holds up to 24 items. The last item you cut or copy is always added to both clipboards.

5. **Place the insertion point before pesticides (but after the space) in the second line of the fourth paragraph, then click the Paste button in the Clipboard group**

   The text is pasted at the location of the insertion point, as shown in FIGURE 2-1. The Paste Options button appears below text when you first paste it in a document. For now you can ignore the Paste Options button.

QUICK TIP
As you drag, the pointer changes to ▷, and a black vertical line, which is the insertion point, moves with the pointer.

6. **Press and hold [Ctrl], click the sentence Ticket prices include lunch. in the third paragraph, then release [Ctrl]**

   The entire sentence is selected. You will drag the selected text to a new location using the mouse.

7. **Press and hold the mouse button over the selected text, then drag the pointer's vertical line to the end of the fifth paragraph (between the period and the paragraph mark) as shown in FIGURE 2-2**

   You drag the insertion point to where you want the text to be inserted when you release the mouse button.

QUICK TIP
If you make a mistake, click the Undo button ↶ on the Quick Access toolbar, then try again.

8. **Release the mouse button**

   The selected text is moved to the location of the insertion point. Text is not placed on the Clipboard when you drag and drop it.

9. **Deselect the text, then click the Save button 🖫 on the Quick Access toolbar**

Editing Documents

FIGURE 2-1: Moved text with Paste Options button

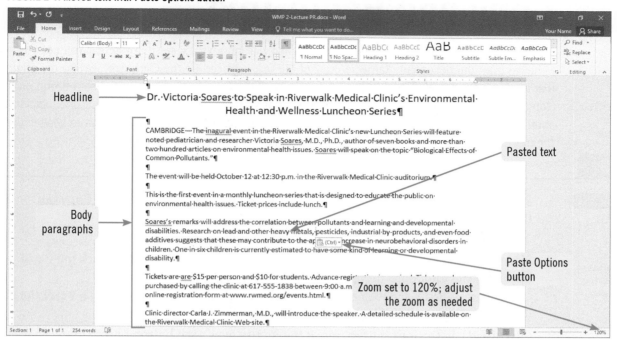

Headline

Body paragraphs

Pasted text

Paste Options button

Zoom set to 120%; adjust the zoom as needed

FIGURE 2-2: Dragging and dropping text in a new location

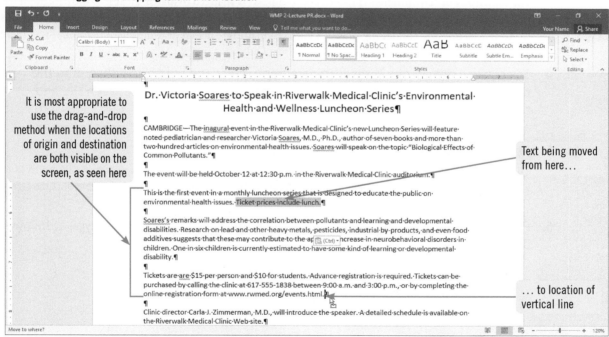

It is most appropriate to use the drag-and-drop method when the locations of origin and destination are both visible on the screen, as seen here

Text being moved from here...

... to location of vertical line

Using keyboard shortcuts

A **shortcut key** is a function key, such as [F1], or a combination of keys, such as [Ctrl][S], that you press to perform a command. For example, instead of using the Cut, Copy, and Paste commands on the Ribbon or the Mini toolbar, you can use the **keyboard shortcuts** [Ctrl][X] to cut text, [Ctrl][C] to copy text, and [Ctrl][V] to paste text. You can also press [Ctrl][S] to save changes to a document instead of clicking the Save button on the Quick Access toolbar or clicking Save on the File tab. Becoming skilled at using keyboard shortcuts can help you quickly accomplish many of the tasks you perform in Word. If a keyboard shortcut is available for a command, then it is listed in the ScreenTip for that command.

Copy and Paste Text

Learning Outcomes
• Copy and paste text
• Format pasted text with the Paste Options button

Copying and pasting text is similar to cutting and pasting text, except that the text you **copy** is not removed from the document. Rather, a copy of the text is placed on the Clipboard, leaving the original text in place. You can copy text to the Clipboard using the Copy button in the Clipboard group on the Home tab, or you can copy text by pressing [Ctrl] as you drag the selected text from one location to another. **CASE** *You continue to edit the press release by copying text from one location to another using the copy-and-paste and drag-and-drop methods.*

STEPS

QUICK TIP
You can also cut or copy text by right-clicking the selected text, and then clicking the Cut or Copy command on the menu that opens.

1. **Select Environmental Health and Wellness in the headline, then click the Copy button in the Clipboard group on the Home tab**

   A copy of the selected text is placed on the Clipboard, leaving the original text you copied in place.

2. **Place the insertion point before Luncheon in the first paragraph, then click the Paste button in the Clipboard group**

   "Environmental Health and Wellness" is inserted before "Luncheon," as shown in FIGURE 2-3. Notice that the pasted text is formatted differently than the paragraph in which it was inserted.

3. **Click the Paste Options button, move the mouse over each button on the menu that opens to read its ScreenTip, then click the Keep Text Only (T) button**

   The formatting of "Environmental Health and Wellness" is changed to match the rest of the paragraph. The buttons on the Paste Options menu allow you to change the formatting of pasted text. You can choose to keep the original formatting (Keep Source Formatting), match the destination formatting (Merge Formatting), or paste as unformatted text (Keep Text Only).

TROUBLE
Be sure you can see the last two paragraphs on your screen before completing this step.

4. **Select www.rwmed.org in the fifth paragraph, press and hold [Ctrl], then drag the pointer's vertical line to the end of the last paragraph, placing it between site and the period**

   As you drag, the pointer changes to ⬚, indicating that the selected text is being copied and moved.

TROUBLE
If you move the text instead of copying it, click the Undo button ↶ on the Quick Access toolbar and repeat Steps 4 and 5.

5. **Release the mouse button, then release [Ctrl]**

   The text is copied to the last paragraph. Since the formatting of the text you copied is the same as the formatting of the destination paragraph, you can ignore the Paste Options button. Text is not copied to the Clipboard when you copy it using the drag-and-drop method.

6. **Place the insertion point before www.rwmed.org in the last paragraph, type at followed by a space, then save the document**

   Compare your document with FIGURE 2-4.

Splitting the document window to copy and move items in a long document

If you want to copy or move items between parts of a long document, it can be useful to split the document window into two panes. This allows you to display the item you want to copy or move in one pane and the destination for the item in the other pane. To split a window, click the Split button in the Window group on the View tab, and then drag the horizontal split bar that appears to the location you want to split the window. Once the document window is split into two panes, you can use the scroll bars in each pane to display different parts of the document. To copy or move an item from one pane to another, you can use the Cut, Copy, and Paste commands, or you can drag the item between the panes. When you are finished editing the document, double-click the split bar to restore the window to a single pane, or click the Remove Split button in the Window group on the View tab.

FIGURE 2-3: Text pasted in document

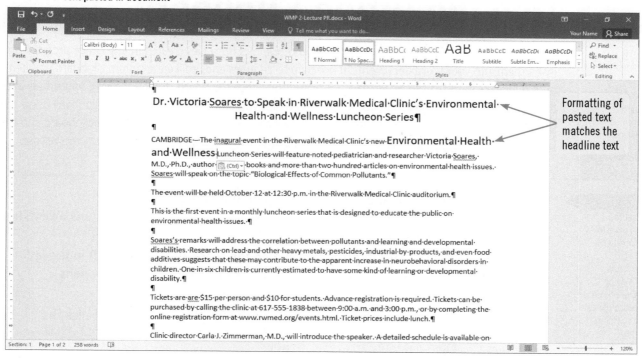

FIGURE 2-4: Copied text in document

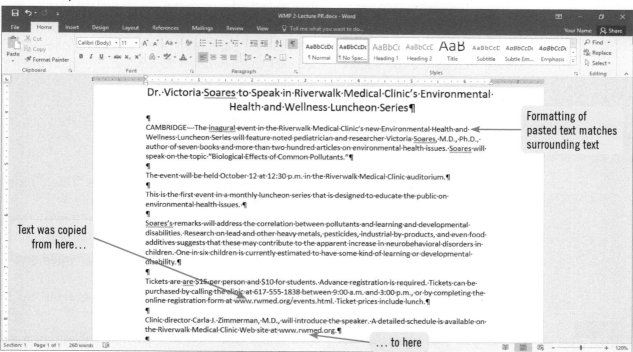

Use the Office Clipboard

Learning Outcomes
- Copy and cut items to the Clipboard
- Paste items from the Clipboard

The Office Clipboard allows you to collect text and graphics from files created in any Office program and insert them into your Word documents. It holds up to 24 items and, unlike the system clipboard, the items on the Office Clipboard can be viewed. To display the Office Clipboard (the Clipboard), you simply click the launcher in the Clipboard group on the Home tab. You add items to the Office Clipboard using the Cut and Copy commands. The last item you collect is always added to both the system clipboard and the Office Clipboard. **CASE** *You use the Office Clipboard to move several sentences in your press release.*

STEPS

QUICK TIP
You can set the Clipboard pane to open automatically when you cut or copy two items consecutively by clicking Options on the Clipboard pane, and then selecting Show Office Clipboard Automatically.

1. **Click the launcher ⬚ in the Clipboard group on the Home tab**
   The Office Clipboard opens in the Clipboard pane. It contains the Environmental Health and Wellness item you copied in the last lesson.

2. **Select the sentence Clinic director... (including the space after the period) in the last paragraph, right-click the selected text, then click Cut on the menu that opens**
   The sentence is cut to the Clipboard.

3. **Select the sentence A detailed schedule is... (including the ¶ mark), right-click the selected text, then click Cut**
   The Clipboard displays the items you cut or copied, as shown in FIGURE 2-5. The icon next to each item indicates the items are from a Word document. The last item collected is displayed at the top of the Clipboard pane. As new items are collected, the existing items move down the Clipboard.

QUICK TIP
If you add a 25th item to the Clipboard, the first item you collected is deleted.

4. **Place the insertion point at the end of the second paragraph (after "auditorium." but before the ¶ mark), then click the Clinic director... item on the Clipboard**
   Clicking an item on the Clipboard pastes the item in the document at the location of the insertion point. Items remain on the Clipboard until you delete them or close all open Office programs.

5. **Place the insertion point at the end of the third paragraph (after the space following "issues." but before the ¶ mark.), then click the A detailed schedule is... item on the Clipboard**
   The sentence is pasted into the document.

6. **Select the fourth paragraph, which begins with the sentence Soares's remarks... (including the ¶ mark), right-click the selected text, then click Cut**
   The paragraph is cut to the Clipboard.

7. **Place the insertion point at the beginning of the third paragraph (before "This..."), click the Paste button in the Clipboard group on the Home tab, then press [Enter]**
   The sentences from the "Soares's remarks..." paragraph are pasted at the beginning of the "This is the first..." paragraph. You can paste the last item collected using either the Paste command or the Clipboard.

8. **Place the insertion point at the end of the fourth paragraph (after "www.rwmed.org." and before the ¶ mark), then press [Delete] twice**
   Two ¶ symbols and the corresponding blank lines between the fourth and fifth paragraphs are deleted.

9. **Click the Show/Hide ¶ button ¶ on in the Paragraph group**
   Compare your press release with FIGURE 2-6. Note that many Word users prefer to work with formatting marks on at all times. Experiment to see which method you prefer.

QUICK TIP
To delete an individual item from the Clipboard, click the list arrow next to the item, then click Delete.

10. **Click the Clear All button on the Clipboard pane to remove the items from the Clipboard, click the Close button ✕ on the Clipboard pane, press [Ctrl][Home], then save the document**
    Pressing [Ctrl][Home] moves the insertion point to the top of the document.

Word 2016

FIGURE 2-5: Office Clipboard in Clipboard pane

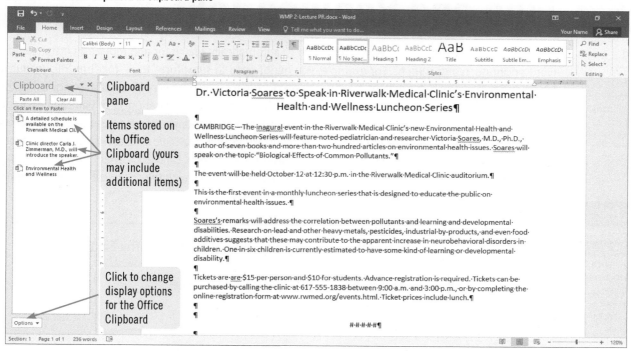

FIGURE 2-6: Revised press release

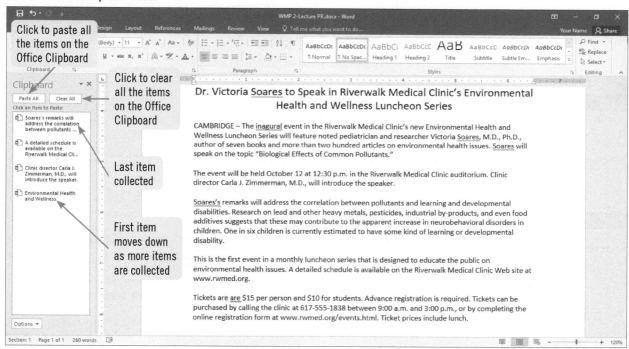

Copying and moving items between documents

You can also use the Clipboard to copy and move items between documents. To do this, open both documents and the Clipboard pane. With multiple documents open, copy or cut an item from one document and then switch to the other document and paste the item. To switch between open documents, point to the Word icon on the taskbar, and then click the document you want to appear in the document window. You can also display more than one document at the same time by clicking the Arrange All button or the View Side by Side button in the Window group on the View tab.

Find and Replace Text

Learning Outcomes
- Replace text
- Find text with the Navigation pane
- Navigate a document

The Find and Replace feature in Word allows you to automatically search for and replace all instances of a word or phrase in a document. For example, you might need to substitute "tour" for "trip." To manually locate and replace each instance of "trip" in a long document would be very time-consuming. Using the Replace command, you can find and replace all occurrences of specific text at once, or you can choose to find and review each occurrence individually. Using the Find command, you can locate and highlight every occurrence of a specific word or phrase in a document. **CASE** ➤ *The clinic director has decided to change the name of the lecture series from "Environmental Health and Wellness Luncheon Series" to "Environmental Health and Wellness Lecture Series." You use the Replace command to search the document for all instances of "Luncheon" and replace them with "Lecture."*

STEPS

TROUBLE

If any of the Search Options check boxes are selected in your Find and Replace dialog box, deselect them. If Format appears under the Find what or Replace with text box, click in the text box, then click the No Formatting button.

1. **Click the Replace button in the Editing group, then click More in the Find and Replace dialog box**

   The Find and Replace dialog box opens and expands, as shown in FIGURE 2-7.

2. **Type Luncheon in the Find what text box**

   "Luncheon" is the text that will be replaced.

3. **Press [Tab], then type Lecture in the Replace with text box**

   "Lecture" is the text that will replace "Luncheon."

4. **Click the Match case check box in the Search Options section to select it**

   Selecting the Match case check box tells Word to find only exact matches for the uppercase and lowercase characters you entered in the Find what text box. You want to replace all instances of "Luncheon" in the proper name "Environmental Health and Wellness Luncheon Series." You do not want to replace "luncheon" when it refers to a lunchtime event.

QUICK TIP

To find, review, and replace each occurrence individually, click Find Next.

5. **Click Replace All**

   Clicking Replace All changes all occurrences of "Luncheon" to "Lecture" in the press release. A message box reports two replacements were made.

6. **Click OK to close the message box, then click the Close button in the Find and Replace dialog box**

   Word replaced "Luncheon" with "Lecture" in two locations, but did not replace "luncheon."

QUICK TIP

Alternately, you can also use the Find tab in the Find and Replace dialog box to find text in a document.

7. **Click the Find button in the Editing group**

   Clicking the Find button opens the Navigation pane, which is used to browse a longer document by headings, by pages, or by specific text. The Find command allows you to quickly locate all instances of text in a document. You use it to verify that Word did not replace "luncheon."

8. **Type luncheon in the search text box in the Navigation pane, then scroll up until the headline is at the top of the document window**

   The word "luncheon" is highlighted and selected in the document, as shown in FIGURE 2-8.

9. **Click the Close button in the Navigation pane**

   The highlighting is removed from the text when you close the Navigation pane.

10. **Press [Ctrl][Home], then save the document**

FIGURE 2-7: Find and Replace dialog box

Replace only exact matches of uppercase and lowercase characters

Find only complete words

Use wildcards (*) in a search string

Find words that sound like the Find what text

Find and replace all forms of a word

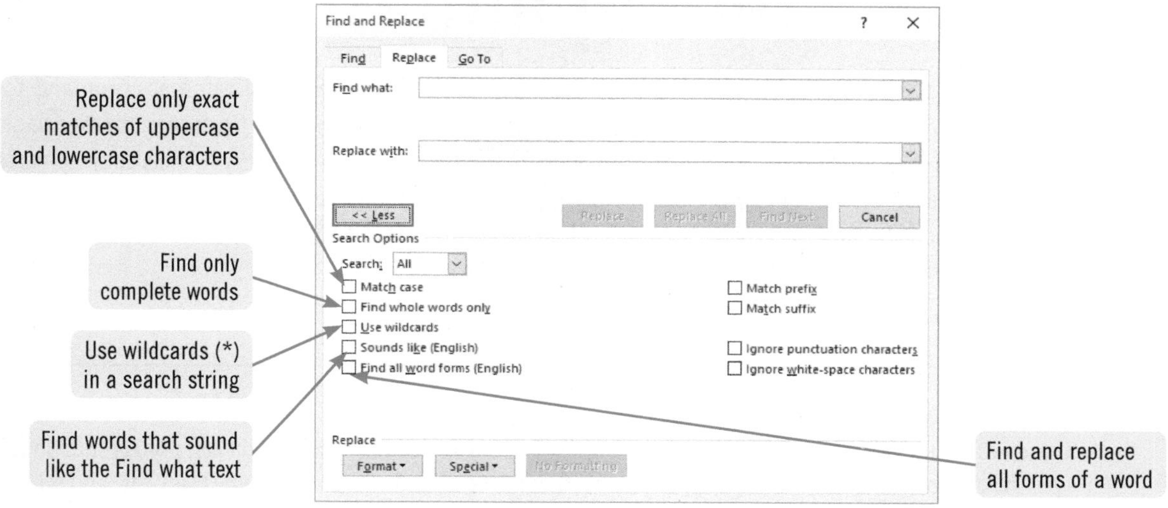

FIGURE 2-8: Found text highlighted in document

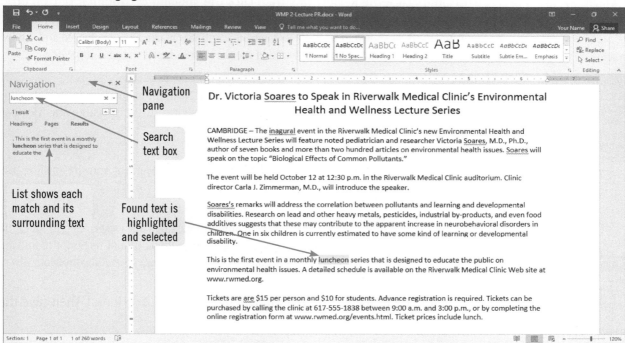

Navigation pane

Search text box

List shows each match and its surrounding text

Found text is highlighted and selected

Navigating a document using the Navigation pane and the Go To command

Rather than scrolling to move to a different place in a longer document, you can use the Navigation pane to quickly move the insertion point to a specific page or a specific heading. One way to open the Navigation pane is by clicking the Page number button on the status bar, then clicking the link in the Navigation pane for the type of item you want to use to navigate the document.

To move to a specific page, section, line, table, graphic, or other item in a document, you use the Go To tab in the Find and Replace dialog box. On the Go To tab in the Find and Replace dialog box, select the type of item you want to find in the Go to what list box, enter the relevant information about that item, and then click Next to move the insertion point to the item.

Check Spelling and Grammar

Learning Outcomes
- Ignore correctly spelled words
- Correct spelling errors
- Correct grammar errors

When you finish typing and revising a document, you can use the Spelling and Grammar command to search the document for misspelled words and grammar errors. The Spelling and Grammar checker flags possible mistakes, suggests correct spellings, and offers remedies for grammar errors such as subject–verb agreement, repeated words, and punctuation. **CASE** *You use the Spelling and Grammar checker to search your press release for errors. Before beginning the search, you set the Spelling and Grammar checker to ignore words, such as Soares, that you know are spelled correctly.*

STEPS

TROUBLE
If Word flags your name as misspelled, right-click it, then click Ignore All. If Soares is not flagged as misspelled, skip to Step 3.

1. **Right-click** Soares **in the headline**

   A menu that includes suggestions for correcting the spelling of "Soares" opens. You can correct individual spelling and grammar errors by right-clicking text that is underlined with a red or blue wavy line and selecting a correction. Although "Soares" is not in the Word dictionary, it is spelled correctly in the document.

2. **Click** Ignore All

   Clicking Ignore All tells Word not to flag "Soares" as misspelled.

QUICK TIP
To change the language used by the Word proofing tools, click the Language button in the Language group on the Review tab, click Set Proofing Language, select the language you prefer in the dialog box that opens, then click OK.

3. **Press** [Ctrl][Home], **click the** Review tab, **then click the** Spelling & Grammar button **in the Proofing group**

   The Spelling pane opens, as shown in **FIGURE 2-9**. The pane identifies "inagural" as misspelled and suggests a possible correction for the error. The word selected in the suggestions box is the correct spelling.

4. **Click** Change

   Word replaces the misspelled word with the correctly spelled word. Next, the word "Soares's" is highlighted as a misspelled word and possible replacement suggestions are shown in the Spelling pane. However, "Soares's" is spelled correctly in the document so no change is needed.

5. **Click** Ignore

   Word ignores the spelling. Next, the word "are" is highlighted in the document and the Spelling pane indicates that "are" is repeated in the sentence.

6. **Click** Delete

   Word deletes the second occurrence of the repeated word and the Spelling pane closes. Keep in mind that the Spelling and Grammar checker identifies many common errors, but you cannot rely on it to find and correct all spelling and grammar errors in your documents or to always suggest a valid correction. Always proofread your documents carefully.

QUICK TIP
If Word flags a grammar error, the suggested correction is shown in the Grammar pane.

7. **Click** OK **to complete the spelling and grammar check, press** [Ctrl][Home], **then save the document**

Using Smart Lookup

The Smart Lookup feature gives you quick access to information about document text, including definitions, images, and other material from online sources. For example, you might use Smart Lookup to see the definition of a word used in a document or to hear the word pronounced. To use Smart Lookup, select the text you want to look up in your document, then click the Smart Lookup button in the Insights group on the Review tab. The Insights pane opens and includes the Explore and Define tabs. The Explore tab includes images and web links related to the selected text. The Define tab includes a dictionary definition of the selected text and a link you can click to hear the selected text pronounced.

FIGURE 2-9: Spelling pane

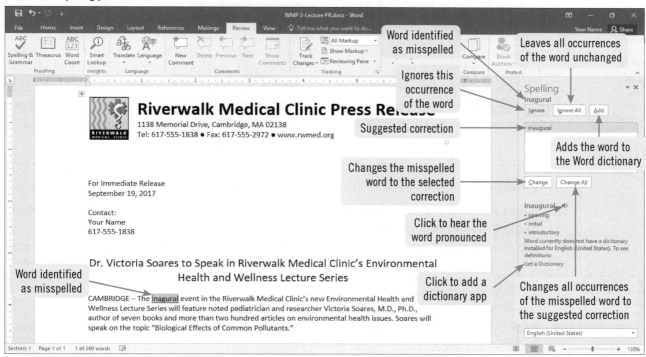

Inserting text with AutoCorrect

As you type, AutoCorrect automatically corrects many commonly misspelled words. By creating your own AutoCorrect entries, you can set Word to insert text that you type often, such as your name or contact information, or to correct words you misspell frequently. For example, you could create an AutoCorrect entry so that the name "Mary T. Watson" is automatically inserted whenever you type "mtw" followed by a space. You create AutoCorrect entries and customize other AutoCorrect and AutoFormat options using the AutoCorrect dialog box. To open the AutoCorrect dialog box, click the File tab, click Options, click Proofing in the Word Options dialog box that opens, and then click AutoCorrect Options. On the AutoCorrect tab in the AutoCorrect dialog box, type the text you want to be corrected

automatically in the Replace text box (such as "mtw"), type the text you want to be inserted in its place automatically in the With text box (such as "Mary T. Watson"), and then click Add. The AutoCorrect entry is added to the list. Click OK to close the AutoCorrect dialog box, and then click OK to close the Word Options dialog box. Word inserts an AutoCorrect entry in a document when you press [Spacebar] or a punctuation mark after typing the text you want Word to correct. For example, Word inserts "Mary T. Watson" when you type "mtw" followed by a space. If you want to remove an AutoCorrect entry you created, simply open the AutoCorrect dialog box, select the AutoCorrect entry you want to remove in the list, click Delete, click OK, and then click OK to close the Word Options dialog box.

Research Information

Learning Outcomes
• Find synonyms using the Thesaurus
• Check word count

The Word research features allow you to quickly search reference sources and the web for information related to a word or phrase. Among the reference sources available are a Thesaurus, which you can use to look up synonyms for awkward or repetitive words, as well as dictionary and translation sources. **CASE** ▸ *After proofreading your document for errors, you decide the press release would read better if several adjectives were more descriptive. You use the Thesaurus to find synonyms.*

STEPS

1. **Scroll until the headline is displayed at the top of your screen**

2. **Select noted in the first sentence of the first paragraph, then click the Thesaurus button in the Proofing group on the Review tab**

   The Thesaurus pane opens, as shown in FIGURE 2-10. "Noted" appears in the search text box, and possible synonyms for "noted" are listed under the search text box.

QUICK TIP
To look up synonyms for a different word, type the word in the search text box, then click the search button.

3. **Point to prominent in the list of synonyms**

   A shaded box containing a list arrow appears around the word.

4. **Click the list arrow, click Insert on the menu that opens, then close the Thesaurus pane**

   "Prominent" replaces "noted" in the press release.

5. **Right-click currently in the last sentence of the third paragraph, point to Synonyms on the menu that opens, then click now**

   The word "now" replaces "currently" in the press release.

6. **Select the five paragraphs of body text, then click the Word Count button in the Proofing group**

   The Word Count dialog box opens, as shown in FIGURE 2-11. The dialog box lists the number of pages, words, characters, paragraphs, and lines included in the selected text. Notice that the status bar also displays the number of words included in the selected text and the total number of words in the entire document. If you want to view the page, character, paragraph, and line count for the entire document, make sure nothing is selected in your document, and then click Word Count in the Proofing group.

7. **Click Close, press [Ctrl][Home], then save the document**

8. **Click the File tab, click Save As, navigate to the location where you store your files, type WMP 2-Lecture PR Public in the File name text box, then click Save**

   The WMP 2-Lecture PR file closes, and the WMP 2-Lecture PR Public file is displayed in the document window. You will modify this file to prepare it for electronic release to the public.

Publishing a blog directly from Word

A **blog**, which is short for weblog, is an informal journal that is created by an individual or a group and available to the public on the Internet. A blog usually conveys the ideas, comments, and opinions of the blogger and is written using a strong personal voice. The person who creates and maintains a blog, the **blogger**, typically updates the blog regularly. If you have or want to start a blog, you can configure Word to link to your blog site so that you can write, format, and publish blog entries directly from Word.

To create a new blog post, click the File tab, click New, then double-click Blog post to open a predesigned blog post document that you can customize with your own text, formatting, and images. You can also publish an existing document as a blog post by opening the document, clicking the File tab, clicking Share, and then clicking Post to Blog. In either case, Word prompts you to log onto your personal blog account. To blog directly from Word, you must first obtain a blog account with a blog service provider. Resources, such as the Word Help system and online forums, provide detailed information on obtaining and registering your personal blog account with Word.

FIGURE 2-10: Thesaurus pane

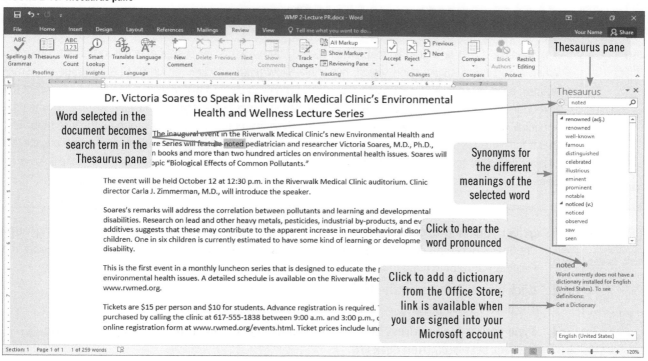

Thesaurus pane

Word selected in the document becomes search term in the Thesaurus pane

Dr. Victoria Soares to Speak in Riverwalk Medical Clinic's Environmental Health and Wellness Lecture Series

The inaugural event in the Riverwalk Medical Clinic's new Environmental Health and ...re Series will featu...e noted pediatrician and researcher Victoria Soares, M.D., Ph.D., ...n books and more than two hundred articles on environmental health issues. Soares will ...opic "Biological Effects of Common Pollutants."

The event will be held October 12 at 12:30 p.m. in the Riverwalk Medical Clinic auditorium. Clinic director Carla J. Zimmerman, M.D., will introduce the speaker.

Soares's remarks will address the correlation between pollutants and learning and developmental disabilities. Research on lead and other heavy metals, pesticides, industrial by-products, and ev... additives suggests that these may contribute to the apparent increase in neurobehavioral disor... children. One in six children is currently estimated to have some kind of learning or developme... disability.

This is the first event in a monthly luncheon series that is designed to educate the p... environmental health issues. A detailed schedule is available on the Riverwalk Med... www.rwmed.org.

Tickets are $15 per person and $10 for students. Advance registration is required. ... purchased by calling the clinic at 617-555-1838 between 9:00 a.m. and 3:00 p.m., o... online registration form at www.rwmed.org/events.html. Ticket prices include lunc...

Synonyms for the different meanings of the selected word

Thesaurus

noted

renowned (adj.)
renowned
well-known
famous
distinguished
celebrated
illustrious
eminent
prominent
notable
noticed (v.)
noticed
observed
saw
seen

Click to hear the word pronounced

noted

Word currently does not have a dictionary installed for English (United States). To see definitions:

Get a Dictionary

Click to add a dictionary from the Office Store; link is available when you are signed into your Microsoft account

English (United States)

Section: 1   Page 1 of 1   1 of 259 words

FIGURE 2-11: Word Count dialog box

Word Count	?	X
Statistics:		
Pages		1
Words		211
Characters (no spaces)		1,222
Characters (with spaces)		1,429
Paragraphs		5
Lines		20

☑ Include textboxes, footnotes and endnotes

Close

Using a dictionary and other add-ins for Word

Instead of a built-in dictionary, Word includes the ability to install a free dictionary add-in from the Office Store that you can use to see definitions of words. A dictionary add-in is just one of many add-ins that are available in Word. **Add-ins** are small programs embedded in Word that allow you to access information on the web without having to leave Word. For example, you can look up something on Wikipedia, insert an online map in one of your documents, or access dictionaries and other reference sources, all from within Word using an add-in. To install a free dictionary add-in from the Office Store, click the Thesaurus button In the Proofing group on the Review tab, click the Get a Dictionary link to open the Dictionaries pane, decide which dictionary you want, review the Terms & Conditions as well as the Privacy Policy associated with the add-in you want, and then click the Download button associated with the dictionary you want in order to install that dictionary. If you want to download other dictionaries or other add-ins, click the Store button in the Add-ins group on the Insert tab, find the add-in you want, and then follow the prompts to install the add-in. Some add-ins are free, and some require purchase. To use an add-in, click the My Add-ins button in the Add-ins group to see your list of add-ins, and then click the add-in you want to use.

Add Hyperlinks

Learning Outcomes
- Insert a hyperlink
- Test hyperlinks
- E-mail a document from Word

A **hyperlink** is text or a graphic that, when clicked, "jumps" the viewer to a different location or program. When a document is viewed on screen, hyperlinks allow readers to link (or jump) to a webpage, an e-mail address, a file, or a specific location in a document. When you create a hyperlink in a document, you select the text or graphic you want to use as a hyperlink and then you specify the location you want to jump to when the hyperlink is clicked. You create a hyperlink using the Hyperlink button in the Links group on the Insert tab. Text that is formatted as a hyperlink appears as colored, underlined text. **CASE** ▶ *Hundreds of people on your lists of press and client contacts will receive the press release by e-mail or view it on your website. To make it easier for these people to access additional information about the series, you add several hyperlinks to the press release.*

STEPS

QUICK TIP
By default, Word automatically creates a hyperlink to an e-mail address or URL when you type an e-mail address or a URL in a document.

1. **Select your name, click the Insert tab, then click the Hyperlink button in the Links group**

   The Insert Hyperlink dialog box opens, as shown in FIGURE 2-12. You use this dialog box to specify the location you want to jump to when the hyperlink—in this case, your name—is clicked.

2. **Click E-mail Address in the Link to section**

   The Insert Hyperlink dialog box changes so you can create a hyperlink to your e-mail address.

3. **Type your e-mail address in the E-mail address text box, type Lecture Series in the Subject text box, then click OK**

   As you type, Word automatically adds mailto: in front of your e-mail address. After you close the dialog box, the hyperlink text—your name—is formatted in blue and underlined.

TROUBLE
If an e-mail message does not open, close the window that opens and continue with Step 6.

4. **Press and hold [Ctrl], then click the your name hyperlink**

   An e-mail message addressed to you with the subject "Lecture Series" opens in the default e-mail program. People can use this hyperlink to send you an e-mail message.

5. **Close the e-mail message window, clicking No if you are prompted to save**

   The hyperlink text changes to purple, indicating the hyperlink has been followed.

QUICK TIP
To remove a hyperlink, right-click it, then click Remove Hyperlink. Removing a hyperlink removes the link, but the text remains.

6. **Scroll down, select environmental health in the fourth paragraph, click the Hyperlink button, click Existing File or Web Page in the Link to section, type www.cdc.gov/nceh in the Address text box, then click OK**

   As you type the web address, Word automatically adds "http://" in front of "www." The text "environmental health" is formatted as a hyperlink to the Centers for Disease Control and Prevention's National Center for Environmental Health home page at www.cdc.gov/nceh. When clicked, the hyperlink will open the webpage in the default browser window. If you point to a hyperlink in Word, the link to location appears in a ScreenTip. You can edit ScreenTip text to make it more descriptive.

QUICK TIP
You can also edit the hyperlink destination or the hyperlink text.

7. **Right-click health in the environmental health hyperlink, click Edit Hyperlink, click ScreenTip in the Edit Hyperlink dialog box, type Information related to environmental health issues in the ScreenTip text box, click OK, click OK, save your changes, then point to the environmental health hyperlink in the document**

   The ScreenTip you created appears above the environmental health hyperlink, as shown in FIGURE 2-13.

TROUBLE
If you are not working with an active Internet connection, skip this step.

8. **Press [Ctrl], click the environmental health hyperlink, verify the link opened in your browser, then click the Word icon 📄 on the taskbar to return to the press release**

   Before distributing a document, it's important to test each hyperlink to verify it works as you intended.

FIGURE 2-12: Insert Hyperlink dialog box

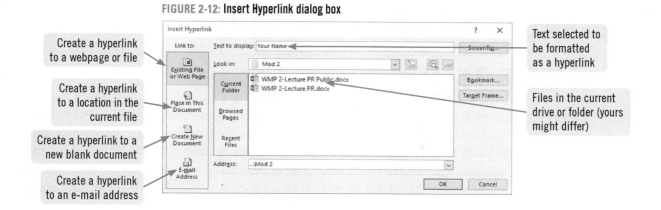

Create a hyperlink to a webpage or file

Create a hyperlink to a location in the current file

Create a hyperlink to a new blank document

Create a hyperlink to an e-mail address

Text selected to be formatted as a hyperlink

Files in the current drive or folder (yours might differ)

FIGURE 2-13: Hyperlinks in the document

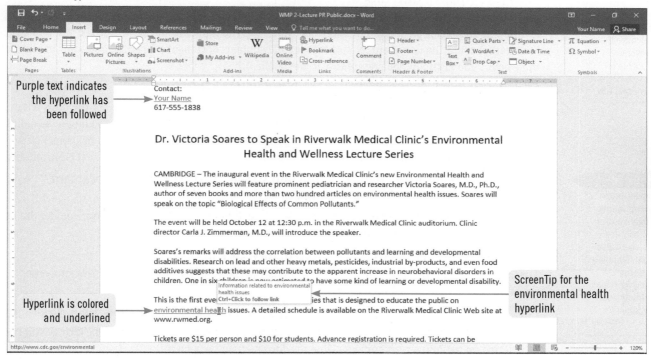

Purple text indicates the hyperlink has been followed

Hyperlink is colored and underlined

ScreenTip for the environmental health hyperlink

Sharing documents directly from Word, including e-mailing

Word includes several options for distributing and sharing documents over the Internet directly from within Word, including saving a document to OneDrive for others to view and edit, e-mailing a document, presenting a document online so others can view it in a web browser, sending it by Instant Message, and posting a document to a blog. To share a document, open the file in Word, click the File tab, click Share, and then click one of the Share options. You can also use the Share button on the title bar to save a document to an online location.

When you e-mail a document from within Word, the document is sent as an attachment to an e-mail message using your default e-mail program. You can choose to attach the document as a Word file, a .pdf file, or an .xps file, or to send it as an Internet fax. When you click an option, a message window opens that includes the filename of the current file as the message subject and the file as an attachment. Type the e-mail address(es) of the recipient(s) in the To and Cc text boxes, any message you want in the message window, and then click Send to send the message. The default e-mail program sends a copy of the document to each recipient. Note that faxing a document directly from Word requires registration with a third-party Internet fax service.

Work with Document Properties

Before you distribute a document electronically to people outside your organization, it's wise to make sure the file does not include embedded private or confidential information. The Info screen in Backstage view includes tools for stripping a document of sensitive information, for securing its authenticity, and for guarding it from unwanted changes once it is distributed to the public. One of these tools, the Document Inspector, detects and removes unwanted private or confidential information from a document. **CASE** *Before sending the press release to the public, you remove all identifying information from the file.*

STEPS

1. **Press [Ctrl][Home], then click the File tab**

   Backstage view opens with the Info screen displayed. The left side of the Info screen includes options related to stripping the file of private information. See TABLE 2-1. The right side of the Info screen displays basic information about the document. Notice that the file contains document properties. You want to remove these before you distribute the press release to the public.

2. **Click the Show All Properties link at the bottom of the Info screen**

   The Properties section expands on the Info screen. It shows the document properties for the press release. **Document properties** are user-defined details about a file that describe its contents and origin, including the name of the author, the title of the document, and keywords that you can assign to help organize and search your files. You decide to remove this information from the file before you distribute it electronically.

3. **Click the Check for Issues button on the Info screen, then click Inspect Document, clicking Yes if prompted to save changes**

   The Document Inspector dialog box opens. You use this dialog box to indicate which private or identifying information you want to search for and remove from the document.

4. **Make sure all the check boxes are selected, then click Inspect**

   After a moment, the Document Inspector dialog box indicates the file contains document properties, as shown in FIGURE 2-14.

5. **Click Remove All next to Document Properties and Personal Information, then click Close**

   The document property information is removed from the press release document, but the change will not be reflected on the Info screen until you close the document and reopen it.

6. **Click Save on the Info screen, close the document, open the document again in Word, then click the File tab**

   The Info screen shows the document properties have been removed from the file.

7. **Save the document, submit it to your instructor, close the file, then exit Word**

   The completed press release is shown in FIGURE 2-15.

TABLE 2-1: Options on the Info screen

option	use to
Protect Document	Mark a document as final so that it is read-only and cannot be edited; encrypt a document so that a password is required to open it; restrict what kinds of changes can be made to a document and by whom; restrict access to editing, copying, and printing a document and add a digital signature to a document to verify its integrity
Check for Issues	Detect and remove unwanted information from a document, including document properties and comments; check for content that people with disabilities might find difficult to read; and check the document for features that are not supported by previous versions of Microsoft Word
Manage Document	Browse and recover draft versions of unsaved files

FIGURE 2-14: **Results after inspecting a document**

Removes document property information from the file

FIGURE 2-15: **Completed press release for electronic distribution**

Viewing and modifying advanced document properties

The Properties section of the Info screen includes summary information about the document that you enter. To view more detailed document properties, click the Properties button on the Info screen, and then click Advanced Properties to open the Properties dialog box. The General, Statistics, and Contents tabs of the Properties dialog box display information about the file that is automatically created and updated by Word. The General tab shows the file type, location, size, and date and time the file was created and last modified; the Statistics tab displays information about revisions to the document along with the number of pages, words, lines, paragraphs, and characters in the file; and the Contents tab shows the title of the document.

You can define other document properties using the Summary and Custom tabs in the Properties dialog box. The Summary tab shows information similar to the information shown on the Info screen. The Custom tab allows you to create new document properties, such as client, project, or date completed. To create a custom property, select a property name in the Name list box on the Custom tab, use the Type list arrow to select the type of data you want for the property, type the identifying detail (such as a project name) in the Value text box, and then click Add. When you are finished viewing or modifying the document properties, click OK to close the Properties dialog box.

Practice

Concepts Review

Label the elements of the Word program window shown in FIGURE 2-16.

FIGURE 2-16

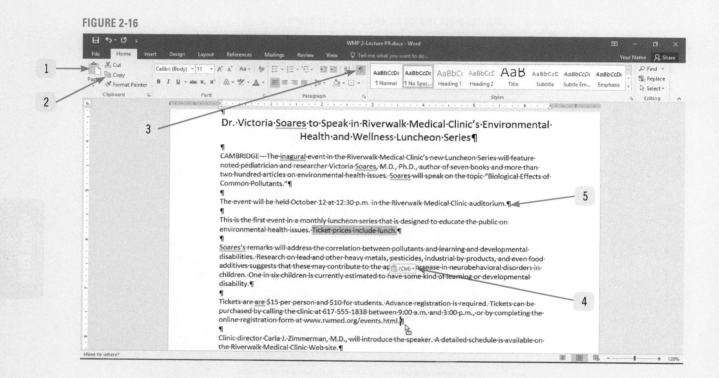

Match each term with the statement that best describes it.

6. Office Clipboard
7. Paste
8. Hyperlink
9. Thesaurus
10. Shortcut Key
11. Smart Lookup
12. Cut
13. System clipboard
14. Document properties

a. Command used to insert text stored on the Clipboard into a document
b. Temporary storage area for up to 24 items collected from Office files
c. Temporary storage area for only the last item cut or copied from a document
d. A function key or a combination of keys that perform a command when pressed
e. Text or a graphic that jumps the reader to a different location or program when clicked
f. A program that accesses information on the web from within Word
g. User-defined details about a file that describe its contents and origin
h. Feature used to suggest synonyms for words
i. Command used to remove text from a document and place it on the Clipboard

Select the best answer from the list of choices.

15. What is the keyboard shortcut for the Cut command?

   a. [Ctrl][V]   **c.** [Ctrl][P]

   b. [Ctrl][C]   **d.** [Ctrl][X]

16. Which command is used to display a document in two panes in the document window?

   a. Split   **c.** Arrange All

   b. New Window   **d.** Two pages

17. Which of the following statements is *not* true?

   a. You can view the contents of the Office Clipboard.

   b. The last item cut or copied from a document is stored on the system clipboard.

   c. The Office Clipboard can hold more than one item.

   d. When you move text by dragging it, a copy of the text you move is stored on the system clipboard.

18. To locate and select all instances of a word in a document, which command do you use?

   a. Highlight   **c.** Find

   b. Show/Hide   **d.** Search

19. Which of the following is an example of a document property?

   a. URL   **c.** Permission

   b. Keyword   **d.** Language

20. A hyperlink *cannot* be linked to which of the following?

   a. Document   **c.** ScreenTip

   b. E-mail address   **d.** Webpage

Skills Review

1. Cut and paste text.

   a. Start Word, click the Open Other Documents link, open the file WMP 2-2.docx from the location where you store your Data Files, then save the document with the filename **WMP 2-2017 PR**.

   b. Select **Your Name** and replace it with your name.

   c. Display paragraph and other formatting marks in your document if they are not already displayed.

   d. Use the Cut and Paste buttons to switch the order of the two sentences in the fourth body paragraph (which begins The famous children's entertainer…).

   e. Use the drag-and-drop method to switch the order of the second and third paragraphs.

   f. Adjust the spacing if necessary so that there is one blank line between paragraphs, then save your changes.

2. Copy and paste text.

   a. Use the Copy and Paste buttons to copy **NHF 2015** from the headline and paste it before the word **map** in the third paragraph.

   b. Change the formatting of the pasted text to match the formatting of the third paragraph, then insert a space between **2015** and **map** if necessary.

   c. Use the drag-and-drop method to copy **NHF** from the third paragraph and paste it before the word **stage** in the second sentence of the fourth paragraph, then save your changes.

3. Use the Office Clipboard.

   a. Use the launcher in the Clipboard group to open the Clipboard pane.

   b. Scroll so that the first body paragraph is displayed at the top of the document window.

   c. Select the fifth paragraph (which begins Health fair maps…) and cut it to the Clipboard.

   d. Select the third paragraph (which begins Newburyport is easily accessible…) and cut it to the Clipboard.

   e. Use the Clipboard to paste the Health fair maps… item as the new fourth paragraph.

   f. Use the Clipboard to paste the Newburyport is easily accessible… item as the new fifth paragraph.

   g. Adjust the spacing if necessary so there is one blank line between each of the six body paragraphs.

   h. Turn off the display of formatting marks, clear and close the Clipboard pane, then save your changes.

Skills Review (continued)

4. **Find and replace text.**
   a. Using the Replace command, replace all instances of **2015** with **2017**.
   b. Replace all instances of **tenth** with **twelfth**.
   c. Replace all instances of the abbreviation **st** with **street**, taking care to replace whole words only when you perform the replace. (*Hint*: Deselect Match case if it is selected.)
   d. Click the Find tab, deselect the Find whole words only check box, click the Reading Highlight button, click Highlight All, close the dialog box, then view all instances of **st** in the document to make sure no errors occurred when you replaced st with street.
   e. Click the Find button to open the Navigation pane, notice the results and the highlighted text, close the Navigation pane, then save your changes to the press release. (*Note: You can see the highlighted results using either the Reading Highlight button in the Find and Replace dialog box or the Navigation pane.*)

5. **Check spelling and grammar and research information.**
   a. Switch to the Review tab.
   b. Move the insertion point to the top of the document, then use the Spelling & Grammar command to search for and correct any spelling and grammar errors in the press release.
   c. Use the Thesaurus to replace **famous** in the third paragraph with a different suitable word, then close the Thesaurus pane.
   d. Check the word count of the press release.
   e. Proofread your press release, correct any errors, then save your changes.

6. **Add hyperlinks.**
   a. Save the document as **WMP 2-2017 PR Public**, then switch to the Insert tab.
   b. Select your name, then open the Insert Hyperlink dialog box.
   c. Create a hyperlink to your e-mail address with the subject **NHF 2017**.
   d. Test the your name hyperlink, then close the message window that opens and click No if a message window opens. (*Hint*: Press [Ctrl], then click the hyperlink.)
   e. Select **NIH** in the last paragraph of the press release, then create a hyperlink to the webpage with the URL **www.nih.gov**.
   f. Right-click the NIH hyperlink, then edit the hyperlink ScreenTip to become **Information on the National Institutes of Health**.
   g. Point to the NIH hyperlink to view the new ScreenTip, then save your changes.
   h. If you are working with an active Internet connection, press [Ctrl], click the NIH hyperlink, view the NIH home page in the browser window, then close the browser window and return to Word. The finished press release is shown in FIGURE 2-17.

FIGURE 2-17

PRESS RELEASE

For Immediate Release
August 20, 2017

Contact:
Your Name
978-555-3984

NHF 2017
Newburyport Health Fair to Focus on Child Health Issues

NEWBURYPORT, MA -- A variety of health and safety information for parents will be available at the Newburyport Health Fair, to be held Saturday, September 22 from 10 a.m. to 4 p.m. at Waterfront Park. More than 60 exhibitors, health care providers, and entertainers will be on hand for this annual event, now in its twelfth year. The Newburyport Health Fair is free and open to the public.

Pediatricians will be available to answer questions and distribute information about many child and adolescent health and safety topics, including healthy eating, injury prevention, and immunizations. In addition, adult screenings for blood pressure, cholesterol, vision, hearing, skin cancer, body strength, flexibility, and posture alignment will be available to the public free of charge.

Emergency vehicle tours, massage workshops, nutrition counseling, and tai chi demonstrations will be held throughout the day. The renowned children's entertainer Adam Apple will perform on the NHF stage at 1:00 p.m.

Health fair maps will be available prior to the event at businesses and public libraries, and on the day of the event at Waterfront Park. Waterfront Park is bordered by College Street, Battery Street, and the harbor.

Newburyport is easily accessible from all points in New England by car or bus, and from Boston by train. On Saturday, non-Newburyport residents may park in permit-only areas provided they display a copy of the NHF 2017 map on the dashboard.

NHF 2017 receives funds from Fletcher Allen Hospital of Massachusetts, Newburyport City Council, New England Healthy Kids, and the NIH, with valuable support from local businesses.

#####

Skills Review (continued)

7. Work with document properties.

    a. Click the File tab, click the Properties button on the Info screen, then click Advanced Properties to open the Properties dialog box and view the document properties for the press release on the Summary tab.

    b. Close the Properties dialog box, then use the Check for Issues command to run the Document Inspector.

    c. Remove the document property and personal information data, close the Document Inspector, save your changes, then close the file.

    d. Open the file WMP 2017 PR Public, then verify that the document properties have been removed both on the Info screen and in the Properties dialog box. Save the document, submit it to your instructor, close the file, then exit Word.

Independent Challenge 1

Dr. Chen, a physician in your office, is leaving her practice at Erie Medical Center for a practice at another hospital in Buffalo. She asks you to draft a letter to her patients informing them of the move. You'll create a change of address letter for Dr. Chen by modifying a letter you wrote for another doctor.

    a. Start Word, open the file WMP 2-3.docx from the location where you store your Data Files, then save it as **WMP 2-Change of Address Letter**.

    b. Replace the doctor's name and address, the date, the inside address, and the salutation with the text shown in FIGURE 2-18.

    c. Use the Replace command to replace all instances of **St. Mary's** with **Memorial**.

    d. In the second body paragraph, replace **1478 Portland Street** with **327 Westside Avenue**.

    e. Use the Find command to locate the word **superb**, then use the Thesaurus to replace the word with a synonym.

FIGURE 2-18

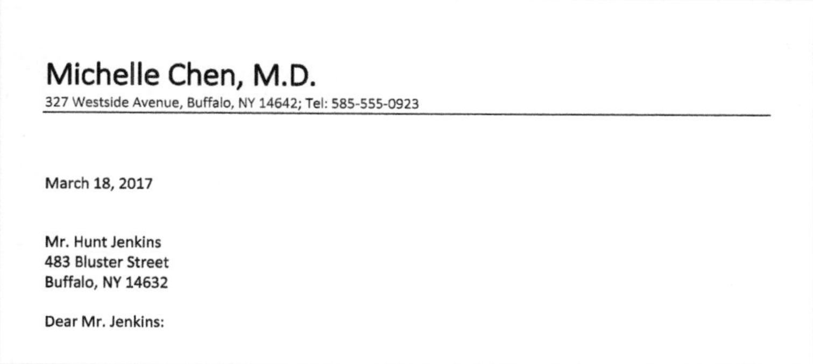

Michelle Chen, M.D.
327 Westside Avenue, Buffalo, NY 14642; Tel: 585-555-0923

March 18, 2017

Mr. Hunt Jenkins
483 Bluster Street
Buffalo, NY 14632

Dear Mr. Jenkins:

    f. Create an AutoCorrect entry that inserts **Erie Medical Center at the University of Buffalo** whenever you type **emc** followed by a space.

    g. Select each instance of Highland Hospital, type **emc** followed by a space, then delete the extra space before the period.

    h. Move the last sentence of the first body paragraph so it becomes the first sentence of the third body paragraph, adjusting the space as needed.

    i. Replace James Sharlet with **Michelle Chen** in the signature block, then replace the typist's initials yi with your initials.

    j. Use the Spelling and Grammar command to check for and correct spelling and grammar errors.

    k. Delete the AutoCorrect entry you created for emc. (*Hint*: Open the AutoCorrect dialog box, select the AutoCorrect entry you created, then click [Delete].)

    l. Open the Properties dialog box, add your name as the author, change the title to **Michelle Chen, M.D.**, add the keywords **address change**, then add the comment **Change of address letter**.

    m. Review the paragraph, line, word, and character count on the Statistics tab.

    n. On the Custom tab, add a property named **Office** with the value **Address Change**, then close the dialog box.

    o. Proofread the letter, correct any errors, save your changes, submit a copy to your instructor, close the document, then exit Word.

Independent Challenge 2

An advertisement for job openings in San Francisco caught your eye and you have decided to apply. The ad, shown in FIGURE 2-19, was printed in last weekend's edition of your local newspaper. Instead of writing a cover letter from scratch, you revise a draft of a cover letter you wrote several years ago for a summer internship position.

FIGURE 2-19

San Francisco Health
The Neighborhood Health Center

San Francisco Comprehensive Community Health Center (SFCCHC), offering quality health care to the San Francisco community for over thirty years, is seeking candidates for the following positions:

Registered Nurses
Openings in Adult Medicine and Pediatrics. Must have two years of nursing experience. Current RN license and CPR required. Position B12C6

Laboratory Technician
Perform a variety of routine laboratory tests and procedures. Certification as MLT (ASCP) required, plus two years work experience. Position C14B5

Correspondence Coordinator
Process all correspondence mail in our medical records department. Must have knowledge of HIPAA regulations. Fluency with Microsoft Word required. Position C13D4

Medical Assistant
Maintain patient flow, assist physicians using sterile techniques, and educate patients on health issues. Must enjoy interacting with patients and be proficient with Microsoft Word. MA certification preferred. CPR required. Position B16F5

Positions offer salary, excellent benefits, and career opportunities.

Send resume and cover letter referencing position code to:

Maxine Sorbello
Director of Human Resources
San Francisco Comprehensive Community Health Center
3826 Sacramento Street
San Francisco, CA 94118
Fax to 415-555-2939 or Email to hr@sfcchc.com

a. Read the ad shown in FIGURE 2-19 and decide which position to apply for. Choose the position that most closely matches your qualifications.

b. Start Word, open WMP 2-4.docx from the location where you store your Data Files, then save it as **WMP 2-Cover Letter**.

c. Replace the name, address, telephone number, and e-mail address in the letterhead with your own information.

d. Remove the hyperlink from the e-mail address.

e. Replace the date with today's date, then replace the inside address and the salutation with the information shown in FIGURE 2-19.

f. Read the draft cover letter to get a feel for its contents.

g. Rework the text in the body of the letter to address your qualifications for the job you have chosen to apply for in the following ways:

- Delete the third paragraph.
- Adjust the first sentence of the first paragraph as follows: specify the job you are applying for, including the position code, and indicate where you saw the position advertised.
- Move the first sentence in the last paragraph, which briefly states your qualifications and interest in the position, to the end of the first paragraph, then rework the sentence to describe your current qualifications.
- Adjust the second paragraph as follows: describe your work experience and skills. Add a third paragraph if your qualifications are extensive.
- Adjust the final paragraph as follows: politely request an interview for the position and provide your phone number and e-mail address.

h. Include your name in the signature block.

i. When you are finished revising the letter, check it for spelling and grammar errors, and correct any mistakes. Make sure to remove any hyperlinks. Save your changes to the letter, submit the file to your instructor, close the document, then exit Word.

Independent Challenge 3

As director of public education at Atlantic Community Hospital, you drafted a memo to the nursing staff asking them to help you finalize the schedule for the Healthy Living seminar series. Today, you'll examine the draft and make revisions before distributing it as an e-mail attachment.

a. Start Word, open the file WMP 2-5.docx from the drive and folder where you store your Data Files, then save it as **WMP 2-Healthy Living Memo**.

Independent Challenge 3 (continued)

b. Replace Your Name with your name in the From line, then scroll until the first body paragraph is at the top of the screen.

c. Use the Split command on the View tab to split the window under the first body paragraph, then scroll until the last paragraph of the memo is displayed in the bottom pane.

d. Use the Cut and Paste buttons to move the sentence **If you are planning to lead…** from the first body paragraph to become the first sentence in the last paragraph of the memo.

e. Double-click the split bar to restore the window to a single pane.

f. Use the [Delete] key to merge the first two paragraphs into one paragraph.

g. Use the Clipboard to reorganize the brown bag lunch topics so that the topics are listed in alphabetical order, then clear and close the Clipboard.

h. Use drag-and-drop to reorganize the list of Saturday morning lectures so that the lectures are listed in alphabetical order.

i. Select the phrase "website" in the first paragraph, then create a hyperlink to the URL **www.cengage.com** with the ScreenTip **2018 Healthy Living Series Schedule**.

j. Select "e-mail me" in the last paragraph, then create a hyperlink to your e-mail address with the subject **Healthy Living Series Schedule**.

k. Use the Spelling and Grammar command to check for and correct spelling and grammar errors.

l. Use the Document Inspector to strip the document of document property information, ignore any other content that is flagged by the Document Inspector, then close the Document Inspector.

m. Proofread the memo, correct any errors, save your changes, submit a copy to your instructor, close the document, then exit Word.

Independent Challenge 4: Explore

Reference sources—dictionaries, thesauri, style and grammar guides, and guides to business etiquette and procedure—are essential for day-to-day use in the workplace. Much of this reference information is available on the web. In this independent challenge, you will locate reference sources that might be useful to you, including the Office Add-ins resources that are available for Word. Your goal is to familiarize yourself with online reference sources and Office Add-ins for Word so you can use them later in your work. You will insert a screenshot of an Office Add-in webpage in your document.

a. Start Word, open the file WMP 2-6.docx from the location where you store your Data Files, then save it as **WMP 2-References**. This document contains the questions you will answer about the web reference sources you find and Office Add-ins. You will type your answers to the questions in the document.

b. Replace the placeholder text at the top of the WMP 2-References document with your name and the date.

c. Use your favorite search engine to search the web for grammar and style guides, dictionaries, and thesauri. Use the keywords **grammar**, **usage**, **dictionary**, **glossary**, or **thesaurus** to conduct your search.

d. Complete question 1 of the WMP 2-References document, making sure to format each website name as a hyperlink to that website.

e. Read question 2 of the WMP 2-References document, then move the insertion point under question 2.

f. Click the Store button in the Add-ins group on the Insert tab. Explore the add-ins available through the Office Add-ins window, click one add-in to select it, then click the hyperlink for that add-in to open it in a new browser window. (*Hint*: The hyperlink for an add-in is located under the icon for the add-in.)

g. Switch to the WMP 2-References document in Word. Close the Office Add-ins window if it is still open.

h. With the insertion point below question 2, click the Screenshot button in the Illustrations group on the Insert tab. The Available Windows gallery opens.

i. Read the ScreenTip for each thumbnail in the gallery, find the Add-in browser window thumbnail in the gallery, click it, then click Yes in the dialog box that opens. A screenshot of the Add-in you selected is inserted in the WMP 2-References document.

j. Save the document, submit a copy to your instructor, close the document, then exit Word.

Visual Workshop

Open WMP 2-7.docx from the drive and folder where you store your Data Files, then save the document as **WMP 2-Termination Letter**. Replace the placeholders for the date, letterhead, inside address, salutation, and closing with the information shown in FIGURE 2-20, then use the Office Clipboard to reorganize the sentences to match FIGURE 2-20. Correct spelling and grammar errors, remove the document property information from the file, then submit a copy to your instructor.

FIGURE 2-20

Your Name, M.D.
8890 Harbor Avenue, Providence, RI 02904; Tel: 401-555-3523

9/8/2017

Mr. Jackson Earle
77 East Street
Providence, RI 02918

Dear Mr. Earle:

As a result of a change in our insurance affiliations, I am no longer able to provide medical care to you as your podiatrist. Consequently, you should identify another physician to assume your care.

If you have not received a referral to another provider or if you wish to contact a provider who has not previously cared for you, contact your primary care physician. You may also contact the Providence County Medical Society at 401-555-2983.

I will remain available to treat you for a limited time, not to exceed thirty (30) days from the date of this letter. Please try to transfer your care as soon as possible within this period. In the event you have an emergency prior to your transfer of care to another provider, you may contact me through my office.

Copies of your medical record will be sent to the new provider you have selected, upon receipt of your written authorization. A copy of a release form is enclosed for you to complete and return to this office, allowing the record to be transferred.

Sincerely,

Your Name, M.D.

Enc.
Certified Mail, Return Receipt Request
Mailed on September 8, 2017

Formatting Text and Paragraphs

CASE You have finished drafting the text for an information sheet on the flu to distribute to patients. Now, you need to format the information sheet so it is attractive and highlights the significant information.

Module Objectives

After completing this module, you will be able to:

- Format with fonts
- Use the Format Painter
- Change line and paragraph spacing
- Align paragraphs
- Work with tabs

- Work with indents
- Add bullets and numbering
- Add borders and shading
- Insert online pictures

Files You Will Need

WMP 3-1.docx	WMP 3-4.docx
WMP 3-2.docx	WMP 3-5.docx
WMP 3-3.docx	WMP 3-6.docx

Format with Fonts

Learning Outcomes
• Change font and font size
• Change font color
• Select an entire document

Formatting text with fonts is a quick and powerful way to enhance the appearance of a document. A **font** is a complete set of characters with the same typeface or design. Arial, Times New Roman, Courier, Tahoma, and Calibri are some of the more common fonts, but there are hundreds of others, each with a specific design and feel. Another way to change the appearance of text is to increase or decrease its **font size**. Font size is measured in points. A **point** is 1/72 of an inch. **CASE** *You change the font and font size of the body text, title, and headings in the information sheet. You select fonts and font sizes that enhance the positive tone of the document and help to structure the information visually for readers.*

STEPS

1. **Start Word, open the file** WMP 3-1.docx **from the location where you store your Data Files, save it as** WMP 3-Flu Info Sheet, **then change the zoom level to 120%**

   Notice that the name of the font used in the document, Calibri, is displayed in the Font list box in the Font group. The word "(Body)" in the Font list box indicates Calibri is the font used for body text in the current theme, the default theme. A **theme** is a related set of fonts, colors, styles, and effects that is applied to an entire document to give it a cohesive appearance. The font size, 11, appears in the Font Size list box in the Font group.

QUICK TIP
There are two types of fonts: **serif fonts** have a small stroke, called a serif, at the ends of characters; **sans serif fonts** do not have a serif. Garamond is a serif font. Trebuchet MS is a sans serif font.

2. **Scroll the document to get a feel for its contents, press [Ctrl][Home], press [Ctrl][A] to select the entire document, then click the** Font list arrow **in the Font group**

   The Font list, which shows the fonts available on your computer, opens as shown in FIGURE 3-1. The font names are formatted in the font. Font names can appear in more than one location on the Font list.

3. **Drag the pointer slowly down the font names in the Font list, drag the scroll box to scroll down the Font list, then click** Garamond

   As you drag the pointer over a font name, a preview of the font is applied to the selected text. Clicking a font name applies the font. The font of the flyer changes to Garamond.

QUICK TIP
You can also type a font size in the Font Size text box.

4. **Click the** Font Size list arrow **in the Font group, drag the pointer slowly up and down the Font Size list, then click** 12

   As you drag the pointer over a font size, a preview of the font size is applied to the selected text. Clicking 12 increases the font size of the selected text to 12 points.

5. **Select the title** Riverwalk Medical Clinic Influenza Information Sheet, **click the** Font list arrow, **scroll to and click** Trebuchet MS, **click the** Font Size list arrow, **click 22, then click the** Bold button B **in the Font group**

   The title is formatted in 22-point Trebuchet MS bold.

QUICK TIP
To use a different set of theme colors, click the Design tab, click the Colors button in the Document Formatting group, then select a different color set.

6. **Click the** Font Color list arrow A ▾ **in the Font group**

   A gallery of colors opens. It includes the set of theme colors in a range of tints and shades as well as a set of standard colors. You can point to a color in the gallery to preview it applied to the selected text.

7. **Click the** Green, Accent 6 **color as shown in** FIGURE 3-2, **then deselect the text**

   The color of the title text changes to green. The active color on the Font Color button also changes to green.

TROUBLE
If the mini toolbar closes, select the text again.

8. **Scroll down, select the heading** Flu Vaccine, **then, using the Mini toolbar, click the** Font list arrow, **click** Trebuchet MS, **click the** Font Size list arrow, **click 14, click** B, **click** A, **then deselect the text**

   The heading is formatted in 14-point Trebuchet MS bold with a green color.

9. **Press [Ctrl][Home], then click the** Save button **on the Quick Access toolbar**

   Compare your document to FIGURE 3-3.

FIGURE 3-1: **Font list**

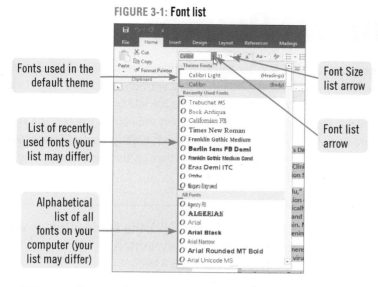

Fonts used in the default theme

List of recently used fonts (your list may differ)

Alphabetical list of all fonts on your computer (your list may differ)

Font Size list arrow

Font list arrow

FIGURE 3-2: **Font Color Palette**

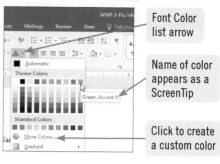

Font Color list arrow

Name of color appears as a ScreenTip

Click to create a custom color

FIGURE 3-3: **Document formatted with fonts**

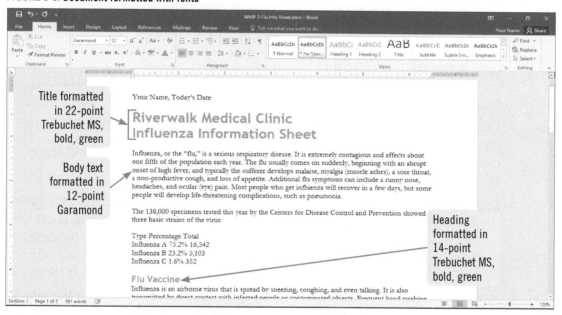

Title formatted in 22-point Trebuchet MS, bold, green

Body text formatted in 12-point Garamond

Heading formatted in 14-point Trebuchet MS, bold, green

Adding a drop cap

A fun way to illustrate a document with fonts is to add a drop cap to a paragraph. A **drop cap** is a large initial capital letter, often used to set off the first paragraph of an article. To create a drop cap, place the insertion point in the paragraph you want to format, click the Insert tab, and then click the Drop Cap button in the Text group to open a menu of Drop cap options. Preview and select one of the options on the menu, or click Drop Cap Options to open the Drop Cap dialog box, shown in FIGURE 3-4. In the Drop Cap dialog box, select the position, font, number of lines to drop, and the distance you want the drop cap to be from the paragraph text, and then click OK. The drop cap is added to the paragraph as a graphic object.

Once a drop cap is inserted in a paragraph, you can modify it by selecting it and then changing the settings in the Drop Cap dialog box. For even more interesting effects, you can enhance a drop cap with font color, font styles, or font effects. You can also fill the graphic object with shading or add a border around it. To enhance a drop cap, first select it, and then experiment with the formatting options available in the Font dialog box and in the Borders and Shading dialog box.

FIGURE 3-4: **Drop Cap dialog box**

Drop Cap   ? ×

Position

None   Dropped   In margin

Options

Font:
Garamond

Lines to drop: 3

Distance from text: 0"

OK   Cancel

Use the Format Painter

Learning
Outcomes
• Apply font styles
  and effects
• Add a shadow to
  text
• Change character
  spacing

You can dramatically change the appearance of text by applying different font styles, font effects, and character-spacing effects. For example, you can use the buttons in the Font group to make text darker by applying **bold** or to make text slanted by applying *italic*. When you are satisfied with the formatting of certain text, you can quickly apply the same formats to other text using the Format Painter. The **Format Painter** is a powerful Word feature that allows you to copy all the format settings applied to selected text to other text that you want to format the same way. **CASE** *You spice up the appearance of the text in the document by applying different font styles and text effects.*

STEPS

1. **Select extremely contagious in the first body paragraph, click the Bold button B on the Mini toolbar, select the entire paragraph, then click the Italic button I**

   The words "extremely contagious" are bold, and the entire paragraph is italic.

2. **Select Influenza Information Sheet, then click the launcher ⌧ in the Font group**

   The Font dialog box opens, as shown in FIGURE 3-5. You can use the options on the Font tab to change the font, font style, size, and color of text, and to add an underline and apply font effects to text.

3. **Scroll down the Size list, click 48, click the Font color list arrow, click the Orange, Accent 2 color in the Theme Colors, then click the Text Effects button**

   The Format Text Effects dialog box opens with the options for Text Fill & Outline active. You can also use this dialog box to apply text effects such as shadow, reflection, and 3-D effects to selected text.

4. **Click the white Text Effects icon in the dialog box, click Shadow, click the Presets list arrow, click Offset Diagonal Bottom Right in the Outer section, click OK, click OK, then deselect the text**

   The text is larger, orange, and has a shadow effect.

5. **Select Influenza Information Sheet, right-click, click Font on the menu that opens, click the Advanced tab, click the Scale list arrow, click 66%, click OK, then deselect the text**

   You use the Advanced tab in the Font dialog box to change the scale, or width, of the selected characters, to alter the spacing between characters, or to raise or lower the characters. Decreasing the scale of the characters makes them narrower and gives the text a tall, thin appearance, as shown in FIGURE 3-6.

6. **Scroll down, select the subheading When To Be Vaccinated, then, using the Mini toolbar, click the Font list arrow, click Trebuchet MS, click B, click I, click the Font Color list arrow A ▾, click the Orange, Accent 2 color in the Theme Colors, then deselect the text**

   The subheading is formatted in Trebuchet MS, bold, italic, and orange.

7. **Select When To Be Vaccinated, then click the Format Painter button in the Clipboard group**

   The pointer changes to 🖌I.

8. **Scroll down, select Who Should Be Vaccinated with the 🖌I pointer, then deselect the text**

   The subheading is formatted in Trebuchet MS, bold, italic, and orange, as shown in FIGURE 3-7.

9. **Scroll up, select Flu Vaccine, then double-click the Format Painter button**

   Double-clicking the Format Painter button allows the Format Painter to remain active until you turn it off. By keeping the Format Painter active, you can apply formatting to multiple items.

10. **Scroll down, select the headings Prevention, Treatment, and Medications with the pointer, click the Format Painter button to turn off the Format Painter, then save your changes**

    The headings are formatted in 14-point Trebuchet MS bold with a green font color.

FIGURE 3-5: Font tab in Font dialog box

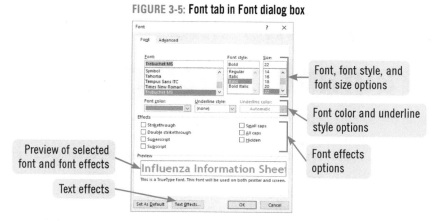

Font, font style, and font size options

Font color and underline style options

Font effects options

Preview of selected font and font effects

Text effects

FIGURE 3-6: Font and character spacing effects applied to text

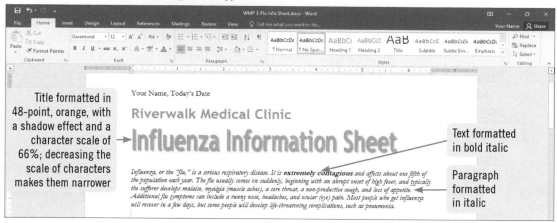

Title formatted in 48-point, orange, with a shadow effect and a character scale of 66%; decreasing the scale of characters makes them narrower

Text formatted in bold italic

Paragraph formatted in italic

FIGURE 3-7: Formats copied and applied using the Format Painter

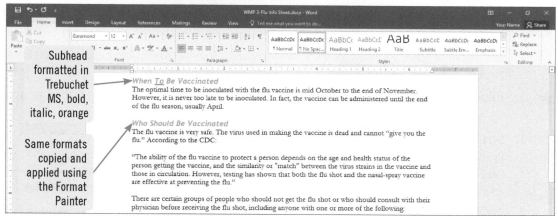

Subhead formatted in Trebuchet MS, bold, italic, orange

Same formats copied and applied using the Format Painter

Underlining text

Another creative way to call attention to text and to jazz up the appearance of a document is to apply an underline style to words you want to highlight. The Underline list arrow in the Font group displays straight, dotted, wavy, dashed, and mixed underline styles, along with a gallery of colors to choose from. To apply an underline to text, simply select it, click the Underline list arrow, and then select an underline style from the list. For a wider variety of underline styles, click More Underlines in the list, and then select an underline style in the Font dialog box. You can change the color of an underline at any time by selecting the underlined text, clicking the Underline list arrow, pointing to Underline Color, and then choosing from the options in the color gallery. If you want to remove an underline from text, select the underlined text, and then click the Underline button.

Word 2016

Change Line and Paragraph Spacing

Learning
Outcomes
• Add spacing under
  paragraphs
• Change line spac-
  ing in paragraphs
• Apply styles to text

Increasing the amount of space between lines adds more white space to a document and can make it easier to read. Adding space before and after paragraphs can also open up a document and improve its appearance. You use the Line and Paragraph Spacing list arrow in the Paragraph group on the Home tab to quickly change line spacing. To change paragraph spacing, you use the Spacing options in the Paragraph group on the Layout tab. Both line and paragraph spacing are measured in points. **CASE** *You increase the line spacing of several paragraphs and add extra space under each heading to give the information sheet a more open feel. You work with formatting marks turned on, so you can see the paragraph marks (¶).*

STEPS

1. **Press [Ctrl][Home], click the Show/Hide ¶ button ¶ in the Paragraph group, place the insertion point in the italicized paragraph under the title, then click the Line and Paragraph Spacing list arrow ≣▾ in the Paragraph group on the Home tab**
   The Line Spacing list opens. This list includes options for increasing the space between lines. The check mark on the Line Spacing list indicates the current line spacing.

2. **Click 1.15**
   The space between the lines in the paragraph increases to 1.15 lines. Notice that you do not need to select an entire paragraph to change its paragraph formatting; simply place the insertion point in the paragraph.

3. **Scroll down, select the four-line list that begins with "Type Percentage Total", click ≣▾, then click 1.5**
   The line spacing between the selected paragraphs changes to 1.5. To change the paragraph-formatting features of more than one paragraph, you must select the paragraphs.

4. **Scroll down, place the insertion point in the heading Flu Vaccine, then click the Layout tab**
   The paragraph spacing settings for the active paragraph are shown in the Before and After text boxes in the Paragraph group on the Layout tab.

5. **Click the After up arrow in the Spacing section in the Paragraph group until 6 pt appears**
   Six points of space are added after the Flu Vaccine heading paragraph.

6. **Scroll down, place the insertion point in the heading Prevention, then press [F4]**
   Pressing [F4] repeats the last action you took. In this case, six points of space are added after the Prevention heading. Note that using [F4] is not the same as using the Format Painter. Pressing [F4] repeats only the last action you took, and using the Format Painter applies multiple format settings at the same time.

7. **Scroll down, select Treatment, press and hold [Ctrl], select Medications, release [Ctrl], then press [F4]**
   When you press [Ctrl] as you select items, you can select and format multiple items at once. Six points of space are added after each heading.

8. **Press [Ctrl][Home], place the insertion point in Influenza Information Sheet, then click the Before up arrow in the Spacing section in the Paragraph group twice so that 12 pt appears**
   The second line of the title has 12 points of space before it, as shown in FIGURE 3-8.

9. **Click the Home tab, click ¶, then save your changes**

FIGURE 3-8: Line and paragraph spacing applied to document

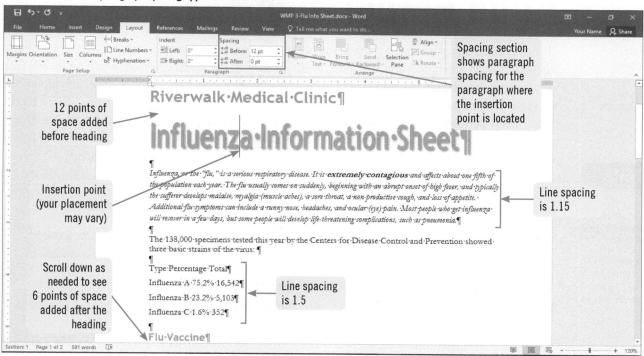

12 points of space added before heading

Spacing section shows paragraph spacing for the paragraph where the insertion point is located

Insertion point (your placement may vary)

Line spacing is 1.15

Scroll down as needed to see 6 points of space added after the heading

Line spacing is 1.5

Formatting with Quick Styles

You can also apply multiple format settings to text in one step by applying a style. A **style** is a set of formats, such as font, font size, and paragraph alignment, that is named and stored together. Formatting a document with styles is a quick and easy way to give it a professional appearance. To make it even easier, Word includes sets of styles, called **Quick Styles**, that are designed to be used together in a document to make it attractive and readable. A Quick Style set includes styles for a title, several heading levels, body text, quotes, and lists. The styles in a Quick Style set use common fonts, colors, and formats so that using the styles together in a document gives the document a cohesive look.

To view the active set of Quick Styles, click the More button ▼ in the Styles group on the Home tab to expand the Quick Styles gallery, shown in FIGURE 3-9. As you move the pointer over each style in the gallery, a preview of the style is applied to the selected text. To apply a style to the selected text, you simply click the style in the Quick Styles gallery. To remove a style from

FIGURE 3-9: Quick Styles gallery

AaBbCcDc	AaBbCcDc	AaBbCc	AaBbCcD	AaB	AaBbCcD	AaBbCcDc	AaBbCcDc
¶ Normal	No Spacing	Heading 1	Heading 2	Title	Subtitle	Subtle Em...	Emphasis

AaBbCcDc	AaBbCcDc	AaBbCcDc	AaBbCcDc	AABBCCDC	AABBCCDC	AaBbCcDc	AaBbCcDc
Intense E...	Strong	Quote	Intense Q...	Subtle Ref...	Intense R...	Book Title	¶ List Para...

🖉 Create a Style

🖋 Clear Formatting

🖉 Apply Styles...

selected text, you click the Clear All Formatting button in the Font group or the Clear Formatting command in the Quick Styles gallery.

If you want to change the active set of Quick Styles to a Quick Style set with a different design, click the Design tab, click the More button ▼ in the Document Formatting group, and then select the Quick Style set that best suits your document's content, tone, and audience. When you change the Quick Style set, a complete set of new fonts and colors is applied to the entire document. You can also change the color scheme or font used in the active Quick Style set by clicking the Colors or Fonts buttons, and then selecting from the available color schemes or font options.

Align Paragraphs

Changing paragraph alignment is another way to enhance a document's appearance. Paragraphs are aligned relative to the left and right margins in a document. By default, text is **left-aligned**, which means it is flush with the left margin and has a ragged right edge. Using the alignment buttons in the Paragraph group, you can **right-align** a paragraph—make it flush with the right margin—or **center** a paragraph so that it is positioned evenly between the left and right margins. You can also **justify** a paragraph so that both the left and right edges of the paragraph are flush with the left and right margins. **CASE** ▶ *You change the alignment of several paragraphs at the beginning of the information sheet to make it more visually interesting.*

STEPS

1. **Replace** Your Name, Today's Date **with your name, a comma, and the date**

2. **Select your name, the comma, and the date, then click the** Align Right button ☰ **in the Paragraph group**

   The text is aligned with the right margin. In Page Layout view, the place where the white and shaded sections on the horizontal ruler meet shows the left and right margins.

3. **Place the insertion point between your name and the comma, press** [Delete] **to delete the comma, then press** [Enter]

   The new paragraph containing the date is also right-aligned. Pressing [Enter] in the middle of a paragraph creates a new paragraph with the same text and paragraph formatting as the original paragraph.

4. **Select the** two-line title, **then click the** Center button ☰ **in the Paragraph group**

   The two paragraphs that make up the title are centered between the left and right margins.

5. **Scroll down as needed, place the insertion point in the** Flu Vaccine **heading, then click** ☰

   The Flu Vaccine heading is centered.

6. **Place the insertion point in the italicized paragraph under the title, then click the** Justify button ☰ **in the Paragraph group**

   The paragraph is aligned with both the left and right margins, as shown in FIGURE 3-10. When you justify a paragraph, Word adjusts the spacing between words so that each line in the paragraph is flush with the left and the right margins.

7. **Scroll down, place the insertion point in** Flu Vaccine, **then click the** launcher ▣ **in the Paragraph group**

   The Paragraph dialog box opens, as shown in FIGURE 3-11. The Indents and Spacing tab shows the paragraph format settings for the paragraph where the insertion point is located. You can check or change paragraph format settings using this dialog box.

8. **Click the** Alignment list arrow, **click** Left, **click** OK, **then save your changes**

   The Flu Vaccine heading is left-aligned.

FIGURE 3-10: Modified paragraph alignment

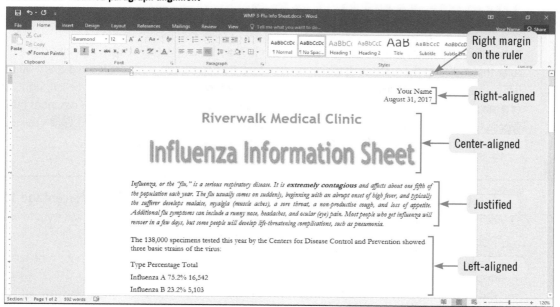

FIGURE 3-11: Indents and Spacing tab in Paragraph dialog box

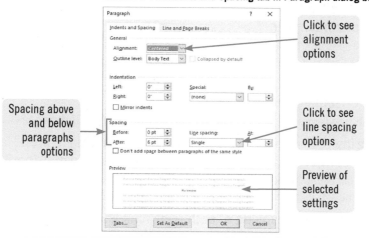

Formatting a document using themes

Changing the theme applied to a document is another powerful and efficient way to tailor a document's look and feel, particularly when a document is formatted with a Quick Style set. By default, all documents created in Word are formatted with the default Office theme—which uses Calibri as the font for the body text—but you can change the theme at any time to fit the content, tone, and purpose of a document. When you change the theme for a document, a complete set of new theme colors, fonts, and effects is applied to the whole document.

To preview how various themes look when applied to the current document, click the Themes button in the Document Formatting group on the Design tab, and then move the pointer over each theme in the gallery and notice how the document changes. When you click the theme you like, all document content that uses theme colors, all text that is formatted with a style, including default body text, and all table styles and graphic effects change to the colors, fonts, and effects used by the theme. In addition, the gallery of colors changes to display the set of theme colors, and the active Quick Style set changes to employ the theme colors and fonts. Note that changing the theme does not change the non-theme-based font formatting that has already been applied. For example, if you changed the font of text, applied bold to text, or changed the font color of text to a standard or custom color, that formatting remains in place.

If you want to tweak the document design further, you can modify it by applying a different set of theme colors, heading and body text fonts, or graphic effects. To do this, simply click the Colors, Fonts, or Effects button in the Document Formatting group, move the pointer over each option in the gallery to preview it in the document, and then click the option you like best.

Work with Tabs

Learning
Outcomes
• Set tab stops and
  tab leaders
• Modify tabs
• Use tabs to align
  text

Tabs allow you to align text at a specific location in a document. A **tab stop** is a point on the horizontal ruler that indicates the location at which to align text. By default, tab stops are located every 1/2" from the left margin, but you can also set custom tab stops. Using tabs, you can align text to the left, right, or center of a tab stop, or you can align text at a decimal point or insert a bar character. TABLE 3-1 describes the different types of tab stops. You set tabs using the horizontal ruler or the Tabs dialog box. **CASE** > *You use tabs to format the statistical information on the flu so it is easy to read.*

STEPS

1. **Scroll as needed, then select the four-line list beginning with "Type Percentage Total"**
   Before you set tab stops for existing text, you must select the paragraphs for which you want to set tabs.

2. **Point to the tab indicator ⌊ at the left end of the horizontal ruler**
   The icon that appears in the tab indicator indicates the active type of tab; pointing to the tab indicator displays a ScreenTip with the name of the active tab type. By default, left tab is the active tab type. Clicking the tab indicator scrolls through the types of tabs and indents.

QUICK TIP
To remove a tab
stop, drag it off the
ruler.

3. **Click the tab indicator to see each of the available tab and indent types, make Left Tab ⌊ the active tab type, click the 1" mark on the horizontal ruler, then click the 3½" mark on the horizontal ruler**
   A left tab stop is inserted at the 1" mark and the 3½" mark on the horizontal ruler. Clicking the horizontal ruler inserts a tab stop of the active type for the selected paragraph or paragraphs.

4. **Click the tab indicator twice so the Right Tab icon ⌟ is active, then click the 5" mark on the horizontal ruler**
   A right tab stop is inserted at the 5" mark on the horizontal ruler, as shown in FIGURE 3-12.

5. **Place the insertion point before Type in the first line in the list, press [Tab], place the insertion point before Percentage, press [Tab], place the insertion point before Total, then press [Tab]**
   Inserting a tab before "Type" left-aligns the text at the 1" mark, inserting a tab before "Percentage" left-aligns the text at the 3½" mark, and inserting a tab before "Total" right-aligns "Total" at the 5" mark.

6. **Insert a tab at the beginning of each remaining line in the list**
   The paragraphs left-align at the 1" mark.

QUICK TIP
Place the insertion
point in a paragraph
to see the tab stops
for that paragraph
on the horizontal
ruler.

7. **Insert a tab before each percentage, then insert a tab before each total number**
   The percentages left-align at the 3½" mark. The total numbers right-align at the 5" mark.

8. **Select the four lines of tabbed text, drag the right tab stop to the 5½" mark on the horizontal ruler, then deselect the text**
   Dragging the tab stop moves it to a new location. The total numbers right-align at the 5½" mark.

QUICK TIP
Double-click a tab
stop on the ruler
to open the Tabs
dialog box.

9. **Select the last three lines of tabbed text, click the launcher ⌐ in the Paragraph group, then click the Tabs button at the bottom of the Paragraph dialog box**
   The Tabs dialog box opens, as shown in FIGURE 3-13. You can use the Tabs dialog box to set tab stops, change the position or alignment of existing tab stops, clear tab stops, and apply tab leaders to tabs. **Tab leaders** are lines that appear in front of tabbed text.

10. **Click 3.5" in the Tab stop position list box, click the 2 option button in the Leader section, click Set, click 5.5" in the Tab stop position list box, click the 2 option button in the Leader section, click Set, click OK, deselect the text, then save your changes**
    A dotted tab leader is added before each 3.5" and 5.5" tab stop in the last three lines of tabbed text, as shown in FIGURE 3-14.

Formatting Text and Paragraphs

FIGURE 3-12: Left and right tab stops on the horizontal ruler

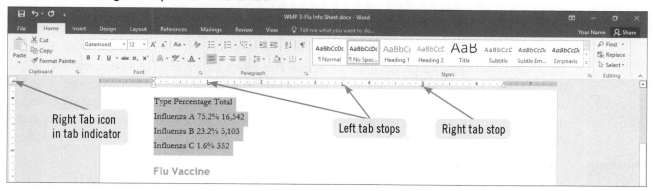

FIGURE 3-13: Tabs dialog box

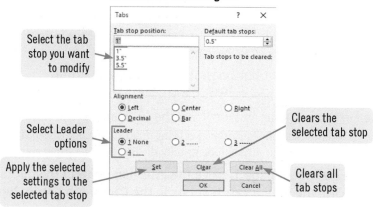

FIGURE 3-14: Tab leaders

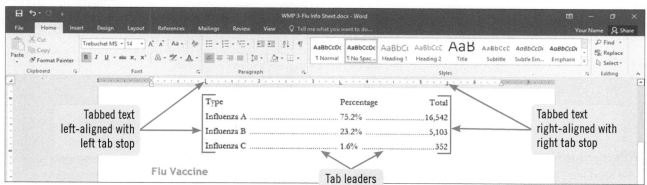

TABLE 3-1: Types of tabs

tab	use to
Left tab	Set the start position of text so that text runs to the right of the tab stop as you type
Center tab	Set the center align position of text so that text stays centered on the tab stop as you type
Right tab	Set the right or end position of text so that text moves to the left of the tab stop as you type
Decimal tab	Set the position of the decimal point so that numbers align around the decimal point as you type
Bar tab	Insert a vertical bar at the tab position

Work with Indents

Learning Outcomes
- Indent a paragraph
- Indent the first line of a paragraph

When you **indent** a paragraph, you move its edge in from the left or right margin. You can indent the entire left or right edge of a paragraph, just the first line, or all lines except the first line. The **indent markers** on the horizontal ruler indicate the indent settings for the paragraph in which the insertion point is located. Dragging an indent marker to a new location on the ruler is one way to change the indentation of a paragraph; changing the indent settings in the Paragraph group on the Layout tab is another; and using the indent buttons in the Paragraph group on the Home tab is a third. TABLE 3-2 describes different types of indents and some of the methods for creating each. **CASE** *You indent several paragraphs in the document.*

STEPS

1. **Press [Ctrl][Home], place the insertion point in the italicized paragraph under the title, then click the Increase Indent button ⊞ in the Paragraph group on the Home tab**
   The entire paragraph is indented ½" from the left margin, as shown in FIGURE 3-15. The indent marker also moves to the ½" mark on the horizontal ruler. Each time you click the Increase Indent button, the left edge of a paragraph moves another ½" to the right.

2. **Click the Decrease Indent button ⊞ in the Paragraph group**
   The left edge of the paragraph moves ½" to the left, and the indent marker moves back to the left margin.

3. **Drag the First Line Indent marker ▽ to the ¼" mark on the horizontal ruler**
   FIGURE 3-16 shows the First Line Indent marker being dragged. The first line of the paragraph is indented ¼". Dragging the First Line Indent marker indents only the first line of a paragraph.

4. **Scroll to the bottom of page 1, place the insertion point in the quotation, click the Layout tab, click the Indent Left text box in the Paragraph group, type .5, click the Indent Right text box, type .5, then press [Enter]**
   The left and right edges of the paragraph are indented ½" from the margins, as shown in FIGURE 3-17.

5. **Press [Ctrl][Home], place the insertion point in the italicized paragraph, then click the launcher ⊡ in the Paragraph group**
   The Paragraph dialog box opens. You can use the Indents and Spacing tab to check or change the alignment, indentation, and paragraph and line spacing settings applied to a paragraph.

6. **Click the Special list arrow, click (none), click OK, then save your changes**
   The first line indent is removed from the paragraph.

Applying text effects and clearing formatting

The Word Text Effects and Typography feature allows you to add visual appeal to your documents by adding special text effects to text, including outlines, shadows, reflections, and glows. The feature also includes a gallery of preformatted combined text effect styles, called **WordArt**, that you can apply to your text to format it quickly and easily. To apply a WordArt style or a text effect to text, simply select the text, click the Text Effects and Typography button in the Font group on the Home tab, and select a WordArt style from the gallery or point to a type of text effect, such as reflection or shadow, to open a gallery of styles related to that type of text effect. Experiment with combining text effect styles to give your text a striking appearance.

If you are unhappy with the way text is formatted, you can click the Clear All Formatting button to return the text to the default format settings. The default format includes font and paragraph formatting: text is formatted in 11-point Calibri, and paragraphs are left-aligned with 1.08 point line spacing, 8 points of space after, and no indents. To clear formatting from text and return it to the default format, select the text you want to clear, and then click the Clear All Formatting button in the Font group on the Home tab. If you prefer to return the text to the default font and remove all paragraph formatting, making the text 11-point Calibri, left-aligned, single spaced, with no paragraph spacing or indents, select the text and then simply click the No Spacing button in the Styles group on the Home tab.

FIGURE 3-15: Indented paragraph

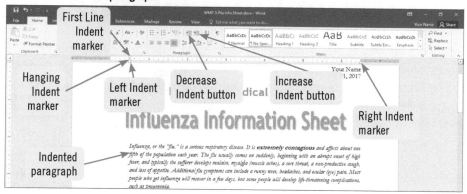

FIGURE 3-16: Dragging the First Line Indent marker

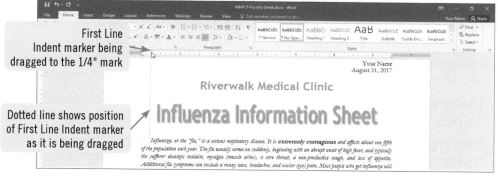

FIGURE 3-17: Paragraph indented from the left and right

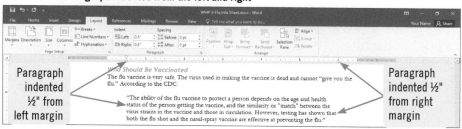

TABLE 3-2: Types of indents

indent type: description	to create
Left indent: The left edge of a paragraph is moved in from the left margin	Drag the Left Indent marker ▭ on the ruler to the right to the position where you want the left edge of the paragraph to align; when you drag the left indent marker, all the indent markers move as one
Right indent: The right edge of a paragraph is moved in from the right margin	Drag the Right Indent marker △ on the ruler to the left to the position where you want the right edge of the paragraph to align
First line indent: The first line of a paragraph is indented more than the subsequent lines	Drag the First Line Indent marker ▽ on the ruler to the right to the position where you want the first line of the paragraph to begin; or activate the First Line Indent marker ▽ in the tab indicator, and then click the ruler at the position where you want the first line of the paragraph to begin
Hanging indent: The subsequent lines of a paragraph are indented more than the first line	Drag the Hanging Indent marker △ on the ruler to the right to the position where you want the hanging indent to begin; or activate the Hanging Indent marker △ in the tab indicator, and then click the ruler at the position where you want the second and remaining lines of the paragraph to begin; when you drag the hanging indent marker, the left indent marker moves with it
Negative indent (or Outdent): The left edge of a paragraph is moved to the left of the left margin	Drag the Left Indent marker ▭ on the ruler left to the position where you want the negative indent to begin; when you drag the left indent marker, all markers move as one

Add Bullets and Numbering

Learning Outcomes
- Apply bullets or numbering to lists
- Renumber a list
- Change bullet or numbering styles

Formatting a list with bullets or numbering can help to organize the ideas in a document. A **bullet** is a character, often a small circle, that appears before the items in a list to add emphasis. Formatting a list as a numbered list helps illustrate sequences and priorities. You can quickly format a list with bullets or numbering by using the Bullets and Numbering buttons in the Paragraph group on the Home tab. **CASE** *You format the lists in the information sheet with numbers and bullets.*

STEPS

1. **Scroll until the top of page 2 is at the top of your screen**

2. **Select the four-line list above the Prevention heading, click the Home tab, then click the Numbering list arrow ▤ in the Paragraph group**

   The Numbering Library opens, as shown in FIGURE 3-18. You use this list to choose or change the numbering style applied to a list. You can drag the pointer over the numbering styles to preview how the selected text will look if the numbering style is applied.

3. **Click the numbering style called out in FIGURE 3-18**

   The paragraphs are formatted as a numbered list.

QUICK TIP
To remove a bullet or number, select the paragraph(s), then click ▤ or ▤.

4. **Place the insertion point after vaccine at the end of the third line, press [Enter], then type An active neurological disorder**

   Pressing [Enter] in the middle of the numbered list creates a new numbered paragraph and automatically renumbers the remainder of the list. Similarly, if you delete a paragraph from a numbered list, Word automatically renumbers the remaining paragraphs.

5. **Click 1 in the list**

   Clicking a number in a list selects all the numbers, as shown in FIGURE 3-19.

6. **Click the Bold button B in the Font group**

   The numbers are all formatted in bold. Notice that the formatting of the items in the list does not change when you change the formatting of the numbers. You can also use this technique to change the formatting of bullets in a bulleted list.

QUICK TIP
To use a symbol or a picture for a bullet character, click the Bullets list arrow, click Define New Bullet, and then select from the options in the Define New Bullet dialog box.

7. **Select the list of items under the Prevention heading, then click the Bullets button ▤ in the Paragraph group**

   The five paragraphs are formatted as a bulleted list using the most recently used bullet style.

8. **Click a bullet in the list to select all the bullets, click the Bullets list arrow ▤ in the Paragraph group, click the check mark bullet style, click the document to deselect the text, then save your changes**

   The bullet character changes to a check mark, as shown in FIGURE 3-20.

Creating multilevel lists

You can create lists with hierarchical structures by applying a multilevel list style to a list. To create a **multilevel list**, also called an outline, begin by applying a multilevel list style using the Multilevel List list arrow ▤ in the Paragraph group on the Home tab, then type your outline, pressing [Enter] after each item. To demote items to a lower level of importance in the outline, place the insertion point in the item, then click the Increase Indent button ▤ in the Paragraph group on the Home tab. Each time you indent a paragraph, the item is demoted to a lower level in the outline. Similarly, you can use the Decrease Indent button ▤ to promote an item to a higher level in the outline. You can also create a hierarchical structure in any bulleted or numbered list by using ▤ and ▤ to demote and promote items in the list. To change the multilevel list style applied to a list, select the list, click ▤ and then select a new style.

FIGURE 3-18: Numbering list

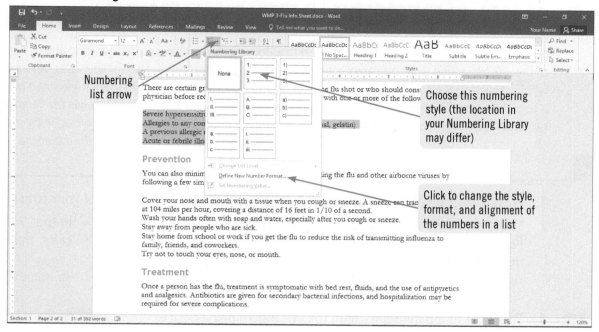

Numbering list arrow

Choose this numbering style (the location in your Numbering Library may differ)

Click to change the style, format, and alignment of the numbers in a list

FIGURE 3-19: Numbered list

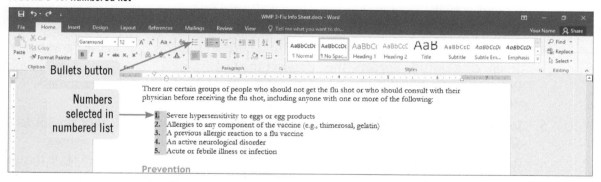

Bullets button

Numbers selected in numbered list

FIGURE 3-20: Check mark bullets applied to list

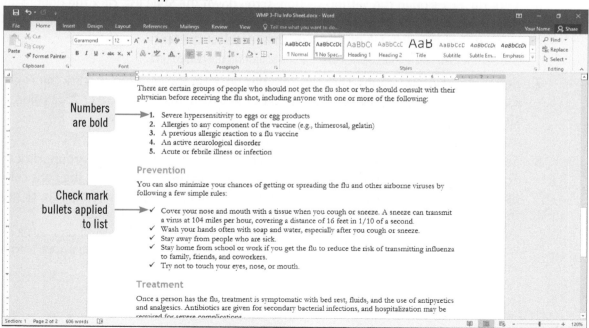

Numbers are bold

Check mark bullets applied to list

Add Borders and Shading

Borders and shading can add color and splash to a document. **Borders** are lines you add above, below, to the side, or around words or paragraphs. You can format borders using different line styles, colors, and widths. **Shading** is a color or pattern you apply behind words or paragraphs to make them stand out on a page. You apply borders and shading using the Borders button and the Shading button in the Paragraph group on the Home tab. **CASE** ▶ *You enhance the tabbed text of the flu statistics information by adding shading to it. You also apply a border around the tabbed text to set it off from the rest of the document.*

STEPS

1. **Press [Ctrl][Home], then scroll down until the tabbed text is at the top of your screen**

2. **Select the four paragraphs of tabbed text, click the Shading list arrow 🖉 ⋅ in the Paragraph group on the Home tab, click the Green, Accent 6, Lighter 60% color, then deselect the text**

   Light green shading is applied to the four paragraphs. Notice that the shading is applied to the entire width of the paragraphs, despite the tab settings.

3. **Select the four paragraphs, drag the Left Indent marker ▢ to the ¾" mark on the horizontal ruler, drag the Right Indent marker △ to the 5¾" mark, then deselect the text**

   The shading for the paragraphs is indented from the left and right, which makes it look more attractive, as shown in **FIGURE 3-21**.

4. **Select the four paragraphs, click the Bottom Border list arrow ⊞ ⋅ in the Paragraph group, click Outside Borders, then deselect the text**

   A black outside border is added around the selected text. The style of the border added is the most recently used border style, in this case the default, a thin black line.

5. **Select the four paragraphs, click the Outside Borders list arrow ⊞ ⋅, click No Border, click the No Border list arrow ⊞ ⋅, then click Borders and Shading**

   The Borders and Shading dialog box opens, as shown in **FIGURE 3-22**. You use the Borders tab to change the border style, color, and width, and to add boxes and lines to words or paragraphs.

6. **Click the Box icon in the Setting section, scroll down the Style list, click the double-line style, click the Color list arrow, click the Green, Accent 6, Darker 25% color, click the Width list arrow, click 1½ pt, click OK, then deselect the text**

   A 1½-point dark green double-line border is added around the tabbed text.

7. **Select the four paragraphs, click the Bold button B in the Font group, click the Font Color list arrow A ⋅ in the Font group, click the Green, Accent 6, Darker 25% color, then deselect the text**

   The text changes to bold dark green.

8. **Select the first line in the tabbed text, click the launcher 🖅 in the Font group, click the Font tab if it is not the active tab, scroll and click 14 in the Size list, click the Font color list arrow, click the Orange, Accent 2, Darker 25% color, click the Small caps check box in the Effects section, click OK, deselect the text, then save your changes**

   The text in the first line of the tabbed text is enlarged and changed to orange small caps, as shown in **FIGURE 3-23**. When you change text to small caps, the lowercase letters are changed to uppercase letters in a smaller font size.

FIGURE 3-21: Shading applied to the tabbed text

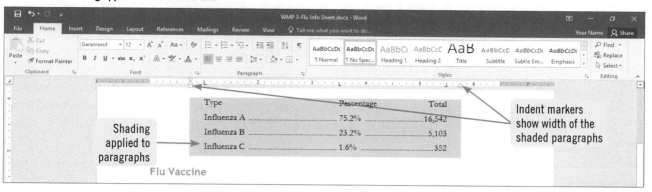

Shading applied to paragraphs

Indent markers show width of the shaded paragraphs

FIGURE 3-22: Borders tab in Borders and Shading dialog box

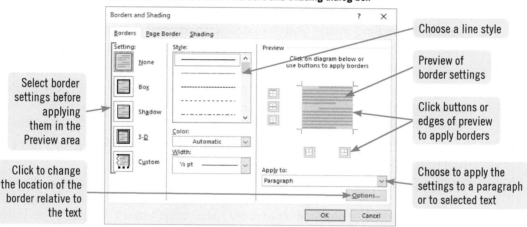

Select border settings before applying them in the Preview area

Click to change the location of the border relative to the text

Choose a line style

Preview of border settings

Click buttons or edges of preview to apply borders

Choose to apply the settings to a paragraph or to selected text

FIGURE 3-23: Borders and shading applied to the document

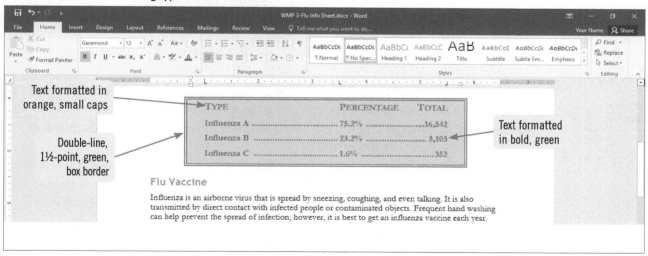

Text formatted in orange, small caps

Double-line, 1½-point, green, box border

Text formatted in bold, green

Word 2016

Highlighting text in a document

The Highlight tool allows you to mark and find important text in a document. **Highlighting** is transparent color that is applied to text using the Highlight pointer. To highlight text, click the Text Highlight Color list arrow in the Font group on the Home tab, select a color, then use the I-beam part of the pointer to select the text you want to highlight. Click to turn off the Highlight pointer. To remove highlighting, select the highlighted text, click then click No Color. Highlighting prints, but it is used most effectively when a document is viewed on screen.

Insert Online Pictures

A **clip** is a media file, such as a graphic, photograph, sound, movie, or animation, that can be inserted into a document. **Clip art** is a collection of graphic images that you can insert into a document. Bing Image Search clip art images are images that you can add to a document using the Online Pictures command on the Insert tab. Once you insert a clip art image, you can wrap text around it, resize it, enhance it, and move it to a different location. **CASE** ▶ *You illustrate the second page of the document with an online clip art image.*

STEPS

1. **Scroll to the top of page 2, place the insertion point before** Prevention, **click the** Insert tab, **then click the** Online Pictures button **in the Illustrations group**

   The Insert Pictures window opens. You can use this to search for images related to a keyword.

2. **Type** flu **in the Bing Image Search text box, then press** [Enter]

   Images that have the keyword "flu" associated with them appear in the Bing Image Search window.

3. **Scroll down the gallery of images, click the clip called out in** FIGURE 3-24, **then click** Insert

   The clip is inserted at the location of the insertion point. When a graphic is selected, the active tab changes to the Picture Tools Format tab. This tab contains commands used to adjust, enhance, arrange, and size graphics. The white circles that appear on the square edges of the graphic are the **sizing handles**.

4. **Type** 1.8 **in the Shape Height text box in the Size group on the Picture Tools Format tab, then press** [Enter]

   The size of the graphic is reduced. When you decreased the height of the graphic, the width decreased proportionally. You can also resize a graphic proportionally by dragging a corner sizing handle. Until you apply text wrapping to a graphic, it is part of the line of text in which it was inserted (an **inline graphic**). To move a graphic independently of text, you must make it a **floating graphic**.

5. **Click the** Position button **in the Arrange group, then click** Position in Middle Center with Square Text Wrapping

   The graphic is moved to the middle of the page and the text wraps around it. Applying text wrapping to the graphic made it a floating graphic. A floating graphic can be moved anywhere on a page. You can also wrap text around a graphic using the Layout Options button.

6. **Scroll up until the top of page 2 is at the top of your screen, position the pointer over the graphic, when the pointer changes to** ⬚ **drag the graphic up and to the left so its edges align with the left margin and the top of the first line of text on the page as shown in** FIGURE 3-25, **then release the mouse button**

   The graphic is moved to the upper-left corner of the page. Green alignment guides may appear to help you align the image with the margins.

7. **Click the** Position button **in the Arrange group, then click** Position in Top Right with Square Text Wrapping

   The graphic is moved to the upper-right corner of the page.

8. **Click the** Picture Effects button **in the Picture Styles group, point to** Shadow, **point to each style to see a preview applied to the graphic, then click** Offset Center

   A shadow effect is applied to the graphic.

9. **Press** [Ctrl][Home], **click the** View tab, **then click the** Multiple Pages button **in the Zoom group to view the completed document as shown in** FIGURE 3-26.

10. **Save your changes, submit the document to your instructor, then close the document and exit Word**

Formatting Text and Paragraphs

FIGURE 3-24: Insert Pictures window

Click the All Images list arrow to see more options

Select this clip (or a similar clip if this clip is not available)

Source: Bing

FIGURE 3-25: Graphic being moved to a new location

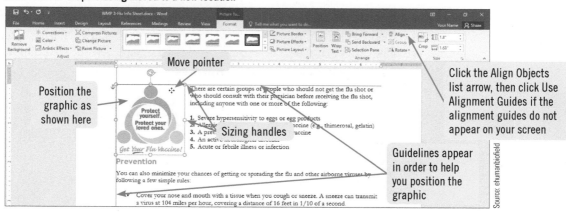

Move pointer

Position the graphic as shown here

Sizing handles

Click the Align Objects list arrow, then click Use Alignment Guides if the alignment guides do not appear on your screen

Guidelines appear in order to help you position the graphic

Source: ehumanbiofield

FIGURE 3-26: Completed Document

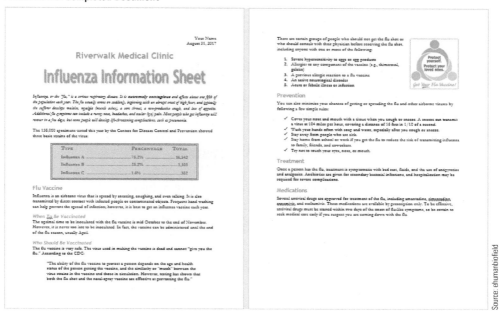

Source: ehumanbiofield

Practice

Concepts Review

Label each element of the Word program window shown in FIGURE 3-27.

FIGURE 3-27

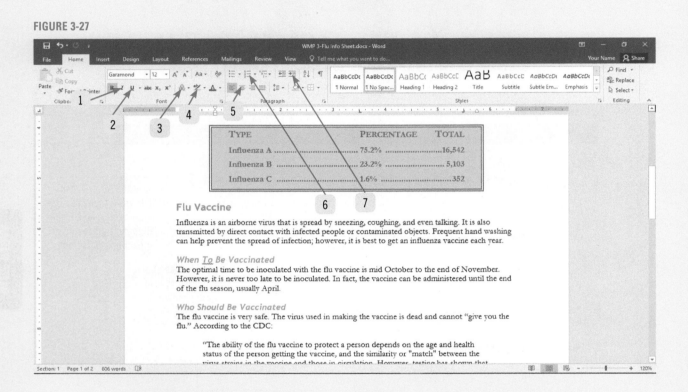

Match each term with the statement that best describes it.

8. **Inline graphic**
9. **Style**
10. **Shading**
11. **Border**
12. **Floating graphic**
13. **Highlight**
14. **Point**
15. **Bullet**

  a. A graphic symbol that appears at the beginning of a paragraph in a list
  b. Transparent color that is applied to text to mark it in a document
  c. A set of format settings
  d. An image that text wrapping has been applied to
  e. An image that is inserted as part of a line of text
  f. A line that can be applied above, below, or to the sides of a paragraph
  g. A unit of measurement equal to $1/72$ of an inch
  h. Color or pattern that is applied behind text to make it look attractive

Select the best answer from the list of choices.

16. **Which dialog box is used to change the scale of characters?**
    - **a.** Paragraph
    - **b.** Font
    - **c.** Tabs
    - **d.** Borders and Shading

17. **What is Calibri?**
    - **a.** A font
    - **b.** A style
    - **c.** A text effect
    - **d.** A character format

18. **What is the most precise way to increase the amount of white space between two paragraphs?**
    - **a.** Indent the paragraphs
    - **b.** Change the line spacing of the paragraphs
    - **c.** Change the before spacing for the second paragraph
    - **d.** Change the font size

19. **Which type of indent results in subsequent lines of a paragraph being indented more than the first line?**
    - **a.** Right indent
    - **b.** First line indent
    - **c.** Negative indent
    - **d.** Hanging indent

20. **Which command is used to add a reflection or an outline to text?**
    - **a.** Underline
    - **b.** Text Effects and Typography
    - **c.** Strikethrough
    - **d.** Change Case

Skills Review

1. **Format with fonts.**
   a. Start Word, open the file WMP 3-2.docx from the location where you store your Data Files, save it as **WMP 3-Scheduling Guidelines**, then scroll through the document to get a feel for its contents.
   b. Press [Ctrl][A], then format the text in 12-point Californian FB. Choose a different serif font if Californian FB is not available to you.
   c. Press [Ctrl][Home], format the report title **Saint Joan Family Health** in 36-point Berlin Sans FB Demi. Choose a different sans serif font if Berlin Sans FB Demi is not available to you.
   d. Change the font color of the report title to Blue, Accent 5, Darker 25%.
   e. Format the subtitle **Guidelines for Scheduling and Processing Patients** in 16-point Berlin Sans FB Demi with a Gold, Accent 4, Darker 25% font color, then press [Enter] before Processing in the subtitle.
   f. Format the heading **Our policy** in 14-point Berlin Sans FB Demi with a Gold, Accent 4, Darker 25% font color.
   g. Press [Ctrl][Home], then save your changes to the report.

2. **Use the Format Painter.**
   a. Use the Format Painter to copy the format of the Our policy heading to the following headings: **Five-step approach..., Determining the time..., Processing new patients**.
   b. Show formatting marks, then format the paragraph under the Our policy heading in italic.
   c. Format **Appointment Time**, the first line in the six-line list under the Determining the time... heading, in bold, small caps, with a Blue, Accent 5, Darker 25% font color.
   d. Change the font color of the next five lines under Appointment Time to Blue, Accent 5, Darker 25%.
   e. Scroll to the top of the report, change the character scale of Saint Joan Family Health to 66%, then save your changes.

3. **Change line and paragraph spacing.**
   a. Change the line spacing of the three-line list under the first body paragraph to 1.5 lines.
   b. Add 12 points of space after the title Saint Joan Family Health. Add 6 points of space after the Processing Patients line in the subtitle.
   c. Add 12 points of space after the Our policy heading, then add 12 points of space after each additional heading in the report (Five-step approach..., Determining the time..., Processing new patients).
   d. Add 6 points of space after each paragraph in the list under the Five-step approach... heading, except the last paragraph.

Skills Review (continued)

    e. Change the line spacing of the six-line list under the Determining the time... heading that begins with Appointment Time to 1.15.

    f. Add 6 points of space after each paragraph under the Processing new patients heading.

    g. Press [Ctrl][Home], then save your changes to the report.

4. Align paragraphs.

    a. Press [Ctrl][A] to select the entire document, then justify all the paragraphs.

    b. Center the report title and subtitle.

    c. Press [Ctrl][End], press [Enter], type your name, press [Enter], type the current date, then right-align your name and the date.

    d. Save your changes to the report.

5. Work with tabs.

    a. Scroll up and select the six-line list with appointment time information under the Determining the time... heading.

    b. Set left tab stops at the 1¾" mark and the 3¾" mark.

    c. Insert a tab at the beginning of each line in the list.

    d. In the first line, insert a tab before Time. In the second line, insert a tab before 45 minutes. In the remaining lines, insert a tab before each number.

    e. Select all the lines, then drag the first tab stop to the 2" mark on the horizontal ruler.

    f. Select the last five lines, insert dotted line tab leaders before the 3¾" tab stop, press [Ctrl][Home], then save your changes to the report.

6. Work with indents.

    a. Indent the paragraph under the Our policy heading ½" from the left and ½" from the right.

    b. Indent the first line of the three body paragraphs under the Determining the time... heading ½".

    c. Press [Ctrl][Home], then save your changes to the report.

7. Add bullets and numbering.

    a. Apply bullets to the three-line list under the first body paragraph. Change the bullet style to small black circles if that is not the current bullet symbol.

    b. Change the font color of the bullets to Blue, Accent 5, Darker 25%.

    c. Scroll down until the Five-step approach... heading is at the top of your screen.

    d. Format the five-paragraph list under the Five-step approach... heading as a numbered list.

    e. Format the numbers in 14-point Berlin Sans FB Demi, then change the font color to Blue, Accent 5, Darker 25%.

    f. Scroll down until the Processing new patients heading is at the top of your screen, then format the paragraphs under the heading as a bulleted list using check marks as the bullet style.

    g. Change the font color of the bullets to Blue, Accent 5, Darker 25%, press [Ctrl][Home], then save your changes to the report.

8. Add borders and shading.

    a. Add a 1-point Blue, Accent 5, Darker 25% bottom border below the Our policy heading.

    b. Use the Format Painter or the [F4] key to add the same border to the other headings in the report (Five-step approach..., Determining the time..., Processing new patients).

    c. Under the Determining the time... heading, select the six lines of tabbed text, which are formatted in blue, then apply Gold, Accent 4, Lighter 60% shading to the paragraphs.

    d. Select the six lines of tabbed text again if necessary, then add a 1½ -point Blue, Accent 5, Darker 25% single line box border around the paragraphs.

    e. Indent the shading and border around the paragraphs 1¾" from the left and 1¾" from the right.

    f. Turn off formatting marks, then save your changes.

Skills Review (continued)

9. Insert online pictures. *(Note: To complete these steps, your computer must be connected to the Internet.)*

a. Press [Ctrl][Home], then open the Insert Pictures window.

b. Search using Bing Image Search to find images related to the keyword **schedule**.

c. Insert the image shown in FIGURE 3-28. *(Note:* Select a different image if this one is not available to you. It is best to select an image that is similar in shape to the image shown in FIGURE 3-28.)

d. Use the Shape Width text box in the Size group on the Picture Tools Format tab to change the width of the image to 1.5".

e. Use the Position command to position the image in the top left with square text wrapping.

f. Left-align the title and the subtitle.

g. View your document in two-page view and compare it to the document shown in FIGURE 3-28. Adjust the size or position of the image as needed so that your document resembles the document shown in the figure.

h. Save your changes to the document, submit it to your instructor, close the file, and then exit Word.

FIGURE 3-28

Saint Joan Family Health

Guidelines for Scheduling and Processing Patients

A well-managed schedule of appointments is an important factor in delivering quality health care to patients, and is critical to the smooth and efficient running of Saint Joan Family Health. With that in mind, there are several factors to consider when scheduling patients for appointments:

- The specialty and personal preferences of each physician.
- The type of appointment required by the patient's condition.
- The urgency with which the patient needs to see a physician.

Our policy

Our patients have entrusted us with their health care. Many physicians charge patients who fail to keep appointments. At Saint Joan Family Health, we extend equal consideration to patients who take time out of their busy work day to allow us to participate in their health care. We respect that patients make every effort to arrive on time for appointments, and we endeavor to be available to them when they arrive.

Five-step approach to scheduling appointments

1. When a patient calls to schedule an appointment, assess the reason for the appointment and determine the urgency and how much time will be needed.

2. Ask the patient when he or she is not available for the appointment. This demonstrates a willingness to accommodate the patient's needs.

3. Offer the patient at least two choices of available times, if possible. Always state the day of the week, the date, and the time. This enables the patient to choose between alternatives and demonstrates the importance of the patient's input.

4. Repeat the agreed upon time to the patient. If the patient is present at the time of the booking, write down the day, date, and time of the appointment on an appointment reminder card and give it to the patient.

5. Close with an expression of anticipation of the next visit, such as "We'll see you at 10:00 a.m. on March 1st." This provides further verification of the date.

Determining the time required for an appointment

The time allotted for an appointment is particular to each physician's specialty and the patient's condition. Physicians are as frustrated as patients if appointments do not run smoothly, or if not enough time has been allowed to adequately address the patient's needs. The following table offers general guidelines for determining the amount of time to book for each type of appointment:

APPOINTMENT	TIME
New patient	45 minutes
Complete physical	30 minutes
Counseling	30 minutes
Sick visit	15 minutes
Other	15 minutes

In addition, it is important to schedule into each day several "emergency" booking slots that can be used to accommodate patients who need same day appointments. This is particularly critical during flu season. Be sure to analyze the appointment schedule regularly to ensure that it is meeting the needs of patients and physicians.

When a patient telephones to book an appointment, it is important to obtain his/her full name (ask for correct spelling), current home and work phone numbers (for contact purposes), and the reason for the visit. Patients sometimes object to providing this personal information. When this happens, you can explain to the patient that you require this information to schedule an adequate amount of time for the appointment, and so that any paperwork or special equipment that might be required will be ready when he/she arrives. Also, reassure the patient that all information he/she provides to Saint Joan Family Health remains confidential.

Processing new patients

- ✓ Gather as much information as you can from the new patient over the telephone when he/she calls to book an appointment.
- ✓ Ask the patient to complete a patient information form as soon as he/she arrives at the office, and check the form for completeness.
- ✓ Photocopy the patient's insurance card(s).
- ✓ Ask the patient to read and sign a copy of our privacy notice.
- ✓ Enter the information from the patient information form into our database.

Your Name
Today's Date

Source: edhat

Independent Challenge 1

You work for Grand River Neurology Associates. Your boss has given you the text for a Notice of Patient Rights and Responsibilities and has asked you to format it on letterhead. It's important that the Notice has a clean, striking design, and reflects the practice's professionalism.

a. Start Word, open the file WMP 3-3.docx from the drive and folder where you store your Data Files, save it as **WMP 3-Notice of Rights**, then read the document to get a feel for its contents. FIGURE 3-29 shows how you will format the letterhead.

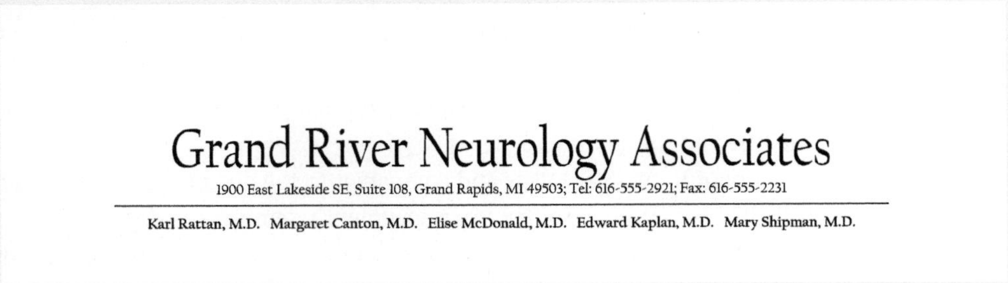

FIGURE 3-29

Grand River Neurology Associates
1900 East Lakeside SE, Suite 108, Grand Rapids, MI 49503; Tel: 616-555-2921; Fax: 616-555-2231

Karl Rattan, M.D.   Margaret Canton, M.D.   Elise McDonald, M.D.   Edward Kaplan, M.D.   Mary Shipman, M.D.

b. Select the entire document, change the style to No Spacing, then change the font to 11-point Californian FB.

c. In the first line of the letterhead, format **Grand River Neurology Associates** in 36-point Californian FB, then change the character spacing to 80%.

d. Change the font size of the next two paragraphs—the address and the physician information—to 9 point, then bold the paragraph that lists the physicians.

e. Center the three-line letterhead.

f. Add 6 points of space after the address line paragraph, then add a ½ point black border below the address line paragraph.

g. With the insertion point in the address line, open the Borders and Shading dialog box, click Options to open the Border and Shading Options dialog box, change the Bottom setting to **5** points, then click OK twice to close the dialog boxes and to adjust the location of the border relative to the line of text.

h. Format the title **Patient Rights and Responsibilities** in 14-point Arial, bold, then center the title.

i. Format the following headings (including the colons) in 12-point Arial, bold: **Your Rights as a Patient**, **Your Responsibilities as a Patient**, **Advance Directives**, **Financial Concerns**, **Income Guidelines**, and **Acknowledgement of Receipt....**

j. Format the lists under Your Rights as a Patient and Your Responsibilities as a Patient as bulleted lists, using a bullet style of your choice.

k. Apply bold italic to Living Wills and Durable Powers of Attorney for Healthcare under the Advance Directives heading.

l. Center the Income Guidelines heading, select the 9-line list under the heading, then set a left tab stop at the 1¾" mark and right tab stops at the 3½" and 4¾" marks. Insert tabs before every line in the list, then insert tabs before every $.

m. Select the text in the first line of tabbed text, then apply an underline. Select the remaining eight lines of tabbed text, then add dotted line tab leaders to the 3½" and 4¾" tab stops.

n. Type your name as the patient name, then type the current date.

o. Examine the document carefully for formatting errors, and make any necessary adjustments.

p. Save the document, submit it to your instructor, then close the file and exit Word.

Independent Challenge 2

Your employer, Learn and Be Healthy, is a nonprofit organization devoted to educating the public on health issues. Your boss has written the text for a flyer about Peripheral Artery Disease, and asks you to format it so that it is eye catching and attractive.

a. Open the file WMP 3-4.docx from the drive and folder where you store your Data Files, save it as **WMP 3-PAD Flyer**, then read the document. FIGURE 3-30 shows how you will format the first several paragraphs of the flyer.

FIGURE 3-30

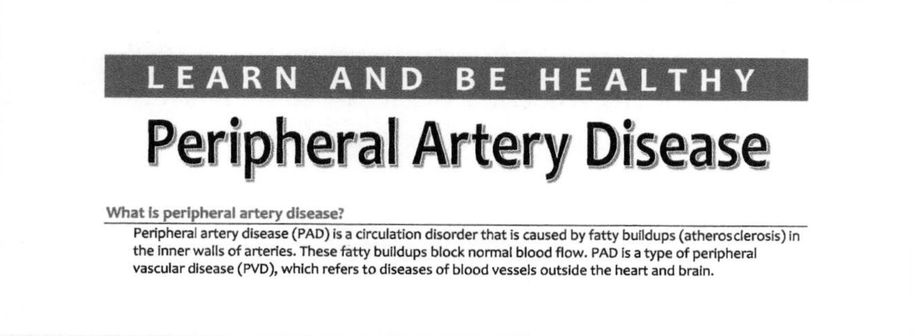
LEARN AND BE HEALTHY

Peripheral Artery Disease

What is peripheral artery disease?

Peripheral artery disease (PAD) is a circulation disorder that is caused by fatty buildups (atherosclerosis) in the inner walls of arteries. These fatty buildups block normal blood flow. PAD is a type of peripheral vascular disease (PVD), which refers to diseases of blood vessels outside the heart and brain.

b. Select the entire document, change the style to No Spacing, then change the font to 10-point Candara.

c. Center the first line, **Learn and Be Healthy**, and apply shading to the paragraph. Choose a dark custom shading color of your choice for the shading color. (*Hint*: Click More Colors, then select a color from the Standard or Custom tab.) Format the text in 24-point Candara, bold, with a white font color. Expand the character spacing by 8 points. (*Hint*: Use the Advanced tab in the Font dialog box. Set the Spacing to Expanded, and then type **8** in the By text box.)

d. Format the second line, **Peripheral Artery Disease**, in 48-point Candara. Apply the Fill - Black, Text 1, Outline - Background 1, Hard Shadow - Background 1 text effect style to the text. (*Hint*: Use the Text Effects and Typography button.) Change the character scale to 80% and center the line.

e. Format each **question** heading in 11-point Candara, bold. Change the font color to the same custom color used for shading the title. (*Note*: The color now appears in the Recent Colors section of the Font Color gallery.) Add a single-line ½-point black border under each heading.

f. Format each subheading (**PAD may require...** and **Lifestyle changes...**) in 10-point Candara, bold. Add 3 points of spacing before each paragraph. (*Hint*: Select 0 in the Before text box, type 3, then press [Enter].)

g. Indent each body paragraph ¼", except for the last two lines in the document.

h. Format the three lines under the **PAD may require...** subheading as a bulleted list. Use a bullet symbol of your choice, and format the bullets in the custom font color.

i. Format the six lines under the **Lifestyle changes...** subheading as a bulleted list. If necessary, use the Format Painter to copy the bullet style you just applied to the three-line list.

j. Format the **For more information...** heading in 12-point Candara, bold, with the custom font color, then center the heading.

k. Format the last line in 11-point Candara, center the line, replace Your Name with your name, then apply bold to your name.

l. Examine the document carefully for formatting errors, and make any necessary adjustments.

m. Save the flyer, submit it to your instructor, then close the file and exit Word.

Independent Challenge 3

One of your responsibilities as patient care coordinator at Metropolitan Healthcare is to facilitate patient-staff interactions to achieve excellent care for patients at the facility. You have drafted a memo to the Metropolitan Healthcare staff in order to outline several ways that can encourage patients to be involved in their own healthcare. You need to format the memo so it is professional looking and easy to read.

a. Start Word, open the file WMP 3-5.docx from the drive and folder where you store your Data Files, then save it as **WMP 3-Metropolitan Memo**.

b. Select the **Metropolitan Healthcare Memorandum** heading, apply the Quick Style Title to it, then center the heading. (*Hint*: Open the Quick Style gallery, then click the Title style.)

c. In the memo header, replace Today's Date and Your Name with the current date and your name.

d. Select the four-line memo header, set a left tab stop at the ¾" mark, then insert tabs before the date, the recipient's name, your name, and the subject of the memo.

e. Apply the Quick Style Strong to **Date:**, **To:**, **From:**, and **Re:**.

f. Apply the Quick Style Heading 2 to the headings **Encourage questions**, **Offer an interpreter**, **Identify yourself**, and **Ensure medication safety**.

g. Under the Offer an interpreter heading, apply the Quick Style Emphasis to the words **Interpreters' hours** and **Languages**.

h. On the second page of the document, format the list under the **Ensure medication safety** heading as a multilevel list. FIGURE 3-31 shows the hierarchical structure of the outline. (*Hints*: The list is on pages 2 and 3 so be sure to select the entire list before applying the multilevel style. Apply a multilevel list style, then use the Increase Indent and Decrease Indent buttons to change the level of importance of each item.)

i. Change the outline numbering style to the bullet numbering style shown in FIGURE 3-31 if a different style is used in your outline.

j. Change the font color of each bullet level in the list to a theme font color of your choice. (*Hint*: Select one bullet of each level to select all the bullets at that level, then apply a font color.)

k. Zoom out on the memo so that two pages are displayed in the document window, then, using the Change Case button, change the title Metropolitan Healthcare Memorandum so that only the initial letter of each word is capitalized.

FIGURE 3-31

❖ Information patients need to share with healthcare providers
- ➤ Details about everything they take
  - ▪ Prescription medications
  - ▪ Non-prescription medications
    - • Aspirin
    - • Antacids
    - • Laxatives
    - • Etc.
  - ▪ Vitamins
  - ▪ Herbs or other supplements
    - • St. John's Wort
    - • Ginko biloba
    - • Etc.
- ➤ Information about allergic reactions to medications
  - ▪ Rashes
  - ▪ Difficulty breathing
  - ▪ Etc.
- ➤ Details of illnesses or medical conditions
  - ▪ High blood pressure
  - ▪ Glaucoma
  - ▪ Diabetes
  - ▪ Thyroid disease
  - ▪ Etc.

❖ Information healthcare providers need to share with patients
- ➤ What each prescribed medication is and what it is used for
  - ▪ Name of medication
  - ▪ Purpose of medication
  - ▪ Dosage
  - ▪ Side effects
  - ▪ Drug interactions
- ➤ Written directions for the dosage and purpose
  - ▪ "Take once a day for high blood pressure"

Independent Challenge 3 (continued)

l. Using the Fonts button on the Design tab, change the fonts to a font set of your choice. Choose fonts that allow the document to fit on two pages.

m. Using the Colors button on the Design tab, change the colors to a color palette of your choice.

n. Apply different styles and adjust other formatting elements as necessary to make the memo attractive, eye catching, and readable. The finished memo should fit on two pages.

o. Save the document, submit it to your instructor, then close the file and exit Word.

Independent Challenge 4: Explore

The fonts you choose for a document can have a major effect on the document's tone. Not all fonts are appropriate for use in a business document, and some fonts, especially those with a definite theme, are appropriate only for specific purposes. In this Independent Challenge, you will use font formatting and other formatting features to design a letterhead and a fax coversheet for yourself or your business. The letterhead and coversheet should not only look professional and attract interest, but also say something about the character of your business or your personality. FIGURE 3-32 shows an example of a business letterhead.

a. Start Word, and save a new blank document as **WMP 3-Personal Letterhead** to the drive and folder where you store your Data Files.

b. Type your name or the name of your business, your address, your phone number, your fax number, and your website or e-mail address.

c. Format your name or the name of your business in a font that expresses your personality or says something about the nature of your business. Use fonts, font colors, text effects and typography, borders, shading, paragraph formatting, and other formatting features to design a letterhead that is appealing and professional.

d. Save your changes, submit the document to your instructor, then close the file.

e. Open a new blank document, and save it as **WMP 3-Personal Fax Coversheet**. Type FAX, your name or the name of your business, your address, your phone number, your fax number, and your website or e-mail address at the top of the document.

f. Type a fax header that includes the following: Date:, To:, From:, Re:, Pages:, and Comments:.

g. Format the information in the fax coversheet using fonts, font effects, borders, paragraph formatting, and other formatting features. Since a fax coversheet is designed to be faxed, all fonts and other formatting elements should be black or grey.

h. Save your changes, submit the document to your instructor, close the file, then exit Word.

FIGURE 3-32

Santa Fe Healing Arts

443 Sanchez Street, 6th floor, Santa Fe, NM 87501   Tel: 505-555-9767   Fax: 505-555-2992   www.sfhealingarts.com

Visual Workshop

Open the file WMP 3-6.docx from the drive and folder where you store your Data Files. Create the flyer shown in FIGURE 3-33. (*Hints*: Find the clip art image using the keyword yoga. Choose a different image if the image shown in the figure is not available. Use Footlight MT Light or another similar font for the text. Use the Gradient Fill, Blue, Accent 1, Reflection text effect, and change the font color of the text to orange. Align the text in the box using a right and then a left tab stop. Use paragraph spacing to adjust the spacing between paragraphs so that all the text fits on one page. Make other adjustments as needed so your flyer is similar to the one shown in FIGURE 3-33.) Save the flyer as **WMP 3-Fresh Start Yoga**, then submit a copy to your instructor.

FIGURE 3-33

Fresh Start Yoga

12 Week Weight Management and Exercise Program

This series will help you find a balanced approach to healthy eating and consistent activity through yoga. The program includes group exercise, behavioral nutrition classes, and individual counseling.

Free information session
Thursday, June 20th, 6 p.m.

The Wellness Center at Valley Community Hospital

Program participants receive:
- A free fitness assessment
- An individualized yoga plan

Register by:	June 27th
Classes begin:	July 6th

Fee for the program is $259. The cost may be reimbursed by insurance.
For more information, contact Your Name at 555-3374.

Formatting Text and Paragraphs

Creating and Formatting Tables

CASE You are preparing a summary budget for an advertising campaign aimed at the greater Cambridge market. The goal of the ad campaign is to educate the community about the services provided by the Riverwalk Medical Clinic and to attract new patients. You decide to format the budget information as a table so that it is easy to read and analyze.

Module Objectives

After completing this module, you will be able to:

- Insert a table
- Insert and delete rows and columns
- Modify rows and columns
- Sort table data
- Split and merge cells
- Perform calculations in tables
- Apply a table style
- Customize a table format

Files You Will Need

WMP 4-1.docx   WMP 4-2.docx

Insert a Table

Learning Outcomes
• Insert a table
• Type text in a table
• Add rows

A **table** is a grid made up of rows and columns of cells that you can fill with text and graphics. A **cell** is the box formed by the intersection of a column and a row. The lines that divide the columns and rows and help you see the grid-like structure of a table are called **borders**. You can create a table in a document by using the Table command in the Tables group on the Insert tab. Once you have created a table, you can add text and graphics to it. **CASE** ▸ *You begin by inserting a blank table and adding text to it.*

STEPS

1. **Start** Word, **click** Blank document, **click the** View tab, **then click the** Page Width button **in the Zoom group**

2. **Click the** Insert tab, **then click the** Table button **in the Tables group**

   The Table menu opens. It includes a grid for selecting the number of columns and rows you want the table to contain, as well as several commands for inserting a table. TABLE 4-1 describes these commands. As you move the pointer across the grid, a preview of the table with the specified number of columns and rows appears in the document at the location of the insertion point.

3. **Point to the** second box **in the fourth row to select 2x4 Table, then click**

   A table with two columns and four rows is inserted in the document, as shown in FIGURE 4-1. Black borders surround the table cells. The insertion point is in the first cell in the first row.

4. **Type** Location, **then press** [Tab]

   Pressing [Tab] moves the insertion point to the next cell in the row.

5. **Type** Cost, **press** [Tab], **then type** The Boston Globe

   Pressing [Tab] at the end of a row moves the insertion point to the first cell in the next row.

6. **Press** [Tab], **type** 6,200, **press** [Tab], **then type the following text in the table, pressing** [Tab] **to move from cell to cell**

Boston.com	1,300
Cambridge River Festival	750

7. **Press** [Tab]

   Pressing [Tab] at the end of the last cell of a table creates a new row at the bottom of the table, as shown in FIGURE 4-2. The insertion point is located in the first cell in the new row.

8. **Type the following, pressing** [Tab] **to move from cell to cell and to create new rows**

Cambridge Chronicle	1,950
Wickedlocal.com	1,250
Mass mailing	1,560
Boston Magazine	1,860

9. **Click the** Save button 💾 **on the Quick Access toolbar, then save the document as** WMP 4-Clinic Ad Budget **to the location where you store your Data Files**

   The table is shown in FIGURE 4-3.

TABLE 4-1: Table menu commands

command	use to
Insert Table	Create a table with any number of columns and rows and select an AutoFit behavior
Draw Table	Create a complex table by drawing the table columns and rows
Convert Text to Table	Convert text that is separated by tabs, commas, or another separator character into a table
Excel Spreadsheet	Insert a blank Excel worksheet into the document as an embedded object
Quick Tables	Insert a preformatted table template and replace the placeholder data with your own data

FIGURE 4-1: **Blank table**

FIGURE 4-2: **New row in table**

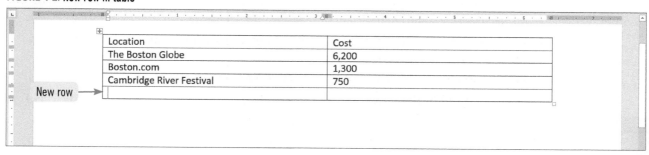

FIGURE 4-3: **Text in the table**

Location	Cost
The Boston Globe	6,200
Boston.com	1,300
Cambridge River Festival	750
Cambridge Chronicle	1,950
Wickedlocal.com	1,250
Mass mailing	1,560
Boston Magazine	1,860

Converting text to a table and a table to text

Starting with a blank table is just one way to create a table. You can also convert text that is separated by a tab, a comma, or another separator character into a table. For example, to create a two-column table of last and first names, you could type the names as a list with a comma separating the last and first name in each line, and then convert the text to a table. The separator character—a comma in this example—indicates where you want to divide the table into columns, and a paragraph mark indicates where you want to begin a new row. To convert text to a table, select the text, click the Table button in the Tables group on the Insert tab, and then click Convert Text to Table. In the Convert Text to Table dialog box, select from the options for structuring and formatting the table, and then click OK to create the table.

Conversely, you can convert a table to text that is separated by tabs, commas, or some other character by selecting the table, clicking the Table Tools Layout tab, and then clicking the Convert to Text button in the Data group.

Insert and Delete Rows and Columns

Learning Outcomes
• Select rows and columns
• Insert and delete rows and columns

You can easily modify the structure of a table by adding and removing rows and columns. First, you must click or select an existing row or column in the table to indicate where you want to insert or delete. You can select any element of a table using the Select command on the Table Tools Layout tab, but it is often easier to select, add, and delete rows and columns using the mouse. **CASE** *You add new rows and columns to the table, and delete unnecessary rows.*

STEPS

1. **Click the** Home tab, **click the** Show/Hide ¶ button ¶ **in the Paragraph group to display formatting marks, then move the pointer up and down the left edge of the table**
   An end of cell mark appears at the end of each cell and an end of row mark appears at the end of each row. When you move the pointer to the left of two existing rows, an Insert Control appears outside the table.

> **QUICK TIP**
> You can also insert a row by right-clicking a row, clicking the Insert button on the Mini toolbar, and then clicking Insert Above or Insert Below.

2. **Move the pointer to the left of the border above the Wickedlocal.com row, then click the** Insert Control
   A new row is inserted directly above the Wickedlocal.com row, as shown in **FIGURE 4-4**.

3. **Click the** first cell **of the new row, type** Bostonherald.com, **press [Tab], then type** 1,530

4. **Place the pointer in the margin to the left of the** Boston.com **row until the pointer changes to** ⌐, **click to select the row, press and hold the mouse button, drag down to select the** Cambridge River Festival row, **then release the mouse button**
   The two rows are selected, including the end of row marks.

> **QUICK TIP**
> If the end of row mark is not selected, you have selected only the text in the row, not the row itself.

5. **Click the** Table Tools Layout tab, **then click the** Insert Below button **in the Rows & Columns group**
   Two new rows are added below the selected rows. To insert multiple rows, you select the number of rows you want to insert before inserting the rows, and then click an Insert Control or use the buttons on the Ribbon.

> **QUICK TIP**
> If you select a row and press [Delete], you delete only the contents of the row, not the row itself.

6. **Click the** Cambridge Chronicle row, **click the** Delete button **in the Rows & Columns group, click** Delete Rows, **select the two** blank rows, **click the** Delete button **on the Mini toolbar, then click** Delete Rows
   The Cambridge Chronicle row and the two blank rows are deleted.

7. **Place the pointer over the top border of the** Location column **until the pointer changes to** ↓, **then click**
   The entire column is selected.

> **QUICK TIP**
> To select a cell, place the pointer near the left border of the cell, then click.

8. **Click the** Insert Left button **in the Rows & Columns group, then type** Type
   A new column is inserted to the left of the Location column, as shown in **FIGURE 4-5**.

9. **Place the pointer over the border between the Location and Cost columns at the top of the table, click the** Insert Control, **then type** Details **in the first cell of the new column**
   A new column is added between the Location and Cost columns.

10. **Press [↓] to move the insertion point to the next cell in the Details column, click the** Home tab, **click** ¶ **to turn off the display of formatting marks, enter the text shown in** FIGURE 4-6 **in each cell in the Details and Type columns, then save your changes**
    You can use the arrow keys to move the insertion point from cell to cell. Notice that text wraps to the next line in the cell as you type. Compare your table to **FIGURE 4-6**.

FIGURE 4-4: **Inserted row**

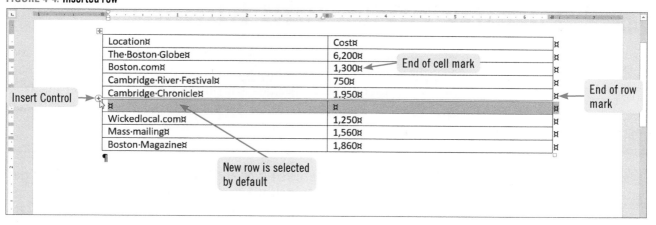

FIGURE 4-5: **Inserted column**

Type¤	Location¤	Cost¤	¤
¤	The·Boston·Globe¤	6,200¤	¤
¤	Boston.com¤	1,300¤	¤
¤	Cambridge·River·Festival¤	750¤	¤
¤	Bostonherald.com¤	1,530¤	¤
¤	Wickedlocal.com¤	1,250¤	¤
¤	Mass·mailing¤	1,560¤	¤
¤	Boston·Magazine¤	1,860¤	¤

New column

FIGURE 4-6: **Text in Type and Details columns**

Type	Location	Details	Cost
Print	The Boston Globe	¼ page, 4 times	6,200
Web	Boston.com	Premium placement, 1 year	1,300
Misc.	Cambridge River Festival	1500 brochures	750
Web	Bostonherald.com	Premium placement, 1 year	1,530
Web	Wickedlocal.com	Live link, premium placement, multiple listings, 1 year	1,250
Misc.	Mass mailing	2000 brochures, including postage	1,560
Print	Boston Magazine	½ page, 3 times	1,860

Copying and moving rows and columns

You can copy and move rows and columns within a table in the same manner you copy and move text. Select the row or column you want to move, then use the Copy or Cut button to place the selection on the Clipboard. Place the insertion point in the location where you want to insert the row or column, then click the Paste button to paste the selection. Rows are inserted above the row containing the insertion point; columns are inserted to the left of the column containing the insertion point. You can also copy or move columns and rows by selecting them and using the pointer to drag them to a new location in the table.

Modify Rows and Columns

Once you create a table, you can easily adjust the size of columns and rows to make the table easier to read. You can change the width of columns and the height of rows by dragging a border, by using the AutoFit command, or by setting precise measurements in the Cell Size group on the Table Tools Layout tab. **CASE** *You adjust the size of the columns and rows to make the table more attractive and easier to read. You also center the text vertically in each table cell.*

STEPS

1. **Position the pointer over the border between Type and Location until the pointer changes to ⊣⊢, then drag the border to approximately the ½" mark on the horizontal ruler**

   The dotted line that appears as you drag represents the border. Dragging the column border changes the width of the first and second columns: the first column is narrower and the second column is wider. When dragging a border to change the width of an entire column, make sure no cells are selected in the column. You can also drag a row border to change the height of the row above it.

2. **Position the pointer over the right border of the Location column until the pointer changes to ⊣⊢, then double-click**

   Double-clicking a column border automatically resizes the column to fit the text.

3. **Double-click the right border of the Details column with the ⊣⊢ pointer, then double-click the right border of the Cost column with the ⊣⊢ pointer**

   The widths of the Details and Cost columns are adjusted.

4. **Move the pointer over the table, then click the table move handle ⊞ that appears outside the upper-left corner of the table**

   Clicking the table move handle selects the entire table. You can also use the Select button in the Table group on the Table Tools Layout tab to select an entire table.

5. **With the table still selected, click the Table Tools Layout tab, click the Distribute Rows button ☷ in the Cell Size group, then click in the table to deselect it**

   All the rows in the table become the same height, as shown in FIGURE 4-7. You can also use the Distribute Columns button to make all the columns the same width, or you can use the AutoFit button to make the width of the columns fit the text, to adjust the width of the columns so the table is justified between the margins, or to set fixed column widths.

6. **Click in the Details column, click the Table Column Width text box in the Cell Size group, type 3.5, then press [Enter]**

   The width of the Details column changes to 3.5".

7. **Click the Select button in the Table group, click Select Table, click the Align Center Left button ▤ in the Alignment group, deselect the table, then save your changes**

   The text is centered vertically in each table cell, as shown in FIGURE 4-8. You can use the alignment buttons in the Alignment group to change the vertical and horizontal alignment of the text in selected cells or in the entire table.

Creating and Formatting Tables

FIGURE 4-7: **Resized columns and rows**

Table move handle:
click to select
the table; drag to
move the table

Rows are all
the same
height

Table resize handle; drag
to change the size of all
the rows and columns

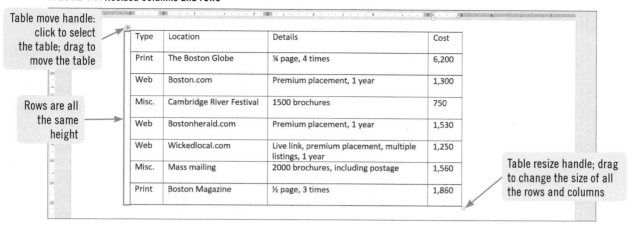

Type	Location	Details	Cost
Print	The Boston Globe	¼ page, 4 times	6,200
Web	Boston.com	Premium placement, 1 year	1,300
Misc.	Cambridge River Festival	1500 brochures	750
Web	Bostonherald.com	Premium placement, 1 year	1,530
Web	Wickedlocal.com	Live link, premium placement, multiple listings, 1 year	1,250
Misc.	Mass mailing	2000 brochures, including postage	1,560
Print	Boston Magazine	½ page, 3 times	1,860

FIGURE 4-8: **Text centered vertically in cells**

Text is centered
vertically in the cell

Column is widened

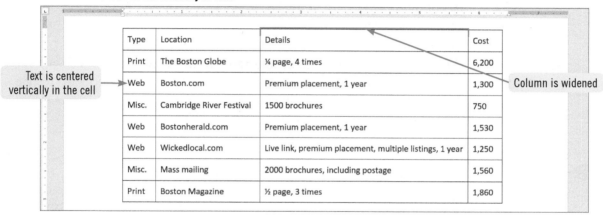

Type	Location	Details	Cost
Print	The Boston Globe	¼ page, 4 times	6,200
Web	Boston.com	Premium placement, 1 year	1,300
Misc.	Cambridge River Festival	1500 brochures	750
Web	Bostonherald.com	Premium placement, 1 year	1,530
Web	Wickedlocal.com	Live link, premium placement, multiple listings, 1 year	1,250
Misc.	Mass mailing	2000 brochures, including postage	1,560
Print	Boston Magazine	½ page, 3 times	1,860

Setting advanced table properties

When you want to wrap text around a table, indent a table, or set other advanced table properties, you click the Properties command in the Table group on the Table Tools Layout tab to open the Table Properties dialog box, shown in **FIGURE 4-9**. Using the Table tab in this dialog box, you can set a precise width for the table, change the horizontal alignment of the table between the margins, indent the table, and set text wrapping options for the table. You can also click Options on the Table tab to open the Table Options dialog box, which you use to customize the table's default cell margins and the spacing between table cells. Alternatively, click Borders and Shading on the Table tab to open the Borders and Shading dialog box, which you can use to create a custom format for the table.

The Column, Row, and Cell tabs in the Table Properties dialog box allow you to set an exact width for columns, to specify an exact height for rows, and to indicate an exact size for individual cells. The Alt Text tab is used to add alternative text for a table that will appear on a webpage, such as a title and a description.

FIGURE 4-9: **Table Properties dialog box**

Table Properties dialog box with tabs: Table, Row, Column, Cell, Alt Text. Size: Preferred width: 6.08" Measure in: Inches. Alignment: Left, Center, Right; Indent from left: 0". Text wrapping: None, Around. Positioning. Borders and Shading... Options... OK Cancel.

Sort Table Data

Learning Outcomes
- Sort table data by one or more criteria
- Sort lists and paragraphs

Tables are often easier to interpret and analyze when the data is **sorted**, which means the rows are organized in alphabetical or sequential order based on the data in one or more columns. When you sort a table, Word arranges all the table data according to the criteria you set. You set sort criteria by specifying the column (or columns) you want to sort by and indicating the sort order—ascending or descending— you want to use. **Ascending order** lists data alphabetically or sequentially (from A to Z, 0 to 9, or earliest to latest). **Descending order** lists data in reverse alphabetical or sequential order (from Z to A, 9 to 0, or latest to earliest). You can sort using the data in one column or multiple columns. When you sort by multiple columns you must select primary, secondary, and tertiary sort criteria. You use the Sort command in the Data group on the Table Tools Layout tab to sort a table. **CASE** *You sort the table so that all ads of the same type are listed together. You also add secondary sort criteria so that the ads within each type are listed in descending order by cost.*

STEPS

1. **Place the insertion point anywhere in the table**

   To sort an entire table, you simply need to place the insertion point anywhere in the table. If you want to sort specific rows only, then you must select the rows you want to sort.

2. **Click the Sort button in the Data group on the Table Tools Layout tab**

   The Sort dialog box opens, as shown in FIGURE 4-10. You use this dialog box to specify the column or columns you want to sort by, the type of information you are sorting (text, numbers, or dates), and the sort order (ascending or descending). Column 1 is selected by default in the Sort by list box. Since you want to sort your table first by the information in the first column—the type of ad (Print, Web, or Misc.)—you don't change the Sort by criteria.

3. **Click the Header row option button in the My list has section to select it**

   The table includes a **header row**, which is the first row of a table that contains the column headings. You must select the Header row option button first when you do not want the header row included in the sort.

4. **Click the Descending option button in the Sort by section**

   The information in the Type column will be sorted in descending—or reverse alphabetical—order, so that the "Web" ads will be listed first, followed by the "Print" ads, and then the "Misc." ads.

5. **Click the Then by list arrow in the first Then by section, click Cost, verify that Number appears in the Type list box, then click the Descending option button**

   Within the Web, Print, and Misc. groups, the rows will be sorted by the cost of the ad, which is the information contained in the Cost column. The rows will appear in descending order within each group, with the most expensive ad listed first.

6. **Click OK, then deselect the table**

   The rows in the table are sorted first by the information in the Type column and second by the information in the Cost column, as shown in FIGURE 4-11. The first row of the table, which is the header row, is not included in the sort.

7. **Save your changes to the document**

FIGURE 4-10: Sort dialog box

Click to select the primary sort column

Click to select the type of data in the sort column

Choose the sort order

Include or exclude the header row in the sort

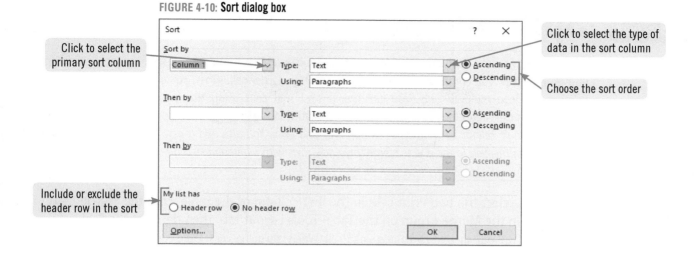

FIGURE 4-11: Sorted table

Header row is not included in the sort

First, rows are sorted by type in descending order

Second, within each type, rows are sorted by cost in descending order

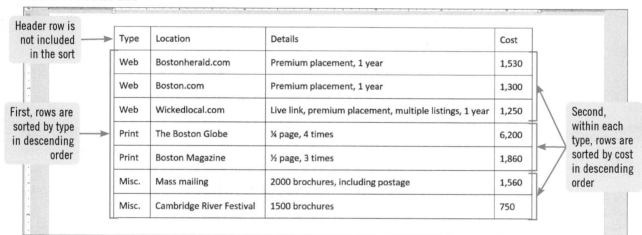

Type	Location	Details	Cost
Web	Bostonherald.com	Premium placement, 1 year	1,530
Web	Boston.com	Premium placement, 1 year	1,300
Web	Wickedlocal.com	Live link, premium placement, multiple listings, 1 year	1,250
Print	The Boston Globe	¼ page, 4 times	6,200
Print	Boston Magazine	½ page, 3 times	1,860
Misc.	Mass mailing	2000 brochures, including postage	1,560
Misc.	Cambridge River Festival	1500 brochures	750

Sorting lists and paragraphs

In addition to sorting table data, you can use the Sort command to alphabetize text or sort numerical data. When you want to sort data that is not formatted as a table, such as lists and paragraphs, you use the Sort command in the Paragraph group on the Home tab. To sort lists and paragraphs, select the items you want included in the sort, then click the Sort button. In the Sort Text dialog box, use the Sort by list arrow to select the sort by criteria (such as paragraphs or fields), use the Type list arrow to select the type of data (text, numbers, or dates), and then click the Ascending or Descending option button to choose a sort order.

When sorting text information in a document, the term "fields" refers to text or numbers that are separated by a character, such as a tab or a comma. For example, you might want to sort a list of names alphabetically. If the names you want to sort are listed in "Last name, First name" order, then last name and first name are each considered a field. You can choose to sort the list in alphabetical order by last name or by first name. Use the Options button in the Sort Text dialog box to specify the character that separates the fields in your lists or paragraphs, along with other sort options.

Split and Merge Cells

A convenient way to change the format and structure of a table is to merge and split the table cells. When you **merge** cells, you combine adjacent cells into a single larger cell. When you **split** a cell, you divide an existing cell into multiple cells. You can merge and split cells using the Merge Cells and Split Cells commands in the Merge group on the Table Tools Layout tab. **CASE** ▶ *You merge cells in the first column to create a single cell for each ad type—Web, Print, and Misc. You also add a new row to the bottom of the table, and split the cells in the row to create three new rows with a different structure.*

STEPS

1. **Drag to select the two** Print cells **in the first column of the table, click the** Merge Cells button **in the Merge group on the Table Tools Layout tab, then deselect the text**
   The two Print cells merge to become a single cell. When you merge cells, Word converts the text in each cell into a separate paragraph in the merged cell.

2. **Select the first** Print **in the cell, then press [Delete]**

3. **Select the three** Web cells **in the first column, click the** Merge Cells button, **type** Web, **select the two** Misc. cells, **click the** Merge Cells button, **then type** Misc.
   The three Web cells merge to become one cell and the two Misc. cells merge to become one cell.

4. **Click the** Cambridge River Festival cell, **then click the** Insert Below button **in the Rows & Columns group**
   A row is added to the bottom of the table.

5. **Select the** first three cells **in the new last row of the table, click the** Merge Cells button, **then deselect the cell**
   The three cells in the row merge to become a single cell.

6. **Click the** first cell in the last row, **then click the** Split Cells button **in the Merge group**
   The Split Cells dialog box opens, as shown in FIGURE 4-12. You use this dialog box to split the selected cell or cells into a specific number of columns and rows.

7. **Type** 1 **in the Number of columns text box, press [Tab], type** 3 **in the Number of rows text box, click** OK, **then deselect the cells**
   The single cell is divided into three rows of equal height. When you split a cell into multiple rows, the width of the original column does not change. When you split a cell into multiple columns, the height of the original row does not change. If the cell you split contains text, all the text appears in the upper-left cell.

8. **Click the** last cell **in the Cost column, click the** Split Cells button, **repeat Step 7, then save your changes**
   The cell is split into three rows, as shown in FIGURE 4-13. The last three rows of the table now have only two columns.

Changing cell margins

By default, table cells have .08" left and right cell margins with no spacing between the cells, but you can adjust these settings for a table using the Cell Margins button in the Alignment group on the Table Tools Layout tab. First, place the insertion point in the table, and then click the Cell Margins button to open the Table Options dialog box. Enter new settings for the top, bottom, left, and right cell margins in the text boxes in the Default cell margins section of the dialog box, or select the Allow spacing between cells check box and then enter a setting in the Default cell spacing section to increase spacing between table cells. You can also deselect the Automatically resize to fit contents check box in the Options section of the dialog box to turn off the setting that causes table cells to widen to fit the text as you type. Any settings you change in the Table Options dialog box are applied to the entire table.

FIGURE 4-12: Split Cells dialog box

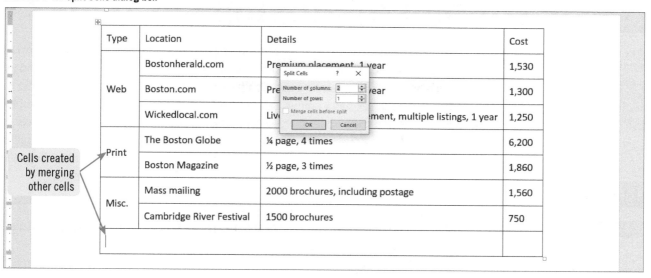

Cells created by merging other cells

FIGURE 4-13: Cells split into three rows

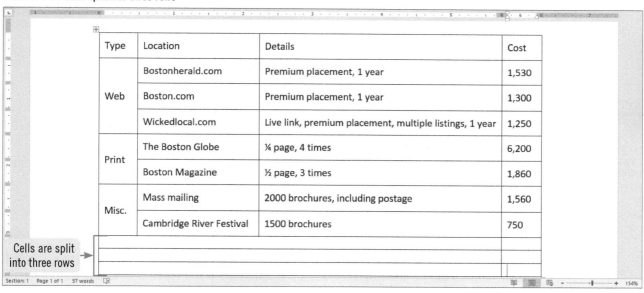

Cells are split into three rows

Using tables to lay out a page

Tables are often used to display information for quick reference and analysis, but you can also use tables to structure the layout of a page. You can insert any kind of information in the cell of a table—including graphics, bulleted lists, charts, and other tables (called **nested tables**). For example, you might use a table to lay out a résumé, a newsletter, or a webpage. When you use a table to lay out a page, you generally remove the table borders to hide the table structure from the reader. After you remove borders,

it can be helpful to display the table gridlines on screen while you work. **Gridlines** are dotted lines that show the boundaries of cells, but do not print. If your document will be viewed online—for example, if you are planning to e-mail your résumé to potential employers—you should turn off the display of gridlines before you distribute the document so that it looks the same online as it looks when printed. To turn gridlines off or on, click the View Gridlines button in the Table group on the Table Tools Layout tab.

Perform Calculations in Tables

Learning Outcomes
- Sum numbers in a table
- Update a field
- Insert a formula

If your table includes numerical information, you can perform simple calculations in the table. The Formula command allows you to quickly total the numbers in a column or row, and to perform other standard calculations, such as averages. When you calculate data in a table using formulas, you use cell references to refer to the cells in the table. Each cell has a unique **cell reference** composed of a letter and a number; the letter represents its column and the number represents its row. For example, the cell in the third row of the fourth column is cell D3. **FIGURE 4-14** shows the cell references in a simple table. **CASE** *You use the Formula command to calculate the total cost of the Clinic ad campaign. You also add information about the budgeted cost, and create a formula to calculate the difference between the total and budgeted costs.*

STEPS

QUICK TIP

You must type a zero in any blank cell in a row or column before using the SUM function.

1. **Click the first blank cell in column 1, type Total Cost, press [Tab], then click the Formula button in the Data group on the Table Tools Layout tab**

   The Formula dialog box opens, as shown in **FIGURE 4-15**. The SUM function appears in the Formula text box followed by the reference for the cells to include in the calculation, (ABOVE). The formula =SUM(ABOVE) indicates that Word will sum the numbers in the cells above the active cell.

2. **Click OK**

   Word totals the numbers in the cells above the active cell and inserts the sum as a field. You can use the SUM function to quickly total the numbers in a column or a row. If the cell you select is at the bottom of a column of numbers, Word totals the column. If the cell is at the right end of a row of numbers, Word totals the row.

3. **Select 750 in the cell above the total, then type 850**

   If you change a number that is part of a calculation, you must recalculate the field result.

QUICK TIP

To change a field result to regular text, click the field to select it, then press [Ctrl][Shift][F9].

4. **Press [↓], right-click the cell, then click Update Field**

   The information in the cell is updated. When the insertion point is in a cell that contains a formula, you can also press [F9] or [Fn][F9], depending on your keyboard, to update the field result.

5. **Press [Tab], type Budgeted, press [Tab], type 13,950, press [Tab], type Difference, then press [Tab]**

   The insertion point is in the last cell of the table.

6. **Click the Formula button**

   The Formula dialog box opens. Word proposes to sum the numbers above the active cell, but you want to insert a formula that calculates the difference between the total and budgeted costs. You can type simple custom formulas using a plus sign (+) for addition, a minus sign (–) for subtraction, an asterisk (*) for multiplication, and a slash (/) for division.

QUICK TIP

Cell references are determined by the number of columns in each row, not by the number of columns in the table. Rows 9 and 10 have only two columns: A and B.

7. **Select =SUM(ABOVE) in the Formula text box, then type =B9–B10**

   You must type an equal sign (=) to indicate that the text following the equal sign (=) is a formula. You want to subtract the budgeted cost in the second column of row 10 from the total cost in the second column of row 9; therefore, you type a formula to subtract the value in cell B10 from the value in cell B9.

8. **Click OK, then save your changes**

   The difference appears in the cell, as shown in **FIGURE 4-16**.

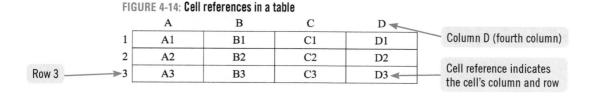

FIGURE 4-14: Cell references in a table

	A	B	C	D
1	A1	B1	C1	D1
2	A2	B2	C2	D2
3	A3	B3	C3	D3

Column D (fourth column)

Row 3

Cell reference indicates the cell's column and row

FIGURE 4-15: Formula dialog box

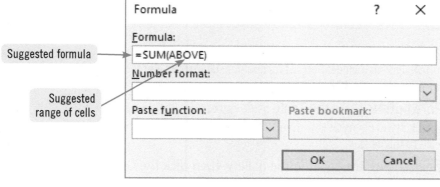

Suggested formula — =SUM(ABOVE)

Suggested range of cells

FIGURE 4-16: Difference calculated

Type	Location	Details	Cost
Web	Bostonherald.com	Premium placement, 1 year	1,530
	Boston.com	Premium placement, 1 year	1,300
	Wickedlocal.com	Live link, premium placement, multiple listings, 1 year	1,250
Print	The Boston Globe	¼ page, 4 times	6,200
	Boston Magazine	½ page, 3 times	1,860
Misc.	Mass mailing	2000 brochures, including postage	1,560
	Cambridge River Festival	1500 brochures	850
Total Cost			14,550
Budgeted			13,950
Difference			600

Cell A9

Cell A10

Cell B9

Cell B10

B9-B10=600

Working with formulas

In addition to the SUM function, Word includes formulas for averaging, counting, and rounding data, to name a few. To use a Word formula, delete any text in the Formula text box, type =, click the Paste function list arrow in the Formula dialog box, select a function, and then insert the cell references of the cells you want to include in the calculation in parentheses after the name of the function. When entering formulas, you must separate cell references by a comma. For example, if you want to average the values in cells A1, B3, and C4, enter the formula =AVERAGE(A1,B3,C4). You must separate cell ranges by a colon. For example, to total the values in cells A1 through A9, enter the formula =SUM(A1:A9). To display the result of a calculation in a particular number format, such as a decimal percentage (0.00%), click the Number format list arrow in the Formula dialog box and select a number format. Word inserts the result of a calculation as a field in the selected cell.

Apply a Table Style

Learning Outcomes
• Customize a table style
• Change theme colors

Adding shading and other design elements to a table can help give it a polished appearance and make the data easier to read. Word includes predefined, built-in table styles that you can apply to a table to format it quickly. Table styles include borders, shading, fonts, alignment, colors, and other formatting effects. You can apply a table style to a table using the buttons in the Table Styles group on the Table Tools Design tab. **CASE** *You want to enhance the appearance of the table with shading, borders, and other formats, so you apply a table style to the table. After applying a style, you change the theme colors.*

STEPS

1. **Click the Table Tools Design tab**

   The Table Tools Design tab includes buttons for applying table styles and for adding, removing, and customizing borders and shading in a table.

2. **Click the More button ▼ in the Table Styles group**

   The gallery of table styles opens, as shown in FIGURE 4-17. You point to a table style in the gallery to preview the style applied to the table.

3. **Move the pointer over the styles in the gallery, then click the Grid Table 4 – Accent 5 style**

   The Grid Table 4 – Accent 5 style is applied to the table, as shown in FIGURE 4-18. Because of the structure of the table, this style neither enhances the table nor helps make the data more readable.

4. **Click the More button ▼ in the Table Styles group, scroll down, then click the List Table 3 – Accent 5 style**

   This style works better with the structure of the table, and makes the table data easier to read.

5. **In the Table Style Options group, click the First Column check box to clear it, then click the Banded Columns check box to select it**

   The bold formatting is removed from the first column, and column borders are added to the table. When the banded columns or banded rows setting is active, the odd columns or rows are formatted differently from the even columns or rows to make the table data easier to read.

6. **Click the Design tab, click the Colors list arrow in the Document Formatting group, then scroll down and click Slipstream in the gallery that opens**

   The color palette for the document changes to the colors used in the Slipstream theme, and the table color changes to orange.

7. **Click the Table Tools Design tab, then click the List Table 3 – Accent 6 style in the Table Styles group**

   The table color changes to red.

8. **Click the Table Tools Layout tab, click the table move handle ⊞, click the Align Center Left button ▤ in the Alignment group, select the Type column, click the Align Center button ▤, select the Cost column, then click the Align Center Right button ▤**

   First, the data in the table is left-aligned and centered vertically, then the data in the Type column is centered, and finally the data in the Cost column is right-aligned.

9. **Select the last three rows of the table, click the Bold button B on the Mini toolbar, then click the Align Center Right button ▤ in the Alignment group on the Table Tools Layout tab on the Ribbon**

   The text in the last three rows is right-aligned and bold is applied.

10. **Select the first row of the table, click the Center button ≡ on the Mini toolbar, click the Font Size list arrow on the Mini toolbar, click 14, deselect the row, then save your changes**

    The text in the header row is centered and enlarged, as shown in FIGURE 4-19.

Creating and Formatting Tables

FIGURE 4-17: Gallery of table styles

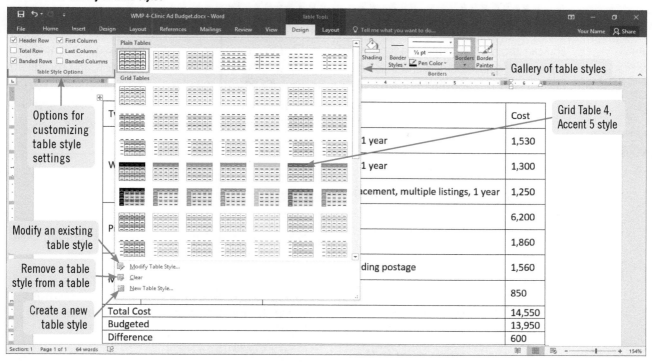

Options for customizing table style settings

Gallery of table styles

Grid Table 4, Accent 5 style

Modify an existing table style

Remove a table style from a table

Create a new table style

FIGURE 4-18: Grid Table 4, Accent 5 style applied to table

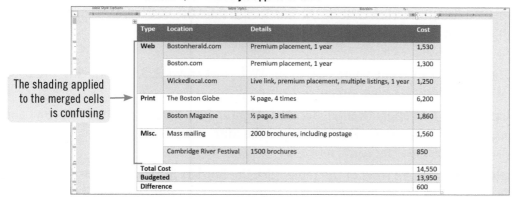

The shading applied to the merged cells is confusing

FIGURE 4-19: List Table 3, Accent 6 style (Slipstream theme) applied to table

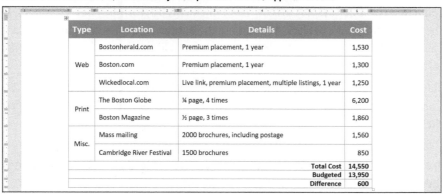

Word 2016

Creating and Formatting Tables

Customize a Table Format

You can also use the formatting tools available in Word to create your own table designs. For example, you can add or remove borders and shading; vary the line style, thickness, and color of borders; and change the orientation of text from horizontal to vertical. In addition, if a table is located at the top of a document, you can press [Enter] at the beginning of a table to move the table down one line in the document. **CASE** ▸ *You adjust the text direction, shading, and borders in the table to make it easier to understand at a glance.*

STEPS

1. **Select the Type and Location cells in the first row, click the Merge Cells button in the Merge group on the Table Tools Layout tab, then type Ad Location**
   The two cells are combined into a single cell containing the text "Ad Location."

2. **Select the Web, Print, and Misc. cells, click the Bold button B on the Mini toolbar, click the Text Direction button in the Alignment group twice, then deselect the cells**
   The text is rotated 270 degrees.

3. **Position the pointer over the right border of the Web cell until the pointer changes to +‖+, then drag the border to approximately the ¼" mark on the horizontal ruler**
   The width of the column containing the vertical text narrows.

> **QUICK TIP**
> In cells with vertical text, the I-beam pointer is rotated 90 degrees, and the buttons in the Alignment group change to vertical alignment.

4. **Place the insertion point in the Web cell, click the Table Tools Design tab, then click the Shading list arrow in the Table Styles group**
   The gallery of shading colors for the Slipstream theme opens.

5. **Click Blue, Accent 1 in the gallery as shown in FIGURE 4-20, click the Print cell, click the Shading list arrow, click Orange, Accent 5, click the Misc. cell, click the Shading list arrow, then click Green, Accent 3**
   Shading is applied to each cell.

6. **Drag to select the Nine white cells in the Web rows (rows 2, 3, and 4), click the Shading list arrow, then click Blue, Accent 1, Lighter 40%**

7. **Repeat Step 6 to apply Orange, Accent 5, Lighter 40% shading to the Print rows and Green, Accent 3, Lighter 40% shading to the Misc. rows**
   Shading is applied to all the cells in rows 1–8.

> **TROUBLE**
> If gridlines appear, click the Borders list arrow, then click View Gridlines to turn off the display.

8. **Select the last three rows of the table, click the Borders list arrow in the Borders group, click No Border on the Borders menu, then click in the table to deselect the rows**
   The top, bottom, left, and right borders are removed from each cell in the selected rows. You use the Borders menu to both add and remove borders.

> **QUICK TIP**
> To change the color, line weight, line style, or border style of an existing border, adjust the active settings in the Borders group, click the Border Painter button, then click the border with the Border Painter pointer 🖌.

9. **Select the Total Cost row, click the Borders list arrow, click Top Border, click the 13,950 cell, click the Borders list arrow, then click the Bottom Border**
   The active border color is black. You can use the buttons in the Borders group to change the active color, line weight, line style, and border style settings before adding a border to a table. A black top border is added to the Total Cost row, and a black bottom border is added below 13,950.

10. **Select the Total Cost row, click the Borders list arrow, click Borders and Shading, click the Color list arrow, click Red, Accent 6, click the top border button in the Preview area, then click OK**
    The top border changes to red. The completed table is shown in FIGURE 4-21.

11. **Press [Ctrl][Home], press [Enter] to move the table down one line, type your name, save, submit the document, close the document, then exit Word**

Creating and Formatting Tables

FIGURE 4-20: Gallery of shading colors from the Slipstream theme

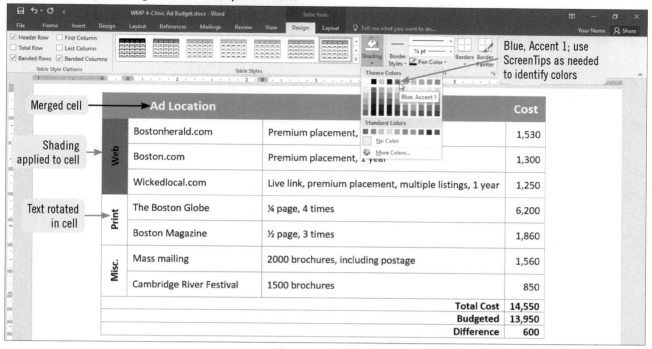

FIGURE 4-21: Completed table

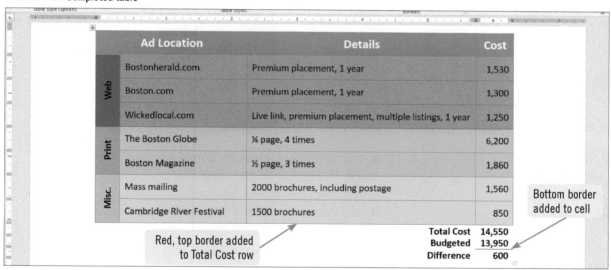

Drawing a table

The Word Draw Table feature allows you to draw table cells exactly where you want them. To draw a table, click the Table button on the Insert tab, and then click Draw Table. If a table is already started, you can click the Draw Table button in the Draw group on the Table Tools Layout tab to turn on the Draw pointer ⌀, and then click and drag to draw a cell. Using the same method, you can draw borders within the cell to create columns and rows, or draw additional cells attached to the first cell. Click the Draw Table button to turn off the draw feature. The borders

you draw are added using the active line style, line weight, and pen color settings found in the Borders group on the Table Tools Design tab.

If you want to remove a border from a table, click the Eraser button in the Draw group to activate the Eraser pointer ⌀, and then click the border you want to remove. Click the Eraser button to turn off the erase feature. You can use the Draw pointer and the Eraser pointer to change the structure of any table, not just the tables you draw from scratch.

Practice

Concepts Review

Label each element shown in FIGURE 4-22.

FIGURE 4-22

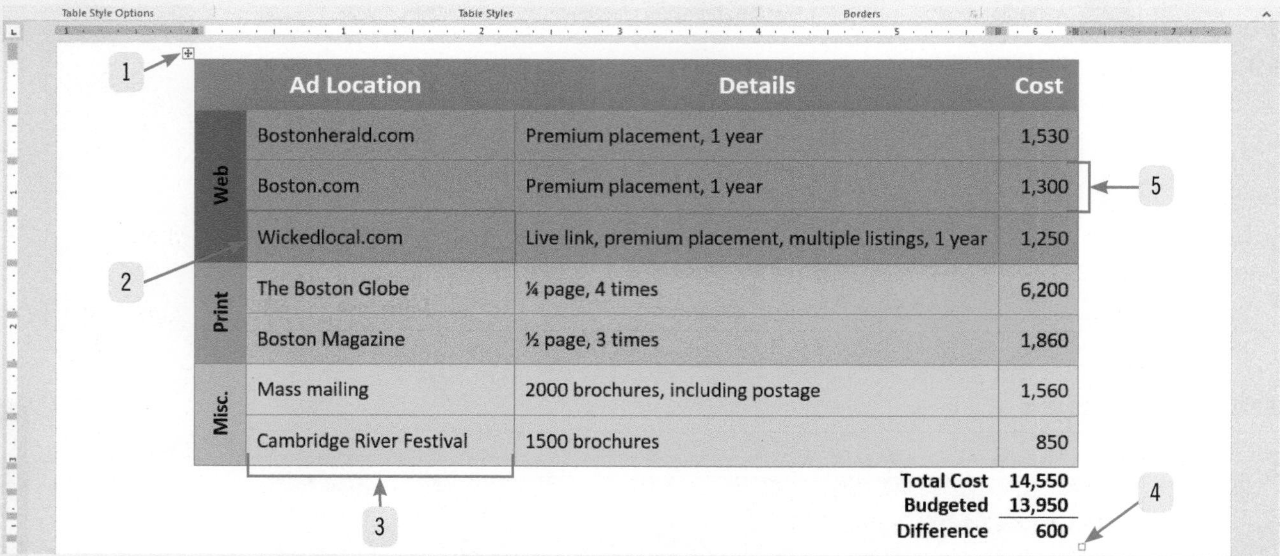

Match each term with the statement that best describes it.

6. Cell	a. Sort order that organizes text from A to Z
7. Descending order	b. The box formed by the intersection of a column and a row
8. Ascending order	c. An object inserted in a table cell
9. Header row	d. The first row of a table that contains the column headings
10. Cell reference	e. To combine two or more adjacent cells into one larger cell
11. Borders	f. Lines that separate columns and rows in a table that print
12. Split	g. To divide an existing cell into multiple cells
13. Merge	h. Lines that show columns and rows in a table that do not print
14. Gridlines	i. A cell address composed of a column letter and a row number
15. Nested table	j. Sort order that organizes text from Z to A

Select the best answer from the list of choices.

16. **Which of the following is the cell reference for the third cell in the second column?**

   a. C2
   b. 2C

   c. 3B
   d. B3

17. **Which button do you use to change the alignment of text in a cell?**

   a. ▤
   b. ▦

   c. ↕↓
   d. ▤

18. Which of the following is *not* a valid way to add a new row to the bottom of a table?

  a. Click in the bottom row, then click the Insert Below button in the Rows & Columns group on the Table Tools Layout tab.

  b. Click in the bottom row, open the Properties dialog box, then insert a new row using the options on the Row tab.

  c. Place the insertion point in the last cell of the last row, then press [Tab].

  d. Right-click the bottom row, point to Insert, then click Insert Rows Below.

19. Which of the following is *not* a correct formula for adding the values in cells A1, A2, and A3?

  a. =SUM(A1,A2,A3)

  b. =SUM(A1~A3)

  c. =A1+A2+A3

  d. =SUM(A1:A3)

20. What happens when you double-click a column border?

  a. The column width is adjusted to fit the text.

  b. The columns in the table are distributed evenly.

  c. A new column is added to the left.

  d. A new column is added to the right.

Skills Review

1. Insert a table.

  a. Start Word, then save a new blank document as **WMP 4-Flu Mortality** to the drive and folder where you store your Data Files.

  b. Type your name, press [Enter] three times, type **Influenza Mortality in Selected Major Cities**, then press [Enter].

  c. Insert a table that contains four columns and four rows.

  d. Type the text shown in FIGURE 4-23, pressing [Tab] to add rows as necessary. (*Note: Do not format the text or the table at this time.*)

  e. Save your changes.

FIGURE 4-23

City	>=65	25-64	<25
Boston	301	113	9
San Diego	125	58	3
Philadelphia	534	196	28
Detroit	225	148	18
Miami	176	96	10
Phoenix	141	62	9

2. Insert and delete rows and columns.

  a. Insert a row above the Miami row, then type the following text in the new row:

Dallas	312	115	16

  b. Delete the Boston row.

  c. Insert a column to the right of the <25 column, type **Date Reported** in the header row, then enter a date in each cell in the column using the format MM/DD/YY (for example, 06/27/16).

  d. Move the Date Reported column to the right of the City column, then save your changes.

3. Modify rows and columns.

  a. Double-click the border between the first and second columns to resize the columns.

  b. Drag the border between the second and third columns precisely to the 1¾" mark on the horizontal ruler.

  c. Double-click the right border of the >=65, 25-64, and <25 columns.

  d. Select the >=65, 25-64, and <25 columns, then distribute the columns evenly.

  e. Select rows 2–7, set the row height to exactly .3", then save your changes.

4. Sort table data.

  Perform three separate sorts, making sure to select that your list has a header row, as follows:

  a. Sort the table data in descending order by the information in the >=65 column, then click OK.

  b. Sort the table data in ascending order by date reported, then click OK.

  c. Sort the table data by city name in alphabetical order, click OK, then save your changes.

5. Split and merge cells.

  a. Insert a row above the header row, then merge the first cell in the new row with the City cell.

  b. Merge the second cell in the new row with the Date Reported cell.

  c. Merge the three remaining blank cells in the first row into a single cell, then type **Mortality by Age** in the merged cell.

Skills Review (continued)

   d. Add a new row to the bottom of the table.

   e. Merge the first two cells in the new row, then type **Average Mortality by Age** in the merged cell.

   f. Select the first seven cells in the first column (from City to San Diego), open the Split Cells dialog box, clear the Merge cells before split check box, then split the cells into two columns.

   g. Type **State** as the heading for the new column, then enter the following text in the remaining cells in the column: **TX, MI, FL, PA, AZ, CA.**

   h. Click the AutoFit button in the Cell Size group, click AutoFit Contents to autofit the table to the contents, then save your changes.

6. Perform calculations in tables.

   a. Place the insertion point in the last cell in the >=65 column.

   b. Open the Formula dialog box, delete the text in the Formula text box, type **=average(above)**, click the Number format list arrow, scroll down, click 0.00, then click OK.

   c. Repeat Step b to insert the average mortality rate by age in the last cell in the 25-64 and <25 columns.

   d. Change the value of the >=65 mortality rate by age for Phoenix to 190.

   e. Recalculate the average mortality rate by age for >=65, then save your changes. (*Hint*: Right-click the cell and select Update Field, or use [F9].)

7. Apply a table style.

   a. Click the Table Tools Design tab, preview table styles applied to the table, and then apply an appropriate style. Was the style you chose effective?

   b. Apply the Grid Table 1 Light style to the table, then remove the style from First Column and Banded Rows.

   c. Apply bold to the >=65, 25-64, and <25 column headings, and to the bottom row of the table.

   d. Center the table between the margins, center the table title **Influenza Mortality in Selected Major Cities**, increase the font size of the title to 14 points, apply bold, then save your changes.

8. Customize a table format.

   a. Select the entire table, then use the Align Center button in the Alignment group on the Table Tools Layout tab to center the text in every cell vertically and horizontally.

   b. Center right-align the dates in column 3 and the numbers in columns 4–6.

   c. Center left-align the city names and state abbreviations in columns 1 and 2, but not the column headings.

   d. Center right-align the text in the bottom row. Make sure the text in the header row is still centered.

   e. Change the theme colors to Marquee.

   f. Select all the cells in the header row, including the >=65, 25-64, and <25 column headings, apply Green, Accent 2 shading, then change the font color to White, Background 1.

   g. Apply Green, Accent 2, Lighter 40% shading to the cells containing the city names and state abbreviations, and Green, Accent 2, Lighter 60% shading to the cells containing the dates.

   h. To the cells containing the >=65, 25-64, and <25 data (excluding the Average Mortality by Age data), apply Gold, Accent 5, Lighter 40% shading; Orange, Accent 3, Lighter 40% shading; and Green, Accent 2, Lighter 40% shading, respectively.

   i. Apply Green, Accent 2 shading to the last row of the table, then change the font color to White, Background 1.

FIGURE 4-24

   j. Change all the table borders to a 1/2-point white border. (*Hint*: Select the table, then, using the buttons in the Borders group on the Table Tools Design tab, verify that the line style is a single line, verify that the weight is ½ pt, change the pen color to white, click the Border Painter button to turn off the Border Painter, then use the Borders list arrow to apply all borders.)

   k. Compare your table to FIGURE 4-24, make any necessary adjustments, save your changes, submit a copy to your instructor, close the file, then exit Word.

Influenza Mortality in Selected Major Cities

City	State	Date Reported	Mortality by Age		
			>=65	25-64	<25
Dallas	TX	06/28/17	312	115	16
Detroit	MI	07/23/17	225	148	18
Miami	FL	07/06/17	176	96	10
Philadelphia	PA	07/04/17	534	196	28
Phoenix	AZ	06/29/17	190	62	9
San Diego	CA	06/11/17	125	58	3
Average Mortality by Age			260.33	112.50	14.00

Independent Challenge 1

You are the office manager for a dental office. In preparation for a meeting about the anticipated growth of the practice's business, you create a table showing projected quarterly expenditures for the fiscal year 2019.

a. Start Word, then save a new blank document as **WMP 4-2019 Expenditures** to the location where you store your Data Files.

b. Type the table title **Projected Quarterly Expenditures, Fiscal Year 2019** at the top of the document, then press [Enter].

c. Insert a table with five columns and four rows, then enter the data shown in FIGURE 4-25 into the table, adding rows as necessary. (*Note: Do not format the text or the table at this time.*)

d. Resize the columns to fit the text.

e. Sort the table rows in alphabetical order by Item.

FIGURE 4-25

Item	Q1	Q2	Q3	Q4
Impression Products	1367	1438	1295	1635
Instruments	916	893	991	802
Anesthetics	1154	959	996	1100
Cements and Liners	829	902	948	1080
Finishing and Polishing	463	394	472	289
Pins and Posts	730	695	463	586

f. Add a new row to the bottom of the table, type **Total** in the first cell, then enter a formula in each remaining cell in the new row to calculate the sum of the cells above it.

g. Add a new column to the right side of the table, type **Total** in the first cell, then enter a formula in each remaining cell in the new column to calculate the sum of the cells to the left of it. (*Hint*: Make sure the formula you insert in each cell sums the cells to the left, not the cells above. In the last cell in the last column, you can sum the cells to the left or the cells above; either way the total should be the same.)

h. Apply a table style to the table. Select a style that enhances the information contained in the table, and adjust the Table Style Options to suit the content.

i. Center the text in the header row, left-align the remaining text in the first column, then right-align the numerical data in the table.

j. Enhance the table with fonts, font colors, shading, and borders to make the table attractive and easy to read at a glance.

k. Increase the font size of the table title to 14 points, then center the table title and the table on the page.

l. Press [Ctrl][End], press [Enter], type your name, save your changes, submit the file to your instructor, close the file, then exit Word.

Independent Challenge 2

You are a medical assistant in a busy family practice. One of your responsibilities at the office is to create a list of all scheduled appointments for the day. You find it easiest to format this information as a table.

a. Start Word, open the file WMP 4-1.docx, then save it as **WMP 4-September 26 Appointments** to the location where you store your Data Files.

b. Center the table title, then increase the font size to 18 points.

c. Turn on formatting marks, select the tabbed text in the document, then convert the text to a table.

d. Add a row above the first row in the table, then enter the following column headings in the new header row: **Last Name, First Name, DOB, Phone, Physician, Time**.

e. Apply an appropriate table style to the table. Add or remove the style from various elements of the table using the options in the Table Style Options group, as necessary.

f. Adjust the column widths so that the table is attractive and readable.

g. Make the height of each row at least .25".

h. Center left-align the text in each cell in the Last Name, First Name, and Physician columns, including the column heads.

i. Center right-align the text in each cell in the Time column, then center align the text in each cell in the DOB and Phone columns, including the column heads.

j. Center the column headings, then center the entire table on the page.

Independent Challenge 2 (continued)

k. Sort the table by last name and then by first name in alphabetical order.

l. Sort the entire table by physician in alphabetical order.

m. Change the shading of the Chen, Groot, and Wilson rows, each to a different color.

n. Sort the table by Time, and then by Physician, in ascending order.

o. Move the Time column to become the first column in the table, then adjust the column width to fit the text. Move the rows for the appointments from 9:00 to 12:30 to the beginning of the table.

p. Enhance the table with borders, shading, fonts, and other formats, if necessary, to make it attractive and readable.

q. Type your name at the bottom of the document or in the footer, save your changes, submit a copy of the table to your instructor, close the document, then exit Word.

Independent Challenge 3

You work in a pediatrician's office. Your boss has given you data on appropriate Ibuprofen and Acetaminophen doses for children and has asked you to format the information for parents. You'll use tables to lay out the information so it is easily understandable.

a. Start Word, open the file WMP 4-2.docx from the drive and folder where you store your Data Files, then save it as **WMP 4-Dosages**. Read the document to get a feel for its contents.

b. Merge the cell in the first row of the table, then merge the cells in the Acetaminophen Doses row.

c. Insert a new row under the first row. Type **One dose lasts 6-8 hours** in the new cell.

d. Insert a new row under the Acetaminophen Doses row. Type **One dose lasts 4-6 hours** in the new row.

e. Change all the text in the table to 10-point Arial, then center all the text horizontally and vertically in the cells. (*Hint*: Use the Center Align button.)

f. Make the height of each row at least **.25"**.

g. Select the third row of the table, copy it, then paste the row below the One dose lasts 4-6 hours row.

h. Split the table above the Acetaminophen Doses row, then press [Enter].

i. Refer to FIGURE 4-26 and follow the steps below as you format the Ibuprofen and Acetaminophen tables. (*Hint*: Turn on gridlines to help you see the structure of the table as you format it.)

j. Format the header row in 14-point Arial, bold, then remove all the borders.

k. Format the second row in 12-point Arial, then remove all the borders.

l. In each column, merge the cells in rows 3 and 4. Remove the left border from the first cell in the new row 3. In the remaining cells in the row, apply bold to the text, then add a top border.

m. Apply bold to the text in the fourth row, then apply Gold, Accent 4, Lighter 40% shading to the cells.

FIGURE 4-26

Ibuprofen Doses (Brand names Motrin or Advil)
One dose lasts 6-8 hours

	Infants' concentrated drops 50 mg/1.25 ml	Children's suspension 100 mg/5 ml	Children's chewable tablets 50 mg	Children's chewable tablets 100 mg	Junior caplets 100 mg
Weight	**Dropperful**	**Teaspoon**	**Tablet**	**Tablet**	**Caplet**
Under 6 months	Consult your doctor				
12-16 lbs.	1 dropperful				
17-21 lbs.	1½ droppersful				
22-32 lbs.		1 teaspoon			
33-43 lbs.		1½ teaspoons	3 tablets		
44-54 lbs.		2 teaspoons	4 tablets	2 tablets	2 caplets
55-65 lbs.		2½ teaspoons	5 tablets	2½ tablets	2½ caplets
66-95 lbs.		3 teaspoons	6 tablets	3 tablets	3 caplets

Acetaminophen Doses (Brand names Tylenol or Tempra)
One dose lasts 4-6 hours

	Infants' concentrated drops 80 mg/0.8 ml	Children's suspension 160 mg/5 ml	Children's chewable tablets 80 mg	Children's chewable tablets 160 mg	Junior caplets 160 mg
Weight	**Dropperful**	**Teaspoon**	**Tablet**	**Tablet**	**Caplet**
Under 6 months	Consult your doctor				
12-17 lbs.	1 dropperful				
18-22 lbs.	1½ droppersful				
23-34 lbs.		1 teaspoon			
35-46 lbs.		1½ teaspoons	3 tablets		
47-57 lbs.		2 teaspoons	4 tablets	2 tablets	2 caplets
58-69 lbs.		2½ teaspoons	5 tablets	2½ tablets	2½ caplets
70-95 lbs.		3 teaspoons	6 tablets	3 tablets	3 caplets

Independent Challenge 3 (continued)

n. In the fifth row, merge the cells in columns 2-6, then apply bold to the text in the merged cell.

o. In columns 2-5, merge all adjoining blank cells, then remove the borders between the blank cells. (*Hint*: You might need to reapply borders to some adjacent cells after you remove the borders between the blank cells.)

p. Repeat steps j-o to format the Acetaminophen table.

q. In the Ibuprofen table, apply Green, Accent 6 shading to the cells in row 3, columns 2-6 and to the cells in column 1, rows 5-12.

r. Apply Green, Accent 6, Lighter 80% shading to the blank cells in columns 2-5.

s. Apply Green, Accent 6, Lighter 40% shading to the remaining table cells in columns 2-5.

t. Repeat steps q-s to apply shading to the Acetaminophen table, using shades of Blue, Accent 5 shading.

u. Examine the document for errors, then make any necessary adjustments.

v. Press [Ctrl][End], press [Enter], type your name, save your changes to the document, preview it, submit the file to your instructor, close the file, then exit Word.

Independent Challenge 4: Explore

A well-written and well-formatted résumé gives you an advantage when it comes to getting a job interview. In a winning résumé, the content and format support your career objective and effectively present your background and qualifications. One simple way to create a résumé is to lay out the page using a table. In this exercise you research guidelines for writing and formatting résumés. You then create your own résumé using a table for its layout.

a. Use your favorite search engine to search the web for information on writing and formatting résumés. Use the keywords **resume advice**.

b. Find helpful advice on writing and formatting résumés from at least two websites.

c. Think about the information you want to include in your résumé. The header should include your name, address, telephone number, and e-mail address. The body should include your career objective and information on your education, work experience, and skills. You may want to add additional information.

d. Sketch a layout for your résumé using a table as the underlying grid. Include the table rows and columns in your sketch.

e. Start Word, open a new blank document, then save it as **WMP 4-My Resume** to the location where you store your Data Files.

f. Set appropriate margins, then insert a table to serve as the underlying grid for your résumé. Split and merge cells, and adjust the size of the table columns as necessary.

g. Type your résumé in the table cells. Take care to use a professional tone and keep your language to the point.

h. Format your résumé with fonts, bullets, and other formatting features. Adjust the spacing between sections by resizing the table columns and rows.

i. When you are satisfied with the content and format of your résumé, remove the borders from the table, then hide the gridlines if they are visible. You may want to add some borders back to the table to help structure the résumé for readers.

j. Check your résumé for spelling and grammar errors.

k. Save your changes, preview your résumé, submit a copy to your instructor, close the file, then exit Word.

Visual Workshop

Create the calendar shown in FIGURE 4-27 using a table to lay out the entire page. (*Hint*: The font is Century Gothic.) Type your name in the last empty cell, save the calendar with the file name **WMP 4-August 2017** to the location where you store your Data Files, then print a copy.

FIGURE 4-27

Lakeside General Hospital
Community Education Calendar

August 2017

Sunday	Monday	Tuesday	Wednesday	Thursday	Friday	Saturday
		1 Diabetes Mgmt. Education 1:30 p.m.	**2**	**3**	**4** Yoga 9:00 a.m.	**5** Women's AA 9:00 a.m. AA 8:00 p.m.
6 OA 6:30 p.m.	**7**	**8** Diabetes Mgmt. Education 1:30 p.m.	**9**	**10** Nursing Mother's Support Group 10:00 a.m.	**11** Yoga 9:00 a.m.	**12** Women's AA 9:00 a.m. AA 8:00 p.m.
13 OA 6:30 p.m.	**14** Cancer Support Group 7:00 p.m.	**15** Diabetes Mgmt. Education 1:30 p.m.	**16**	**17**	**18** Yoga 9:00 a.m.	**19** Women's AA 9:00 a.m. AA 8:00 p.m.
20 OA 6:30 p.m.	**21**	**22** Diabetes Mgmt. Education 1:30 p.m.	**23** Stroke Support Group 1:30 p.m.	**24** Nursing Mother's Support Group 10:00 a.m.	**25** Yoga 9:00 a.m.	**26** Women's AA 9:00 a.m. AA 8:00 p.m.
27 OA 6:30 p.m.	**28** Cancer Support Group 7:00 p.m.	**29** Diabetes Mgmt. Education 1:30 p.m.	**30**	**31**		Your Name

All groups meet in Conference Room 1.
For more information, call 555-4745

Formatting Documents

CASE You have written and formatted the text for an informational report for Riverwalk Medical Clinic patients about staying healthy while traveling. You are now ready to format the pages. You plan to organize the text in columns, to illustrate the report with a table, and to add footnotes and a bibliography.

Module Objectives

After completing this module, you will be able to:

- Set document margins
- Create sections and columns
- Insert page breaks
- Insert page numbers
- Add headers and footers

- Insert a table
- Add footnotes and endnotes
- Insert citations
- Manage sources and create a bibliography

Files You Will Need

WMP 5-1.docx   WMP 5-5.docx
WMP 5-2.docx   WMP 5-6.docx
WMP 5-3.docx   WMP 5-7.docx
WMP 5-4.docx

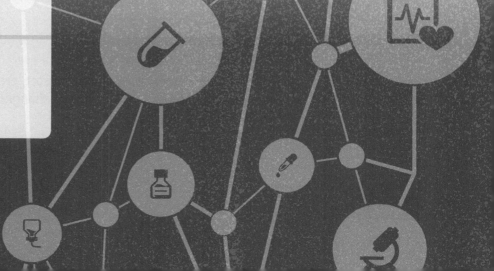

Set Document Margins

Learning Outcomes
- Set custom margins
- Change paper size
- Change page orientation

Changing a document's margins is one way to change the appearance of a document and control the amount of text that fits on a page. The **margins** of a document are the blank areas between the edge of the text and the edge of the page. When you create a document in Word, the default margins are 1" at the top, bottom, left, and right sides of the page. You can adjust the size of a document's margins using the Margins command on the Layout tab or using the rulers. **CASE** *The report should be a four-page document when finished. You begin by reducing the size of the document margins so that more text fits on each page.*

STEPS

1. **Start Word, open the file** WMP 5-1.docx **from the location where you store your Data Files, then save it as** WMP 5-Healthy Traveler

   The report opens in Print Layout view.

2. **Scroll through the report to get a feel for its contents, then press** [Ctrl][Home]

   The report is currently five pages long. Notice that the status bar indicates the page where the insertion point is located and the total number of pages in the document.

3. **Click the** Layout tab, **then click the** Margins button **in the Page Setup group**

   The Margins menu opens. You can select predefined margin settings from this menu, or you can click Custom Margins to create different margin settings.

4. **Click** Custom Margins

   The Page Setup dialog box opens with the Margins tab displayed, as shown in FIGURE 5-1. You can use the Margins tab to change the top, bottom, left, or right document margin, to change the orientation of the pages from portrait to landscape, and to alter other page layout settings. **Portrait orientation** means a page is taller than it is wide; **landscape orientation** means a page is wider than it is tall. This report uses portrait orientation. You can also use the Orientation button in the Page Setup group on the Layout tab to change the orientation of a document.

5. **Click the** Top down arrow **three times until** 0.7" **appears, then click the** Bottom down arrow **until** 0.7" **appears**

   The top and bottom margins of the report will be .7".

6. **Press** [Tab], **type** .7 **in the Left text box, press** [Tab], **then type** .7 **in the Right text box**

   The left and right margins of the report will also be .7". You can change the margin settings by using the arrows or by typing a value in the appropriate text box.

7. **Click** OK

   The document margins change to .7", as shown in FIGURE 5-2. The location of each margin (right, left, top, and bottom) is shown on the horizontal and vertical rulers at the intersection of the white and shaded areas. You can also change a margin setting by using the ⟷ pointer to drag the intersection to a new location on the ruler.

8. **Click the** View tab, **then click the** Multiple Pages button **in the Zoom group**

   The first three pages of the document appear in the document window.

9. **Scroll down to view all five pages of the report, press** [Ctrl][Home], **click the** 100% **button in the Zoom group, then save your changes**

FIGURE 5-1: Margins tab in Page Setup dialog box

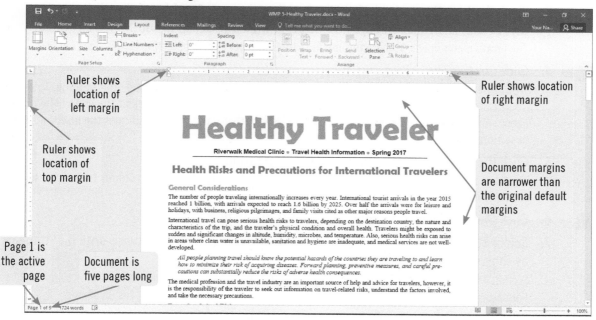

Default margin settings

Set gutter margin

Select page orientation

Select gutter position

Set mirror margins and other page layout options

Preview of margin settings

Select part of document to apply settings to

FIGURE 5-2: Report with smaller margins

Ruler shows location of left margin

Ruler shows location of top margin

Page 1 is the active page

Document is five pages long

Ruler shows location of right margin

Document margins are narrower than the original default margins

Changing orientation, margin settings, and paper size

By default, the documents you create in Word use an 8½" x 11" paper size in portrait orientation with the default margin settings. You can change the orientation, margin settings, and paper size to common settings using the Orientation, Margins, and Size buttons in the Page Setup group on the Layout tab. You can also adjust these settings and others in the Page Setup dialog box. For example, to change the layout of multiple pages, use the Multiple pages list arrow on the Margins tab to create pages that use mirror margins, that include two pages per sheet of paper, or that are formatted using a book fold. **Mirror margins** are used in a document with facing pages, such as a magazine, where the margins on the left page of the document are a mirror image of the margins on the right page. Documents with mirror margins have inside and outside margins, rather than right and left margins. Another type of margin is a gutter margin, which is used in documents that are bound, such as books. A **gutter** adds extra space to the left, top, or inside margin to allow for the binding. Add a gutter to a document by adjusting the setting in the Gutter position text box on the Margins tab. To change the size of the paper used, use the Paper size list arrow on the Paper tab to select a standard paper size, or enter custom measurements in the Width and Height text boxes.

Create Sections and Columns

Learning Outcomes
- Customize the status bar
- Insert section breaks
- Format text in columns

Dividing a document into sections allows you to format each section of the document with different page layout settings. A **section** is a portion of a document that is separated from the rest of the document by section breaks. **Section breaks** are formatting marks that you insert in a document to show the end of a section. Once you have divided a document into sections, you can format each section with different column, margin, page orientation, header and footer, and other page layout settings. By default, a document is formatted as a single section, but you can divide a document into as many sections as you like. **CASE** *You insert a section break to divide the document into two sections, and then format the text in the second section in two columns. First, you customize the status bar to display section information.*

STEPS

1. **Right-click the status bar, click Section on the Customize Status Bar menu that opens (if it is not already checked), then click the document to close the menu**
   The status bar indicates the insertion point is located in section 1 of the document.

2. **Click the Home tab, then click the Show/Hide ¶ button ¶ in the Paragraph group**
   Turning on formatting marks allows you to see the section breaks you insert in a document.

3. **Place the insertion point before the heading General Considerations, click the Layout tab, then click the Breaks button in the Page Setup group**
   The Breaks menu opens. You use this menu to insert different types of section breaks. See TABLE 5-1.

4. **Click Continuous**
   Word inserts a continuous section break, shown as a dotted double line, above the heading. When you insert a section break at the beginning of a paragraph, Word inserts the break at the end of the previous paragraph. The document now has two sections. Notice that the status bar indicates the insertion point is in section 2.

5. **Click the Columns button in the Page Setup group**
   The columns menu opens. You use this menu to format text using preset column formats or to create custom columns.

6. **Click More Columns to open the Columns dialog box**

7. **Select Two in the Presets section, click the Spacing down arrow twice until 0.3" appears as shown in FIGURE 5-3, then click OK**
   Section 2 is formatted in two columns of equal width with .3" of spacing between, as shown in FIGURE 5-4. Formatting text in columns is another way to increase the amount of text that fits on a page.

8. **Click the View tab, click the Multiple Pages button in the Zoom group, scroll down to examine all four pages of the document, press [Ctrl][Home], then save the document**
   The text in section 2—all the text below the continuous section break—is formatted in two columns. Text in columns flows automatically from the bottom of one column to the top of the next column.

TABLE 5-1: Types of section breaks

section	function
Next Page	Begins a new section and moves the text following the break to the top of the next page
Continuous	Begins a new section on the same page
Even Page	Begins a new section and moves the text following the break to the top of the next even-numbered page
Odd Page	Begins a new section and moves the text following the break to the top of the next odd-numbered page

FIGURE 5-3: Columns dialog box

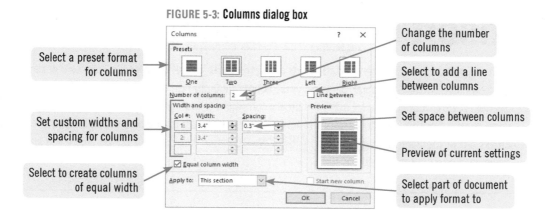

Select a preset format for columns →

Set custom widths and spacing for columns →

Select to create columns of equal width →

Change the number of columns

Select to add a line between columns

Set space between columns

Preview of current settings

Select part of document to apply format to

FIGURE 5-4: Continuous section break and columns

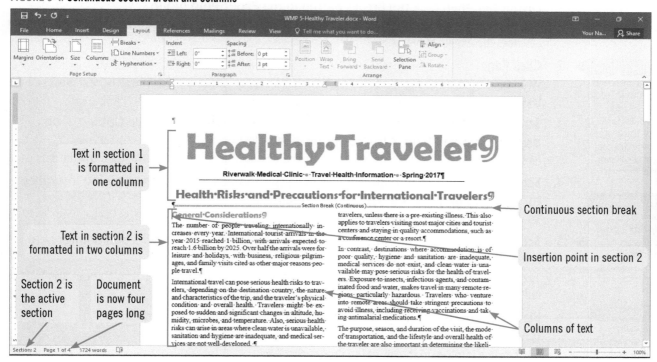

Text in section 1 is formatted in one column →

Text in section 2 is formatted in two columns →

Section 2 is the active section

Document is now four pages long

Continuous section break

Insertion point in section 2

Columns of text

Changing page layout settings for a section

Dividing a document into sections allows you to vary the layout of a document. In addition to applying different column settings to sections, you can apply different margins, page orientation, paper size, vertical alignment, header and footer, page numbering, footnotes, endnotes, and other page layout settings. For example, if you are formatting a report that includes a table with many columns, you might want to change the table's page orientation to landscape so that it is easier to read. To do this, you would insert a section break before and after the table to create a section that contains only the table, and then you would change the page orientation of the section that contains the table to landscape. If the table does not fill the page, you could also change the vertical alignment of the table so that it is centered vertically on the page. To do this, use the Vertical alignment list arrow on the Layout tab of the Page Setup dialog box.

To check or change the page layout settings for an individual section, place the insertion point in the section, then open the Page Setup dialog box. Select any options you want to change, click the Apply to list arrow, click This section, then click OK. When you select This section in the Apply to list box, the settings are applied to the current section only. When you select This point forward, the settings are applied to the current section and all sections that follow it. If you select Whole document in the Apply to list box, the settings are applied to all the sections in the document. Use the Apply to list arrow in the Columns dialog box or the Footnote and Endnote dialog box to change those settings for a section.

Insert Page Breaks

Learning Outcomes
• Insert and delete page breaks
• Insert a column break
• Balance columns

As you type text in a document, Word inserts an **automatic page break** (also called a soft page break) when you reach the bottom of a page, allowing you to continue typing on the next page. You can also force text onto the next page of a document by using the Breaks command to insert a **manual page break** (also called a hard page break). Another way to control the flow of text is to apply pagination settings using the Line and Page Breaks tab in the Paragraph dialog box. **CASE** ▶ *You insert manual page breaks where you know you want to begin each new page of the report.*

STEPS

1. **Click the 100% button in the Zoom group on the View tab, scroll to the bottom of page 1, place the insertion point before the heading Malaria: A Serious..., click the Layout tab, then click the Breaks button in the Page Setup group**
   The Breaks menu opens. You also use this menu to insert page, column, and text-wrapping breaks. TABLE 5-2 describes these types of breaks.

2. **Click Page**
   Word inserts a manual page break before "Malaria: A Serious Health Risk for Travelers" and moves all the text following the page break to the beginning of the next page, as shown in FIGURE 5-5.

3. **Scroll down, place the insertion point before the heading Preventive Options... on page 2, press and hold [Ctrl], then press [Enter]**
   Pressing [Ctrl][Enter] is a fast way to insert a manual page break. The heading is forced to the top of the third page.

4. **Scroll to the bottom of page 3, place the insertion point before the heading Insurance for Travelers on page 3, then press [Ctrl][Enter]**
   The heading is forced to the top of the fourth page.

5. **Scroll up, click to the left of the page break on page 2 with the selection pointer ⇗ to select the page break, then press [Delete]**
   The manual page break is deleted and the text from pages 2 and 3 flows together. You can also use the selection pointer to click to the left of a section or a column break to select it.

6. **Place the insertion point before the heading Medical Kit... on page 2, then press [Ctrl] [Enter]**
   The heading is forced to the top of the third page.

7. **Click the View tab, click the Multiple Pages button in the Zoom group, scroll to view all four pages of the document, then save your changes**
   Pages 1, 2, and 3 are shown in FIGURE 5-6. Your screen might show a different number of pages.

Controlling automatic pagination

Another way to control the flow of text between pages (or between columns) is to apply pagination settings to specify where Word positions automatic page breaks. To apply automatic pagination settings, simply select the paragraphs(s) or line(s) you want to control, click the launcher in the Paragraph group on the Home or Layout tab, click the Line and Page Breaks tab in the Paragraph dialog box, and then select one or more of the following settings in the Pagination section before clicking OK.

• Keep with next: Apply to any paragraph you want to appear together with the next paragraph in order to prevent the page or column from breaking between the paragraphs.

• Keep lines together: Apply to selected paragraph or lines to prevent a page or column from breaking in the middle of a paragraph or between certain lines.

• Page break before: Apply to add an automatic page break before a specific paragraph.

• Widow/Orphan control: Turned on by default; ensures at least two lines of a paragraph appear at the top and bottom of every page or column by preventing a page or column from beginning with only the last line of a paragraph (a **widow**), or ending with only the first line of a new paragraph (an **orphan**).

FIGURE 5-5: Manual page break in document

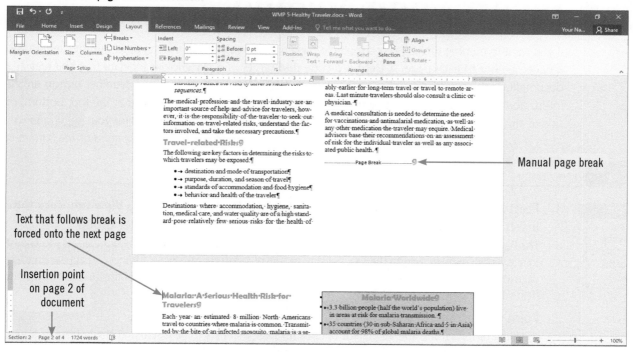

Manual page break

Text that follows break is forced onto the next page

Insertion point on page 2 of document

FIGURE 5-6: Pages 1, 2, and 3

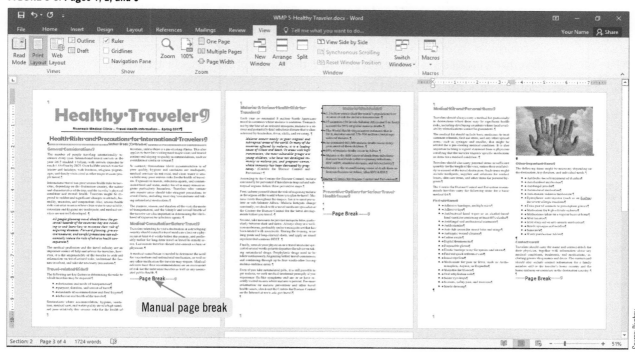

Manual page break

Source: Pixabay

Word 2016

TABLE 5-2: Types of breaks

break	function
Page	Forces the text following the break to begin at the top of the next page
Column	Forces the text following the break to begin at the top of the next column
Text Wrapping	Forces the text following the break to begin at the beginning of the next line

Insert Page Numbers

If you want to number the pages of a multiple-page document, you can insert a page number field to add a page number to each page. A **field** is a code that serves as a placeholder for data that changes in a document, such as a page number or the current date. When you use the Page Number button on the Insert tab to add page numbers to a document, you insert the page number field at the top, bottom, or side of any page, and Word automatically numbers all the pages in the document for you. **CASE** *You insert a page number field so that page numbers will appear centered between the margins at the bottom of each page in the document.*

STEPS

1. **Press [Ctrl][Home], click the 100% button in the Zoom group on the View tab, click the Insert tab, then click the Page Number button in the Header & Footer group**

   The Page Number menu opens. You use this menu to select the position for the page numbers. If you choose to add a page number field to the top, bottom, or side of a document, a page number will appear on every page in the document. If you choose to insert it in the document at the location of the insertion point, the field will appear on that page only.

2. **Point to Bottom of Page**

   A gallery of formatting and alignment options for page numbers to be inserted at the bottom of a page opens, as shown in FIGURE 5-7.

3. **Scroll down the gallery to view the options, scroll to the top of the gallery, then click Plain Number 2 in the Simple section**

   A page number field containing the number 1 is centered in the Footer area at the bottom of page 1 of the document, as shown in FIGURE 5-8. The document text is gray, or dimmed, because the Footer area is open. Text that is inserted in a Footer area appears at the bottom of every page in a document.

4. **Double-click the document text**

   Double-clicking the document text closes the Footer area. The page number is now dimmed because it is located in the Footer area, which is no longer the active area. When the document is printed, the page numbers appear as normal text. You will learn more about working with the Footer area in the next lesson.

5. **Scroll down the document to see the page number at the bottom of each page**

   Word numbered each page of the report automatically, and each page number is centered at the bottom of the page. If you want to change the numbering format or start page numbering with a different number, you can simply click the Page Number button, click Format Page Numbers, and then choose from the options in the Page Number Format dialog box.

6. **Press [Ctrl][Home], click the View tab, click the Page Width button in the Zoom group, then save the document**

Moving around in a long document

Rather than scrolling to move to a different place in a long document, you can use the Navigation pane to move the insertion point to the top of a specific page. To open the Navigation pane, click the Find button in the Editing group on the Home tab, and then click Pages in the Navigation pane to display a thumbnail of each document page in the Navigation pane. Use the scroll box in the Navigation pane to scroll through the thumbnails. Click a thumbnail in the Navigation pane to move the insertion point to the top of that page in the document window.

FIGURE 5-7: **Page Number gallery**

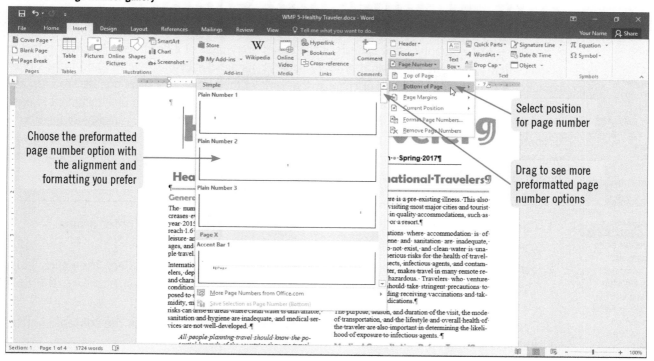

Choose the preformatted page number option with the alignment and formatting you prefer

Select position for page number

Drag to see more preformatted page number options

FIGURE 5-8: **Page number in document**

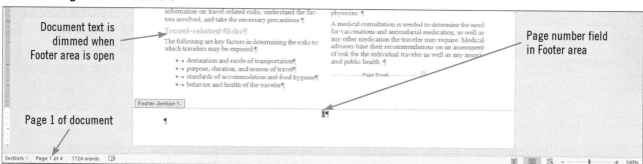

Document text is dimmed when Footer area is open

Page 1 of document

Page number field in Footer area

Inserting Quick Parts

The Word Quick Parts feature makes it easy to insert reusable pieces of content into a document quickly. The **Quick Parts** items you can insert include fields, such as for the current date or the total number of pages in a document; document property information, such as the author and title of a document; and building blocks, which are customized content that you create, format, and save for future use.

To insert a Quick Part into a document at the location of the insertion point, click the Quick Parts button in the Text group on the Insert tab (or, if headers and footers are open, click the Quick Parts button in the Insert group on the Header & Footer Tools Design tab), and then select the type of Quick Part you want to insert. To insert a field into a document, click Field on the Quick Parts menu that opens, click the name of the field you want to insert in the Field dialog box, and then click OK. Field information is updated automatically each time the document is opened or saved.

To insert a document property, point to Document Property on the Quick Parts menu, and then click the property you want to insert. The property is added to the document as a content control and contains the document property information shown in the Properties dialog box. If you did not assign a document property, the content control contains a placeholder, which you can replace with your own text. Once you replace the placeholder text—or edit the document property information that appears in the content control—this text replaces the property information in the Properties dialog box.

To insert a building block, click Building Blocks Organizer on the Quick Parts menu, select the building block you want, and then click Insert. You can learn more about working with building blocks in the next lesson.

Add Headers and Footers

Learning Outcomes
- Create and format headers and footers
- Create a different first page header or footer

A **header** is text or graphics that appears at the top of every page of a document. A **footer** is text or graphics that appears at the bottom of every page. In longer documents, headers and footers often contain the title of the publication or chapter, the name of the author, or a page number. You can add headers and footers to a document by double-clicking the top or bottom margin of a document to open the Header and Footer areas, and then inserting text and graphics into them. You can also use the Header or Footer command on the Insert tab to insert predesigned headers and footers that you can modify with your information. When the header and footer areas are open, the document text is dimmed and cannot be edited. **CASE** *You create a header that describes the report.*

STEPS

1. **Click the Insert tab, then click the Header button in the Header & Footer group**
   A gallery of built-in header designs opens.

2. **Scroll down the gallery to view the header designs, scroll up the gallery, then click Blank**
   The Header & Footer Tools Design tab opens and is the active tab, as shown in FIGURE 5-9. This tab is available whenever the Header and Footer areas are open.

3. **Type Health Information for Travelers from Riverwalk Medical Clinic in the content control in the Header area**
   This text will appear at the top of every page in the document.

4. **Select the header text (but not the paragraph mark below it), click the Home tab, click the Font list arrow in the Font group, click Berlin Sans FB Demi, click the Font Color list arrow A·, click Blue, Accent 5, click the Center button in the Paragraph group, click the Bottom Border button, then click in the Header area to deselect the text**
   The text is formatted in blue Berlin Sans FB Demi and centered in the Header area with a bottom border.

5. **Click the Header & Footer Tools Design tab, then click the Go to Footer button in the Navigation group**
   The insertion point moves to the Footer area, where a page number field is centered in the Footer area.

6. **Select the page number field in the footer, use the Mini toolbar to change the formatting to Berlin Sans FB Demi and Blue, Accent 5, then click in the Footer area to deselect the text and field**
   The footer text is formatted in blue Berlin Sans FB Demi.

7. **Click the Close Header and Footer button in the Close group, then scroll down until the bottom of page 1 and the top of page 2 appear in the document window**
   The Header and Footer areas close, and the header and footer text is dimmed, as shown in FIGURE 5-10.

8. **Press [Ctrl][Home]**
   The report already includes the document name at the top of the first page. You can modify headers and footers so that the header and footer text does not appear on the first page of a document.

9. **Position the pointer over the header text at the top of page 1, then double-click**
   The Header and Footer areas open. The Options group on the Header & Footer Tools Design tab includes options for creating a different header and footer for the first page of a document, and for creating different headers and footers for odd- and even-numbered pages.

10. **Click the Different First Page check box to select it, click the Close Header and Footer button, scroll to see the header and footer on pages 2, 3, and 4, then save the document**
    The header and footer text is removed from the Header and Footer areas on the first page.

FIGURE 5-9: Header area

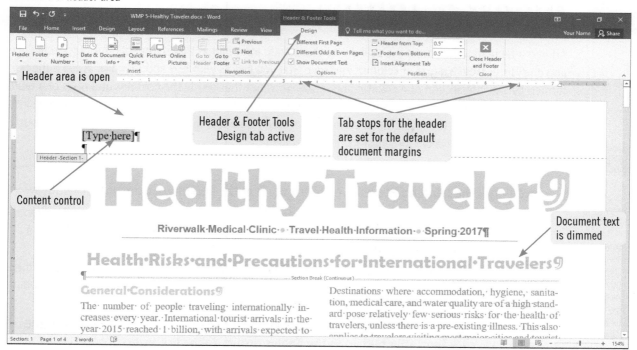

FIGURE 5-10: Header and footer in document

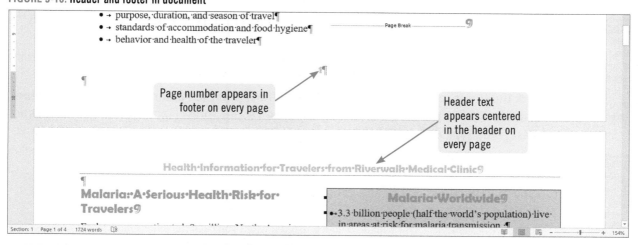

Adding a custom header or footer to the gallery

When you design a header that you want to use again in other documents, you can add it to the Header gallery by saving it as a building block. **Building blocks** are reusable pieces of formatted content or document parts, including headers and footers, page numbers, and text boxes, that are stored in galleries. Building blocks include predesigned content that comes with Word, as well as content that you create and save for future use. For example, you might create a custom header that contains your company name and logo and is formatted using the fonts, border, and colors you use in all company documents.

To add a custom header to the Header gallery, select all the text in the header, including the last paragraph mark, click the Header button, and then click Save Selection to Header Gallery.

In the Create New Building Block dialog box that opens, type a unique name for the header in the Name text box, click the Gallery list arrow and select the appropriate gallery, verify that the Category is General, and then type a brief description of the new header design in the Description text box. This description appears in a ScreenTip when you point to the custom header in the gallery. When you are finished, click OK. The new header appears in the Header gallery under the General category.

To remove a custom header from the Header gallery, right-click it, click Organize and Delete, make sure the appropriate building block is selected in the Building Blocks Organizer that opens, click Delete, click Yes, and then click Close. You can follow the same process to add or remove a custom footer to the Footer gallery.

Formatting Documents

Word 111

Word 2016

Insert a Table

Learning Outcomes
• Create a table
• Delete a table
• Apply a table style

Adding a table to a document is a useful way to illustrate information that is intended for quick reference and analysis. A table is a grid of columns and rows that you can fill with text and graphics. A cell is the box formed by the intersection of a column and a row. The lines that divide the columns and rows of a table and help you see the grid-like structure of the table are called borders. A simple way to insert a table into a document is to use the Insert Table command on the Insert tab. **CASE** ▸ *You add a table to page 2 showing the preventive options for serious travel health diseases.*

STEPS

1. **Scroll until the heading Preventive Options... is at the top of your document window**

TROUBLE
If the final line in the blue shaded box on your screen wraps differently than that shown in the figure, click the References tab, click the Style list arrow in the Citations & Bibliography group, then click MLA Seventh Edition.

2. **Select the heading Preventive Options... and the two paragraph marks below it, click the Layout tab, click the Columns button in the Page Setup group, click One, click the heading to deselect the text, then scroll down to see the bottom half of page 2**
   A continuous section break is inserted before the heading and after the second paragraph mark, creating a new section, section 3, as shown in FIGURE 5-11. The document now includes four sections, with the heading Preventive Options... in Section 3. Section 3 is formatted as a single column.

3. **Place the insertion point before the first paragraph mark below the heading, click the Insert tab, click the Table button in the Tables group, then click Insert Table**
   The Insert Table dialog box opens. You use this dialog box to create a blank table.

QUICK TIP
To delete a table, click in the table, click the Table Tools Layout tab, click the Delete button in the Rows & Columns group, then click Delete Table.

4. **Type 5 in the Number of columns text box, press [Tab], type 6 in the Number of rows text box, make sure the Fixed column width option button is selected, then click OK**
   A blank table with five columns and six rows is inserted in the document. The insertion point is in the upper-left cell of the table, and the Table Tools Design tab becomes the active tab.

5. **Click the Home tab, click the Show/Hide ¶ button ¶ in the Paragraph group, type Disease in the first cell in the first row, press [Tab], type Vaccine, press [Tab], type Prophylaxis Drug, press [Tab], type Eat and Drink Safely, press [Tab], type Avoid Insects, then press [Tab]**
   Don't be concerned if the text wraps to the next line in a cell as you type. Pressing [Tab] moves the insertion point to the next cell in the row or to the first cell in the next row.

QUICK TIP
You can also click in a cell to move the insertion point to it.

6. **Type Malaria, press [Tab][Tab], click the Bullets list arrow ☰ · in the Paragraph group, click the check mark style, press [Tab][Tab], then click the Bullets button ☰**
   The active bullet style, a check mark, is added to a cell when you click the Bullets button.

TROUBLE
If you pressed [Tab] after the last row, click the Undo button ↶ on the Quick Access toolbar to remove the blank row.

7. **Type the text shown in FIGURE 5-12 in the table cells**

8. **Click the Table Tools Layout tab, click the AutoFit button in the Cell Size group, click AutoFit Contents, click the AutoFit button again, then click AutoFit Window**
   The width of the table columns is adjusted to fit the text and then the window.

QUICK TIP
You can also format table text using the buttons on the Mini toolbar or the Home tab.

9. **Click the Select button in the Table group, click Select Table, click the Align Center button ▤ in the Alignment group, click Disease in the table, click the Select button, click Select Column, click the Align Center Left button ▤, then click in the table to deselect the column**
   The text in the table is centered in each cell, and then the text in the first column is left-aligned.

10. **Click the Table Tools Design tab, click the More button ▾ in the Table Styles group, scroll down, click the List Table 3 – Accent 5 style, then save your changes**
    The List Table 3 - Accent 5 table style is applied to the table, as shown in FIGURE 5-13. A **table style** includes format settings for the text, borders, and shading in a table.

FIGURE 5-11: New section

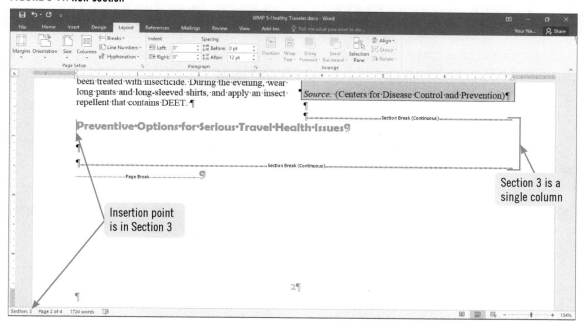

FIGURE 5-12: Text in table

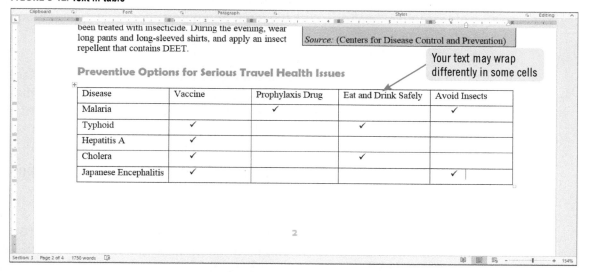

FIGURE 5-13: Completed table

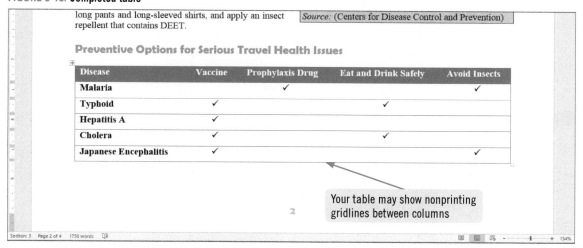

Add Footnotes and Endnotes

Learning
Outcomes
• Insert and delete
  a footnote
• Modify note
  reference marks
• Convert footnotes
  to endnotes

Footnotes and endnotes are used in documents to provide further information, explanatory text, or references for text in a document. A **footnote** or **endnote** is an explanatory note that consists of two linked parts: the **note reference mark** that appears next to text to indicate that additional information is offered in a footnote or endnote, and the corresponding footnote or endnote text. Word places footnotes at the end of each page and endnotes at the end of the document. You insert and manage footnotes and endnotes using the tools in the Footnotes group on the References tab. **CASE** *You add several footnotes to the report.*

STEPS

1. **Press [Ctrl][Home], place the insertion point at the end of the first body paragraph in the second column of text (after "resort."), click the References tab, then click the Insert Footnote button in the Footnotes group**

   A note reference mark, in this case a superscript 1, appears after "resort.", and the insertion point moves below a separator line at the bottom of the page. A note reference mark can be a number, a symbol, a character, or a combination of characters.

2. **Type Behavior is a critical factor. For example, going outdoors in a malaria-endemic area could result in becoming infected., place the insertion point at the end of the second column of text (after "health."), click the Insert Footnote button, then type It is best to consult a travel medicine specialist.**

   The footnote text appears below the separator line at the bottom of page 1, as shown in FIGURE 5-14.

3. **Scroll down until the bottom half of page 3 appears in the document window, place the insertion point at the end of "Medications taken on a regular basis at home" in the second column, click the Insert Footnote button, then type All medications should be stored in carry-on luggage, in their original containers and labeled clearly.**

   The footnote text for the third footnote appears at the bottom of the first column on page 3.

4. **Place the insertion point at the end of "Sunscreen" in the bulleted list in the second column, click the Insert Footnote button, then type SPF 15 or greater.**

   The footnote text for the fourth footnote appears at the bottom of page 3.

5. **Place the insertion point after "Disposable gloves" in the first column, click the Insert Footnote button, type At least two pairs., place the insertion point after "Scissors, safety pins, and tweezers" in the first column, click the Insert Footnote button, then type Pack these items in checked luggage.**

   Notice that when you inserted new footnotes between existing footnotes, Word automatically renumbered the footnotes and wrapped the footnote text to the next column. The new footnotes appear at the bottom of the first column on page 3, as shown in FIGURE 5-15.

6. **Press [Ctrl][Home], then click the Next Footnote button in the Footnotes group**

   The insertion point moves to the first reference mark in the document.

7. **Click the Next Footnote button twice, press [Delete] to select the number 3 reference mark, then press [Delete] again**

   The third reference mark and associated footnote are deleted from the document and the footnotes are renumbered automatically. You must select a reference mark to delete a footnote; you can not simply delete the footnote text itself.

8. **Press [Ctrl][Home], then save your changes**

FIGURE 5-14: Footnotes in the document

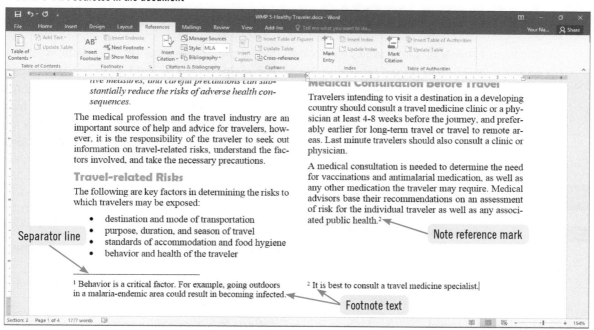

FIGURE 5-15: Renumbered footnotes in the document

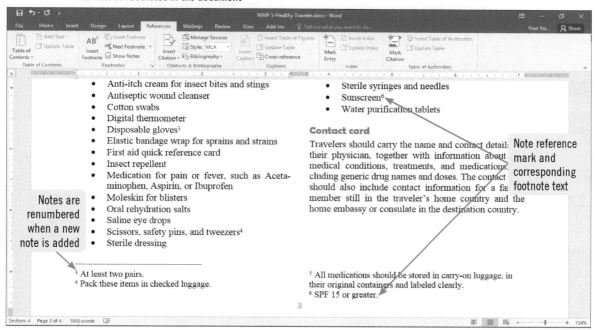

Customizing the layout and formatting of footnotes and endnotes

You can change the location, formatting, and numbering options for footnotes and endnotes in a document using the Footnote and Endnote dialog box. To open the dialog box, click the launcher in the Footnotes group on the References tab. Use the list arrows in the Location section of the dialog box to locate footnotes at the bottom of the page (the default) or directly below the text on a page, and to locate endnotes at the end of a document or at the end of a section. Use the Columns list arrow in the Footnote layout section to format footnote text in one or more columns, or to match section layout (the default). Use the options in the Format section of the dialog box to change the number format of the note reference marks, to use a symbol instead of a character, and to change the numbering of footnotes and endnotes. You can choose to apply the settings to a section or to the document as a whole. When you are finished, click Apply.

Insert Citations

Learning Outcomes
- Add a source to a document
- Insert a citation
- Edit a citation

The Word References feature allows you to keep track of the reference sources you consult when writing research papers, reports, and other documents, and makes it easy to insert a citation in a document. A **citation** is a parenthetical reference in the document text that gives credit to the source for a quotation or other information used in a document. Citations usually include the name of the author and, for print sources, a page number. When you insert a citation you can use an existing source or create a new source. Each time you create a new source, the source information is saved on your computer so that it is available for use in any document. **CASE** ▶ *The report already includes two citations. You add several more citations to the report.*

STEPS

QUICK TIP
Make sure the References tab is the active tab.

1. **Scroll down, place the insertion point after "people travel" but before the period at the end of the first paragraph in the first column of text, click the** Style list arrow **in the Citations & Bibliography group, then click** MLA Seventh Edition

   You will format the sources and citations in the report using the style recommended by the Modern Language Association (MLA).

QUICK TIP
When you create a new source for a document, it appears automatically in the bibliography when you generate it.

2. **Click the** Insert Citation button **in the Citations & Bibliography group**

   A list of the sources already used in the document opens. You can choose to cite one of these sources, create a new source, or add a placeholder for a source. When you add a new citation to a document, the source is added to the list of master sources that is stored on the computer. The new source is also associated with the document.

3. **Click** Add New Source, **click the** Type of Source list arrow **in the Create Source dialog box, scroll down to view the available source types, click** Report, **then click the** Corporate Author check box

   You select the type of source and enter the source information in the Create Source dialog box. The fields available in the dialog box change, depending on the type of source selected.

QUICK TIP
Only sources that you associate with a document stay with the document when you move it to another computer. The master list of sources remains on the computer where it was created.

4. **Enter the data shown in** FIGURE 5-16 **in the Create Source dialog box, then click** OK

   The citation (World Tourism Organization) appears at the end of the paragraph. Because the source is a print publication, it needs to include a page number.

5. **Click the citation to select it, click the** Citation Options list arrow **on the right side of the citation, then click** Edit Citation

   The Edit Citation dialog box opens, as shown in FIGURE 5-17.

QUICK TIP
You can also choose to add or remove the author, year, or title from a citation.

6. **Type** 19 **in the Pages text box, then click** OK

   The page number 19 is added to the citation.

7. **Scroll down, place the insertion point at the end of the quotation (after ...consequences.), click the** Insert Citation button, **click** Add New Source, **enter the information shown in** FIGURE 5-18, **then click** OK

   A citation for the web publication that the quotation was taken from is added to the report. No page number is used in this citation because the source is a website.

8. **Scroll to the bottom of page 2, click under the table, type** Source:, **italicize** Source:, **click after** Source:, **click the** Insert Citation button, **then click** Johnson, Margaret **in the list of sources**

   The citation (Johnson) appears under the table.

9. **Click the citation, click the** Citation Options list arrow, **click** Edit Citation, **type** 55 **in the Pages text box, click** OK, **then save your changes**

   The page number 55 is added to the citation.

FIGURE 5-16: Adding a Report source

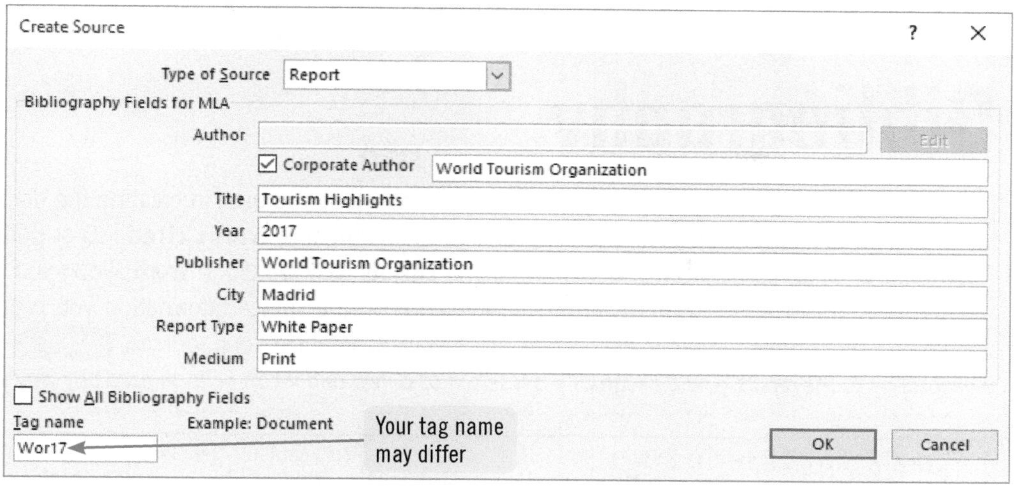

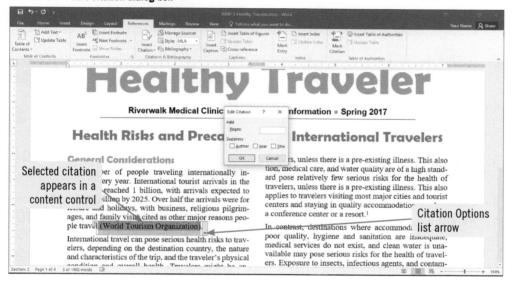

FIGURE 5-17: Edit Citation dialog box

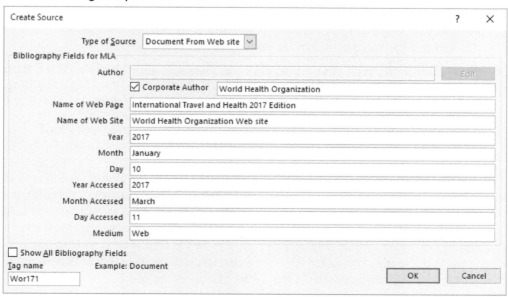

FIGURE 5-18: Adding a web publication source

Manage Sources and Create a Bibliography

Learning Outcomes
- Add and delete sources
- Edit a source
- Insert a bibliography field

Many documents require a **bibliography**, a list of sources that you used in creating the document. The list of sources can include only the works cited in your document (a **works cited** list) or both the works cited and the works consulted (a bibliography). The Bibliography feature in Word allows you to generate a works cited list or a bibliography automatically based on the source information you provide for the document. The Source Manager dialog box helps you to organize your sources. **CASE** ▶ *You add a bibliography to the report. The bibliography is inserted as a field and it can be formatted any way you choose.*

STEPS

1. **Press [Ctrl][End] to move the insertion point to the end of the document, then click the Manage Sources button in the Citations & Bibliography group**

   The Source Manager dialog box opens, as shown in FIGURE 5-19. The Master List shows the two sources you added and any other sources available on your computer. The Current List shows the sources available in the current document. A check mark next to a source indicates the source is cited in the document. You use the tools in the Source Manager dialog box to add, edit, and delete sources from the lists, and to copy sources between the Master and Current Lists. The sources that appear in the Current List will appear in the bibliography.

2. **Click the Baker, Mary source in the Current List**

   A preview of the citation and bibliographical entry for the source in MLA style appears in the Preview box. You do not want this source to be included in your bibliography for the report.

3. **Click Delete**

   The source is removed from the Current List but remains on the Master List on the computer where it originated.

4. **Click Close, click the Bibliography button in the Citations & Bibliography group, click References, then scroll up to see the heading References at the top of the field**

   A Bibliography field labeled "References" is added at the location of the insertion point. The bibliography includes all the sources associated with the document, formatted in the MLA style for bibliographies. The text in the Bibliography field is formatted with the default styles.

5. **Select References; apply the following formats: Berlin Sans FB Demi and the Green, Accent 6 font color; drag down the list of sources to select the entire list and change the font size to 11; then click outside the bibliography field to deselect it**

   The format of the bibliography text now matches the rest of the report.

6. **Press [Ctrl][End], type your name, click the View tab, click Multiple Pages, then scroll up and down to view each page in the report**

   The completed report is shown in FIGURE 5-20.

7. **Save your changes, submit your document, close the file, then exit Word**

Working with web sources

Publications found on the web can be challenging to document. Many websites can be accessed under multiple domains, URLs change, and electronic publications are often updated frequently, making each visit to a website potentially unique. For these reasons, it's best to rely on the author, title, and publication information for a web publication when citing it as a source in a research document. If possible, you can include a URL as supplementary information only, along with the date the website was last updated and the date you accessed the site. Since websites are often removed, it's also a good idea to download or print any web source you use so that it can be verified later.

FIGURE 5-19: Source Manager dialog box

Your Master List will contain the two sources you added and either no additional sources or different additional sources

List of sources associated with the document

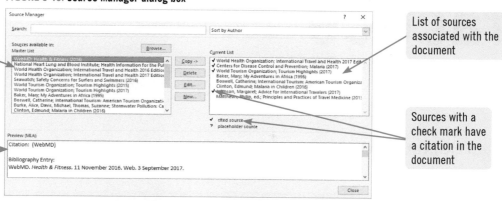

Preview of the citation and bibliography entry for the selected source in MLA style (as defined by Word)

Sources with a check mark have a citation in the document

FIGURE 5-20: Completed report

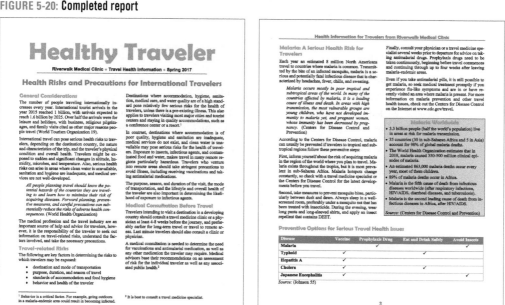

Word 2016

Practice

Concepts Review

Label each element shown in FIGURE 5-21.

FIGURE 5-21

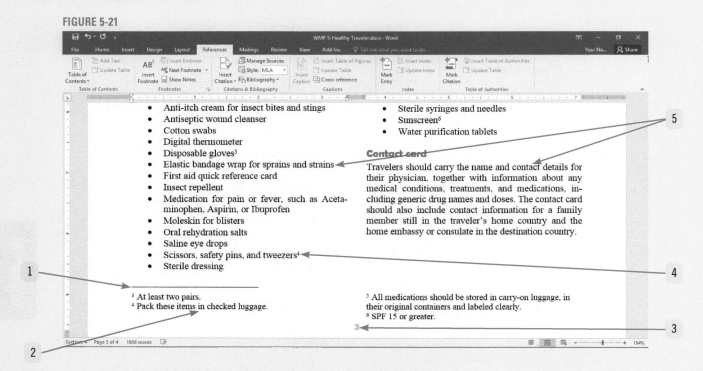

Match each term with the statement that best describes it.

6. **Bibliography**
7. **Header**
8. **Margin**
9. **Table**
10. **Citation**
11. **Manual page break**
12. **Field**
13. **Footer**
14. **Section break**

a. A grid of columns and rows that you can fill with text and graphics

b. A list of the sources used to create a document

c. Text or graphics that appear at the top of every page in a document

d. A formatting mark that forces the text following the mark to begin at the top of the next page

e. Text or graphics that appear at the bottom of every page in a document

f. A placeholder for information that changes

g. A formatting mark that divides a document into parts that can be formatted differently

h. The blank area between the edge of the text and the edge of the page

i. A parenthetical reference in the document text that gives credit to a source

Formatting Documents

Select the best answer from the list of choices.

15. **Which type of break can you insert if you want to force text to begin on the next page?**
    a. Column break
    b. Continuous section break
    c. Next page section break
    d. Text wrapping break

16. **Which type of break do you insert if you want to balance the columns in a section?**
    a. Text wrapping break
    b. Manual page break
    c. Column break
    d. Continuous section break

17. **Which of the following do documents with mirror margins always have?**
    a. Inside and outside margins
    b. Sections
    c. Portrait orientation
    d. Different first page headers and footers

18. **Which of the following cannot be inserted using the Quick Parts command?**
    a. AutoText building block
    b. Page number field
    c. Page break
    d. Document property

19. **Which appears at the end of a document?**
    a. Endnote
    b. Citation
    c. Page break
    d. Footnote

20. **What name describes formatted pieces of content that are stored in galleries?**
    a. Field
    b. Endnote
    c. Property
    d. Building Block

Skills Review

1. **Set document margins.**
    a. Start Word, open the file WMP 5-2.docx from the location where you store your Data Files, then save it as **WMP 5-Seaside Fitness**.
    b. Change the top and bottom margin settings to Moderate: 1" top and bottom, and .75" left and right.
    c. Save your changes to the document.

2. **Create sections and columns.**
    a. Turn on the display of formatting marks, then customize the status bar to display sections if they are not displayed already.
    b. Insert a continuous section break before the **Welcome to the Seaside Fitness Center** heading.
    c. Format the text in section 2 in two columns, then save your changes to the document.

3. **Insert page breaks.**
    a. Scroll to page 3, then insert a manual page break before the heading **Facilities and Services**. (*Hint*: The page break will appear at the bottom of page 2.)
    b. Scroll down and insert a manual page break before the heading **Membership**, then press [Ctrl][Home].
    c. On page 1, select the heading **Welcome to the Seaside Fitness Center** and the paragraph mark below it, use the Columns button to format the selected text as one column, then center the heading on the page.
    d. Follow the direction in step c to format the heading **Facilities and Services** and the paragraph mark below it on page 3, and the heading **Membership** and the paragraph mark below it on page 4, as one column, with centered text, then save your changes to the document.

4. **Insert page numbers.**
    a. Insert page numbers in the document at the bottom of the page. Select the Plain Number 2 page number style from the gallery.
    b. Close the Footer area, scroll through the document to view the page number on each page, then save your changes to the document.

Skills Review (continued)

5. Add headers and footers.

   a. Double-click the margin at the top of a page to open the Header and Footer areas.

   b. With the insertion point in the Header area, click the Quick Parts button in the Insert Group on the Header & Footer Tools Design tab, point to Document Property, then click Author.

   c. Replace the text in the Author content control with your name, press [End] to move the insertion point out of the content control, then press [Spacebar]. (*Note*: If your name does not appear in the header, right-click the Author content control, click Remove Content Control, then type your name in the header.)

   d. Click the Insert Alignment Tab button in the Position group, select the Right option button and keep the alignment relative to the margin, then click OK in the dialog box to close the dialog box and move the insertion point to the right margin.

   e. Use the Date & Time button in the Insert group to insert the current date using a format of your choice as static text. (*Hint*: Be sure the Update automatically check box is not checked.)

   f. Apply italic to the text in the header.

   g. Move the insertion point to the Footer area.

   h. Double-click the page number to select it, then format the page number in bold and italic.

   i. Move the insertion point to the header on page 1, use the Header & Footer Tools Design tab to create a different header and footer for the first page of the document, type your name in the First Page Header area, then apply italic to your name.

   j. Close headers and footers, scroll to view the header and footer on each page, then save your changes to the document.

6. Insert a table.

   a. On page 4, double-click the word **Table** at the end of the Membership Rates section to select it, press [Delete], open the Insert Table dialog box, then create a table with two columns and five rows.

   b. Apply the List Table 2 table style to the table.

   c. Press [Tab] to leave the first cell in the header row blank, then type **Rate**.

   d. Press [Tab], then type the following text in the table, pressing [Tab] to move from cell to cell.

Enrollment/Individual	**$100**
Enrollment/Couple	**$150**
Monthly membership/Individual	**$125**
Monthly membership/Couple	**$200**

   e. Select the table, use the AutoFit command on the Table Tools Layout tab to select the AutoFit to Contents option, and then select the AutoFit to Window option. (*Note*: In this case, AutoFit to Window fits the table to the width of the column of text.)

   f. Save your changes to the document.

7. Add footnotes and endnotes.

   a. Press [Ctrl][Home], scroll down, place the insertion point at the end of the first body paragraph, insert a footnote, then type **People who are active live longer and feel better.**

   b. Place the insertion point at the end of the first paragraph under the Benefits of Exercise heading, insert a footnote, then type **There are 1,440 minutes in every day. Schedule 30 of them for physical activity.**

   c. Place the insertion point at the end of the first paragraph under the Tips for Staying Motivated heading, insert a footnote, type **Always consult your physician before beginning an exercise program.**, then save your changes.

8. Insert citations.

   a. Place the insertion point at the end of the second paragraph under the Benefits of Exercise heading (after "down from 52% in 2015" but before the period), then be sure the style for citations and bibliography is set to MLA Seventh Edition.

Skills Review (continued)

b. Insert a citation, add a new source, enter the source information shown in the Create Source dialog box in FIGURE 5-22, then click OK.

c. Place the insertion point at the end of the italicized quotation in the second column of text, insert a citation, then select Jason, Laura from the list of sources.

d. Edit the citation to include the page number **25**.

e. Scroll to page 2, place the insertion point at the end of the "Be a morning exerciser" paragraph but before the ending period, insert a citation for WebMD, then save your changes.

FIGURE 5-22

Create Source		?	X
Type of **S**ource	Web site		

Bibliography Fields for MLA

Author			Edit
	☑ Corporate Author	WebMD	
Name of Web Page	Health & Fitness		
Year	2016		
Month	November		
Day	11		
Year Accessed	2017		
Month Accessed	September		
Day Accessed	3		
Medium	Web		

☐ Show **A**ll Bibliography Fields

Tag name: Web16   Example: Document

[OK] [Cancel]

9. Manage sources and create a bibliography.

a. Press [Ctrl][End], then open the Source Manager dialog box.

b. Select the source Health, National Institute of: ... in the Current List, click Edit, click the Corporate Author check box, edit the entry so it reads **National Institute of Health**, click OK, then click Close.

c. Insert a bibliography labeled References.

d. Select References, then change the font to 14-point Tahoma with a black font color. Pages 1 and 4 of the formatted document are shown in FIGURE 5-23.

e. Save your changes to the document, submit it to your instructor, then close the document and exit Word.

FIGURE 5-23

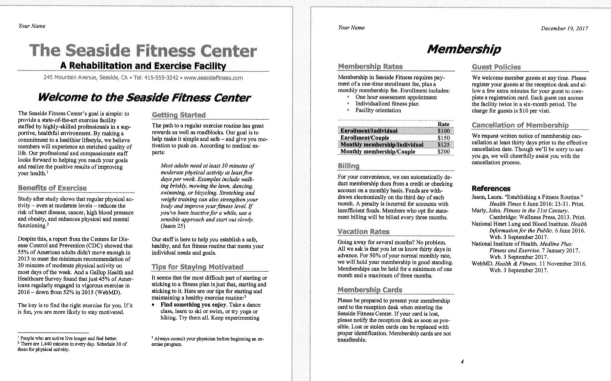

Independent Challenge 1

You are the owner of the Muscular Therapy Center, which offers a variety of massage services to clients. You have begun work on the text for a brochure advertising your business and you are now ready to lay out the pages and prepare the final copy. The brochure will be printed on both sides of an 8½" x 11" sheet of paper, and folded in thirds.

a. Start Word, open the file WMP 5-3.docx from the location where you store your Data Files, then save it as **WMP 5-Massage Brochure**. Read the document to get a feel for its contents.

b. Change the page orientation to landscape, and change all four margins to .5".

c. Format the document in three columns of equal width.

d. Insert a next page section break before the heading **Welcome to the Muscular Therapy Center**.

e. On page 1, insert column breaks before the headings **Menu of Massage Services** and **Shiatsu Massage**.

f. Change the column spacing in section 1 (which is the first page) to .4", add lines between the columns on the first page.

FIGURE 5-24

g. Double-click the bottom margin to open the footer area, create a different header and footer for the first page, then type **A variety of choices to meet your needs.** in the First Page Footer -Section 1- area.

h. Center the text in the footer area, format it in 14-point Papyrus, bold, all caps, with a Blue-Gray, Text 2 font color, then close headers and footers.

i. On page 2, insert a column break before Your Name, then press [Enter] 21 times to move the contact information to the bottom of the second column.

j. Replace Your Name with your name, then center the contact information in the column.

k. Press [Ctrl][End], insert a column break at the bottom of the second column. Type the text shown in FIGURE 5-24 in the third column, then apply the No Spacing style to the text. Refer to the figure as you follow the instructions for formatting the text in the third column.

l. Format Therapeutic Massage in 28-point Papyrus, bold, then format Muscular Therapy Center in 20-point Papyrus bold.

m. Format the remaining text in 12-point Papyrus. Center the text in the third column, then change the font color to Blue-Gray, Text 2.

n. Insert an online picture similar to the image shown in FIGURE 5-24. Do not be concerned if the image you select is not the same image as that shown in the figure. Do not wrap text around the graphic.

o. Resize the graphic and add or remove blank paragraphs in the third column of your brochure so that the spacing between elements roughly matches the spacing shown in FIGURE 5-24.

p. Save your changes, then submit a copy to your instructor. If possible, you can print the brochure with the two pages back to back so that the brochure can be folded in thirds.

q. Close the document and exit Word.

Therapeutic Massage

at the

Muscular Therapy Center

The Skill of Massage
The Art of Healing

Source: Bing.com

Independent Challenge 2

You work in the Campus Safety Department at Valley State University Hospital. You have written the text for an informational flyer about parking regulations on the hospital campus, and now you need to format the flyer so it is attractive and readable.

a. Start Word, open the file WMP 5-4.docx from the drive and folder where you store your Data Files, then save it as **WMP 5-Parking FAQ**. Read the document to get a feel for its contents.

b. Change all four margins to .7".

c. Insert a continuous section break before **1. May I drive a car to work at the hospital?** (*Hint*: Place the insertion point before the word May.)

d. Scroll down and insert a next page section break before **Sample Parking Permit**.

e. Format the text in section 2 in three columns of equal width with .3" of space between the columns.

f. Hyphenate the document using the automatic hyphenation feature. (*Hint*: Use the Hyphenation button in the Page Setup group on the Layout tab.)

g. Add a 3-point dotted-line bottom border to the blank paragraph under Valley State University Hospital (VSUH). (*Hint*: Place the insertion point before the paragraph mark under Valley State...)

h. Open the Header area, and type your name in the header. Right-align your name, and format it in 10-point Arial.

i. Add the following text to the footer, inserting symbols between words as indicated: **Parking and Shuttle Service Office • 54 Buckley Street • VSUH • 942-555-2227**. (*Hint*: Use the Symbol button in the Symbols group on the Insert tab to insert a symbol. To find a small circle symbol, be sure the font is set to (normal text) and the subset is set to General Punctuation.)

j. Format the footer text in 9-point Arial Black, and center it in the footer.

k. Apply a 3-point dotted-line border above the footer text. Make sure to apply the border to the paragraph.

l. Add a continuous section break at the end of section 2 to balance the columns in section 2.

m. Place the insertion point on page 2 (which is section 4). Change the left and right margins in section 4 to 1". Also change the page orientation of section 4 to landscape.

n. Change the vertical alignment of section 4 to center. (*Hint*: Use the Vertical alignment list arrow on the Layout tab in the Page Setup dialog box.)

o. Apply an appropriate table style to the table, such as the style shown in FIGURE 5-25. (*Hint*: Check and uncheck the options in the Table Style Options group on the Table Tools Design tab to customize the style so it enhances the table data.)

p. Save your changes, submit your work, close the document, then exit Word.

FIGURE 5-25

Sample Parking Permit

Valley State University Hospital
Office of Parking and Shuttle Service

2017-18 Parking Permit

License number:	VT 623 487
Make:	Subaru
Model:	Forester
Year:	2013
Color:	Silver
Permit Issue Date:	September 6, 2017
Permit Expiration Date:	June 4, 2018

Restrictions:
Parking is permitted in the Valley State University Hospital Greene Street lot 24 hours a day, 7 days a week. Shuttle service is available from the Greene Street lot to the hospital and other campus locations from 6 a.m. to 11 p.m. Monday through Friday. Parking is also permitted in any on-campus lot from 4:30 p.m. Friday to midnight Sunday.

Independent Challenge 3

A book publisher would like to publish an article you wrote on stormwater pollution in Australia as a chapter in a forthcoming book called *Environmental Issues for the New Millennium*. The publisher has requested that you format your article like a book chapter before submitting it for publication and has provided you with a style sheet. According to the style sheet, the citations and bibliography should be formatted in Chicago style. You have already created the sources for the chapter, but you need to insert the citations.

a. Start Word, open the file WMP 5-5.docx from the location where you store your Data Files, then save it as **WMP 5-Chapter 8**. You will format the first page as shown in FIGURE 5-26.

b. Change the font of the entire document to 10-point Book Antigua. If this font is not available to you, select a different font suitable for the pages of a book. Change the alignment to justified.

c. Use the Page Setup dialog box to change the paper size to a custom setting of 6" x 9".

d. Create mirror margins. (*Hint*: Use the Multiple pages list arrow.) Change the top and bottom margins to .8", change the inside margin to .4", change the outside margin to .6", and create a .3" gutter to allow room for the book's binding.

e. Change the Zoom level to Page Width, open the Header and Footer areas, then apply the setting to create different headers and footers for odd- and even-numbered pages.

f. In the odd-page header, type **Chapter 8**, insert a symbol of your choice, type **The Silver Creek Catchment and Stormwater Pollution**, then format the header text in 9-point Book Antigua italic and right-align the text.

g. In the even-page header, type your name, then format the header text in 9-point Book Antigua italic. (*Note*: The even-page header should be left-aligned.)

h. Insert a left-aligned page number field in the even-page footer area, format it in 10-point Book Antigua, insert a right-aligned page number field in the odd-page footer area, then format it in 10-point Book Antigua.

i. Format the page numbers so that the first page of your chapter, which is Chapter 8 in the book, begins on page 167. (*Hint*: Select a page number field, click the Page Number button, then click Format Page Numbers.)

j. Go to the beginning of the document, press [Enter] 10 times, type **Chapter 8: The Silver Creek Catchment and Stormwater Pollution**, press [Enter] twice, type your name, then press [Enter] twice.

k. Format the chapter title in 16-point Book Antigua bold, format your name in 14-point Book Antigua, then left-align the title text and your name.

l. Click the References tab, make sure the citations and bibliography style is set to Chicago Sixteenth Edition, place the insertion point at the end of the first body paragraph on page 1 but before the ending period, insert a citation for Alice Burke, et. al., then add the page number **40** to the citation.

m. Add the citations listed in TABLE 5-3 to the document using the sources already associated with the document.

FIGURE 5-26

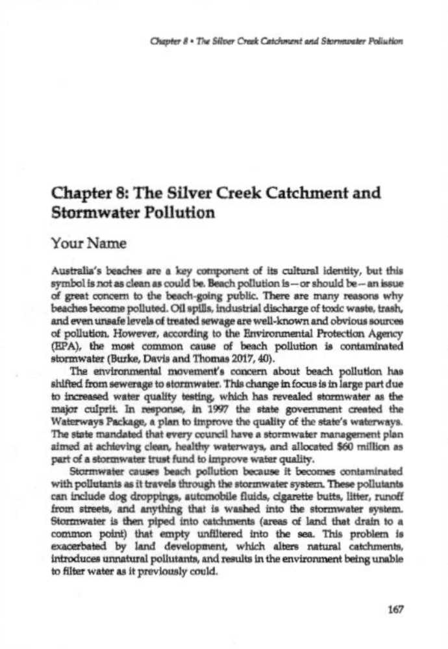

Chapter 8 • The Silver Creek Catchment and Stormwater Pollution

Chapter 8: The Silver Creek Catchment and Stormwater Pollution

Your Name

Australia's beaches are a key component of its cultural identity, but this symbol is not as clean as could be. Beach pollution is—or should be—an issue of great concern to the beach-going public. There are many reasons why beaches become polluted. Oil spills, industrial discharge of toxic waste, trash, and even unsafe levels of treated sewage are well-known and obvious sources of pollution. However, according to the Environmental Protection Agency (EPA), the most common cause of beach pollution is contaminated stormwater (Burke, Davis and Thomas 2017, 40).

The environmental movement's concern about beach pollution has shifted from sewerage to stormwater. This change in focus is in large part due to increased water quality testing, which has revealed stormwater as the major culprit. In response, in 1997 the state government created the Waterways Package, a plan to improve the quality of the state's waterways. The state mandated that every council have a stormwater management plan aimed at achieving clean, healthy waterways, and allocated $60 million as part of a stormwater trust fund to improve water quality.

Stormwater causes beach pollution because it becomes contaminated with pollutants as it travels through the stormwater system. These pollutants can include dog droppings, automobile fluids, cigarette butts, litter, runoff from streets, and anything that is washed into the stormwater system. Stormwater is then piped into catchments (areas of land that drain to a common point) that empty unfiltered into the sea. This problem is exacerbated by land development, which alters natural catchments, introduces unnatural pollutants, and results in the environment being unable to filter water as it previously could.

167

TABLE 5-3

page	location for citation	source	page number
2	End of the first complete paragraph (after ...WCSMP, but before the period)	City of Weston	3
3	End of the first complete paragraph (after ...pollution, but before the colon)	Jensen	135
4	End of first paragraph (after ...health effects, but before the period)	City of Weston	5
4	End of fourth bulleted list item (after 1 month.)	Seawatch	None
5	End of second paragraph (after ...problem arises, but before the period)	Burke, et. al.	55
5	End of paragraph before Conclusion (after ...stormwater system, but before the period)	City of Weston	7
6	End of first paragraph under Conclusion (after ...include, but before the colon)	Jensen	142

Independent Challenge 3 (continued)

n. Press [Ctrl][End], insert a Works Cited list, format the Works Cited heading in 11-point Book Antigua, black font color, bold, then format the list of works cited in 10-point Book Antigua.

o. Scroll to page 4 in the document, place the insertion point at the end of the paragraph above the Potential health effects... heading, press [Enter] twice, type **Table 1: Total annual pollutant loads per year in the Silver Creek Catchment**, press [Enter] twice, then format the text you just typed as bold if it is not bold.

p. Insert a table with four columns and four rows.

q. Type the text shown in FIGURE 5-27 in the table. Do not be concerned when the text wraps to the next line in a cell.

r. Apply the Grid Table 1 Light table style. Make sure the text in the header row is bold, then remove any bold formatting from the text in the remaining rows.

FIGURE 5-27

Area	Nitrogen	Phosphorus	Suspended solids
Silver Creek	9.3 tonnes	1.2 tonnes	756.4 tonnes
Durras Arm	6.2 tonnes	.9 tonnes	348.2 tonnes
Cabbage Tree Creek	9.8 tonnes	2.3 tonnes	485.7 tonnes

s. Use AutoFit to make the table fit the contents, then use AutoFit to make the table fit the window.

t. Save your changes, submit your work, then close the document and exit Word.

Independent Challenge 4: Explore

One of the most common opportunities to use the page layout features of Word is when formatting a research paper. The format recommended by the *Publication Manual of the American Psychological Association*, a style guide that includes information on preparing, writing, and formatting research papers, is the standard format used by many programs for medical professionals. In this independent challenge, you will research the APA guidelines for formatting a research paper and use the guidelines you find to format the pages of a sample research report.

a. Use your favorite search engine to search the web for information on the APA guidelines for formatting a research report. Use the keywords **APA Style** and **research paper format** to conduct your search.

b. Look for information on the proper formatting for the following aspects of a research paper: paper size, margins, line spacing, paragraph indentation, page numbers, short title, abstract, and first page of the body of the report. Also find information on proper formatting for citations and a works cited page. Print the information you find.

c. Start Word, open the file WMP 5-6.docx from the drive and folder where you store your Data Files, then save it as **WMP 5-APA Research Paper**. Using the information you learned, format this document as a research report.

d. Adjust the margins, set the line spacing, and add a short title and page numbers to the document in the format recommended by the APA. Use **Advances in the Treatment of Type 1 Diabetes** as the title for your sample report, use your name as the author name, use **Diabetes Advancements** as the running head, and make up information about your affiliation (for example, your school or class). Make sure to format the title page exactly as the APA style dictates.

e. Format the remaining text as the abstract and body of the research report.

f. Create three sources, insert three citations in the document—a book, a journal article, and a website—and create a works cited page, following APA style. If necessary, edit the format of the citations and works cited page to conform to APA format. (*Note*: For this practice document, you are allowed to make up sources. Never make up sources for real research papers.)

g. Save the document, submit a copy to your instructor, close the document, then exit Word.

Word 2016

Visual Workshop

Open the file WMP 5-7.docx from the location where you store your Data Files, then modify it to create the article shown in FIGURE 5-28. (*Hint*: Change all four margins to .6". Add the footnotes as shown in the figure.) Save the document with the filename **WMP 5-Lyme Disease**, then print a copy.

FIGURE 5-28

TRAVELER'S HEALTH WATCH

Protect Yourself from Lyme Disease

By Your Name

Lyme disease, an inflammatory disease transmitted by the bite of a deer tick, has become a serious public health risk in certain areas of the United States and Canada. Campers, hikers, fishermen, outdoor enthusiasts, and other travelers or residents in endemic areas who have frequent or prolonged exposure to tick habitats during the spring and summer months are at increased risk for Lyme disease.

How ticks spread the disease

The bacterium that causes Lyme disease is spread by the bite of infected *Ixodes* ticks, commonly known as deer ticks. Ticks can attach to any part of the human body, but are most often found in hairy areas such as the scalp, groin, and armpit. In most cases the tick must be attached for at least 48 hours before the bacteria can be transmitted. During the spring and summer months, when people spend more time outdoors, the young (nymphal) ticks are most often responsible for spreading the disease. These ticks are tiny (about the size of the head of a pin) and rarely noticed, making it difficult for people to find and remove an infected tick.

Tick habitat and distribution

The risk of exposure to infected ticks is greatest in woods and in thick brush or long grass, but ticks can also be carried by animals into lawns and gardens and into houses by pets. In the United States, most infections occur in the:
- Northeast, from Maryland to Massachusetts.
- North central states, especially Wisconsin and Minnesota.
- West coast, particularly California.

Symptoms and signs

Early Lyme disease is characterized initially by *erythema migrans*, the bull's eye rash that often occurs on the skin around a tick bite. The rash usually appears within three days to one month after being bitten. Other flulike symptoms of early Lyme disease include fatigue, headache, chills and fever, muscle and joint pain, and swollen lymph nodes.

Treatment and prognosis

Lyme disease can usually be cured by antibiotics if treatment begins in the early stages of infection. Most people who are treated in the later stages also respond well to antibiotics, although some may have persistent or recurring symptoms.[1]

Protection from tick bites

Here are some precautions to decrease the chances of being bitten by a tick:
- Avoid tick-infested areas, particularly in May, June, and July.[2]
- Wear light-colored clothing, including long pants, socks, and long-sleeved shirts.
- Tuck pant legs into socks or boots and shirt into pants so ticks cannot crawl under clothing.
- Wear a hat.
- Spray insect repellent containing a 20-30% concentration of DEET on clothes and exposed skin other than the face.
- Walk in the center of trails to avoid contact with overgrown brush and grass.
- Wash and dry clothing at a high temperature, inspect body surfaces carefully, and remove attached ticks with tweezers. Make sure to remove the head of the tick. ■

---

[1] If left untreated, Lyme disease can result in chronic arthritis and nerve and heart dysfunction.

[2] Ticks are especially common near deer trails.

Source: Pixabay

Merging Word Documents

CASE ▶ You need to send a letter to patients who recently had a routine mammogram screening, informing them that their mammogram showed no evidence of cancer. You also need to send a reminder card to patients who need to schedule an appointment for a routine mammogram. You use mail merge to create a personalized form letter about the mammogram and mailing labels for the reminder cards.

Module Objectives

After completing this module, you will be able to:

- Understand mail merge
- Create a main document
- Design a data source
- Enter and edit records
- Add merge fields
- Merge data
- Create labels
- Sort and filter records

Files You Will Need

WMP 6-1.docx   WMP 6-3.docx
WMP 6-2.mdb   WMP 6-4.mdb

Understand Mail Merge

Learning Outcomes
- Identify the elements of a mail merge
- State the benefits of performing a mail merge

When you perform a **mail merge**, you merge a standard Word document with a file that contains customized information for many individuals or items. The standard document is called the **main document**. The file with the unique data for individual people or items is called the **data source**. Merging the main document with a data source results in a **merged document** that contains customized versions of the main document, as shown in FIGURE 6-1. The Mail Merge pane steps you through the process of setting up and performing a mail merge. You can also perform a mail merge using the commands on the Mailings tab. **CASE** ➤ *You decide to use the Mail Merge pane to create your form letters and the commands on the Mailings tab to create your mailing labels. Before beginning, you explore the steps involved in performing a mail merge.*

DETAILS

- **Create the main document**

  The main document contains the text—often called **boilerplate text**—that appears in every version of the merged document. The main document also includes the merge fields, which indicate where the customized information is inserted when you perform the merge. You insert the merge fields in the main document after you have created or selected the data source. You can create a main document using one of the following: a new blank document, the current document, a template, or an existing document.

- **Create a data source or select an existing data source**

  The data source is a file that contains the unique information for each individual or item, such as a person's name. It provides the information that varies in every version of the merged document. A data source is composed of data fields and data records. A **data field** is a category of information, such as last name, first name, street address, city, or postal code. A **data record** is a complete set of related information for an individual or an item, such as one person's name and address. It is easiest to think of a data source file as a table: the header row contains the names of the data fields (the **field names**), and each row in the table is an individual data record. You can create a new data source, or you can use an existing data source, such as a data source created in Word, an Outlook contact list, an Access database, or an Excel worksheet.

- **Identify the fields to include in the data source and enter the records**

  When you create a new data source, you must first identify the fields to include, such as first name, last name, and street address if you are creating a data source that will include addresses. It is also important to think of and include all the fields you will need (not just the obvious ones) before you begin to enter data. For example, if you are creating a data source that includes names and addresses, you might need to include fields for a person's middle name, title, apartment number, department name, or country, even if some records in the data source will not include that information. Once you have identified the fields and set up your data source, you are ready to enter the data for each record.

- **Add merge fields to the main document**

  A **merge field** is a placeholder that you insert in the main document to indicate where the data from each record should be inserted when you perform the merge. For example, you insert a ZIP Code merge field in the location where you want to insert a ZIP Code. The merge fields in a main document must correspond with the field names in the associated data source. Merge fields must be inserted, not typed, in the main document. The Mail Merge pane and the Mailings tab provide access to the dialog boxes you use to insert merge fields.

- **Merge the data from the data source into the main document**

  Once you have established your data source and inserted the merge fields in the main document, you are ready to perform the merge. You can merge to a new file, which contains a customized version of the main document for each record in the data source, or you can merge directly to a printer or e-mail message.

FIGURE 6-1: Mail merge process

Data source document

	Date	Title	First Name	Last Name	Address Line 1	City	State	Zip Code	Country
Data record →	11/2/17	Ms.	Erica	Bass	62 Cloud St.	Somerville	MA	02144	US
	11/3/17	Ms.	Claudia	Beck	23 Plum St.	Boston	MA	02483	US
	10/30/17	Ms.	Kate	Gans	456 Elm St.	Arlington	MA	02474	US
	11/2/17	Ms.	Lauren	Miller	48 East Ave.	Vancouver	BC	V6F 1AH	CANADA
	11/1/17	Ms.	Monica	Bright	56 Pearl St.	Cambridge	MA	02139	US

Field name

Main document

![Riverwalk Medical Clinic logo]
Riverwalk Medical Clinic
1138 Memorial Drive • Cambridge, MA 02138 • Tel: (617) 555-1838 • Fax: (617) 555-2972 • www.rwmed.org
Carla J. Zimmerman, MD • Anna Wolf-Rosenbaum, MD • Forrest P. Quinn, MD • Lan Nguyen, MD • Heather L. Nordgren, MD • Jeffrey Patrick, MD

December 9, 2017

Merge fields

«AddressBlock»

«GreetingLine»

We are happy to inform you that your «Date» mammogram showed no evidence of cancer.

Routine screening mammography is the most sensitive way to detect the early signs of cancer, and significantly reduces breast cancer mortality. However, not all breast cancers are detected by the mammogram. Some can be felt before they can be seen. Thus, to complete the screening procedure and detect all breast cancers as early as possible, you must be examined by your physician annually and perform proper breast self examinations monthly. The enclosed brochure details the proper method of breast self-examination.

If you develop any lumps or other significant breast problems, contact your physician immediately. Do not wait for your next routine check up.

Your imaging results will be stored at the Riverwalk Medical Clinic, and made available upon your written request.

Sincerely,

Lan Nguyen, M.D.

LN/yn
Enclosure

Boilerplate text

Merged document

![Riverwalk Medical Clinic logo]
Riverwalk Medical Clinic
1138 Memorial Drive • Cambridge, MA 02138 • Tel: (617) 555-1838 • Fax: (617) 555-2972 • www.rwmed.org
Carla J. Zimmerman, MD • Anna Wolf-Rosenbaum, MD • Forrest P. Quinn, MD • Lan Nguyen, MD • Heather L. Nordgren, MD • Jeffrey Patrick, MD

December 9, 2017

Ms. Eliza Bass
62 Cloud St.
Somerville, MA 02144

Dear Ms. Bass:

We are happy to inform you that your 11/2/17 mammogram showed no evidence of cancer.

Routine screening mammography is the most sensitive way to detect the early signs of cancer, and significantly reduces breast cancer mortality. However, not all breast cancers are detected by the mammogram. Some can be felt before they can be seen. Thus, to complete the screening procedure and detect all breast cancers as early as possible, you must be examined by your physician annually and perform proper breast self examinations monthly. The enclosed brochure details the proper method of breast self-examination.

If you develop any lumps or other significant breast problems, contact your physician immediately. Do not wait for your next routine check up.

Your imaging results will be stored at the Riverwalk Medical Clinic, and made available upon your written request.

Sincerely,

Lan Nguyen, M.D.

LN/yn
Enclosure

Customized information

Create a Main Document

Learning Outcomes
• Start a mail merge
• Create a letter main document

The first step in performing a mail merge is to create the main document—the file that contains the boilerplate text. You can create a main document from scratch, save an existing document as a main document, or use a mail merge template to create a main document. The Mail Merge pane walks you through the process of selecting the type of main document to create. **CASE** ▶ *You use an existing form letter for your main document. You begin by opening the Mail Merge pane.*

STEPS

TROUBLE
A document, blank or otherwise, must be open in the program window for the commands on the Mailings tab to be available.

1. **Start Word, open a blank document, click the Mailings tab, click the Start Mail Merge button in the Start Mail Merge group, then click Step-by-Step Mail Merge Wizard**

   The Mail Merge pane opens, as shown in FIGURE 6-2, and displays information for the first step in the mail merge process: Select document type, which is the type of merge document to create.

2. **Make sure the Letters option button is selected, then click Next: Starting document to continue with the next step**

   The Mail Merge pane displays the options for the second step: Select starting document, which is the main document. You can use the current document, start with a mail merge template, or use an existing file.

QUICK TIP
If you choose "Use the current document" and the current document is blank, you can create a main document from scratch. Either type the boilerplate text at this step, or wait until the Mail Merge pane prompts you to do so.

3. **Select the Start from existing document option button, make sure (More files...) is selected in the Start from existing list box, then click Open**

   The Open dialog box opens.

4. **Navigate to the location where you store your Data Files, select the file WMP 6-1.docx, then click Open**

   The letter that opens contains the boilerplate text for the main document. Notice the filename in the title bar is Document1. When you create a main document that is based on an existing document, Word gives the main document a default temporary filename.

5. **Click the Save button on the Quick Access toolbar, then save the document with the filename WMP 6-Mammogram Results Letter Main to the location where you store your Data Files**

   It's a good idea to include "main" in the filename so that you can easily recognize the file as a main document.

6. **Select September 24, 2017 in the letter, type today's date, scroll down, select Lan Nguyen, type your name, press [Ctrl][Home], then save your changes**

   The edited main document is shown in FIGURE 6-3.

7. **Click Next: Select recipients to continue with the next step**

   You continue with Step 3 of 6 in the next lesson.

Using a mail merge template

If you are creating letters or faxes, you can use a mail merge template to start your main document. Each template includes placeholder text, which you can replace, and merge fields, which you can match to the field names in your data source. To create a main document that is based on a mail merge template, click the File tab, click New, type "mail merge" in the Search for online templates text box, click the Start searching button, select one of the mail merge templates to use as your main document, and then click Create. You can then use the Mail Merge pane or the Ribbon to begin a mail merge using the current document. In the Step 2 of 6 Mail Merge pane, click the Use the current document option button, and then click Next. Once you have created the main document, you can customize the main document with your own information: edit the placeholder text; change the document format; or add, remove, or modify the merge fields.

Before performing the merge, make sure to match the names of the merge fields used in the template with the field names used in your data source. To match the field names, click the Match Fields button in the Write & Insert Fields group on the Mailings tab, and then use the list arrows in the Match Fields dialog box to select the field name in your data source that corresponds to each address field component in the main document.

FIGURE 6-2: Step 1 of 6 Mail Merge task pane

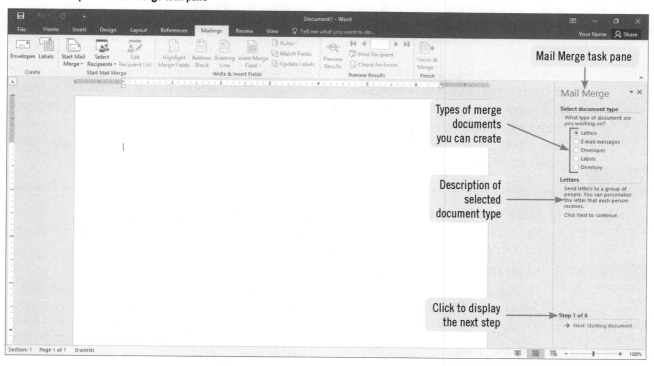

Types of merge documents you can create

Mail Merge task pane

Description of selected document type

Click to display the next step

FIGURE 6-3: Main document with Step 2 of 6 Mail Merge task pane

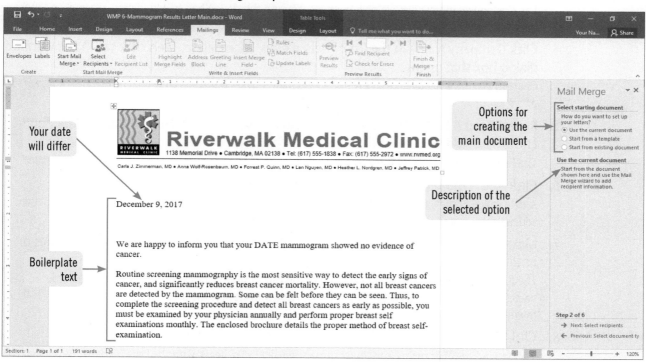

Your date will differ

Boilerplate text

Options for creating the main document

Description of the selected option

Design a Data Source

Learning
Outcomes
• Create a data
  source
• Add and remove
  fields in a data
  source

Once you have identified the main document, the next step in the mail merge process is to identify the data source, the file that contains the information that is used to customize each version of the merge document. You can use an existing data source that already contains the records you want to include in your merge, or you can create a new data source. When you create a new data source, you must determine the fields to include—the categories of information, such as a first name, last name, city, or ZIP Code—and then add the records. **CASE** ▸ *You create a new data source that includes fields for the patient name, patient address, and exam date of the patient's most recent mammogram.*

STEPS

1. **Make sure Step 3 of 6 is displayed at the bottom of the Mail Merge pane**

   Step 3 of 6 involves selecting a data source to use for the merge. You can use an existing data source, use a list of contacts created in Microsoft Outlook, or create a new data source.

2. **Select the Type a new list option button, then click Create**

   The New Address List dialog box opens, as shown in FIGURE 6-4. You use this dialog box both to design your data source and to enter records. The column headings in the Type recipient information... section of the dialog box are fields that are commonly used in form letters, but you can customize your data source by adding and removing columns (fields) from this table. A data source can be merged with more than one main document, so it's important to design a data source to be flexible. The more fields you include in a data source, the more flexible it is. For example, if you include separate fields for a person's title, first name, middle name, and last name, you can use the same data source to create an envelope addressed to "Mr. John Montgomery Smith" and a form letter with the greeting "Dear John".

3. **Click Customize Columns**

   The Customize Address List dialog box opens. You use this dialog box to add, delete, rename, and reorder the fields in the data source.

4. **Click Company Name in the list of field names, click Delete, then click Yes in the warning dialog box that opens**

   Company Name is removed from the list of field names. The Company Name field is no longer a part of the data source.

5. **Repeat Step 4 to delete the following fields: Address Line 2, Home Phone, Work Phone, and E-mail Address**

   The fields are removed from the data source.

6. **Click Add, type Date in the Add Field dialog box, then click OK**

   A field called "Date", which you will use to indicate the date of the patient's most recent mammogram, is added to the data source.

7. **Make sure Date is selected in the list of field names, then click Move Up eight times or until Date is at the top of the list**

   The field name "Date" is moved to the top of the list, as shown in FIGURE 6-5. Although the order of field names does not matter in a data source, it's convenient to arrange the field names logically to make it easier to enter and edit records.

8. **Click OK**

   The New Address List dialog box shows the customized list of fields, with the Date field first in the list. The next step is to enter each record you want to include in the data source. You add records to the data source in the next lesson.

FIGURE 6-4: New Address List dialog box

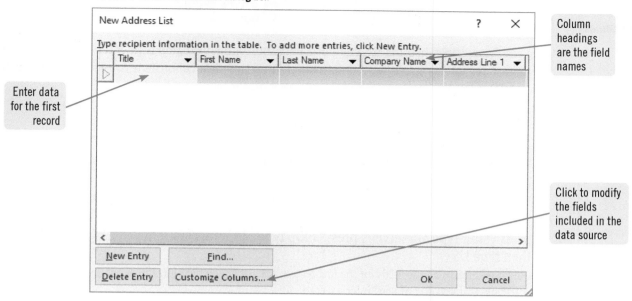

FIGURE 6-5: Customize Address List dialog box

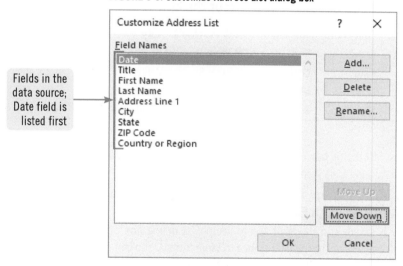

Merging with an Outlook data source

If you maintain lists of contacts in Microsoft Outlook, you can use one of your Outlook contact lists as a data source for a merge. To merge with an Outlook data source, click the Select from Outlook contacts option button in the Step 3 of 6 Mail Merge pane, then click Choose Contacts Folder to open the Choose Profile dialog box. In this dialog box, use the Profile Name list arrow to select the profile you want to use, then click

OK to open the Select Contacts dialog box. In this dialog box, select the contact list you want to use as the data source, and then click OK. All the contacts included in the selected folder appear in the Mail Merge Recipients dialog box. Here you can refine the list of recipients to include in the merge by sorting and filtering the records. When you are satisfied, click OK in the Mail Merge Recipients dialog box.

Enter and Edit Records

Learning Outcomes
• Add a record
• Edit a record

Once you have established the structure of a data source, the next step is to enter the records. Each record includes the complete set of information for each individual or item you include in the data source. **CASE** ▸ *You create a record for each recent mammogram patient.*

STEPS

QUICK TIP
Be careful not to add spaces or extra punctuation after an entry in a field, or these will appear when the data is merged.

1. **Verify the insertion point is in the Date text box in the New Address List dialog box, type** 11/02/17, **then press** [Tab]

   "11/02/17" appears in the Date field, and the insertion point moves to the next column, the Title field.

2. **Type** Ms., **press** [Tab], **type** Erica, **press** [Tab], **type** Bass, **press** [Tab], **type** 62 Cloud St., **press** [Tab], **type** Somerville, **press** [Tab], **type** MA, **press** [Tab], **type** 02144, **press** [Tab], **then type** US

   Data is entered in all the fields for the first record. You used each field for this record, but it's okay to leave a field blank if you do not need it for a record.

3. **Click** New Entry

   The record for Erica Bass is added to the data source, and the New Address List dialog box displays empty fields for the next record, as shown in FIGURE 6-6.

QUICK TIP
You can also press [Tab] at the end of the last field to start a new record.

4. **Enter the following four records, pressing** [Tab] **to move from field to field, and clicking** New Entry **at the end of each record except the last:**

Date	Title	First Name	Last Name	Address Line 1	City	State	ZIP Code	Country
11/03/17	Ms.	Claudia	Beck	23 Plum St.	Boston	MA	02483	US
10/30/17	Ms.	Kate	Gans	456 Elm St.	Arlington	MA	02474	US
11/02/17	Ms.	Lauren	Miller	48 East Ave.	Vancouver	BC	V6F 1AH	CANADA
11/01/17	Ms.	Monica	Bright	56 Pearl St.	Cambridge	MA	02139	US

5. **Click** OK

   The Save Address List dialog box opens. Data sources are saved by default in the My Data Sources folder in Microsoft Office Address Lists (*.mdb) format.

TROUBLE
If a check mark appears in the blank record under Monica Bright, click the check mark to eliminate the blank record from the merge.

6. **Type** WMP 6-Mammogram Patients **in the File name text box, navigate to the location where you store your Data Files, then click** Save

   The data source is saved, and the Mail Merge Recipients dialog box opens, as shown in FIGURE 6-7. The dialog box shows the records in the data source in table format. You can use the dialog box to sort and filter records, and to select the recipients to include in the mail merge. The check marks in the second column indicate the records that will be included in the merge.

7. **Click** WMP 6-Mammogram Patients.mdb **in the Data Source list box at the bottom of the dialog box, then click** Edit **to open the Edit Data Source dialog box, as shown in** FIGURE 6-8

   You use this dialog box to edit a data source, including adding and removing fields, editing field names, adding and removing records, and editing existing records.

QUICK TIP
If you want to add new records or modify existing records, click Edit recipient list in the Mail Merge pane.

8. **Click** Ms. **in the Title field of the Kate Gans record to select it, type** Dr., **click** OK **in the Edit Data Source dialog box, then click** Yes

   The data in the Title field for Kate Gans changes from "Ms." to "Dr.", and the dialog box closes.

9. **Click** OK **in the Mail Merge Recipients dialog box**

   The dialog box closes. The file type and filename of the data source attached to the main document now appear under Use an existing list heading in the Mail Merge pane.

FIGURE 6-6: **Record in New Address List dialog box**

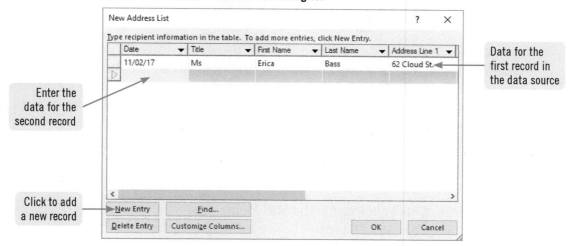

Enter the data for the second record

Data for the first record in the data source

Click to add a new record

FIGURE 6-7: **Mail Merge Recipients dialog box**

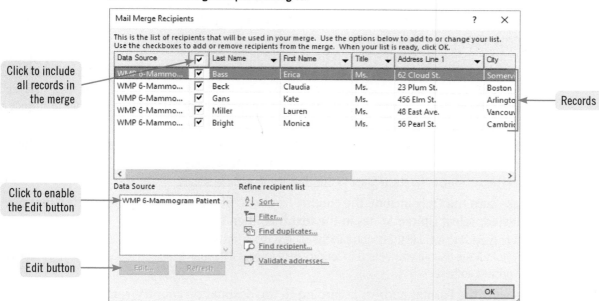

Click to include all records in the merge

Records

Click to enable the Edit button

Edit button

FIGURE 6-8: **Edit Data Source dialog box**

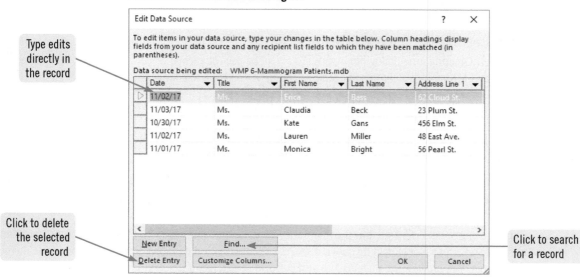

Type edits directly in the record

Click to delete the selected record

Click to search for a record

Add Merge Fields

Learning Outcomes
- Insert merge fields
- Customize an address block or greeting field

After you have created and identified the data source, the next step is to insert the merge fields in the main document. Merge fields serve as placeholders for text that is inserted when the main document and the data source are merged. The names of merge fields correspond to the field names in the data source. You can insert merge fields using the Mail Merge pane or the Address Block, Greeting Line, and Insert Merge Field buttons in the Write & Insert Fields group on the Mailings tab. You cannot type merge fields into the main document. **CASE** ▶ *You use the Mail Merge pane to insert merge fields for the inside address and greeting of the letter. You also insert a merge field for the exam date in the body of the letter.*

STEPS

1. **Click Next: Write your letter in the Mail Merge pane**

   The Mail Merge pane shows the options for Step 4 of 6: Write your letter. During this step, you write or edit the boilerplate text and insert the merge fields in the main document. Since your form letter is already written, you are ready to add the merge fields to it.

   QUICK TIP
   You can also click the Address Block button in the Write & Insert Fields group on the Mailings tab to insert an address block.

2. **Click the blank line above the first body paragraph, then click Address block in the Mail Merge pane**

   The Insert Address Block dialog box opens, as shown in FIGURE 6-9. You use this dialog box to specify the fields you want to include in an address block. In this merge, the address block is the inside address of the form letter. An address block automatically includes fields for the recipient's name, street, city, state, and postal code, but you can select the format for the recipient's name and indicate whether to include a company name or country in the address.

3. **Scroll the list of formats for a recipient's name to get a feel for the kinds of formats you can use, then click Mr. Joshua Randall Jr. if it is not already selected**

   The selected format uses the recipient's title, first name, and last name.

4. **Make sure the Only include the country/region if different than: option button is selected, select United States in the text box, then type US**

   You only need to include the country in the address block if the country is different than the United States, so you indicate that all entries in the Country field in your data source, except "US", should be included in the printed address.

   QUICK TIP
   You cannot simply type chevrons around a field name. You must insert merge fields using the Mail Merge pane or the buttons in the Write & Insert Fields group on the Mailings tab.

5. **Deselect the Format address according to the destination country/region check box, click OK, then press [Enter] twice**

   The merge field AddressBlock is added to the main document. Chevrons (<< and >>) surround a merge field to distinguish it from the boilerplate text.

6. **Click Greeting line in the Mail Merge pane**

   The Insert Greeting Line dialog box opens. You want to use the format "Dear Mr. Randall:" for a greeting. The default format uses a comma instead of a colon, so you have to change the comma to a colon.

7. **Click the , list arrow, click :, click OK, then press [Enter]**

   The merge field GreetingLine is added to the main document.

   QUICK TIP
   You can also click the Insert Merge Field button or list arrow in the Write & Insert Fields group on the Mailings tab to insert a merge field.

8. **In the body of the letter select DATE, then click More items in the Mail Merge pane**

   The Insert Merge Field dialog box opens and displays the list of field names included in the data source.

9. **Make sure Date is selected in the dialog box, click Insert, click Close, press [Spacebar] to add a space between the merge field and "mammogram" if there is no space, then save your changes**

   The Date merge field is inserted in the main document, as shown in FIGURE 6-10. You must type spaces and punctuation after a merge field if you want spaces and punctuation to appear in that location in the merged documents. You preview the merged data and perform the merge in the next lesson.

FIGURE 6-9: Insert Address Block dialog box

Formats for the
recipient's name

Click to match the
default address
field names to the
field names used
in your data source

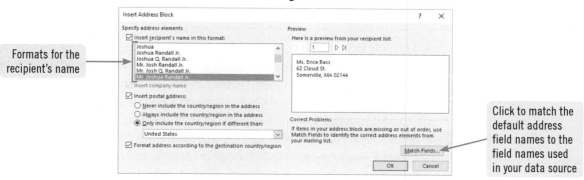

FIGURE 6-10: Merge fields in the main document

Merge fields

Space after
merge field

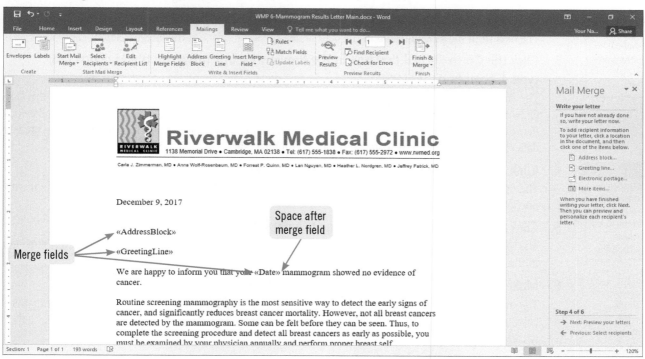

Matching fields

The merge fields you insert in a main document must correspond with the field names in the associated data source. If you are using the Address Block merge field, you must make sure that the default address field names correspond with the field names used in your data source. If the default address field names do not match the field names in your data source, click Match Fields in the Insert Address Block dialog box, then use the list arrows in the Match Fields dialog box to select the field name in the data source that corresponds to each default address field name. You can also click the Match Fields button in the Write & Insert Fields group on the Mailings tab to open the Match Fields dialog box.

Merge Data

Learning Outcomes
- Preview a merge
- Merge data to a new document
- Customize a merged document

Once you have added records to your data source and inserted merge fields in the main document, you are ready to perform the merge. Before merging, it's a good idea to preview the merged data to make sure the printed documents will appear as you want them to. You can preview the merge using the Mail Merge pane or the Preview Results button in the Preview Results group on the Mailings tab. When you merge the main document with the data source, you must choose between merging to a new file or directly to a printer. **CASE** *Before merging the form letter with the data source, you preview the merge to make sure the data appears in the letter as you intended. You then merge the two files to a new document.*

STEPS

QUICK TIP
To adjust the main document, click the Preview Results button in the Preview Results group on the Mailings tab, then make any necessary changes. Click the Preview Results button again to preview the merged data.

1. **Click Next: Preview your letters in the Mail Merge pane, then scroll down as necessary to see the date of the mammogram in the document**

   The data from the first record in the data source appears in place of the merge fields in the main document, as shown in FIGURE 6-11. Always preview a document to verify that the merge fields, punctuation, page breaks, and spacing all appear as you intend before you perform the merge.

2. **Click the Next Recipient button ⟩⟩ in the Mail Merge pane**

   The data from the second record in the data source appears in place of the merge fields.

3. **Click the Go to Record text box in the Preview Results group on the Mailings tab, type 4, then press [Enter]**

   The data for the fourth record appears in the document window. The non-U.S. country name, in this case CANADA is included in the address block, just as you specified. You can also use the First Record 🄚, Previous Record ◄, Next Record ▶ and Last Record ▶🄘 buttons in the Preview Results group to preview the merged data. TABLE 6-1 describes other commands on the Mailings tab.

QUICK TIP
If your data source contains many records, you can merge directly to a printer to avoid creating a large file.

4. **Click Next: Complete the merge in the Mail Merge pane**

   The options for Step 6 of 6 appear in the Mail Merge pane. Merging to a new file creates a document with one letter for each record in the data source. This allows you to edit the individual letters.

5. **Click Edit individual letters to merge the data to a new document**

   The Merge to New Document dialog box opens. You can use this dialog box to specify the records to include in the merge.

6. **Make sure the All option button is selected, then click OK**

   The main document and the data source are merged to a new document called Letters1, which contains a customized form letter for each record in the data source. You can now further personalize the letters without affecting the main document or the data source.

7. **Scroll to the fourth letter (addressed to Ms. Lauren Miller), place the insertion point before V6F in the address block, then press [Enter]**

   The postal code is now consistent with the proper format for a Canadian address.

8. **Click the Save button 🖫 on the Quick Access toolbar to open the Save As dialog box, then save the merged document as WMP 6-Mammogram Results Letter Merge to the location where you store your Data Files**

   You may decide not to save a merged file if your data source is large. Once you have created the main document and the data source, you can create the letters by performing the merge again.

QUICK TIP
Print only one letter if you are required to submit a printed document to your instructor.

9. **Submit the document to your instructor, then close all open Word files without closing Word, saving changes to the files if prompted**

FIGURE 6-11: Preview of merged data

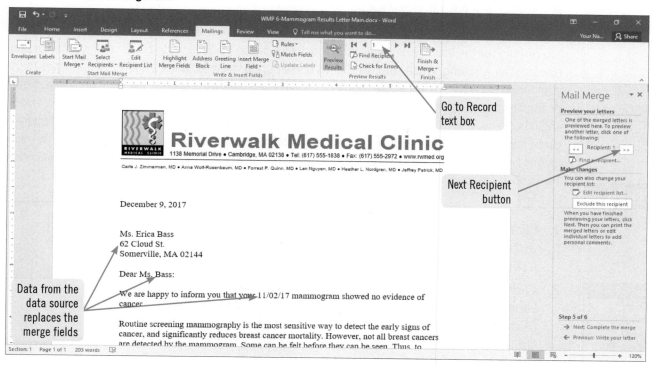

TABLE 6-1: Commands on the Mailings tab

command	use to
Envelopes	Create and print an individual envelope
Labels	Create and print an individual label
Start Mail Merge	Select the type of mail merge document to create and start the mail merge process
Select Recipients	Attach an existing data source to a main document or create a new data source
Edit Recipient List	Edit, sort, and filter the associated data source
Highlight Merge Fields	Highlight the merge fields in the main document
Address Block	Insert an Address Block merge field in the main document
Greeting Line	Insert a Greeting Line merge field in the main document
Insert Merge Field	Insert a merge field from the data source in the main document
Rules	Set rules to control how Word merges the data in the data source with the main document
Match Fields	Match the names of address or greeting fields used in a main document with the field names used in the data source
Update Labels	Update all the labels in a label main document to match the content and formatting of the first label
Preview Results	Switch between viewing the main document with merge fields or with merged data
Find Recipient	Search for a specific record in the merged document
Check for Errors	Check for and report errors in the merge
Finish & Merge	Specify whether to merge to a new document or directly to a printer or to e-mail, then complete the merge

Create Labels

Learning
Outcomes
• Create a label
  main document
• Merge with an
  existing data
  source

You can also use the Mail Merge pane or the commands on the Mailings tab to create mailing labels or print envelopes for a mailing. When you create labels or envelopes, you must select a label or envelope size to use as the main document, select a data source, and then insert the merge fields in the main document before performing the merge. In addition to mailing labels, you can use mail merge to create labels for CDs, videos, and other items, and to create documents that are based on standard or custom label sizes, such as business cards, name tags, and postcards. **CASE** *You decide to use the commands on the Mailings tab to create mailing labels for the reminder cards you need to send to patients who need to schedule a routine mammogram. You create a new label main document and attach an existing data source.*

STEPS

1. **Click the File tab, click New, click Blank document, make sure the zoom level is set to 120%, then click the Mailings tab**

   A blank document must be open for the commands on the Mailings tab to be available.

QUICK TIP

To create an envelope mail merge, click Envelopes to open the Envelope Options dialog box, and then select from the options.

2. **Click the Start Mail Merge button in the Start Mail Merge group, click Labels, click the Label vendors list arrow in the Label Options dialog box, then click Microsoft if Microsoft is not already displayed**

   The Label Options dialog box opens, as shown in FIGURE 6-12. You use this dialog box to select a label size for your labels and to specify the type of printer you plan to use. The name Microsoft appears in the Label vendors list box. You can use the Label vendors list arrow to select other brand name label vendors, such as Avery or Office Depot. Many standard-sized labels for mailings, business cards, postcards, and other types of labels are listed in the Product number list box. The type, height, width, and page size for the selected product are displayed in the Label information section.

QUICK TIP

If your labels do not match FIGURE 6-13, click the Undo button ↺ on the Quick Access toolbar, then repeat Step 3, making sure to click the second instance of 30 Per Page.

3. **Click the second instance of 30 Per Page in the Product number list, click OK, click the Table Tools Layout tab, click View Gridlines in the Table group to turn on the display of gridlines if they are not displayed, then click the Mailings tab**

   A table with gridlines appears in the main document, as shown in FIGURE 6-13. Each table cell is the size of a label for the label product you selected.

4. **Save the label main document with the filename WMP 6-Mammogram Reminder Labels Main to the location where you store your Data Files**

   Next, you need to select a data source for the labels.

5. **Click the Select Recipients button in the Start Mail Merge group, then click Use an Existing List**

   The Select Data Source dialog box opens.

QUICK TIP

To create or change the return address for an envelope mail merge, click the File tab, click Options, click Advanced in the left pane of the Word Options dialog box, then scroll down the right pane and enter the return address in the Mailing address text box in the General section.

6. **Navigate to the location where you store your Data Files, open the file WMP 6-2.mdb, then save your changes**

   The data source file is attached to the label main document and <<Next Record>> appears in every cell in the table except the first cell, which is blank. In the next lesson, you sort and filter the records before performing the mail merge.

FIGURE 6-12: **Label Options dialog box**

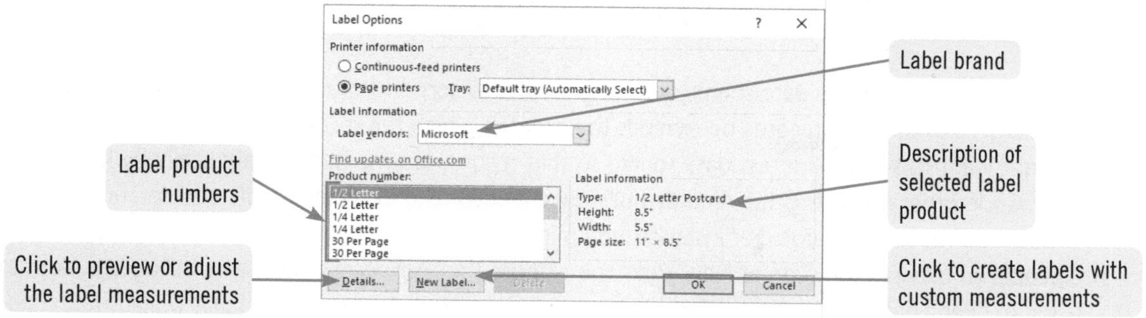

Label brand

Label product numbers

Description of selected label product

Click to preview or adjust the label measurements

Click to create labels with custom measurements

FIGURE 6-13: **Label main document**

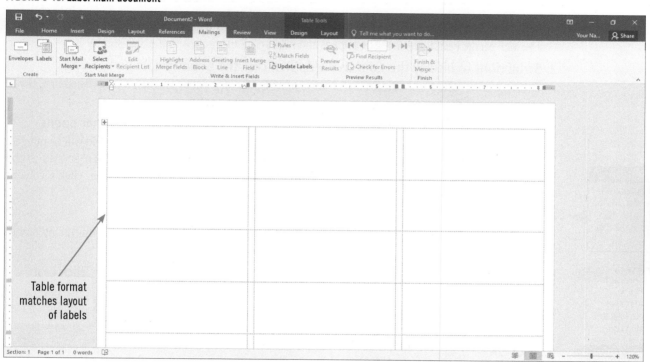

Table format matches layout of labels

Printing individual envelopes and labels

The Mail Merge feature enables you to easily print envelopes and labels for mass mailings, but you can also quickly format and print individual envelopes and labels using the Envelopes or Labels commands in the Create group on the Mailings tab. Simply click the Envelopes button or Labels button to open the Envelopes and Labels dialog box. On the Envelopes tab, shown in FIGURE 6-14, type the recipient's address in the Delivery address box and the return address in the Return address box. Click Options to open the Envelope Options dialog box, which you use to select the envelope size, change the font and font size of the delivery and return addresses, and change the printing options. When you are ready to print the envelope, click Print in the Envelopes and Labels dialog box. The procedure for printing an individual label is similar to printing an individual envelope: enter the label text in the Address box on the Labels tab, click Options to select a label product number, click OK, and then click Print.

FIGURE 6-14: **Envelopes and Labels dialog box**

Word 2016

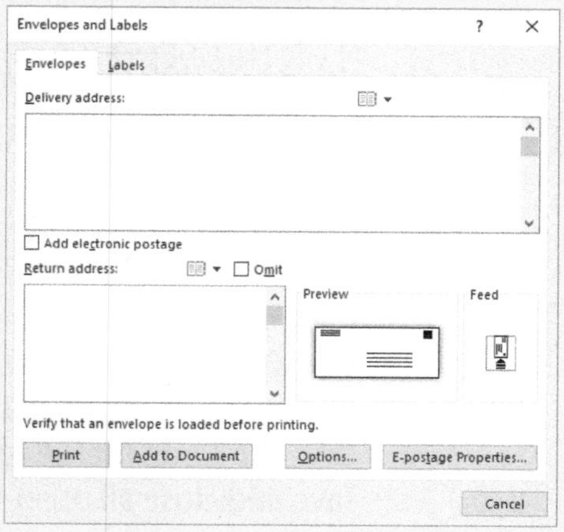

Sort and Filter Records

Learning Outcomes
- Filter a data source
- Sort records in a data source
- Add merge fields to a label main document

If you are using a large data source, you might want to sort and/or filter the records before performing a merge. **Sorting** the records determines the order in which the records are merged. For example, you might want to sort an address data source so that records are merged alphabetically by last name or in ZIP Code order. **Filtering** the records pulls out the records that meet specific criteria and includes only those records in the merge. For instance, you might want to filter a data source to send a mailing only to people who live in the state of New York. You can use the Mail Merge Recipients dialog box both to sort and to filter a data source. **CASE** ▶ *You apply a filter to the data source so that only United States addresses are included in the merge. You then sort those records so that they merge in ZIP Code order.*

STEPS

1. **Click the** Edit Recipient List button **in the Start Mail Merge group**

   The Mail Merge Recipients dialog box opens and displays all the records in the data source.

2. **Scroll right to display the Country field, then click the** Country column heading

   The records are sorted in ascending alphabetical order by country, with Canadian records listed first. If you want to reverse the sort order, you can click the column heading again.

3. **Click the** Country column heading list arrow, **then click** US **on the menu that opens**

   A filter is applied to the data source so that only the records with "US" in the Country field will be merged. The grayish-blue arrow in the Country column heading indicates that a filter has been applied to the column. You can filter a data source by as many criteria as you like. To remove a filter, click a column heading list arrow, then click (All).

QUICK TIP

Use the options on the Filter Records tab to apply more than one filter to the data source.

4. **Click** Sort **in the Refine recipient list section of the dialog box**

   The Filter and Sort dialog box opens with the Sort Records tab displayed. You can use this dialog box to apply more advanced sort and filter options to the data source.

TROUBLE

Make sure the Ascending option buttons are selected in the dialog box.

5. **Click the** Sort by list arrow, **click** ZIP Code, **click the first** Then by list arrow, **click** Last Name, **then click** OK

   The Mail Merge Recipients dialog box (shown in FIGURE 6-15) now displays only the records with a U.S. address sorted first in ZIP Code order, and then alphabetically by last name.

QUICK TIP

Sorting and filtering a data source does not alter the records in a data source; it simply reorganizes the records for the current merge only.

6. **Click** OK

   The sort and filter criteria you set are saved for the current merge.

7. **Click the** Address Block button **in the Write & Insert Fields group, then click** OK **in the Insert Address Block dialog box**

   The Address Block merge field is added to the first label.

8. **Click the** Update Labels button **in the Write & Insert Fields group**

   The merge field is copied from the first label to every label in the main document.

QUICK TIP

To change the font or paragraph formatting of merged data, format the merge fields, including the chevrons, before performing a merge.

9. **Click the** Preview Results button **in the Preview Results group**

   A preview of the merged label data appears in the main document, as shown in FIGURE 6-16. Only U.S. addresses are included, and the labels are organized in ZIP Code order, with recipients with the same ZIP Code listed in alphabetical order by last name.

10. **Click the** Finish & Merge button **in the Finish group, click** Edit Individual Documents, **click** OK **in the Merge to New Document dialog box, replace** Ms. Julia Packer **with your name in the first label, save the document as** WMP 6-Mammogram Reminder Labels US Only Zip Code Merge **to the location where you store your Data Files, submit the labels, save and close all open files, then exit Word**

FIGURE 6-15: US records sorted in ZIP Code order

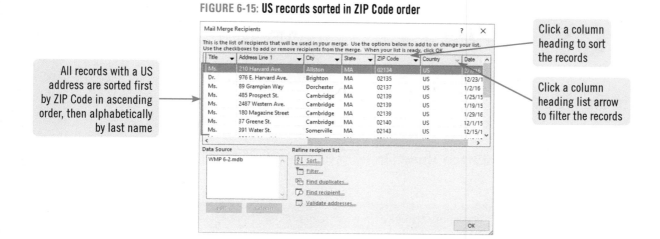

All records with a US address are sorted first by ZIP Code in ascending order, then alphabetically by last name

Click a column heading to sort the records

Click a column heading list arrow to filter the records

FIGURE 6-16: Merged labels

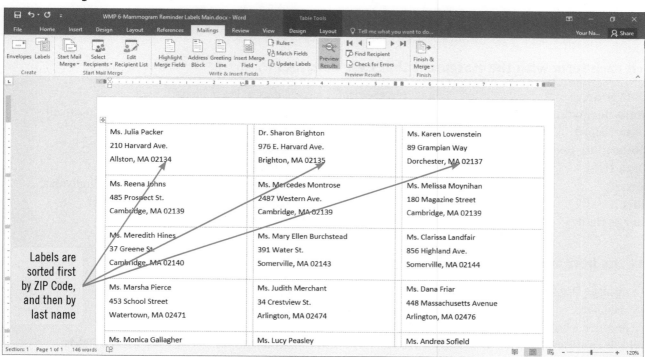

Labels are sorted first by ZIP Code, and then by last name

Inserting individual merge fields

You must include proper punctuation, spacing, and blank lines between the merge fields in a main document if you want punctuation, spaces, and blank lines to appear between the data in the merge documents. For example, to create an address line with a city, state, and ZIP Code, you insert the City merge field, type a comma and a space, insert the State merge field, type a space, and then insert the ZIP Code merge field: <<City>>, <<State>> <<ZIP Code>>.

You can insert an individual merge field by clicking the Insert Merge Field list arrow in the Write & Insert Fields group

and then selecting the field name from the menu that opens. Alternatively, you can click the Insert Merge Field button to open the Insert Merge Field dialog box, which you can use to insert several merge fields at once by clicking a field name in the dialog box, clicking Insert, clicking another field name, clicking Insert, and so on. When you have finished inserting the merge fields, click Close to close the dialog box. You can then add spaces, punctuation, and lines between the merge fields you inserted in the main document.

Practice

Concepts Review

Describe the function of each button shown in FIGURE 6-17.

FIGURE 6-17

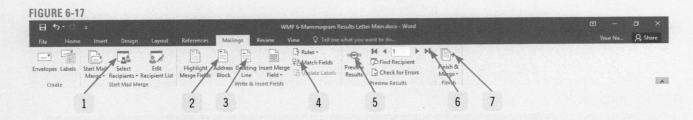

Match each term with the statement that best describes it.

8. Data source
9. Main document
10. Data record
11. Boilerplate text
12. Data field
13. Filter
14. Sort
15. Merge field

a. A placeholder for merged data in the main document
b. The standard text that appears in every version of a merged document
c. A file that contains boilerplate text and merge fields
d. To pull out records that meet certain criteria
e. To organize records in a sequence
f. A file that contains customized information for each item or individual
g. A complete set of information for one item or individual
h. A category of information in a data source

Select the best answer from the list of choices.

16. To change the font of merged data, which element should you format?
    a. Field name
    b. Boilerplate text
    c. Merge field
    d. Data record

17. Which command is used to synchronize the field names in a data source with the merge fields in a document?
    a. Match Fields
    b. Highlight Merge Fields
    c. Rules
    d. Update Labels

18. In a mail merge, which type of file contains the information that varies for each individual or item?
    a. Filtered document
    b. Sorted document
    c. Main document
    d. Data source

19. Which action do you perform on a data source to reorganize the order of the records for a merge?
    a. Edit records
    b. Sort records
    c. Filter records
    d. Delete records

20. Which action do you perform on a data source in order to merge only certain records?
    a. Edit records
    b. Sort records
    c. Filter records
    d. Delete records

Skills Review

1. Create a main document.

a. Start Word, open a new blank document, change the style of the document to No Spacing, then open the Mail Merge pane.

b. Use the Mail Merge pane to create a letter main document, click Next: Starting document, then select the Use the current document option button.

c. At the top of the blank document, type **Atlantic Health and Life**, press [Enter], then type **1233 Wharf Street, Portsmouth, NH 03828; Tel: 603-555-8457; www.atlantichealthandlife.net**.

d. Press [Enter] five times, type today's date, press [Enter] five times, then type **We are writing to confirm your choice of a Primary Care Physician in STATE. According to our records, you selected PCP, as your Primary Care Physician.**

e. Press [Enter] twice, then type **It's important that you contact your Primary Care Physician to coordinate all your medical care. If you need to see a specialist, your Primary Care Physician will refer you to one who is affiliated with his or her hospital or medical group.**

f. Press [Enter] twice, then type **If the physician listed above is not the one you selected, please call Member Services at 1-800-555-1328.**

g. Press [Enter] twice, type **Sincerely,**, press [Enter] four times, type your name, press [Enter], then type **Member Services**.

h. Center the first two lines of text, change the font used for Atlantic Health and Life to 20 point Berlin Sans FB Demi, then remove the hyperlink in the second line of text. (*Hint*: Right-click the hyperlink.)

i. Save the main document as **WMP 6-Subscriber PCP Letter Main** to the location where you store your Data Files.

2. Design a data source.

a. Click Next: Select recipients, select the Type a new list option button in the Step 3 of 6... pane, then click Create.

b. Click Customize Columns in the New Address List dialog box, then remove these fields from the data source: Company Name, Address Line 2, Country or Region, Home Phone, Work Phone, and E-mail Address.

c. Add an **ID** field and a **PCP** field to the data source. Be sure these fields follow the ZIP Code field.

d. Rename the Address Line 1 field **Street**, then click OK to close the Customize Address List dialog box.

3. Enter and edit records.

a. Add the records shown in TABLE 6-2 to the data source.

TABLE 6-2

Title	First Name	Last Name	Street	City	State	ZIP Code	ID	PCP
Mr.	John	Sargent	34 Mill St.	Exeter	NH	03833	MT3948	Susan Trifilio, M.D.
Mr.	Tom	Jenkins	289 Sugar Hill Rd.	Franconia	NH	03632	CZ2846	Richard Pattavina, M.D.
Ms.	Nancy	Curtis	742 Main St.	Derby	VT	04634	MT1928	Edwin March, M.D.
Mr.	Peter	Field	987 Ocean Rd.	Portsmouth	NH	03828	CF8725	Rebecca Keller, M.D.
Ms.	Lisa	Juarez	73 Bay Rd.	Durham	NH	03814	MK2991	Anna Doherty, M.D.
Ms.	Willa	Reed	67 Apple St.	Northfield	MA	01360	CG8231	Bruce Dewey, M.D.
Ms.	Mia	Suzuki	287 Mountain Rd.	Dublin	NH	03436	MT1878	Lisa Giaimo, M.D.

b. Save the data source as **WMP 6-Subscriber Data** to the location where you store your Data Files.

c. Change the PCP for record 2 (Tom Jenkins) from Richard Pattavina, M.D. to **Diana Ray, M.D.**

d. Click OK as needed to close all dialog boxes.

4. Add merge fields.

a. Click Next: Write your letter, then in the blank line above the first body paragraph, insert an Address block merge field.

b. In the Insert Address Block dialog box, click Match Fields.

Skills Review (continued)

c. Click the list arrow next to Address 1 in the Match Fields dialog box, click Street, then click OK.

d. Press [Enter] twice, type **Member ID:**, insert a space, then insert the ID merge field.

e. Press [Enter] twice, insert a Greeting Line merge field using the default greeting line format, then press [Enter].

f. In the first body paragraph, replace STATE with the State merge field and PCP with the PCP merge field. (*Note*: Make sure to insert a space before or after each merge field as needed.) Save your changes to the main document.

5. **Merge data.**

a. Click Next: Preview your letters to preview the merged data, then use the Next Record button to scroll through each letter, examining it carefully for errors.

b. Click the Preview Results button on the Mailings tab, make any necessary adjustments to the main document, save your changes, then click the Preview Results button to return to the preview of the document.

c. Click Next: Complete the merge, click Edit individual letters, then merge all the records to a new file.

d. Save the merged document as **WMP 6-Subscriber PCP Letter Merge** to the location where you store your Data Files. The fifth letter is shown in FIGURE 6-18. Submit the file or a copy of the last letter per your instructor's directions, then save and close all open files but not Word.

FIGURE 6-18

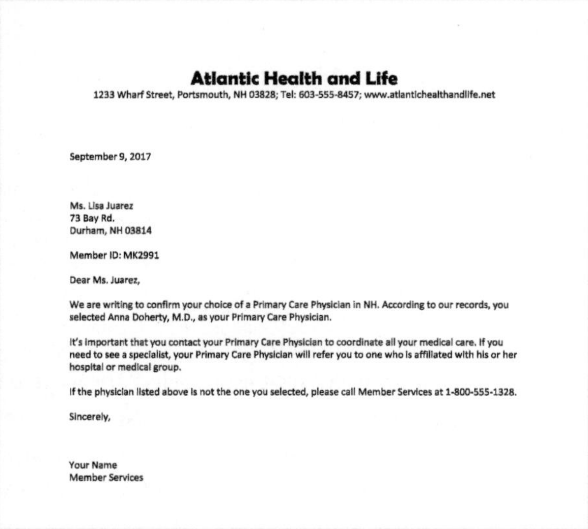

6. **Create labels.**

a. Open a new blank document, click the Start Mail Merge button in the Start Mail Merge group on the Mailings tab, then create a Labels main document.

b. In the Label Options dialog box, select Avery US Letter 5160 Easy Peel Address Labels, then click OK.

c. Click the Select Recipients button, then open the WMP 6-Subscriber Data.mdb file you created.

d. Save the label main document as **WMP 6-Subscriber Labels Main** to the location where you store your Data Files.

7. **Sort and filter records.**

a. Click the Edit Recipient List button, filter the records so that only the records with NH in the State field are included in the merge, sort the records in ZIP Code order, then click OK as needed to return to the labels document.

b. Insert an Address Block merge field using the default settings, click the Preview Results button, then notice that the street address is missing and the address block includes the region. (*Hint*: To preview all labels, click the Next Record button.)

c. Click the Preview Results button, then click the Match Fields button to open the Match Fields dialog box.

d. Click the list arrow next to Address 1, click Street, then click OK.

e. Click the Preview Results button to preview the merged data, and notice that the address block now includes the street address.

f. Click the Update Labels button, examine the merged data for errors, then correct any mistakes.

g. Click the Finish & Merge button, then click the Edit Individual Documents to merge all the records to an individual document, shown in FIGURE 6-19.

h. Save the merged file as **WMP 6-Subscriber Labels NH Only Merge** to the location where you store your Data Files.

i. In the first label, change Ms. Mia Suzuki to your name, submit the document to your instructor, save and close all open Word files, then exit Word.

FIGURE 6-19

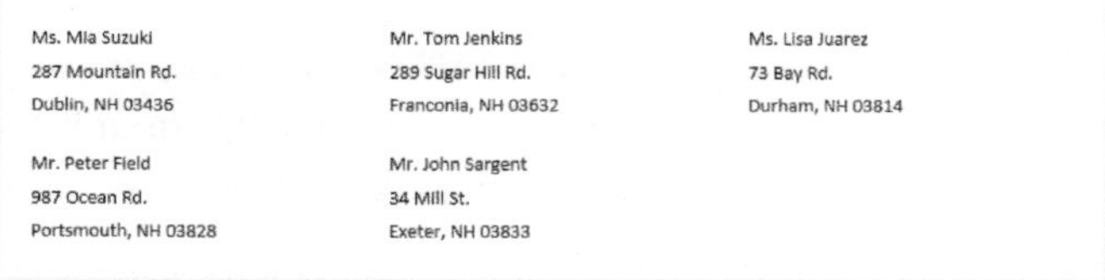

Independent Challenge 1

You work for Rocky Mountain Eye Care. Your office has designed a maintenance program for gas permeable (GP) contact lenses, and you want to send a letter introducing the program to all patients who wear GP lenses. You'll use Mail Merge to create the letter and create an envelope for one letter.

a. Start Word, open a blank document, then using either the Mailings tab or the Mail Merge pane, create a letter main document using the file WMP 6-3.docx from the location where you store your Data Files.

b. Replace Your Name with your name in the signature block, then save the main document as **WMP 6-GP Letter Main**.

c. Use the file WMP 6-4.mdb from the location where you store your Data Files as the data source.

d. Sort the data source by last name, then filter the data so that only records with GP as the lens are included in the merge.

e. Insert an Address Block and a Greeting Line merge field in the main document, then preview the merged letters.

f. Merge all the records to a new document, then save it as **WMP 6-GP Letter Merge**.

g. Select the inside address in the first merge letter, then click the Envelopes button in the Create group on the Mailings tab to open the Envelopes and Labels dialog box. (*Note*: You will create one envelope and include it as part of the merge document. If you were doing a mailing merge, you would create a separate envelope merge.)

h. On the Envelopes tab in the Envelopes and Labels dialog box, verify that the Omit check box is not selected, then type your name in the Return address text box along with the address **Rocky Mountain Eye Care, 60 Crandall Street, Boulder, CO 80306**.

i. Click Options to open the Envelope Options dialog box, click the Envelope Options tab if it is not the active tab, make sure the Envelope size is set to Size 10, then change the font of the Delivery address and the Return address to Times New Roman.

j. Click the Printing Options tab, select the appropriate Feed method for your printer, then click OK.

k. Click Add to Document, click No if a message box opens asking if you want to save the new return address as the default return address. (*Note*: The dialog box closes without printing the envelope and the envelope is added as the first page of the merge document.)

l. Submit the file or a copy of the envelope and the first merge letter per your instructor's directions, close all open Word files, saving changes, and then exit Word.

Independent Challenge 2

One of your responsibilities at Northwest Family Health, a growing family health clinic, is to create business cards for the staff. You use mail merge to create the cards so that you can easily produce standard business cards for future employees.

a. Start Word, open a blank document, then use the Mailings tab or the Mail Merge pane to create labels using the current blank document.

b. Select Microsoft North American Size, which is described as Horizontal Card, 2" high x 3.5" wide. (*Hint*: Select the second instance of North American Size in the Product number list box.)

c. Create a new data source that includes the fields and records shown in TABLE 6-3: (*Hint*: Customize the Address List fields before adding data.)

TABLE 6-3

Title	First Name	Last Name	Phone	Fax	E-mail	Hire Date
Medical Director	Helen	Callaghan	(503) 555-3982	(503) 555-6654	hcallaghan@nwfh.com	1/12/13
Nurse Practitioner	Seamus	Gallagher	(503) 555-2323	(503) 555-4956	sgallagher@nwfh.com	3/18/14

Independent Challenge 2 (continued)

d. Add six more records to the data source, including records for a Medical Assistant, an Immunization Coordinator, three Physicians, and an Administrative Assistant. Add your name as the Administrative Assistant. (*Hint*: Be careful not to add a blank row at the bottom of the data source.)

FIGURE 6-20

Northwest Family Health

Helen Callaghan
Medical Director

984 Grant Street, Portland, OR 97209
Tel: (503) 555-3982
Fax: (503) 555-6654
E-mail: hcallaghan@nwfh.com
Web: www.nwfh.com

Source: Pixabay

e. Save the data source with the filename **WMP 6-NWFH Employee Data** to the location where you store your Data Files, then sort the data by Title.

f. In the first table cell, create the Northwest Family Health business card. **FIGURE 6-20** shows a sample business card, but you should create your own design. Include the company name, a street address, and the website address **www.nwfh.com**. Also include First Name, Last Name, Title, Phone, Fax, and E-mail merge fields. (*Hint*: If your design includes a graphic, insert the graphic before inserting the merge fields. Insert each merge field individually, adjusting the spacing between merge fields as necessary.)

g. Format the business card with fonts, colors, and other formatting features. (*Hint*: Make sure to select the entire merge field, including the chevrons, before formatting.)

h. Update all the labels, preview the data, make any necessary adjustments, then merge all the records to a new document.

i. Save the merge document as **WMP 6-NWFH Business Cards Merge** to the location where you store your Data Files, submit a copy to your instructor, then close the file.

j. Save the main document as **WMP 6-NWFH Business Cards Main** to the location where you store your Data Files, close the file, then exit Word.

Independent Challenge 3

You need to create a class list for a fitness and nutrition class you teach for children who are overweight. You want the class list to include contact information for the children, as well as their age and body mass index (BMI) at the time they registered for the class. You decide to use mail merge to create the class list.

a. Start Word, open a new document, then use the Mailings tab or the Mail Merge pane to create a directory using the current blank document.

b. Create a new data source that includes the following fields: First Name, Last Name, Age, BMI, Parent First Name, Parent Last Name, Address, City, State, ZIP Code, and Home Phone.

c. Enter the records shown in **TABLE 6-4** in the data source:

TABLE 6-4

First Name	Last Name	Age	BMI	Parent First Name	Parent Last Name	Address	City	State	ZIP Code	Home Phone
Ellie	Wright	8	25.32	Kerry	Wright	58 Main St.	Camillus	NY	13031	555-2345
Liam	Jacob	7	20.02	Bob	Jacob	32 North Way	Camillus	NY	13031	555-9827
Dwayne	Rule	8	22.52	Sylvia	Rule	289 Sylvan Way	Marcellus	NY	13032	555-9724
Caroline	Herman	7	21.89	Sarah	Thomas	438 Lariat St.	Marcellus	NY	13032	555-8347

Independent Challenge 3 (continued)

d. Add five additional records to the data source using the following last names and positions:

O'Keefe, 24.03   Goleman, 21.17   Choy, 23.45

George, 26.12   Siebert, 21.63

Make up the remaining information for these five records.

e. Save the data source as **WMP 6-Kids Fitness Class Data** to the location where you store your Data Files, then sort the records by last name.

f. Insert a table that includes six columns and one row in the main document.

g. In the first table cell, insert the First Name and Last Name merge fields, separated by a space.

h. In the second cell, insert the Age merge field, and in the third cell, insert the BMI merge field.

i. In the fourth cell, insert the Address and City merge fields, separated by a comma and a space.

j. In the fifth cell, insert the Home Phone merge field.

k. In the sixth cell, insert the Parent First Name and Parent Last Name merge fields, separated by a space.

l. Preview the merged data and make any necessary adjustments. (*Hint*: Only one record is displayed at a time when you preview the data. Click the Next Record button to see more records.)

m. Merge all the records to a new document, then save the document as **WMP 6-Kids Fitness Class List Merge** to the location where you store your Data Files.

n. Press [Ctrl][Home], press [Enter], type **Fitness and Nutrition for Children** at the top of the document, press [Enter], type **Instructor:** followed by your name, then center the two lines.

o. Insert a new row at the top of the table, then type the following column headings in the new row: **Name, Age, BMI, Address, Phone, Parent Name**.

p. Format the class list to make it attractive and readable, save your changes, submit a copy to your instructor, close the file, close the main document without saving changes, then exit Word.

Independent Challenge 4: Explore

Mail merge can be used not only for mailings but also to create CD/DVD labels, labels for file folders, phone directories, business cards, and many other types of documents. In this independent challenge, you design and create a data source that you can use at work or in your personal life, and then you merge the data source with a main document that you create. Your data source might include contact information for your friends and associates, inventory for your business, details for an event such as a wedding (guests invited, responses, gifts received), data on one of your collections (such as music or photos), or some other type of information.

a. Determine the content of your data source, list the fields you want to include, and then determine the logical order of the fields. Be sure to select your fields carefully so that your data source is flexible and can be merged with many types of documents. Generally it is better to include more fields, even if you don't enter data in them for each record.

b. Start Word, open a blank document, start a mail merge for the type of document you want to create (such as a directory or a label), then create a new data source.

c. Customize the columns in the data source to include the fields and organization you determined in Step a.

d. Add at least five records to the data source, then save it as **WMP 6-Your Name Data** to the location where you store your Data Files.

e. Write and format the main document, insert the merge fields, preview the merge, make any necessary adjustments, then merge the files to a document.

f. Adjust the formatting of the merge document as necessary, add your name to the header, save the merge document as **WMP 6-Your Name Merge** to the location where you store your Data Files, submit a copy to your instructor, close the file, close the main document without saving changes, then exit Word.

Visual Workshop

Using mail merge, create the postcards shown in FIGURE 6-21. Use Avery US Letter 3263 Postcards labels for the main document, and create a data source that contains at least four records, including your name in the first record. Save the data source as **WMP 6-Patient Data**, save the merge document as **WMP 6-Patient Reminder Card Merge**, and save the main document as **WMP 6-Patient Reminder Card Main**, all to the location where you store your Data Files. (*Hints*: Notice that the postcard label main document is formatted as a table. To lay out the postcard, insert a nested table with two columns and one row in the upper-left cell; add the text, graphic, and merge field to the nested table; and then remove the outside borders on the nested table. Use a different online image if the image shown is not available to you. The font is Book Antiqua.) Submit a copy of the postcards to your instructor.

FIGURE 6-21

Sylvia C. Ponce, M.D.

124 East 16th Street, Suite 400
New York, NY 10003

Telephone: 212-555-8634

Our records indicate it is time for your annual eye exam. Please call our office to schedule an appointment.

Mr. Philip Pope

3902 Broadway

Apt. 2C

New York, NY 10025

Sylvia C. Ponce, M.D.

124 East 16th Street, Suite 400
New York, NY 10003

Telephone: 212-555-8634

Our records indicate it is time for your annual eye exam. Please call our office to schedule an appointment.

Ms. Zadie Sloan

414 W. 107th St.

Apt. 112

New York, NY 10027

Source: Pixabay

Merging Word Documents

Getting Started with Excel 2016

CASE ▶ You have been hired as an assistant at Riverwalk Medical Clinic (RMC), a large outpatient medical facility staffed by family physicians, specialists, nurses, and other allied health professionals. You report to Tony Sanchez, R.N., the office manager. As Tony's assistant, you create worksheets to analyze data from various departments, so you can help him make sound decisions on clinic expansion and investments, as well as day-to-day operations.

Module Objectives

After completing this module, you will be able to:

- Understand spreadsheet software
- Identify Excel 2016 window components
- Understand formulas
- Enter labels and values and use the AutoSum button
- Edit cell entries
- Enter and edit a simple formula
- Switch worksheet views
- Choose print options

Files You Will Need

EMP 1-1.xlsx	EMP 1-4.xlsx
EMP 1-2.xlsx	EMP 1-5.xlsx
EMP 1-3.xlsx	

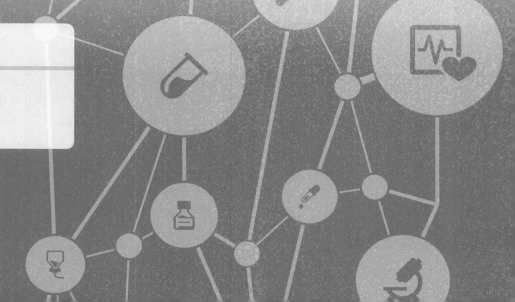

Understand Spreadsheet Software

Learning Outcomes
- Describe the uses of Excel
- Define key spreadsheet terms

Microsoft Excel is the electronic spreadsheet program within the Microsoft Office suite. An **electronic spreadsheet** is an app you use to perform numeric calculations and to analyze and present numeric data. One advantage of a spreadsheet program over pencil and paper is that your calculations are updated automatically, so you can change entries without having to manually recalculate. TABLE 1-1 shows some of the common business tasks people accomplish using Excel. In Excel, the electronic spreadsheet you work in is called a **worksheet**, and it is contained in a file called a **workbook**, which has the file extension .xlsx. **CASE** ▶ *At RMC, you use Excel extensively to track finances and manage clinic data.*

DETAILS

When you use Excel, you have the ability to:

- **Enter data quickly and accurately**

  With Excel, you can enter information faster and more accurately than with pencil and paper. FIGURE 1-1 shows a payroll worksheet created using pencil and paper. FIGURE 1-2 shows the same worksheet created using Excel. Equations were added to calculate the hours and pay. You can use Excel to recreate this information for each week by copying the worksheet's structure and the information that doesn't change from week to week, then entering unique data and formulas for each week.

- **Recalculate data easily**

  Fixing typing errors or updating data is easy in Excel. In the payroll example, if you receive updated hours for an employee, you just enter the new hours and Excel recalculates the pay.

- **Perform what-if analysis**

  The ability to change data and quickly view the recalculated results gives you the power to make informed business decisions. For instance, if you're considering raising the hourly rate for an entry-level patient transporter from $12.50 to $15.00, you can enter the new value in the worksheet and immediately see the impact on the overall payroll as well as on the individual employee. Any time you use a worksheet to ask the question "What if?" you are performing **what-if analysis**. Excel also includes a Scenario Manager where you can name and save different what-if versions of your worksheet.

- **Change the appearance of information**

  Excel provides powerful features, such as the Quick Analysis tool, for making information visually appealing and easier to understand. Format text and numbers in different fonts, colors, and styles to make them stand out.

- **Create charts**

  Excel makes it easy to create charts based on worksheet information. Charts are updated automatically in Excel whenever data changes. The worksheet in FIGURE 1-2 includes a 3-D pie chart.

- **Share information**

  It's easy for everyone at RMC to collaborate in Excel using the company intranet, the Internet, or a network storage device. For example, you can complete the weekly payroll that your boss, Tony Sanchez, started creating. You can also take advantage of collaboration tools such as shared workbooks so that multiple people can edit a workbook simultaneously.

- **Build on previous work**

  Instead of creating a new worksheet for every project, it's easy to modify an existing Excel worksheet. When you are ready to create next week's payroll, you can open the file for last week's payroll, save it with a new filename, and modify the information as necessary. You can also use predesigned, formatted files called **templates** to create new worksheets quickly. Excel comes with many templates that you can customize.

FIGURE 1-1: Traditional paper worksheet

Riverwalk Medical Clinic
Health Professionals Payroll Calculator

Name	Position	Hours	O/T Hrs	Hrly Rate	Reg Pay	O/T Pay
Brucker, Pieter	Patient Transporter	40	4	17.50	700.00	140.00
Cucci, Livia	Renal Dialysis Technician	35	0	16.00	560.00	-
Klimt, Gustave	Physician Assistant	40	2	41.50	1,660.00	166.00
La Pen, Jean-Marie	Anesthesia Technician	29	0	16.75	485.75	-
Martinez, Juan	Medical Records Coding Technician	37	0	19.63	726.31	-
Mioshi, Keiko	Medical Records Technician	39	0	17.95	700.05	-
Shernwood, Burt	Massage Therapist	40	1	22.75	910.00	45.50
Strano, Riccardo	Medical Laboratory Technician	40	8	19.00	760.00	304.00
Wadsworth, Alicia	Interventional Radiology Technician	40	5	29.00	1,160.00	290.00
Yamamoto, Johji	Electroencephalograph Technician	38	0	21.00	798.00	-

FIGURE 1-2: Excel worksheet

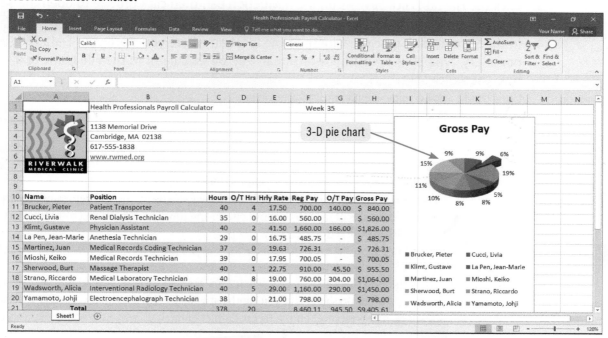

TABLE 1-1: Business tasks you can accomplish using Excel

you can use spreadsheets to	by
Perform calculations	Adding formulas and functions to worksheet data; for example, adding a list of sales results or calculating a car payment
Represent values graphically	Creating charts based on worksheet data; for example, creating a chart that displays expenses
Generate reports	Creating workbooks that combine information from multiple worksheets, such as summarized sales information from multiple stores
Organize data	Sorting data in ascending or descending order; for example, alphabetizing a list of products or customer names, or prioritizing orders by date
Analyze data	Creating data summaries and short lists using PivotTables or AutoFilters; for example, making a list of the top 10 customers based on spending habits
Create what-if data scenarios	Using variable values to investigate and sample different outcomes, such as changing the interest rate or payment schedule on a loan

Identify Excel 2016 Window Components

Learning Outcomes
• Open and save an Excel file
• Identify Excel window elements

To start Excel, Microsoft Windows must be running. Similar to starting any app in Office, you can use the Start button on the Windows taskbar, the Start button on your keyboard, or you may have a shortcut on your desktop you prefer to use. If you need additional assistance, ask your instructor or technical support person.

CASE *You decide to start Excel and familiarize yourself with the worksheet window.*

STEPS

1. **Start Excel, click** Open Other Workbooks **on the navigation bar, click** This PC, **then click** Browse **to open the Open dialog box**

2. **In the Open dialog box, navigate to the location where you store your Data Files, click** EMP 1-1.xlsx, **then click** Open

   The file opens in the Excel window.

3. **Click the** File tab, **click** Save As **on the navigation bar, then click** Browse **to open the Save As dialog box**

4. **In the Save As dialog box, navigate to the location where you store your Data Files if necessary, type** EMP 1-Health Professionals Payroll Calculator **in the File name text box, then click** Save

   Using **FIGURE 1-3** as a guide, identify the following items:

   • The **Name box** displays the active cell address. "A1" appears in the Name box.

   • The **formula bar** allows you to enter or edit data in the worksheet.

   • The **worksheet window** contains a grid of columns and rows. Columns are labeled alphabetically and rows are labeled numerically. The worksheet window can contain a total of 1,048,576 rows and 16,384 columns. The intersection of a column and a row is called a **cell**. Cells can contain text, numbers, formulas, or a combination of all three. Every cell has its own unique location or **cell address**, which is identified by the coordinates of the intersecting column and row. The column and row indicators are shaded to make identifying the cell address easy.

   • The **cell pointer** is a dark rectangle that outlines the cell you are working in. This cell is called the **active cell**. In **FIGURE 1-3**, the cell pointer outlines cell A1, so A1 is the active cell.

   • **Sheet tabs** below the worksheet grid let you switch from sheet to sheet in a workbook. By default, a workbook file contains one worksheet—but you can have as many sheets as your computer's memory allows, in a workbook. The New sheet button to the right of Sheet 1 allows you to add worksheets to a workbook. **Sheet tab scrolling buttons** let you navigate to additional sheet tabs when available.

   • You can use the **scroll bars** to move around in a worksheet that is too large to fit on the screen at once.

   • The **status bar** is located at the bottom of the Excel window. It provides a brief description of the active command or task in progress. The **mode indicator** in the lower-left corner of the status bar provides additional information about certain tasks.

5. **Click cell** D4

   Cell D4 becomes the active cell. To activate a different cell, you can click the cell or press the arrow keys on your keyboard to move to it.

6. **Click cell** C11, **press and hold the mouse button, drag** ✥ **to cell** C20, **then release the mouse button**

   Your selected cells are highlighted, as shown in **FIGURE 1-4**. A selection of two or more cells is called a **range**; you select a range when you want to perform an action on a group of cells at once, such as moving or formatting. When you select a range, the status bar displays the average, count (or number of items selected), and sum of the selected cells as a quick reference.

FIGURE 1-3: Open workbook

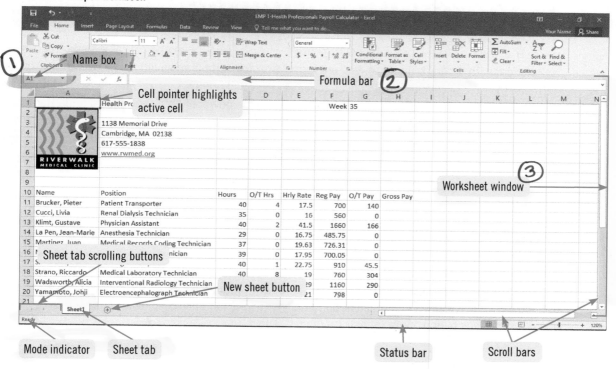

Name box · Formula bar · Cell pointer highlights active cell · Worksheet window · Sheet tab scrolling buttons · New sheet button · Mode indicator · Sheet tab · Status bar · Scroll bars

FIGURE 1-4: Selected range

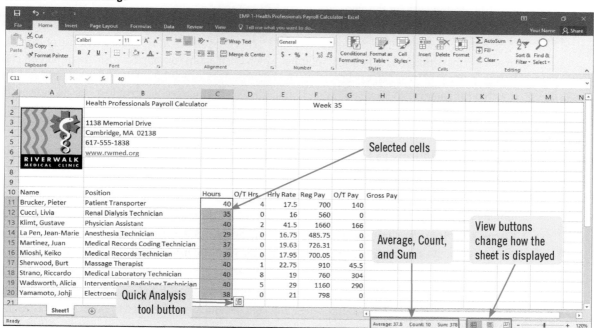

Selected cells · Average, Count, and Sum · View buttons change how the sheet is displayed · Quick Analysis tool button

Using OneDrive and Office Online

If you have a Microsoft account, you can save your Excel files and photos in OneDrive, a cloud-based service from Microsoft. When you save files in OneDrive, you can access them on other devices—such as a tablet or smartphone. OneDrive is available as an app on smartphones and tablets, making access simple. You can open files to view them on any device, and you can even make edits to them using **Office Online**, which includes simplified versions of the apps found in the Office 2016 suite. Because Office Online is web-based, the apps take up no computer disk space and you can use them on any Internet-connected device.

Excel 2016
Module 1

Learning
Outcomes
• Explain how a
  formula works
• Identify Excel
  arithmetic operators

Understand Formulas

Excel is a truly powerful program because users at every level of mathematical expertise can make calculations with accuracy. To do so, you use formulas. A **formula** is an equation in a worksheet. You use formulas to make calculations as simple as adding a column of numbers, or as complex as creating profit-and-loss projections for a global corporation. To tap into the power of Excel, you should understand how formulas work. **CASE** ▶ *Managers at RMC use the Health Professionals Payroll Calculator workbook to keep track of employee hours prior to submitting them to the Payroll Department. You'll be using this workbook regularly, so you need to understand the formulas it contains and how Excel calculates the results.*

1. **Click cell F11**

   The active cell contains a formula, which appears on the formula bar. All Excel formulas begin with the equal sign (=). If you want a cell to show the result of adding 4 plus 2, the formula in the cell would look like this: =4+2. If you want a cell to show the result of multiplying two values in your worksheet, such as the values in cells C11 and E11, the formula would look like this: =C11*E11, as shown in **FIGURE 1-5**. While you're entering a formula in a cell, the cell references and arithmetic operators appear on the formula bar. See **TABLE 1-2** for a list of commonly used arithmetic operators. When you're finished entering the formula, you can either click the Enter button on the formula bar or press [Enter].

2. **Click cell G11**

   This cell contains an example of a more complex formula, which calculates overtime pay. At RMC, overtime pay is calculated at twice the regular hourly rate times the number of overtime hours. The formula used to calculate overtime pay for the employee in row 5 is:

   O/T Hrs times (2 times Hrly Rate)

   In the worksheet cell, you would enter: =D11*(2*E11), as shown in **FIGURE 1-6**. The use of parentheses creates groups within the formula and indicates which calculations to complete first—an important consideration in complex formulas. In this formula, first the hourly rate is multiplied by 2, because that calculation is within the parentheses. Next, that value is multiplied by the number of overtime hours. Because overtime is calculated at twice the hourly rate, managers are aware that they need to closely watch this expense.

In creating calculations in Excel, it is important to:

- **Know where the formulas should be**

  An Excel formula is created in the cell where the formula's results should appear. This means that the formula calculating Gross Pay for the employee in row 5 will be entered in cell G5.

- **Know exactly what cells and arithmetic operations are needed**

  Don't guess; make sure you know exactly what cells are involved before creating a formula.

- **Create formulas with care**

  Make sure you know exactly what you want a formula to accomplish before it is created. An inaccurate formula may have far-reaching effects if the formula or its results are referenced by other formulas, as shown in the payroll example in **FIGURE 1-6**.

- **Use cell references rather than values**

  The beauty of Excel is that whenever you change a value in a cell, any formula containing a reference to that cell is automatically updated. For this reason, it's important that you use cell references in formulas, rather than actual values, whenever possible.

- **Determine what calculations will be needed**

  Sometimes it's difficult to predict what data will be needed within a worksheet, but you should try to anticipate what statistical information may be required. For example, if there are columns of numbers, chances are good that both column and row totals should be present.

FIGURE 1-5: Viewing a formula

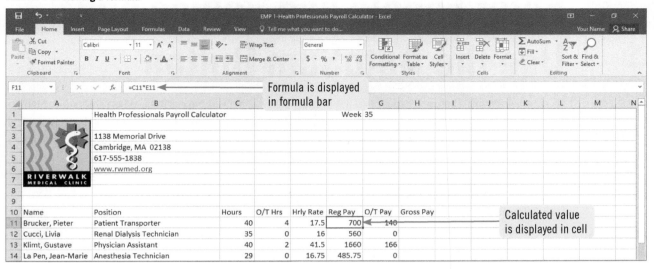

Formula is displayed in formula bar

Calculated value is displayed in cell

FIGURE 1-6: Formula with multiple operators

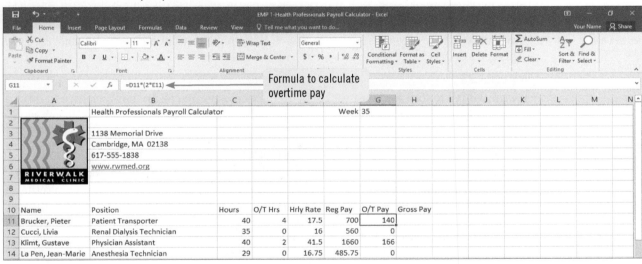

Formula to calculate overtime pay

TABLE 1-2: Excel arithmetic operators

operator	purpose	example
+	Addition	=A5+A7
-	Subtraction or negation	=A5-10
*	Multiplication	=A5*A7
/	Division	=A5/A7
%	Percent	=35%
^ (caret)	Exponent	=6^2 (same as 6^2)

Excel 2016

Enter Labels and Values and Use the AutoSum Button

Learning Outcomes
- Build formulas with the AutoSum button
- Copy formulas with the fill handle

To enter content in a cell, you can type in the formula bar or directly in the cell itself. When entering content in a worksheet, you should start by entering all the labels first. **Labels** are entries that contain text and numerical information not used in calculations, such as "2019 Sales" or "Travel Expenses". Labels help you identify data in worksheet rows and columns, making your worksheet easier to understand. **Values** are numbers, formulas, and functions that can be used in calculations. To enter a calculation, you type an equal sign (=) plus the formula for the calculation; some examples of an Excel calculation are "=2+2" and "=C5+C6". Functions are built-in formulas; you learn more about them in the next module. **CASE** *You want to enter some information in the Health Professionals Payroll Calculator workbook and use a very simple function to total a range of cells.*

STEPS

1. **Click cell A21, then click in the formula bar**

   Notice that the **mode indicator** on the status bar now reads "Edit," indicating you are in Edit mode. You are in Edit mode any time you are entering or changing the contents of a cell.

2. **Type Totals, then click the Enter button ✓ on the formula bar**

   Clicking the Enter button accepts the entry. The new text is left-aligned in the cell. Labels are left-aligned by default, and values are right-aligned by default. Excel recognizes an entry as a value if it is a number or it begins with one of these symbols: +, -, =, @, #, or $. When a cell contains both text and numbers, Excel recognizes it as a label.

3. **Click cell C21**

   You want this cell to total the hours worked by all the employees. You might think you need to create a formula that looks like this: =C11+C12+C13+C14+C15+C16+C17+C18+C19+C20. However, there's an easier way to achieve this result.

4. **Click the AutoSum button ∑ in the Editing group on the Home tab on the Ribbon**

   The SUM function is inserted in the cell, and a suggested range appears in parentheses, as shown in FIGURE 1-7. A **function** is a built-in formula; it includes the **arguments** (the information necessary to calculate an answer) as well as cell references and other unique information. Clicking the AutoSum button sums the adjacent range (that is, the cells next to the active cell) above or to the left, although you can adjust the range if necessary by selecting a different range before accepting the cell entry. Using the SUM function is quicker than entering a formula, and using the range C11:C20 is more efficient than entering individual cell references.

5. **Click ✓ on the formula bar**

   Excel calculates the total contained in cells C11:C20 and displays the result, 378, in cell C21. The cell actually contains the formula =SUM(C11:C20), and the result is displayed.

6. **Click cell D19, type 6, then press [Enter]**

   The number 6 replaces the cell's contents, the cell pointer moves to cell D20, and the value in cell G19 changes.

7. **Scroll down to cell D24, type Average Gross Pay, then press [Enter]**

   The new label is entered in cell D24. The contents appear to spill into the empty cells to the right.

8. **Click cell C21, position the pointer on the lower-right corner of the cell (the fill handle) so that the pointer changes to +, drag + to cell H21, then release the mouse button**

   Dragging the fill handle across a range of cells copies the contents of the first cell into the other cells in the range. In the range C21:H21, each filled cell now contains a function that sums the range of cells above, as shown in FIGURE 1-8.

9. **Save your work**

FIGURE 1-7: Creating a formula using the AutoSum button

FIGURE 1-7: **Creating a formula using the AutoSum button**

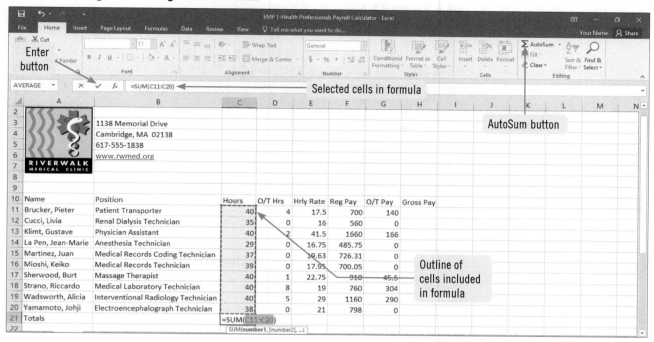

FIGURE 1-8: **Results of copied SUM functions**

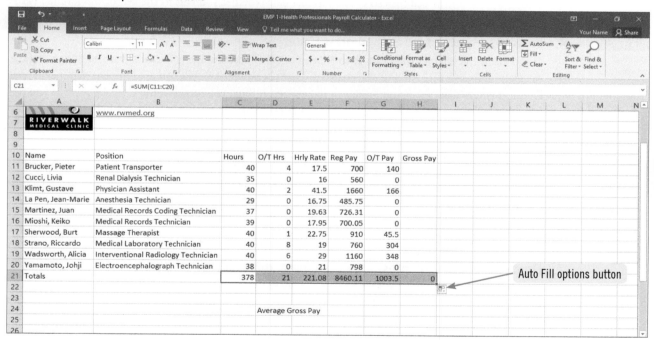

Navigating a worksheet

With over a million cells available in a worksheet, it is important to know how to move around in, or **navigate**, a worksheet. You can use the arrow keys on the keyboard ↑, ↓, →, or ← to move one cell at a time, or press [Page Up] or [Page Down] to move one screen at a time. To move one screen to the left, press [Alt][Page Up]; to move one screen to the right, press [Alt][Page Down]. You can also use the mouse pointer to click the desired cell. If the desired cell is not visible in the worksheet window, use the scroll bars or use the Go To command by clicking the Find & Select button in the Editing group on the Home tab on the Ribbon. To quickly jump to the first cell in a worksheet, press [Ctrl][Home]; to jump to the last cell, press [Ctrl][End].

Edit Cell Entries

You can change, or **edit**, the contents of an active cell at any time. To do so, double-click the cell, and then click in the formula bar or just start typing. Excel switches to Edit mode when you are making cell entries. Different pointers, shown in TABLE 1-3, guide you through the editing process. **CASE** *You noticed some errors in the worksheet and want to make corrections. The first error is in cell A11, which contains a misspelled name.*

STEPS

1. **Click cell A11, then click to the right of P in the formula bar**

   As soon as you click in the formula bar, a blinking vertical line called the **insertion point** appears on the formula bar at the location where new text will be inserted. See FIGURE 1-9. The mouse pointer changes to I when you point anywhere in the formula bar.

2. **Press [Delete], then click the Enter button ✓ on the formula bar**

   Clicking the Enter button accepts the edit, and the spelling of the employee's first name is corrected. You can also press [Enter] or [Tab] to accept an edit. Pressing [Enter] to accept an edit moves the cell pointer down one cell, and pressing [Tab] to accept an edit moves the cell pointer one cell to the right.

3. **Click cell C12, then press [F2]**

   Excel switches to Edit mode, and the insertion point blinks in the cell. Pressing [F2] activates the cell for editing directly in the cell instead of the formula bar. Whether you edit in the cell or the formula bar is simply a matter of preference; the results in the worksheet are the same.

4. **Press [Backspace], type 8, then press [Enter]**

   The value in the cell changes from 35 to 38, and cell C13 becomes the active cell. Did you notice that the calculations in cells C21 and F12 also changed? That's because those cells contain formulas that include cell C12 in their calculations. If you make a mistake when editing, you can click the Cancel button ✕ on the formula bar *before* pressing [Enter] to confirm the cell entry. The Enter and Cancel buttons appear only when you're in Edit mode. If you notice the mistake *after* you have confirmed the cell entry, click the Undo button ↶ ▾ on the Quick Access Toolbar.

5. **Click cell A15, then double-click the word Juan in the formula bar**

   Double-clicking a word in a cell selects it. When you selected the word, the Mini toolbar was automatically displayed.

6. **Type Javier, then press [Enter]**

   When text is selected, typing deletes it and replaces it with the new text.

7. **Double-click cell D18, press [Delete], type 4, then click ✓**

   Double-clicking a cell activates it for editing directly in the cell. Compare your screen to FIGURE 1-10.

8. **Save your work**

Recovering unsaved changes to a workbook file

You can use Excel's AutoRecover feature to automatically save (Autosave) your work as often as you want. This means that if you suddenly lose power or if Excel closes unexpectedly while you're working, you can recover all or some of the changes you made since you saved it last. (Of course, this is no substitute for regularly saving your work: this is just added insurance.) To customize the AutoRecover settings, click the File tab, click Options, then click

Save. AutoRecover lets you decide how often and into which location it should Autosave files. When you restart Excel after losing power, a Document Recovery pane opens and provides access to the saved and Autosaved versions of the files that were open when Excel closed. You can also click the File tab, click Open on the navigation bar, then click any file in the Recover Unsaved Workbooks list to open Autosaved workbooks.

FIGURE 1-9: Worksheet in Edit mode

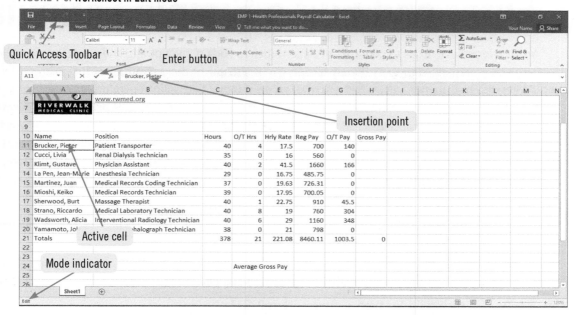

FIGURE 1-10: Edited worksheet

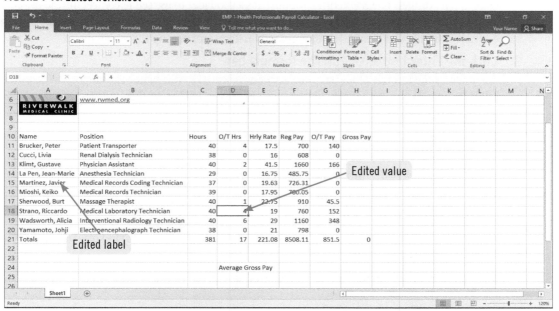

TABLE 1-3: Common pointers in Excel

name	pointer	use to	visible over the
Normal	⊕	Select a cell or range; indicates Ready mode	Active worksheet
Fill handle	+	Copy cell contents to adjacent cells	Lower-right corner of the active cell or range
I-beam	I	Edit cell contents in active cell or formula bar	Active cell in Edit mode or over the formula bar
Move	✛	Change the location of the selected cell(s)	Perimeter of the active cell(s)
Copy	▷⁺	Create a duplicate of the selected cell(s)	Perimeter of the active cell(s) when [Ctrl] is pressed
Column resize	↔	Change the width of a column	Border between column heading indicators

Enter and Edit a Simple Formula

Learning
Outcomes
• Enter a formula
• Use cell references
  to create a formula

You use formulas in Excel to perform calculations such as adding, multiplying, and averaging. Formulas in an Excel worksheet start with the equal sign (=), also called the **formula prefix**, followed by cell addresses, range names, values, and **calculation operators**. Calculation operators indicate what type of calculation you want to perform on the cells, ranges, or values. They can include **arithmetic operators**, which perform mathematical calculations (see TABLE 1-2 in the "Understand Formulas" lesson); **comparison operators**, which compare values for the purpose of true/false results; **text concatenation operators**, which join strings of text in different cells; and **reference operators**, which enable you to use ranges in calculations. **CASE** *You want to create a formula in the worksheet that calculates gross pay for each employee.*

STEPS

1. **Click cell H11**

   This is the first cell where you want to insert the formula. To calculate gross pay, you need to add regular pay and overtime pay. For employee Peter Brucker, regular pay appears in cell F11 and overtime pay appears in cell G11.

QUICK TIP
You can reference a
cell in a formula
either by typing the
cell reference or
clicking the cell in
the worksheet; when
you click a cell to add
a reference, the
Mode indicator
changes to "Point."

2. **Type =, click cell F11, type +, then click cell G11**

   Compare your formula bar to FIGURE 1-11. The blue and red cell references in cell H11 correspond to the colored cell outlines. When entering a formula, it's a good idea to use cell references instead of values whenever you can. That way, if you later change a value in a cell (if, for example, Peter's regular pay changes to 690), any formula that includes this information reflects accurate, up-to-date results.

3. **Click the Enter button ✓ on the formula bar**

   The result of the formula =F11+G11, 840, appears in cell H11. This same value appears in cell H21 because cell H21 contains a formula that totals the values in cells H11:H20, and there are no other values at this time.

4. **Click cell G11**

   The formula in this cell calculates overtime pay by multiplying overtime hours (D11) times twice the regular hourly rate (2*E11). You want to edit this formula to reflect a new overtime pay rate.

5. **Click to the right of 2 in the formula bar, then type .5 as shown in FIGURE 1-12**

   The formula that calculates overtime pay has been edited.

6. **Click ✓ on the formula bar**

   Compare your screen to FIGURE 1-13. Notice that the calculated values in cells G21, H11, and H21 have all changed to reflect your edits to cell G11.

7. **Save your work**

Understanding named ranges

It can be difficult to remember the cell locations of critical information in a worksheet, but using cell names can make this task much easier. You can name a single cell or range of contiguous, or touching, cells. For example, you might name a cell that contains data on average gross pay "AVG_GP" instead of trying to remember the cell address C18. A named range must begin with a letter or an underscore. It cannot contain any spaces or be the same as a built-in name, such as a function or another object (such as a different named range) in the workbook. To name a range, select the cell(s) you want to name, click the Name box in the formula bar, type the name you want to use, then press [Enter]. You can also name a range by clicking the Formulas tab, then clicking the Define Name button in the Defined Names group. Type the new range name in the Name text box in the New Name dialog box, verify the selected range, then click OK. When you use a named range in a formula, the named range appears instead of the cell address. You can also create a named range using the contents of a cell already in the range. Select the range containing the text you want to use as a name, then click the Create from Selection button in the Defined Names group. The Create Names from Selection dialog box opens. Choose the location of the name you want to use, then click OK.

FIGURE 1-11: **Simple formula in a worksheet**

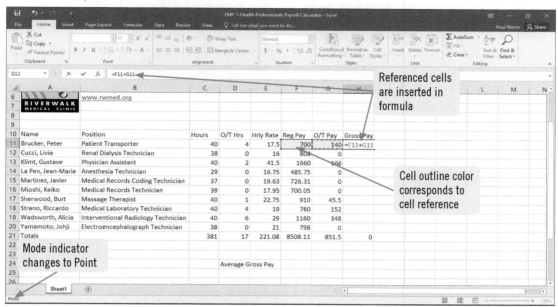

Referenced cells are inserted in formula

Cell outline color corresponds to cell reference

Mode indicator changes to Point

FIGURE 1-12: **Edited formula in a worksheet**

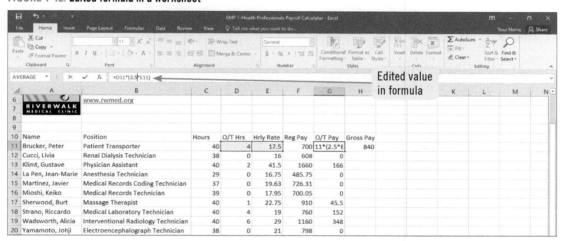

Edited value in formula

FIGURE 1-13: **Edited formula with changes**

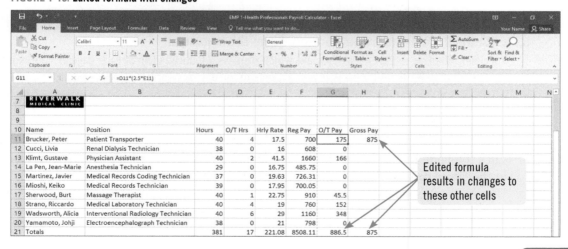

Edited formula results in changes to these other cells

Excel 2016

Switch Worksheet Views

You can change your view of the worksheet window at any time, using either the View tab on the Ribbon or the View buttons on the status bar. Changing your view does not affect the contents of a worksheet; it just makes it easier for you to focus on different tasks, such as entering content or preparing a worksheet for printing. The View tab includes a variety of viewing options, such as View buttons, zoom controls, and the ability to show or hide worksheet elements such as gridlines. The status bar offers fewer View options but can be more convenient to use. **CASE** *You want to make some final adjustments to your worksheet, including adding a header so the document looks more polished.*

STEPS

1. **Click the View tab on the Ribbon, then click the Page Layout button in the Workbook Views group**

   The view switches from the default view, Normal, to Page Layout view. **Normal view** shows the worksheet without including certain details like headers and footers, or tools like rulers and a page number indicator; it's great for creating and editing a worksheet, but may not be detailed enough when you want to put the finishing touches on a document. **Page Layout view** provides a more accurate view of how a worksheet will look when printed, as shown in **FIGURE 1-14**. The margins of the page are displayed, along with a text box for the header. A footer text box appears at the bottom of the page, but your screen may not be large enough to view it without scrolling. Above and to the left of the page are rulers. Part of an additional page appears to the right of this page. If the contents fit on a single page, the page to the right would appear dimmed, indicating that it does not contain any data. A page number indicator on the status bar tells you the current page and the total number of pages in this worksheet.

2. **Move the pointer ⓚ over the header *without clicking***

   The header is made up of three text boxes: left, center, and right. Each text box is outlined as you pass over it with the pointer.

3. **Click the left header text box, type Riverwalk Medical Clinic, click the center header text box, type Health Prof Payroll Calculator, click the right header text box, then type Week 35**

   The new text appears in the text boxes, as shown in **FIGURE 1-15**. You can also press the [Tab] key to advance from one header box to the next.

4. **Select the range B1:G1, then press [Delete]**

   The duplicate information you just entered in the header is deleted from cells in the worksheet.

5. **Click the View tab if necessary, click the Ruler check box in the Show group, then click the Gridlines check box in the Show group to deselect these options**

   The rulers and the gridlines are hidden. By default, gridlines in a worksheet do not print, so hiding them gives you a more accurate image of your final document.

6. **Click the Page Break Preview button ⊞ on the status bar**

   Your view changes to Page Break Preview, which displays a reduced view of each page of your worksheet, along with page break indicators that you can drag to include more or less information on a page.

7. **Drag the pointer ↔ from the bottom page break indicator to the right of column I**

   See **FIGURE 1-16**. When you're working on a large worksheet with multiple pages, sometimes you need to adjust where pages break; in this worksheet, however, the information all fits comfortably on one page.

8. **Click the Page Layout button in the Workbook Views group, click the Ruler check box in the Show group, then click the Gridlines check box in the Show group**

   The rulers and gridlines are no longer hidden. You can show or hide View tab items in any view.

9. **Save your work**

FIGURE 1-14: Page Layout view

Turns ruler on/off

Workbook Views group

Turns gridlines on/off

Vertical ruler

Horizontal ruler

Header text box

Additional page

Current page and total number of pages

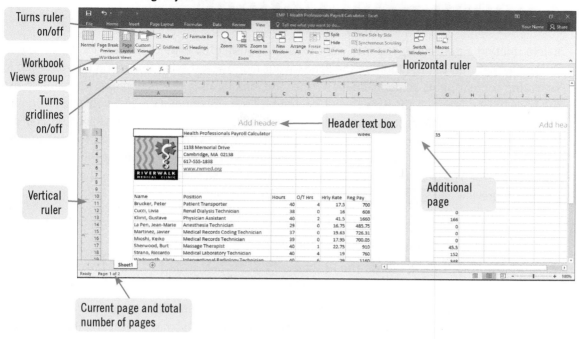

FIGURE 1-15: Header text entered

Header & Footer Tools Design tab

Header text boxes

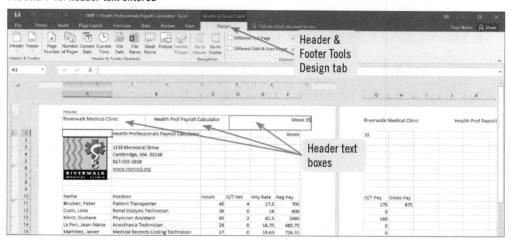

FIGURE 1-16: Page Break Preview

Blue outline indicates print area

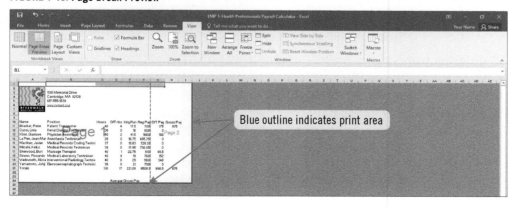

Choose Print Options

Before printing a document, you may want to review it using the Page Layout tab to fine-tune your printed output. You can use tools on the Page Layout tab to adjust print orientation (the direction in which the content prints across the page), paper size, and location of page breaks. You can also use the Scale to Fit options on the Page Layout tab to fit a large amount of data on a single page without making changes to individual margins, and to turn gridlines and column/row headings on and off. When you are ready to print, you can set print options such as the number of copies to print and the correct printer, and you can preview your document in Backstage view using the File tab. You can also adjust page layout settings from within Backstage view and immediately see the results in the document preview. **CASE** *You are ready to prepare your worksheet for printing.*

STEPS

1. **Click cell A24, type your name, then click** ✓

2. **Click the Page Layout tab on the Ribbon**
   Compare your screen to FIGURE 1-17. The solid outline indicates the default **print area**, the area to be printed.

QUICK TIP
You can use the Zoom slider on the status bar at any time to enlarge your view of specific areas of your worksheet.

3. **Click the Orientation button in the Page Setup group, then click Landscape**
   The paper orientation changes to **landscape**, so the contents will print across the length of the page instead of across the width. Notice how the margins of the worksheet adjust. You could return to the **portrait** orientation, so the contents would print across the width of the page, by clicking the Orientation button in the Page Setup group, then clicking Portrait.

4. **Click the Gridlines View check box in the Sheet Options group on the Page Layout tab, click the Gridlines Print check box to select it if necessary, then save your work**
   Printing gridlines makes the data easier to read, but the gridlines will not print unless the Gridlines Print check box is checked.

QUICK TIP
To change the active printer, click the current printer in the Printer section in Backstage view, then choose a different printer.

5. **Click the File tab, click Print on the navigation bar, then select an active printer if necessary**
   The Print tab in Backstage view displays a preview of your worksheet exactly as it will look when it is printed. To the left of the worksheet preview, you can also change a number of document settings and print options. To open the Page Setup dialog box and adjust page layout options, click the Page Setup link in the Settings section. Compare your preview screen to FIGURE 1-18. You can print from this view by clicking the Print button, or return to the worksheet without printing by clicking the Back button ⬅. You can also print an entire workbook from the Backstage view by clicking the Print button in the Settings section, then selecting the active sheet or entire workbook.

QUICK TIP
If the Quick Print button 🖨 appears on the Quick Access Toolbar, you can click it to print a worksheet using the default settings.

6. **Compare your settings to FIGURE 1-18, then click the Print button**
   One copy of the worksheet prints.

7. **Submit your work to your instructor as directed, then exit Excel**

Printing worksheet formulas

Sometimes you need to keep a record of all the formulas in a worksheet. You might want to do this to see exactly how you came up with a complex calculation, so you can explain it to others. To prepare a worksheet to show formulas rather than results when printed, open the workbook containing the formulas you want to

print. Click the Formulas tab, then click the Show Formulas button in the Formula Auditing group to select it. When the Show Formulas button is selected, formulas rather than resulting values are displayed in the worksheet on screen and when printed. (The Show Formulas button is a toggle: click it again to hide the formulas.)

FIGURE 1-17: Worksheet with Portrait orientation

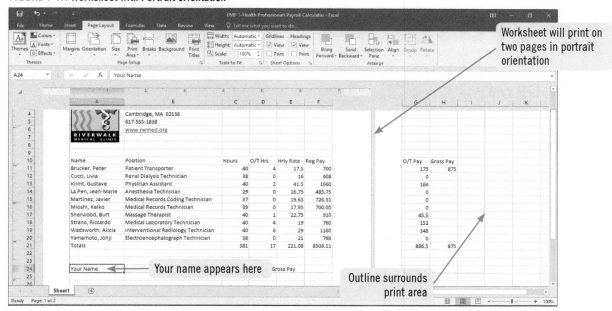

Worksheet will print on two pages in portrait orientation

Your name appears here

Outline surrounds print area

FIGURE 1-18: Worksheet in Backstage view

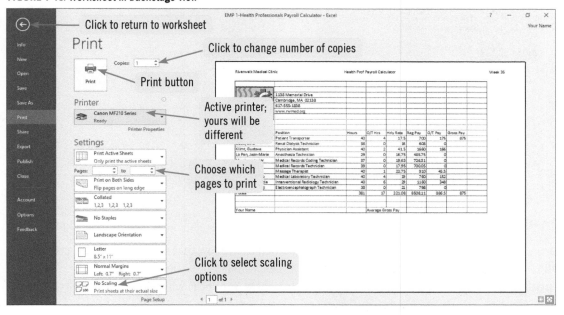

Click to return to worksheet

Click to change number of copies

Print button

Active printer; yours will be different

Choose which pages to print

Click to select scaling options

Scaling to fit

If you have a large amount of data that you want to fit to a single sheet of paper, but you don't want to spend a lot of time trying to adjust the margins and other settings, you have several options. You can easily print your work on a single sheet by clicking the No Scaling list arrow in the Settings section on the Print place in Backstage view, then clicking Fit Sheet on One Page. Another method for fitting worksheet content onto one page is to click the Page Layout tab, then change the Width and Height settings in the Scale to Fit group each to 1 page. You can also use the Fit to option in the Page Setup dialog box to fit a worksheet on one page. To open the Page Setup dialog box, click the dialog box launcher in the Scale to Fit group on the Page Layout tab, or click the Page Setup link in the Print place in Backstage view. Make sure the Page tab is selected in the Page Setup dialog box, then click the Fit to option button.

Excel 2016

Practice

Concepts Review

Label the elements of the Excel worksheet window shown in FIGURE 1-19.

FIGURE 1-19

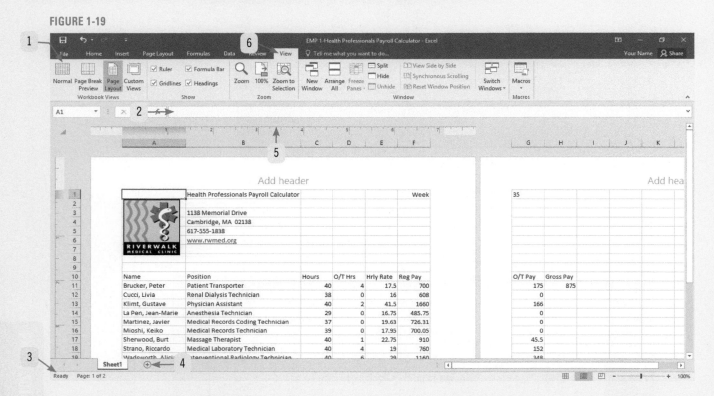

Match each term with the statement that best describes it.

7. **Name box**
8. **Workbook**
9. **Formula prefix**
10. **Orientation**
11. **Cell**
12. **Normal view**

a. Part of the Excel program window that displays the active cell address
b. Default view in Excel
c. Direction in which contents of page will print
d. Equal sign preceding a formula
e. File consisting of one or more worksheets
f. Intersection of a column and a row

Select the best answer from the list of choices.

13. Which feature could be used to print a very long worksheet on a single sheet of paper?

  a. Show Formulas

  b. Scale to Fit

  c. Page Break Preview

  d. Named Ranges

14. In which area can you see a preview of your worksheet?

  a. Page Setup

  b. Backstage view

  c. Printer Setup

  d. View tab

15. A selection of multiple cells is called a:

  a. Group.

  b. Range.

  c. Reference.

  d. Package.

16. Using a cell address in a formula is known as:

  a. Formularizing.

  b. Prefixing.

  c. Cell referencing.

  d. Cell mathematics.

17. Which worksheet view shows how your worksheet will look when printed?

  a. Page Layout

  b. Data

  c. Review

  d. View

18. Which key can you press to switch to Edit mode?

  a. [F1]

  b. [F2]

  c. [F4]

  d. [F6]

19. In which view can you see the header and footer areas of a worksheet?

  a. Normal view

  b. Page Layout view

  c. Page Break Preview

  d. Header/Footer view

20. Which view shows you a reduced view of each page of your worksheet?

  a. Normal

  b. Page Layout

  c. Thumbnail

  d. Page Break Preview

21. The maximum number of worksheets you can include in a workbook is:

  a. 3.

  b. 250.

  c. 255.

  d. Unlimited.

Skills Review

1. Understand spreadsheet software.

  a. What is the difference between a workbook and a worksheet?

  b. Identify five common business uses for electronic spreadsheets.

  c. What is what-if analysis?

2. Identify Excel 2016 window components.

  a. Start Excel.

  b. Open EMP 1-2.xlsx from the location where you store your Data Files, then save it as **EMP 1-Weather Data**.

  c. Locate the formula bar, the Sheet tabs, the mode indicator, and the cell pointer.

3. Understand formulas.

  a. What is the average high temperature of the listed cities? (*Hint*: Select the range B5:G5 and use the status bar.)

  b. What formula would you create to calculate the difference in altitude between Atlanta and Dallas? Enter your answer (as an equation) in cell D13.

Skills Review (continued)

4. Enter labels and values and use the AutoSum button.

   a. Click cell H8, then use the AutoSum button to calculate the total snowfall.

   b. Click cell H7, then use the AutoSum button to calculate the total rainfall.

   c. Save your changes to the file.

5. Edit cell entries.

   a. Use [F2] to correct the spelling of SanteFe in cell G3 (the correct spelling is Santa Fe).

   b. Click cell A17, then type your name.

   c. Save your changes.

6. Enter and edit a simple formula.

   a. Change the value 41 in cell C8 to **52**.

   b. Change the value 37 in cell D6 to **35.4**.

   c. Select cell J4, then use the fill handle to copy the formula in cell J4 to cells J5:J8.

   d. Save your changes.

7. Switch worksheet views.

   a. Click the View tab on the Ribbon, then switch to Page Layout view.

   b. Add the header **Average Annual Weather Data** to the center header text box.

   c. Add your name to the right header box.

   d. Add the multi-line header **Potential Medical Research Locations** to the left header box (press [Enter] where you want the new line to begin), as shown in FIGURE 1-20.

   e. Delete the contents of the range A1:H1 and cell A17.

   f. Save your changes.

8. Choose print options.

   a. Use the Page Layout tab to change the orientation to Portrait.

   b. Turn off gridlines by deselecting both the Gridlines View and Gridlines Print check boxes (if necessary) in the Sheet Options group.

   c. Scale the worksheet so all the information fits on one page. If necessary, scale the worksheet so all the information fits on one page. (*Hint*: Click the Width list arrow in the Scale to Fit group, click 1 page, click the Height list arrow in the Scale to Fit group, then click 1 page.) Compare your screen to FIGURE 1-20.

   d. Preview the worksheet in Backstage view, then print the worksheet.

   e. Save your changes, submit your work to your instructor as directed, then close the workbook and exit Excel.

FIGURE 1-20

	Atlanta	Boston	Dallas	Orlando	Phoenix	Santa Fe	Total		Average
Altitude	1050	20	430	91	1110	7000			1616.83
High Temp	89	69	92	82	86	70			81.3333
Low Temp	33.5	44	35.4	62	59	43			46.15
Rain (in.)	50.19	42.53	21.32	47.7	7.3	14	183.04		30.5067
Snow (in.)	0	52	6	0	0	32	90		15

Potential Medical Research Locations

Average Annual Weather Data

Your Name

Alt. Diff. ->   Atlanta & Dallas   620

Independent Challenge 1

The Human Resources division of Allied Cardiology Associates has just notified you that they hired two new physicians who will be relocating to your area. They would like you to create a workbook that contains real estate properties for their consideration. You've started a worksheet for this project that contains labels but no data.

   a. Open the file EMP 1-3.xlsx from the location where you store your Data Files, then save it as **EMP 1-Property Listings**.

   b. Enter the data shown in TABLE 1-4 in columns A, C, D, and E (the property address information should spill into column B).

TABLE 1-4

Property Address	Price	Bedrooms	Bathrooms	Area
1507 Pinon Lane	525500	4	2.5	NE
32 Zanzibar Way	325000	3	4	SE
60 Pottery Lane	475500	2	2	NE
902 Excelsior Drive	310000	4	3	NW

   c. Use Page Layout view to create a header with the following components: the title **Property Listings** in the center and your name on the right.

   d. Create formulas for totals in cells C6:E6.

   e. Save your changes, then compare your worksheet to FIGURE 1-21.

   f. Submit your work to your instructor as directed.

   g. Close the worksheet and exit Excel.

FIGURE 1-21

Independent Challenge 2

You are the general manager for Top Flight Medical Supplies, a small supplier of medical products. Although the company is just five years old, it is expanding rapidly, and you are continually looking for ways to save time. You recently began using Excel to manage and maintain data on inventory and sales, which has greatly helped you to track information accurately and efficiently.

   a. Start Excel.

   b. Save a new workbook as **EMP 1-Top Flight Medical Supplies** in the location where you store your Data Files.

   c. Switch to an appropriate view, then add a header that contains your name in the left header text box and the title **Top Flight Medical Supplies** in the center header text box.

Independent Challenge 2 (continued)

d. Using FIGURE 1-22 as a guide, create labels for at least seven medical supply manufacturers and sales for three months in Quarter 2. Include other labels as appropriate. The manufacturer should be in column A and the months should be in columns B, C, and D. A Total row should be beneath the data, and a Total column should be in column E.

FIGURE 1-22

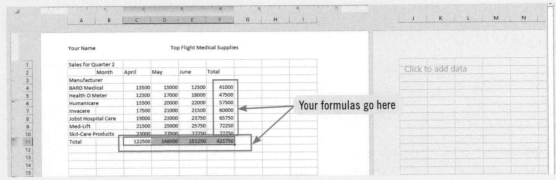

e. Enter values of your choice for the monthly sales for each manufacturer.
f. Add formulas in the Total column to calculate total quarterly sales for each manufacturer. Add formulas at the bottom of each column of values to calculate the total for that column. Remember that you can use the AutoSum button and the fill handle to save time.
g. Save your changes, preview the worksheet in Backstage view, then submit your work to your instructor as directed.
h. Close the workbook and exit Excel.

Independent Challenge 3

This Independent Challenge requires an Internet connection.

Some of the research staff at Great Plains Hospital prefer to use Fahrenheit rather than Celsius temperatures, so you think it would be helpful to create a worksheet that can be used to convert Celsius temperatures to Fahrenheit, to help employees who are unfamiliar with this type of temperature measurement.

a. Start Excel, then save a blank workbook as **EMP 1-Temperature Conversions** in the location where you store your Data Files.
b. Create column headings using FIGURE 1-23 as a guide. (*Hint*: You can widen column C by clicking cell C1, clicking the Format button in the Cells group on the Home tab, then clicking AutoFit Column Width.)

FIGURE 1-23

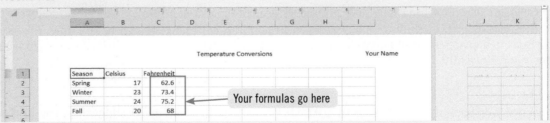

c. Create row labels for each of the seasons.
d. In the appropriate cells, enter what you determine to be a reasonable indoor temperature for each season.
e. Use your web browser to find out the conversion rate for Celsius to Fahrenheit. (*Hint*: Use your favorite search engine to search on a term such as **temperature conversion formula**.)

Independent Challenge 3 (continued)

f. In the appropriate cells, create a formula that calculates the conversion of the Celsius temperature you entered into a Fahrenheit temperature.

g. In Page Layout View, add your name and the title **Temperature Conversions** to the header.

h. Save your work, then submit your work to your instructor as directed.

i. Close the file, then exit Excel.

Independent Challenge 4: Explore

You recently started working as a bookkeeper at the Cuba Clinic, a physical therapy clinic in Cuba, New Mexico. You are setting up a sample invoice to bill patients for physical therapy services and equipment.

a. Start Excel, open the file EMP 1-4.xlsx from the location where you store your Data Files, then save it as **EMP 1-Cuba Clinic Invoice**.

b. There is an error in cell E5: please use the Help feature to find out what is wrong. If you need additional assistance, search Help on *overview of formulas*.

c. Correct the error in the formula in cell E5, then copy the corrected formula into cells E6:E7.

d. Correct the error in the formula in cell E11, then copy the corrected formula into cells E12 and E13.

e. Cells E8 and E14 also contain incorrect formulas. Cell E8 should contain a formula that calculates the total physical therapy services, and cell E14 should calculate the total equipment cost.

f. Cell F17 should contain a formula that adds the total services and total equipment.

g. Cell F18 should calculate the sales tax by multiplying the Subtotal (F17) and the sales tax (cell B18).

h. The Invoice total (cell F19) should contain a formula that adds the Subtotal (cell F17) and Sales tax (cell F18).

i. Add the following to cell A21: **Terms**, then add the following to cell B21: **Net 10**.

j. Switch to Page Layout view and make the following changes to the Header: Patient 43 (in the left header box), Cuba Clinic Invoice (in the center header box), and your name (in the right header box).

k. Delete the contents of A1:A2, switch to Normal view, then compare your worksheet to FIGURE 1-24.

l. Save your work.

FIGURE 1-24

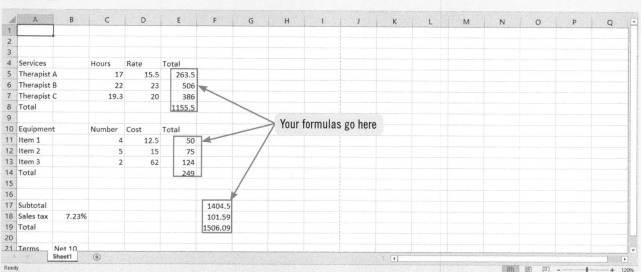

Visual Workshop

Open the file EMP 1-5.xlsx from the location where you store your Data Files, then save it as **EMP 1-Gold Coast Clinic Inventory Items**. Using the skills you learned in this module, modify your worksheet so it matches FIGURE 1-25. Enter formulas in cells D4 through D13 and in cells B14 and C14. Use the AutoSum button and fill handle to make entering your formulas easier. Add your name in the left header text box, then print one copy of the worksheet with the formulas displayed.

FIGURE 1-25

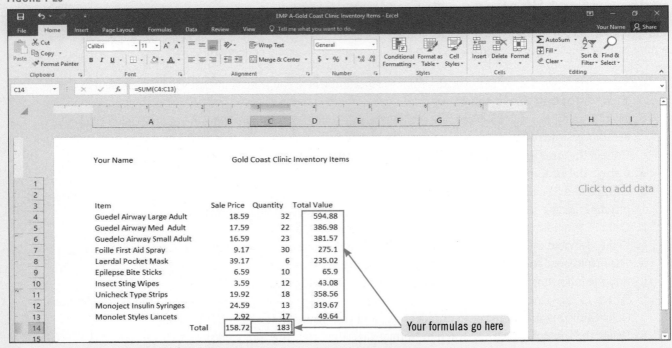

Working with Formulas and Functions

CASE Tony Sanchez, R.N., the office manager at Riverwalk Medical Clinic, needs to analyze departmental insurance reimbursements for the current year. He has asked you to prepare a worksheet that summarizes this reimbursement data and includes some statistical analysis. He would also like you to perform some what-if analysis to see what quarterly revenues would look like with various projected increases.

Module Objectives

After completing this module, you will be able to:

- Create a complex formula
- Insert a function
- Type a function
- Copy and move cell entries
- Understand relative and absolute cell references
- Copy formulas with relative cell references
- Copy formulas with absolute cell references
- Round a value with a function

Files You Will Need

EMP 2-1.xlsx   EMP 2-3.xlsx

EMP 2-2.xlsx   EMP 2-4.xlsx

Create a Complex Formula

A **complex formula** is one that uses more than one arithmetic operator. You might, for example, need to create a formula that uses addition and multiplication. In formulas containing more than one arithmetic operator, Excel uses the standard **order of precedence** rules to determine which operation to perform first. You can change the order of precedence in a formula by using parentheses around the part you want to calculate first. For example, the formula =4+2*5 equals 14, because the order of precedence dictates that multiplication is performed before addition. However, the formula =(4+2)*5 equals 30, because the parentheses cause 4+2 to be calculated first. **CASE** *You want to create a formula that calculates a 20% increase in insurance reimbursements.*

STEPS

1. **Start Excel, open the file EMP 2-1.xlsx from the location where you store your Data Files, then save it as EMP 2-Insurance Reimbursement Analysis**

2. **Select the range B9:B16, click the Quick Analysis tool 📊 that appears below the selection, then click the Totals tab**

   The Totals tab in the Quick Analysis tool displays commonly used functions, as seen in FIGURE 2-1.

3. **Click the AutoSum button 📊 in the Quick Analysis tool**

   The newly calculated value is displayed in cell B17 and has bold formatting automatically applied, helping to set it off as a sum.

4. **Click cell B17, then drag the fill handle to cell E17**

   The formula in cell B17, as well as the bold formatting, is copied to cells C17:E17.

5. **Click cell B19, type =, click cell B17, then type +**

   In this first part of the formula, you are inserting a reference to the cell that contains total insurance reimbursements for Quarter 1.

6. **Click cell B17, then type *.2**

   The second part of this formula adds a 20% increase (B17*.2) to the original value of the cell (the total insurance reimbursements for Quarter 1).

7. **Click the Enter button ✓ on the formula bar**

   The result, 428695.56, appears in cell B19.

8. **Press [Tab], type =, click cell C17, type +, click cell C17, type *.2, then click ✓**

   The result, 422048.64, appears in cell C19.

9. **Drag the fill handle from cell C19 to cell E19, then save your work**

   The calculated values appear in the selected range, as shown in FIGURE 2-2. Dragging the fill handle on a cell copies the cell's contents or continues a series of data (such as Quarter 1, Quarter 2, etc.) into adjacent cells. This feature is called **Auto Fill**.

Using Add-ins to improve worksheet functionality

Excel has more functionality than simple and complex math computations. Using the My Add-ins feature (found in the Add-ins group in the Insert tab), you can insert an add-in into your worksheet that accesses the web and adds functionality. Many of the add-ins are free or available for a small fee and can be used to create an email, appointment, meeting, contact, or task, or be a reference source, such as the Mini Calendar or Date Picker. When you click the My Add-ins button list arrow, you'll see any Recently Used Add-ins. Click See All to display the featured Add-ins for Office and to go to the Store to view available add-ins. When you find one you want, make sure you're logged in to Office.com, click the add-in, click Trust It, and the add-in will be installed. Click the My Add-ins button and your add-in should appear under Recently Used Add-ins. Click it, then click Insert. The add-in is displayed in the Recently Used Add-ins pane when you click the My Add-ins button.

FIGURE 2-1: Formula containing multiple arithmetic operators

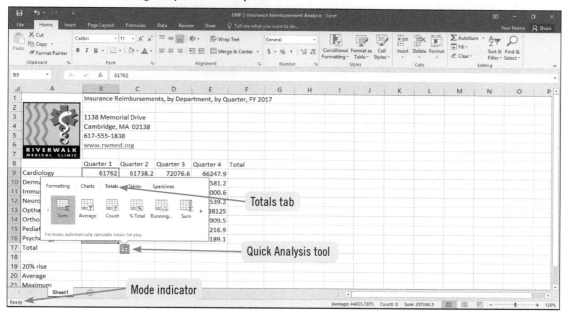

FIGURE 2-2: Complex formulas in worksheet

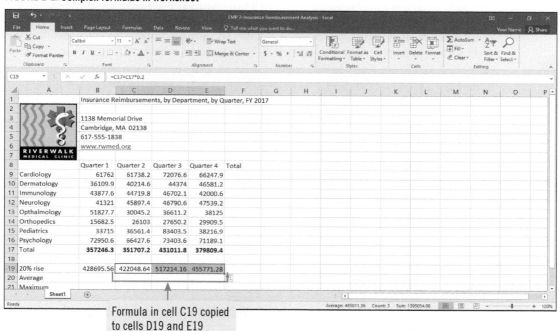

Formula in cell C19 copied to cells D19 and E19

Reviewing the order of precedence

When you work with formulas that contain more than one operator, the order of precedence is very important because it affects the final value. If a formula contains two or more operators, such as 4+.55/4000*25, Excel performs the calculations in a particular sequence based on the following rules: Operations inside parentheses are calculated before any other operations. Reference operators (such as ranges) are calculated first. Exponents are calculated next, then any multiplication and division—progressing from left to right. Finally, addition and subtraction are calculated from left to right. In the example 4+.55/4000*25, Excel performs the arithmetic operations by first dividing .55 by 4000, then multiplying the result by 25, then adding 4. You can change the order of calculations by using parentheses. For example, in the formula (4+.55)/4000*25, Excel would first add 4 and .55, then divide that amount by 4000, then finally multiply by 25.

Insert a Function

Functions are predefined worksheet formulas that enable you to perform complex calculations easily. You can use the Insert Function button on the formula bar to choose a function from a dialog box. You can quickly insert the SUM function using the AutoSum button on the Ribbon, or you can click the AutoSum list arrow to enter other frequently used functions, such as **AVERAGE**. You can also use the Quick Analysis tool to calculate commonly used functions. Functions are organized into categories, such as Financial, Date & Time, and Statistical, based on their purposes. You can insert a function on its own or as part of another formula. For example, you have used the SUM function on its own to add a range of cells. You could also use the SUM function within a formula that adds a range of cells and then multiplies the total by a decimal. If you use a function alone, it always begins with an equal sign (=) as the formula prefix. **CASE** *You need to calculate the average reimbursements for the first quarter of the year and decide to use a function to do so.*

STEPS

1. **Click cell B20**

   This is the cell where you want to enter a calculation that averages reimbursements per department for the first quarter.

2. **Click the Insert Function button 𝑓ₓ on the formula bar**

   An equal sign (=) is inserted in the active cell and in the formula bar, and the Insert Function dialog box opens, as shown in **FIGURE 2-3**. In this dialog box, you specify the function you want to use by clicking it in the Select a function list. The Select a function list initially displays recently used functions. If you don't see the function you want, you can click the Or select a category list arrow to choose the desired category. If you're not sure which category to choose, you can type the function name or a description in the Search for a function field. The AVERAGE function is a statistical function, but you don't need to open the Statistical category because this function already appears in the Most Recently Used category.

3. **Click AVERAGE in the Select a function list if necessary, read the information that appears under the list, then click OK**

   The Function Arguments dialog box opens, in which you define the range of cells you want to average.

4. **Click the Collapse button 🔲 in the Number1 field of the Function Arguments dialog box, select the range B9:B16 in the worksheet, then click the Expand button 🔲 in the Function Arguments dialog box**

   Clicking the Collapse button minimizes the dialog box so that you can select cells in the worksheet. When you click the Expand button, the dialog box is restored, as shown in **FIGURE 2-4**. You can also begin dragging in the worksheet to automatically minimize the dialog box; after you select the desired range, the dialog box is restored.

5. **Click OK**

   The Function Arguments dialog box closes, and the calculated value is displayed in cell B20. The average reimbursements per department for Quarter 1 is 44655.788.

6. **Click cell C20, click the AutoSum list arrow Σ ˙ in the Editing group on the Home tab, then click Average**

   A ScreenTip beneath cell C20 displays the arguments needed to complete the function. The text "number1" is in boldface, telling you that the next step is to supply the first cell in the group you want to average.

7. **Select the range C9:C16 in the worksheet, then click the Enter button ✓ on the formula bar**

   The average reimbursements per department for the second quarter appear in cell C20.

8. **Drag the fill handle from cell C20 to cell E20**

   The formula in cell C20 is copied to the rest of the selected range, as shown in **FIGURE 2-5**.

9. **Save your work**

FIGURE 2-3: **Insert Function dialog box**

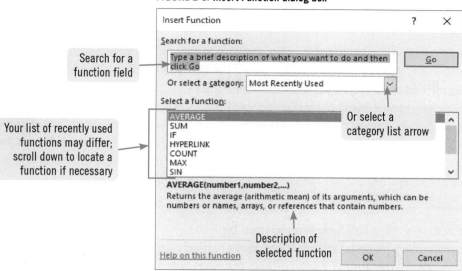

Search for a function field

Your list of recently used functions may differ; scroll down to locate a function if necessary

Or select a category list arrow

Description of selected function

FIGURE 2-4: **Expanded Function Arguments dialog box**

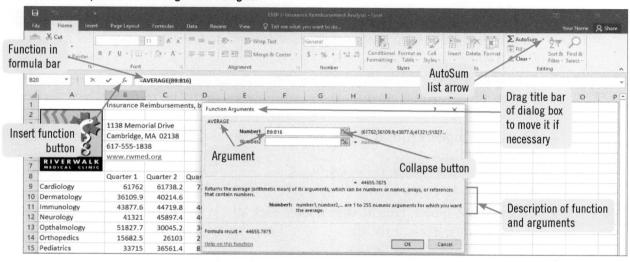

Function in formula bar

Insert function button

Argument

AutoSum list arrow

Drag title bar of dialog box to move it if necessary

Collapse button

Description of function and arguments

FIGURE 2-5: **Average functions used in worksheet**

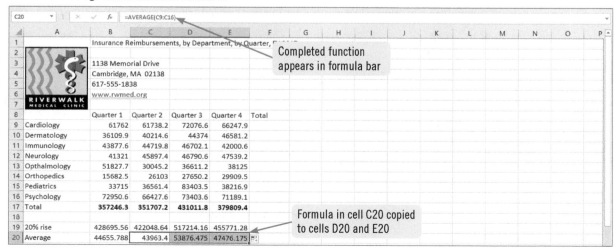

Completed function appears in formula bar

Formula in cell C20 copied to cells D20 and E20

Type a Function

Learning
Outcomes
• Copy a range to
  the Clipboard
• Paste a Clipboard
  entry
• Empty cell contents
• Copy cell contents

In addition to using the Insert Function dialog box, the AutoSum button, or the AutoSum list arrow on the Ribbon to enter a function, you can manually type the function into a cell and then complete the arguments needed. This method requires that you know the name and initial characters of the function, but it can be faster than opening several dialog boxes. Experienced Excel users often prefer this method, but it is only an alternative, not better or more correct than any other method. The Excel **Formula AutoComplete** feature makes it easier to enter function names by typing, because it suggests functions depending on the first letters you type. **CASE** *You want to calculate the maximum and minimum quarterly reimbursements in your worksheet, and you decide to manually enter these statistical functions.*

STEPS

1. **Scroll up if necessary, click cell B21, type =, then type m**

   Because you are manually typing this function, it is necessary to begin with the equal sign (=). The Formula AutoComplete feature displays a list of function names beginning with "M" beneath cell B21. Once you type an equal sign in a cell, each letter you type acts as a trigger to activate the Formula AutoComplete feature. This feature minimizes the amount of typing you need to do to enter a function and reduces typing and syntax errors.

2. **Click MAX in the list**

   Clicking any function in the Formula AutoComplete list opens a ScreenTip next to the list that describes the function.

3. **Double-click MAX**

   The function is inserted in the cell, and a ScreenTip appears beneath the cell to help you complete the formula. See **FIGURE 2-6**.

4. **Select the range B9:B16, as shown in FIGURE 2-7, then click the Enter button ✓ on the formula bar**

   The result, 72950.6, appears in cell B21. When you completed the entry, the closing parenthesis was automatically added to the formula.

5. **Click cell B22, type =, type m, then double-click MIN in the list of function names**

   The MIN function appears in the cell.

6. **Select the range B9:B16, then press [Enter]**

   The result, 15682.5, appears in cell B22.

7. **Select the range B21:B22, then drag the fill handle from cell B22 to cell E22**

   The maximum and minimum values for all of the quarters appear in the selected range, as shown in **FIGURE 2-8**.

8. **Save your work**

Using the COUNT and COUNTA functions

When you select a range, a count of cells in the range that are not blank appears in the status bar. You can use this information to determine things such as how many team members entered project hours in a worksheet. For example, if you select the range A1:A5 and only cells A1, A4, and A5 contain data, the status bar displays "Count: 3." To count nonblank cells more precisely, or to incorporate these calculations in a worksheet, you can use the COUNT and COUNTA functions. The COUNT function returns the number of cells in a range that contain numeric data, including numbers, dates, and formulas. The COUNTA function returns the number of cells in a range that contain any data at all, including numeric data, labels, and even a blank space. For example, the formula =COUNT(A1:A5) returns the number of cells in the range that contain numeric data, and the formula =COUNTA(A1:A5) returns the number of cells in the range that are not empty. If you use the COUNT functions in the Quick Analysis tool, the calculation is entered in the cell immediately beneath the selected range.

FIGURE 2-6: **MAX function in progress**

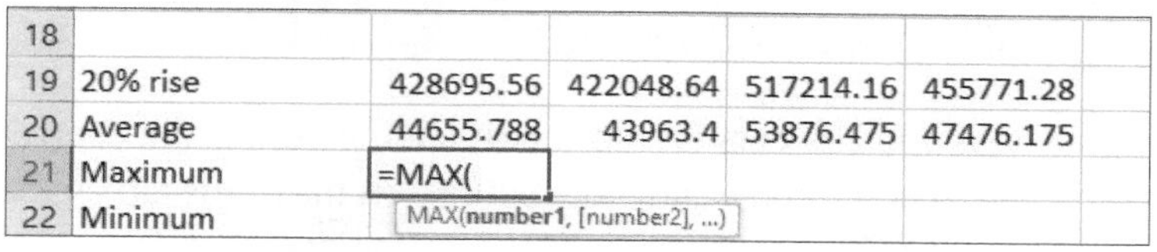

18						
19	20% rise	428695.56	422048.64	517214.16	455771.28	
20	Average	44655.788	43963.4	53876.475	47476.175	
21	Maximum	=MAX(				
22	Minimum	MAX(**number1**, [number2], ...)				

FIGURE 2-7: **Completing the MAX function**

	A	B	C	D	E	F
4	RIVERWALK MEDICAL CLINIC	Cambridge, MA 02138				
5		617-555-1838				
6		www.rwmed.org				
7						
8		Quarter 1	Quarter 2	Quarter 3	Quarter 4	Total
9	Cardiology	61762	61738.2	72076.6	66247.9	
10	Dermatology	36109.9	40214.6	44374	46581.2	
11	Immunology	43877.6	44719.8	46702.1	42000.6	
12	Neurology	41321	45897.4	46790.6	47539.2	
13	Opthalmology	51827.7	30045.2	36611.2	38125	
14	Orthopedics	15682.5	26103	27650.2	29909.5	
15	Pediatrics	33715	36561.4	83403.5	38216.9	
16	Psychology	72950.6	66427.6	73403.6	71189.1	
17	Total	**357246.3**	**351707.2**	**431011.8**	**379809.4**	
18						
19	20% rise	428695.56	422048.64	517214.16	455771.28	
20	Average	44655.788	43963.4	53876.475	47476.175	
21	Maximum	=MAX(B9:B16				

FIGURE 2-8: **Completed MAX and MIN functions**

	A	B	C	D	E	F
4	RIVERWALK MEDICAL CLINIC	Cambridge, MA 02138				
5		617-555-1838				
6		www.rwmed.org				
7						
8		Quarter 1	Quarter 2	Quarter 3	Quarter 4	Total
9	Cardiology	61762	61738.2	72076.6	66247.9	
10	Dermatology	36109.9	40214.6	44374	46581.2	
11	Immunology	43877.6	44719.8	46702.1	42000.6	
12	Neurology	41321	45897.4	46790.6	47539.2	
13	Opthalmology	51827.7	30045.2	36611.2	38125	
14	Orthopedics	15682.5	26103	27650.2	29909.5	
15	Pediatrics	33715	36561.4	83403.5	38216.9	
16	Psychology	72950.6	66427.6	73403.6	71189.1	
17	Total	**357246.3**	**351707.2**	**431011.8**	**379809.4**	
18						
19	20% rise	428695.56	422048.64	517214.16	455771.28	
20	Average	44655.788	43963.4	53876.475	47476.175	
21	Maximum	72950.6	66427.6	83403.5	71189.1	
22	Minimum	15682.5	26103	27650.2	29909.5	
23						

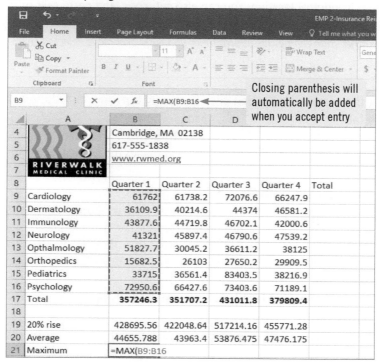

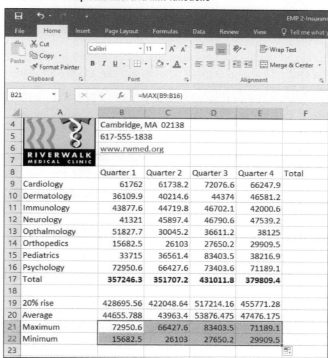

Copy and Move Cell Entries

Learning Outcomes
- Copy a range to the Clipboard
- Paste a Clipboard entry
- Empty cell contents
- Copy cell contents

There are three ways you can copy or move cells and ranges (or the contents within them) from one location to another: the Cut, Copy, and Paste buttons on the Home tab on the Ribbon; the fill handle in the lower-right corner of the active cell or range; or the drag-and-drop feature. When you copy cells, the original data remains in the original location; when you cut or move cells, the original data is deleted from its original location. You can also cut, copy, and paste cells or ranges from one worksheet to another. **CASE** *In addition to the 20% rise in insurance reimbursements, you also want to show a 30% rise. Rather than retype this information, you copy and move selected cells.*

STEPS

QUICK TIP
To cut or copy selected cell contents, activate the cell, then select the characters within the cell that you want to cut or copy.

1. **Select the range B8:E8, then click the Copy button 📋 in the Clipboard group on the Home tab**

   The selected range (B8:E8) is copied to the **Clipboard**, a temporary Windows storage area that holds the selections you copy or cut. A moving border surrounds the selected range until you press [Esc] or copy an additional item to the Clipboard.

2. **Click the launcher 🔲 in the Clipboard group**

   The Office Clipboard opens in the Clipboard task pane, as shown in FIGURE 2-9. When you copy or cut an item, it is cut or copied both to the Clipboard provided by Windows and to the Office Clipboard. Unlike the Windows Clipboard, which holds just one item at a time, the Office Clipboard contains up to 24 of the most recently cut or copied items from any Office program. Your Clipboard task pane may contain more items than shown in the figure.

QUICK TIP
Once the Office Clipboard contains 24 items, the oldest existing item is automatically deleted each time you add an item.

3. **Scroll down so row 27 is visible, click cell B25, then click the Paste button in the Clipboard group**

   A copy of the contents of range B8:E8 is pasted into the range B25:E25. When pasting an item from the Office Clipboard or Clipboard into a worksheet, you only need to specify the upper-left cell of the range where you want to paste the selection. Notice that the information you copied remains in the original range B8:E8; if you had cut instead of copied, the information would have been deleted from its original location once it was pasted.

4. **Press [Delete]**

   The selected cells are empty. You have decided to paste the cells in a different row. You can repeatedly paste an item from the Office Clipboard as many times as you like, as long as the item remains in the Office Clipboard.

QUICK TIP
You can also close the Office Clipboard pane by clicking the launcher in the Clipboard group.

5. **Click cell B24, click the first item in the Office Clipboard, then click the Close button ✖ on the Clipboard task pane**

   Cells B24:E24 contain the copied labels.

6. **Click cell A19, press and hold [Ctrl], point to any edge of the cell until the pointer changes to ⬚, drag cell A19 to cell A25, release the mouse button, then release [Ctrl]**

   The copy pointer ⬚ continues to appear as you drag, as shown in FIGURE 2-10. When you release the mouse button, the contents of cell A19 are copied to cell A25.

7. **Click to the right of 2 in the formula bar, press [Backspace], type 3, then click the Enter button ✔**

8. **Click cell B25, type =, click cell B17, type *1.3, click ✔ on the formula bar, then save your work**

   This new formula calculates a 30% increase of the expenses for Quarter 1, though using a different method from what you previously used. Anything you multiply by 1.3 returns an amount that is 130% of the original amount, or a 30% increase. Compare your screen to FIGURE 2-11.

FIGURE 2-9: Copied data in Office Clipboard

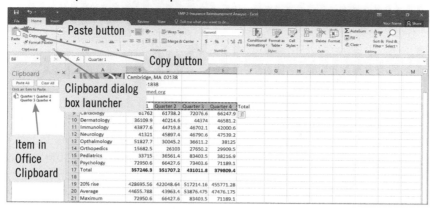

FIGURE 2-10: Copying cell contents with drag-and-drop

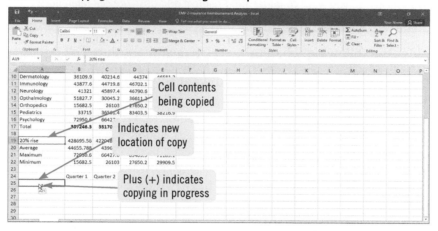

FIGURE 2-11: Formula entered to calculate a 30% increase

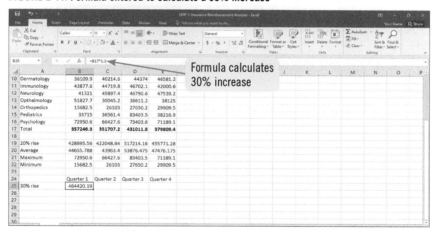

Inserting and deleting selected cells

As you add formulas to your workbook, you may need to insert or delete cells. When you do this, Excel automatically adjusts cell references to reflect their new locations. To insert cells, click the Insert list arrow in the Cells group on the Home tab, then click Insert Cells. The Insert dialog box opens, asking if you want to insert a cell and move the current active cell down or to the right of the new one. To delete one or more selected cells,

click the Delete list arrow in the Cells group, click Delete Cells, and in the Delete dialog box, indicate which way you want to move the adjacent cells. When using this option, be careful not to disturb row or column alignment that may be necessary to maintain the accuracy of cell references in the worksheet. Click the Insert button or Delete button in the Cells group to insert or delete a single cell.

Excel 2016
Module 2

Learning
Outcomes
• Identify cell
 referencing
• Identify when to
 use absolute or
 relative cell
 references

Understand Relative and Absolute Cell References

As you work in Excel, you may want to reuse formulas in different parts of a worksheet to reduce the amount of data you have to retype. For example, you might want to include a what-if analysis in one part of a worksheet showing a set of sales projections if sales increase by 10%. To include another analysis in another part of the worksheet showing projections if sales increase by 50%, you can copy the formulas from one section to another and simply change the "1" to a "5". But when you copy formulas, it is important to make sure that they refer to the correct cells. To do this, you need to understand the difference between relative and absolute cell references. **CASE** ▶ *You plan to reuse formulas in different parts of your worksheets, so you want to understand relative and absolute cell references.*

DETAILS

Consider the following when using relative and absolute cell references:

• **Use relative references when you want to preserve the relationship to the formula location**

When you create a formula that references another cell, Excel normally does not "record" the exact cell address for the cell being referenced in the formula. Instead, it looks at the relationship that cell has to the cell containing the formula. For example, in FIGURE 2-12, cell F5 contains the formula: =SUM(B5:E5). When Excel retrieves values to calculate the formula in cell F5, it actually looks for "the four cells to the left of the formula," which in this case is cells B5:E5. This way, if you copy the cell to a new location, such as cell F6, the results will reflect the new formula location and will automatically retrieve the values in cells B6, C6, D6, and E6. These are **relative cell references**, because Excel is recording the input cells *in relation to* or *relative to* the formula cell.

In most cases, you want to use relative cell references when copying or moving, so this is the Excel default. In FIGURE 2-12, the formulas in cells F5:F12 and cells B13:F13 contain relative cell references. They total the "four cells to the left of" or the "eight cells above" the formulas.

• **Use absolute cell references when you want to preserve the exact cell address in a formula**

There are times when you want Excel to retrieve formula information from a specific cell, and you don't want the cell address in the formula to change when you copy it to a new location. For example, you might have a price in a specific cell that you want to use in all formulas, regardless of their location. If you use relative cell referencing, the formula results would be incorrect, because the formula would reference a different cell every time you copy it. Therefore, you need to use an **absolute cell reference**, which is a reference that does not change when you copy the formula.

You create an absolute cell reference by placing a $ (dollar sign) in front of both the column letter and the row number of the cell address. You can either type the dollar sign when typing the cell address in a formula (for example, "=C12*B16") or you can select a cell address on the formula bar and then press [F4], and the dollar signs are added automatically. FIGURE 2-13 shows formulas containing both absolute and relative references. The formulas in cells B19 to E26 use absolute cell references to refer to a potential sales increase of 50%, shown in cell B16.

FIGURE 2-12: Formulas containing relative references

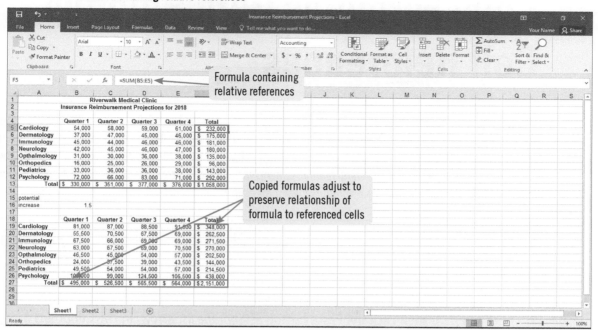

Formula containing relative references

Copied formulas adjust to preserve relationship of formula to referenced cells

FIGURE 2-13: Formulas containing absolute and relative references

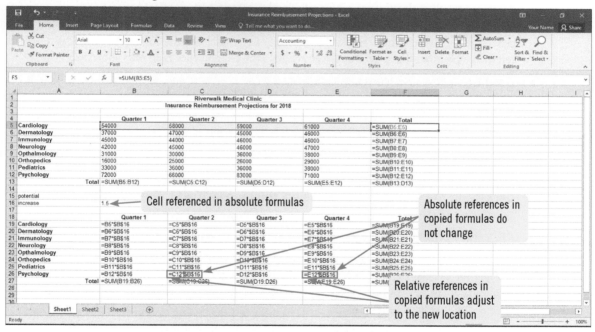

Cell referenced in absolute formulas

Absolute references in copied formulas do not change

Relative references in copied formulas adjust to the new location

Using a mixed reference

Sometimes when you copy a formula, you want to change the row reference, but keep the column reference the same. This type of cell referencing combines elements of both absolute and relative referencing and is called a **mixed reference**. For example, when copied, a formula containing the mixed reference C$14 would change the column letter relative to its new location, but not the row number. In the mixed reference $C14, the column letter would not change, but the row number would be updated relative to its location. Like an absolute reference, a mixed reference can be created by pressing the [F4] function key with the cell reference selected. With each press of the [F4] key, you cycle through all the possible combinations of relative, absolute, and mixed references (C14, C14, C$14, and $C14).

Copy Formulas with Relative Cell References

Learning Outcomes
- Copy and paste formulas with relative cell references
- Examine Auto Fill and Paste Options
- Use the Fill button

Copying and moving a cell allow you to reuse a formula you've already created. Copying cells is usually faster than retyping the formulas in them and helps to prevent typing errors. If the cells you are copying contain relative cell references and you want to maintain the relative referencing, you don't need to make any changes to the cells before copying them. **CASE** ▶ *You want to copy the formula in cell B25, which calculates the 30% increase in quarterly reimbursements for Quarter 1, to cells C25 through E25. You also want to create formulas to calculate total reimbursements for each department.*

STEPS

1. **Click cell B25 if necessary, then click the Copy button 📋 in the Clipboard group on the Home tab**

   The formula for calculating the 30% expense increase during Quarter 1 is copied to the Clipboard. Notice that the formula =B17*1.3 appears in the formula bar, and a moving border surrounds the active cell.

2. **Click cell C25, then click the Paste button 📋 *(not the list arrow)* in the Clipboard group**

   The formula from cell B25 is copied into cell C25, where the new result of 457219.36 appears. Notice in the formula bar that the cell references have changed so that cell C17 is referenced instead of B17. This formula contains a relative cell reference, which tells Excel to substitute new cell references within the copied formulas as necessary. This maintains the same relationship between the new cell containing the formula and the cell references within the formula. In this case, Excel adjusted the formula so that cell C17—the cell reference nine rows above C25—replaced cell B17, the cell reference nine rows above B25.

3. **Drag the fill handle from cell C25 to cell E25**

   A formula similar to the one in cell C25 now appears in cells D25 and E25. After you use the fill handle to copy cell contents, the **Auto Fill Options button** appears, as shown in FIGURE 2-14. You can use the Auto Fill Options button to fill the cells with only specific elements of the copied cell if you wish.

4. **Scroll up, click cell F9, click the AutoSum button Σ in the Editing group, then click the Enter button ✓ on the formula bar**

5. **Click 📋 in the Clipboard group, select the range F10:F11, then click 📋**

   See FIGURE 2-15. After you click the Paste button, the **Paste Options button** appears.

6. **Click the Paste Options button 📋 (Ctrl) ▾ adjacent to the selected range**

   You can use the Paste Options list to paste only specific elements of the copied selection if you wish. The formula for calculating total expenses for the Dermatology department appears in the formula bar. You would like totals to appear in cells F12:F16. The Fill button in the Editing group can be used to copy the formula into the remaining cells.

7. **Press [Esc] to close the Paste Options list, then select the range F11:F16**

8. **Click the Fill button 🔽 in the Editing group, then click Down**

   The formulas containing relative references are copied to each cell. Compare your worksheet to FIGURE 2-16.

9. **Save your work**

FIGURE 2-14: Formula copied using the fill handle

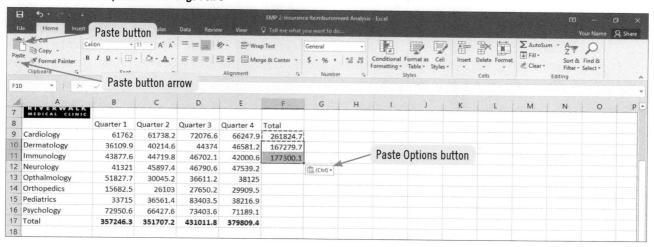

		Quarter 1	Quarter 2	Quarter 3	Quarter 4	
23						
24						Auto Fill Options button
25	30% rise	464420.19	457219.36	560315.34	493752.22	
26						

FIGURE 2-15: Formulas pasted in the range F5:F6

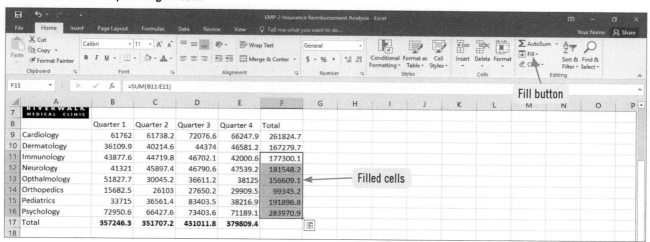

FIGURE 2-16: Formula copied using Fill Down

Using Paste Preview

You can selectively copy formulas, values, or other choices using the Paste list arrow, and you can see how the pasted contents will look using the Paste Preview feature. When you click the Paste list arrow, a gallery of paste option icons opens. When you point to an icon, a preview of how the content will be pasted using that option is shown in the worksheet. Options include pasting values only, pasting values with number formatting, pasting formulas only, pasting formatting only, pasting transposed data so that column data appears in rows and row data appears in columns, and pasting with no borders (to remove any borders around pasted cells).

Excel 2016

Copy Formulas with Absolute Cell References

Learning Outcomes
• Create an absolute cell reference
• Use the fill handle to copy absolute cell references

When copying cells, you might want one or more cell references in a formula to remain unchanged. In such an instance, you need to apply an absolute cell reference before copying the formula to preserve the specific cell address when the formula is copied. You create an absolute reference by placing a dollar sign ($) before the column letter and row number of the address (for example, A1). **CASE** ▶ *You need to do some what-if analysis to see how various percentage increases might affect total reimbursements. You decide to add a column that calculates a possible increase in the total insurance reimbursements, and then change the percentage to see various potential results.*

STEPS

1. **Press [Ctrl][Home], click cell G6, type Change, then press [Enter]**

2. **Type 1.1, then press [Enter]**
   You store the increase factor that will be used in the what-if analysis in this cell (G7). The value 1.1 can be used to calculate a 10% increase: anything you multiply by 1.1 returns an amount that is 110% of the original amount.

3. **Click cell H8, type What if?, then press [Enter]**

4. **In cell H9, type =, click cell F9, type *, click cell G7, then click the Enter button ✓ on the formula bar**
   The result, 288007, appears in cell H9. This value represents the total annual reimbursements for Cardiology if there is a 10% increase. You want to perform a what-if analysis for all the departments.

> **QUICK TIP**
> Before you copy or move a formula, always check to see if you need to use an absolute cell reference.

5. **Drag the fill handle from cell H9 to cell H16**
   The resulting values in the range H9:H16 are all zeros, which is not the result you wanted. Because you used relative cell addressing in cell H9, the copied formula adjusted so that the formula in cell H10 is =F10*G8; because there is no value in cell G8, the result is 0, an error. You need to use an absolute reference in the formula to keep the formula from adjusting itself. That way, it will always reference cell G7.

> **QUICK TIP**
> When changing a cell reference to an absolute reference, make sure the reference is selected or the insertion point is next to it in the cell before pressing [F4].

6. **Click cell H9, press [F2] to change to Edit mode, then press [F4]**
   When you press [F2], the range finder outlines the arguments of the equation in blue and red. The insertion point appears next to the G7 cell reference in cell H9. When you press [F4], dollar signs are inserted in the G7 cell reference, making it an absolute reference. See **FIGURE 2-17**.

7. **Click ✓, then drag the fill handle from cell H9 to cell H16**
   Because the formula correctly contains an absolute cell reference, the correct values for a 10% increase appear in cells H9:H16. You now want to see what a 20% increase in reimbursements looks like.

8. **Click cell G7, type 1.2, then click ✓**
   The values in the range H9:H16 change to reflect the 20% increase. Compare your worksheet to **FIGURE 2-18**.

9. **Save your work**

FIGURE 2-17: Absolute reference created in formula

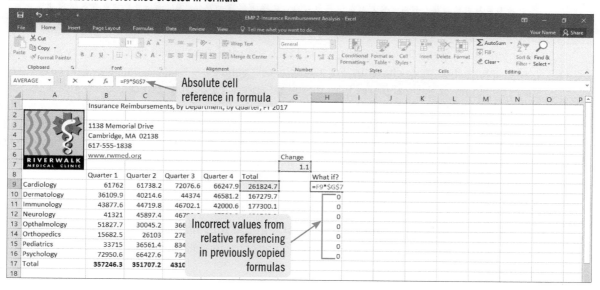

FIGURE 2-18: What-if analysis with modified change factor

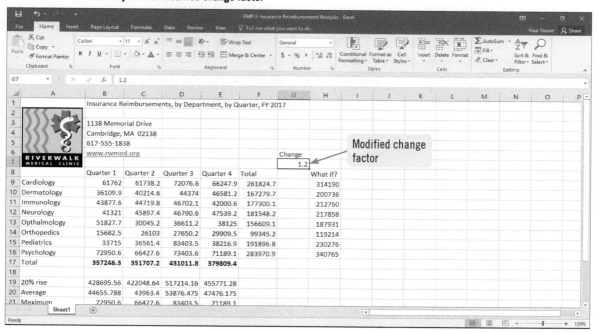

Using the fill handle for sequential text or values

Often, you need to fill cells with sequential text: months of the year, days of the week, years, or text plus a number (Quarter 1, Quarter 2,...). For example, you might want to create a worksheet that calculates data for every month of the year. Using the fill handle, you can quickly and easily create labels for the months of the year just by typing "January" in a cell. Drag the fill handle from the cell containing "January" until you have all the monthly labels you need. You can also easily fill cells with a date sequence by dragging the fill handle on a single cell containing a date. You can

fill cells with a number sequence (such as 1, 2, 3,...) by dragging the fill handle on a selection of two or more cells that contain the sequence. To create a number sequence using the value in a single cell, press and hold [Ctrl] as you drag the fill handle of the cell. As you drag the fill handle, Excel automatically extends the existing sequence into the additional cells. (The content of the last filled cell appears in the ScreenTip.) To choose from all the fill series options for the current selection, click the Fill button in the Editing group on the Home tab, then click Series to open the Series dialog box.

Round a Value with a Function

Learning Outcomes
- Use Formula AutoComplete to insert a function
- Copy an edited formula

The more you explore features and tools in Excel, the more ways you'll find to simplify your work and convey information more efficiently. For example, cells containing financial data are often easier to read if they contain fewer decimal places than those that appear by default. You can round a value or formula result to a specific number of decimal places by using the ROUND function. **CASE** *In your worksheet, you'd like to round the cells showing the 20% rise in reimbursements to show fewer digits; after all, it's not important to show cents in the projections, only whole dollars. You want Excel to round the calculated value to the nearest integer. You decide to edit cell B19 so it includes the ROUND function, and then copy the edited formula into the other formulas in this row.*

STEPS

1. **Click cell B19, then click to the right of = in the formula bar**

   You want to position the function at the beginning of the formula, before any values or arguments.

QUICK TIP

In the Insert Function dialog box, the ROUND function is in the Math & Trig category.

2. **Type RO**

   Formula AutoComplete displays a list of functions beginning with RO beneath the formula bar.

3. **Double-click ROUND in the functions list**

   The new function and an opening parenthesis are added to the formula, as shown in FIGURE 2-19. A few additional modifications are needed to complete your edit of the formula. You need to indicate the number of decimal places to which the function should round numbers, and you also need to add a closing parenthesis around the set of arguments that comes after the ROUND function.

TROUBLE

If you have too many or too few parentheses, the extraneous parenthesis is displayed in red, or a warning dialog box opens with a suggested solution to the error.

4. **Press [END], type ,0), then click the Enter button ✓ on the formula bar**

   The comma separates the arguments within the formula, and 0 indicates that you don't want any decimal places to appear in the calculated value. When you complete the edit, the parentheses at either end of the formula briefly become bold, indicating that the formula has the correct number of open and closed parentheses and is balanced.

5. **Drag the fill handle from cell B19 to cell E19**

   The formula in cell B19 is copied to the range C19:E19. All the values are rounded to display no decimal places. Compare your worksheet to FIGURE 2-20.

6. **Scroll down so row 27 is visible, click cell A27, type your name, then click ✓**

7. **Save your work, preview the worksheet in the Print place in Backstage view, then submit your work to your instructor as directed**

8. **Exit Excel**

Using Auto Fill options

When you use the fill handle to copy cells, the Auto Fill Options button appears. Auto Fill options differ depending on what you are copying. If you had selected cells containing a series (such as "Monday" and "Tuesday") and then used the fill handle, you would see options for continuing the series (such as "Wednesday" and "Thursday") or for simply pasting the copied cells. Clicking the Auto Fill Options button opens a list that lets you choose from the following options: Copy Cells, Fill Series (if applicable), Fill Formatting Only, Fill Without Formatting, or Flash Fill. Choosing Copy Cells means that the cell's contents and its formatting will be copied. The Fill Formatting Only option copies only the formatting attributes, but not cell contents. The Fill Without Formatting option copies the cell contents, but no formatting attributes. Copy Cells is the default option when using the fill handle to copy a cell, so if you want to copy the cell's contents and its formatting, you can ignore the Auto Fill Options button. The Flash Fill option allows you to create customized fill ranges on the fly, such as 2, 4, 6, 8, 10, by entering at least two values in a pattern: Excel automatically senses the pattern.

FIGURE 2-19: ROUND function added to an existing formula

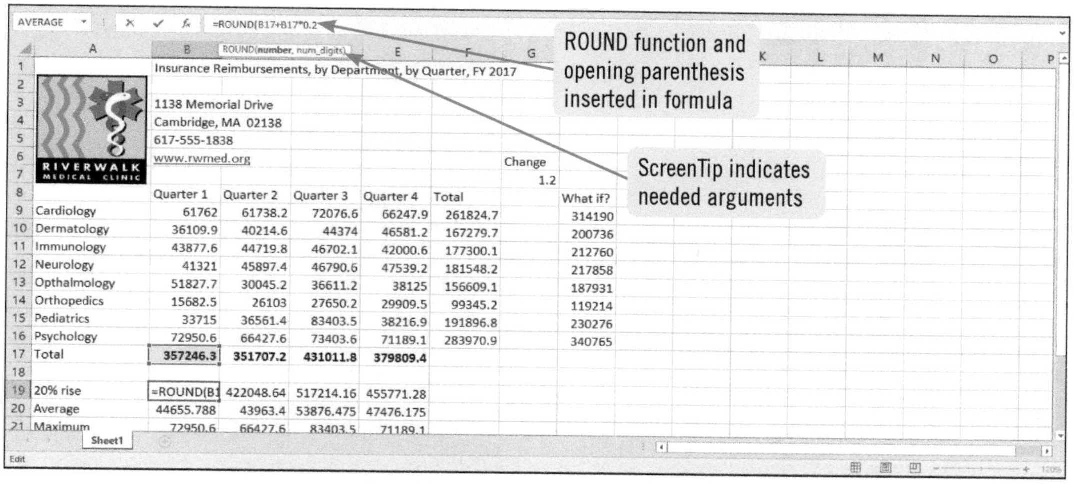

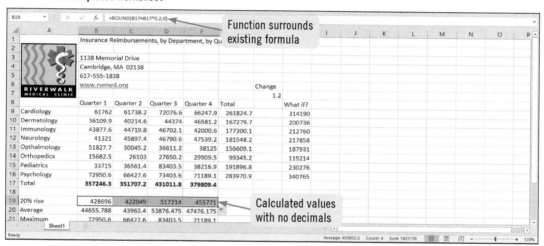

ROUND function and opening parenthesis inserted in formula

ScreenTip indicates needed arguments

FIGURE 2-20: Completed worksheet

Function surrounds existing formula

Calculated values with no decimals

Creating a new workbook using a template

Excel **templates** are predesigned workbook files intended to save time when you create common documents such as balance sheets, budgets, or time cards. Templates contain labels, values, formulas, and formatting, so all you have to do is customize them with your own information. Excel comes with many templates, and you can also create your own or find additional templates on the web. Unlike a typical workbook, which has the file extension .xlsx, a template has the extension .xltx. To create a workbook using a template, click the File tab, then click New on the navigation bar. The New place in Backstage view displays thumbnails of some of the many templates available. The Blank workbook template is selected by default and is used to create a blank workbook with no content or special formatting. To select a different template, click one of the selections in the New place, view the preview, then click Create. FIGURE 2-21 shows an example. (Your available templates may differ.) When you click

Create, a new workbook is created based on the template; when you save the new file in the default format, it has the regular .xlsx extension. To save a workbook of your own as a template, open the Save As dialog box, click the Save as type list arrow, then change the file type to Excel Template.

FIGURE 2-21: Budget Planner template selected in Backstage view

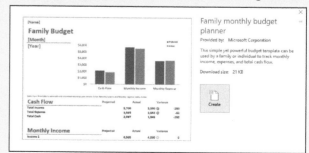

Practice

Concepts Review

Label each element of the Excel worksheet window shown in FIGURE 2-22.

FIGURE 2-22

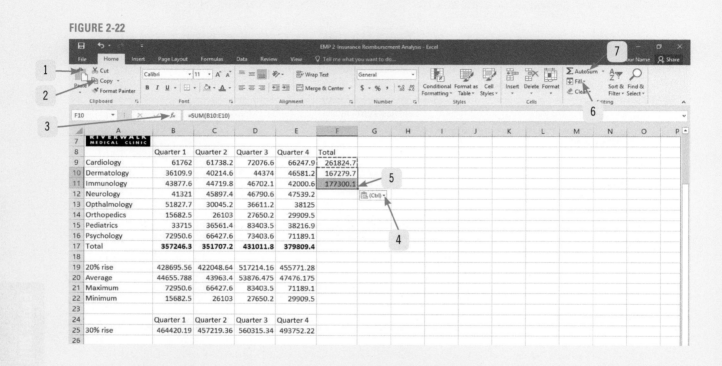

Match each term or button with the statement that best describes it.

8. Launcher
9. Fill handle
10. Drag-and-drop method
11. Formula AutoComplete
12. [Delete] key

a. Clears the contents of selected cells
b. Item on the Ribbon that opens a dialog box or task pane
c. Lets you move or copy data from one cell to another without using the Clipboard
d. Displays an alphabetical list of functions from which you can choose
e. Lets you copy cell contents or continue a series of data into a range of selected cells

Select the best answer from the list of choices.

13. You can use any of the following features to enter a new function *except*:

a. Insert Function button.

b. Formula AutoComplete.

c. AutoSum list arrow.

d. Clipboard.

14. Which key do you press and hold to copy while dragging and dropping selected cells?

a. [Alt]

b. [Ctrl]

c. [F2]

d. [Tab]

15. What type of cell reference is C$19?

a. Relative

b. Absolute

c. Mixed

d. Certain

16. Which key do you press to convert a relative cell reference to an absolute cell reference?

a. [F2]

b. [F4]

c. [F5]

d. [F6]

17. What type of cell reference changes when it is copied?

a. Circular

b. Absolute

c. Relative

d. Specified

Skills Review

1. Create a complex formula.

a. Open EMP 2-2.xlsx from the location where you store your Data Files, then save it as **EMP 2-Medical Supply Company Inventory**.

b. Select the range B4:B8, click the Totals tab in the Quick Analysis tool, then click the AutoSum button.

c. Use the fill handle to copy the formula in cell B9 to cells C9:E9.

d. In cell B11, create a complex formula that calculates a 30% decrease in the total number of cases of oxygen masks.

e. Use the fill handle to copy this formula into cell C11 through cell E11.

f. Save your work.

2. Insert a function.

a. Use the AutoSum list arrow to create a formula in cell B13 that averages the number of cases of oxygen masks in each storage area.

b. Use the Insert Function button to create a formula in cell B14 that calculates the maximum number of cases of oxygen masks in a storage area.

c. Use the AutoSum list arrow to create a formula in cell B15 that calculates the minimum number of cases of oxygen masks in a storage area.

d. Save your work.

Skills Review (continued)

3. Type a function.

    a. In cell C13, type a formula that includes a function to average the number of cases of oxygen tubes in each storage area. (*Hint*: Use Formula AutoComplete to enter the function.)

    b. In cell C14, type a formula that includes a function to calculate the maximum number of cases of oxygen tubes in a storage area.

    c. In cell C15, type a formula that includes a function to calculate the minimum number of cases of oxygen tubes in a storage area.

    d. Save your work.

4. Copy and move cell entries.

    a. Select the range B3:F3.

    b. Copy the selection to the Clipboard.

    c. Open the Clipboard task pane, then paste the selection into cell B17.

    d. Close the Clipboard task pane, then select the range A4:A9.

    e. Use the drag-and-drop method to copy the selection to cell A18. (*Hint*: The results should fill the range A18:A23.)

    f. Save your work.

5. Understand relative and absolute cell references.

    a. Write a brief description of the difference between relative and absolute references.

    b. List at least three situations in which you think a business might use an absolute reference in its calculations. Examples can include calculations for different types of worksheets, such as time cards, invoices, and budgets.

6. Copy formulas with relative cell references.

    a. Calculate the total in cell F4.

    b. Use the Fill button to copy the formula in cell F4 down to cells F5:F8.

    c. Select the range C13:C15.

    d. Use the fill handle to copy these cells to the range D13:E15.

    e. Save your work.

7. Copy formulas with absolute cell references.

    a. In cell H1, change the existing value to **1.575**.

    b. In cell H4, create a formula that multiplies F4 and an absolute reference to cell H1.

    c. Use the fill handle to copy the formula in cell H4 to cells H5 and H6.

    d. Use the Copy and Paste buttons to copy the formula in cell H4 to cells H7 and H8.

    e. Change the amount in cell H1 to **2.3**.

    f. Save your work.

Skills Review (continued)

8. **Round a value with a function.**
   a. Click cell H4.
   b. Edit this formula to include the ROUND function showing one decimal place.
   c. Use the fill handle to copy the formula in cell H4 to the range H5:H8.
   d. Enter your name in cell A25, then compare your work to FIGURE 2-23.
   e. Save your work, preview the worksheet in Backstage view, then submit your work to your instructor as directed.
   f. Close the workbook, then exit Excel.

FIGURE 2-23

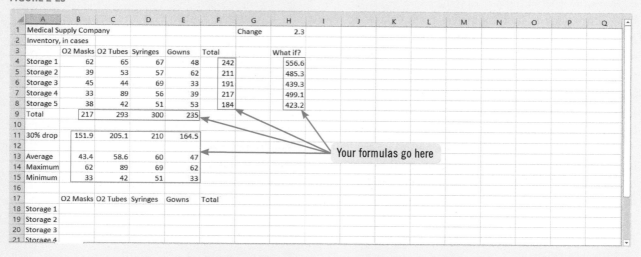

Independent Challenge 1

You keep the accounts for a local charity that wants to start a small clinic in an underserved area. Before you begin, you need to evaluate what you think your monthly expenses will be. You've started a workbook, but need to complete the entries and add formulas.

a. Open EMP 2-3.xlsx from the location where you store your Data Files, then save it as **EMP 2-Estimated Clinic Expenses**.

b. Make up your own expense data, and enter it in cells B4:B10.

c. Create a formula in cell C4 that calculates the annual rent.

d. Copy the formula in cell C4 to the range C5:C10.

e. Move the label in cell A15 to cell A14.

f. Use the Quick Analysis tool to create formulas in cells B11 and C11 that total the monthly and annual expenses.

g. Create a formula in cell C13 that calculates annual reimbursed expenses.

h. Create a formula in cell B14 that determines whether you will make a profit or loss, then copy the formula into cell C14.

i. Copy the labels in cells B3:C3 to cells E3:F3.

j. Type **Projection increase** in cell G1, then type **.2** in cell I1.

k. Create a formula in cell E4 that calculates an increase in the monthly rent by the amount in cell I1. You will be copying this formula to other cells, so you'll need to use an absolute reference.

l. Create a formula in cell F4 that calculates the increased annual rent expense based on the calculation in cell E4.

m. Copy the formulas in cells E4:F4 into cells E10:F10 to calculate the remaining monthly and annual expenses.

n. Create a formula in cell E11 that calculates the total monthly expenses, then copy that formula to cell F11.

o. Copy the contents of cells B13:C13 into cells E13:F13.

p. Create formulas in cells E14 and F14 that calculate profit/loss based on the projected increase in monthly and annual expenses.

q. Change the projected increase to **.17**, then compare your work to the sample in FIGURE 2-24.

r. Enter your name in a cell in the worksheet.

s. Save your work, preview the worksheet in Backstage view, submit your work to your instructor as directed, close the workbook, and exit Excel.

FIGURE 2-24

	A	B	C	D	E	F	G	H	I
1	Estim	Your formulas go here (your formula results will differ)					Projection increase		0.17
2									
3		Monthly	Annually		Monthly	Annually			
4	Rent	4200	50400		4914	58968			
5	Supplies	2000	24000		2340	28080			
6	Pharmacy	3000	36000		3510	42120			
7	Oxygen	1000	12000		1170	14040			
8	Coffee	600	7200		702	8424			
9	Walkers	750	9000		877.5	10530			
10	Utilities	650	7800		760.5	9126			
11	Total	12200	146400		14274	171288			
12									
13	Reimbursed	25000	300000		25000	300000			
14	Profit/Loss	12800	153600		10726	128712			

Independent Challenge 2

The Flight Nurse Training Academy is a small, growing nursing education center. They have hired you to organize their accounting records using Excel. The owners want you to track the school's expenses. Before you were hired, one of the bookkeepers began entering last year's expenses in a workbook, but the analysis was never completed.

a. Start Excel, open EMP 2-4.xlsx from the location where you store your Data Files, then save it as **EMP 2-Flight Nurse Training Academy**. The worksheet includes labels for functions such as the average, maximum, and minimum amounts of each of the expenses in the worksheet.

b. Think about what information would be important for the bookkeeping staff to know.

c. Using the Quick Analysis tool, create a formula in the Quarter 1 column that uses the SUM function, then copy that formula into the Total row for the remaining quarters.

d. Use the SUM function to create formulas for each expense and the total expenses in the Total column.

e. Create formulas for each expense and each quarter in the Average, Maximum, and Minimum columns and rows using the method of your choice.

f. Compare your worksheet to the sample shown in FIGURE 2-25.

g. Enter your name in cell A25, then save your work.

h. Preview the worksheet, then submit your work to your instructor as directed.

i. Close the workbook and exit Excel.

FIGURE 2-25

	A	B	C	D	E	F	G	H	I	J
1	Flight Nurse Training Academy									
2										
3	Operating Expenses for 2017									
4										
5	Expense	Quarter 1	Quarter 2	Quarter 3	Quarter 4	Total	Average	Maximum	Minimum	
6	Rent	11240	11240	11240	11240	44960	11240	11240	11240	
7	Utilities	9700	8982	7729	8696	35107	8776.75	9700	7729	
8	Payroll	27456	28922	26876	29915	113169	28292.3	29915	26876	
9	Insurance	9000	8594	8472	8523	34589	8647.25	9000	8472	
10	Education	3500	3581	6952	4506	18539	4634.75	6952	3500	
11	Inventory	29986	27115	25641	32465	115207	28801.8	32465	25641	
12	Total	**90882**	**88434**	**86910**	**95345**	361571				
13										
14	Average	15147	14739	14485	15890.8					
15	Maximum	29986	28922	26876	32465			Your formulas go here		
16	Minimum	3500	3581	6952	4506					

Excel 2016

Independent Challenge 3

As the accounting manager of a locally owned medical supply business with multiple locations, it is your responsibility to calculate accrued sales tax payments on a monthly basis and then submit the payments to the state government. You've decided to use an Excel workbook to make these calculations.

a. Start Excel, then save a new, blank workbook to the drive and folder where you store your Data Files as
EMP 2-Medical Supply Sales Tax Calculations.

b. Decide on the layout for all columns and rows. The worksheet will contain data for six stores, which you can name by store number, neighborhood, or another method of your choice. For each store, you will calculate total sales tax based on the local sales tax rate. You'll also calculate total tax owed for all six locations.

c. Make up sales data for all six stores.

d. Enter the rate to be used to calculate the sales tax, using your own local rate.

e. Create formulas to calculate the sales tax owed for each location. If you don't know the local tax rate, use **6.5%**.

f. Create a formula to total all the accrued sales tax.

g. Use the ROUND function to eliminate any decimal places in the sales tax figures for each location and in the total due.

h. Add your name to the header, then compare your work to the sample shown in FIGURE 2-26.

i. Save your work, preview the worksheet, and submit your work to your instructor as directed.

j. Close the workbook and exit Excel.

FIGURE 2-26

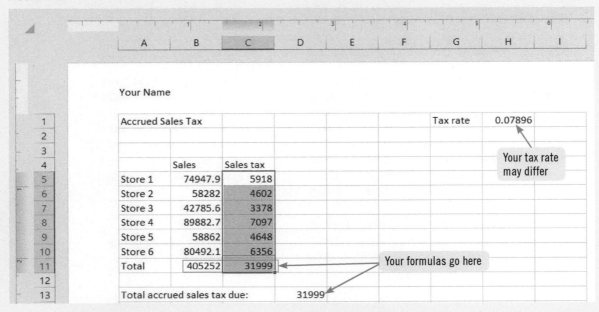

Independent Challenge 4: Explore

Since your recent promotion at work, you have started thinking about purchasing a home. As you begin looking at open houses and realtors' listings, you notice that there are many fees associated with buying a home. Some fees are based on a percentage of the purchase price, and others are a flat fee; overall, they seem to represent a substantial amount above the purchase prices you see listed. You have seen five houses so far that interest you; one is easily affordable, and the remaining four are all nice, but increasingly more expensive. You decide to create an Excel workbook to help figure out the real cost of each home.

a. Find out the typical cost or percentage rate of at least three fees that are usually charged when buying a home and taking out a mortgage. (*Hint*: If you have access to the Internet, you can research the topic of home buying on the web, or you can ask friends about standard rates or percentages for items such as title insurance, credit reports, and inspection fees.)

b. Start Excel, then save a new, blank workbook to the location where you store your Data Files as **EMP 2-Home Purchase Fees**.

c. Create labels and enter data for at least five homes. If you enter this information across the columns in your worksheet, you should have one column for each house, with the purchase price in the cell below each label. Be sure to enter a different purchase price for each house.

d. Create labels for the Fees column and for an Amount or Rate column. Enter the information for each of the fees you have researched.

e. In each house column, enter formulas that calculate the fee for each item. The formulas (and use of absolute or relative referencing) will vary depending on whether the charges are a flat fee or based on a percentage of the purchase price. Make sure that the formulas for items that are based on a percentage of the purchase price (such as the fees for the Title Insurance Policy, Loan Origination, and Underwriter) contain absolute references. A sample of what your workbook might look like is shown in FIGURE 2-27.

f. Total the fees for each house, then create formulas that add the total fees to the purchase price.

g. Enter a title for the worksheet and include your name in the header.

h. Save your work, preview the worksheet, then submit your work to your instructor as directed.

i. Close the file and exit Excel.

FIGURE 2-27

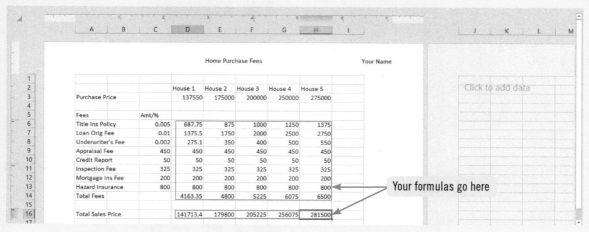

Visual Workshop

Create the worksheet shown in FIGURE 2-28 using the skills you learned in this module. Save the workbook as **EMP 2-Health Insurance Cost Analysis** to the location where you store your Data Files. Enter your name and worksheet title in the header as shown, hide the gridlines, preview the worksheet, and then submit your work to your instructor as directed. (*Hint:* Change the Zoom factor to 90% by using the Zoom out button.)

FIGURE 2-28

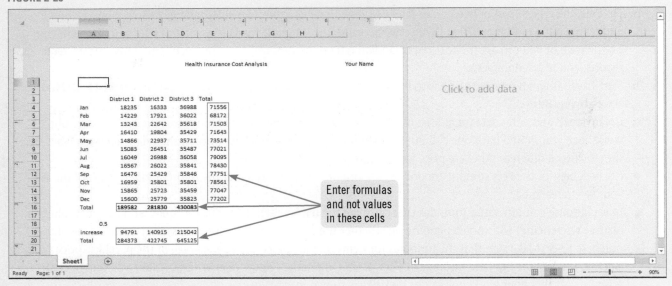

Working with Formulas and Functions

Formatting a Worksheet

CASE The administrators at Riverwalk Medical Clinic have requested data from all RMC departments for emergency room expenses incurred during the first quarter of this year. Tony Sanchez has created a worksheet listing this information. He asks you to format the worksheet to make it easier to read and to call attention to important data.

Module Objectives

After completing this module, you will be able to:

- Format values
- Change font and font size
- Change font styles and alignment
- Adjust column width
- Insert and delete rows and columns

- Apply colors, patterns, and borders
- Apply conditional formatting
- Rename and move a worksheet
- Check spelling

Files You Will Need

EMP 3-1.xlsx	EMP 3-4.xlsx
EMP 3-2.xlsx	EMP 3-5.xlsx
EMP 3-3.xlsx	

Format Values

The **format** of a cell determines how the labels and values look—for example, whether the contents appear boldfaced, italicized, or with dollar signs and commas. Formatting changes only the appearance of a value or label; it does not alter the actual data in any way. To format a cell or range, first you select it, then you apply the formatting using the Ribbon, Mini toolbar, or a keyboard shortcut. You can apply formatting before or after you enter data in a cell or range. **CASE** *Tony has provided you with a worksheet that details emergency room expenses, and you're ready to improve its appearance and readability. You start by formatting some of the values so they are displayed as currency, percentages, and dates.*

STEPS

1. **Start Excel, open the file** EMP 3-1.xlsx **from the location where you store your Data Files, then save it as** EMP 3-RMC Emergency Room Expenses

   This worksheet is difficult to interpret because all the information is crowded and looks the same. In some columns, the contents appear cut off because there is too much data to fit given the current column width. You decide not to widen the columns yet, because the other changes you plan to make might affect column width and row height. The first thing you want to do is format the data showing the cost of each expense.

2. **Select the range** D11:D39, **then click the** Accounting Number Format button $ **in the Number group on the Home tab**

   The default Accounting **number format** adds dollar signs and two decimal places to the data, as shown in FIGURE 3-1. Formatting this data in Accounting format makes it clear that its values are monetary values. Excel automatically resizes the column to display the new formatting. The Accounting and Currency number formats are both used for monetary values, but the Accounting format aligns currency symbols and decimal points of numbers in a column.

3. **Select the range** F11:H39, **then click the** Comma Style button 🔸 **in the Number group**

   The values in columns F, G, and H display the Comma Style format, which does not include a dollar sign but can be useful for some types of accounting data.

4. **Select the range** J11:J39, **click the** Number Format list arrow, **click** Percentage, **then click the** Increase Decimal button ⬆ **in the Number group**

   The data in the % of Total column is now formatted with a percent sign (%) and three decimal places. The Number Format list arrow lets you choose from popular number formats and shows an example of what the selected cell or cells would look like in each format (when multiple cells are selected, the example is based on the first cell in the range). Each time you click the Increase Decimal button, you add one decimal place; clicking the button twice would add two decimal places.

5. **Click the** Decrease Decimal button ⬇ **in the Number group** twice

   Two decimal places are removed from the percentage values in column J.

6. **Select the range** B11:B38, **then click the** launcher 🔲 **in the Number group**

   The Format Cells dialog box opens with the Date category already selected on the Number tab.

7. **Select the first** 14-Mar-12 **format in the Type list box as shown in** FIGURE 3-2, **then click** OK

   The dates in column B appear in the 14-Mar-12 format. The second 14-Mar-12 format in the list (visible if you scroll down the list) displays all days in two digits (it adds a leading zero if the day is only a single-digit number), while the one you chose displays single-digit days without a leading zero.

8. **Select the range** C11:C38, **right-click the range, click** Format Cells **on the shortcut menu, click** 14-Mar **in the Type list box in the Format Cells dialog box, then click** OK

   Compare your worksheet to FIGURE 3-3.

9. **Press** [Ctrl][Home], **then save your work**

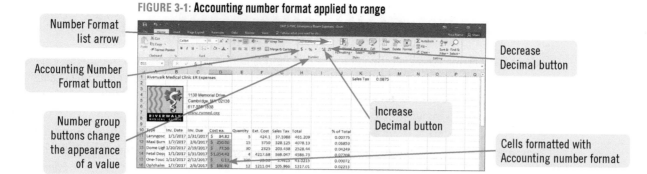

FIGURE 3-1: **Accounting number format applied to range**

Number Format list arrow

Accounting Number Format button

Number group buttons change the appearance of a value

Decrease Decimal button

Increase Decimal button

Cells formatted with Accounting number format

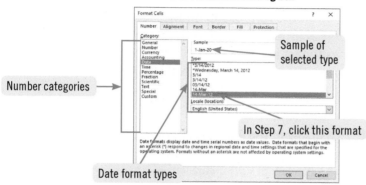

FIGURE 3-2: **Format Cells dialog box**

Number categories

Sample of selected type

In Step 7, click this format

Date format types

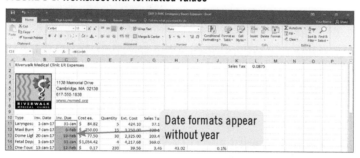

FIGURE 3-3: **Worksheet with formatted values**

Date formats appear without year

Formatting as a table

Excel includes 60 predefined **table styles** to make it easy to format selected worksheet cells as a table. You can apply table styles to any range of cells that you want to format quickly, or even to an entire worksheet, but they're especially useful for those ranges with labels in the left column and top row, and totals in the bottom row or right column. To apply a table style, select the data to be formatted or click anywhere within the intended range (Excel can automatically detect a range of cells filled with data), click the Format as Table button in the Styles group on the Home tab, then click a style in the gallery, as shown in **FIGURE 3-4**. Table styles are organized in three categories: Light, Medium, and Dark. Once you click a style, Excel asks you to confirm the range selection, then applies the style. Once you have formatted a range as a table, you can use Live Preview to preview the table in other styles by pointing to any style in the Table Styles gallery.

FIGURE 3-4: **Table Styles gallery**

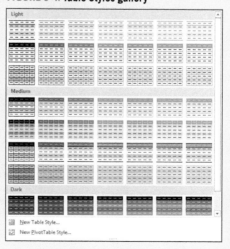

Change Font and Font Size

Learning
Outcomes
• Change a font
• Change a font size
• Use the Mini
   toolbar

A **font** is the name for a collection of characters (letters, numbers, symbols, and punctuation marks) with a similar, specific design. The **font size** is the physical size of the text, measured in units called points. A **point** is equal to 1/72 of an inch. The default font and font size in Excel is 11-point Calibri. TABLE 3-1 shows several fonts in different font sizes. You can change the font and font size of any cell or range using the Font and Font Size list arrows. The Font and Font Size list arrows appear on the Home tab on the Ribbon and on the Mini toolbar, which opens when you right-click a cell or range. **CASE** *You want to change the font and font size of the labels and the worksheet title so that they stand out more from the data.*

STEPS

1. **Click the** Font list arrow **in the Font group on the Home tab, scroll down in the Font list to see an alphabetical listing of the fonts available on your computer, then click** Times New Roman, **as shown in** FIGURE 3-5

   The font in cell A1 changes to Times New Roman. Notice that the font names on the list are displayed in the font they represent.

2. **Click the** Font Size list arrow **in the Font group, then click** 20

   The worksheet title appears in 20-point Times New Roman, and the Font and Font Size list boxes on the Home tab display the new font and font size information.

3. **Click the** Increase Font Size button **A˄ in the Font group** twice

   The font size of the title increases to 24 point.

4. **Select the range A10:J10, right-click the selection, then click the** Font list arrow **on the Mini toolbar**

   The Mini toolbar includes the most commonly used formatting tools, so it's great for making quick formatting changes.

5. **Scroll down in the Font list and click** Times New Roman, **click the** Font Size list arrow **on the Mini toolbar, then click** 14

   The Mini toolbar closes when you move the pointer away from the selection. Compare your worksheet to FIGURE 3-6. Notice that some of the column labels are now too wide to appear fully in the column. Excel does not automatically adjust column widths to accommodate cell formatting; you have to adjust column widths manually. You'll learn to do this in a later lesson.

6. **Save your work**

TABLE 3-1: Examples of fonts and font sizes

font	12 point	24 point
Calibri	Excel	Excel
Playbill	Excel	Excel
Comic Sans MS	Excel	Excel
Times New Roman	Excel	Excel

FIGURE 3-5: Font list

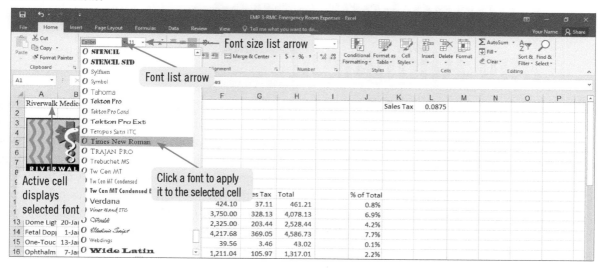

FIGURE 3-6: Worksheet with formatted title and column labels

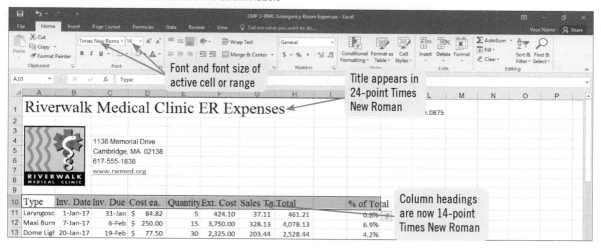

Inserting and adjusting online pictures and other images

You can illustrate your worksheets using online pictures and other images. Office.com makes many photos and animations available for your use. To add a picture to a worksheet, click the Online Pictures button in the Illustrations group on the Insert tab. The Insert Pictures window opens. Here you can search for online pictures (or Clip Art) from a variety of popular sources such as Facebook and Flickr, through the Bing search engine, or on OneDrive. To search, type one or more **keywords** (words related to your subject) in the appropriate Search text box, then press [Enter]. For example, pictures that relate to the keyword health in a search of Office.com appear in the Office.com window, as shown in **FIGURE 3-7**. When you double-click the image you want in the window, the image is inserted at the location of the active cell. To add images on your computer (or computers on your network) to a worksheet, click the Insert tab on the Ribbon, then click the Pictures button in the Illustrations group. Navigate to

the file you want, then click Insert. To resize an image, drag any corner sizing handle. To move an image, point inside the clip until the pointer changes to ✣, then drag it to a new location.

FIGURE 3-7: Results of Online Picture search

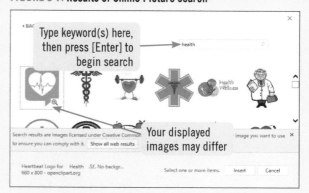

Change Font Styles and Alignment

Font styles are formats such as bold, italic, and underlining that you can apply to affect the way text and numbers look in a worksheet. You can also change the **alignment** of labels and values in cells to position them in relation to the cells' edges—such as left-aligned, right-aligned, or centered. You can apply font styles and alignment options using the Home tab, the Format Cells dialog box, or the Mini toolbar. See TABLE 3-2 for a description of common font style and alignment buttons that are available on the Home tab and the Mini toolbar. Once you have formatted a cell the way you want it, you can "paint" or copy the cell's formats into other cells by using the Format Painter button in the Clipboard group on the Home tab. This is similar to using copy and paste, but instead of copying cell contents, it copies only the cell's formatting. **CASE** *You want to further enhance the worksheet's appearance by adding bold and underline formatting and centering some of the labels.*

STEPS

1. **Press [Ctrl][Home], then click the Bold button B in the Font group on the Home tab**
   The title in cell A1 appears in bold.

2. **Click cell A10, then click the Underline button U in the Font group**
   The column label is now underlined.

3. **Click the Italic button I in the Font group, then click B**
   The heading now appears in boldface, underlined, italic type. Notice that the Bold, Italic, and Underline buttons in the Font group are all selected.

4. **Click the Italic button I to deselect it**
   The italic font style is removed from cell A10, but the bold and underline font styles remain.

5. **Click the Format Painter button 🖌 in the Clipboard group, then select the range B10:J10**
   The formatting in cell A10 is copied to the rest of the column labels. To paint the formats on more than one selection, double-click the Format Painter button to keep it activated until you turn it off. You can turn off the Format Painter by pressing [Esc] or by clicking 🖌. You decide the title would look better if it were centered over the data columns.

6. **Select the range A1:H1, then click the Merge & Center button 🔲 in the Alignment group**
   The Merge & Center button creates one cell out of the eight cells across the row, then centers the text in that newly created, merged cell. The title "Riverwalk Medical Clinic ER Expenses" is centered across the eight columns you selected. To split a merged cell into its original components, select the merged cell, then click the Merge & Center button to deselect it. Occasionally, you may find that you want cell contents to wrap within a cell. You can do this by selecting the cells containing the text you want to wrap, then clicking the Wrap Text button 🔲 in the Alignment group on the Home tab on the Ribbon.

7. **Select the range A10:J10, right-click the selection, then click the Center button ☰ on the Mini toolbar**
   Compare your screen to FIGURE 3-8. Although they may be difficult to read, notice that all the headings are centered within their cells.

8. **Save your work**

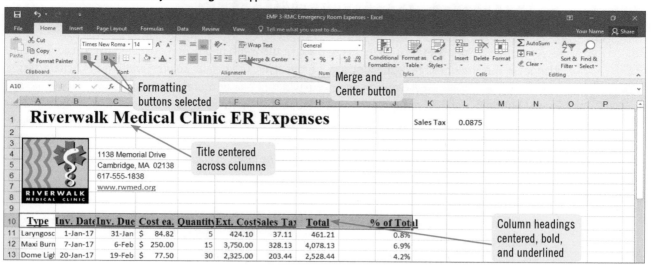

FIGURE 3-8: Worksheet with font styles and alignment applied

TABLE 3-2: Common font style and alignment buttons

button	description
B	Bolds text
I	Italicizes text
U	Underlines text
	Centers text across columns, and combines two or more selected, adjacent cells into one cell
	Aligns text at the left edge of the cell
	Centers text horizontally within the cell
	Aligns text at the right edge of the cell
	Wraps long text into multiple lines

Rotating and indenting cell entries

In addition to applying fonts and font styles, you can rotate or indent data within a cell to further change its appearance. You can rotate text within a cell by altering its alignment. Click the Home tab, select the cells you want to modify, then click the launcher in the Alignment group to open the Alignment tab of the Format Cells dialog box. Click a position in the Orientation box or type a number in the Degrees text box to rotate text from its default horizontal orientation, then click OK. You can indent cell contents using the Increase Indent button in the Alignment group, which moves cell contents to the right one space, or the Decrease Indent button , which moves cell contents to the left one space.

Adjust Column Width

As you format a worksheet, you might need to adjust the width of one or more columns to accommodate changes in the amount of text, the font size, or font style. The default column width is 8.43 characters, a little less than 1". With Excel, you can adjust the width of one or more columns by using the mouse, the Format button in the Cells group on the Home tab, or the shortcut menu. Using the mouse, you can drag or double-click the right edge of a column heading. The Format button and shortcut menu include commands for making more precise width adjustments. TABLE 3-3 describes common column formatting commands. **CASE** *You have noticed that some of the labels in columns A through J don't fit in the cells. You want to adjust the widths of the columns so that the labels appear in their entirety.*

STEPS

1. **Position the mouse pointer on the line between the column A and column B headings until it changes to ↔**

   See FIGURE 3-9. The **column heading** is the box at the top of each column containing a letter. Before you can adjust column width using the mouse, you need to position the pointer on the right edge of the column heading for the column you want to adjust. The cell entry "Monoject Syringes" is the widest in the column.

2. **Click and drag the ↔ to the right until the column displays the "Monoject Syringes" cell entries fully (approximately 16.43 characters, 1.31", or 120 pixels)**

   As you change the column width, a ScreenTip is displayed listing the column width. In Normal view, the ScreenTip lists the width in characters and pixels; in Page Layout view, the ScreenTip lists the width in inches and pixels.

3. **Position the pointer on the line between columns B and C until it changes to ↔, then double-click**

   Double-clicking the right edge of a column heading activates the **AutoFit** feature, which automatically resizes the column to accommodate the widest entry in the column. Column B automatically widens to fit the widest entry, which is the column label "Inv. Date".

4. **Use AutoFit to resize columns D and J, and resize column C so it has a width of 10 characters**

5. **Select the range E12:H12**

   You can change the width of multiple columns at once, by first selecting either the column headings or at least one cell in each column.

6. **Click the Format button in the Cells group, then click Column Width**

   The Column Width dialog box opens. Column width measurement is based on the number of characters that will fit in the column when formatted in the Normal font and font size (in this case, 11-point Calibri).

7. **Drag the dialog box by its title bar if its placement obscures your view of the worksheet, type 11 in the Column width text box, then click OK**

   The widths of columns E, F, G, and H change to reflect the new setting. See FIGURE 3-10.

8. **Save your work**

TABLE 3-3: Common column formatting commands

command	description	available using
Column Width	Sets the width to a specific number of characters	Format button; shortcut menu
AutoFit Column Width	Fits to the widest entry in a column	Format button; mouse
Hide & Unhide	Hides or displays hidden column(s)	Format button; shortcut menu
Default Width	Resets column to worksheet's default column width	Format button

FIGURE 3-9: Preparing to change the column width

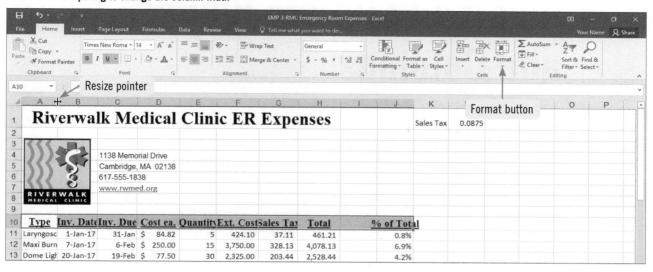

FIGURE 3-10: Worksheet with column widths adjusted

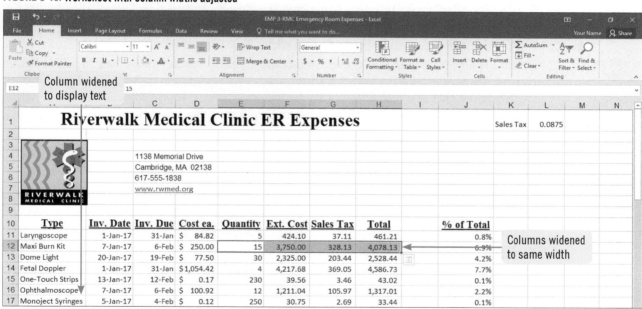

Changing row height

Changing row height is as easy as changing column width. Row height is calculated in points, the same units of measure used for fonts. The row height must exceed the size of the font you are using. Normally, you don't need to adjust row heights manually, because row heights adjust automatically to accommodate font size changes. If you format something in a row to be a larger point size, Excel adjusts the row to fit the largest point size in the row. However, you have just as many options for changing row height as you do column width. Using the mouse, you can place the ✛ pointer on the line dividing a row heading from the heading below, and then drag to the desired height; double-clicking the line AutoFits the row height where necessary. You can also select one or more rows, then use the Row Height command on the shortcut menu, or click the Format button on the Home tab and click the Row Height or AutoFit Row Height command.

Excel 2016

Insert and Delete Rows and Columns

Learning
Outcomes
• Use the Insert dialog box
• Use column and row heading buttons to insert and delete

As you modify a worksheet, you might find it necessary to insert or delete rows and columns to keep your worksheet current. For example, you might need to insert rows to accommodate new inventory products or remove a column of yearly totals that are no longer necessary. When you insert a new row, the row is inserted above the cell pointer and the contents of the worksheet shift down from the newly inserted row. When you insert a new column, the column is inserted to the left of the cell pointer and the contents of the worksheet shift to the right of the new column. To insert multiple rows, select the same number of row headings as you want to insert before using the Insert command. **CASE** *You want to improve the overall appearance of the worksheet by inserting a row between the last row of data and the totals. Also, you have learned that row 34 and column J need to be deleted from the worksheet.*

STEPS

1. Right-click cell A39, then click Insert on the shortcut menu

The Insert dialog box opens. See FIGURE 3-11. You can choose to insert a column or a row; insert a single cell and shift the cells in the active column to the right; or insert a single cell and shift the cells in the active row down. An additional row between the last row of data and the totals will visually separate the totals.

2. Click the Entire row option button, then click OK

A blank row appears between the Otoscope Set data and the totals, and the formula result in cell E40 has not changed. The Insert Options button ⬛ appears beside cell A40. Pointing to the button displays a list arrow, which you can click and then choose from the following options: Format Same As Above (the default setting, already selected), Format Same As Below, or Clear Formatting.

3. Click the row 34 heading

All of row 34 is selected, as shown in FIGURE 3-12.

4. Click the Delete button in the Cells group; *do not click the list arrow*

Excel deletes row 34, and all rows below it shift up one row. You must use the Delete button or the Delete command on the shortcut menu to delete a row or column; pressing [Delete] on the keyboard removes only the *contents* of a selected row or column.

5. Click the column J heading

The percentage information is calculated elsewhere and is no longer necessary in this worksheet.

6. Click the Delete button in the Cells group

Excel deletes column J. The remaining columns to the right shift left one column.

7. Use AutoFit to resize columns F and H, then save your work

Hiding and unhiding columns and rows

When you don't want data in a column or row to be visible, but you don't want to delete it, you can hide the column or row. To hide a selected column, click the Format button in the Cells group on the Home tab, point to Hide & Unhide, then click Hide Columns. A hidden column is indicated by a dark green vertical line in its original position. This green line disappears when you click elsewhere in the worksheet. You can display a hidden column by selecting the columns on either side of the hidden column, clicking the Format button in the Cells group, pointing to Hide & Unhide, and then clicking Unhide Columns. (To hide or unhide one or more rows, substitute Hide Rows and Unhide Rows for the Hide Columns and Unhide Columns commands.)

FIGURE 3-11: Insert dialog box

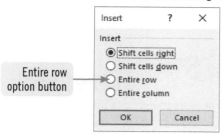

Entire row option button

FIGURE 3-12: Worksheet with row 34 selected

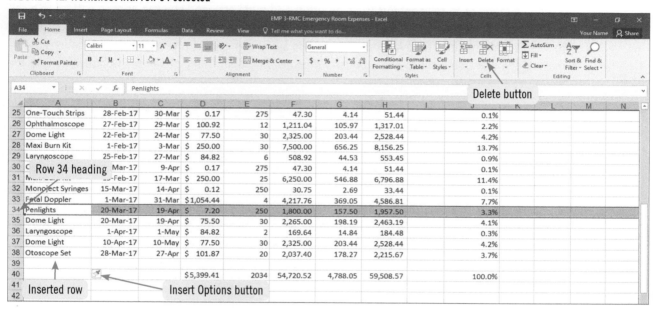

Adding and editing comments

Much of your work in Excel may be in collaboration with teammates with whom you share worksheets. You can share ideas with other worksheet users by adding comments within selected cells. To include a comment in a worksheet, click the cell where you want to place the comment, click the Review tab on the Ribbon, then click the New Comment button in the Comments group. You can type your comments in the resizable text box that opens containing the computer user's name. A small, red triangle appears in the upper-right corner of a cell containing a comment. If comments are not already displayed in a workbook, other users can point to the triangle to display the comment. To see all worksheet comments, as shown in FIGURE 3-13, click the Show All Comments button in the Comments group. To edit a comment, click the cell containing the comment, then click the Edit Comment button in the Comments

group. To delete a comment, click the cell containing the comment, then click the Delete button in the Comments group.

FIGURE 3-13: Comments displayed in a worksheet

19	Otoscope Set	12-Jan-17	11-Feb	$ 101.87	20	2,037.40
20	Laryngoscope	25-Jan-17	24-Feb	$ 72.34	6	434.04
21	Laryngoscope	1-Feb-17	3-Mar	$ 23.91	2	47.82
22	Ring Cutter	3-Feb-17	5-Mar	$ 5.67		
23	Fetal Doppler	1-Feb-17	3-Mar	$ 1,054.42		
24	Laryngoscope	1-Mar-17	31-Mar	$ 23.91		
25	One-Touch Strips	28-Feb-17	30-Mar	$ 0.17		
26	Ophthalmoscope	27-Feb-17	29-Mar	$ 100.92	12	1,211.04
27	Dome Light	22-Feb-17	24-Mar	$ 77.50	30	2,265.00
28	Maxi Burn Kit	1-Feb-17	3-Mar	$ 250.00	30	7,500.00
29	Laryngoscope	25-Feb-17	27-Mar	$ 72.34		
30	One-Touch Strips	10-Mar-17	9-Apr	$ 0.17		
31	Maxi Burn Kit	15-Mar-17	17-Mar	$ 250.00		
32	Monoject Syringes	15-Mar-17	14-Apr	$ 0.12		
33	Fetal Doppler	1-Mar-17	31-Mar	$ 1,054.44	4	4,217.76
34	Dome Light	20-Mar-17	19-Apr	$ 75.50	30	2,265.00
35	Laryngoscope	1-Apr-17	1-May	$ 23.91	2	47.82

Tony Sanchez:
These items are very costly. How can we economize?

Tony Sanchez:
We've gotten a great price on these!

Apply Colors, Patterns, and Borders

Learning Outcomes
- Use Live Preview to apply color to cells
- Format cells using the shortcut menu
- Apply a border and pattern to a cell

You can use colors, patterns, and borders to enhance the overall appearance of a worksheet and make it easier to read. You can add these enhancements by using the Borders, Font Color, and Fill Color buttons in the Font group on the Home tab of the Ribbon and on the Mini toolbar, or by using the Fill tab and the Border tab in the Format Cells dialog box. You can open the Format Cells dialog box by clicking the dialog box launcher in the Font, Alignment, or Number group on the Home tab, or by right-clicking a selection, then clicking Format Cells on the shortcut menu. You can apply a color to the background of a cell or a range or to cell contents (such as letters and numbers), and you can apply a pattern to a cell or range. You can apply borders to all the cells in a worksheet or only to selected cells to call attention to selected information. To save time, you can also apply **cell styles**, predesigned combinations of formats. **CASE** *You want to add a pattern, a border, and color to the title of the worksheet to give the worksheet a more professional appearance.*

STEPS

1. **Select cell** A1, **click the** Fill Color list arrow 🖌 **in the Font group, then hover the pointer over the** Turquoise, Accent 2 color **(first row, sixth column from the left)**

   See **FIGURE 3-14**. Live Preview shows you how the color will look *before* you apply it. (Remember that cell A1 spans columns A through H because the Merge & Center command was applied.)

2. **Click the** Turquoise, Accent 2 color

   The color is applied to the background (or fill) of this cell. When you change fill or font color, the color on the Fill Color or Font Color button changes to the last color you selected.

QUICK TIP
Use fill colors and patterns sparingly. Too many colors can be distracting or make it hard to see which information is important.

3. **Right-click cell** A1, **then click** Format Cells **on the shortcut menu**

   The Format Cells dialog box opens.

4. **Click the** Fill tab, **click the** Pattern Style list arrow, **click the** 6.25% Gray style **(first row, sixth column from the left), then click** OK

5. **Click the** Borders list arrow ⊞ **in the Font group, then click** Thick Bottom Border

   Unlike underlining, which is a text-formatting tool, borders extend to the width of the cell, and can appear at the bottom of the cell, at the top, on either side, or on any combination of the four sides. It can be difficult to see a border when the cell is selected.

QUICK TIP
You can also create custom cell borders. Click the Borders list arrow in the Font group, click More Borders, then click the individual border buttons to apply the borders you want to the selected cell(s).

6. **Select the range** A10:H10, **click the** Font Color list arrow 🅰 **in the Font group, then click the** Blue, Accent 1 color **(first Theme Colors row, fifth column from the left) on the palette**

   The new color is applied to the labels in the selected range.

7. **Select the range** J1:K1, **click the** Cell Styles button **in the Styles group, click the** Neutral cell style **(first row, fourth column from the left) in the gallery, then** AutoFit column J

   The font and color change in the range, as shown in **FIGURE 3-15**.

8. **Save your work**

Formatting a Worksheet

FIGURE 3-14: Live Preview of fill color

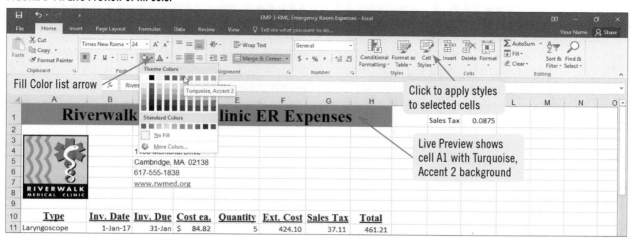

Fill Color list arrow

Click to apply styles to selected cells

Live Preview shows cell A1 with Turquoise, Accent 2 background

FIGURE 3-15: Worksheet with color, patterns, border, and style applied

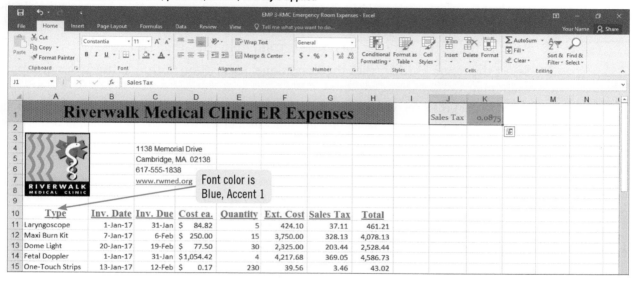

Font color is Blue, Accent 1

Working with themes and cell styles

Using themes and cell styles makes it easier to ensure that your worksheets are consistent. A **theme** is a predefined set of formats that gives your Excel worksheet a professional look. Formatting choices included in a theme are colors, fonts, and line and fill effects. To apply a theme, click the Themes button in the Themes group on the Page Layout tab to open the Themes gallery, as shown in FIGURE 3-16, then click a theme in the gallery. **Cell styles** are automatically updated if you change a theme. For example, if you apply the 20% - Accent1 cell style to cell A1 in a worksheet that has no theme applied, the fill color changes to light blue with no pattern, and the font changes to Calibri. If you change the theme of the worksheet to Ion Boardroom, cell A1's fill color changes to red and the font changes to Century Gothic, because these are the new theme's associated formats.

FIGURE 3-16: Themes gallery

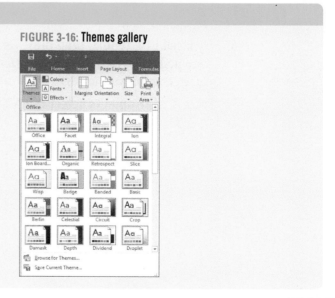

Apply Conditional Formatting

Learning Outcomes
- Create conditional formatting in a range
- Change formatting and parameters in conditional formatting

So far, you've used formatting to change the appearance of different types of data, but you can also use formatting to highlight important aspects of the data itself. For example, you can apply formatting that changes the font color to red for any cells where the value is greater than $100 and to green where the value is below $50. This is called **conditional formatting** because Excel automatically applies different formats to data if the data meets conditions you specify. The formatting is updated if you change data in the worksheet. You can also copy conditional formats the same way you copy other formats. **CASE** ▶ *Tony is concerned about emergency room expenses exceeding the yearly budget. You decide to use conditional formatting to highlight certain trends and patterns in the data so that it's easy to spot the most expensive expenses.*

STEPS

1. **Select the range H11:H37, click the Conditional Formatting button in the Styles group on the Home tab, point to Data Bars, then point to the Light Blue Data Bar (second row, second from left)**

   Data bars are colored horizontal bars that visually illustrate differences between values in a range of cells. Live Preview shows how this formatting will appear in the worksheet, as shown in FIGURE 3-17.

2. **Point to the Green Data Bar (first row, second from left), then click it**

3. **Select the range F11:F37, click the Conditional Formatting button in the Styles group, then point to Highlight Cells Rules**

   The Highlight Cells Rules submenu displays choices for creating different formatting conditions. For example, you can create a rule for values that are greater than or less than a certain amount, or between two amounts.

4. **Click Between on the submenu**

   The Between dialog box opens, displaying input boxes you can use to define the condition and a default format (Light Red Fill with Dark Red Text) selected for cells that meet that condition. Depending on the condition you select in the Highlight Cells Rules submenu (such as "Greater Than" or "Less Than"), this dialog box displays different input boxes. You define the condition using the input boxes and then assign the formatting you want to use for cells that meet that condition. Values used in input boxes for a condition can be constants, formulas, cell references, or dates.

5. **Type 2000 in the first text box, type 4000 in the second text box, click the with list arrow, click Light Red Fill, compare your settings to FIGURE 3-18, then click OK**

   All cells with values between 2000 and 4000 in column F appear with a light red fill.

6. **Click cell E14, type 3, then press [Enter]**

   When the value in cell E14 changes, the formatting also changes because the new value meets the condition you set. Compare your results to FIGURE 3-19.

7. **Press [Ctrl][Home] to select cell A1, then save your work**

FIGURE 3-17: Previewing data bars in a range

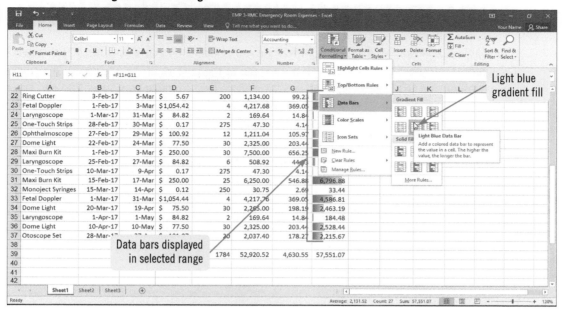

FIGURE 3-18: Between dialog box

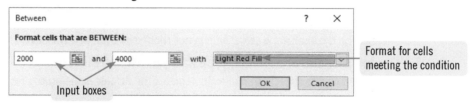

FIGURE 3-19: Worksheet with conditional formatting

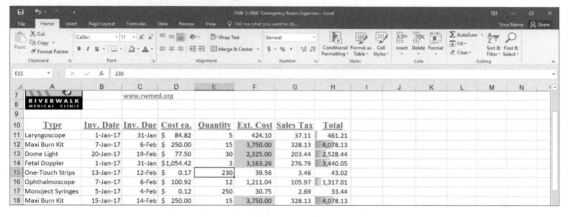

Managing conditional formatting rules

If you create a conditional formatting rule and then want to change a condition, you don't need to create a new rule; instead, you can modify the rule using the Rules Manager. Click the Conditional Formatting button in the Styles group, then click Manage Rules. The Conditional Formatting Rules Manager dialog box opens. Select the rule you want to edit, click Edit Rule, and then modify the settings in the Edit the Rule Description area in the Edit Formatting Rule dialog box. To change the formatting for a rule, click the Format Style button in the Edit the Rule Description area, select the formatting styles you want the text to have, then click OK three times to close the Format Cells dialog box, the Edit Formatting Rule dialog box, and the Conditional Formatting Rules Manager dialog box. The rule is modified, and the new conditional formatting is applied to the selected cells. To delete a rule, select the rule in the Conditional Formatting Rules Manager dialog box, then click the Delete Rule button.

Rename and Move a Worksheet

Learning Outcomes
- Rename a sheet
- Apply color to a sheet tab
- Reorder sheets in a workbook

By default, an Excel workbook initially contains one worksheet named Sheet1, although you can add sheets at any time. Each sheet name appears on a sheet tab at the bottom of the worksheet. When you open a new workbook, the first worksheet, Sheet1, is the active sheet. To move from sheet to sheet, you can click any sheet tab at the bottom of the worksheet window. The sheet tab scrolling buttons, located to the left of the sheet tabs, are useful when a workbook contains too many sheet tabs to display at once. To make it easier to identify the sheets in a workbook, you can rename each sheet and add color to the tabs. You can also organize them in a logical way. For instance, to better track performance goals, you could name each workbook sheet for an individual salesperson, and you could move the sheets so they appear in alphabetical order. **CASE** *In the current worksheet, Sheet1 contains information about actual emergency room expenses. Sheet2 contains an expenses budget, and Sheet3 contains no data. You want to rename the two sheets in the workbook to reflect their contents, add color to a sheet tab to easily distinguish one from the other, and change their order, then delete the empty sheet.*

STEPS

1. **Click the** Sheet2 tab

   Sheet2 becomes active, appearing in front of the Sheet1 tab; this is the worksheet that contains the budgeted emergency room expenses. See FIGURE 3-20.

2. **Click the** Sheet1 tab

   Sheet1, which contains the actual emergency room expenses, becomes active again.

3. **Double-click the** Sheet2 tab, **type** Budget, **then press** [Enter]

   The new name for Sheet2 automatically replaces the default name on the tab. Worksheet names can have up to 31 characters, including spaces and punctuation.

4. **Right-click the** Budget tab, **point to** Tab Color **on the shortcut menu, then click the** Bright Green, Accent 4, Lighter 40% color **(fourth row, third column from the right) as shown in** FIGURE 3-21

5. **Double-click the** Sheet1 tab, **type** Actual, **then press** [Enter]

   Notice that the color of the Budget tab changes depending on whether it is the active tab; when the Actual tab is active, the color of the Budget tab changes to the green tab color you selected. You decide to rearrange the order of the sheets so that the Budget tab is to the left of the Actual tab.

6. **Click the** Budget tab, **hold down the mouse button, drag it to the left of the** Actual tab, **as shown in** FIGURE 3-22, **then release the mouse button**

   As you drag, the pointer changes to ▨, the sheet relocation pointer, and a small, black triangle just above the tabs shows the position the moved sheet will be in when you release the mouse button. The first sheet in the workbook is now the Budget sheet. See FIGURE 3-23. You can move multiple sheets by pressing and holding [Shift] while clicking the sheets you want to move, then dragging the sheets to their new location.

7. **Click the** Actual sheet tab, **click the** Page Layout button 🔲 **on the status bar to open Page Layout view, enter your name in the left header text box, then click anywhere in the worksheet to deselect the header**

8. **Click the** Page Layout tab **on the Ribbon, click the** Orientation button **in the Page Setup group, then click** Landscape

9. **Right-click the** Sheet3 tab, **click** Delete **on the shortcut menu, press** [Ctrl][Home], **then save your work**

FIGURE 3-20: Sheet tabs in workbook

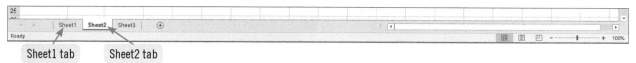

FIGURE 3-21: Tab Color palette

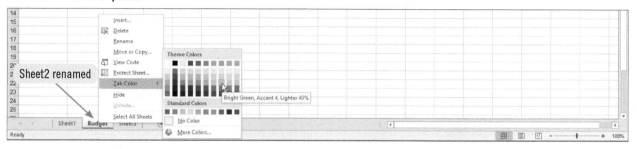

FIGURE 3-22: Moving the Budget sheet

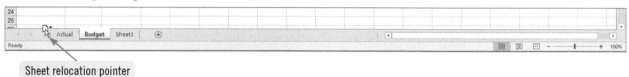

FIGURE 3-23: Reordered sheets

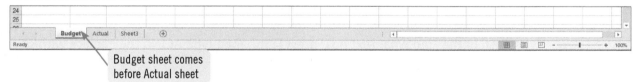

Copying, adding, and deleting worksheets

There are times when you may want to copy a worksheet. For example, a workbook might contain a sheet with Quarter 1 expenses, and you want to use that sheet as the basis for a sheet containing Quarter 2 expenses. To copy a sheet within the same workbook, press and hold [Ctrl], drag the sheet tab to the desired tab location, release the mouse button, then release [Ctrl]. A duplicate sheet appears with the same name as the copied sheet followed by "(2)" indicating that it is a copy. You can then rename the sheet to a more meaningful name. To copy a sheet to a different workbook, both the source and destination workbooks must be open. Select the sheet to copy or move, right-click the sheet tab, then click Move or Copy in the shortcut menu. Complete the information in the Move or Copy dialog box. Be sure to click the Create a copy check box if you are copying rather than moving the worksheet. Carefully check your calculation results whenever you move or copy a worksheet. You can add multiple worksheets to a workbook by clicking the Home tab on the Ribbon, pressing and holding [Shift], then clicking the number of existing worksheet tabs that correspond with the number of sheets you want to add, clicking the Insert list arrow in the Cells group on the Home tab, then clicking Insert Sheet. You can delete multiple worksheets from a workbook by clicking the Home tab, pressing and holding [Shift], clicking the sheet tabs of the worksheets you want to delete, clicking the Delete list arrow in the Cells group on the Home tab, then clicking Delete Sheet.

Check Spelling

Excel includes a spell checker to help you ensure that the words in your worksheet are spelled correctly. The spell checker scans your worksheet, displays words it doesn't find in its built-in dictionary, and suggests replacements when they are available. To check all of the sheets in a multiple-sheet workbook, you need to display each sheet individually and run the spell checker for each one. Because the built-in dictionary cannot possibly include all the words that anyone needs, you can add words to the dictionary, such as your company name, an acronym, or an unusual technical term. Once you add a word or term, the spell checker no longer considers that word misspelled. Any words you've added to the dictionary using Word, Access, or PowerPoint are also available in Excel. **CASE** ▶ *Before you distribute this workbook to Tony, you check the spelling.*

STEPS

1. **Click the Review tab on the Ribbon, then click the Spelling button in the Proofing group**

   The Spelling: English (United States) dialog box opens, as shown in FIGURE 3-24, with "Monoject" selected as the first misspelled word in the worksheet. For any word, you have the option to Ignore this case of the flagged word, Ignore All cases of the flagged word, Change the word to the selected suggestion, Change All instances of the flagged word to the selected suggestion, or add the flagged word to the dictionary using Add to Dictionary.

2. **Click Ignore All**

   Next, the spell checker finds the word "Laryngoscoope" and suggests "Laryngoscope" as an alternative.

3. **Verify that the word Laryngoscope is selected in the Suggestions list, then click Change**

   When no more incorrect words are found, Excel displays a message indicating that the spell check is complete.

4. **Click OK**

5. **Click the Home tab, click Find & Select in the Editing group, then click Replace**

   The Find and Replace dialog box opens. You can use this dialog box to replace a word or phrase. It might be a misspelling of a proper name that the spell checker didn't recognize as misspelled, or it could simply be a term that you want to change throughout the worksheet. Tony has just told you that each instance of "Maxi" in the worksheet should be changed to "ACE."

6. **Type Maxi in the Find what text box, press [Tab], then type ACE in the Replace with text box**

   Compare your dialog box to FIGURE 3-25.

7. **Click Replace All, click OK to close the Microsoft Excel dialog box, then click Close to close the Find and Replace dialog box**

   Excel has made four replacements.

8. **Click the File tab, click Print on the navigation bar, click the No Scaling setting in the Settings section on the Print tab, then click Fit Sheet on One Page**

9. **Click the Return button ⊙ to return to your worksheet, save your work, submit it to your instructor as directed, close the workbook, then exit Excel**

   The completed worksheet is shown in FIGURE 3-26.

Emailing a workbook

You can send an entire workbook from within Excel using your installed email program, such as Microsoft Outlook. To send a workbook as an email message attachment, open the workbook, click the File tab, then click Share on the navigation bar. With the Email option selected in the Share section in Backstage view, click Send as Attachment in the right pane. An email message opens in your default email program with the workbook automatically attached; the filename appears in the Attached field. Complete the To and optional Cc fields, include a message if you wish, then click Send.

FIGURE 3-24: **Spelling: English (U.S.) dialog box**

Misspelled word →

Suggested replacement for misspelled word →

Click to ignore all occurrences of misspelled word

Click to add word to dictionary

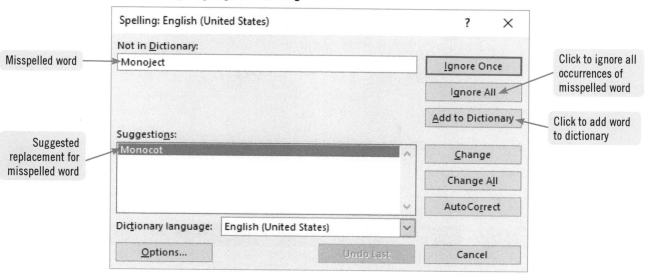

FIGURE 3-25: **Find and Replace dialog box**

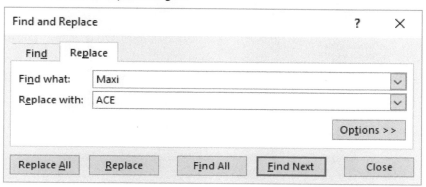

FIGURE 3-26: **Completed worksheet**

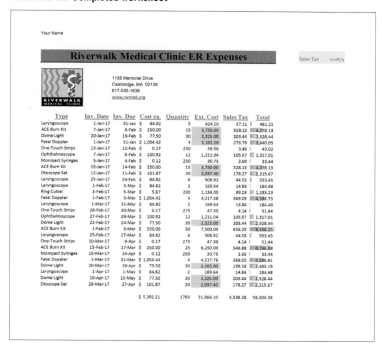

Practice

Concepts Review

Label each element of the Excel worksheet window shown in FIGURE 3-27.

FIGURE 3-27

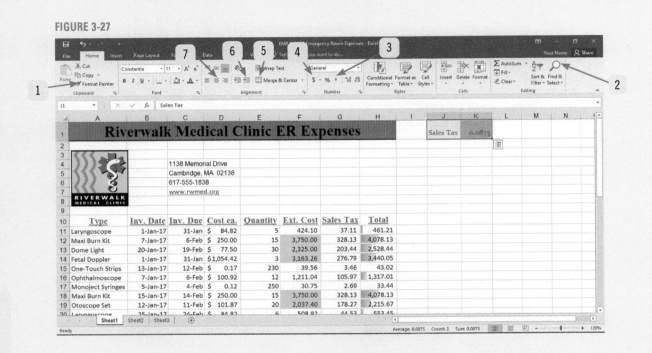

Match each command or button with the statement that best describes it.

8. **Spelling button**
9. $
10. ⬧ ▾
11. **[Ctrl][Home]**
12. ⬧
13. **Conditional formatting**

a. Checks for apparent misspellings in a worksheet
b. Adds dollar signs and two decimal places to selected data
c. Displays fill color options for a cell
d. Moves cell pointer to cell A1
e. Centers cell contents across multiple cells
f. Changes formatting of a cell that meets a certain rule

Select the best answer from the list of choices.

14. **Which of the following is an example of Accounting number format?**
    a. 5555
    b. $5,555.55
    c. 55.55%
    d. 5,555.55

15. **What is the name of the feature used to resize a column to accommodate its widest entry?**
    a. AutoFormat
    b. AutoFit
    c. AutoResize
    d. AutoRefit

16. **Which button copies multiple formats from selected cells to other cells?**
    a.
    b.
    c.
    d.

17. **Which button increases the number of decimal places in selected cells?**
    a.
    b.
    c.
    d.

18. **Which button removes the italic font style from selected cells?**
    a.
    b.
    c.
    d.

19. **What feature is used to delete a conditional formatting rule?**
    a. Rules Reminder
    b. Conditional Formatting Rules Manager
    c. Condition Manager
    d. Format Manager

Skills Review

1. **Format values.**
   a. Start Excel, open the file EMP 3-2.xlsx from the location where you store your Data Files, then save it as **EMP 3-Health Insurance Premiums**.
   b. Use the Sum function to enter a formula in cell B10 that totals the number of employees.
   c. Create a formula in cell C5 that calculates the monthly insurance premium for the accounting department. (*Hint*: Make sure you use the correct type of cell reference in the formula. To calculate the department's monthly premium, multiply the number of employees by the monthly premium in cell B14.)
   d. Copy the formula in cell C5 to the range C6:C10.
   e. Format the range C5:C10 using Accounting number format.
   f. Change the format of the range C6:C9 to the Comma Style.
   g. Reduce the number of decimals in cell B14 to 0 using a button in the Number group on the Home tab.
   h. Save your work.

2. **Change font and font sizes.**
   a. Select the range of cells containing the column labels (in row 4).
   b. Change the font of the selection to Times New Roman.
   c. Increase the font size of the selection to 12 points.
   d. Increase the font size of the label in cell A1 to 14 points.
   e. Save your changes.

3. **Change font styles and alignment.**
   a. Apply the bold and italic font styles to cell A1, then Merge & Center its contents from columns A–D.
   b. Use the Merge & Center button to center the Health Insurance Premiums label over columns A–D.
   c. Apply the italic font style to the Health Insurance Premiums label.
   d. Add the bold font style to the labels in row 4.
   e. Use the Format Painter to copy the format in cell A4 to the range A5:A10.
   f. Apply the format in cell C10 to cell B14.
   g. Change the alignment of cell A10 to Align Right using a button in the Alignment group.

Skills Review (continued)

    h. Select the range of cells containing the column labels, then center them.

    i. Remove the italic font style from the Health Insurance Premiums label, then increase the font size to 14.

    j. Move the Health Insurance Premiums label to cell A3, then add the bold and underline font styles.

    k. Save your changes.

4. Adjust column width.

    a. Resize column C to a width of 10.71 characters.

    b. Use the AutoFit feature to resize columns A and B.

    c. Clear the contents of cell A13 (do not delete the cell).

    d. Change the text in cell A14 to **Monthly Premium**, then change the width of the column to 25 characters.

    e. Save your changes.

5. Insert and delete rows and columns.

    a. Insert a new row between rows 5 and 6.

    b. Add a new department, **Donations**, in the newly inserted row. Enter **6** as the number of employees in the department.

    c. Copy the formula in cell C7 to C6.

    d. Add the following comment to cell A6: **New Department**. Display the comment, then drag to move it out of the way, if necessary.

    e. Add a new column between the Department and Employees columns with the title **Family Coverage**, then resize the column using AutoFit.

    f. Delete the Legal row from the worksheet.

    g. Move the value in cell C14 to cell B14.

    h. Save your changes.

6. Apply colors, patterns, and borders.

    a. Add Outside Borders around the range A4:D10.

    b. Add a Bottom Double Border to cells C9 and D9 (above the calculated employee and premium totals).

    c. Apply the Aqua, Accent 5, Lighter 80% fill color to the labels in the Department column (do not include the Total label).

    d. Apply the Orange, Accent 6, Lighter 60% fill color to the range A4:D4.

    e. Change the color of the font in the range A4:D4 to Red, Accent 2, Darker 25%.

    f. Add a 12.5% Gray pattern style to cell A1.

    g. Format the range A14:B14 with a fill color of Dark Blue, Text 2, Lighter 40%, change the font color to White, Background 1, then apply the bold font style.

    h. Save your changes.

7. Apply conditional formatting.

    a. Select the range D5:D9, then create a conditional format that changes cell contents to green fill with dark green text if the value is between 150 and 275.

    b. Select the range C5:C9, then create a conditional format that changes cell contents to red text if the number of employees exceeds 10.

    c. Apply a purple gradient-filled data bar to the range C5:C9. (*Hint*: Click Purple Data Bar in the Gradient Fill section.)

    d. Use the Rules Manager to modify the conditional format in cells C5:C9 to display values greater than 10 in bold dark red text.

    e. Save your changes.

8. Rename and move a worksheet.

    a. Name the Sheet1 tab **Insurance Data**.

    b. Add a sheet to the workbook, then name the new sheet **Employee Data**.

    c. Change the Insurance Data tab color to Red, Accent 2, Lighter 40%.

Skills Review (continued)

d. Change the Employee Data tab color to Aqua, Accent 5, Lighter 40%.

e. Move the Employee Data sheet so it comes before (to the left of) the Insurance Data sheet.

f. Make the Insurance Data sheet active, enter your name in cell A20, then save your work.

9. Check spelling.

a. Move the cell pointer to cell A1.

b. Use the Find & Select feature to replace the Accounting label with **Accounting/Legal**.

c. Check the spelling in the worksheet using the spell checker, and correct any spelling errors if necessary.

d. Save your changes, then compare your Insurance Data sheet to FIGURE 3-28.

e. Preview the Insurance Data sheet in Backstage view, submit your work to your instructor as directed, then close the workbook and exit Excel.

FIGURE 3-28

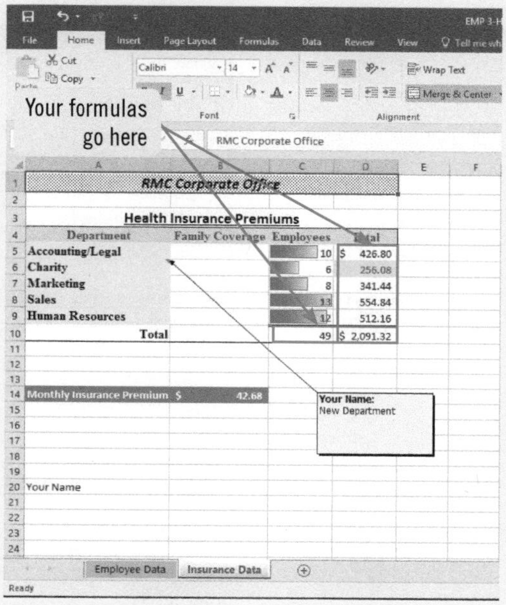

Independent Challenge 1

You run a wholesale medical supply distribution business, and one of your newest clients is Montbello, a small assisted living facility. Now that you've converted the facility's accounting records to Excel, the manager would like you to work on an analysis of the inventory. Although more items will be added later, the worksheet has enough items for you to begin your modifications.

a. Start Excel, open the file EMP 3-3.xlsx from the location where you store your Data Files, then save it as **EMP 3-Medical Supply Inventory**.

b. Create a formula in cell E4 that calculates the value of the items in stock based on the price paid per item in cell B4. Format the cell in the Comma Style.

c. In cell F4, calculate the sale value of the items in stock using an absolute reference to the markup value shown in cell I1.

d. Copy the formulas created above into the range E5:F14; first convert any necessary cell references to absolute so that the formulas work correctly.

e. Apply bold to the column labels, and italicize the inventory items in column A.

f. Make sure that all columns are wide enough to display the data and labels.

g. Format the values in the Sale Value column as Accounting number format with two decimal places.

h. Format the values in the Price Paid column as Comma Style with two decimal places.

Independent Challenge 1 (continued)

i. Add a row under Thera-Band Assists for **Nail files**, price paid **0.31**, sold individually (**each**), with **24** on hand. Copy the appropriate formulas to cells E5:F5.

j. Verify that all the data in the worksheet is visible and formulas are correct. Adjust any items as needed, and check the spelling of the entire worksheet.

k. Use conditional formatting to apply yellow fill with dark yellow text to items with a quantity of less than 20 on hand.

l. Use an icon set of your choosing in the range D4:D15 to illustrate the relative differences between values in the range.

m. Add an outside border around the data in the Item column (*do not* include the Item column label).

n. Delete the row containing the Pins entry.

o. Enter your name in an empty cell below the data, then save the file. Compare your worksheet to the sample in FIGURE 3-29.

p. Preview the worksheet in Backstage view, submit your work to your instructor as directed, close the workbook, then exit Excel.

FIGURE 3-29

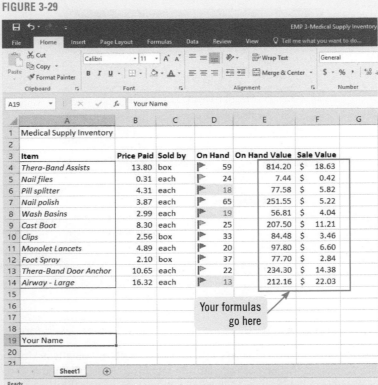

Independent Challenge 2

You volunteer several hours each week with the Memphis Association of Medical Clinics, and you are in charge of maintaining the membership list. You're currently planning a mailing campaign to members in certain regions of the city. You also want to create renewal letters for members whose membership expires soon. You decide to format the list to enhance the appearance of the worksheet and make your upcoming tasks easier to plan.

a. Start Excel, open the file EMP 3-4.xlsx from the location where you store your Data Files, then save it as **EMP 3-Memphis Association of Medical Clinics**.

b. Remove any blank columns.

c. Create a conditional format in the Zip Code column so that entries greater than 38249 appear in light red fill with dark red text.

d. Make all columns wide enough to fit their data and labels. (*Hint*: You can use any method to size the columns.)

e. Use formatting enhancements, such as fonts, font sizes, font styles, and fill colors, to make the worksheet more attractive.

Independent Challenge 2 (continued)

f. Center the column labels.

g. Use conditional formatting so that entries for Year of Membership Expiration that are between 2021 and 2023 appear in green fill with bold black text. (*Hint*: Create a custom format for cells that meet the condition.)

h. Adjust any items as necessary, then check the spelling.

i. Change the name of the Sheet1 tab to one that reflects the sheet's contents, then add a tab color of your choice.

j. Enter your name in an empty cell, then save your work.

k. Preview the worksheet, make any final changes you think necessary, then submit your work to your instructor as directed. Compare your work to the sample shown in FIGURE 3-30.

l. Close the workbook, then exit Excel.

FIGURE 3-30

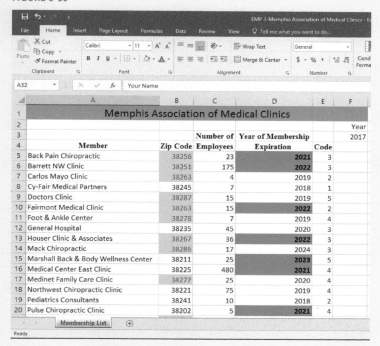

Independent Challenge 3

Emergent Health Care Systems is a Boston-based healthcare provider that offers clinic and urgent-care services. As the finance manager for the company, one of your responsibilities is to analyze the monthly reports from the five district clinics. Your boss, Joanne Bennington, has just asked you to prepare a quarterly revenue report for an upcoming meeting. Because several top executives will be attending this meeting, Joanne reminds you that the report must look professional. In particular, she asks you to highlight the fact that the Northeastern district continues to outpace the other districts.

a. Plan a worksheet that shows the company's revenue during the first quarter. Assume that all client visits are the same price. Make sure you include the following:

• The number of patients seen (clients sold) and the associated revenues (revenue) for each of the five district clinics. The five districts are Northeastern, Midwestern, Southeastern, Southern, and Western.

• Calculations that show month-by-month totals for January, February, and March, and a 3-month cumulative total.

• Calculations that show each district's share of sales (percent of Total Revenue).

• Labels that reflect the month-by-month data as well as the cumulative data.

• Formatting enhancements such as data bars that emphasize the recent month's revenue surge and the Northeastern district's revenue leadership.

b. Ask yourself the following questions about the organization and formatting of the worksheet: What worksheet title and labels do you need, and where should they appear? How can you calculate the totals? What formulas can you copy to save time and keystrokes? Do any of these formulas need to use an absolute reference? How do you show dollar amounts? What information should be shown in bold? Do you need to use more than one font? Should you use more than one point size?

c. Start Excel, then save a new, blank workbook as **EMP 3-Emergent Health Care Systems** to the location where you store your Data Files.

Excel 2016

Independent Challenge 3 (continued)

d. Build the worksheet with your own price and revenue data. Enter the titles and labels first, then enter the numbers and formulas. You can use the information in TABLE 3-4 to get started.

TABLE 3-4

Emergent Health Care Systems										
1st Quarter Sales Report										
		January		February		March		Total		
Office	Price	Units Sold	Sales	Units Sold	Sales	Units Sold	Sales	Units Sold	Sales	25% Increase in Revenue
Northeastern										
Midwestern										
Southeastern										
Southern										
Western										

e. Add a row beneath the data containing the totals for each column.

f. Adjust the column widths as necessary.

g. Change the height of row 1 to 33 points.

h. Format labels and values to enhance the look of the worksheet, and change the font styles and alignment if necessary.

i. Resize columns and adjust the formatting as necessary.

j. Add data bars for the monthly Clients Seen columns.

k. Add a column that calculates a 25% increase in total revenue. Use an absolute cell reference in this calculation. (*Hint:* Make sure that the current formatting is applied to the new information.)

l. Delete the contents of cells J4:K4 if necessary, then merge and center cell I4 over column I:K.

m. Add a bottom double border to cells I10:L10.

n. Enter your name in an empty cell.

o. Check the spelling in the workbook, change to a landscape orientation, save your work, then compare your work to FIGURE 3-31.

p. Preview the worksheet in Backstage view, then submit your work to your instructor as directed.

q. Close the workbook file, then exit Excel.

FIGURE 3-31

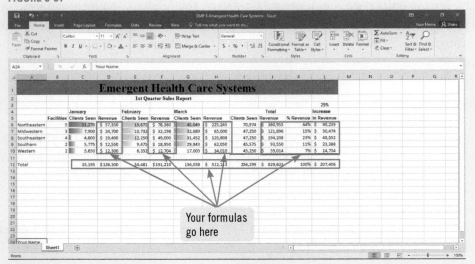

Formatting a Worksheet

Independent Challenge 4: Explore

This Independent Challenge requires an Internet connection.

You have been notified that your research grant to study the spread of airborne diseases has been approved. You plan to visit seven different countries over the course of 2 months, and you have budgeted an identical spending allowance in each country. You want to create a worksheet that calculates the amount of native currency you will have in each country based on the budgeted amount. You want the workbook to reflect the currency information for each country.

a. Start Excel, then save a new, blank workbook as **EMP 3-Research Grant Travel Budget** to the location where you store your Data Files.

b. Add a title at the top of the worksheet.

c. Think of seven countries that each use a different currency, then enter column and row labels for your worksheet. (*Hint*: You may wish to include row labels for each country, plus column labels for the country, the $1 equivalent in native currency, the total amount of native currency employees will have in each country, and the name of each country's monetary unit.)

d. Decide how much money you want to bring to each country (for example, $1,000), and enter that in the worksheet.

e. Use your favorite search engine to find your own information sources on currency conversions for the countries you have listed.

f. Enter the cash equivalent to $1 in U.S. dollars for each country in your list.

g. Create an equation that calculates the amount of native currency you will have in each country, using an absolute cell reference in the formula.

h. Format the entries in the column containing the native currency $1 equivalent as Number number format with three decimal places, and format the column containing the total native currency budget with two decimal places, using the correct currency number format for each country. (*Hint*: Use the Number tab in the Format cells dialog box; choose the appropriate currency number format from the Symbol list.)

i. Create a conditional format that changes the font style and color of the calculated amount in the $1,000 US column to light red fill with dark red text if the amount exceeds **1000** units of the local currency.

j. Merge and center the worksheet title over the column headings.

k. Add any formatting you want to the column headings, and resize the columns as necessary.

l. Add a background color to the title and change the font color if you choose.

m. Enter your name in the header of the worksheet.

n. Spell check the worksheet, save your changes, compare your work to FIGURE 3-32, then preview the worksheet, and submit your work to your instructor as directed.

o. Close the workbook and exit Excel.

FIGURE 3-32

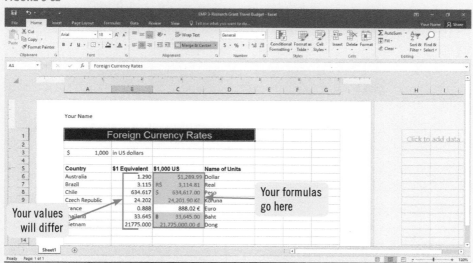

Visual Workshop

Open the file EMP 3-5.xlsx from the location where you store your Data Files, then save it as **EMP 3-Bellingham General Hospital Administrative Staff**. Use the skills you learned in this module to format the worksheet so it looks like the one shown in FIGURE 3-33. Create a conditional format in the Level column so that entries greater than 3 appear in yellow fill with dark red text. Create an additional conditional format in the Review Cycle column so that any value equal to 3 appears in black fill with white bold text. Replace the Accounting department label with **Legal**. (*Hint*: The only additional font used in this exercise is 18-point Times New Roman in row 1.) Enter your name in the upper-right part of the header, check the spelling in the worksheet, save your changes, then submit your work to your instructor as directed. (*Hint*: To match the figure exactly, remember to match the zoom level.)

FIGURE 3-33

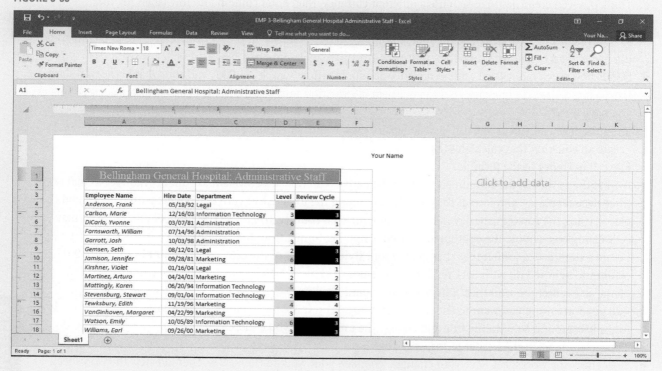

Formatting a Worksheet

Working with Charts

CASE ▶ At the upcoming annual meeting, Tony Sanchez wants to discuss spending patterns at Riverwalk Medical Clinic. He asks you to create a chart showing the trends in insurance reimbursements over the past four quarters.

Module Objectives

After completing this module, you will be able to:

- Plan a chart
- Create a chart
- Move and resize a chart
- Change the chart design

- Change the chart format
- Format a chart
- Annotate and draw on a chart
- Create a pie chart

Files You Will Need

EMP 4-1.xlsx   EMP 4-4.xlsx

EMP 4-2.xlsx   EMP 4-5.xlsx

EMP 4-3.xlsx   EMP 4-6.xlsx

Plan a Chart

Before creating a chart, you need to plan the information you want your chart to show and how you want it to look. Planning ahead helps you decide what type of chart to create and how to organize the data. Understanding the parts of a chart makes it easier to format and change specific elements so that the chart best illustrates your data. **CASE** *In preparation for creating the chart for Tony's presentation, you identify your goals for the chart and plan its layout.*

DETAILS

Use the following guidelines to plan the chart:

- **Determine the purpose of the chart, and identify the data relationships you want to communicate graphically**

  You want to create a chart that shows quarterly insurance reimbursements throughout Riverwalk Medical Clinic. This worksheet data is shown in FIGURE 4-1. In the first quarter, the Ophthalmology department settled a dispute with a large insurance carrier, which resulted in greatly increased reimbursements starting in the third quarter. You also want the chart to illustrate whether the quarterly expenses for each department increased or decreased from quarter to quarter.

- **Determine the results you want to see, and decide which chart type is most appropriate**

  Different chart types display data in distinctive ways. For example, a pie chart compares parts to the whole, so it's useful for showing what proportion of a budget amount was spent on tours in one country relative to what was spent on tours in other countries. A line chart, in contrast, is best for showing trends over time. To choose the best chart type for your data, you should first decide how you want your data displayed and interpreted. TABLE 4-1 describes several different types of charts you can create in Excel and their corresponding buttons on the Insert tab on the Ribbon. Because you want to compare RMC reimbursements in multiple departments over a period of four quarters, you decide to use a column chart.

- **Identify the worksheet data you want the chart to illustrate**

  Sometimes you use all the data in a worksheet to create a chart, while at other times you may need to select a range within the sheet. The worksheet from which you are creating your chart contains reimbursement data for each of the past four quarters and the totals for the past year. You will need to use all the quarterly data except the quarterly totals.

- **Understand the elements of a chart**

  The chart shown in FIGURE 4-2 contains basic elements of a chart. In the figure, RMC departments are on the horizontal axis (also called the **x-axis**) and reimbursement dollar amounts are on the vertical axis (also called the **y-axis**). The horizontal axis is also called the **category axis** because it often contains the names of data groups, such as locations, months, or years. The vertical axis is also called the **value axis** because it often contains numerical values that help you interpret the size of chart elements. (3-D charts also contain a **z-axis**, for comparing data across both categories and values.) The area inside the horizontal and vertical axes is the **plot area**. The **tick marks**, on the vertical axis, and **gridlines** (extending across the plot area) create a scale of measure for each value. Each value in a cell you select for your chart is a **data point**. In any chart, a **data marker** visually represents each data point, which in this case is a column. A collection of related data points is a **data series**. In this chart, there are four data series (Quarter 1, Quarter 2, Quarter 3, and Quarter 4). Each is made up of column data markers of a different color, so a **legend** is included to make it easy to identify them.

FIGURE 4-1: Worksheet containing reimbursement data

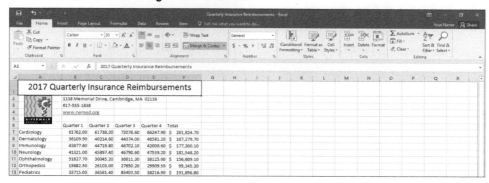

FIGURE 4-2: Chart elements

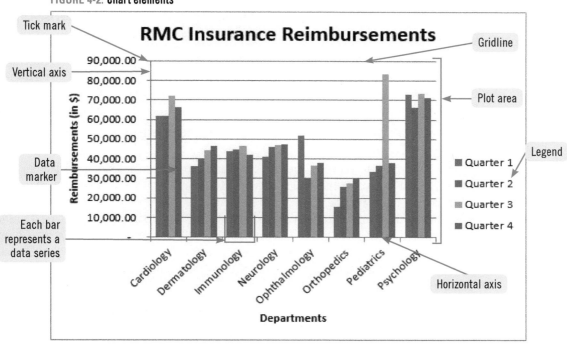

TABLE 4-1: Common chart types

type	button	description
Column		Compares data using columns; the Excel default; sometimes referred to as a bar chart in other spreadsheet programs
Line		Compares trends over even time intervals; looks similar to an area chart, but does not emphasize total
Pie		Compares sizes of pieces as part of a whole; used for a single series of numbers
Bar		Compares data using horizontal bars; sometimes referred to as a horizontal bar chart in other spreadsheet programs
Area		Shows how individual volume changes over time in relation to total volume
Scatter		Compares trends over uneven time or measurement intervals; used in scientific and engineering disciplines for trend spotting and extrapolation
Combo		Displays two or more types of data using different chart types; illustrates mixed or widely varying types of data

Create a Chart

To create a chart in Excel, you first select the range in a worksheet containing the data you want to chart. Once you've selected a range, you can use the Quick Analysis tool or the Insert tab on the Ribbon to create a chart based on the data in the range. **CASE** *Using the worksheet containing the quarterly insurance reimbursement data, you create a chart that shows how the reimbursements in each department varied across the quarters.*

STEPS

QUICK TIP
When charting data for a particular time period, make sure that all series are for the same time period.

1. **Start Excel, open the file EMP 4-1.xlsx from the location where you store your Data Files, then save it as EMP 4-Quarterly Insurance Reimbursements**
   You want the chart to include the quarterly insurance reimbursement values, as well as quarter and department labels. You don't include the Total column and row because the figures in these cells would skew the chart.

2. **Select the range A6:E14, click the Quick Analysis tool 📧 in the lower-right corner of the range, then click Charts**
   The Charts tab on the Quick Analysis tool recommends commonly used chart types based on the range you have selected. The Charts tab also includes a More Charts button for additional chart types, such as stock charts for charting stock market data.

QUICK TIP
To base a chart on data in nonadjacent ranges, press and hold [Ctrl] while selecting each range, then use the Insert tab to create the chart.

3. **On the Charts tab, verify that Clustered Column is selected, as shown in FIGURE 4-3, then click Clustered Column**
   The chart is inserted in the center of the worksheet, and two contextual Chart Tools tabs appear on the Ribbon: Design and Format. On the Design tab, which is currently active, you can quickly change the chart type, chart layout, and chart style, and you can swap how the columns and rows of data in the worksheet are represented in the chart. When seen in the Normal view, three tools appear to the right of the chart: these enable you to add, remove, or change chart elements ➕ , set a style and color scheme 🖌 , and filter the results shown in a chart 🔽 . Currently, the departments are charted along the horizontal x-axis, with the quarterly reimbursement dollar amounts charted along the y-axis. This lets you easily compare the quarterly reimbursements for each department.

4. **Click the Switch Row/Column button in the Data group on the Chart Tools Design tab**
   The quarters are now charted along the x-axis. The reimbursement amounts per department are charted along the y-axis, as indicated by the updated legend. See FIGURE 4-4.

5. **Click the Undo button 🔄 ▾ on the Quick Access Toolbar**
   The chart returns to its original design.

QUICK TIP
You can also triple-click to select the chart title text.

6. **Click the Chart Title placeholder to show the text box, click anywhere in the Chart Title text box, press [Ctrl][A] to select the text, type Quarterly Insurance Reimbursements, then click anywhere in the chart to deselect the title**
   Adding a title helps identify the chart. The border around the chart and the **sizing handles**, the small series of dots at the corners and sides of the chart's border, indicate that the chart is selected. See FIGURE 4-5. Your chart might be in a different location on the worksheet and may look slightly different; you will move and resize it in the next lesson. Any time a chart is selected, as it is now, a blue border surrounds the worksheet data range on which the chart is based, a purple border surrounds the cells containing the category axis labels, and a red border surrounds the cells containing the data series labels. This chart is known as an **embedded chart** because it is inserted directly in the current worksheet and doesn't exist in a separate file. Embedding a chart in the current sheet is the default selection when creating a chart, but you can also embed a chart on a different sheet in the workbook, or on a newly created chart sheet. A **chart sheet** is a sheet in a workbook that contains only a chart that is linked to the workbook data.

7. **Save your work**

FIGURE 4-3: Charts tab in Quick Analysis tool

FIGURE 4-4: Clustered Column chart with different configuration of rows and columns

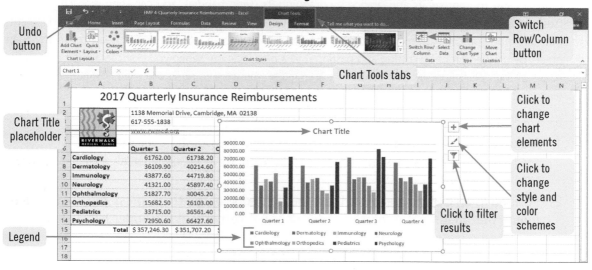

FIGURE 4-5: Chart with original configuration restored and title added

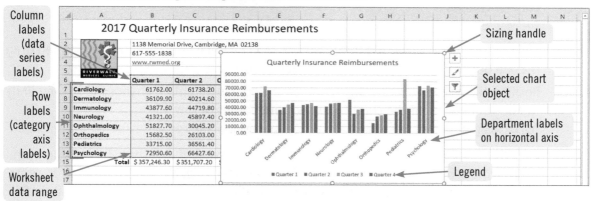

Creating sparklines

You can quickly create a miniature chart called a **sparkline** that serves as a visual indicator of data trends. You can create a sparkline by selecting a range of data, clicking the Quick Analysis tool, clicking the Sparklines tab, then clicking the type of sparkline you want. (The sparkline appears in the cell immediately adjacent to the selected range.) You can also select a range, click the Insert tab, then click the Line, Column, or Win/Loss button in the Sparklines group. In the Create Sparklines dialog box that opens, enter the cell in which you want the sparkline to appear,

then click OK. **FIGURE 4-6** shows a sparkline created in a cell. Any changes to data in the range are reflected in the sparkline. To delete a selected sparkline from a cell, click the Clear button in the Group group on the Sparkline Tools Design tab.

FIGURE 4-6: Sparklines in a cell

Move and Resize a Chart

Learning Outcomes
- Reposition a chart
- Resize a chart
- Modify a legend
- Modify chart data

A chart is an **object**, or an independent element on a worksheet, and is not located in a specific cell or range. You can select an object by clicking it; sizing handles around the object indicate it is selected. (When a chart is selected in Excel, the Name box, which normally tells you the address of the active cell, tells you the chart number.) You can move a selected chart anywhere on a worksheet without affecting formulas or data in the worksheet. Any data changed in the worksheet is automatically updated in the chart. You can even move a chart to a different sheet in the workbook, and it will still reflect the original data. You can resize a chart to improve its appearance by dragging its sizing handles. You can reposition chart objects (such as a title or legend) to predefined locations using commands available from the Chart Elements button or the Add Chart Element button on the Chart Tools Design tab, or you can freely move any chart object by dragging it or by cutting and pasting it to a new location. When you point to a chart object, the name of the object appears as a ScreenTip. **CASE** ▶ *You want to resize the chart, position it below the worksheet data, and move the legend.*

STEPS

QUICK TIP
To delete a selected chart, press [Delete].

1. **Make sure the chart is still selected, then position the pointer over the chart**

   The pointer shape ⬚ indicates that you can move the chart. For a table of commonly used object pointers, refer to TABLE 4-2.

TROUBLE
Dragging a chart element instead of a blank area moves the element instead of the chart; if this happens, undo the action and try again.

2. **Position ⬚ on a blank area near the upper-left edge of the chart, press and hold the left mouse button, drag the chart until its upper-left corner is at the upper-left corner of cell A18, then release the mouse button**

   When you release the mouse button, the chart appears in the new location.

3. **Scroll down so you can see the whole chart, position the pointer on the right-middle sizing handle until it changes to ↔, then drag the right border of the chart to the right edge of column F**

   The chart is widened. See FIGURE 4-7.

QUICK TIP
To resize a selected chart to an exact size, click the Chart Tools Format tab, then enter the desired height and width in the Size group.

4. **Position the pointer over the upper-middle sizing handle until it changes to ↕, then drag the top border of the chart to the top edge of row 17**

5. **Position the pointer over the lower-middle sizing handle until it changes to ↕, then drag the bottom border of the chart to the bottom border of row 30**

   You can move any object on a chart. You want to align the top of the legend with the top of the plot area.

QUICK TIP
You can move a legend to the right, top, left, or bottom of a chart by clicking Legend in the Add Chart Element button in the Chart Layouts group on the Chart Tools Design tab, then clicking a location option.

6. **Click the Quick Layout button in the Chart Layouts group of the Chart Tools Design tab, click Layout 1 (in the upper-left corner of the palette), click the legend to select it, press and hold [Shift], drag the legend up using ⬚ so the dotted outline is approximately 1/4" above the top of the plot area, then release [Shift]**

   When you click the legend, sizing handles appear around it and "Legend" appears as a ScreenTip when the pointer hovers over the object. As you drag, a dotted outline of the legend border appears. Pressing and holding the [Shift] key holds the horizontal position of the legend as you move it vertically. Although the sizing handles on objects within a chart look different from the sizing handles that surround a chart, they function the same way.

7. **Click cell A14, type Psychiatry, click the Enter button ✓ on the formula bar, use AutoFit to resize column A, then save your work**

   The axis label changes to reflect the updated cell contents, as shown in FIGURE 4-8. Changing any data in the worksheet modifies corresponding text or values in the chart. Because the chart is no longer selected, the Chart Tools tabs no longer appear on the Ribbon.

FIGURE 4-7: **Moved and resized chart**

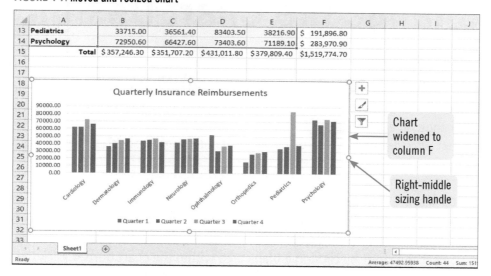

FIGURE 4-8: **Worksheet with modified legend and label**

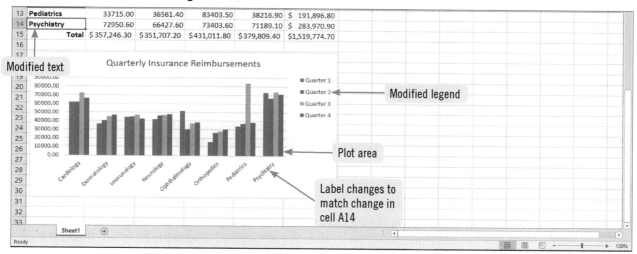

TABLE 4-2: **Common object pointers**

name	pointer	use	name	pointer	use
Diagonal resizing	⤢ or ⤡	Change chart shape from corners	I-beam	I	Edit object text
Draw	+	Draw an object	Move	⤧	Move object
Horizontal resizing	⟷	Change object width	Vertical resizing	↕	Change object height

Moving an embedded chart to a sheet

Suppose you have created an embedded chart that you decide would look better on a chart sheet or in a different worksheet. You can make this change without recreating the entire chart. To do so, first select the chart, click the Chart Tools Design tab, then click the Move Chart button in the Location group. The Move Chart dialog box opens. To move the chart to its own chart sheet, click the New sheet option button, type a name for the new sheet if desired, then click OK. If the chart is already on its own sheet or you want to move it to a different existing sheet, click the Object in option button, click the desired worksheet, then click OK.

Change the Chart Design

Learning
Outcomes
• Change the chart
  design
• Change the chart
  type
• Apply a chart style

Once you've created a chart, you can change the chart type, modify the data range and column/row configuration, apply a different chart style, and change the layout of objects in the chart. The layouts in the Chart Layouts group on the Chart Tools Design tab offer arrangements of objects in your chart, such as its legend, title, or gridlines; choosing one of these layouts is an alternative to manually changing how objects are arranged in a chart. **CASE** ➤ *You discovered that the data for Pediatrics and Psychiatry in Quarter 2 is incorrect. After the correction, you want to see how the data looks using different chart layouts and types.*

STEPS

1. **Click cell C13, type 40462.01, press [Enter], type 61947.18, then press [Enter]**
   In the chart, the Quarter 2 data markers for Pediatrics and Psychiatry reflect the adjusted reimbursement figures. See FIGURE 4-9.

> **QUICK TIP**
> You can see more layout choices by clicking the More button ⏷ in the Chart Styles group.

2. **Select the chart by clicking a blank area within the chart border, click the Chart Tools Design tab on the Ribbon, click the Quick Layout button in the Chart Layouts group, then click Layout 3**
   The legend moves to the bottom of the chart. You prefer the original layout.

3. **Click the Undo button ↶ on the Quick Access Toolbar, then click the Change Chart Type button in the Type group**
   The Change Chart Type dialog box opens, as shown in FIGURE 4-10. The left pane of the dialog box lists the available categories, and the right pane shows the individual chart types. A pale gray border surrounds the currently selected chart type.

4. **Click Bar in the left pane of the Change Chart Type dialog box, confirm that the first Clustered Bar chart type is selected in the right pane, then click OK**
   The column chart changes to a clustered bar chart. See FIGURE 4-11. You decide to see how the data looks in a three-dimensional column chart.

5. **Click the Change Chart Type button in the Type group, click Column in the left pane of the Change Chart Type dialog box, click 3-D Clustered Column (fourth from the left in the top row) in the right pane, verify that the left-most 3-D chart is selected, then click OK**
   A three-dimensional column chart appears. You notice that the three-dimensional column format gives you a sense of volume, but it is more crowded than the two-dimensional column format.

> **QUICK TIP**
> If you plan to print a chart on a black-and-white printer, you may wish to apply a black-and-white chart style to your chart so you can see how the output will look as you work.

6. **Click the Change Chart Type button in the Type group, click Clustered Column (first from the left in the top row) in the right pane of the Change Chart Type dialog box, then click OK**

7. **Click the Style 3 chart style in the Chart Styles group**
   The columns change to lighter shades of color. You prefer the previous chart style's color scheme.

8. **Click ↶ on the Quick Access Toolbar, then save your work**

Creating a combo chart

A **combo chart** presents two or more charts in one; a column chart with a line chart, for example. This type of chart is helpful when charting dissimilar but related data. For example, you can create a combo chart based on home price and home size data, showing home prices in a column chart and related home sizes in a line chart. Here a **secondary axis** (such as a vertical axis on the right side of the chart) would supply the scale for the home sizes.

To create a combo chart, select all the data you want to plot, click the Combo chart button 📊▾ in the Charts group in the Insert tab, click a suggested type or Create Custom Combo Chart, supply additional series information if necessary, then click OK. To change an existing chart to a combo chart, select the chart, click Change Chart Type in the Type group on the Chart Tools Design tab, click Combo in the left pane, then follow the same procedure.

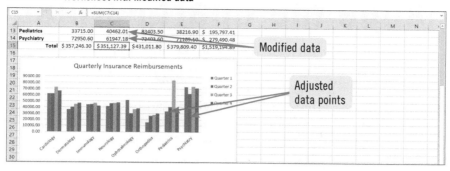

FIGURE 4-9: Worksheet with modified data

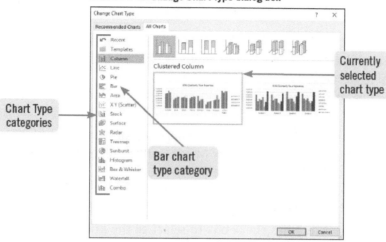

FIGURE 4-10: Change Chart Type dialog box

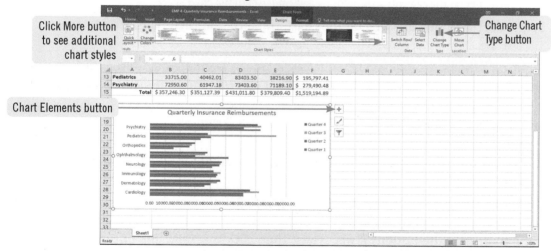

FIGURE 4-11: Column chart changed to bar chart

Working with a 3-D chart

Excel includes two kinds of 3-D chart types. In a true 3-D chart, a third axis, called the **z-axis**, lets you compare data points across both categories and values. The z-axis runs along the depth of the chart, so it appears to advance from the back of the chart. To create a true 3-D chart, look for chart types that begin with "3-D," such as 3-D Column. In a 3-D chart, data series can sometimes obscure other columns or bars in the same chart, but you can rotate the chart to obtain a better view. Right-click the chart, then click 3-D Rotation. The Format Chart Area pane opens with the 3-D Rotation category active. The 3-D Rotation options let you change the orientation and perspective of the chart area, plot area, walls, and floor. The 3-D Format category lets you apply three-dimensional effects to selected chart objects. (Not all 3-D Rotation and 3-D Format options are available on all charts.)

Change the Chart Format

Learning
Outcomes
• Change the
  gridlines display
• Add axis titles
• Change the
  border color
• Add a shadow
  to an object

While the Chart Tools Design tab contains preconfigured chart layouts you can apply to a chart, the Chart Elements button makes it easy to add, remove, and modify individual chart objects such as a chart title or legend. Using options on this shortcut menu (or using the Add Chart Element button on the Chart Tools Design tab), you can also add text to a chart, add and modify labels, change the display of axes, modify the fill behind the plot area, create titles for the horizontal and vertical axes, and eliminate or change the look of gridlines. You can format the text in a chart object using the Home tab or the Mini toolbar, just as you would the text in a worksheet. **CASE** *You want to change the layout of the chart by creating titles for the horizontal and vertical axes. To improve the chart's appearance, you'll add a drop shadow to the chart title.*

STEPS

1. **With the chart still selected, click the Add Chart Element button in the Chart Layouts group on the Chart Tools Design tab, point to Gridlines, then click Primary Major Horizontal to deselect it**

   The gridlines that extend from the value axis tick marks across the chart's plot area are removed as shown in FIGURE 4-12.

2. **Click the Chart Elements button [+] in the upper-right corner *outside* the chart border, click the Gridlines arrow, click Primary Major Horizontal, click Primary Minor Horizontal, then click [+] to close the Chart Elements fly-out menu**

   Both major and minor gridlines now appear in the chart. **Major gridlines** represent the values at the value axis tick marks, and **minor gridlines** represent the values between the tick marks.

QUICK TIP
You can move any
title to a new
position by clicking
one of its edges,
then dragging it.

QUICK TIP
You can also edit text
in a chart or axis title
by positioning the
pointer over the
selected title until it
changes to ⌶, click-
ing the title, then
editing the text.

3. **Click [+], click the Axis Titles check box to select all the axis titles options, triple-click the vertical axis title on the chart, then type Revenue (in $)**

   Descriptive text on the category axis helps readers understand the chart.

4. **Select the horizontal axis title on the chart, triple-click it, then type Departments**

   The text "Departments" appears on the horizontal axis, as shown in FIGURE 4-13.

5. **Right-click the horizontal axis labels ("Cardiology", "Dermatology", etc.), click Font on the shortcut menu, click the Latin text font list arrow in the Font dialog box, click Times New Roman, click the Size down arrow until 8 is displayed, then click OK**

   The font of the horizontal axis labels changes to Times New Roman, and the font size decreases, making more of the plot area visible.

6. **Right-click the vertical axis labels, then use the procedures in step 5 to change the font to 8 pt Times New Roman**

QUICK TIP
You can also apply a
border to a selected
chart object by
clicking the Shape
Outline list arrow on
the Chart Tools
Format tab, and then
selecting from the
available options.

7. **Right-click the Chart Title ("Quarterly Insurance Reimbursement"), click Format Chart Title on the shortcut menu, click the Border arrow [▸] in the Format Chart Title pane to display the options if necessary, then click the Solid line option button in the pane**

   A solid border appears around the chart title with the default blue color.

QUICK TIP
You can also apply a
shadow to a selected
chart object by
clicking the Shadow
arrow, then clicking a
shadow effect.

8. **Click the Effects button [⬠] in the Format Chart Title pane, click Shadow, click the Presets list arrow, click Offset Diagonal Bottom Right in the Outer group (first row, first from the left), click the Format Chart Title pane Close button [✕], then save your work**

   A blue border with a drop shadow surrounds the title. Compare your work to FIGURE 4-14.

Working with Charts

FIGURE 4-12: Gridlines removed from chart

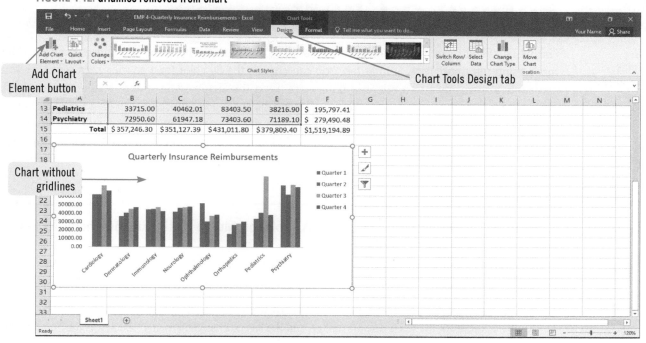

Add Chart Element button

Chart Tools Design tab

Chart without gridlines

FIGURE 4-13: Axis titles added to chart

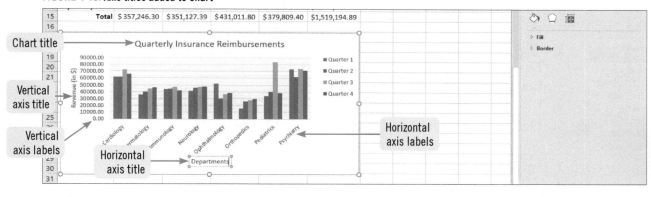

Chart title

Vertical axis title

Vertical axis labels

Horizontal axis title

Horizontal axis labels

FIGURE 4-14: Enhanced chart

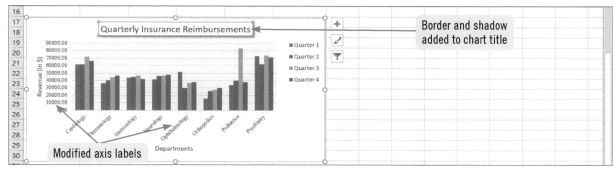

Border and shadow added to chart title

Modified axis labels

Adding data labels to a chart

There are times when your audience might benefit by seeing data labels on a chart. These labels appear next to the data markers in the chart and can indicate the series name, category name, and/or the value of one or more data points. Once your chart is selected, you can add this information to your chart by clicking the Chart Elements button in the upper-right corner outside the selected chart, clicking the Data Labels arrow, and then clicking a display option for the data labels. Once you have added the data labels, you can format them or delete individual data labels. To delete a data label, select it and then press [Delete].

Format a Chart

Formatting a chart can make it easier to read and understand. Many formatting enhancements can be made using the Chart Tools Format tab. You can change the fill color for a specific data series, or you can apply a shape style to a title or a data series using the Shape Styles group. Shape styles make it possible to apply multiple formats, such as an outline, fill color, and text color, all with a single click. You can also apply different fill colors, outlines, and effects to chart objects using arrows and buttons in the Shape Styles group. **CASE** *You want to use a different color for one data series in the chart and apply a shape style to another, to enhance the look of the chart.*

STEPS

1. **With the chart selected, click the Chart Tools Format tab on the Ribbon, then click any column in the Quarter 4 data series**

   Handles appear on each column in the Quarter 4 data series, indicating that the entire series is selected.

2. **Click the Shape Fill list arrow in the Shape Styles group on the Chart Tools Format tab**

3. **Click Orange, Accent 6 (first row, 10th from the left) as shown in FIGURE 4-15**

   All the columns for the series become orange, and the legend changes to match the new color. You can also change the color of selected objects by applying a shape style.

4. **Click any column in the Quarter 3 data series**

   Handles appear on each column in the Quarter 3 data series.

5. **Click the More button ▼ on the Shape Styles gallery, then *hover the pointer* over the Moderate Effect – Olive Green, Accent 3 shape style (fifth row, fourth from the left) in the gallery, as shown in FIGURE 4-16**

   Live Preview shows the data series in the chart with the shape style applied.

6. **Click the Subtle Effect – Olive Green, Accent 3 shape style**

   The style for the data series changes, as shown in FIGURE 4-17.

7. **Save your work**

Previewing a chart

To print or preview just a chart, select the chart (or make the chart sheet active), click the File tab, then click Print on the navigation bar. To reposition a chart by changing the page's margins, click the Show Margins button ⊞ in the lower-right corner of the Print tab to display the margins in the preview. You can drag the margin lines to the exact settings you want; as the margins change, the size and placement of the chart on the page change too.

FIGURE 4-15: New shape fill applied to data series

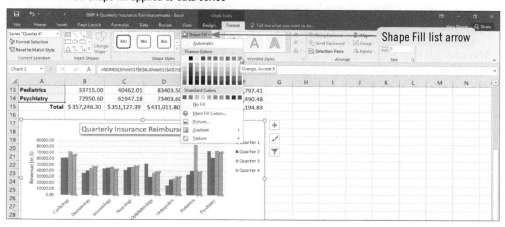

FIGURE 4-16: Live Preview of new style applied to data series

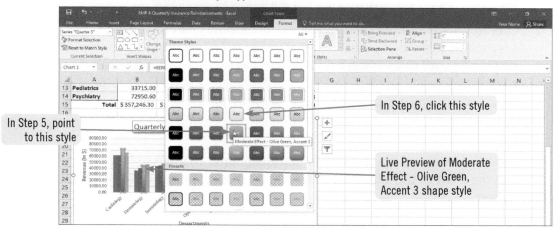

FIGURE 4-17: Style of data series changed

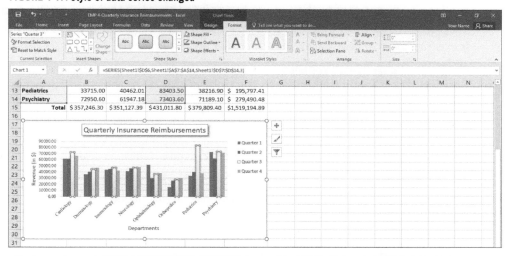

Changing alignment and angle in axis labels and titles

The buttons on the Chart Tools Design tab provide a few options for positioning axis labels and titles, but you can customize their position and rotation to exact specifications using the Format Axis pane or Format Axis Title pane. With a chart selected, right-click the axis text you want to modify, then click Format Axis or Format Axis Title on the shortcut menu. In the pane that opens, click the Size & Properties button, then select the appropriate option. You can also create a custom angle by clicking the Custom angle up and down arrows. When you have made the desired changes, close the pane.

Annotate and Draw on a Chart

Learning Outcomes
- Type text in a text box
- Draw an arrow on a chart
- Modify a drawn object

You can use text annotations and graphics to point out critical information in a chart. **Text annotations** are labels that further describe your data. You can also draw lines and arrows that point to the exact locations you want to emphasize. Shapes such as arrows and boxes can be added from the Illustrations group on the Insert tab or from the Insert Shapes group on the Chart Tools Format tab on the Ribbon. The Insert group is also used to insert pictures into worksheets and charts. **CASE** *You want to call attention to the Orthopedics revenue increases, so you decide to add a text annotation and an arrow to this information in the chart.*

STEPS

1. **With the chart selected and the Chart Tools Format tab active, click the** Text Box **button** 🔲 **in the Insert Shapes group, then move the pointer over the worksheet**

   The pointer changes to ↓, indicating that you will insert a text box where you next click.

QUICK TIP

You can also insert a text box by clicking the Text Box button in the Text group in the Insert tab, then clicking in the worksheet.

2. **Click to the** right of the chart **(anywhere** *outside* **the chart boundary)**

   A text box is added to the worksheet, and the Drawing Tools Format tab appears on the Ribbon so that you can format the new object. First you need to type the text.

3. **Type** Great Improvement

   The text appears in a selected text box on the worksheet, and the chart is no longer selected, as shown in FIGURE 4-18. Your text box may be in a different location; this is not important because you'll move the annotation in the next step.

4. **Point to an edge of the text box so that the pointer changes to** ⇱, **drag the** text box **into the chart to the left of the chart title, as shown in** FIGURE 4-19, **then release the mouse button**

   The text box is a text annotation for the chart. You also want to add a simple arrow shape in the chart.

QUICK TIP

To annotate a chart using a callout, click the Shapes button in the Illustrations group on the Insert tab or the More button on the Insert Shapes group on the Chart Tools Format tab, then click a shape in the Callouts category of the Shapes gallery.

5. **Click the** chart **to select it, click the** Chart Tools Format tab, **click the** Arrow button ⬉ **in the Insert Shapes group, then move the pointer over the text box on the chart**

   The pointer changes to ➕, and the status bar displays "Click and drag to insert an AutoShape." When ➕ is over the text box, black handles appear around the text in the text box. A black handle can act as an anchor for the arrow.

6. **Position** ➕ **on the** black handle **to the right of the "t" in the word "Improvement" (in the text box), press and hold the** left mouse button, **drag the** line **to the** Quarter 2 column **for the Orthopedics category in the chart, then release the mouse button**

   An arrow points to the Quarter 2 revenue for Orthopedics, and the Drawing Tools Format tab displays options for working with the new arrow object. You can resize, format, or delete it just like any other object in a chart.

7. **Click the** Shape Outline list arrow **in the Shape Styles group, click the** Automatic color, **click the** Shape Outline list arrow **again, point to** Weight, **then click** 1½ pt

   Compare your finished chart to FIGURE 4-20.

8. **Save your work**

FIGURE 4-18: **Text box added**

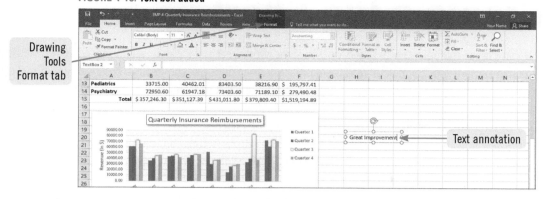

FIGURE 4-19: **Text annotation on the chart**

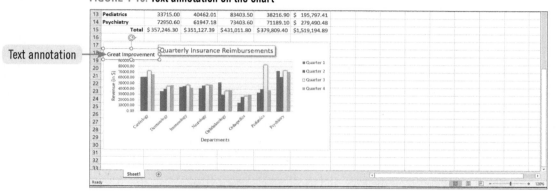

FIGURE 4-20: **Arrow shape added to chart**

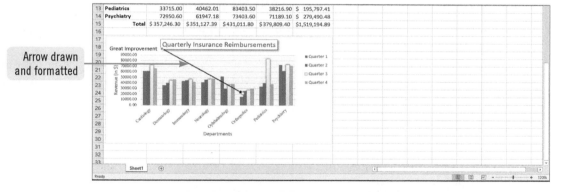

Adding SmartArt graphics

In addition to charts, annotations, and drawn objects, you can create a variety of diagrams using SmartArt graphics. **SmartArt graphics** are available in List, Process, Cycle, Hierarchy, Relationship, Matrix, Pyramid, Picture, and Office.com categories. To insert SmartArt, click the Insert a SmartArt Graphic button in the Illustrations group on the Insert tab to open the Choose a SmartArt Graphic dialog box. Click a SmartArt category in the left pane, then click a layout for the graphic in the right pane. The right pane shows sample layouts for the selected SmartArt, as shown in FIGURE 4-21. The SmartArt graphic appears in the worksheet as an embedded object with sizing handles. Depending on the type of SmartArt graphic you selected, a text pane opens next to the graphic; you can enter text into the graphic using the text pane or by typing directly in the shapes in the diagram.

FIGURE 4-21: **Choose a SmartArt Graphic dialog box**

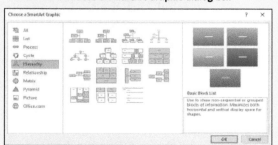

Create a Pie Chart

Learning Outcomes
- Create a pie chart
- Explode a pie chart slice

You can create multiple charts based on the same worksheet data. While a column chart may illustrate certain important aspects of your worksheet data, you may find that you want to create an additional chart to emphasize a different point. Depending on the type of chart you create, you have additional options for calling attention to trends and patterns. For example, if you create a pie chart, you can emphasize one data point by **exploding**, or pulling that slice away from, the pie chart. When you're ready to print a chart, you can preview it just as you do a worksheet to check the output before committing it to paper. You can print a chart by itself or as part of the worksheet. **CASE** *At an upcoming meeting, Tony plans to discuss the total reimbursement revenue and which departments need improvement. You want to create a pie chart he can use to illustrate total revenue. Finally, you want to fit the worksheet and the charts onto one worksheet page.*

STEPS

1. **Select the range A7:A14, press and hold [Ctrl], select the range F7:F14, click the** Insert **tab, click the** Insert Pie or Doughnut Chart button **in the Charts group, then click** 3-D Pie **in the chart gallery**

   The new chart appears in the center of the worksheet. You can move the chart and quickly format it using a chart layout.

2. **Drag the** chart **so its upper-left corner is at the upper-left corner of cell** G1, **click the** Quick Layout button **in the Chart Layouts group of the Chart Tools Design tab, then click** Layout 2

   The chart is repositioned on the page, and its layout changes so that a chart title is added, the percentages are displayed on each slice, and the legend appears just below the chart title.

3. **Select the** Chart Title text, **then type** Total Reimbursements, by Department

4. **Click the slice for the** Orthopedics data point, **click it again so it is the only slice selected, right-click it, then click** Format Data Point

   The Format Data Point pane opens, as shown in FIGURE 4-22. You can use the Point Explosion slider to control the distance a pie slice moves away from the pie, or you can type a value in the Point Explosion text box.

   TROUBLE
   If the Format Data Series command appears on the shortcut menu instead of Format Data Point, double-click the slice you want to explode to make sure it is selected by itself, then right-click it again.

5. **Double-click 0 in the** Point Explosion text box, **type** 40, **then click the** Close button ☒

   Compare your chart to FIGURE 4-23. You decide to preview the chart and data before you print.

6. **Click cell A1, switch to** Page Layout view, **type your name in the left header text box, then click cell** A1

   You decide the chart and data would fit better on the page if they were printed in landscape orientation.

7. **Click the** Page Layout tab, **click the** Orientation button **in the Page Setup group, then click** Landscape

8. **Click the** File tab, **click** Print **on the navigation bar, verify that the correct printer is selected, click the** No Scaling setting **in the Settings section on the Print tab, then click** Fit Sheet on One Page

   The data and chart are positioned horizontally on a single page, as shown in FIGURE 4-24. The printer you have selected may affect the appearance of your preview screen.

9. **Save and close the workbook, submit your work to your instructor as directed, then exit Excel**

FIGURE 4-22: Format Data Point pane

Format Data Point

Series Options ▼

◢ Series Options

Angle of first slice

0°

Point Explosion

0%

Point Explosion slider

Point Explosion text box

FIGURE 4-23: Exploded pie slice

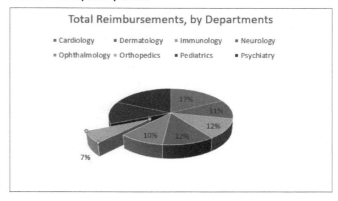

Total Reimbursements, by Departments

- Cardiology - Dermatology - Immunology - Neurology
- Ophthalmology - Orthopedics - Pediatrics - Psychiatry

FIGURE 4-24: Preview of worksheet with charts in Backstage view

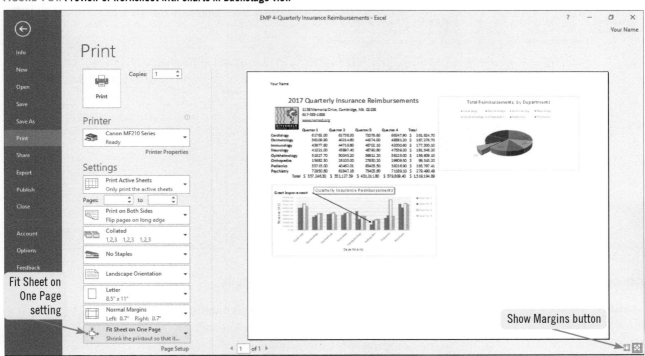

Fit Sheet on One Page setting

Show Margins button

Excel 2016

Using the Insert Chart dialog box to discover new chart types

Excel 2016 includes five new chart types. You can explore these charts by clicking the Insert tab on the Ribbon, clicking Recommended Charts, then clicking the All Charts tab in the Insert Chart dialog box. Near the bottom of the list in the left panel are the new chart types: Treemap (which has nine variations), Sunburst, Histogram, Box & Whisker, and Waterfall. If cells are selected prior to opening the Insert Chart dialog box, you will see a sample of the chart type when you click each chart type; the sample will be magnified when you hover the mouse over the sample. The Treemap and Sunburst charts both offer visual comparisons of relative sizes. The Histogram looks like a column chart, but each column (or bin) represents a range of values. The Box & Whisker chart shows distribution details as well as the mean, quartiles, and outliers. The Waterfall chart shows results above and below an imaginary line.

Practice

Concepts Review

Label each element of the Excel chart shown in FIGURE 4-25.

FIGURE 4-25

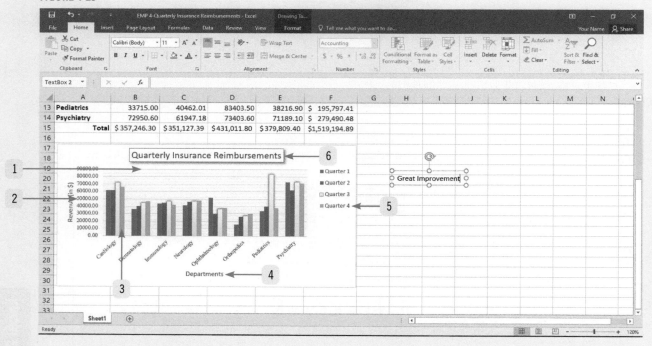

Match each chart type with the statement that best describes it.

7. Combo
8. Pie
9. Area
10. Column
11. Line

a. Displays different chart types within one chart
b. Compares trends over even time intervals
c. Compares data using columns
d. Compares data as parts of a whole
e. Shows how volume changes over time

Select the best answer from the list of choices.

12. **Which tab on the Ribbon do you use to create a chart?**
    a. Design
    b. Insert
    c. Page Layout
    d. Format

13. **A collection of related data points in a chart is called a:**
    a. Data series.
    b. Data tick.
    c. Cell address.
    d. Value title.

14. **The object in a chart that identifies the colors used for each data series is a(n):**
    a. Data marker.
    b. Data point.
    c. Organizer.
    d. Legend.

15. **How do you move an embedded chart to a chart sheet?**
    a. Click a button on the Chart Tools Design tab.
    b. Drag the chart to the sheet tab.
    c. Delete the chart, switch to a different sheet, then create a new chart.
    d. Use the Copy and Paste buttons on the Ribbon.

16. **Which is *not* an example of a SmartArt graphic?**
    a. Sparkline
    b. Basic Matrix
    c. Organization Chart
    d. Basic Pyramid

17. **Which tab appears only when a chart is selected?**
    a. Insert
    b. Chart Tools Format
    c. Review
    d. Page Layout

Skills Review

1. **Plan a chart.**
   a. Start Excel, open the Data File EMP 4-2.xlsx from the location where you store your Data Files, then save it as **EMP 4-Departmental Software Usage Polling Results**.
   b. Describe the type of chart you would use to plot this data.
   c. What chart type would you use to compare the number of Excel users in each type of business?

2. **Create a chart.**
   a. In the worksheet, select the range containing all the data and headings.
   b. Click the Quick Analysis tool.
   c. Create a Clustered Column chart, then add the chart title **Software Usage, by Department** above the chart.
   d. If necessary, click the Switch Row/Column button so the departments (Cardiology, Dermatology, etc.) appear as the x-axis.
   e. Save your work.

Skills Review (continued)

3. Move and resize a chart.

    a. Make sure the chart is still selected, and close any open panes if necessary.

    b. Move the chart beneath the worksheet data.

    c. Widen the chart so it extends to the right edge of column H.

    d. Use the Quick Layout button on the Chart Tools Design tab to move the legend to the right of the charted data. (*Hint*: Use Layout 1.)

    e. Resize the chart so its bottom edge is at the top of row 25.

    f. Save your work.

4. Change the chart design.

    a. Change the value in cell B3 to **8**. Observe the change in the chart.

    b. Select the chart.

    c. Use the Quick Layout button in the Chart Layouts group on the Chart Tools Design tab to apply the Layout 10 layout to the chart, then undo the change.

    d. Use the Change Chart Type button on the Chart Tools Design tab to change the chart to a Clustered Bar chart.

    e. Change the chart to a 3-D Clustered Column chart, then change it back to a Clustered Column chart.

    f. Save your work.

5. Change the chart layout.

    a. Use the Chart Elements button to turn off the primary major horizontal gridlines in the chart.

    b. Change the font used in the horizontal and vertical axis labels to Times New Roman.

    c. Turn on the primary major gridlines for both the horizontal and vertical axes.

    d. Change the chart title's font to Times New Roman if necessary, with a font size of 20 and font color of Black, Text 1, then make the chart title bold.

    e. Insert **Departments** as the primary horizontal axis title.

    f. Insert **Number of Users** as the primary vertical axis title.

    g. Change the font size of the horizontal and vertical axis titles to 10 and the font to Times New Roman in bold, if necessary.

    h. Change "Personnel" in the worksheet column heading to **Human Resources**, then AutoFit column E, and any other columns as necessary.

    i. Change the font size of the legend to 14.

    j. Add a solid line border in the default color and a (preset) Offset Diagonal Bottom Right shadow to the chart title.

    k. Save your work.

6. Format a chart.

    a. Make sure the chart is selected, then select the Chart Tools Format tab, if necessary.

    b. Change the shape fill of the Excel data series to Dark Blue, Text 2.

    c. Change the shape style of the Excel data series to Subtle Effect – Orange, Accent 6.

    d. Save your work.

7. Annotate and draw on a chart.

    a. Make sure the chart is selected, then create the text annotation **Needs more users**.

    b. Position the text annotation so the word "Needs" is just below the word "Software" in the chart title.

    c. Select the chart, then use the Chart Tools Format tab to create a 1½ pt weight Automatic (black) arrow that points from the bottom center of the text box to the Excel users in the Neurology category.

    d. Deselect the chart.

    e. Save your work.

Skills Review (continued)

8. Create a pie chart.

   a. Select the range A1:F2, then create a 3-D Pie chart.

   b. Drag the 3-D pie chart beneath the existing chart.

   c. Change the chart title to **Excel Users**.

   d. Apply the Style 7 chart style to the chart, then apply Layout 6 using the Quick Layout button.

   e. Explode the Human Resources slice from the pie chart at **25%**.

   f. In Page Layout view, enter your name in the left section of the worksheet header.

   g. Preview the worksheet and charts in Backstage view, make sure all the contents fit on one page, then submit your work to your instructor as directed. When printed, the worksheet should look like FIGURE 4-26. (Note that certain elements such as the title may look slightly different when printed.)

   h. Save your work, close the workbook, then exit Excel.

FIGURE 4-26

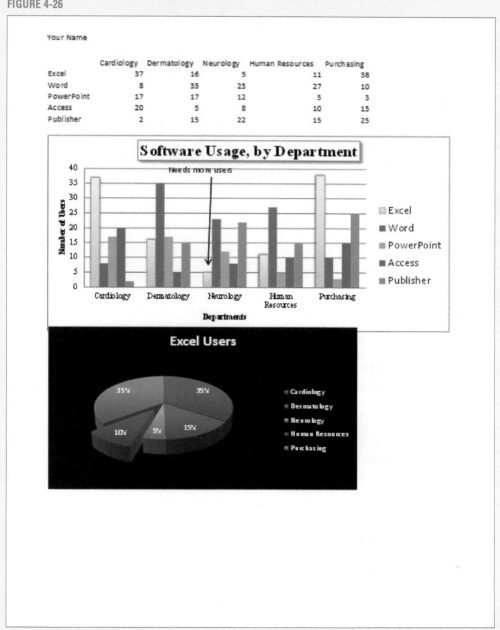

Your Name

	Cardiology	Dermatology	Neurology	Human Resources	Purchasing
Excel	37	16	5	11	38
Word	8	35	23	27	10
PowerPoint	17	17	12	5	3
Access	20	5	8	10	15
Publisher	2	15	22	15	25

Independent Challenge 1

You are the operations manager for the Chicago Medical Research Group. Each year the group revisits the number and types of activities they support to better manage their budgets. For this year's budget, you need to create charts to document the number of grants in previous years.

a. Start Excel, open the file EMP 4-3.xlsx from the location where you store your Data Files, then save it as **EMP 4-Chicago Medical Research Group**.

b. Take some time to plan your charts. Which type of chart or charts might best illustrate the information you need to display? What kind of chart enhancements do you want to use? Will a 3-D effect make your chart easier to understand?

c. Create a Clustered Column chart for the data.

d. Change at least one of the colors used in a data series.

e. Make the appropriate modifications to the chart to make it visually attractive and easier to read and understand. Include a legend to the right of the chart, and add a chart title and horizontal and vertical axis titles using the text shown in TABLE 4-3.

TABLE 4-3

title	text
Chart title	Number of Research Grants
Vertical axis title	Number of Grants
Horizontal axis title	Departments

f. Create at least two additional charts for the same data to show how different chart types display the same data. Reposition each new chart so that all charts are visible in the worksheet. One of the additional charts should be a pie chart for an appropriate data set; the other is up to you.

g. Modify each new chart as necessary to improve its appearance and effectiveness. A sample worksheet containing three charts based on the worksheet data is shown in FIGURE 4-27.

h. Enter your name in the worksheet header.

i. Save your work. Before printing, preview the worksheet in Backstage view, then adjust any settings as necessary so that all the worksheet data and charts will print on a single page.

j. Submit your work to your instructor as directed.

k. Close the workbook, then exit Excel.

FIGURE 4-27

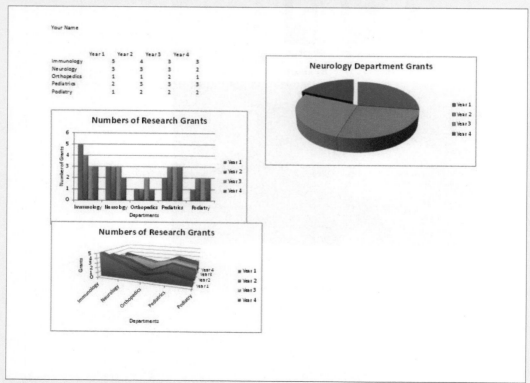

Independent Challenge 2

You work at Pinnacle Medical Consultants, a locally owned medical consortium. One of your responsibilities is to manage the company's revenues and expenses using Excel. As part of your efforts, you want to help the staff better understand and manage the largest sources of both expenses and revenue. To do this, you've decided to create charts using the previous year's operating expenses including rent, utilities, and payroll. The manager will use these charts at the next monthly meeting.

a. Start Excel, open EMP 4-4.xlsx from the location where you store your Data Files, then save it as **EMP 4-Pinnacle Medical Consultants**.

b. Decide which data in the worksheet should be charted. What chart types are best suited for the information you need to show? What kinds of chart enhancements are necessary?

c. Create a 3-D Clustered Column chart in the worksheet showing the expense data for all four quarters. (*Hint*: The expense categories should appear on the x-axis. Do not include the totals.)

d. Change the vertical axis labels (Expenses data) so that no decimals are displayed. (*Hint*: Use the Number category in the Format Axis pane.)

e. Using the revenue data, create two charts on this worksheet that compare the revenue amounts. (*Hint*: Move each chart to a new location on the worksheet, then deselect it before creating the next one.)

f. In one chart of the revenue data, add data labels, then add chart titles as you see fit.

g. Make any necessary formatting changes to make the charts look more attractive, then enter your name in a worksheet cell.

h. Save your work.

i. Preview each chart in Backstage view, and adjust any items as needed. Fit the worksheet to a single page, then submit your work to your instructor as directed. A sample of a printed worksheet is shown in FIGURE 4-28.

j. Close the workbook, then exit Excel.

FIGURE 4-28

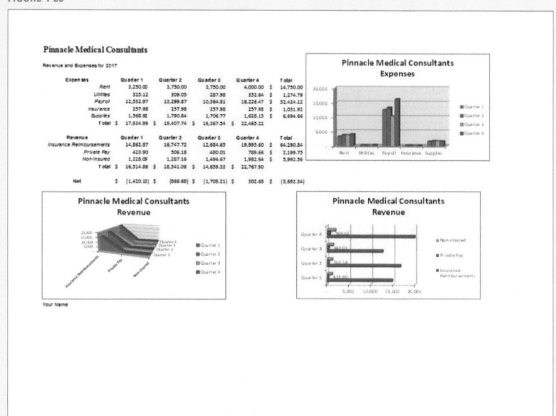

Independent Challenge 3

You are reviewing expenses for the Bethesda Medical Hospital's operating room and have been examining the most recent expenses. The board of directors wants to examine expenses and has asked you to prepare charts that can be used in this evaluation. In particular, you want to see how dollar amounts compare among the different expenses, and you also want to see how expenses compare with each other proportionally to the total budget.

a. Start Excel, open the Data File EMP 4-5.xlsx from the location where you store your Data Files, then save it as **EMP 4-OR Expenses**.

b. Identify three types of charts that seem best suited to illustrate the data in the range A16:B24. What kinds of chart enhancements are necessary?

c. Create at least two different types of charts that show the distribution of operating room expenses. (*Hint*: Move each chart to a new location on the same worksheet.) One of the charts should be a 3-D pie chart.

d. In at least one of the charts, add annotated text and an arrow highlighting important data, such as the largest expense.

e. Change the color of at least one data series in at least one of the charts.

f. Add chart titles and category and value axis titles where appropriate. Format the titles with a font of your choice. Apply a shadow to the chart title in at least one chart.

g. Add your name to a section of the header, then save your work.

h. Explode a slice from the 3-D pie chart.

i. Add a data label to the exploded pie slice.

j. Preview the worksheet in Backstage view. Adjust any items as needed. Be sure the charts are all visible on one page. Compare your work to the sample in FIGURE 4-29.

k. Submit your work to your instructor as directed, close the workbook, then exit Excel.

FIGURE 4-29

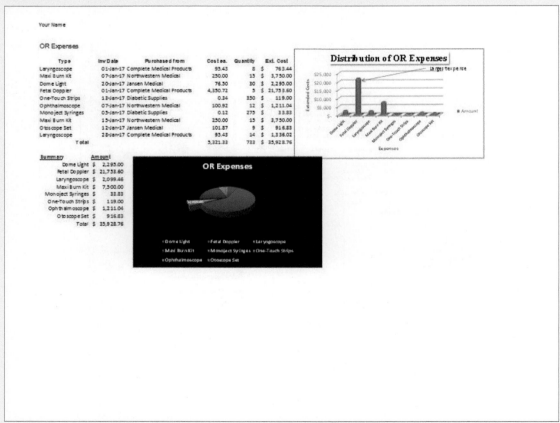

Independent Challenge 4: Explore

This Independent Challenge requires an Internet connection.

As financial manager at the Good Health Clinic, you have worked hard and saved money, and you have decided to purchase a home. The clinic wants to move you and your family to its new location, which you get to choose. You have a good idea where you'd like to live, and you decide to use the web to find out more about houses that are currently available. A worksheet would be a great place to compare the features and prices of potential homes.

a. Start Excel, then save a new, blank workbook as **EMP 4-My Dream House** to the location where you save your Data Files.

b. Decide on where you would like to live, and use your favorite search engine to find information sources on homes for sale in that area. (*Hint*: Try using realtor.com or other realtor-sponsored sites.)

c. Determine a price range and features within the home. Find data for at least five homes that meet your location and price requirements, and enter them in the worksheet. See TABLE 4-4 for a suggested data layout.

TABLE 4-4

suggested data layout		House 1	House 2	House 3	House 4	House 5
Location						
Price range						
		House 1	House 2	House 3	House 4	House 5
Asking price						
Bedrooms						
Bathrooms						
Year built						
Size (in sq. ft.)						

d. Format the data so it looks attractive and professional.

e. Create any type of column chart using only the House and Asking Price data. Place it on the same worksheet as the data. Include a descriptive title.

f. Change the colors in the chart using the chart style of your choice.

g. Enter your name in a section of the header.

h. Create an additional chart: a combo chart that plots the asking price on one axis and the size of the home on the other axis. (*Hint*: Use the Tell me what you want to do text box above the Ribbon to get more guidance on creating a Combo Chart.)

i. Save the workbook. Preview the worksheet in Backstage view and make adjustments if necessary to fit all of the information on one page. See FIGURE 4-30 for an example of what your worksheet might look like.

j. Submit your work to your instructor as directed.

k. Close the workbook, then exit Excel.

FIGURE 4-30

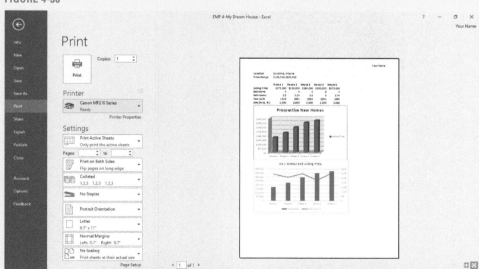

Excel 2016

Visual Workshop

Open the Data File EMP 4-6.xlsx from the location where you store your Data Files, then save it as **EMP 4-Projected Diagnostics Laboratory Revenue**. Format the worksheet data so it looks like FIGURE 4-31, then create and modify two charts to match the ones shown in the figure. You will need to make formatting, layout, and design changes once you create the charts. (*Hint*: The shadow used in the 3-D pie chart title is made using the Outer Offset Diagonal Bottom Right shadow.) Enter your name in the left text box of the header, then save and preview the worksheet. Submit your work to your instructor as directed, then close the workbook and exit Excel.

FIGURE 4-31

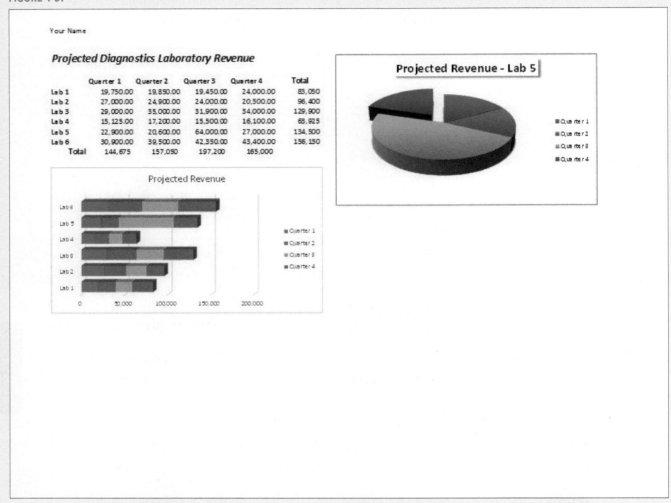

Getting Started with Access 2016

CASE ▶ Kristen Royal, R.N., is the new office assistant for Riverwalk Medical Center, a large family practice clinic. She uses Microsoft Access 2016 to store, maintain, and analyze patient information. She has hired you to help her use Access to support an electronic medical record for each patient.

Module Objectives

After completing this module, you will be able to:

- Understand relational databases
- Explore a database
- Create a database
- Create a table
- Create primary keys
- Relate two tables
- Enter data
- Edit data

Files You Will Need

AMP 1-1.accdb   AMP 1-3.accdb
AMP 1-2.accdb   AMP 1-4.accdb

Access 2016
Module 1

Learning
Outcomes
• Describe relational
database concepts
• Explain when to
use a database

Understand Relational Databases

Microsoft Access 2016 is relational database software that runs on the Windows operating system. You use **relational database software** to manage data—such as information about patients, medical procedures, medical diagnosis codes, medicines, employees, doctors, or insurance—that is organized into lists. Many small clinics and medical companies track some of this information in a spreadsheet program such as Microsoft Excel. Although Excel offers some list-management features and is more commonly used than Access, Access provides many more tools and advantages for managing data. The advantages are mainly due to the "relational" nature of the lists that Access manages. TABLE 1-1 compares the two programs. **CASE** *You and Kristen Royal review the advantages of database software over spreadsheets for managing lists of information.*

DETAILS

The advantages of using Access for database management include

- **Duplicate data is minimized**
  FIGURES 1-1 and 1-2 compare how you might store sales data in a single Excel spreadsheet list versus three related Access tables. With Access, you do not have to reenter information such as a patient's name and date of birth or doctor name every time the patient visits the clinic, because lists can be linked, or "related," in relational database software.

- **Information is more accurate, reliable, and consistent because duplicate data is minimized**
  The relational nature of data stored in an Access database allows you to minimize duplicate data entry, which creates more accurate, reliable, and consistent information. For example, patient data in a Patients table is entered only once, not every time a patient seeks medical help at the clinic.

- **Data entry is faster and easier using Access forms**
  Data entry forms (screen layouts) make data entry faster, easier, and more accurate than entering data in a spreadsheet.

- **Information can be viewed and sorted in many ways using Access queries, forms, and reports**
  In Access, you can save queries (questions about the data), data entry forms, and reports, allowing you to use them over and over without performing extra work to re-create a particular view of the data.

- **Information is more secure using Access passwords and security features**
  Access databases can be encrypted and password protected.

- **Several users can share and edit information at the same time**
  Unlike spreadsheets or word-processing documents, more than one person can enter, update, and analyze data in an Access database at the same time.

FIGURE 1-1: **Using a spreadsheet to organize patient data**

	A	B	C	D	E	F	G
1	PtLastName	PtFirstName	DOB	DateOfService	DiagDescription	DrLastName	DrFirstName
2	Clark	Beth	8/6/1975	5/9/2017	Pain in limb	Zimmerman	Carla
3	Clark	Beth	8/6/1975	6/8/2017	Sunburn	Zimmerman	Carla
4	Clark	Kelsey	4/4/1989	8/4/2017	Pain in limb	Nguyen	Lan
5	Clark	Kelsey	4/4/1989	5/4/2017	Knee meniscus injury	Nguyen	Lan
6	Color	Arnold	1/6/1972	5/16/2017	Sinusitis, acute	Rosenbaum	Anna
7	Creek	Lynn	7/8/1971	4/12/2017	Hypertension	Rosenbaum	Anna
8	Czerski	Sven	7/16/1961	6/2/2017	Drug withdrawal	Rosenbaum	Anna
9	Czerski	Sven	7/16/1961	7/15/2017	Psychosis	Rosenbaum	Anna
10	Czerski	Sven	7/16/1961	5/2/2017	Plantar fasciitis	Rosenbaum	Anna
11	Daniels	Hector	9/8/1957	5/10/2017	Hemorrhoids	Quinn	Forrest
12	Dao	Chin	8/1/1949	5/21/2017	Bronchitis	Patrick	Jeffery
		Chin	8/1/1949	5/21/2017	Hypoglycemia, diabetes I	Patrick	Jeffery
		Daniels	1/5/1983	6/8/2017	Spring/strain: neck	Zimmerman	Carla
		Daniels	1/5/1983	5/7/2017	Hypoglycemia, diabetes I	Zimmerman	Carla

Doctor information is duplicated for each patient visit to that doctor

Patient information is duplicated each time the patient visits the clinic

FIGURE 1-2: **Using a relational database to organize patient data**

Patients table

Patient ID	PtLastName	PtFirstName	DOB
1	Clark	Beth	08/06/1975
2	Clark	Kelsey	04/04/1989
3	Color	Arnold	01/06/1972
4	Creek	Lynn	07/08/1971

Visits table

Patient ID	DrCode	DateOfService	Diagnosis
1	CJZ	05/09/17	Pain in limb
2	LN	05/04/17	Knee meniscus injury
3	AWR	05/16/17	Sinusitis, acute

Doctors table

DrCode	DrFirstName	DrMiddleName	DrLastName	DrDegree
CJZ	Carla	J	Zimmerman	MD
LN	Lan		Nguyen	MD
AWR	Anna	Wolf	Rosenbaum	MD

TABLE 1-1: **Comparing Excel with Access**

feature	Excel	Access
Layout	Provides a natural tabular layout for easy data entry	Provides a natural tabular layout as well as the ability to create customized data entry screens called forms
Storage	Restricted to a file's limitations	Virtually unlimited when coupled with the ability to use Microsoft SQL Server to store data
Linked tables	Manages single lists of information—no relational database capabilities	Relates lists of information to reduce data redundancy and create a relational database
Reporting	Limited	Provides the ability to create an unlimited number of reports
Security	Limited to file security options such as marking the file "read-only" or protecting a range of cells	When used with SQL Server, provides extensive security down to the user and data level
Multiuser capabilities	Not allowed	Allows multiple users to simultaneously enter and update data
Data entry	Provides limited data entry screens	Provides the ability to create an unlimited number of data entry forms

Access 2016

Explore a Database

Learning Outcomes
- Start Access and open a database
- Identify Access components
- Open and define Access objects

You can start Access in many ways. If you double-click an existing Access database icon or shortcut, that specific database will open directly within Access. This is the fastest way to open an *existing* Access database. If you start Access on its own, however, you see a window that requires you to make a choice between opening a database and creating a new database. **CASE** *Kristen Royal has developed a database to start building an electronic medical record for each patient. She asks you to start Access 2016 and review this database.*

STEPS

1. **Start Access**

   Access starts, as shown in FIGURE 1-3. This window allows you to open an existing database, create a new database from a template, or create a new blank database.

   TROUBLE
   If a yellow Security Warning bar appears below the Ribbon, click Enable Content.

2. **Click the Open Other Files link, navigate to the location where you store your Data Files, click the AMP 1-1.accdb database file, click Open, click the File tab, click Save As, click the Save As button, type AMP 1-Riverwalk in the File name box, click Save, then click Enable Content if prompted**

   The AMP 1-Riverwalk database opens and contains six tables of data named Diagnosis, Insurance, Patients, ProcedureCodes, Providers, and Visits. It also contains four queries, two forms, and one report. Each of these items (table, query, form, and report) is a different type of **object** in an Access database and is displayed in the **Navigation Pane**. The purpose of each object is defined in TABLE 1-2. To learn about an Access database, you explore its objects.

   TROUBLE
   If the Navigation Pane is not open, click the Shutter Bar Open/Close button ⟫ to open it and view the database objects.

3. **In the Navigation Pane, double-click the Providers table to open it, double-click the Insurance table to open it, then double-click the Patients table to open it**

   The Providers, Insurance, and Patients tables open to display the data they store. A **table** is the fundamental building block of a relational database because it stores all of the data. You can enter or edit data in a table.

4. **In the Navigation Pane, double-click the InsuranceCharges query to open it, double-click any occurrence of Shield in "Blue Shield", type Cross then click any other row**

   A **query** selects a subset of data from one or more tables. In this case, the InsuranceCharges query selects data from the Patients, Visits, and Insurance tables. Editing data in one object changes that information in every other object of the database, which demonstrates the power and productivity of a relational database.

5. **Double-click the ElectronicMedicalRecord form to open it, type Aaron to replace Matthew in the First Name box, then click the Close button at the bottom of the form to close the form**

   An Access **form** is a data entry screen. Users prefer forms for data entry (rather than editing and entering data in tables and queries) because information can be presented in an easy-to-use layout.

   TROUBLE
   Be sure to close the ElectronicMedical-Record form before opening the Patients report so that the data is updated.

6. **Double-click the Patients report to open it**

   An Access **report** is a professional printout. A report is for printing purposes only, not data entry. As shown in FIGURE 1-4, changing Matthew's name to Aaron in the form automatically updated the report as well.

7. **Click the Close button ☒ in the upper-right corner of the window**

   Clicking the Close button in the upper-right corner of the window closes Access as well as the database on which you are working. Changes to data are automatically saved as you work. Access will prompt you to save *design* changes to objects before it closes.

FIGURE 1-3: Opening the Microsoft Access 2016 window

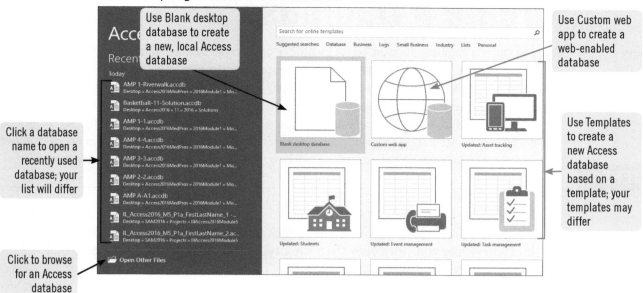

Use Blank desktop database to create a new, local Access database

Use Custom web app to create a web-enabled database

Click a database name to open a recently used database; your list will differ

Use Templates to create a new Access database based on a template; your templates may differ

Click to browse for an Access database

FIGURE 1-4: Objects in the AMP 1-Riverwalk database

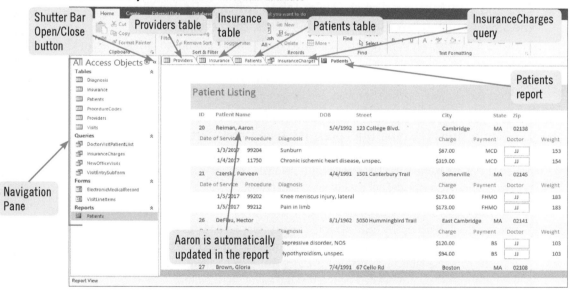

Shutter Bar Open/Close button

Providers table

Insurance table

Patients table

InsuranceCharges query

Navigation Pane

Patients report

Aaron is automatically updated in the report

TABLE 1-2: Access objects and their purpose

object	icon	purpose
Table		Contains all of the raw data within the database in a spreadsheet-like view; tables are linked with a common field to create a relational database, which minimizes redundant data
Query		Allows you to select a subset of fields or records from one or more tables; queries are created when you have a question about the data
Form		Provides an easy-to-use data entry screen
Report		Provides a professional printout of data that can contain enhancements such as headers, footers, graphics, and calculations on groups of records

Create a Database

You can create a database using an Access **template** or a sample database provided within the Microsoft Access program, or you can start with a blank database to create a database from scratch. Your decision depends on whether Access has a template that closely resembles the type of data you plan to manage. If it does, building your own database from a template might be faster than creating the database from scratch. Regardless of which method you use, you can always modify the database later, tailoring it to meet your specific needs. **CASE** ► *Kristen Royal reasons that the best way for you to learn Access is to start a new database from scratch, so she asks you to create a new database that will track staff communication.*

STEPS

1. **Start Access**

2. **Click the** Blank desktop database icon, **click the** Browse button 📁, **navigate to the location where you store your Data Files, type** AMP 1-Staff **in the File name box, click** OK, **then click the** Create button

   A new, blank database file with a single table named Table1 is created, as shown in FIGURE 1-5. Although you might be tempted to start entering data into the table, a better way to build a table is to first define the columns, or **fields**, of data that the table will store. **Table Design View** provides the most options for defining fields.

3. **Click the** View button 🖉 **on the Fields tab to switch to Design View, type** Employees **in the Save As dialog box as the new table name, then click** OK

   The table name changes from Table1 to Employees, and you are positioned in Table Design View, a window you use to name and define the fields of a table. Access created a field named ID with an AutoNumber data type. The **data type** is a significant characteristic of a field because it determines what type of data the field can store such as text, dates, or numbers. See TABLE 1-3 for more information about data types.

4. **Press [↓] to move to the first blank Field Name cell, type** FirstName, **press [↓], type** LastName, **press [↓], type** Title, **press [↓], type** DateOfBirth, **then press [↓]**

   Be sure to separate the first and last names into two fields so that you can easily sort, find, and filter on either part of the name later. The DateOfBirth field will contain only dates, so you should change its data type from Short Text (the default data type) to Date/Time.

5. **Click** Short Text **in the DateOfBirth row, click the** list arrow, **then click** Date/Time

   With these five fields properly defined for the new Employees table, as shown in FIGURE 1-6, you're ready to enter data. You switch back to Datasheet View to enter or edit data. **Datasheet View** is a spreadsheet-like view of the data in a table. A **datasheet** is a grid that displays fields as columns and records as rows. The new **field names** you just defined are listed at the top of each column.

6. **Click the** View button 📊 **to switch to Datasheet View, click** Yes **when prompted to save the table, press [Tab] to move to the FirstName field, type** your first name, **press [Tab] to move to the LastName field, type** your last name, **press [Tab] to move to the Title field, type** RN, **press [Tab], type** 1/32/90, **then press [Tab]**

   Because 1/32/1990 is not a valid date, Access does not allow you to make that entry and displays an error message, as shown in FIGURE 1-7. This shows that selecting the best data type for each field in Table Design View before entering data in Datasheet View helps prevent data entry errors.

7. **Press [Esc], edit the DateOfBirth entry for the first record to** 1/31/90, **press [Tab], enter two more sample records using realistic data, right-click the** Employees table tab, **then click** Close **to close the Employees table**

FIGURE 1-5: Creating a database with a new table

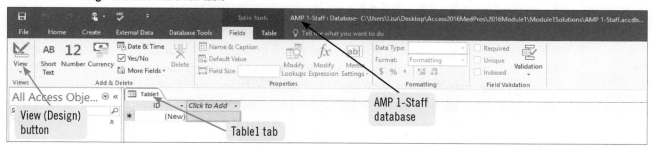

FIGURE 1-6: Defining field names and data types for the Employees table in Table Design View

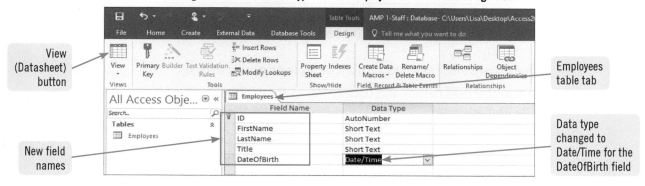

FIGURE 1-7: Entering your first record in the Employees table

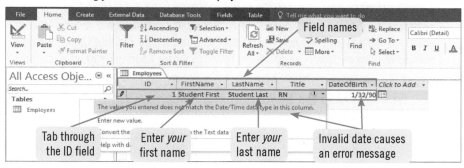

TABLE 1-3: Data types

data type	description of data
Short Text	Text or numbers not used in calculations such as a name, zip code, or phone number
Long Text	Lengthy text greater than 255 characters, such as comments or notes
Number	Numeric data that can be used in calculations, such as quantities
Date/Time	Dates and times
Currency	Monetary values
AutoNumber	Sequential integers controlled by Access
Yes/No	Only two values: Yes or No
Hyperlink	Web and email addresses
Attachment	External files such as .jpg images, spreadsheets, and documents
Calculated	Result of a calculation based on other fields in the table
Lookup Wizard	The Lookup Wizard helps you set Lookup properties, which display a drop-down list of values for the field; after using the Lookup Wizard, the final data type for the field is either Short Text or Number, depending on the values in the drop-down list

Create a Table

Learning
Outcomes
• Create a table in
Table Design View
• Set appropriate
data types for
fields

After creating your database and first table, you need to create new, related tables to build a relational database. Creating a table consists of these essential tasks: defining the fields in the table, selecting an appropriate data type for each field, naming the table, and determining how the table will participate in the relational database. **CASE** *Kristen Royal asks you to create another table to store staff evaluations. The new table will eventually be connected to the Employees table so each employee record in the Employees table may be related to many records in the Evaluations table.*

STEPS

1. **Click the Create tab on the Ribbon, then click the Table Design button in the Tables group**

   In **Design View**, you create and manipulate the structure of an object.

2. **Enter the field names and data types, as shown in** FIGURE 1-8

   The Evaluations table will contain four fields. EvaluationID is set with an AutoNumber data type so each record is automatically numbered by Access. The Notes field has a Long Text data type so a long evaluation can be recorded. EvaluationDate is a Date/Time field to identify the date of the evaluation. EmployeeID has a Number data type and will be used to link the Evaluations table to the Employees table later.

   TROUBLE
   To rename an object, close it, right-click it in the Navigation Pane, then click Rename.

3. **Click the View button ▦ to switch to Datasheet View, click Yes when prompted to save the table, type Evaluations as the table name, click OK, then click No when prompted to create a primary key**

   A **primary key field** contains unique data for each record. You'll identify a primary key field for the Evaluations table later. For now, you'll enter the first record in the Evaluations table in Datasheet View. A **record** is a row of data in a table. Refer to TABLE 1-4 for a summary of important database terminology.

   TROUBLE
   The EvaluationID field is an AutoNumber field, which will automatically increment to provide a unique value. If the number has already incremented beyond 1 for the first record, AutoNumber still works as intended.

4. **Press [Tab] to move to the Notes field, type Good communicator and hard worker, press [Tab], type 1/7/17 in the EvaluationDate field, press [Tab], then type 1 in the EmployeeID field**

   You entered 1 in the EmployeeID field to connect this evaluation with the employee in the Employees table that has an ID value of 1. Knowing which EmployeeID value to enter for each evaluation is difficult. After you relate the tables properly (a task you have not yet performed), Access can make it easier to link each evaluation to the correct employee.

5. **Point to the divider line between the Notes and EvaluationDate field names, and then drag the ◄► pointer to the right to widen the Notes field to read the entire entry, as shown in** FIGURE 1-9

6. **Right-click the Evaluations table tab, click Close, then click Yes if prompted to save the table**

Creating a table in Datasheet View

You can also create a new table in Datasheet View using the commands on the Fields tab of the Ribbon. But if you use Design View to design your table before starting the data entry process, you will probably avoid some common data entry errors. Design View helps you focus on the appropriate data type for each field.

Selecting the best data type for each field before entering any data into that field helps prevent incorrect data and unintended typos. For example, if a field is given a Number, Currency, or Date/Time data type, you will not be able to enter text into that field by mistake.

FIGURE 1-8: **Creating the Evaluations table**

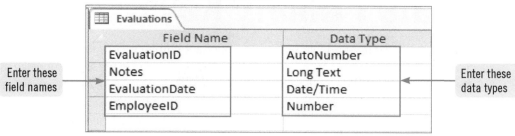

Enter these field names

Field Name	Data Type
EvaluationID	AutoNumber
Notes	Long Text
EvaluationDate	Date/Time
EmployeeID	Number

Enter these data types

FIGURE 1-9: **Entering the first record in the Evaluations table**

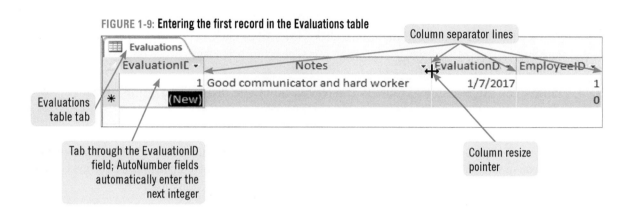

Column separator lines

Evaluations table tab

Tab through the EvaluationID field; AutoNumber fields automatically enter the next integer

Column resize pointer

TABLE 1-4: **Important database terminology**

term	description
Field	A specific piece or category of data such as a first name, last name, city, state, or phone number
Record	A group of related fields that describes a person, place, thing, or transaction such as a patient, prescription, physician, or diagnosis
Key field	A field that contains unique information for each record, such as a patient number for a patient
Table	A collection of records for a single subject such as Patients, Providers, or Insurance
Relational database	Multiple tables that are linked together to address a business process such as an electronic medical record at Riverwalk Medical Clinic
Objects	The parts of an Access database that help you view, edit, manage, and analyze the data: tables, queries, forms, reports, macros, and modules

Create Primary Keys

Learning Outcomes
- Set the primary key field
- Define one-to-many relationships

The **primary key field** of a table serves two important purposes. First, it contains data that uniquely identifies each record. No two records can have the exact same entry in the field designated as the primary key field. Second, the primary key field helps relate one table to another in a **one-to-many relationship**, where one record from one table may be related to many records in the second table. For example, one record in the Employees table may be related to many records in the Evaluations table. (One employee can have many evaluations.) The primary key field is always on the "one" side of a one-to-many relationship between two tables. **CASE** *Kristen Royal asks you to check that a primary key field has been appropriately identified for each table in the new staff database.*

STEPS

1. **Right-click the** Evaluations table **in the Navigation Pane, then click** Design View

   Table Design View for the Evaluations table opens. The field with the AutoNumber data type is generally the best candidate for the primary key field in a table because it automatically contains a unique number for each record.

   > **TROUBLE**
   > Make sure the Design tab is selected on the Ribbon.

2. **Click the** EvaluationID field **if it is not already selected, then click the** Primary Key button **in the Tools group on the Design tab**

   The EvaluationID field is now set as the primary key field for the Evaluations table, as shown in FIGURE 1-10.

   > **QUICK TIP**
   > You can also click the Save button 💾 on the Quick Access Toolbar to save a table.

3. **Right-click the** Evaluations table tab, **click** Close, **then click** Yes **to save the table**

   Any time you must save design changes to an Access object such as a table, Access displays a dialog box to remind you to save the object.

4. **Right-click the** Employees table **in the Navigation Pane, then click** Design View

   Access has already set ID as the primary key field for the Employees table, as shown in FIGURE 1-11.

5. **Right-click the** Employees table tab, **then click** Close

   You were not prompted to save the Employees table because you did not make any design changes. Now that you're sure that each table in the AMP 1-Staff database has an appropriate primary key field, you're ready to link the tables. The primary key field plays a critical role in this relationship.

FIGURE 1-10: Creating a primary key field for the Evaluations table

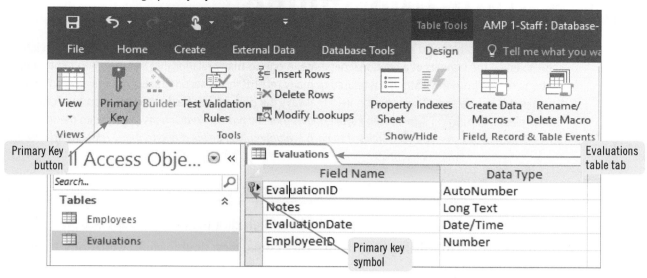

FIGURE 1-11: Confirming the primary key field for the Employees table

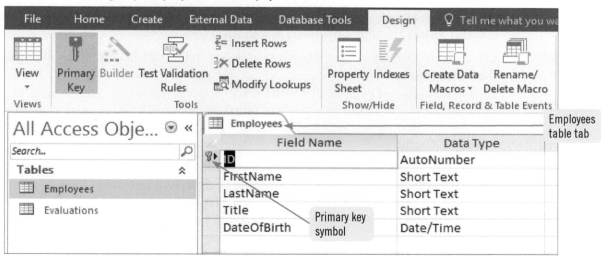

Field properties

Properties are the characteristics that define the field. Two properties are required for every field: Field Name and Data Type. Many other properties, such as Field Size, Format, Caption, and Default Value, are defined in the Field Properties pane in the lower half of a table's Design View. As you add more property entries, you are generally restricting the amount or type of data that can be entered in the field, which increases data entry accuracy. For example, you might change the Field Size property for a State field to 2 to eliminate an incorrect entry such as FLL. Field properties change depending on the data type of the selected field. For example, date fields do not have a Field Size property because Access controls the size of fields with a Date/Time data type.

Relate Two Tables

Learning Outcomes
- Define common field and foreign key field
- Create one-to-many relationships
- Set referential integrity

After you create tables and set primary key fields, you must connect the tables in one-to-many relationships to enjoy the benefits of a relational database. A one-to-many relationship between two tables means that one record from the first table is related to many records in the second table. You use a common field to make this connection. The common field is always the primary key field in the table on the "one" side of the relationship. **CASE** *Kristen Royal explains that she has new evaluations to enter into the staff database. To identify which employee is related to each evaluation, you define a one-to-many relationship between the Employees and Evaluations tables.*

STEPS

1. **Click the Database Tools tab on the Ribbon, then click the Relationships button**

2. **In the Show Table dialog box, double-click Employees, double-click Evaluations, then click Close**

   Each table is represented by a small **field list** window that displays the table's field names. A **key symbol** identifies the primary key field in each table. To relate the two tables in a one-to-many relationship, you connect them using a common field, which is always the primary key field on the "one" side of the relationship.

3. **Drag ID in the Employees field list to the EmployeeID field in the Evaluations field list**

   The Edit Relationships dialog box opens, as shown in FIGURE 1-12. **Referential integrity**, a set of Access rules that governs data entry, helps ensure data accuracy.

4. **Click the Enforce Referential Integrity check box in the Edit Relationships dialog box, then click Create**

   The **one-to-many line** shows the link between the ID field of the Employees table (the "one" side) and the EmployeeID field of the Evaluations table (the "many" side, indicated by the **infinity symbol**), as shown in FIGURE 1-13. The linking field on the "many" side is called the **foreign key field**. Now that these tables are related, it is much easier to enter evaluations for the correct employee.

5. **Right-click the Relationships tab, click Close, click Yes to save changes, then double-click the Employees table in the Navigation Pane to open it in Datasheet View**

   When you relate two tables in a one-to-many relationship, expand buttons ⊞ appear to the left of each record in the table on the "one" side of the relationship. In this case, the Employees table is on the "one" side of the relationship.

6. **Click the expand button ⊞ to the left of the first record**

   A **subdatasheet** shows the related evaluation records for each employee. In other words, the subdatasheet shows the records on the "many" side of a one-to-many relationship. The expand button ⊞ also changed to the collapse button ⊟ for the first employee. Widening the Notes field allows you to see the entire entry in the Evaluations subdatasheet. Now the task of entering evaluations for the correct employee is much more straightforward.

7. **Enter two more evaluations for your second and third employees, as shown in** FIGURE 1-14

   Interestingly, the EmployeeID field in the Evaluations table (the foreign key field) is not displayed in the subdatasheet. Behind the scenes, Access is entering the correct EmployeeID value in the Evaluations table, which is the glue that ties each evaluation to the correct employee.

8. **Close the Employees table, then click Yes if prompted to save changes**

FIGURE 1-12: Edit Relationships dialog box

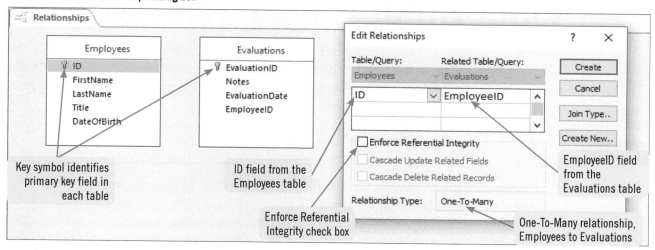

Key symbol identifies primary key field in each table

ID field from the Employees table

Enforce Referential Integrity check box

EmployeeID field from the Evaluations table

One-To-Many relationship, Employees to Evaluations

FIGURE 1-13: Linking the Employees and Evaluations tables

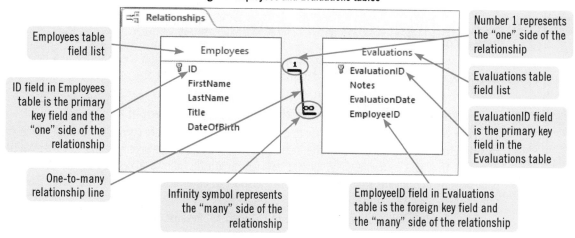

Employees table field list

ID field in Employees table is the primary key field and the "one" side of the relationship

One-to-many relationship line

Infinity symbol represents the "many" side of the relationship

Number 1 represents the "one" side of the relationship

Evaluations table field list

EvaluationID field is the primary key field in the Evaluations table

EmployeeID field in Evaluations table is the foreign key field and the "many" side of the relationship

FIGURE 1-14: Entering evaluations using the subdatasheet

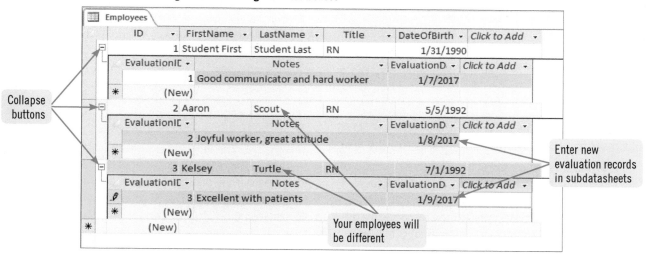

Collapse buttons

Enter new evaluation records in subdatasheets

Your employees will be different

Enter Data

Learning Outcomes
- Navigate records in a datasheet
- Enter records in a datasheet

Your skill in navigating and entering new records is a key to your success with a relational database. You can use many techniques to navigate through the records in the table's datasheet. **CASE** *Even though you have already successfully entered some records, Kristen Royal asks you to master this essential skill by entering several more employees in the staff database.*

STEPS

1. **Double-click the Employees table in the Navigation Pane to open it, press [Tab] three times, then press [Enter] three times**

   The Employees table reopens. The Evaluations subdatasheets are collapsed. Both the [Tab] and [Enter] keys move the focus to the next field. The **focus** refers to which data you would edit if you started typing. When you navigate to the last field of the record, pressing [Tab] or [Enter] advances the focus to the first field of the next record. You can also use the Next record ▶ and Previous record ◀ **navigation buttons** on the navigation bar in the lower-left corner of the datasheet to navigate through the records. The **Current record** text box on the navigation bar tells you the number of the current record as well as the total number of records in the datasheet.

   > **QUICK TIP**
   > Press [Tab] in the ID AutoNumber field.

2. **Click the FirstName field of the fourth record to position the insertion point to enter a new record**

   You can also use the New (blank) record button ▶※ on the navigation bar to move to a new record. You enter new records at the end of the datasheet. You learn how to sort and reorder records later. A complete list of navigation keystrokes is shown in TABLE 1-5.

   > **QUICK TIP**
   > Access databases are multiuser with one important limitation: Two users cannot edit the same record at the same time. In that case, a message explains that the second user must wait until the first user moves to a different record.

3. **At the end of the datasheet, enter the three records shown in FIGURE 1-15**

   The **edit record symbol** 🖉 appears to the left of the record you are currently editing. When you move to a different record, Access saves the data. Therefore, Access never prompts you to save *data* because it performs that task automatically. Saving data automatically allows Access databases to be **multiuser** databases, which means that more than one person can enter and edit data in the same database at the same time.

   Your ID values might differ from those in FIGURE 1-15. Because the ID field is an **AutoNumber** field, Access automatically enters the next consecutive number into the field as it creates the record. If you delete a record or are interrupted when entering a record, Access discards the value in the AutoNumber field and does not reuse it. Therefore, AutoNumber values do not represent the number of records in your table. Instead, they provide a unique value per record, similar to check numbers.

Changing from Navigation mode to Edit mode

If you navigate to another area of the datasheet by clicking with the mouse pointer instead of pressing [Tab] or [Enter], you change from **Navigation mode** to Edit mode. In **Edit mode,** Access assumes that you are trying to make changes to the current field value, so keystrokes such as [Ctrl][End], [Ctrl][Home], [←], and [→] move the insertion point within the field. To return to Navigation mode, press [Tab] or [Enter] (thus moving the focus to the next field), or press [↑] or [↓] (thus moving the focus to a different record).

FIGURE 1-15: New records in the Employees table

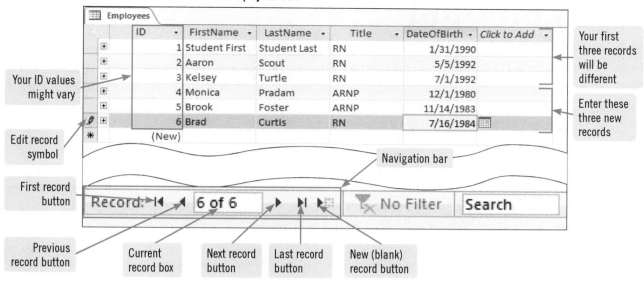

TABLE 1-5: Navigation mode keyboard shortcuts

shortcut key	moves to the
[Tab], [Enter], or [→]	Next field of the current record
[Shift][Tab] or [←]	Previous field of the current record
[Home]	First field of the current record
[End]	Last field of the current record
[Ctrl][Home] or [F5]	First field of the first record
[Ctrl][End]	Last field of the last record
[↑]	Current field of the previous record
[↓]	Current field of the next record

Cloud computing

Using **OneDrive**, a free service from Microsoft, you can store files in the "cloud" and retrieve them anytime you are connected to the Internet. Saving your files to the OneDrive is one example of cloud computing. **Cloud computing** means you are using an Internet resource to complete your work.

Edit Data

Learning Outcomes
• Edit data in a datasheet
• Delete records in a datasheet
• Preview and print a datasheet

Updating existing data in a database is another critical database task. To change the contents of an existing record, navigate to the field you want to change and type the new information. You can delete unwanted data by clicking the field and using [Backspace] or [Delete] to delete text to the left or right of the insertion point. Other data entry keystrokes are summarized in TABLE 1-6. **CASE** ▸ *Kristen Royal asks you to correct two records in the Employees table.*

STEPS

1. **Double-click the name in the FirstName field of the last record, type Mark, press [Enter], type Arno, press [Enter], type PA, press [Enter], type 2/5/82, then press [Enter]**

   You changed the name, title, and birth date of the last employee. When you entered the last two digits of the year value, Access inserted the first two digits after you pressed [Enter]. You'll also change the first employee.

QUICK TIP

The ScreenTip for the Undo button ↺ displays the action you can undo.

2. **Double-click RN in the Title field for the first record, type PAC, then press [Esc]**

   Pressing [Esc] once removes the current field's editing changes, so the Title value changes back to the previous entry. Pressing [Esc] twice removes all changes to the current record. When you move to another record, Access saves your edits, so you can no longer use [Esc] to remove editing changes to the current record. You can, however, click the Undo button ↺ on the Quick Access Toolbar to undo changes to a previous record.

3. **Retype PAC, press [Enter], type 12/1/80 in the DateOfBirth field, press [Enter], click the 12/1/80 date you just entered, click the Calendar icon 🗓, then click December 24, 1980, as shown in FIGURE 1-16**

   When you are working in the DateOfBirth field, which has a Date/Time data type, you can enter a date from the keyboard or use the **Calendar Picker**, a pop-up calendar to find and select a date.

4. **Click the record selector for the second to the last record (Brook Foster), click the Delete button in the Records group on the Home tab, then click Yes**

   A message warns that you cannot undo a record deletion. The Undo button is dimmed, indicating that you cannot use it. The Employees table now has five records, as shown in FIGURE 1-17. Keep in mind that your ID values might differ from those in the figure because they are controlled by Access.

QUICK TIP

If requested to print the Employees datasheet by your instructor, click the Print button, then click OK.

5. **Click the File tab, click Print, then click Print Preview to review the printout of the Employees table before printing**

6. **Click the Close Print Preview button, click the Close button in the upper-right corner of the window to close the AMP 1-Staff.accdb database and Access 2016, then click Yes if prompted to save design changes to the Employees table**

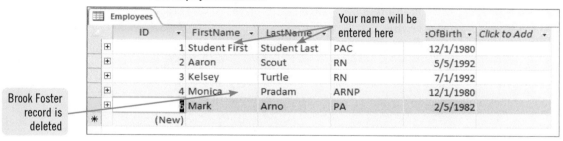

FIGURE 1-16: Editing employee records

Quick Access Toolbar; your buttons might be different

Undo button

Record selector button for Brook Foster record

Delete button

Click the left or right arrow to change the month

Calendar picker for date entries

December 24, 1980

FIGURE 1-17: Final Employees datasheet

Your name will be entered here

	ID	FirstName	LastName		?OfBirth	Click to Add
⊞	1	Student First	Student Last	PAC	12/1/1980	
⊞	2	Aaron	Scout	RN	5/5/1992	
⊞	3	Kelsey	Turtle	RN	7/1/1992	
⊞	4	Monica	Pradam	ARNP	12/1/1980	
⊞	5	Mark	Arno	PA	2/5/1982	
✳	(New)					

Brook Foster record is deleted

TABLE 1-6: Edit mode keyboard shortcuts

editing keystroke	action
[Backspace]	Deletes one character to the left of the insertion point
[Delete]	Deletes one character to the right of the insertion point
[F2]	Switches between Edit and Navigation mode
[Esc]	Undoes the change to the current field
[Esc][Esc]	Undoes all changes to the current record
[F7]	Starts the spell-check feature
[Ctrl][']	Inserts the value from the same field in the previous record into the current field
[Ctrl][;]	Inserts the current date in a Date field

Resizing and moving datasheet columns

You can resize the width of a field in a datasheet by dragging the column separator, the thin line that separates the field names to the left or right. The pointer changes to ✚ as you make the field wider or narrower. Release the mouse button when you have resized the field. To adjust the column width to accommodate the widest entry in the field, double-click the column separator. To move a column, click the field name to select the entire column, then drag the field name left or right.

Practice

Concepts Review

Label each element of the Access window shown in FIGURE 1-18.

FIGURE 1-18: New records in the Employees table

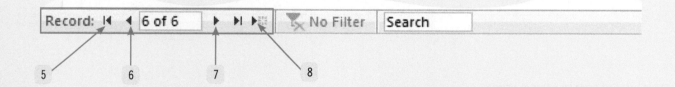

Match each term with the statement that best describes it.

10. **Field**
11. **Record**
12. **Table**
13. **Datasheet**
14. **Query**
15. **Form**
16. **Report**

a. An easy-to-use data entry screen
b. A category of information in a table, such as a company name, city, or state
c. A professional printout of database information
d. A collection of records for a single subject, such as all the patient records
e. A group of related fields for one item, such as all of the information for one patient
f. A subset of data from one or more tables
g. A spreadsheet-like grid that displays fields as columns and records as rows

Select the best answer from the list of choices.

17. Which of the following is *not* a typical benefit of relational databases?

   a. Minimized duplicate data entry   **c.** More accurate data

   b. More common than spreadsheets   **d.** Faster information retrieval

18. Which of the following is *not* an advantage of managing data with relational database software such as Access versus spreadsheet software such as Excel?

   a. Allows multiple users to enter data simultaneously   **c.** Reduces duplicate data entry

   b. Provides data entry forms   **d.** Uses a single table to store all data

19. When you create a new database, which object is created first?

   a. Table   **c.** Query

   b. Form   **d.** Module

Skills Review

1. Understand relational databases.

   a. Write down five advantages of managing database information in Access versus using a spreadsheet.

   b. Write a sentence to explain how the terms *field, record, table,* and *relational database* relate to one another.

2. Explore a database.

   a. Start Access.

   b. Open the AMP 1-2.accdb database from the location where you store your Data Files, then save it as **AMP 1-Diabetes**. Click Enable Content if a yellow Security Warning message appears.

   c. Open each of the five tables to study the data they contain. Complete the following table, then close the tables in Access:

table name	number of records	number of fields

   d. Double-click the ConsultsByEmployee query in the Navigation Pane to open it. Change any occurrence of Molly Frank in the EmployeeFirst and EmployeeLast fields to *your* **name**. Move to another record to save your changes.

   e. Double-click the EmployeeEntry form in the Navigation Pane to open it. Use the navigation buttons to navigate through the 16 employees to observe each employee's information. Find the record with your name and change the Street Address, City, State, and Zip Code information to your school's address. Close the EmployeeEntry form.

   f. Double-click the PatientListing report in the Navigation Pane to open it. Notice the name Tanner Aaron in the first record. Scroll to the bottom of the report to observe the grand total calculation of 67.5 then close the report.

   g. Open the Patients table and find the Tanner Aaron record (29). Change the LastName field value of Aaron to *your* **last name**, then close the Patients table.

   h. Open the PatientListing report again. Find *your* last name. (*Hint:* The records are sorted by the LastName field.) Close the report.

   i. Close the AMP 1-Diabetes database, and then close Access 2016.

3. Create a database.

   a. Start Access, click the Blank desktop database icon, use the Browse button to navigate to the location where you store your Data Files, type **AMP 1-Personnel** as the filename, click OK, and then click Create to create a new database named AMP 1-Personnel.accdb.

Skills Review (continued)

b. Switch to Table Design View, name the table **Nurses**, then enter the following fields and data types:

field name	data type
NurseID	AutoNumber
NurseFirst	Short Text
NurseLast	Short Text
Degree	Short Text
HireDate	Date/Time

c. Save the table, switch to Datasheet View, and enter two records using *your* name in the first record and your instructor's name in the second. Tab through the ID field, an AutoNumber field.

d. Enter **RN** as the value in the Degree field for both records. Use today's date for the DateOfHire value.

e. Widen each column in the Nurses table so that all data is visible, then save and close the Nurses table.

4. Create a table.

a. Click the Create tab on the Ribbon, click the Table Design button in the Tables group, then create a new table with the following two fields and data types:

field name	data type
DegreeAbbreviation	Short Text
DegreeDescription	Short Text

b. Save the table with the name **Degrees**. Click No when asked if you want Access to create the primary key field.

5. Create primary keys.

a. In Table Design View of the Degrees table, set the DegreeAbbreviation as the primary key field.

b. Save the Degrees table, and open it in Datasheet View.

c. Enter one record, using **RN** as the DegreeAbbreviation value and **Registered Nurse** for the DegreeDescription value to match the Degree value of RN that you entered for both records in the Nurses table.

d. Close the Degrees table.

6. Relate two tables.

a. From the Database Tools tab, open the Relationships window.

b. Add the Degrees, then the Nurses table to the Relationships window.

c. Drag the bottom edge of the Nurses table to expand the field list to display all of the fields.

d. Drag the DegreeAbbreviation field from the Degrees table to the Degree field of the Nurses table.

e. In the Edit Relationships dialog box, click the Enforce Referential Integrity check box, then click Create. Your Relationships window should look similar to FIGURE 1-19. If you connect the wrong fields by mistake, right-click the line connecting the two fields, click Delete, then try again.

f. Close the Relationships window, and save changes when prompted.

FIGURE 1-19

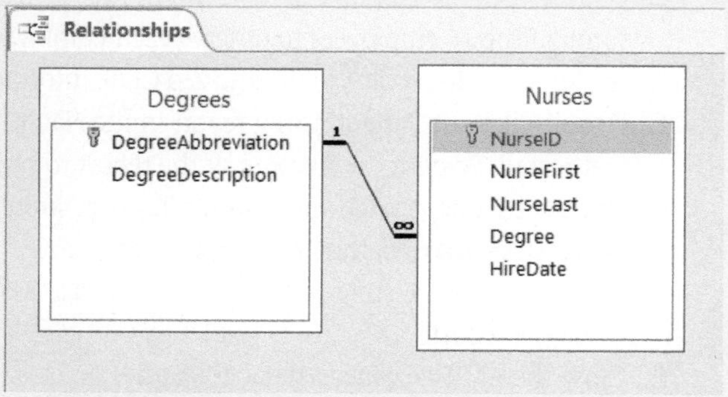

Skills Review (continued)

7. Enter data.

a. Open the Degrees table, widen the DegreeDescription field, and enter the following records:

DegreeAbbreviation	DegreeDescription
LPN	Licensed Practical Nurse
ARNP	Advanced Registered Nurse Practitioner
BSN	Bachelor of Science in Nursing
CNA	Certified Nurse's Assistant

b. Save, close, and reopen the Degrees table. Notice that Access automatically sorts the records by the values in the primary key field, the DegreeAbbreviation field. Double-check abbreviations and spelling for accuracy.

8. Edit data.

a. Click the Expand button for the RN record to see the two related records from the Nurses table.

b. Enter two more nurse records in the RN subdatasheet using any fictitious but realistic data, as shown in FIGURE 1-20. Notice that you are not required to enter a value for the Degree field, the foreign key field in the subdatasheet.

FIGURE 1-20

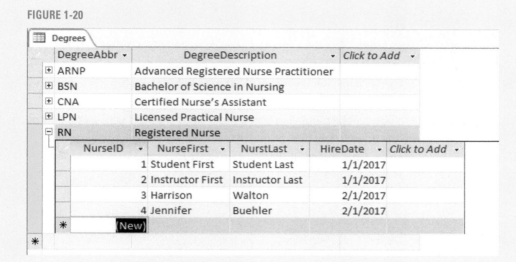

c. If required by your instructor, print the Degrees datasheet and the Nurses datasheet.

d. Click the Close button in the upper-right corner of the Access window to close all open objects as well as the AMP 1-Personnel database and Access 2016. If prompted to save any design changes, click Yes.

Independent Challenge 1

Consider the following four subject areas:

- Telephone directory
- Medications
- Diagnosis Codes
- College Course Offerings

a. For each subject, build a Word table with four to seven columns and four rows. In the first row, enter field names that you would expect to see in a table used to manage that subject.

b. In the other rows of each table, enter three realistic records. The first table, Telephone Directory, is completed as an example to follow.

TABLE: **Telephone Directory**

FirstName	LastName	Street	Zip	Phone
Ted	Polo	111 Oak Street	50846	555-444-3311
Courtney	Born	533 Adams Street	50837	555-444-3322
Michael	Mahring	4400 Wedd Avenue	50847	555-444-9876

Independent Challenge 2

You are working with a medical school's intern placement program. You have started an Access database to track evaluations of interns.

a. Start Access, open the AMP 1-3.accdb database, save it as **AMP 1-Internships** to the location where you store your Data Files, then enable content if prompted.

b. Open the InternNames table to observe the number of fields and records, and add your own name as a new record.

c. Switch to Design View to note the primary key field of the table, InternNo, then close the table.

d. In Table Design View, build the new table shown in FIGURE 1-21 named **Evaluations**. Be sure to enter the field names and data types exactly as shown.

FIGURE 1-21

Field Name	Data Type	
EvaluationNo	AutoNumber	
Prompt	Number	1-5 scale, 5 being the best
Professional	Number	1-5 scale, 5 being the best
Knowledgeable	Number	1-5 scale, 5 being the best
Respectful	Number	1-5 scale, 5 being the best
EvaluatorLastName	Short Text	
EvaluatorFirstName	Short Text	
EvaluationDate	Date/Time	
InternNo	Number	foreign key field to InternNames table

Independent Challenge 2 (continued)

e. Set EvaluationNo as the primary key field, and close the Evaluations table.

f. Open the Relationships window, click the Show Table button to add the field lists for both tables to the Relationships window, and drag the title bars of the field lists to position them as shown in FIGURE 1-22. Resize the field lists to show all fields.

g. Create the one-to-many relationship and enforce referential integrity as shown in FIGURE 1-22. If you create the relationship incorrectly, right-click the line linking the fields, click Delete, and try again.

FIGURE 1-22

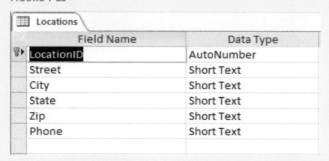

h. Click the Relationship Report button on the Design tab, then print it if required by your instructor.

i. To close the report, right-click the Relationships for AMP 1-Internships tab, and click Close. Click Yes when prompted to save changes to the report, then click OK to accept the report name.

j. Save your changes to the Relationships window, if prompted, close the AMP 1-Internships.accdb database, then exit Access 2016.

Independent Challenge 3

You are working for a pediatric clinic that has several locations. Each location has several physicians assigned to that location. You have created an Access database to help keep track of which physicians work at each location.

a. Start Access, open the AMP 1-4.accdb database, save it as **AMP 1-Pediatrics** to the location where you store your Data Files, then enable content if prompted.

b. Add a new record to the Providers table, using your own first and last names, and a unique entry for the ProviderCode field.

c. In Table Design View, build the new table shown in FIGURE 1-23 named **Locations**. Be sure to enter the field names and data types exactly as shown.

FIGURE 1-23

Field Name	Data Type
LocationID	AutoNumber
Street	Short Text
City	Short Text
State	Short Text
Zip	Short Text
Phone	Short Text

Independent Challenge 3 (continued)

d. Set LocationID as the primary key field, and open it in Datasheet View.

e. Enter two sample records in the Locations table using fictitious but realistic data. Note the value of the LocationID field for both records (probably 1 and 2).

f. Open the Providers table in Table Design View, then add a new field named LocationID with a Number data type. This field will serve as the foreign key field to connect the Locations and Providers tables in a one-to-many relationship. Save the Providers table.

g. Open the Providers table in Datasheet View, and give each record a LocationID value that matches a LocationID value in the Locations table (probably 1 or 2, but these values must match one of the existing values in the LocationID field for the Locations table).

h. Close the Providers and Locations tables.

i. Open the Relationships window, click the Show Table button to add the field lists for both tables to the Relationships window, and drag the title bars of the field lists to position them as shown in FIGURE 1-24.

j. Create the one-to-many relationship between the Locations and Providers tables using the common LocationID field, and enforce referential integrity as shown in FIGURE 1-24. If you create the relationship incorrectly or cannot enforce referential integrity, right-click the link line, click Delete, and try again.

k. Click the Relationship Report button on the Design tab, then if requested by your instructor, click Print to print a copy of the Relationships for AMP 1-Pediatrics report.

l. To close the report, right-click the Relationships for AMP 1-Pediatrics tab and click Close. Click Yes when prompted to save changes to the report, then click OK to accept the report name.

m. Close the AMP 1-Pediatrics.accdb database, and exit Access 2016.

FIGURE 1-24

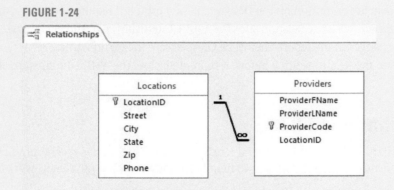

Independent Challenge 4: Explore

Now that you've learned about Microsoft Access and relational databases, brainstorm how you might use an Access database in your daily life or career. Start by visiting the Microsoft website, and explore what's new about Access 2016. (*Note*: To complete this Independent Challenge, make sure you are connected to the Internet.)

a. Using your favorite search engine, look up the keywords *benefits of a relational database* or *benefits of Microsoft Access* to find articles that discuss the benefits of organizing data in a relational database.

b. Read several articles about the benefits of organizing data in a relational database such as Access, identifying three distinct benefits. Use a Word document to record those three benefits. Also, copy and paste the website address of the article you are referencing for each benefit you have identified.

c. In addition, as you read the articles that describe relational database benefits, list any terminology unfamiliar to you, identifying at least five new terms.

d. Using a search engine or a website that provides a computer glossary such as *www.whatis.com* or *www.webopedia.com*, look up the definition of the new terms, and enter both the term and the definition of the term in your document as well as the website address where your definition was found.

e. Finally, based on your research and growing understanding of Access 2016, list three ways you could use an Access database to organize, enhance, or support the activities and responsibilities of your daily life or career. Type your name at the top of the document, and submit it to your instructor as requested.

Visual Workshop

Start Access, then create a database named **AMP 1-Prescriptions** in the drive and folder where you store your Data Files. Create a table named **ScriptAbbreviations** with three Short Text fields shown in FIGURE 1-25. Specify the Abbreviation field to be the primary key field. Then enter the 20 records shown in the figure with common prescription abbreviation codes.

FIGURE 1-25

Abbreviation	Latin	Meaning	Click to Add
ac	ante cibum	before meals	
bid	bis in die	twice a day	
cc		cubic centimeter	
dc		discontinue	
gt	gutta	drop	
hs	hora somni	at bedtime	
im	intramuscular	into the muscle (injected)	
inj	injection	injection	
iv	intravenous	into the vein	
od	oculus dexter	right eye	
os	oculus sinister	left eye	
pc	post cibum	after meals	
po	per os	by mouth	
prn	pro re nata	as needed	
q	quaque	every	
q 3 h	quaque 3 hora	every 3 hours	
qd	quaque die	every day	
qid	quater in die	4 times a day	
sig	signa	write	
tid	ter in die	3 times a day	
*			

Building and Using Queries

CASE   Kristen Royal, R.N. and office assistant for Riverwalk Medical Clinic, has several questions about the patient database. You'll develop queries to provide Kristen with up-to-date answers.

Module Objectives

After completing this module, you will be able to:

- Use the Query Wizard
- Work with data in a query
- Use Query Design View
- Sort and find data

- Filter data
- Apply AND criteria
- Apply OR criteria
- Format a datasheet

Files You Will Need

AMP 2-1.accdb	AMP 2-4.accdb
AMP 2-2.accdb	AMP 2-5.accdb
AMP 2-3.accdb	AMP 2-6.accdb

Use the Query Wizard

Learning Outcomes
- Describe the purpose for a query
- Create a query with the Simple Query Wizard

A **query** answers a question about the information in the database. A query allows you to select a subset of fields and records from one or more tables and then present the selected data as a single datasheet. A major benefit of working with data through a query is that you can focus on only the specific information you need to answer a question, rather than navigating through all the fields and records from many large tables. You can enter, edit, and navigate data in a query datasheet just like a table datasheet. However, keep in mind that Access data is physically stored only in tables, even though you can select, view, and edit it through other Access objects such as queries and forms. Because a query doesn't physically store the data, a query datasheet is sometimes called a **logical view** of the data. Technically, a query is a set of **SQL (Structured Query Language)** instructions, but because you can use Access query tools such as Query Design View to create and modify the query, you are not required to know SQL to build or use Access queries. **CASE** *You use the Simple Query Wizard to create a query that displays fields from the Patients and Visits tables in one datasheet.*

STEPS

1. **Start Access, click the** Open Other Files link, **browse for and select the** AMP 2-1.accdb **database file, click** Open, **click the** File tab, **click** Save As, **click** Save Database As, **click the** Save As button, **type** AMP 2-Riverwalk **in the File name box, click** Save, **then click** Enable Content **if prompted**

    Access provides several tools to create a new query. One way is to use the **Simple Query Wizard**, which prompts you for the information it needs to create a new query.

2. **Click the** Create tab **on the Ribbon, click the** Query Wizard button **in the Queries group, then click** OK **to start the Simple Query Wizard**

    The Simple Query Wizard dialog box opens, prompting you to select the fields you want to view in the new query. You can select fields from one or more existing tables or queries.

3. **Click the** Tables/Queries list arrow, **click** Table: Patients, **double-click** PtLastName, **then double-click** PtFirstName

    So far, you've selected two fields from the Patients table to display the last and then first name of the patient in this query. You also want to add the Diagnosis and DateofService fields from the Visits table.

TROUBLE
Click the Remove Single Field button
[<] if you need to remove a field from the Selected Fields list.

4. **Click the** Tables/Queries list arrow, **click** Table: Visits, **double-click** Diagnosis, **then double-click** DateofService

    You've selected two fields from the Patients table and two from the Visits table for your new query, as shown in FIGURE 2-1.

5. **Click** Next, **click** Next **to select Detail, select** Patients Query **in the title text box, type** PatientDiagnosis **as the name of the query, then click** Finish

    The PatientDiagnosis datasheet opens, displaying two fields from the Patients table and two from the Visits table, as shown in FIGURE 2-2. The query sometimes lists more than one diagnosis and date of service per patient due to the one-to-many relationship between the Patients and Visits tables established in the Relationships window.

FIGURE 2-1: **Selecting fields using the Simple Query Wizard**

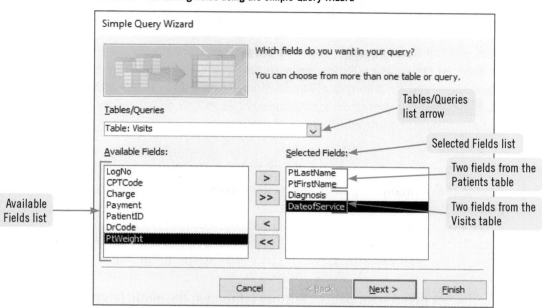

FIGURE 2-2: **PatientDiagnosis datasheet**

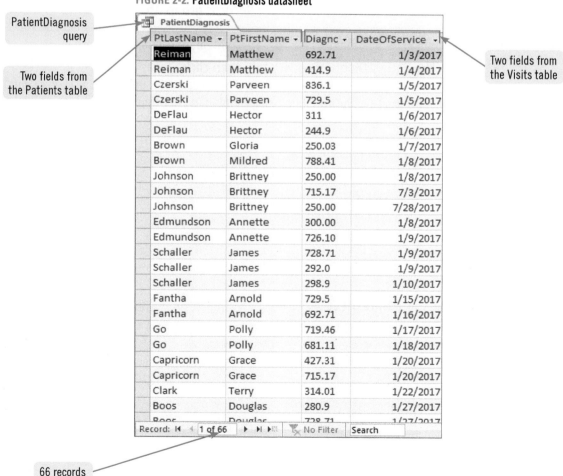

Work with Data in a Query

Learning Outcomes
- Edit records in a query
- Delete records in a query

You enter and edit data in a query datasheet the same way you do in a table datasheet. Because all data is stored in tables, any edits you make to data in a query datasheet are actually stored in the underlying tables and are automatically updated in all views of the data in other queries, forms, and reports. **CASE** ▶ *You want to change the name of two patients and delete one patient record. You can use the PatientDiagnosis query datasheet to make these edits.*

STEPS

1. **Double-click Reiman for patient Aaron Reiman in either the first or second record, type Mitchell, then click any other record**

   All occurrences of Aaron Reiman automatically update to Aaron Mitchell because this patient's name value is stored only once in the Patients table but is related to two records in the Visits table. See FIGURE 2-3. The patient's name is selected from the Patients table and displayed in the PatientDiagnosis query for each patient visit.

2. **Double-click Johnson for patient Brittney Johnson in the ninth, tenth, or eleventh record, type Williams, then click any other record**

   All occurrences of Johnson automatically update to Williams because this value is stored only once in the Patients table. This patient had three visits to the clinic.

3. **Click the record selector button ☐ to the left of the record for Mildred Brown, click the Home tab, click the Delete button in the Records group, then click Yes**

   You can delete records from a query datasheet the same way you delete them from a table datasheet. Notice that the navigation bar now indicates you have 65 records in the datasheet, as shown in FIGURE 2-4.

4. **Right-click the PatientDiagnosis query tab, then click Close**

   Each time a query is opened, it shows a current view of the data. This means that as new patients or visits are recorded in the database, the next time you open this query, the information will include all updates.

Hiding and unhiding fields in a datasheet

To hide a field in a datasheet, right-click the field name at the top of the datasheet, and click the Hide Fields option on the shortcut menu. To unhide a field, right-click any field name, click Unhide Fields, and check the hidden field's check box in the Unhide Columns dialog box.

Freezing and unfreezing fields in a datasheet

In large datasheets, you may want to freeze certain fields so that they remain on the screen at all times. To freeze a field, right-click its field name in the datasheet, and then click Freeze Fields. To unfreeze a field, right-click any field name, and click Unfreeze All Fields.

FIGURE 2-3: Working with data in a query datasheet

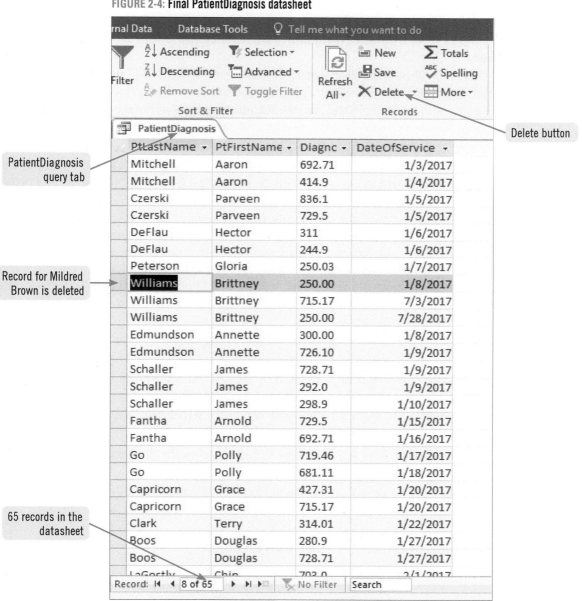

Update Aaron Reiman to Aaron Mitchell

Record selector button for Mildred Brown record

PtLastName	PtFirstName	Diagnc	DateOfService
Mitchell	Aaron	692.71	1/3/2017
Mitchell	Aaron	414.9	1/4/2017
Czerski	Parveen	836.1	1/5/2017
Czerski	Parveen	729.5	1/5/2017
DeFlau	Hector	311	1/6/2017
DeFlau	Hector	244.9	1/6/2017
Brown	Gloria	250.03	1/7/2017
Brown	Mildred	788.41	1/8/2017
Johnson	Brittney	250.00	1/8/2017
Johnson	Brittney	715.17	7/3/2017
Johnson	Brittney	250.00	7/28/2017

FIGURE 2-4: Final PatientDiagnosis datasheet

PatientDiagnosis query tab

Delete button

Record for Mildred Brown is deleted

65 records in the datasheet

PtLastName	PtFirstName	Diagnc	DateOfService
Mitchell	Aaron	692.71	1/3/2017
Mitchell	Aaron	414.9	1/4/2017
Czerski	Parveen	836.1	1/5/2017
Czerski	Parveen	729.5	1/5/2017
DeFlau	Hector	311	1/6/2017
DeFlau	Hector	244.9	1/6/2017
Peterson	Gloria	250.03	1/7/2017
Williams	Brittney	250.00	1/8/2017
Williams	Brittney	715.17	7/3/2017
Williams	Brittney	250.00	7/28/2017
Edmundson	Annette	300.00	1/8/2017
Edmundson	Annette	726.10	1/9/2017
Schaller	James	728.71	1/9/2017
Schaller	James	292.0	1/9/2017
Schaller	James	298.9	1/10/2017
Fantha	Arnold	729.5	1/15/2017
Fantha	Arnold	692.71	1/16/2017
Go	Polly	719.46	1/17/2017
Go	Polly	681.11	1/18/2017
Capricorn	Grace	427.31	1/20/2017
Capricorn	Grace	715.17	1/20/2017
Clark	Terry	314.01	1/22/2017
Boos	Douglas	280.9	1/27/2017
Boos	Douglas	728.71	1/27/2017
LaGortly	Chin	703.0	2/1/2017

Record: 8 of 65   No Filter   Search

Use Query Design View

Learning Outcomes
• Work in Query Design View
• Add criteria to a query

You use **Query Design View** to add, delete, or move the fields in an existing query; to specify sort orders; or to add **criteria** to limit the number of records shown in the resulting datasheet. You can also use Query Design View to create a new query from scratch. Query Design View presents the fields you can use for that query in small windows called **field lists**. If you use the fields of two or more related tables in the query, the relationship between two tables is displayed with a **join line** (also called a **link line**) identifying which fields are used to establish the relationship. **CASE** ▸ *Kristen Royal asks you to add a diagnosis description to the PatientDiagnosis query to limit the records to a specific date of service. You use Query Design View to modify the existing PatientDiagnosis query to meet her request.*

STEPS

1. **Double-click the** PatientDiagnosis query **in the Navigation Pane to review the datasheet**

   The PatientDiagnosis query contains the PtLastName and PtFirstName fields from the Patients table and the Diagnosis and DateofService fields from the Visits table.

QUICK TIP
Drag the lower edge of the field list to view more fields.

2. **Click the** View button 🔍 **on the Home tab to switch to Query Design View, then drag the** Diagnosis table **from the Navigation Pane to the right of the Visits table to add it to the query**

   Query Design View displays the tables used in the query in the upper pane of the window. The link line shows that one record in the Patients table may be related to many records in the Visits table, but when a query is created with the Query Wizard, the one and infinity symbols are not shown on the link line. The lower pane of the window, called the **query design grid** (or query grid for short), displays the field names, sort orders, and criteria used within the query.

3. **Drag the** DiagDescription field **from the Diagnosis table to the** DateofService column **in the query grid as shown in** FIGURE 2-5, **then click the** View button 🔲 **in the Results group to switch to Datasheet View**

   The DateofService field automatically shifted to the right to accommodate the new DiagDescription field in Query Design View. When you double-click a field in a field list, Access inserts it in the next available position in the query design grid. You can also select a field and then drag it to a specific column of the query grid. To select a field in the query grid, you click its field selector. The **field selector** is the thin gray bar above each field in the query grid. If you want to delete a field from a query, click its field selector, then press [Delete]. Deleting a field from a query does not delete it from the underlying table; the field is deleted only from the query's logical view of the data.

   In Datasheet View, the DiagDescription field adds a description for each DiagnosisCode. To limit the datasheet to only records with a 5/15/2017 date of service, you return to Design View and enter criteria.

4. **Click** 🔍 **to switch back to Design View, click the** Criteria cell **for the** DateofService field, **type** 5/15/2017, **then click** 🔲 **to switch to Datasheet View**

   Now only two records are selected, because only two of the records have a date of 5/15/2017 in the DateofService field, as shown in FIGURE 2-6.

5. **Click the** File tab, **click** Save As, **click** Save Object As, **click the** Save As button, **type** May15Visits, **then click** OK

   In Access, the **Save As command** on the File tab allows you to save the entire database (and all objects it contains) or just the current object with a new name. Recall that Access saves *data* automatically as you move from record to record.

6. **Right-click the** May15Visits query tab, **then click** Close

FIGURE 2-5: PatientDiagnosis query in Design View

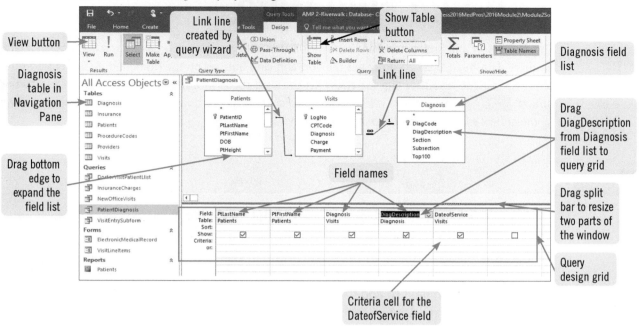

FIGURE 2-6: PatientDiagnosis datasheet with DiagDescription field and 5/15/2017 DateofService criterion

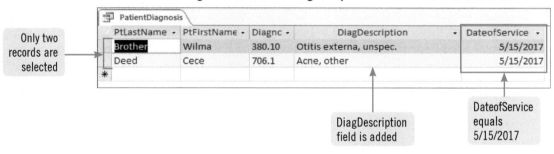

Adding or deleting a table in a query

You might want to add a table's field list to the upper pane of Query Design View to select fields from that table for the query. To add a new table to Query Design View, drag it from the Navigation Pane to Query Design View, or click the Show Table button on the Design tab, then add the desired table(s). To delete an unneeded table from Query Design View, click its title bar, then press [Delete].

Sort and Find Data

The Access sort and find features are handy tools that help you quickly organize and find data in a table or query datasheet. TABLE 2-1 describes the Sort and Find buttons on the Home tab. Besides using these buttons, you can also click the list arrow on the field name in a datasheet and then click a sorting option. **CASE** *Kristen asks you to modify the PatientDiagnosis query to redisplay all the records sorted by the patient's last name and then by date of service.*

STEPS

1. **Double-click the PatientDiagnosis query in the Navigation Pane to open its datasheet**

   It's often helpful to review the data in the datasheet before making modifications in Design View.

2. **Click the View button ⊠ in the Views group to switch to Design View, click the Show Table button, double-click Diagnosis, click the Close button, then double-click the DiagDescription field to add it to the query grid**

   Access evaluates sort orders from left to right. You want to change the sort order so that the records sort first by PtLastName, then by DateofService.

3. **Click the PtLastName Sort cell, click the list arrow, click Ascending, click the DateofService Sort cell, click the list arrow, then click Ascending as shown in FIGURE 2-7**

   The records are now set to be sorted in ascending order, first by PtLastName, then by the values in the DateofService field. Because sort orders always work from left to right, you might need to rearrange the fields before applying a sort order that uses more than one field. To move a field in the query design grid, click its field selector, then drag it to the left or the right.

4. **Click the View button ⊞ in the Results group, then click any value in the DiagDescription field**

   The records are now sorted in ascending order by the PtLastName field. If two records have the same PtLastName value, they are further sorted by DateofService. You can also sort directly in the datasheet using the Ascending and Descending buttons on the Home tab, but to specify multiple sort orders on nonconsecutive fields, it's best to use Query Design View. Your next task is to replace all occurrences of "unspec." with "unspecified" in the DiagDescription field.

5. **Click the Find button on the Home tab, type unspec. in the Find What box, click the Replace tab, click the Replace With box, type unspecified, click the Match list arrow, then click Any Part of Field as shown in FIGURE 2-8**

   The Find and Replace dialog box can be used to find or replace any series of characters in the current field or the entire datasheet.

6. **Click the Find Next button in the Find and Replace dialog box, click Replace as many times as necessary to replace all occurrences, click OK when prompted that Access cannot find the text specified, then click Cancel to close the Find and Replace dialog box**

   Access replaced all occurrences of "unspec." with "unspecified" in the DiagDescription field, as shown in FIGURE 2-9.

7. **Right-click the PatientDiagnosis query tab, click Close, then click Yes to save changes**

FIGURE 2-7: Setting sort orders for the PatientDiagnosis query

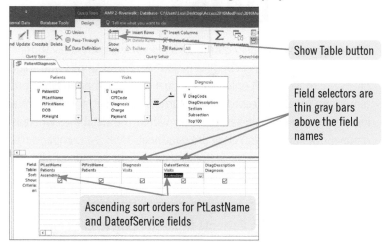

Show Table button

Field selectors are thin gray bars above the field names

Ascending sort orders for PtLastName and DateofService fields

FIGURE 2-8: Find and Replace dialog box

unspec. in the Find What text box

Look In the current field (DiagDescription)

Match any part of the field

unspecified in the Replace With box

Replace button

Replace All button

FIGURE 2-9: Final PatientDiagnosis datasheet with new sort orders

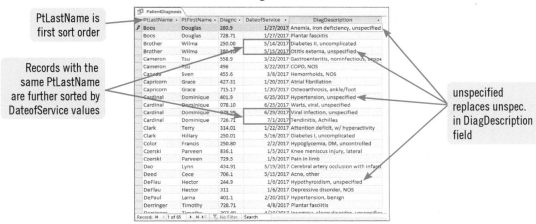

PtLastName is first sort order

Records with the same PtLastName are further sorted by DateofService values

unspecified replaces unspec. in DiagDescription field

TABLE 2-1: Sort and Find buttons

name	button	purpose
Ascending		Sorts records based on the selected field in ascending order (0 to 9, A to Z)
Descending		Sorts records based on the selected field in descending order (Z to A, 9 to 0)
Remove Sort		Removes the current sort order
Find		Opens the Find and Replace dialog box, which allows you to find data in a single field or in the entire datasheet
Replace		Opens the Find and Replace dialog box, which allows you to find and replace data
Go To		Helps you navigate to the first, previous, next, last, or new record
Select		Helps you select a single record or all records in a datasheet

Filter Data

Learning Outcomes
- Apply and remove filters in a query
- Use comparison operators with criteria

Filtering a table or query datasheet *temporarily* displays only those records that match given criteria. Recall that criteria are limiting conditions you set. For example, you might want to show patients from only a given city or visits with only an individual doctor. Although filters provide a quick and easy way to display a temporary subset of records in the current datasheet, they are not as powerful or flexible as queries. Most important, a query is a saved object within the database, whereas filters are temporary because Access removes them when you close the datasheet. TABLE 2-2 compares filters and queries. **CASE** *Kristen asks you to find all patients from Boston and all patients born on or after 1/1/1990. You can filter the Patients table datasheet to provide this information.*

STEPS

1. **Double-click the Patients table to open it, click any occurrence of Boston in the City field, click the Selection button in the Sort & Filter group on the Home tab, then click Equals "Boston"**

   Ten records are selected, as shown in FIGURE 2-10. A filter icon appears to the right of the City field. Filtering by the selected field value, called **Filter By Selection**, is a fast and easy way to filter the records for an exact match. To filter for comparative data (for example, where DOB (date of birth) is *equal to* or *greater than* 1/1/1990), you must use the **Filter By Form** feature. Filter buttons are summarized in TABLE 2-3.

2. **Click the Advanced button in the Sort & Filter group, then click Filter By Form**

   The Filter by Form window opens. The previous Filter By Selection criterion, "Boston" in the City field, is still in the grid. Access distinguishes between text and numeric entries by placing "quotation marks" around text criteria.

3. **Click the DOB cell, then type >=1/1/1990 as shown in FIGURE 2-11**

   Filter By Form also allows you to apply two or more criteria at the same time. In the DOB criterion, >= means greater than or equal to. Comparison operators are further described in the next lesson.

4. **Click the Toggle Filter button in the Sort & Filter group**

   The datasheet selects three records that match both filter criteria, as shown in FIGURE 2-12. Note that filter icons appear next to the DOB and City field names as both fields are involved in the filter.

5. **Close the Patients datasheet, then click Yes when prompted to save the changes**

   Saving changes to the datasheet saves the last sort order and column width changes. Filters are not saved.

Using wildcard characters

To search for a pattern, you can use a **wildcard** character to represent any character in the condition entry. Use a question mark (?) to search for any single character and an asterisk (*) to search for any number of characters. Wildcard characters are often used with the **Like** operator. For example, the criterion Like "12/*/17" would find all dates in December of 2017, and the criterion Like "F*" would find all entries that start with the letter F.

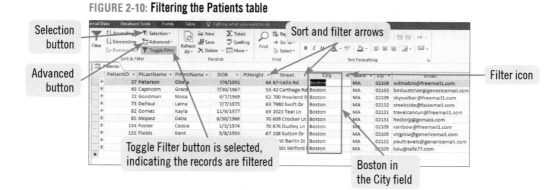

FIGURE 2-10: Filtering the Patients table

FIGURE 2-11: Filtering by Form criteria

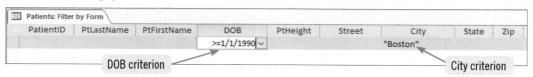

FIGURE 2-12: Results of filtering by form

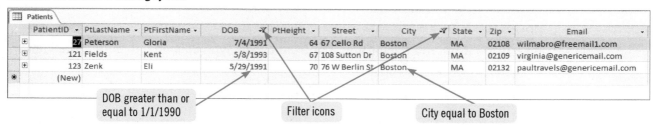

TABLE 2-2: Filters vs. queries

characteristics	filters	queries
Are saved as an object in the database		•
Can be used to select a subset of records in a datasheet	•	•
Can be used to select a subset of fields in a datasheet		•
Resulting datasheet used to enter and edit data	•	•
Resulting datasheet used to sort, filter, and find records	•	•
Commonly used as the source of data for a form or report		•
Can calculate sums, averages, counts, and other types of summary statistics across records		•
Can be used to create calculated fields		•

TABLE 2-3: Filter buttons

name	button	purpose
Filter		Provides a list of values in the selected field that can be used to customize a filter
Selection		Filters records that equal, do not equal, or are otherwise compared with the current value
Advanced		Provides advanced filter features such as Filter By Form, Save As Query, and Clear All Filters
Toggle Filter		Applies or removes the current filter

Apply AND Criteria

Learning Outcomes
• Enter AND criteria in a query
• Define criteria syntax
• Use wildcards in criteria

You can limit the number of records that appear on a query datasheet by entering criteria in Query Design View. **Criteria** are tests, or limiting conditions, for which the record must be true to be selected for the query datasheet. To create **AND criteria**, which means that *all* criteria must be true to select the record, enter two or more criteria on the *same* Criteria row of the query design grid. **CASE** ▶ *Kristen Royal asks you to provide a list of all patient visits for Dr. Babbage in the month of May 2017. Use Query Design View to create the query with AND criteria to meet her request.*

STEPS

1. **Click the Create tab on the Ribbon, click the Query Design button, double-click Providers, double-click Visits, double-click Patients, then click Close in the Show Table dialog box**

   You want four fields in this query.

2. **Drag the bottom edge of the Visits field list down to display all of the fields, double-click DrLastName, double-click DateofService, double-click PtFirstName, then double-click PtLastName to add these fields to the query grid**

   First add criteria to select only those records for Dr. Babbage.

QUICK TIP

Query criteria are not case sensitive, so Babbage equals BABBAGE equals babbage.

3. **Click the first Criteria cell for the DrLastName field, type Babbage, then click the View button 🔲 to display the results**

   Querying for only Dr. Babbage's patients selects 10 records. Next, you add criteria to select only the visits in May of 2017.

4. **Click the View button 🔲, click the first Criteria cell for the DateofService field, then type 5/*/2017 as shown in FIGURE 2-13**

   Criteria added to the same line of the query design grid are AND criteria. When entered on the same line, each criterion must be true for the record to appear in the resulting datasheet. Querying for both Dr. Babbage and a date of service in May of 2017 narrows the selection to seven records. Every time you add AND criteria, you *narrow* the number of records that are selected because the record must be true for *all* criteria. An asterisk (*) in the day position of the date criterion acts as a wildcard to select any date in May 2017. Wildcards can be used to search for a pattern of characters.

   Access assists you with **criteria syntax**, rules that specify how to enter criteria. Access automatically adds "quotation marks" around text criteria in Short Text and Long Text fields ("Babbage") and pound signs (#) around date criteria in Date/Time fields. The criteria in Number, Currency, and Yes/No fields are not surrounded by any characters. See **TABLE 2-4** for more information about comparison operators such as > (greater than).

TROUBLE

If your datasheet doesn't match FIGURE 2-14, return to Query Design View and compare your criteria with that of FIGURE 2-13.

5. **Click the View button 🔲**

   The AND criterion narrows the number of records selected to seven, as shown in FIGURE 2-14.

6. **Click the Save button 🔲 on the Quick Access Toolbar, type BabbageMay as the query name, click OK, then close the query**

   The query is saved with the new name, BabbageMay, as a new object in the AMP 2-Riverwalk database. Criteria entered in Query Design View are permanently saved with the query (as compared with filters in the previous lesson, which are temporary and not saved with the object).

FIGURE 2-13: Query Design View with AND criteria

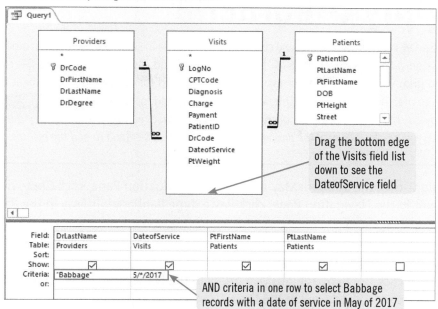

Drag the bottom edge of the Visits field list down to see the DateofService field

AND criteria in one row to select Babbage records with a date of service in May of 2017

FIGURE 2-14: Final datasheet of BabbageMay query

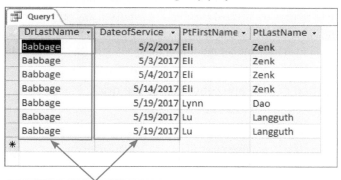

Both criteria are true for these records: Babbage, May 2017

TABLE 2-4: Comparison operators

operator	description	expression	meaning
>	Greater than	>500	Numbers greater than 500
>=	Greater than or equal to	>=500	Numbers greater than or equal to 500
<	Less than	<"Jobs"	Names from A to Jobs, but not Jobs
<=	Less than or equal to	<="Hopper"	Names from A through Hopper, inclusive
<>	Not equal to	<>"Adair"	Any name except for Adair

Searching for blank fields

Is Null and Is Not Null are two other types of common criteria. The **Is Null** criterion finds all records where no entry has been made in the field. **Is Not Null** finds all records where there is any entry in the field, even if the entry is 0. Primary key fields cannot have a null entry.

Access 2016

Apply OR Criteria

Learning
Outcomes
• Enter OR criteria
  in a query
• Rename a query

You use **OR criteria** when *any one* criterion must be true in order for the record to be selected. Enter OR criteria on *different* Criteria rows of the query design grid. As you add rows of OR criteria to the query design grid, you *increase* the number of records selected for the resulting datasheet because the record needs to match *only one* of the Criteria rows to be selected for the datasheet. **CASE** ▸ *Kristen Royal asks you to add criteria to the previous query. She wants to include records for Dr. Jobs during the month of May. To do this, you modify a copy of the BabbageMay query to use OR criteria to add the records.*

STEPS

1. **Right-click the BabbageMay query in the Navigation Pane, click Copy, right-click a blank spot in the Navigation Pane, click Paste, type BabbageJobsMay in the Paste As dialog box, then click OK**

   By copying the BabbageMay query before starting your modifications, you avoid changing the BabbageMay query by mistake.

2. **Right-click the BabbageJobsMay query in the Navigation Pane, click Design View, click the second Criteria cell in the DrLastName field, type Jobs, then click the View button 🔲 to display the query datasheet**

   The query selected 32 records including all of the records with Jobs in the DrLastName field. Note that some of the DateofService values are not in May of 2017. Because each row of the query grid is evaluated separately, all Jobs records are selected regardless of criteria in any other row. In other words, the criteria in one row have no effect on the criteria of other rows. To make sure that the Jobs records are also in the month of May, you need to modify the second row of the query grid (the "or" row) to specify that criteria.

3. **Click the View button 📉, click the second Criteria cell in the DateofService field, type 5/*/2017, then click in any other cell of the grid**

   Query Design View should look like **FIGURE 2-15**.

4. **Click the View button 🔲**

   Eleven records are selected that meet all criteria as entered in row one *or* row two of the query grid, as shown in **FIGURE 2-16**.

5. **Right-click the BabbageJobsMay query tab, click Close, then click Yes to save and close the query datasheet**

FIGURE 2-15: Query Design View with OR criteria

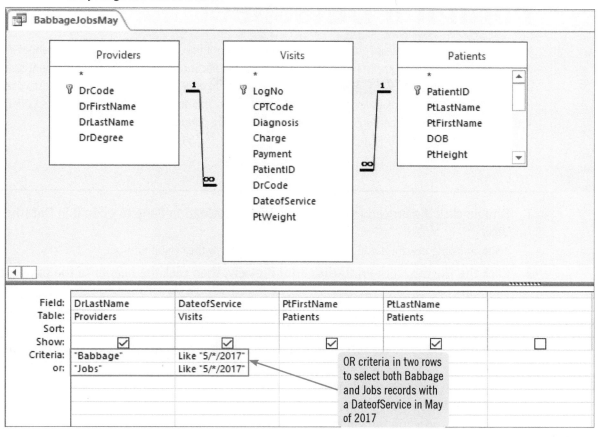

FIGURE 2-16: Final datasheet of the BabbageJobsMay query

DrLastName ▼	DateofService ▼	PtFirstName ▼	PtLastName ▼
Babbage	5/2/2017	Eli	Zenk
Babbage	5/3/2017	Eli	Zenk
Babbage	5/4/2017	Eli	Zenk
Babbage	5/14/2017	Eli	Zenk
Babbage	5/19/2017	Lynn	Dao
Babbage	5/19/2017	Lu	Langguth
Babbage	5/19/2017	Lu	Langguth
Jobs	5/14/2017	Wilma	Brother
Jobs	5/15/2017	Wilma	Brother
Jobs	5/15/2017	Cece	Deed
Jobs	5/16/2017	Hillary	Clark

Both criteria are true for either row:
Babbage *and* May of 2017
Or
Jobs *and* May of 2017

Format a Datasheet

Learning Outcomes
• Zoom in print preview
• Format a datasheet
• Change page orientation

A report is the primary Access tool to create a professional printout, but you can print a datasheet as well. A datasheet allows you to apply some basic formatting modifications such as changing the font size, font face, colors, and gridlines. **CASE** *Kristen Royal asks you to print a list of procedure codes, also called CPT (Current Procedural Terminology) codes, and their descriptions. This data is stored in the ProcedureCodes table. You decide to format the ProcedureCodes table datasheet before printing it.*

STEPS

1. **Double-click the ProcedureCodes table in the Navigation Pane to open it in Datasheet View**

   Before applying new formatting enhancements, you preview the default printout.

2. **Click the File tab, click Print, click Print Preview, then click the header of the printout to zoom in**

   The preview window displays the layout of the printout, as shown in FIGURE 2-17. By default, the printout of a datasheet contains the object name and current date in the header. The page number is in the footer.

3. **Click the Next Page button ▶ in the navigation bar to move to the next page of the printout**

   You decide to switch the report to landscape orientation, then increase the size of the font before printing to make the text easier to read.

4. **Click the Landscape button in the Page Layout group on the Print Preview tab to switch the report to landscape orientation, then click the Close Print Preview button**

   You return to Datasheet View where you can make font face, font size, font color, gridline color, and background color choices.

5. **Click the Font list arrow Calibri (Detail) in the Text Formatting group, click Arial Narrow, click the Font Size list arrow 11 , then click 16**

   With the larger font size applied, you need to resize some columns to accommodate the widest entries.

6. **Use the ↔ pointer to double-click the field separator to the right of the ProcedureDescr field**

   Double-clicking the field separators resizes the columns as needed to display every entry in those fields, as shown in FIGURE 2-18.

QUICK TIP
If you need a printout of this datasheet, click the Print button on the Print Preview tab, then click OK.

7. **Click the File tab, click Print, click Print Preview, click the Portrait button in the Page Layout group to return to portrait orientation, then click anywhere in the preview to zoom out to review the information**

   The preview of the printout is four pages, but with the larger font size, it is easier to read.

8. **Right-click the ProcedureCodes table tab, click Close, click Yes when prompted to save changes, then click the Close button on the title bar to close the AMP 2-Riverwalk.accdb database and Access 2016**

FIGURE 2-17: Preview of the ProcedureCodes datasheet

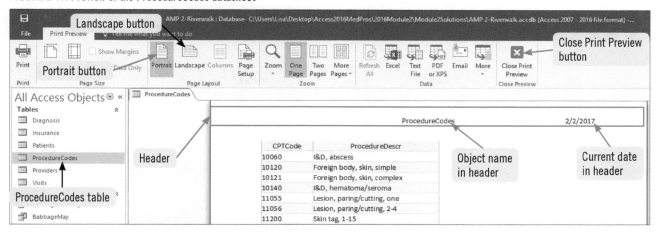

FIGURE 2-18: Formatting the ProcedureCodes datasheet

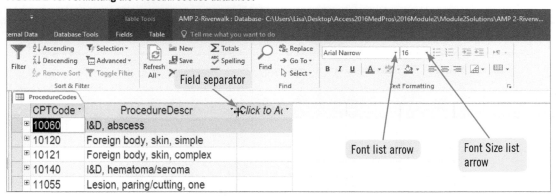

Practice

Concepts Review

Label each element of the Access window shown in FIGURE 2-19.

FIGURE 2-19

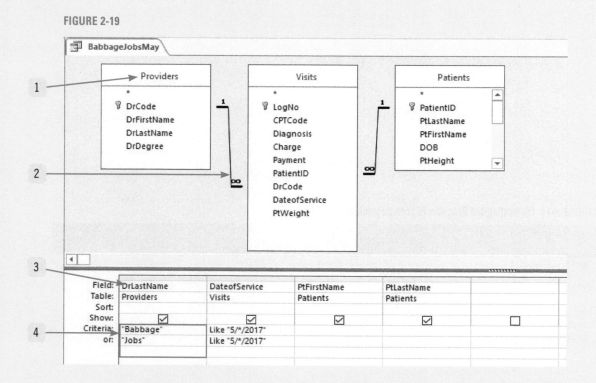

Match each term with the statement that best describes it.

5. **Query grid**
6. **Field selector**
7. **Filter**
8. **Filter By Selection**
9. **Field lists**
10. **Sorting**
11. **Join line**
12. **Is Null**
13. **Criteria**
14. **Syntax**
15. **Wildcard**

a. Limiting conditions used to restrict the number of records that are selected in a query
b. The lower pane in Query Design View
c. Putting records in ascending or descending order based on the values of a field
d. Small windows that display field names
e. Rules that determine how criteria are entered
f. Creates a temporary subset of records
g. Criterion that finds all records where no entry has been made in the field
h. Used to search for a pattern of characters
i. Identifies which fields are used to establish a relationship between two tables
j. A fast and easy way to filter the records for an exact match
k. The thin gray bar above each field in the query grid

Select the best answer from the list of choices.

16. **AND criteria:**
    a. Determine sort orders.
    b. Determine fields selected for a query.
    c. Help set link lines between tables in a query.
    d. Must all be true for the record to be selected.

17. **SQL stands for which of the following?**
    a. Standard Query Language
    b. Special Query Listing
    c. Structured Query Language
    d. Simple Query Listing

18. **A query is sometimes called a logical view of data because:**
    a. Queries do not store data—they only display a view of data.
    b. You can create queries with the Logical Query Wizard.
    c. Queries contain logical criteria.
    d. Query naming conventions are logical.

19. **Which of the following describes OR criteria?**
    a. Selecting a subset of fields and/or records to view as a datasheet from one or more tables
    b. Reorganizing the records in either ascending or descending order based on the contents of one or more fields
    c. Using two or more rows of the query grid to select only those records that meet given criteria
    d. Using multiple fields in the query design grid

20. **Which of the following is *not* true about a query?**
    a. A query can select fields from one or more tables in a relational database.
    b. A query can be created using different tools.
    c. An existing query can be modified in Query Design View.
    d. A query is the same thing as a filter.

Skills Review

1. **Use the Query Wizard.**
   a. Open the AMP 2-2.accdb database from the location where you store your Data Files, then save the database as **AMP 2-Diabetes.accdb**. Enable content if prompted.
   b. Create a new query using the Simple Query Wizard. Select the FirstName, LastName, and City fields from the Patients table, the VisitDate field from the Visits table, and the EFirstName and ELastName fields from the Employees table. Select Detail, then enter **PatientList** as the name of the query.
   c. Open the query in Datasheet View, then change any record with Molly Frank in the EFirstName and ELastName fields to *your* name.

2. **Work with data in a query.**
   a. Delete the first record (James Trusty with a VisitDate of 1/17/2017).
   b. Change any occurrence of Sabrina Santana in the EFirstName and ELastName fields to **Sara Curtis**.
   c. Click any value in the VisitDate field, then click the Descending button on the Home tab to sort the records in descending order on the VisitDate field.
   d. Use the Calendar Picker to choose the date of **6/9/17** for the first record.
   e. Save and close the PatientList query.

Skills Review (continued)

3. Use Query Design View.

    a. Click the Create tab, click the Query Design button, double-click Patients, double-click Medications, double-click MedDescription, then click Close to add these tables to Query Design View.

    b. Drag the bottom edge of the Patients and Medications field lists down to display more of the field names in both tables.

    c. Add the following fields from the Patients table to the query design grid in the following order: FirstName, LastName, TypeOfDiabetes, and DiagnosisDate. Add the following field from the MedDescription table: MedDescrip. View the results in Datasheet View, observing the number of records that are selected.

    d. In Design View, enter criteria to display only those records with a TypeOfDiabetes value of **II** (two capital I's), then observe that 76 records are selected in Datasheet View.

    e. Save the query with the name **TypeII**, then close it.

4. Sort and find data.

    a. In Query Design View of the ConsultsByEmployee query, choose an ascending sort order for the ELastName and VisitDate fields.

    b. Display the query in Datasheet View, noting how the records have been sorted.

    c. Click any value in the ELastName field, then use the Find and Replace dialog box to find all occurrences of Langguth and replace them with **Morris**.

    d. Save and close the ConsultsByEmployee datasheet.

5. Filter data.

    a. Filter the Patients table datasheet for only those records where the City equals **Urbandale**. Three records should be selected.

    b. Apply an advanced Filter By Form or use the filter drop-down arrow for the City field to add the records where the City equals **Clive**. Three additional records should be selected.

    c. Change the name of patient Rosa Verna to *your* name, and if requested by your instructor, print the first page of the filtered Patients datasheet.

    d. Save and close the Patients datasheet.

6. Apply AND criteria.

    a. Right-click the PatientList query, copy it, and then paste it as **DesMoinesFeb2017**.

    b. Open the DesMoinesFeb2017 query in Query Design View.

    c. Modify the criteria to select all of the records with a VisitDate in February of 2017 and a City value equal to **Des Moines**. (*Hint*: Use the asterisk * wildcard character for the day position in the date criteria.)

    d. View the DesMoinesFeb2017 datasheet, which should select 13 records, and if requested by your instructor, print it.

    e. Save and close it the DesMoinesFeb2017 datasheet.

7. Apply OR criteria.

    a. Right-click the ConsultsByEmployee query, copy it, then paste it as **LongConsultsOrMiller**.

    b. Open the LongConsultsOrMiller query in Design View, then add criteria to select the records with a Hrs field value of **>=2**.

Skills Review (continued)

c. Add criteria to also include the records with an ELastName field equal to **Miller**. FIGURE 2-20 shows the resulting datasheet.

d. If requested by your instructor, print the LongConsultsOrMiller datasheet, then save and close it.

8. Format a datasheet.

a. In the MedDescription table datasheet, apply the Georgia font and a 14-point font size.

b. Resize all columns so that all data and field names are visible.

c. Display the MedDescription datasheet in Print Preview, switch the orientation to landscape, click the Margins button in the Page Size group, then click Narrow.

d. If requested by your instructor, print the MedDescription datasheet.

e. Save and close the MedDescription table, then close Access 2016.

FIGURE 2-20

EFirstName ▾	ELastName ▾	FirstName ▾	LastName ▾	VisitDate ▾	Hrs ▾
Sara	Curtis	Grace	Harris	2/6/2017	2.0
Sara	Curtis	Eli	Pietschmann	2/26/2017	2.0
Sara	Curtis	Carlo	Tope	3/29/2017	2.0
Sara	Curtis	Darlene	Harrison	4/11/2017	2.0
Thomas	Miller	Simone	Farris	1/19/2017	2.0
Thomas	Miller	Sonja	Stowe	2/1/2017	1.0
Thomas	Miller	Ruby	Stewart	2/2/2017	1.0
Thomas	Miller	Grace	Towner	2/9/2017	1.0
Thomas	Miller	Ali	Parsons	2/27/2017	1.0
Thomas	Miller	Shen	Warner	3/4/2017	2.0
Thomas	Miller	Darlene	Burnside	3/13/2017	1.8
Thomas	Miller	Sarah	Edmundson	3/18/2017	2.0
Thomas	Miller	Darlene	Howard	3/23/2017	1.5
Thomas	Miller	Vito	Green	4/30/2017	2.0
Thomas	Miller	Hanna	Bellard	5/8/2017	1.5
Thomas	Miller	Cala	McKesson	5/16/2017	1.0
Thomas	Miller	Tanner	Aaron	6/1/2017	1.0
Thomas	Miller	Student First	Student Last	6/2/2017	1.5
Thomas	Miller	Gunner	Lacy	6/9/2017	1.5
Cherry	Morris	Grace	Burnett	2/25/2017	2.0
Cherry	Morris	Sharon	Cooper	3/4/2017	2.0
Cherry	Morris	Sharon	Johnson	3/7/2017	2.0
Cherry	Morris	Rebecca	Grzech	5/6/2017	2.0
Cherry	Morris	Donald	Enga	6/9/2017	2.0
Donald	Roberts	Nada	Howitt	2/5/2017	2.0

Record: I◄ ◄ 1 of 30 ► ►I ►⊕ | No Filter | Search

Independent Challenge 1

You have built an Access database to track nursing assignments at a multilocation dermatology clinic. You will use queries to find specific assignment information.

a. Start Access, open the AMP 2-3.accdb database, save it as **AMP 2-Nurses.accdb** to the location where you store your Data Files, then enable content if prompted.

b. Open each of the five tables, review the fields and records contained in each, then close the tables. Click the Database Tools tab, then click the Relationships button to see how the five tables are joined to create this relational database. Resize the field lists if needed so you can see all of the fields in each table. This database creates a nurse schedule by linking each of the other four tables—Providers, Nurses, Locations, and ScheduleDate—in a one-to-many relationship with the ScheduleItems table.

Independent Challenge 1 (continued)

c. Click the Relationship Report button, then print the report if requested by your instructor. Save and close the report with the default name, Relationships for AMP 2-Nurses. Save and close the Relationships window. Even though you have not created this database, it's important to review the relationships so you can select the correct tables and fields needed for your queries.

d. In Query Design View, build a query with all five tables. Drag the edges of the field lists to resize them and drag the title bars of the field lists so that the link lines do not overlap.

e. Add the following fields to the query grid in the following order: ScheduleDate from the ScheduleDate table, LocationName from the Locations table, NurseLName from the Nurses table, and LastName from the Providers table.

f. View the datasheet, observe the number of records selected, then return to Query Design View.

g. Add sort orders to sort the records in ascending order on the ScheduleDate, LocationName, and NurseLName fields.

h. Add criteria to select only those records where the LastName in the Providers table is **Fletcher** or **Northy**.

i. View the datasheet. Enter *your* last name instead of Manhattan in the NurseLName field, widen all columns so that all data is visible, and save the query with the name **FletcherOrNorthy** as shown in FIGURE 2-21.

j. If requested by your instructor, print the first page of the datasheet.

k. Close the FletcherOrNorthy query and the AMP 2-Nurses.accdb database, then exit Access 2016.

FIGURE 2-21

ScheduleDate	LocationName	NurseLName	LastName
8/27/2017	North	Blago	Northy
8/27/2017	North	Buck	Northy
8/27/2017	North	Fredrick	Northy
8/27/2017	North	Hemmer	Fletcher
8/27/2017	North	Student Last	Fletcher
8/28/2017	North	Blago	Fletcher
8/28/2017	North	Fredrick	Northy
8/28/2017	North	Hemmer	Fletcher
8/28/2017	North	Student Last	Fletcher
8/28/2017	North	Wu	Northy
8/31/2017	North	Buck	Northy
8/31/2017	North	Fredrick	Northy
8/31/2017	North	Hemmer	Fletcher
8/31/2017	North	Student Last	Fletcher
8/31/2017	North	Tharp	Northy
9/4/2017	North	Blago	Northy
9/4/2017	North	Buck	Northy
9/4/2017	North	Fredrick	Northy
9/4/2017	North	Hemmer	Fletcher
9/4/2017	North	Student Last	Fletcher
9/5/2017	North	Blago	Northy
9/5/2017	North	Buck	Northy
9/5/2017	North	Fredrick	Northy
9/5/2017	North	Hemmer	Fletcher
9/5/2017	North	Student Last	Fletcher

Record: 6 of 213   No Filter   Search

Independent Challenge 2

You are working with a medical school's intern placement program. You have started an Access database to track evaluations of interns.

a. Start Access, open the AMP 2-4.accdb database, save it as **AMP 2-InternMgmt** to the location where you store your Data Files, then enable content if prompted.

b. Open the InternName and then the Evaluations tables. Notice that one intern is related to many evaluations as evidenced by the expand buttons to the left of the records in the InternName table.

c. Close both datasheets, then using Query Design View, create a query with the InternFName and InternLName fields from the InternName table, and the EvaluationDate, Prompt, Professional, Knowledgeable, and Respectful fields (in that order) from the Evaluations table.

d. Sort the records in ascending order on the InternLName field, then the EvaluationDate field, and view the datasheet to make sure the sort orders are working correctly.

e. In Query Design View, add criteria to select only the records for interns with the last name of **Barker** or **Lang**, then view the datasheet to make sure the criteria works as desired.

f. In Query Design View, enter the following calculated field in the blank field cell to the right of the Respectful field. To create a larger space to make the entry, right-click the cell, then click Zoom. This calculation will average the four other scores (Prompt, Professional, Knowledgeable, and Respectful). Note that each field name is surrounded by [square brackets], and the addition of the four fields is surrounded by (parentheses) before being divided by 4.

Overall:([Prompt]+[Professional]+[Knowledgeable]+[Respectful])/4

g. Save the query using **OverallScore** as the name, then display the query in Datasheet View, a portion of which is shown in FIGURE 2-22. If you are prompted with a field name, it probably means there is a typo in the calculated field in Step f that you will need to correct in Query Design View.

h. Change the last name of Barker to *your* last name. Resize the columns as needed to view all data.

i. Print the first page of the datasheet if requested by your instructor, then save and close it.

j. Close the OverallScore query and the AMP 2-InternMgmt.accdb database, then exit Access 2016.

FIGURE 2-22

InternFNam	InternLNam	EvaluationD	Prompt	Professional	Knowledgea	Respectful	Overall
Kyle	Barker	1/6/2017	4	5	5	4	4.5
Kyle	Barker	1/6/2017	4	5	5	4	4.5
Kyle	Barker	1/7/2017	4	5	5	4	4.5
Kyle	Barker	1/7/2017	4	5	5	4	4.5
Kyle	Barker	1/8/2017	5	3	5	5	4.5
Kyle	Barker	1/8/2017	5	3	5	5	4.5
Kyle	Barker	1/9/2017	2	3	4	5	3.5
Kyle	Barker	1/9/2017	2	3	4	5	3.5

Independent Challenge 3

You are working for an orthopedic clinic that is highly dependent on patient referrals from primary care physicians. You have created an Access database to keep track of referrals so that you can analyze which physicians refer to your clinic and keep in touch with them regarding patient progress.

a. Start Access, open the AMP 2-5.accdb database, save it as **AMP 2-Referrals.accdb** to the drive and folder where you store your Data Files, then enable content if prompted.

b. Open each of the five tables to observe the number of fields and records in each table, then close the datasheets.

c. On the Database Tools tab, click the Relationships button to view table relationships, then resize the field lists to see all fields in each table. Click the Relationship Report button then print the report if requested by your instructor. Close and save the report with the default name, Relationships for AMP 2-Referrals, then save and close the Relationships window.

d. Create a query in Query Design View and select the ReferringDocs, Visits, and ClinicDocs tables. Select the RFirst and RLast fields from the ReferringDocs table, the DrLast field from the ClinicDocs table, and the VisitDate field from the Visits table.

e. Set an ascending sort order for the RLast, DrLast, and VisitDate fields, then view the datasheet.

f. Find an occurrence of Abbot in the RLast field and replace it with *your* last name.

g. In Query Design View, add criteria to select only those records with your last name or **Bell** in the RLast field, each with a VisitDate greater than or equal to **1/1/2017**. (*Hint*: Use the >= operator.)

h. Save the query with the name **2017Referrals**, display it in Datasheet View as shown in FIGURE 2-23, then print the first page of the datasheet if requested by your instructor.

i. Close the 2017Referrals datasheet, the AMP 2-Referrals.accdb database, and exit Access 2016.

FIGURE 2-23

RFirst	RLast	DrLast	VisitDate
Sheri	Bell	Eagan	1/24/2017
Sheri	Bell	Jefferson	1/1/2017
Sheri	Bell	Jefferson	1/29/2017
Sheri	Bell	Jefferson	5/2/2017
Sheri	Bell	Jefferson	5/26/2017
Sheri	Bell	Thompson	3/3/2017
Sheri	Bell	Thompson	3/7/2017
Sheri	Bell	Thompson	3/25/2017
Sheri	Bell	Thompson	4/25/2017
Sheri	Bell	Thompson	5/13/2017
Sheri	Bell	Thompson	9/9/2017
Sheri	Bell	Thompson	10/13/2017
Sheri	Bell	Thompson	10/20/2017
Sheri	Bell	Thompson	11/28/2017
Sheri	Bell	Wambold	12/2/2017
Joseph	Student Last	Jefferson	1/15/2017
Joseph	Student Last	Jefferson	5/14/2017
Joseph	Student Last	Thompson	10/6/2017
Joseph	Student Last	Wambold	1/30/2017
Joseph	Student Last	Wambold	2/4/2017

Record: 1 of 20   No Filter   Search

Independent Challenge 4: Explore

An Access database is an excellent tool to help record and track job opportunities. For this exercise, you'll create a database from scratch that you can use to enter, edit, and query data in pursuit of a new job or career.

a. Create a new desktop database named **AMP 2-Jobs.accdb** and save it in the location where you store your Data Files.

b. Create a table named **Positions** with the following field names, data types, and descriptions:

Field name	Data type	Description
PositionID	AutoNumber	Primary key field
Title	Short Text	Title of position such as Nurse, Lab Technician, or Clinic Manager
CareerArea	Short Text	Area of the career field such as Biotech, Hospital, or Pharmaceutical
AnnualSalary	Currency	Annual salary
Desirability	Number	Desirability rating of 1 = low to 5 = high to show how desirable the position is to you
EmployerID	Number	Foreign key field to the Employers table

c. Create a table named **Employers** with the following field names, data types, and descriptions:

Field name	Data type	Description
EmployerID	AutoNumber	Primary key field
CompanyName	Short Text	Company name of the employer
EmpStreet	Short Text	Employer's street address
EmpCity	Short Text	Employer's city
EmpState	Short Text	Employer's state
EmpZip	Short Text	Employer's zip code
EmpPhone	Short Text	Employer's phone, such as 913-555-8888

d. Be sure to set EmployerID as the primary key field in the Employers table and the PositionID as the primary key field in the Positions table.

e. Link the Employers and Positions tables together in a one-to-many relationship using the common EmployerID field. One employer record will be linked to many position records. Be sure to enforce referential integrity.

f. Using any valid source of potential employer data, enter 10 records into the Employers table.

g. Using any valid source of job information, enter 10 records into the Positions table for the given employers by using the subdatasheets from within the Employers datasheet. Because one employer may have many positions, all 10 of your Positions records may be linked to the same employer, you may have one position record per employer, or any other combination.

h. Build a query that selects CompanyName from the Employers table, and the Title, CareerArea, Desirability, and AnnualSalary, and fields from the Positions table. Sort the records first in descending order based on Desirability, then in descending order based on AnnualSalary. Save the query as **JobList**, and print it if requested by your instructor.

i. Close the JobList datasheet and the AMP 2-Jobs.accdb database, then exit Access 2016.

Visual Workshop

One of the most challenging aspects of the medical profession is the vast amount of medical terminology you are required to memorize. In this exercise, you will query a database of medical terminology to learn the meanings of common prefixes and suffixes.

Start Access, open the AMP 2-6.accdb database, then save it as a database named **AMP 2-MedicalTerms.accdb** in the location where you store your Data Files. Enable content if prompted. Create a query based on the Terms table with the fields shown in FIGURE 2-24. Criteria have been added to select only those records where the Meaning field contains the word *skin* or *tissue*. (*Hint*: Use wildcard characters in each criterion entry before and after the word *skin* and the word *tissue* to select entries with these words anywhere in the criterion entry, as in *skin* and *tissue*.) Save the query with the name **SkinOrTissue**, then compare the results to FIGURE 2-24, widening columns as needed. Print the datasheet if requested by your instructor. Save and close the query, close the AMP 2-MedicalTerms.accdb database, then exit Access 2016.

FIGURE 2-24

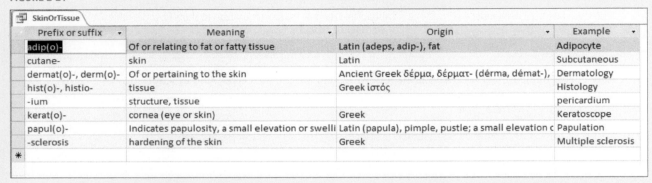

Prefix or suffix	Meaning	Origin	Example
adip(o)-	Of or relating to fat or fatty tissue	Latin (adeps, adip-), fat	Adipocyte
cutane-	skin	Latin	Subcutaneous
dermat(o)-, derm(o)-	Of or pertaining to the skin	Ancient Greek δέρμα, δέρματ- (dérma, démat-),	Dermatology
hist(o)-, histio-	tissue	Greek ἱστός	Histology
-ium	structure, tissue		pericardium
kerat(o)-	cornea (eye or skin)	Greek	Keratoscope
papul(o)-	Indicates papulosity, a small elevation or swelli	Latin (papula), pimple, pustle; a small elevation c	Papulation
-sclerosis	hardening of the skin	Greek	Multiple sclerosis

Creating and Using Forms and Reports

CASE ▶ Kristen Royal, R.N., office manager for Riverwalk Medical Clinic, asks you to create forms and reports to make patient electronic medical records easier to update and analyze.

Module Objectives

After completing this module, you will be able to:

- Manage data with a form
- Use the Form Wizard
- Preview a report
- Use the Report Wizard

- Apply group and sort orders
- Add subtotals and counts
- Add and modify labels
- Back up and secure the database

Files You Will Need

AMP 3-1.accdb	AMP 3-5.accdb
AMP 3-2.accdb	AMP 3-6.accdb
AMP 3-3.accdb	AMP 3-7.accdb
AMP 3-4.accdb	

Manage Data with a Form

Learning Outcomes
- Navigate records in a form
- Enter and edit data in a form
- Describe form controls

Although you can enter and edit data on datasheets, most database designers develop and build forms as the primary method for users to interact with a database. A **form** is an Access database object that allows you to arrange the fields of a record in any layout so you can easily find, enter, edit, and delete records. Forms also provide many productivity and security benefits for the user, who is primarily interested in entering, editing, and analyzing the data in the database. **CASE** *You work with a form previously created for the patient electronic medical record database at Riverwalk Medical Clinic to learn about the uses and benefits of forms.*

STEPS

1. **Start Access, open the AMP 3-1.accdb database from the location where you store your Data Files, click the File tab, click Save As, click the Save As button, type AMP 3-Riverwalk in the File name box, click Save, then enable content if prompted**

   Because forms are often the primary way for users to communicate with the database, they should be as easy to use and intuitive as possible.

2. **Double-click the ElectronicMedicalRecord form to open it, press [Tab] twice to move to the DOB field, click the calendar picker icon, then click 5/1/1992 as shown in FIGURE 3-1**

   Every item on a form is called a **control**. Common controls are summarized In TABLE 3-1, and some controls are identified on FIGURE 3-1. Controls can be **bound**, or tied to an underlying field in a table, or **unbound**, or unattached to data but used to describe or clarify information. Bound controls show data from underlying records as you move from record to record. Unbound controls remain static as you move from record to record.

3. **Click the Next record button ▶ for the main form enough times to move to record 11 of 39**

   The main form navigation buttons identify which patient you are viewing. Some but not all patients have pictures. The subform in the lower half of the form is similar to a subdatasheet because it shows related records. In this case, the subform shows all visits for that patient. Some patients have made one, two, or three visits to the clinic.

4. **Click the Primary Diagnosis combo box arrow for the second record in the subform, then click 305.00 on the list as shown in FIGURE 3-2**

   Selecting 305.00 in the Primary Diagnosis combo box automatically updates the text box with Alcohol abuse, unspec., as shown in FIGURE 3-2. This is just one of the techniques a form can employ to make data entry easy and accurate.

5. **Click the Enter New Patient command button, enter *your first name* in the First Name text box, press [Tab], enter *your last name* in the Last Name text box, and then click the Print This Patient command button**

   Command buttons are common form controls that allow you to simplify and control the actions that the user can take.

6. **Click the Close command button to close the form**

   All data that you edited or entered in the form is saved in the underlying table. In this case, you updated both the Patients and Visits tables.

Creating and Using Forms and Reports

FIGURE 3-1: Record 1 of the Electronic Medical Record form

Labels → Electronic Medical Record

text boxes

Photo

Calendar picker icon

Next record button for main form

Subform

Subform navigation buttons

Combo boxes

Command buttons

Main form navigation buttons

© Photo courtesy of Lisa Friedrichsen

FIGURE 3-2: Record 11 of the Electronic Medical Record form

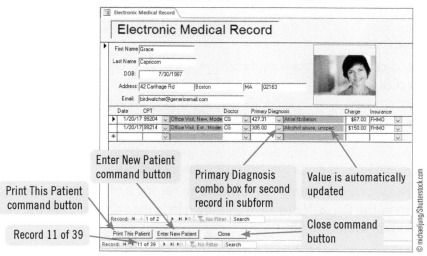

Electronic Medical Record

Enter New Patient command button

Primary Diagnosis combo box for second record in subform

Value is automatically updated

Print This Patient command button

Record 11 of 39

Close command button

© michaeljung/Shutterstock.com

TABLE 3-1: Common form controls

name	used	bound	unbound
Label	Provide consistent descriptive text as you navigate from record to record; the label is the most common type of unbound control and can also be used as a hyperlink to another database object, external file, or webpage		x
Text box	Display, edit, or enter data for each record from an underlying record source; the text box is the most common type of bound control	x	
List box	Display a list of possible data entries	x	
Combo box	Display a list of possible data entries for a field, and provide a text box for an entry from the keyboard; combines the list box and text box controls	x	
Tab control	Create a three-dimensional aspect on a form		x
Check box	Display "yes" or "no" answers for a field; if the box is checked, it means "yes"	x	
Toggle button	Display "yes" or "no" answers for a field; if the button is pressed, it means "yes"	x	
Option button	Display a choice for a field	x	
Option group	Display and organize choices (usually presented as option buttons) for a field	x	
Line and Rectangle	Draw lines and rectangles on the form		x
Command button	Provide an easy way to initiate a command or run a macro		x

Use the Form Wizard

Learning
Outcomes
• Create a form with
  the Form Wizard
• Describe form
  creation tools
• Describe form
  views

As the **database designer**, the person responsible for building and maintaining tables, queries, forms, and reports, you not only use forms, you also need to be able to create forms. The **Form Wizard** prompts you for information it needs to create a form, such as the fields, layout, and title for the form. See TABLE 3-2 for other techniques to create new forms. **CASE** *Kristen Royal asks you to build a form to enter and maintain provider information.*

STEPS

1. **Click the** Create tab **on the Ribbon, then click the** Form Wizard button **in the Forms group**

   The Form Wizard starts, prompting you to select the fields for this form. You want to create a form to enter and update data in the Providers table.

2. **Click the** Tables/Queries list arrow, **click** Table: Providers, **then click the** Select All Fields **button** >>

   You could now select fields from other tables, if necessary, but in this case, you just want to update the data in the Providers table.

3. **Click** Next, **click the** Columnar option button, **click** Next, **type** Provider Entry Form **as the title, then click** Finish

   The Provider Entry Form opens in **Form View**, as shown in FIGURE 3-3. Other form views are summarized in TABLE 3-3. Field names are shown as label controls in the first column of the form. A **label** displays fixed text that doesn't change as you navigate from record to record. In the second column, to the right of the label controls, are text boxes. A **text box** is the most common type of control used to display field values. You enter, edit, find, sort, and filter data by working with the data in a text box control.

4. **Click the** Next record button ▶ **to navigate to record 2 of 6, edit Gutenberg to Guttenberg in the DrLastName field as shown in** FIGURE 3-4, **right-click the** Provider Entry Form tab, **then click** Close

   As you enter or edit data in a form, it is automatically entered and saved in underlying tables.

5. **Double-click the** Providers table **in the Navigation Pane**

   The update to the DrLastName field for Dr. Connie Guttenberg is stored in the Providers table.

6. **Right-click the** Providers table tab, **then click** Close

TABLE 3-2: Form creation tools

tool	icon	creates a form
Form		with one click based on the selected table or query
Form Design		from scratch with access to advanced design changes in Form Design View
Blank Form		with no controls starting in Form Layout View
Form Wizard		by answering a series of questions provided by the Form Wizard dialog boxes
Navigation		used to navigate or move between different areas of the database
More Forms		based on Multiple Items, Datasheet, Split Form, or Modal Dialog arrangements
Split Form		where the upper half displays data as the fields of one record in any arrangement, and the lower half displays data as a datasheet

FIGURE 3-3: **Provider Entry Form in Form View**

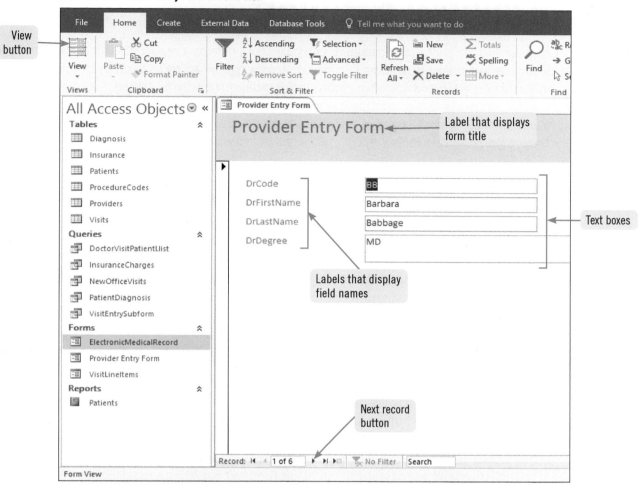

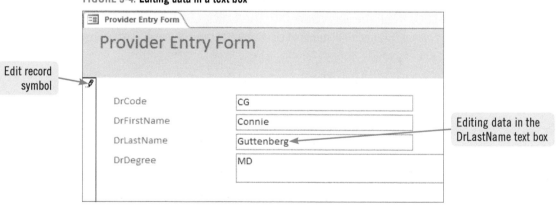

FIGURE 3-4: **Editing data in a text box**

TABLE 3-3: **Form views**

view	primary purpose
Form	To view, enter, edit, and delete data
Layout	To modify the size, position, or formatting of controls; shows data as you modify the form, making it the tool of choice when you want to change the appearance and usability of the form while viewing live data
Design	To modify the Form Header, Detail, and Footer section, or to access the complete range of controls and form properties; Design View does not display data

Preview a Report

Learning
Outcomes
• Preview a report
• Describe report
  sections
• Describe report
  views

Although you can print a table datasheet, query datasheet, or form, a **report** object is the best choice to summarize and distribute database information. Reports provide advanced flexibility by using **sections** that determine where and how often controls in that section print in the final report. For example, controls in the Report Header section print only once at the beginning of the report, but controls in the Detail section print once for every record in the report. TABLE 3-4 describes report sections. **CASE** *You and Kristen Royal preview the Patients report to review and understand report sections.*

STEPS

1. **Double-click the** Patients report **in the Navigation Pane as shown in** FIGURE 3-5

   The first page of the Patients report is displayed in **Report View**, which allows you to preview the data and make some modifications to the report. Other report views are summarized in TABLE 3-5. The first page of the Patients report contains four sections: Report Header, Page Header, Patient Header, and Detail section.

TROUBLE
You may need to
zoom in and out sev-
eral times by clicking
the report to posi-
tion it where you
want.

2. **Right-click the** Patients report tab, **click** Print Preview, **then click the** Next Page **button** ▶ **on the navigation bar to move to the second page**

   Print Preview shows you each individual page of the report as it will be printed on paper and provides an excellent way to learn about report sections. The top of the second page of the report displays the labels in the **Page Header** section, which prints at the top of each page. The **Report Header** section is not repeated on the second and subsequent pages because it prints at the top of only the first page. The **Patient Header** section is printed once for each patient, and the **Detail** section is printed once for every record in the report. In this case, each record represents a patient visit to the clinic.

3. **Click the** Last Page button ▶| **on the navigation bar to move to the last page, then click the report to zoom out, as shown in** FIGURE 3-6

   By looking at the last page of the report in Print Preview, you can see the **Report Footer** section, which prints at the end of the report, as well as the **Page Footer** section, which prints at the end of each page. The Report Footer often contains calculations such as grand totals or a total count of records. The Page Footer section often contains the date and page number.

QUICK TIP
You can also use the
View buttons in the
lower-right corner
of a report to switch
views.

4. **Right-click the** Patients report tab, **then click** Close **to close the Patients report**

   Reports may be printed or distributed electronically through email as attachments using many different file types including Excel (.xlsx) and Portable Document Format (.pdf).

TABLE 3-4: Report sections

section	where does this section print?
Report Header	At the top of the first page
Page Header	At the top of every page (but below the Report Header on the first page)
Group Header	Before every group of records
Detail	Once for every record
Group Footer	After every group of records
Page Footer	At the bottom of every page
Report Footer	At the end of the report

Creating and Using Forms and Reports

FIGURE 3-5: First page of Patients report in Report View

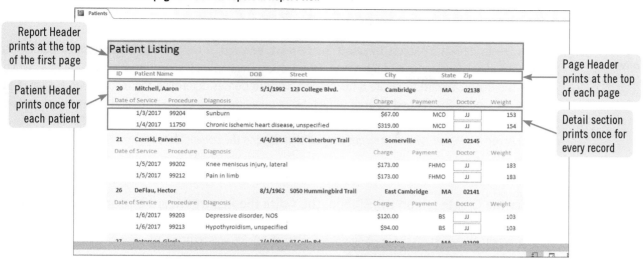

Report Header prints at the top of the first page

Patient Header prints once for each patient

Page Header prints at the top of each page

Detail section prints once for every record

FIGURE 3-6: Last page of Patients report in Print Preview

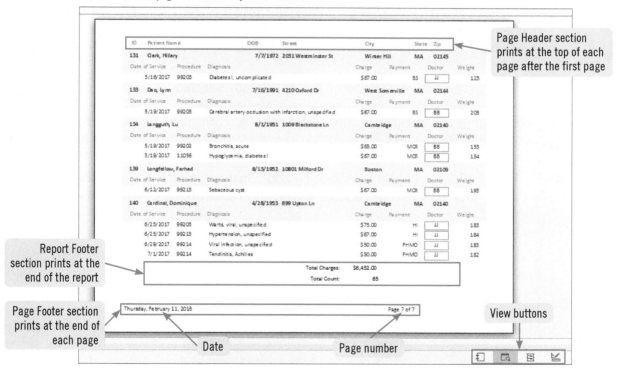

Page Header section prints at the top of each page after the first page

Report Footer section prints at the end of the report

Page Footer section prints at the end of each page

View buttons

Date

Page number

TABLE 3-5: Report views

view	primary purpose
Report View	To quickly review the report without page breaks
Print Preview	To review each page of an entire report as it will appear if printed
Layout View	To modify the size, position, or formatting of controls; shows live data as you modify the report, making it the tool of choice when you want to change the appearance and positioning of controls on a report while also reviewing live data
Design View	To work with report sections or to access the complete range of controls and report properties; Design View does not display data

Use the Report Wizard

Learning Outcomes
- Create a report with the Report Wizard
- Describe report creation tools

You can create reports in Access by using the **Report Wizard**, a tool that asks questions to guide you through the initial development of the report. Other report creation tools are summarized in TABLE 3-6. When you use the Report Wizard to create a new report, your responses determine the record source, style, and layout of the report. The **record source** is the table or query that defines the fields and records displayed on the report. The Report Wizard also helps you sort, group, and analyze the records. **CASE** ▶ *Kristen Royal asks you to use the Report Wizard to create a report that displays the patients for each provider.*

STEPS

1. **Click the** Create tab **on the Ribbon, then click the** Report Wizard button **in the Reports group**

   The Report Wizard starts, prompting you to select the fields you want on the report. You can select fields from one or more tables or queries.

2. **Click the** Tables/Queries list arrow, **click** Table: Providers, **double-click the** DrLastName **field, click the** Tables/Queries list arrow, **click** Table: Patients, **double-click** PtFirstName, **double-click** PtLastName, **click the** Tables/Queries list arrow, **click** Table: Visits, **then double-click the** DateofService field

   By selecting fields from the Providers, Patients, and Visits tables, you have all the fields you need for the report, as shown in FIGURE 3-7.

3. **Click** Next, **then click** by Providers **if it is not already selected**

   Choosing "by Providers" groups together the records for each provider, which will create a header section on the report for each provider. In addition to record-grouping options, the Report Wizard also asks if you want to sort the records within each group. You'll sort the detail records that list each patient in ascending order by their last and then first names.

4. **Click** Next, **click** Next **again to include no additional grouping levels, click the** first sort list arrow, **click** PtLastName, **click the** second sort list arrow, **click** PtFirstName, **then click** Next

   The last questions in the Report Wizard deal with report appearance and creating a report title.

5. **Click** Next **to accept a Stepped layout and Portrait orientation, type** Patient Visits by Provider **for the report title, then click** Finish

   The Patient Visits by Provider report opens in Print Preview in **portrait orientation** (8.5" wide by 11" tall as opposed to **landscape orientation**, 11" wide by 8.5"), as shown in FIGURE 3-8. The records are grouped by provider, and each patient is listed in ascending order in the Detail section. Reports are **read-only** objects, meaning that they read and display data but cannot be used to change (write to) data. As you change data using tables, queries, or forms, reports constantly display those up-to-date edits just like all of the other Access objects.

FIGURE 3-7: Selecting fields for a report using the Report Wizard

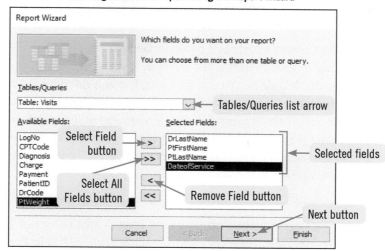

FIGURE 3-8: Patient Visits by Provider report in Print Preview

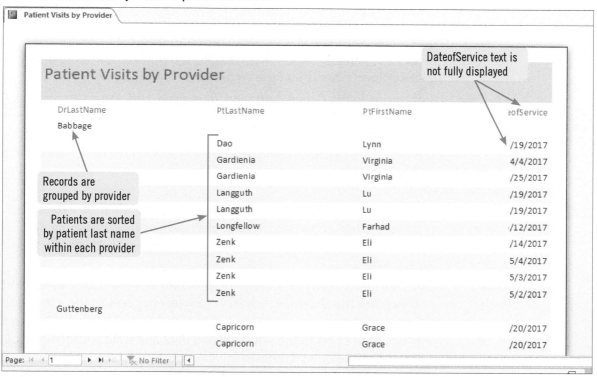

TABLE 3-6: Report creation tools

tool	icon	creates a report
Report		with one click based on the selected table or query
Report Design		from scratch with access to advanced design changes in Report Design View
Blank Report		with no controls starting in Report Layout View
Report Wizard		by answering a series of questions provided by the Report Wizard dialog boxes
Labels		to create labels by using the Label Wizard

Apply Group and Sort Orders

Learning Outcomes
- Group and sort records on a report
- Resize controls in Layout View
- Describe mouse pointer symbols

Grouping means to sort records by a particular field *plus* provide a header and/or footer section before or after each group of sorted records. For example, if you group records by the DrCode field, the Group Header is called the DrCode Header and the Group Footer is called the DrCode Footer. The DrCode Header section appears once for each provider in the report, immediately before the records for that provider. The DrCode Footer section also appears once for each provider in the report, immediately after the records for that provider. You work with grouping and sorting fields in Report Design View. **CASE** ▶ *Kristen Royal asks you to modify the way the records are organized in the Patient Visits by Provider report to more clearly display the data and further sort the patients within each provider.*

STEPS

TROUBLE
If the Field List opens, click the ✕ to close it.

1. **Click the** Design View button ☑ **in the lower-right corner of the window to switch to Report Design View, then click the** Group & Sort button **in the Grouping & Totals group to open the Group, Sort, and Total pane, as shown in** FIGURE 3-9

   The Group, Sort, and Total pane shows you that the records are grouped by the DrCode field (from the Providers table), then sorted by PtLastName and then PtFirstName. A group field varies from a sort field in that a group field also provides the ability to add a Group Header or Group Footer for that field.

   You decide to change the group field from DrCode to DrLastName so that the providers are listed alphabetically by their last name instead of their DrCode value. You also want to add a DrLastName Footer section to calculate the number of patient visits for each provider.

TROUBLE
The More Options button becomes the Less Options button when clicked.

2. **Click the** DrCode arrow **in the Group, Sort, and Total pane, click** DrLastName, **click the** More Options button, **click the** without a footer section arrow, **then click** with a footer section

   The DrLastName Footer section is added to Report Design View as shown in FIGURE 3-10. You will add a calculation to count the number of patient visits for each provider later. For now, you add a third sort order to the detail records.

TROUBLE
You may need to scroll down in the Group, Sort, and Total pane to see the Add a sort button.

3. **Click the** Add a sort button **in the Group, Sort, and Total pane, then click** DateofService

   Now the records for each patient are listed in ascending order based on the DateofService field. You also decide to widen the DateofService field so that the dates are completely visible. **Layout View** is the best place to resize report controls.

4. **Click the** Layout View button ☐ **in the lower-right corner of the window to switch to Report Layout View, click the** DateofService label **to select it, point to the** left edge of the label **and drag with the** ↔ **pointer to the left to view the entire label, click** any date **to select all of them, then point to the** left edge of a date **and drag with the** ↔ **pointer to the left to view the entire dates as shown in** FIGURE 3-11

   Controls can be moved and resized using the mouse pointer symbols shown in TABLE 3-7. Note that the first page of the report now lists Dr. Babbage's patients first because the records are now grouped by the DrLastName field versus the DrCode field. Dr. Babbage's last name is first among providers when sorting the records in ascending order by DrLastName.

5. **Right-click the** Patient Visits by Provider report tab, **click** Close, **then click** Yes **to save the changes to the report**

Creating and Using Forms and Reports

FIGURE 3-9: Patient Visits by Provider report in Design View

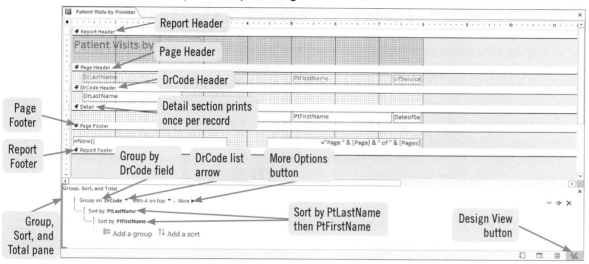

FIGURE 3-10: Modifying the grouping fields in Report Design View

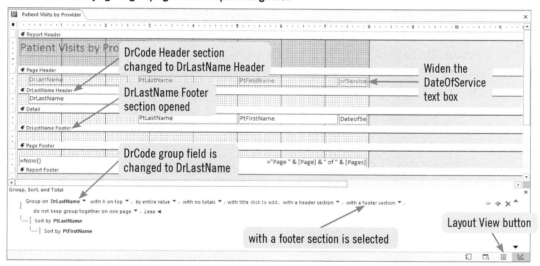

FIGURE 3-11: Resizing the DateofService controls in Report Layout View

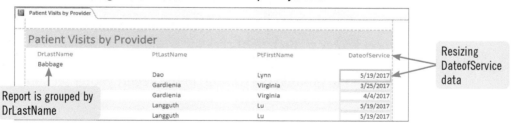

TABLE 3-7: Mouse pointer shapes

shape	when does this shape appear?	action
⬚	When you point to any unselected control on the form or report (the default mouse pointer)	Single-clicking with this mouse pointer selects a control
⬚	When you point to the upper-left corner or edge of a selected control in Form or Report Design View or the middle of the control in Form or Report Layout View	Dragging with this mouse pointer moves the selected control(s)
↔ ↕ ⬉ ⬋	When you point to any sizing handle (except the larger one in the upper-left corner in Form or Report Design View)	Dragging with one of these mouse pointers resizes the control

Add Subtotals and Counts

Learning Outcomes
• Add subtotals to reports
• Copy and paste controls
• Describe expressions

In a report, you create a **calculation** by entering an expression into a text box in Report Design View. When a report is previewed or printed, the expression is evaluated, and the resulting calculation is placed on the report. An **expression** is a combination of field names, operators (such as +, −, /, and *), and functions that results in a single value. A **function** is a built-in formula, such as Sum or Count, that helps you quickly create a calculation. Every expression starts with an equal sign (=), and when it uses a function, the arguments for the function are placed in (parentheses). **Arguments** are the pieces of information that the function needs to create the final answer. When an argument is a field name, the field name must be surrounded by [square brackets]. Common expressions are listed in TABLE 3-8. **CASE** *Kristen Royal asks you to add a calculation to the Patient Visits by Provider report to count the total number of patients for each provider.*

STEPS

1. **Right-click the Patient Visits by Provider report in the Navigation Pane, then click Design View on the shortcut menu**

   A logical place to add subtotals for each group is after the group in the Group Footer section.

2. **Drag the top edge of the Page Footer down about 0.5" to create space in the DrLastName Footer section**

   With the DrLastName Footer section open, you're ready to add a control to count the number of patient visits for each provider. You add calculations to reports by entering an expression into a text box control.

3. **Click the Text Box button ⌗ in the Controls group, then click in the DrLastName Footer section just below the PtFirstName text box**

   Adding a new text box control also adds a new label to its left. First, modify the label to identify the information, then modify the text box to contain the correct expression to sum the number of patients.

4. **Click the Text11 label to select it, double-click Text11, type Total Patients:, click the Unbound text box to select it, click Unbound again, type =Count([PtLastName]), press [Enter], then use the ↔ pointer to widen the text box to view the entire expression, as shown in FIGURE 3-12**

   The expression =Count([PtLastName]) uses the Count function to count the values in the PtLastName field. Because the expression is entered in the DrLastName Footer section, it will count all patient visits values for that provider. To count the number of patient visits for the entire report, the same expression needs to be inserted in the Report Footer section.

5. **Drag the bottom edge of the Report Footer section down about 0.5" to create space in the Report Footer section, right-click the =Count([PtLastName]) text box, click Copy on the shortcut menu, right-click in the Report Footer section, click Paste, then press [→] enough times to position the controls in the Report Footer section just below those in the DrLastName Footer section**

6. **Double-click the DrLastName Footer section bar to open the Property Sheet, click the Format tab, click None in the Force New Page property, click the arrow, then click After Section as shown in FIGURE 3-13**

   This modification will force each provider's information to print on its own page.

7. **Switch to Print Preview, then click the Next Page button ▶ enough times to move through all pages of the report**

   There are six records in the Providers table and hence six pages in this report with Detail records. The seventh and last page of the report prints the Report Footer information, which calculates the total number of patients for the entire report, 65.

FIGURE 3-12: Adding an expression to the DrLastName Footer section

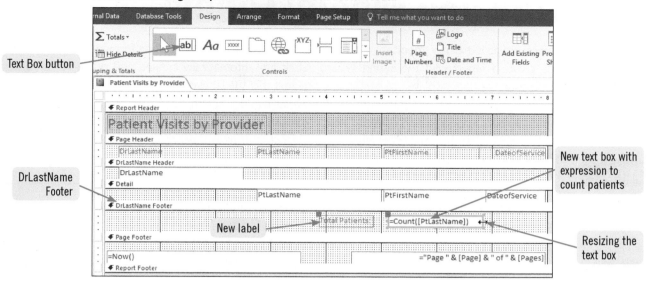

FIGURE 3-13: Adding controls to the Report Footer section and changing section properties

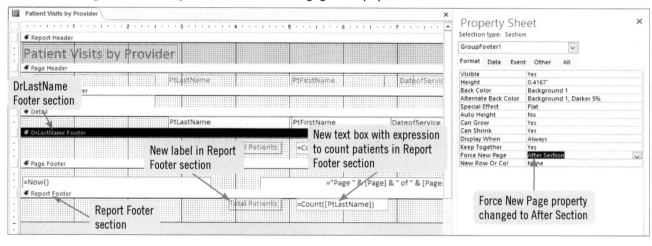

TABLE 3-8: Sample expressions

sample expression	description
=Sum([Salary])	Uses the Sum function to add the values in the Salary field
=[Charge] * 1.05	Multiplies the Charge field by 1.05 (adds 5% to the Charge field)
=[Subtotal] + [Shipping]	Adds the value of the Subtotal field to the value of the Shipping field
=Avg([Weight])	Uses the Avg function to display an average of the values in the Weight field
=Date()	Uses the Date function to display the current date in the form of mm-dd-yy
="Page " &[Page]	Displays the word Page, a space, and the result of the [Page] field, an Access field that contains the current page number
=[FirstName]& " " &[LastName]	Displays the value of the FirstName and LastName fields in one control, separated by a space
=Left([ProductNumber],2)	Uses the Left function to display the first two characters in the ProductNumber field

Add and Modify Labels

Learning
Outcomes
• Add labels to a
  report
• Move and resize
  controls
• Format controls

Labels are an extremely important control because they identify information on forms and reports. When you create a report with the Report Wizard, labels are automatically created and display field names to describe the data displayed by text boxes. The text that the label displays is controlled by its **Caption** property. A **property** is a characteristic of a control such as its Caption, Font Color, or Font Size. Properties are organized in the **Property Sheet**, which you can toggle on and off by clicking the Property Sheet button. **CASE** *You modify the labels on the Patient Visits by Provider report to make them more professional. You also add a label with your name to the Report Header section.*

STEPS

1. **Switch to** Design View, **click the** Property Sheet button **in the Tools group to toggle off the Property Sheet if it is still visible, click the** DrLastName label **in the Page Header section, click** between Dr and LastName **and press the** [Spacebar], **then click** between Last and Name **and press the** [Spacebar] **so the label reads Dr Last Name as shown in** FIGURE 3-14

   Labels may display any text you desire. Text boxes, such as those found in the DrLastName Header and Detail sections, must reference the precise field name as defined in Table Design View. With the first label in the Page Header section modified to include spaces between the words, you'll modify the other three labels in the Page Header section.

2. **In the Page Header section, modify the PtLastName label to read** Pt Last Name, **the PtFirstName label to read** Pt First Name, **and the DateofService label to read** Date of Service

   With the labels in the Page Header section modified to include spaces, your report will be easier to read and more professional. You also want to add a label to the Report Header section with your name. You need to add a new label control to accomplish this.

3. **Click the** Label button **Aa** **in the Controls group, click at about the 5" mark on the ruler in the Report Header section, type** *your name*, **then press** [Enter] **as shown in** FIGURE 3-15

   With the labels in place, you decide to change their text color to black to make them more visible. You can modify each label individually or select all of the labels at the same time to format them more productively. TABLE 3-9 summarizes techniques for selecting multiple controls at the same time.

4. **Click the** Patient Visits by Provider label **in the Report Header section, press and hold** [Shift], **click the label with** *your name* **in the Report Header section, while still holding the** [Shift] **key, click each of the** four labels **in the Page Header section, release** [Shift], **click the** Home tab, **click the** Font Color button arrow **A ·**, **then click** Automatic **to apply a black font color to the six selected controls**

   You are ready to preview your changes.

5. **Switch to** Print Preview **as shown in** FIGURE 3-16, **right-click the** Patient Visits by Provider **report tab, click** Close, **then click** Yes **when prompted to save changes**

Precisely moving and resizing controls

You can move and resize controls using the mouse, but you can move controls more precisely using the keyboard. Pressing the arrow keys while holding [Ctrl] moves selected controls one **pixel (picture element)** at a time in the direction of the arrow. Pressing the arrow keys while holding [Shift] resizes selected controls one pixel at a time.

FIGURE 3-14: Modifying labels in the Page Header section

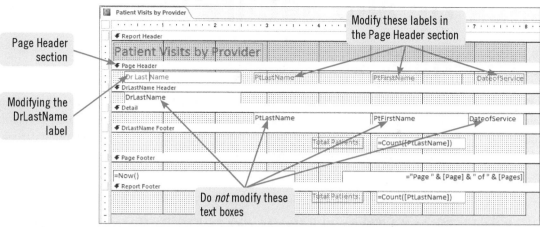

Page Header section

Modify these labels in the Page Header section

Modifying the DrLastName label

Do *not* modify these text boxes

FIGURE 3-15: Adding a label to the Report Header section

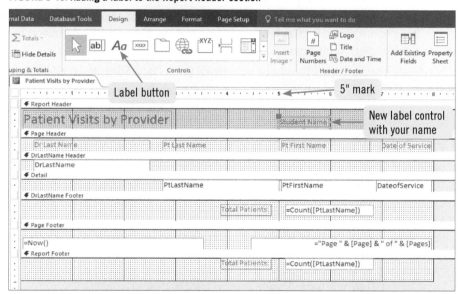

Label button

5" mark

New label control with your name

FIGURE 3-16: Final Patient Visits by Provider report in Print Preview

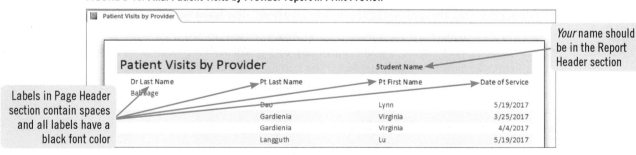

Your name should be in the Report Header section

Labels in Page Header section contain spaces and all labels have a black font color

TABLE 3-9: Selecting more than one control at a time in Report Design View

technique	description
Click, [Shift]+click	Click a control, then press and hold [Shift] while clicking other controls; each one is selected
Drag a selection box	Drag a selection box (an outline box you create by dragging the pointer in Report Design View); every control that is in or is touched by the edges of the box is selected
Click in the ruler	Click in either the horizontal or vertical ruler to select all controls that intersect the selection line
Drag in the ruler	Drag through either the horizontal or vertical ruler to select all controls that intersect the selection line as it is dragged through the ruler

Back Up and Secure the Database

Learning
Outcomes
• Back up a
  database
• Set a database
  password

Backing up a database refers to making a copy of it in a secure location. Backups can be saved on an external hard drive, the hard drive of a second computer, or a web server. A **password** is a combination of uppercase and lowercase letters, numbers, and symbols that the user must enter to open the database. Setting a database password means that anyone who doesn't know the password cannot open the database. **CASE** ▶ *Kristen Royal asks you to back up and secure the AMP 3-Riverwalk database.*

STEPS

1. **Click the** File tab **on the Ribbon, click** Save As**, click** Back Up Database**, click the** Save As **button, then click** Yes **if prompted to close all open objects**

   The Save As dialog box is shown in FIGURE 3-17. When you use the Back Up Database option, the current date is appended to the backup file name. Note that the **Save Object As** option saves only the current object (table, query, form, report, macro, or module).

2. **Navigate to the location where you store your Data Files, then click** Save

   A copy of the database is saved in the location you selected with the name AMP 3-Riverwalk-*current date*.accdb. To set a database password, you must open the database in **exclusive mode**, which means that you are the only person who has the database open, and others cannot open the file during this time.

3. **Click the** File tab**, click** Close**, click the** File tab**, click** Open**, click** Browse**, navigate to the location where you store your Data Files, click** AMP 3-Riverwalk-*current date*.accdb**, click the** Open button arrow**, click** Open Exclusive **as shown in** FIGURE 3-18**, click the** File tab**, click** Info**, then click the** Encrypt with Password button

   Encryption means to make the data in the database unreadable by other software. The Set Database Password dialog box opens. If you lose or forget your password, it cannot be recovered. For security reasons, your password does not appear as you type; for each keystroke, an asterisk appears instead. Passwords are case sensitive. Therefore, you must carefully enter the same password in both the Password and Verify text boxes to make sure you haven't made a typing error.

QUICK TIP
Check to make sure
the Caps Lock key is
not selected before
entering a password.

4. **Type** 4Health!! **in the Password text box, press [Tab], type** 4Health!! **in the Verify text box, click** OK**, then click** OK **if prompted about row level security**

   Passwords should be easy to remember but not as obvious as your name, the word "password," the name of the database, or the name of your company. **Strong passwords** are longer than eight characters and use the entire keyboard, including uppercase and lowercase letters, numbers, and symbols. Microsoft provides an online tool to check the strength of your password. Go to www.microsoft.com, and search for password checker.

5. **Close, then reopen** AMP 3-Riverwalk-*current date*.accdb

   The Password Required dialog box opens.

TROUBLE
Make sure you use
the exact same capi-
talization for the
password as you did
in Step 4.

6. **Type** 4Health!! **then click** OK

   The AMP 3-Riverwalk-*current date*.accdb database opens, giving you full access to all of the objects. To remove a password, you must exclusively open the database, and then go through the same steps used to set the password.

7. **Close the** AMP 3-Riverwalk-*current date*.accdb **database, and exit Access 2016**

Creating and Using Forms and Reports

FIGURE 3-17: Save As dialog box to back up a database

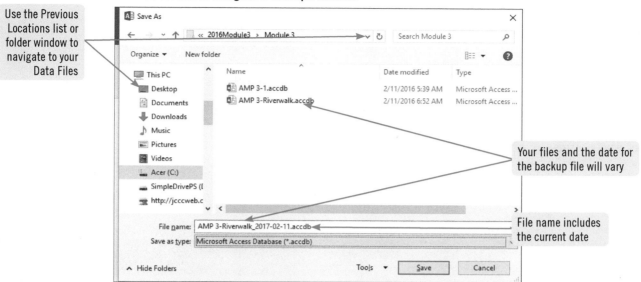

Use the Previous Locations list or folder window to navigate to your Data Files

Your files and the date for the backup file will vary

File name includes the current date

FIGURE 3-18: Opening a database in exclusive mode

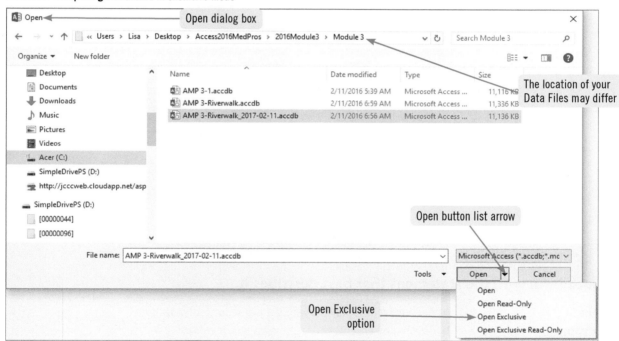

Open dialog box

The location of your Data Files may differ

Open button list arrow

Open Exclusive option

Using portable storage media

Technological advancements continue to make it easier and less expensive to store large files on portable storage devices. **Secure digital (SD)** and **micro SD cards** slip directly into a computer and typically store around 32 to 64 **GB** (**gigabyte**, a million bytes or a thousand megabytes). **CompactFlash (CF) cards** are slightly larger and also store around 16 GB to 64 GB. **USB (Universal Serial Bus) drives** (which plug into a computer's USB port) are also popular. USB drives are also called thumb drives, flash drives, and travel drives. USB devices typically store anywhere from 4 GB to 128 GB of information. Larger still are **external hard drives**, sometimes as small as the size of a cell phone, that store anywhere from 20 GB to about 4 **TB** (**terabyte**, a trillion bytes or a thousand gigabytes) of information and connect to a computer using either a USB or FireWire port.

Practice

Concepts Review

Label each element of Report Design View shown in FIGURE 3-19.

FIGURE 3-19

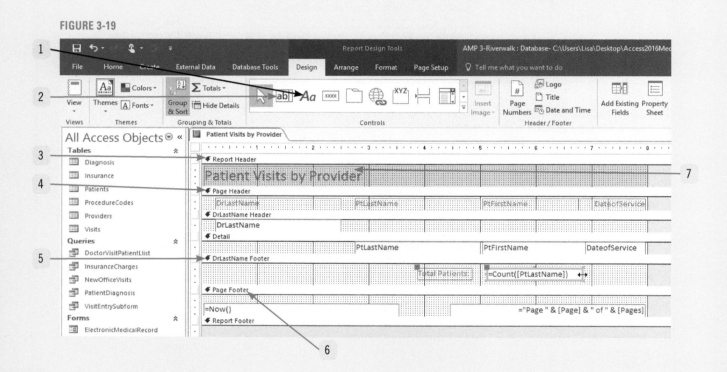

Match each term with the statement that best describes it.

8. Section
9. Expression
10. Detail section
11. Grouping
12. Database designer
13. Calculated control

a. Sorting records *plus* providing a header or footer section
b. Created by entering an expression in a text box
c. Controls placed here print once for every record in the underlying record source
d. Responsible for building and maintaining tables, queries, forms, and reports
e. Determines how controls are positioned on the report
f. A combination of field names, operators, and functions that results in a single value

Select the best answer from the list of choices.

14. Every element on a form is called a(n) _____.
    a. Property
    b. Control
    c. Item
    d. Tool

15. Which of the following is *not* a valid report view?
    a. Section View
    b. Print Preview
    c. Design View
    d. Layout View

16. The most common bound control is the _____.
    a. Label
    b. Text box
    c. Combo box
    d. List box

17. The most common unbound control is the _____.
    a. Command button
    b. Text box
    c. Label
    d. Combo box

18. A title for a report would most commonly be placed in which report section?
    a. Detail
    b. Group Footer
    c. Report Header
    d. Report Footer

19. Which of the following expressions counts the number of records using the FirstName field?
    a. =Count(FirstName)
    b. =Count([FirstName])
    c. =Count[FirstName]
    d. =Count{FirstName}

20. When you enter a calculation in a text box, the first character is a(n) _____.
    a. Left square bracket, [
    b. Left parenthesis, (
    c. Equal sign, =
    d. Asterisk, *

Skills Review

1. **Manage data with a form.**
   a. Open the AMP 3-2.accdb database from the location where you store your Data Files. Save the database as **AMP 3-Diabetes.accdb**. Enable content if prompted.
   b. Open the EmployeeEntry form. Modify the Street Address value for the first record for EmpNo 5 (Kent Moshi) from 201 SW Woodlawn Dr to **505 Grand Ave**. Modify the City from Des Moines to **Ankeny**, and the Zip Code from 50308 to **50021**.
   c. Click the New (blank) record button, and create a new record using the value of **20** as the EmpNo and **your name** for the Last Name and First Name. Enter your school's address and fictitious but realistic data for your Birthday and Hire Date to complete the record.
   d. Close the EmployeeEntry form.

2. **Use the Form Wizard.**
   a. Click the Create tab, then use the Form Wizard to create a form based on all of the fields in the MedDescription table. Use a Columnar layout, and type **Med Entry Form** to title the form.
   b. Navigate through the records to find MedCode 11 (record 21 of 22), as shown in FIGURE 3-20.
   c. Save and close the Med Entry Form.

FIGURE 3-20

3. **Preview a report.**
   a. Open the PatientListing report in Print Preview, then move to the second (the last) page of the report.
   b. Review both pages of the report, identifying the Report Header, Page Header, Detail, and Report Footer sections. If requested by your instructor, print the report and identify the Report Header, Page Header, Detail, and Report Footer sections on the printout.
   c. Close the PatientListing report.

4. **Use the Report Wizard.**
   a. Click the Create tab, then use the Report Wizard to create a report based on the following fields in the Employees table: ELastName, EFirstName, and City. Group the records by City, do not add any sort orders, and use a Stepped layout and a Portrait orientation. Title the report **Employee List by City**.
   b. Preview the report in Print Preview, identifying the Report Header, Page Header, City Header, Detail, and Page Footer sections. If requested by your instructor, print the report, and identify the Report Header, Page Header, Detail, and Report Footer sections on the printout.

5. **Apply group and sort orders.**
   a. Switch to Design View of the Employee List by City report, then open the Group, Sort, and Total pane.
   b. Click the Add a sort button and add ELastName as a sort field under City as a group field.
   c. Click the More Options button for the City group field, then add a City Footer section. (*Hint*: Be careful to add a City Footer section, not an ELastName Footer section.)

Skills Review (continued)

6. Add subtotals and counts.

a. Add a text box control in the City Footer section positioned under the ELastName text box located in the Detail section.

b. Modify the Text9 label to read **Count:**

c. Click Unbound in the text box, and enter the expression **=Count([ELastName])**.

d. Preview the report to make sure the new label and calculation in the City Footer section are working as intended.

7. Add and modify labels.

a. Return to Design View, then modify the ELastName and EFirstName labels in the Page Header section to read **Last Name** and **First Name**. Be careful to modify the labels in the Page Header section rather than the text boxes in the Detail section. (*Hint*: View the report in Print Preview to view how the pages will print on paper to make sure your report is not too wide. If every other page is a blank page, return to Report Design View and narrow controls and the right edge of the report within the 8" mark on the horizontal ruler so that the entire report fits within the width of one page.)

b. Add a new label to the Report Header section with *your name*.

c. Modify all labels in the Report Header and Page Header sections to have a black font color.

d. Preview the updated report. It should look like FIGURE 3-21. Again, be careful to preview multiple pages to make sure your report fits within the width of a single sheet of paper.

e. Save and close the Employee List by City report.

8. Back up and secure the database.

a. Back up the AMP 3-Diabetes.accdb database with the name **AMP 3-Diabetes-*current date*.accdb** in the drive and folder where your Data Files are stored.

b. Close the AMP 3-Diabetes-*current date*.accdb database, reopen it in exclusive mode, and set the following password: **eat123well!**

c. Close the AMP 3-Diabetes-*current date*.accdb database, and reopen it to test the password.

d. Close the AMP 3-Diabetes-*current date*.accdb database, and exit Access 2016.

FIGURE 3-21

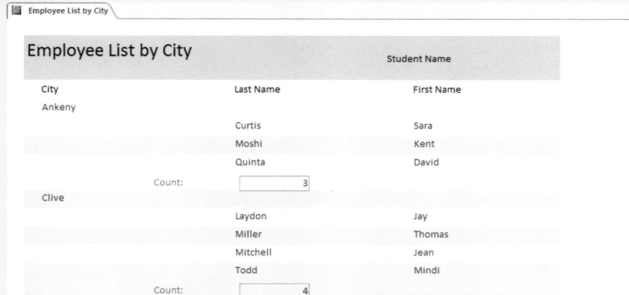

Independent Challenge 1

You have built an Access database to track nursing assignments at a multilocation dermatology clinic. You will create forms and reports to help manage and analyze the information.

a. Start Access, open the AMP 3-3.accdb database from the location where you store your Data Files, then save it as **AMP 3-Nurses.accdb**. Enable content if prompted.

b. Open the ProviderEntry form, and add a new record using **MD** for the title and **your last name** for the Last Name field, as shown in FIGURE 3-22. Close the ProviderEntry form.

c. Open the NurseEntry form, and add a new record using your **instructor's first and last names** in the Nurse First Name and Nurse Last Name fields. Close the NurseEntry form.

d. Open the ScheduleDate form, use the FIND this date list arrow to find the 10/22/2017 date, then enter a new record for **East**, using **your name** in the DoctorNo column and your **instructor's name** in the NurseNo column as shown in FIGURE 3-23.

e. Close the ScheduleDate form, open the Schedule report, and print the first page if requested by your instructor. Your name and your instructor's name will be present on the schedule for 10/22/2017.

f. Close the Schedule report, close the AMP 3-Nurses.accdb database, and exit Access 2016.

FIGURE 3-22

Title	Last Name
PA	Agri
PA	Anderson
PA	Christenson
MD	Fletcher
MD	Gold
MD	Market
MD	Newsome
MD	Northy
MD	Samuelson
MD	Swabe
MD	Student Last

FIGURE 3-23

Work Schedule   FIND this date   10/22/2017

Date 10/22/2017 Sunday   19   Add: Day | Doctor | Nurse   Reports: by Location | by Nurse

LocationNo	DoctorNo	NurseNo
East	Swabe	Jill Kennedy
East	Swabe	Tammy Cavuto
North	Agri	Mary Tharp
North	Anderson	Tina Buck
North	Fletcher	Joyce Johnson
North	Fletcher	Lydia Hemmer
North	Fletcher	Michele Blago
North	Gold	Amberley Stein
North	Gold	Jan Regan
North	Gold	Liz Ducy
North	Gold	Sandy Torrent
North	Northy	Dawn Wu
North	Northy	Sam Fredrick
South	Christenson	Ashley Jackson
South	Christenson	Shannon Kenneth
South	Samuelson	Dana Washington
South	Samuelson	Jennifer McCully
South	Samuelson	Rebecca Rivera
East	Student Last	Instructor First Instructor Last

Record: 19 of 19   No Filter   Search

Record: 12 of 43   No Filter   Search

Independent Challenge 2

You are working with a medical school's intern placement program. You have started an Access database to track evaluations of interns and need to create a report to analyze information.

a. Start Access, open the AMP 3-4.accdb database from the location where you store your Data Files, then save it as **AMP 3-InternMgmt.accdb**. Enable content if prompted.

b. Using the Report Wizard, create a report based on all of the fields from the InternName table, and all of the fields except for EvalNo from the Evaluations table.

c. View the data by InternName, do not add any more grouping levels, choose EvaluationDate as the sorting field, use a Stepped layout and a Landscape orientation, and title the report **Evaluation Report**.

d. In Report Design View, open the Group, Sort, and Total pane, and change the group field to the InternLName field so the records are grouped by the value in the InternLName field vs. the InternNo field.

e. Use Layout View to modify the labels in the Page Header section so that they match the labels shown in FIGURE 3-24. Be careful to modify the labels in the Page Header section and not the text boxes in the InternLName Header or Detail section.

f. Use Layout and Design Views to move and resize controls so that they are all visible and fit within the 10" mark on the horizontal ruler. Delete the last InternNo column by deleting both the label and numbers so that all data is clearly visible, as shown in FIGURE 3-24.

g. In Design View, be sure to narrow all controls in order to drag the right edge of the report to the left of the 10" mark on the horizontal ruler.

h. Preview all pages of the report to make sure all data prints and no blank pages are present. If requested by your instructor, print the first page of the report.

i. Save and close the Evaluation Report, then close the AMP 3-InternMgmt.accdb database and exit Access 2016.

FIGURE 3-24

InternNo	First Name	Last Name	Date	Prompt	Professional	Knowledgeable	Respectful	Evaluator
8	Jill	Clark						
			1/8/2017	4	4	3	5	Bloom
			1/8/2017	4	4	3	5	Bloom
			1/9/2017	5	4	5	4	Reeder
			1/9/2017	5	4	5	4	Reeder
			1/10/2017	4	4	5	5	Waller

Independent Challenge 3

You are working for an orthopedic clinic that is highly dependent on patient referrals from primary care physicians. You have created an Access database to help keep track of referrals so that you can analyze which physicians refer to your clinic and keep in touch with them regarding patient progress. You want to analyze the data with a new report.

a. Start Access, open the AMP 3-5.accdb database from the location where you store your Data Files, then save it as **AMP 3-Referrals.accdb**. Enable content if prompted.

b. Using the Report Wizard, create a new report using the RFirst and RLast fields from the ReferringDocs table and the VisitDate field from the Visits table.

c. View the data by ReferringDocs, do not add any more grouping levels, add the VisitDate field as an ascending sort field, use a Stepped layout and Portrait orientation, and title the report **Referrals**.

d. In Report Design View, open the Group, Sort, and Total pane.

e. Change the Group field from RDocNo to RLast.

f. Add a text box at about the 6.75" mark on the horizontal ruler to the RLast Header section.

g. Delete the Text9 label in the RLast Header section.

h. Change the Unbound text box in the RLast Header section to **=Count([VisitDate])**.

i. Modify the labels in the Page Header section from RFirst and RLast to **Referring Dr First Name** and **Referring Dr Last Name**.

j. In Report Design View, delete the VisitDate text box from the Detail section and the VisitDate label from the Page Header section.

k. Drag the top edge of the Page Footer section up so that there is no space in the Detail section.

l. Preview the report, a portion of which is shown in FIGURE 3-25, and then print the first page if required by your instructor.

m. Save and close the Referrals report, close the AMP 3-Referrals.accdb database, then exit Access 2016.

FIGURE 3-25

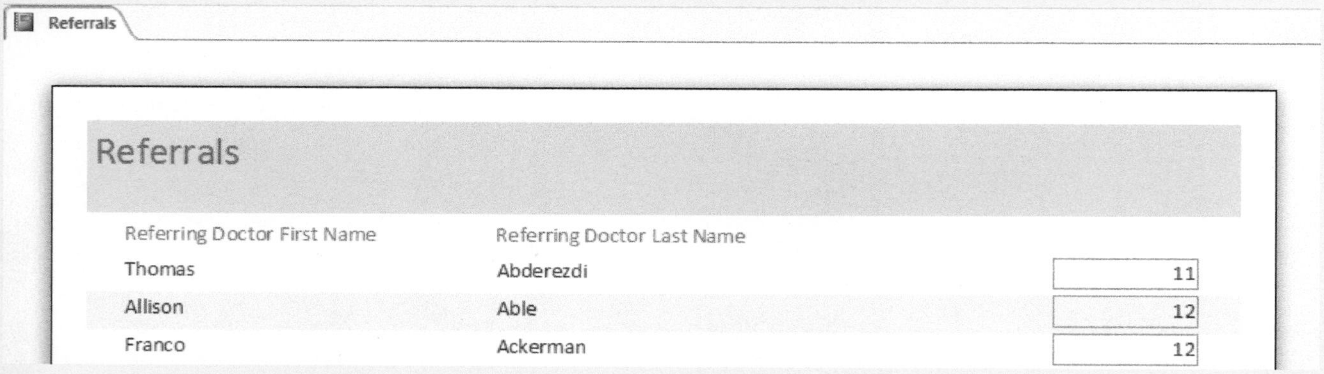

Referrals		
Referring Doctor First Name	Referring Doctor Last Name	
Thomas	Abderezdi	11
Allison	Able	12
Franco	Ackerman	12

Independent Challenge 4: Explore

The medical profession uses a great number of abbreviations. You can use an Access database to organize and learn these abbreviations. In this exercise, you'll create a form and report to manage prescription abbreviations.

a. Start Access, open the AMP 3-6.accdb database from the location where you store your Data Files, then save it as **AMP 3-Prescriptions.accdb**. Enable content if prompted.

b. Click the ScriptAbbreviations table in the Navigation Pane, click the Create tab, then click the Form button to create a new form very quickly.

c. Display the form in Form View, and enter a new record. Enter **aa** in the Abbreviation field, **ana** in the Latin field, and **of each** in the Meaning field. Save the new form with the name **Script Entry**, and close it.

d. Click the ScriptAbbreviations table in the Navigation Pane, click the Create tab, then click the Report button.

e. Switch to Report Design View, delete the controls from the Report Footer section, then open the Group, Sort, and Total pane.

f. Add Abbreviation as a sort field, then display the report in Print Preview, a portion of which is shown in FIGURE 3-26.

g. Close the report, saving it as **ScriptAbbreviations**, close the AMP 3-Prescriptions.accdb database, then exit Access 2016.

FIGURE 3-26

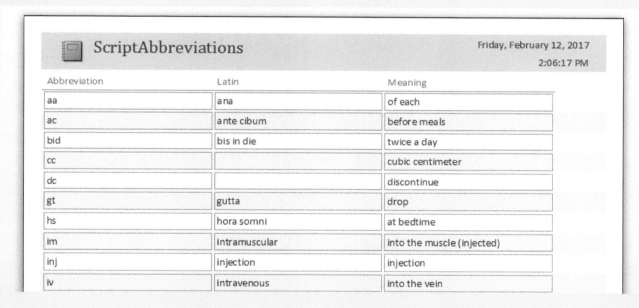

Access 2016

Visual Workshop

One of the most challenging aspects of the medical profession is the vast amount of medical terminology you are required to memorize. In this exercise, you will create a report of medical terminology. Start Access, open the AMP 3-7.accdb database from the location where you store your Data Files, and save it as **AMP 3-MedicalTerms.accdb**. Enable content if prompted. Use the Report Wizard to create a report based on all of the fields in the Terms table except for the ID field. Do not add any grouping levels, sort the records on the Prefix or suffix and then the Meaning fields, choose a Tabular layout and a Portrait orientation, and title the report **Medical Terminology to Learn**. In Report Design View, add your name as a label to the Report Header section and change the font color to black. Preview the report as shown in FIGURE 3-27, and print the first page if requested by your instructor.

Visual Workshop (continued)

FIGURE 3-27

Medical Terminology to Learn

Student Name

Prefix or suffix	Meaning	Origin	Example
a-, an-	Denotes an absence of	Ancient Greek ἀ-/ἀν- (a-/an-),	Apathy, Analgia
ab-	away from	Latin	Abduction
abdomin(o)-	Of or relating to the abdomen	Latin (abdōmen), abdomen, fa	Abdomen
-ac, -acal	pertaining to	Greek -ακός (-akos)	cardiac, hydrophobiac, pha
acanth(o)-	thorn or spine	Ancient Greek ἄκανθα (akanth	acanthion, acanthocyte, ac
acous(io)-	Of or relating to hearing	Greek ἀκουστικός (acoustikos)	acoumeter, acoustician
acr(o)-	extremity, topmost	Greek ἄκρον (akron), highest o	Acrocrany, acromegaly, ac
-acusis	hearing	Greek ἀκουστικός (acoustikos)	paracusis
-ad	toward, in the direction of		dorsad
ad-	increase, adherence, motion t	Latin	Adduction
aden(o)-, aden(i)-	Of or relating to a gland	Ancient Greek ἀδήν, ἀδέν- (ad	Adenocarcinoma, adenolo
adip(o)-	Of or relating to fat or fatty tis	Latin (adeps, adip-), fat	Adipocyte

Page: ◄ ◄ 1 ► ►► ◄ ☒ No Filter ◄

Creating a Presentation in PowerPoint 2016

CASE ▶ You work at Riverwalk Medical Clinic (RMC), a large medical facility in Cambridge, Massachusetts. You have been asked by the Director of Emergency Services, Tallon Carter, to create a training presentation on poisons and their treatment to be used at a future first responder training class.

Module Objectives

After completing this module, you will be able to:

- Define presentation software
- Plan an effective presentation
- Examine the PowerPoint window
- Enter slide text

- Add a new slide
- Apply a design theme
- Compare presentation views
- Print a PowerPoint presentation

Files You Will Need

No files needed.

Define Presentation Software

Presentation software (also called presentation graphics software) is a computer program you use to organize and present information to others. Presentations are typically in the form of a slide show. Whether you are explaining a new product or moderating a meeting, presentation software can help you effectively communicate your ideas. You can use PowerPoint to create informational slides that you print or display on a monitor, share in real time on the web, or save as a video for others to watch. **CASE** *You need to start working on your training presentation. Because you are only somewhat familiar with PowerPoint, you get to work exploring its capabilities. FIGURE 1-1 shows how a presentation looks printed as handouts. FIGURE 1-2 shows how the same presentation might look shared on the Internet with others.*

DETAILS

You can easily complete the following tasks using PowerPoint:

• **Enter and edit text easily**

Text editing and formatting commands in PowerPoint are organized by the task you are performing at the time, so you can enter, edit, and format text information simply and efficiently to produce the best results in the least amount of time.

• **Change the appearance of information**

PowerPoint has many effects that can transform the way text, graphics, and slides appear. By exploring some of these capabilities, you discover how easy it is to change the appearance of your presentation.

• **Organize and arrange information**

Once you start using PowerPoint, you won't have to spend much time making sure your information is correct and in the right order. With PowerPoint, you can quickly and easily rearrange and modify text, graphics, and slides in your presentation.

• **Include information from other sources**

Often, when you create presentations, you use information from a variety of sources. With PowerPoint, you can import text, photographs, videos, numerical data, and other information from files created in programs such as Adobe Photoshop, Microsoft Word, Microsoft Excel, and Microsoft Access. You can also import information from other PowerPoint presentations as well as graphic images from a variety of sources such as the Internet, other computers, a digital camera, or other graphics programs. Always be sure you have permission to use any work that you did not create yourself.

• **Present information in a variety of ways**

With PowerPoint, you can present information using a variety of methods. For example, you can print handout pages or an outline of your presentation for audience members. You can display your presentation as an on-screen slide show using your computer, or if you are presenting to a large group, you can use a video projector and a large screen. If you want to reach an even wider audience, you can broadcast the presentation or upload it as a video to the Internet so people anywhere in the world can use a web browser to view your presentation.

• **Collaborate with others on a presentation**

PowerPoint makes it easy to collaborate or share a presentation with colleagues and coworkers using the Internet. You can use your email program to send a presentation as an attachment to a colleague for feedback. If you have a number of people that need to work together on a presentation, you can save the presentation to a shared workspace such as a network drive or OneDrive so authorized users in your group with an Internet connection can access the presentation.

FIGURE 1-1: PowerPoint handout

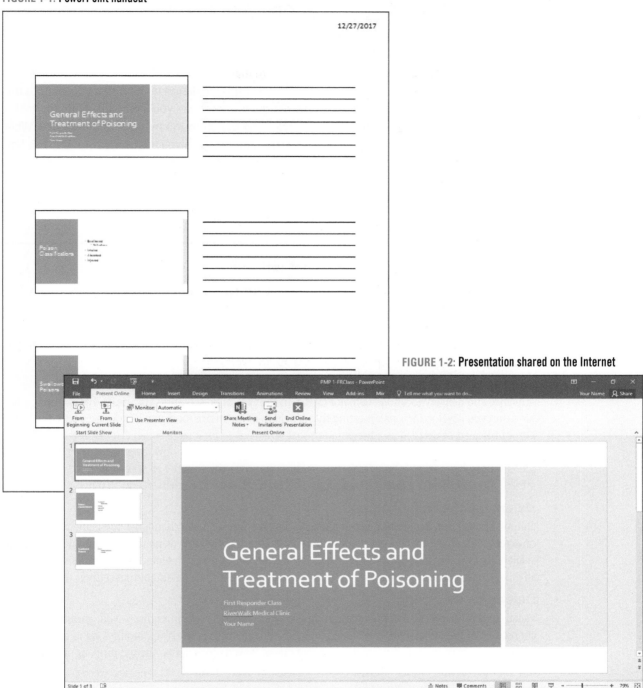

FIGURE 1-2: **Presentation shared on the Internet**

Using PowerPoint on a touch screen

You can use PowerPoint 2016 on a Windows computer with a touch-enabled monitor or any other compatible touch screen, such as a tablet computer. Using your fingers, you can use typical touch gestures to create, modify, and navigate presentations. To enable touch mode capabilities in PowerPoint, you need to add the Touch Mode button to the Quick Access toolbar. Click the Customize Quick Access Toolbar button, click Touch/Mouse Mode, click the on the Quick Access toolbar, then click Touch. In Touch mode, additional space is added around all of the buttons and icons in the Ribbon and the status bar to make them easier to touch. Common gestures that you can use in PowerPoint include double-tapping text to edit it and tapping a slide then dragging it to rearrange it in the presentation.

PowerPoint 2016

Plan an Effective Presentation

Before you create a presentation, you need to have a general idea of the information you want to communicate. PowerPoint is a powerful and flexible program that gives you the ability to start a presentation simply by entering the text of your message. If you have a specific design in mind that you want to use, you can start the presentation by working on the design. In most cases you'll probably enter the text of your presentation into PowerPoint first and then tailor the design to the message and audience. When preparing your presentation, you need to keep in mind not only who you are giving it to, but also how you are presenting it. For example, if you are giving a presentation using a projector, you need to know what other equipment you will need, such as a sound system and a projector. **CASE** *Use the planning guidelines below to help plan an effective presentation.* FIGURE 1-3 *illustrates a storyboard for a well-planned presentation.*

DETAILS

In planning a presentation, it is important to:

• **Determine and outline the message you want to communicate**

The more time you take developing the message and outline of your presentation, the better your presentation will be in the end. A presentation with a clear message that reads like a story and is illustrated with appropriate visual aids will have the greatest impact on your audience. Start the presentation by providing a general description of poisoning classifications. See FIGURE 1-3.

• **Identify your audience and where and how you are giving the presentation**

Audience and delivery location are major factors in the type of presentation you create. For example, a presentation you develop for a staff meeting that is held in a conference room would not necessarily need to be as sophisticated or detailed as a presentation that you develop for a large audience held in an auditorium. Room lighting, natural light, screen position, and room layout all affect how the audience responds to your presentation. You can also broadcast your presentation over the Internet to several people who view the presentation on their computers in real time. This presentation will be delivered in a large room.

• **Determine the type of output**

Output choices for a presentation include black-and-white or color handouts for audience members, on-screen slide show, a video, or an online broadcast. Consider the time demands and computer equipment availability as you decide which output types to produce. Because this presentation will be delivered personally in a large room and you have access to projection equipment, the default output settings work just fine.

• **Determine the design**

Visual appeal, graphics, and presentation design work together to communicate your message. You can choose one of the professionally designed themes that come with PowerPoint, modify one of these themes, or create one of your own. You decide to choose one of PowerPoint's design themes for your presentation.

FIGURE 1-3: Storyboard of the presentation

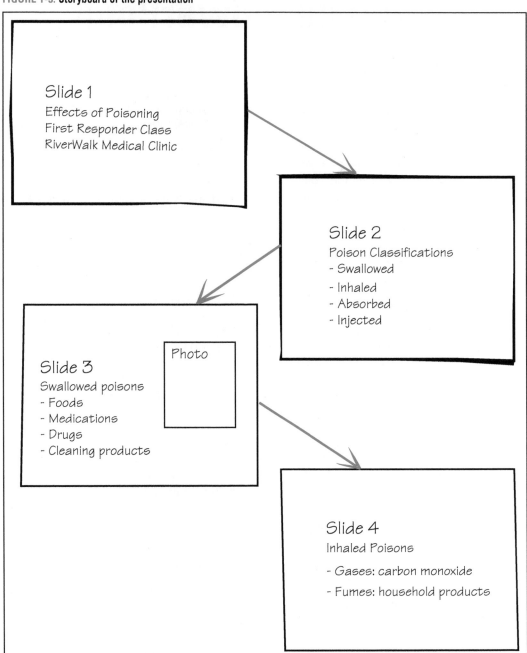

Understanding copyright

Intellectual property is any idea or creation of the human mind. Copyright law is a type of intellectual property law that protects works of authorship, including books, webpages, computer games, music, artwork, and photographs. Copyright protects the expression of an idea, but not the underlying facts or concepts. In other words, the general subject matter is not protected, but how you express it is, such as when several people photograph the same sunset. Copyright attaches to any original work of authorship as soon as it is created; you do not have to register it with the Copyright Office or display the copyright symbol, ©. Fair use is an exception to copyright and permits the public to use copyrighted material for certain purposes without obtaining prior consent from the owner. Determining whether fair use applies to a work depends on its purpose, the nature of the work, how much of the work you want to copy, and the effect on the work's value. Unauthorized use of protected work (such as downloading a photo or a song from the web) is known as copyright infringement and can lead to legal action.

Examine the PowerPoint Window

When you first start PowerPoint, you have the ability to choose what kind of presentation you want to use to start—a blank one, or one with a preformatted design. You can also open and work on an existing presentation. PowerPoint has different **views** that allow you to see your presentation in different forms. By default, the PowerPoint window opens in **Normal view**, which is the primary view that you use to write, edit, and design your presentation. Normal view is divided into areas called **panes**: the pane on the left, called the **Slides tab**, displays the slides of your presentation as small images, called **slide thumbnails**. The large pane is the Slide pane where you do most of your work on the slide. **CASE** *The PowerPoint window and the specific parts of Normal view are described below.*

STEPS

1. **Start** PowerPoint 2016
   PowerPoint starts and the PowerPoint start screen opens, as shown in FIGURE 1-4.
2. **Click the** Blank Presentation slide thumbnail
   The PowerPoint window opens in Normal view, as shown in FIGURE 1-5.

DETAILS

TROUBLE
If you are unsure
how to start
PowerPoint, refer to
the "Getting Started
with Office 2016"
module in this book
for specific instruc-
tions on how to start
the application.

Using FIGURE 1-5 **as a guide, examine the elements of the PowerPoint window, then find and compare the elements described below:**

• The **Ribbon** is a wide band spanning the top of the PowerPoint window and organizes all of PowerPoint's primary commands. Each set of primary commands is identified by a **tab**; for example, the Home tab is selected by default, as shown in FIGURE 1-5. Commands are further arranged into **groups** on the Ribbon based on their function. So, for example, text formatting commands such as Bold, Underline, and Italic are located on the Home tab, in the Font group.

• The **Slides tab** is to the left. You can navigate through the slides in your presentation by clicking the slide thumbnails. You can also add, delete, or rearrange slides using this pane.

• The **Slide pane** displays the current slide in your presentation.

• The **Quick Access toolbar** provides access to common commands such as Save, Undo, Redo, and Start From Beginning. The Quick Access toolbar is always visible no matter which Ribbon tab you select. Click the Customize Quick Access Toolbar button to add or remove buttons.

• The **View Shortcuts** buttons on the status bar allow you to switch quickly between PowerPoint views.

• The **Notes button** on the status bar opens the Notes pane and is used to enter text that references a slide's content. You can print these notes and refer to them when you make a presentation or use them as audience handouts. The Notes pane is not visible in Slide Show view.

• The **Comments button** on the status bar opens the Comments pane. In the Comments pane you can create, edit, select, and delete comments.

• The **status bar**, located at the bottom of the PowerPoint window, shows messages about what you are doing and seeing in PowerPoint, including which slide you are viewing and the total number of slides. In addition, the status bar displays the Zoom slider controls, the Fit slide to current window button 🔳, and other functionality information.

• The **Zoom slider** on the lower-right corner of the status bar is used to zoom the slide in and out.

FIGURE 1-4: PowerPoint start screen

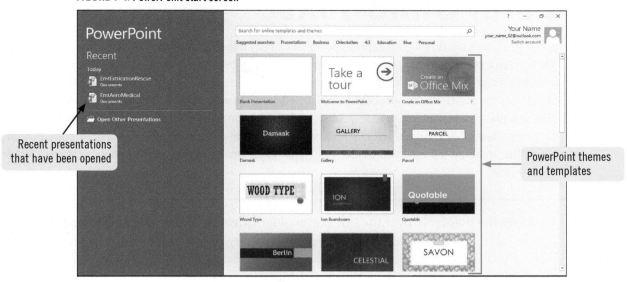

Recent presentations that have been opened

PowerPoint themes and templates

FIGURE 1-5: PowerPoint window in Normal view

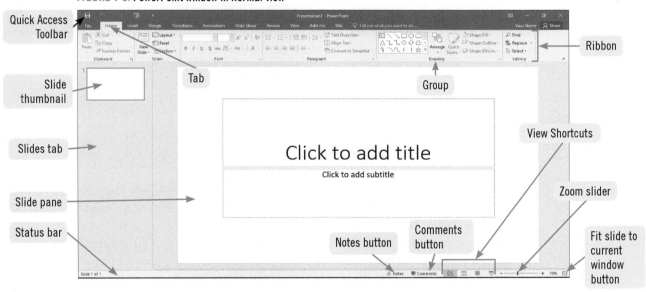

Quick Access Toolbar

Slide thumbnail

Tab

Group

Ribbon

Slides tab

Slide pane

Status bar

View Shortcuts

Zoom slider

Notes button

Comments button

Fit slide to current window button

Viewing your presentation in gray scale or black and white

Viewing your presentation in gray scale (using shades of gray) or pure black and white is very useful when you are printing a presentation on a black-and-white printer and you want to make sure your presentation prints correctly. To see how your color presentation looks in gray scale or black and white, click the View tab, then click either the Grayscale or Black and White button in the Color/Grayscale group. Depending on which button you select, the Grayscale or the Black and White tab appears, and the Ribbon displays different settings that you can customize. If you don't like the way an individual object looks in black and white or gray scale, you can change its color. Click the object while still in Grayscale or Black and White view, then choose an option in the Change Selected Object group on the Ribbon.

Enter Slide Text

Learning Outcomes
- Enter slide text
- Change slide text

When you start a blank PowerPoint presentation, an empty title slide appears in Normal view. The title slide has two **text placeholders**—boxes with dotted borders—where you enter text. The top text placeholder on the title slide is the **title placeholder**, labeled "Click to add title". The bottom text placeholder on the title slide is the **subtitle text placeholder**, labeled "Click to add subtitle". To enter text in a placeholder, click the placeholder and then type your text. After you enter text in a placeholder, the placeholder becomes a text object. An **object** is any item on a slide that can be modified. Objects are the building blocks that make up a presentation slide. **CASE** *Begin working on your presentation by entering text on the title slide.*

STEPS

1. **Move the pointer ⌖ over the title placeholder labeled Click to add title in the Slide pane**
   The pointer changes to I when you move the pointer over the placeholder. In PowerPoint, the pointer often changes shape, depending on the task you are trying to accomplish.

2. **Click the title placeholder in the Slide pane**
   The **insertion point**, a blinking vertical line, indicates where your text appears when you type in the placeholder. A **selection box** with a dashed line border and **sizing handles** appears around the placeholder, indicating that it is selected and ready to accept text. When a placeholder or object is selected, you can change its shape or size by dragging one of the sizing handles. See FIGURE 1-6.

TROUBLE
If you press a wrong key, press [Backspace] to erase the character.

3. **Type General Effects and Treatment of Poisoning**
   PowerPoint wraps the text to a second line and then center-aligns the title text within the title placeholder, which is now a text object. Notice the text also appears on the slide thumbnail on the Slides tab.

4. **Click the subtitle text placeholder in the Slide pane**
   The subtitle text placeholder is ready to accept text.

5. **Type Medical Staff Training, then press [Enter]**
   The insertion point moves to the next line in the text object.

QUICK TIP
To copy text, select the text, click the Home tab, click the Copy button in the Clipboard group, place the insertion point, then click the Paste button in the Clipboard group.

6. **Type First Responder Class, press [Enter], type RiverWalk Medical Clinic, press [Enter], then type your name**
   Notice the AutoFit Options button ⊞ appears near the text object. The AutoFit Options button on your screen indicates that PowerPoint has automatically decreased the font size of all the text in the text object so it fits inside the text object.

7. **Click the AutoFit Options button ⊞, then click Stop Fitting Text to This Placeholder on the shortcut menu**
   The text in the text object changes back to its original size and no longer fits inside the text object.

8. **In the subtitle text object, position I to the right of Training, drag left to select the entire line of text, press [Backspace], then click outside the text object in a blank area of the slide**
   The Medical Staff Training line of text is deleted and the AutoFit Options button menu closes, as shown in FIGURE 1-7. Clicking a blank area of the slide deselects all selected objects on the slide.

9. **Click the Save button 🖫 on the Quick Access toolbar to open Backstage view, then save the presentation as PMP 1-FRClass in the location where you store your Data Files**
   In Backstage view, you have the option of saving your presentation to your computer or OneDrive. Notice that PowerPoint automatically entered the title of the presentation as the filename in the Save As dialog box.

FIGURE 1-6: **Title text placeholder selected**

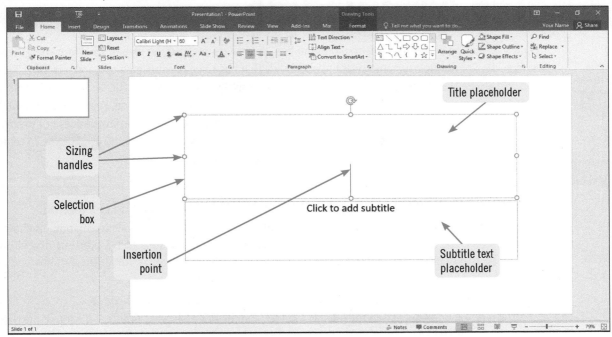

FIGURE 1-7: **Text on title slide**

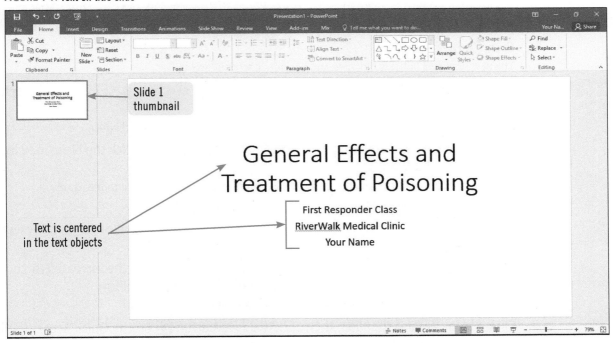

Inking a slide

In Slide View, you can add freehand pen and highlighter marks, also known as **inking**, to the slides of your presentation to emphasize information. To begin inking, go to the slide you want mark up, click the Review tab, then click the Start Inking button in the Ink group. The Pens tab appears on the Ribbon and the Pen tool appears on the slide ready for you to draw using your mouse. To customize your pen, select a different pen color, style, or thickness from options in the Pens group. Click the Highlighter button in the Write group to insert highlighter strokes on your slide. To erase inking on the slide, click the Eraser button in the Write group.

Add a New Slide

Learning
Outcomes
• Add a new slide
• Indent text levels
• Modify slide layout

Usually when you add a new slide to a presentation, you have a pretty good idea of what you want the slide to look like. For example, you may want to add a slide that has a title over bulleted text and a picture. To help you add a slide like this quickly and easily, PowerPoint provides many standard slide layouts. A **slide layout** contains text and object placeholders that are arranged in a specific way on the slide. You have already worked with the Title Slide layout in the previous lesson. In the event that a standard slide layout does not meet your needs, you can modify an existing slide layout or create a new, custom slide layout. **CASE** ▶ *To continue developing the presentation, you create a slide that explains poison classifications.*

STEPS

1. **Click the** New Slide button **in the Slides group on the Home tab on the Ribbon**

   A new blank slide (now the current slide) appears as the second slide in your presentation, as shown in FIGURE 1-8. The new slide contains a title placeholder and a content placeholder. A **content placeholder** can be used to insert text or objects such as tables, charts, videos, or pictures. Notice the status bar indicates Slide 2 of 2 and the Slides tab now contains two slide thumbnails.

2. **Type** Poison Classifications, **then click the** bottom content placeholder

   The text you typed appears in the title placeholder, and the insertion point is now at the top of the bottom content placeholder.

3. **Type** Swallowed, **then press** [Enter]

   The insertion point appears directly below the text when you press [Enter], and a new first-level bullet automatically appears.

4. **Press** [Tab]

   The new first-level bullet is indented and becomes a second-level bullet.

QUICK TIP
You can also press
[Shift][Tab] to
decrease the
indent level.

5. **Type** Medications, **press** [Enter], **click the** Decrease List Level button ◀≣ **in the Paragraph group, then type** Inhaled

   The Decrease List Level button changes the second-level bullet into a first-level bullet.

6. **Press** [Enter], **type** Absorbed, **press** [Enter], **type** Injected, **then click the** New Slide list arrow **in the Slides group**

   The Office Theme layout gallery opens. Each slide layout is identified by a descriptive name.

7. **Click the** Two Content slide layout, **then type** Swallowed Poisons

   A new slide with a title placeholder and two content placeholders appears as the third slide. The text you typed is the title text for the slide.

8. **Click the left content placeholder, type** Foods, **press** [Enter], **click the** Increase List Level button ≣▶, **type** Certain mushrooms, **press** [Enter], **then type** Shellfish

   The Increase List Level button moves the insertion point one level to the right.

9. **Click a blank area of the slide, then click the** Save button ▣ **on the Quick Access toolbar**

   The Save button saves all of the changes to the file. Compare your screen with FIGURE 1-9.

FIGURE 1-8: New blank slide in Normal view

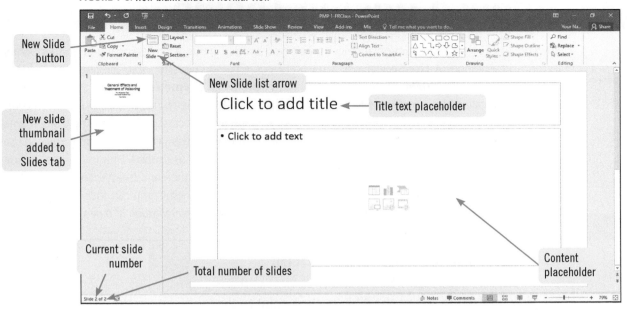

New Slide button

New slide thumbnail added to Slides tab

New Slide list arrow

Click to add title ← Title text placeholder

• Click to add text

Current slide number

Total number of slides

Content placeholder

FIGURE 1-9: New slide with Two Content slide layout

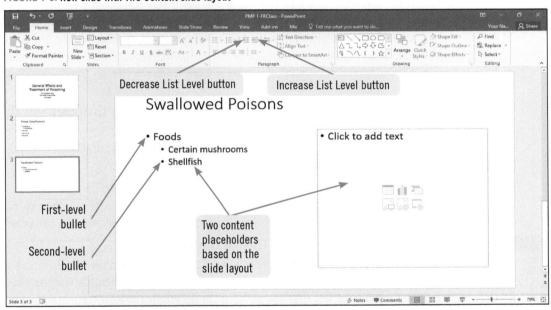

Decrease List Level button

Increase List Level button

Swallowed Poisons

• Foods
  • Certain mushrooms
  • Shellfish

• Click to add text

First-level bullet

Second-level bullet

Two content placeholders based on the slide layout

Entering and printing notes

You can add notes to your slides when there are certain facts you want to remember during a presentation or when there is additional information you want to hand out to your audience. Notes do not appear on the slides when you run a slide show. Use the Notes pane in Normal view or Notes Page view to enter notes for your slides. To open or close the Notes pane, click the Notes button on the status bar. To enter text notes on a slide, click in the Notes pane, then type. If you want to insert graphics as notes, you must use Notes Page view. To open Notes Page view, click the View tab on the Ribbon, then click the Notes Page button in the Presentation Views group. You can print your notes by clicking the File tab on the Ribbon to open Backstage view. Click Print, click the Full Page Slides list arrow in the Settings group (this button retains the last setting for what was printed previously so it might differ) to open the gallery, and then click Notes Pages. Once you verify your print settings, click the Print button. If you don't enter any notes in the Notes pane, and print the notes pages, the slides print as large thumbnails with blank space below the thumbnails to hand write notes.

Apply a Design Theme

Learning Outcome
• Modify the design theme

PowerPoint provides many design themes to help you quickly create a professional and contemporary looking presentation. A **theme** includes a set of 12 coordinated colors for text, fill, line, and shadow, called **theme colors**; a set of fonts for titles and other text, called **theme fonts**; and a set of effects for lines and fills, called **theme effects** to create a cohesive look. Each theme has at least four custom coordinated variants that provide you with additional color options. In most cases, you would apply one theme to an entire presentation; you can, however, apply multiple themes to the same presentation. You can use a design theme as is, or you can alter individual elements of the theme as needed. Unless you need to use a specific design theme, such as a company theme or product design theme, it is faster and easier to use one of the themes supplied with PowerPoint. If you design a custom theme, you can save it to use in the future. **CASE** ▶ *You decide to change the default design theme in the presentation to a new one.*

STEPS

1. **Click the** Slide 1 thumbnail **on the Slides tab**

   Slide 1, the title slide, appears in the Slide pane.

2. **Click the** Design tab **on the Ribbon, then point to the** Ion theme **in the Themes group, as shown in** FIGURE 1-10

   The Design tab appears, and a Live Preview of the Ion theme is displayed on the selected slide. A **Live Preview** allows you to see how your changes affect the slides before actually making the change. The Live Preview lasts about 1 minute, and then your slide reverts back to its original state. The first (far left) theme thumbnail identifies the current theme applied to the presentation, in this case, the default design theme called the Office Theme. The number of themes you can see in the Themes group depends on your monitor resolution and screen size.

3. **Slowly move your pointer** ⌖ **over the other design themes, then click the** Themes group down scroll arrow ▾

   A Live Preview of the theme appears on the slide each time you pass your pointer over the theme thumbnails, and a ScreenTip identifies the theme names.

4. **Move** ⌖ **over the** design themes, **then click the** Berlin theme

   The Berlin design theme is applied to all the slides in the presentation. Notice the new slide background color, graphic elements, fonts, and text color. You decide this theme isn't right for this presentation.

QUICK TIP
One way to apply multiple themes to the same presentation is to click the Slide Sorter button on the status bar, select a slide or a group of slides, then click the theme.

5. **Click the** More button ▾ **in the Themes group**

   The Themes gallery window opens. At the top of the gallery window in the This Presentation section is the current theme applied to the presentation. Notice that just the Berlin theme is listed here because when you changed the theme in the last step, you replaced the default theme with the Berlin theme. The Office section identifies all of the standard themes that come with PowerPoint.

6. **Right-click the** Frame theme **in the Office section, then click** Apply to Selected Slides

   The Frame theme is applied only to Slide 1. You like the Frame theme better, and decide to apply it to all slides.

7. **Right-click the** Frame theme **in the Themes group, then click** Apply to All Slides

   The Frame theme is applied to all three slides. Preview the next slides in the presentation to see how it looks.

8. **Click the** Next Slide button ⬇ **at the bottom of the vertical scroll bar**

   Compare your screen to FIGURE 1-11.

9. **Click the** Previous Slide button ⬆ **at the bottom of the vertical scroll bar, then save your changes**

FIGURE 1-10: Slide showing a different design theme

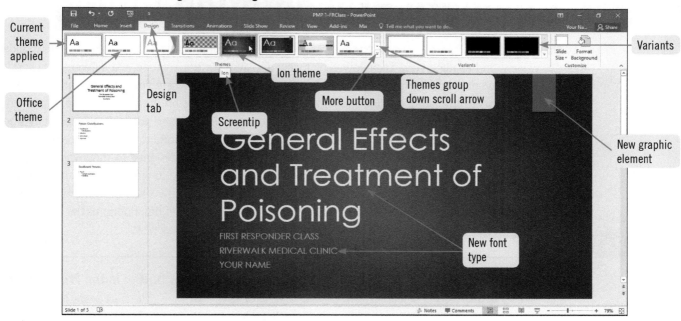

FIGURE 1-10: Slide showing a different design theme

FIGURE 1-11: Presentation with Frame theme applied

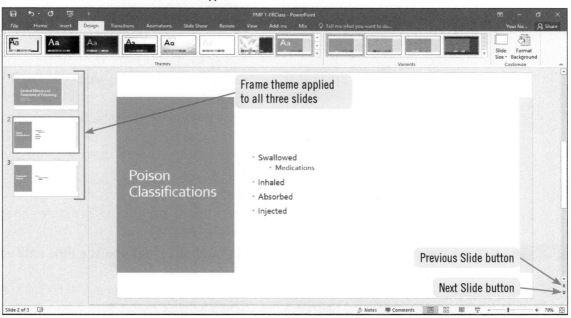

Customizing themes

You are not limited to using the standard themes PowerPoint provides; you can also modify a theme to create your own custom theme. For example, you might want to incorporate your school's or company's colors on the slide background of the presentation or be able to type using fonts your company uses for brand recognition. To change an existing theme, click the View tab on the Ribbon, then click one of the Master buttons in the Master Views group. Click the Theme Colors button, the Theme Fonts button, or the Theme Effects button in the Background group to make changes to the theme, save this new theme for future use by clicking the Themes button in the Edit Theme group, then click Save Current Theme. You also have the ability to create a new font theme or color theme from scratch by clicking the Theme Fonts button or the Theme Colors button and then clicking Customize Fonts or Customize Colors. You work in the Create New Theme Fonts or Create New Theme Colors dialog box to define the custom theme fonts or colors.

PowerPoint 2016

Compare Presentation Views

PowerPoint has six primary views: Normal view, Outline view, Slide Sorter view, Notes Page view, Slide Show view, and Reading view. Each PowerPoint view displays your presentation in a different way and is used for different purposes. Normal view is the primary editing view where you add text, graphics, and other elements to the slides. Outline view is the view you use to focus on the text of your presentation. Slide Sorter view is primarily used to rearrange slides; however, you can also add slide effects and design themes in this view. You use Notes Page view to type notes that are important for each slide. Slide Show view displays your presentation over the whole computer screen and is designed to show your presentation to an audience. Similar to Slide Show view, Reading view is designed to view your presentation on a computer screen. To move easily among the PowerPoint views, use the View Shortcuts buttons located on the status bar and the View tab on the Ribbon. TABLE 1-1 provides a brief description of the PowerPoint views. **CASE** *Examine each of the PowerPoint views, starting with Normal view.*

STEPS

1. **Click the View tab on the Ribbon, then click the Outline View button in the Presentation Views group**

   The presentation text is in the Outline pane on the left side of the window, as shown in FIGURE 1-12. Notice the status bar identifies the number of the slide you are viewing and the total number of slides in the presentation.

2. **Click the small slide icon ▢ next to Slide 2 in the Outline pane, then click the Slide Sorter button ▦ on the status bar**

   Slide Sorter View opens to display a thumbnail of each slide in the presentation in the window. You can examine the flow of your slides and drag any slide or group of slides to rearrange the order of the slides in the presentation.

3. **Double-click the Slide 1 thumbnail, then click the Reading View button ▣ on the status bar**

   The first slide fills the screen, as shown in FIGURE 1-13. Use Reading view to review your presentation or to show your presentation to someone directly on your computer. The status bar controls at the bottom of the window make it easy to move between slides in this view.

4. **Click the Slide Show button ▽ on the status bar**

   The first slide fills the entire screen now without the title bar and status bar. In this view, you can practice running through your slides as they would appear in a slide show.

5. **Click the left mouse button to advance through the slides one at a time until you see a black slide, then click once more to return to Outline view**

   The black slide at the end of the slide show indicates the slide show is finished. At the end of a slide show, you return to the slide and PowerPoint view you were in before you ran the slide show, in this case, Slide 1 in Outline view.

6. **Click the Notes Page button in the Presentation Views group**

   Notes Page view appears, showing a reduced image of the current slide above a large text placeholder. You can enter text in this placeholder and then print the notes page for your own use.

7. **Click the Normal button in the Presentation Views group, then click the Home tab on the Ribbon**

FIGURE 1-12: **Outline view**

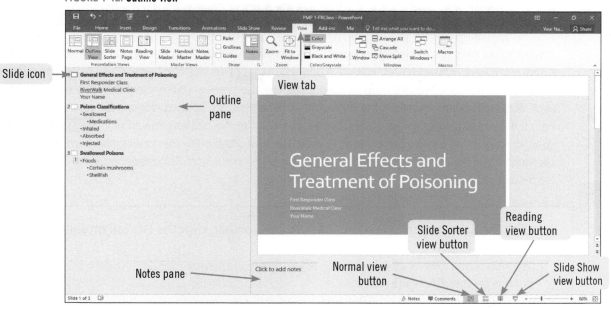

Slide icon

View tab

Outline pane

Slide Sorter view button

Reading view button

Notes pane

Normal view button

Slide Show view button

FIGURE 1-13: **Reading view**

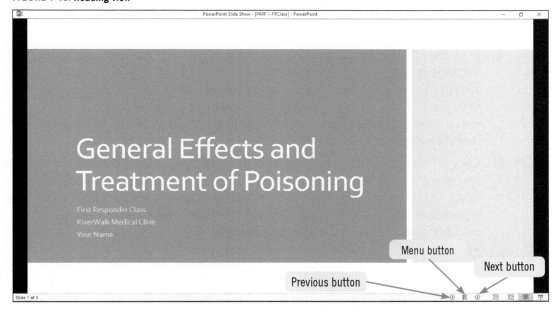

Menu button

Next button

Previous button

TABLE 1-1: **PowerPoint views**

view name	button	button name	displays
Normal	⊞	Normal	The Slide pane and the Slides tab at the same time
Outline View	(no View Shortcuts button)		An outline of the presentation and the Slide pane at the same time
Slide Sorter	⊞	Slide Sorter	Thumbnails of all slides
Slide Show	⊟	Slide Show	Your presentation on the whole computer screen
Reading View	⊞	Reading View	Your presentation in a large window on your computer screen
Notes Page	(no View Shortcuts button)		A reduced image of the current slide above a large text box

Print a PowerPoint Presentation

Learning Outcomes
- Print a presentation
- Set print settings
- Modify color settings

You print your presentation when you want to review your work or when you have completed it and want a hard copy. Reviewing your presentation at different stages of development gives you a better perspective of the overall flow and feel of the presentation. You can also preview your presentation to see exactly how each slide looks before you print the presentation. When you are finished working on your presentation, even if it is not yet complete, you can close the presentation file and exit PowerPoint. **CASE** *You are done working on the training presentation for now. You save and preview the presentation, then you print the slides and notes pages of the presentation so you can review them later. Before leaving for the day, you close the file and exit PowerPoint.*

STEPS

1. **Click the Save button 🔲 on the Quick Access toolbar, click the File tab on the Ribbon, then click Print**

   The Print window opens, as shown in FIGURE 1-14. Notice the preview pane on the right side of the window displays the first slide of the presentation.

2. **Click the Next Page button ▶ at the bottom of the Preview pane, then click ▶ again**

   Each slide in the presentation appears in the preview pane.

3. **Click the Print button**

   Each slide in the presentation prints.

4. **Click the File tab on the Ribbon, click Print, then click the Full Page Slides button in the Settings group**

   The Print Layout gallery opens. In this gallery you can specify what you want to print (slides, handouts, notes pages, or outline), as well as other print options. To save paper when you are reviewing your slides, you can print in handout format, which lets you print up to nine slides per page. The options you choose in the Print window remain there until you change them or close the presentation.

5. **Click 3 Slides, click the Color button in the Settings group, then click Pure Black and White**

   PowerPoint removes the color and displays the slides as thumbnails next to blank lines, as shown in FIGURE 1-15. Using the Handouts with three slides per page printing option is a great way to print your presentation when you want to provide a way for audience members to take notes. Printing pure black-and-white without any gray tones can save printer toner.

6. **Click the Print button**

   The presentation prints one page showing all the slides of the presentation as thumbnails next to blank lines.

7. **Click the File tab on the Ribbon, then click Close**

   If you have made changes to your presentation, a Microsoft PowerPoint alert box opens asking you if you want to save changes you have made to your presentation file.

8. **Click Save, if necessary, to close the alert box**

   Your presentation closes.

9. **Click the Close button ✕ in the title bar**

   The PowerPoint program closes, and you return to the Windows desktop.

FIGURE 1-14: Print window

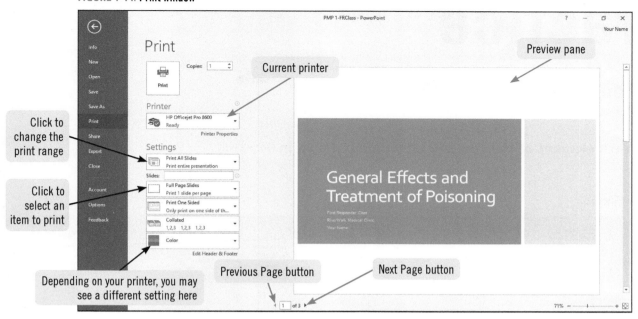

Preview pane

Current printer

Click to change the print range

Click to select an item to print

Depending on your printer, you may see a different setting here

Previous Page button

Next Page button

General Effects and Treatment of Poisoning

FIGURE 1-15: Print window with changed settings

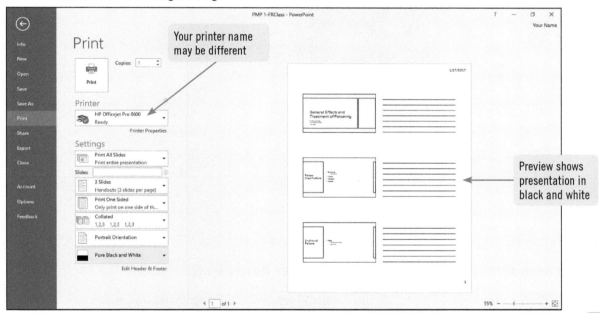

Your printer name may be different

Preview shows presentation in black and white

Microsoft Office Online Apps

Some Office programs, PowerPoint for example, include the capability to incorporate feedback—called online collaboration—across the Internet or a company network. Using **cloud computing** (work done in a virtual environment), you can take advantage of web programs called Microsoft Office Online Apps, which are simplified versions of the programs found in the Microsoft Office 2016 suite. Because these programs are online,

they take up no computer disk space and are accessed using Microsoft OneDrive, a free service from Microsoft. Using Microsoft OneDrive, you and your colleagues can create and store documents in the "cloud" and make the documents available to whomever you grant access. To use Microsoft OneDrive, you need to create a free Microsoft account, which you obtain at the Microsoft website.

PowerPoint 2016

Practice

Concepts Review

Label each element of the PowerPoint window shown in FIGURE 1-16.

FIGURE 1-16

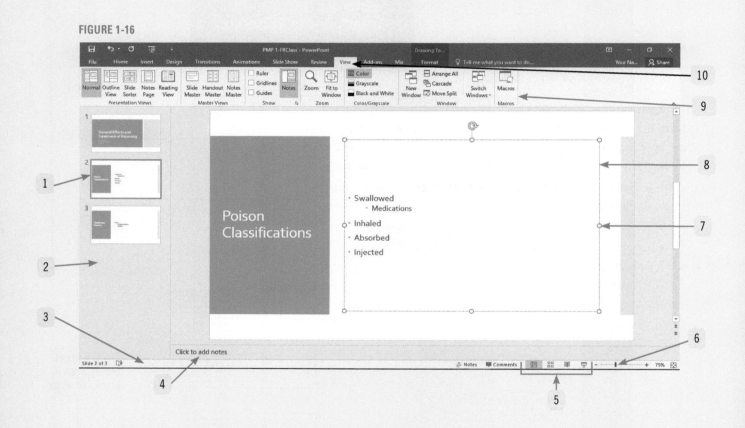

Match each term with the statement that best describes it.

11. **Slide Show view**
12. **Slide Layout**
13. **Inking**
14. **Theme**
15. **Zoom slider**
16. **Text placeholder**

a. Freehand pen and highlighter marks on a slide
b. A view that displays a presentation to show to an audience
c. Allows you to change the size of the slide in the window
d. Set of coordinated colors, fonts, and effects
e. Placeholders arranged in a specific way on the slide
f. Box with dotted border where you enter text

Select the best answer from the list of choices.

17. The view that fills the entire computer screen with each slide in the presentation is called:
    a. Outline view.
    c. Slide Show view.
    b. Normal view.
    d. Fit to window view.

18. You can enter slide text in the Slide Pane and in the _____.
    a. Reading pane
    c. Outline view
    b. Notes Page view
    d. Slides tab

19. What is the function of the slide layout?
    a. Defines how all the elements on a slide are arranged.
    b. Enables you to apply a template to the presentation.
    c. Puts all your slides in order.
    d. Shows you which themes you can apply.

20. Which of the following is not included in a design theme?
    a. Pictures
    c. Fonts
    b. Normal view
    d. Colors

21. Which button indents the insertion point to the right?
    a. Right Indent Level
    c. Decrease Indent Level
    b. Increase List Level
    d. Move Margin

22. Which status bar feature allows you to quickly switch between views?
    a. Zoom slider
    c. Fit slide to current window button
    b. View Shortcuts
    d. Switch view button

23. What can you drag to adjust the size of an object?
    a. Rotate handle
    c. Sizing handle
    b. Object border point
    d. Selection box

24. What are the basic building blocks of any presentation?
    a. Placeholders
    c. Slides
    b. Objects
    d. Graphics

Skills Review

1. **Examine the PowerPoint window.**
   a. Start PowerPoint, if necessary, then open a new blank presentation.
   b. Identify as many elements of the PowerPoint window as you can without referring to the lessons in this module.
   c. Be able to describe the purpose or function of each element.
   d. For any elements you cannot identify, refer to the lessons in this module.

2. **Enter slide text.**
   a. In the Slide pane in Normal view, enter the text **Lancaster Memorial Hospital** in the title placeholder.
   b. In the subtitle text placeholder, enter **Medical Internship Program**.
   c. On the next line of the placeholder, enter your name.
   d. Deselect the text object.
   e. Save the presentation using the filename **PMP 1-Intern** to the location where you store your Data Files.

Skills Review (continued)

3. Add a new slide.
a. Create a new slide.

b. Using FIGURE 1-17, enter text on the slide.

c. Create another new slide.

d. Using FIGURE 1-18, enter text on the slide.

e. Save your changes.

4. Apply a design theme.
a. Click the Design tab.

b. Click the Themes group More button, then point to all of the themes.

c. Locate the Depth theme, then apply it to the selected slide.

d. Select Slide 1.

e. Locate the View theme, then apply it to Slide 1.

f. Apply the View theme to all of the slides in the presentation.

g. Use the Next Slide button to move to Slide 3, then save your changes.

5. Compare presentation views.
a. Click the View tab, then click the Outline View button in the Presentation Views group.

b. Click the Slide Sorter button in the Presentation Views group.

c. Click the Notes Page button in the Presentation Views group, then click the Previous Slide button twice.

d. Click the Reading View button in the Presentation Views group, then click the Next button on the status bar.

e. Click the Normal button on the status bar, then click the Slide Show button.

f. Advance the slides until a black screen appears, then click to end the presentation.

g. Save your changes.

6. Print a PowerPoint presentation.
a. Print all the slides as handouts, 3 Slides, in color.

b. Close the file, saving your changes.

c. Exit PowerPoint.

FIGURE 1-17

Internship Program

- Goals
  - Clinical experience
  - Medical professional standards
  - Advanced study
- Objectives
  - Improve access to quality care statewide
  - Develop appropriate professional practices

FIGURE 1-18

Program Requirements

- Application process
- Associates or bachelors degree
- Oral interview
- Completed or currently enrolled in internship classes
- Join a local medical service team

Independent Challenge 1

You work for the Kansas Health Education Group, which offers courses to certified health professionals throughout the state. One of your jobs is to develop presentations on the certified courses that are offered by the education group. Your supervisor has asked you to create a presentation that describes the latest disaster preparedness and response training course.

a. Start PowerPoint then open a new blank presentation.

b. In the title placeholder on Slide 1, type **Kansas Health Education Group**.

c. In the subtitle placeholder, type **Disaster Preparedness and Response**, press [Enter], type **Certified Training Course**, press [Enter], type your name, press [Enter], then type today's date.

d. Click the AutoFit Options button, then click Stop Fitting Text to This Placeholder.

e. Apply the Gallery design theme to the presentation.

f. Save your presentation with the filename **PMP 1-Kansas** to the location where you store your Data Files.

g. Use FIGURE 1-19 and FIGURE 1-20 to add two more slides to your presentation. (*Hint*: Slide 3 uses the Comparison layout.)

h. Use the buttons on the View tab to switch between all of PowerPoint's views.

i. Print the presentation using handouts, 3 Slides, in black and white.

j. Save and close the file, then exit PowerPoint.

FIGURE 1-19

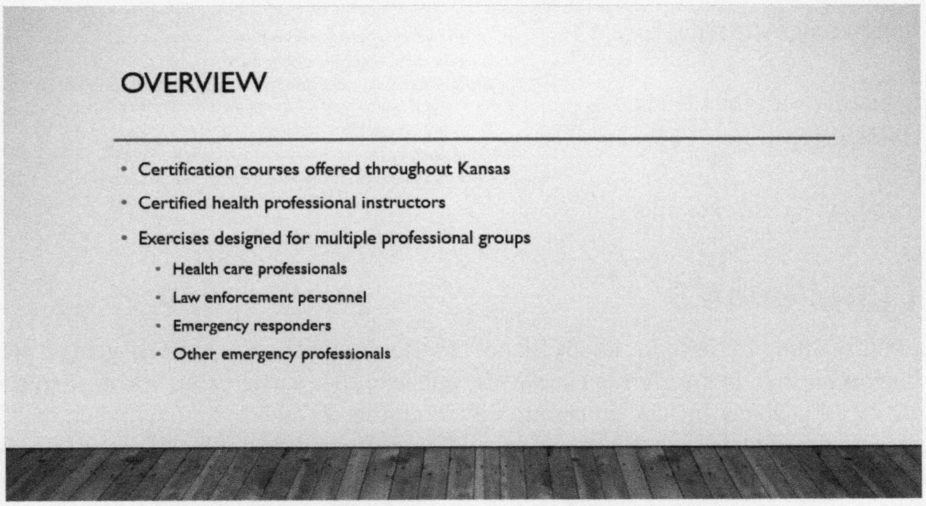

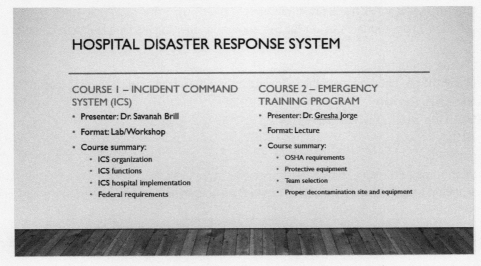

FIGURE 1-20

Independent Challenge 2

You have just been hired by World Medical Relief (WMR), a nonprofit medical organization that provides medical services and disaster relief to impoverished people around the world. You need to create a presentation that describes services offered by WMR. Assume the following: WMR follows internationally accepted health guidelines; need-based assessments are performed by staff in the field; types of programs offered are community health clinics, HIV and AIDS treatment, and basic medical training. The presentation should contain at least four slides. Use the Internet to research appropriate information to help you formulate your ideas.

a. Spend some time planning the slides of your presentation. What is the best way to show the information provided? What other information could you add that might be useful for this presentation?

b. Start PowerPoint and give the presentation an appropriate title on the title slide, then enter today's date and your name in the subtitle placeholder.

c. Add slides and enter appropriate slide text.

d. Create a slide at the end of the presentation with the Section Header layout, then include the following information in the title and text placeholders:
Disaster Relief for the World
World Medical Relief

FIGURE 1-21

e. Apply a design theme. A typical slide might look like the one shown in FIGURE 1-21.

f. Switch views. Run through the slide show at least once.

g. Save your presentation with the filename **PMP 1-WMR** where you store your Data Files.

h. Close the presentation and exit PowerPoint.

DISASTER RESPONSE
- Team commitment to serve those in crisis
- Disaster relief eligibility confirmed
- Situational response depends on nature of disaster and crisis country
  - Ground teams near crisis country given situational priority
- Intervention priorities created
- Crisis country government contact established
- Disaster relief plan proposed and implemented

Independent Challenge 3

You work at Lewiston Dental Group in Newport, Rhode Island. Lewiston Dental Group is a large general practice and surgery facility with six doctors on staff. In an effort to educate the public in the Newport area, you need to create a presentation that provides tooth care guidelines. Include information on tooth care for adults and/or children that covers topics such as infant teething, permanent tooth care, and tooth decay. Your presentation should include at least five slides. Use the Internet to research relevant information to help you formulate your ideas.

a. Spend some time planning the slides of your presentation.

b. Start PowerPoint then open a new blank presentation.

c. Give the presentation an appropriate title on the title slide, and enter today's date and your name in the subtitle placeholder.

d. Add slides and enter appropriate slide text.

e. On the last slide of the presentation, type the following information in the title and text placeholders:
Lewiston Dental Group
General Practice and Dental Surgery
Newport, RI

f. Apply a design theme.

g. Switch views. Run through the slide show at least once.

h. Save your presentation with the filename **PMP 1-Lewiston** to the location where you store your Data Files.

i. Close the presentation and exit PowerPoint.

Independent Challenge 4: Explore

You work for the National Medical Training Center, which produces and delivers certified training courses on subjects such as wound care, cardiac emergencies, injury prevention, and soft tissue injuries. You have been tasked with creating a presentation on wound care that will be used in a certified training course.

a. Spend some time planning the slides of your presentation. Assume the following: the course meets National Alliance of Wound Care requirements; the course is delivered by certified faculty; class topics include wound assessment and wound care. Use the Internet, if possible, to research information that will help you formulate your ideas.

b. Start PowerPoint then open a new blank presentation.

c. Give the presentation an appropriate title on the title slide, then type **NMTC**, your name, and today's date in the subtitle placeholder.

d. Add slides and enter appropriate slide text. You must create at least three slides.

e. Apply a Design Theme. Typical slides might look like the ones shown in FIGURE 1-22 and FIGURE 1-23.

f. View the presentation.

g. Save your presentation with the filename **PMP 1-NMTC,** to the location where you store your Data Files.

h. Close the presentation and exit PowerPoint.

FIGURE 1-22

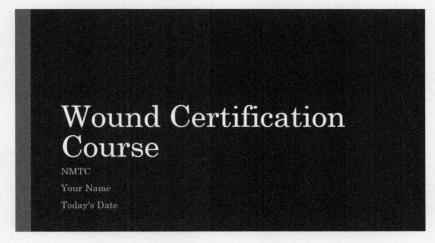

FIGURE 1-23

PowerPoint 2016

Visual Workshop

Create the presentation shown in FIGURE 1-24 and FIGURE 1-25. Make sure you include your name on the title slide. Save the presentation as **PMP 1-Allergy** to the location where you store your Data Files. Print the slides.

FIGURE 1-24

FIGURE 1-25

Basic Facts

- Between 600-1000 deaths caused by severe allergic reactions in U.S. each year
- A person can die from anaphylaxis within 1 minute of exposure
  - Antigen – foreign substance that brings about allergic reaction
- Anaphylaxis signals
  - Swelling of the skin or area of body that comes in contact with substance
  - Hives, itching, rash, weakness, nausea, trouble breathing, vomiting
  - Trouble breathing can lead to obstructed airway

Modifying a Presentation

CASE You continue working on your training presentation on poisons. In this module, you'll enter text using Outline view, then you'll format text, create a SmartArt graphic, draw and modify objects, add slide footer information, and check the spelling in the presentation.

Module Objectives

After completing this module, you will be able to:

- Enter text in Outline view
- Format text
- Convert text to SmartArt
- Insert and modify shapes
- Rearrange and merge shapes

- Edit and duplicate shapes
- Align and group objects
- Add slide footers
- Use Proofing and Language Tools

Files You Will Need

PMP 2-1.pptx   PMP 2-4.pptx
PMP 2-2.pptx   PMP 2-5.pptx
PMP 2-3.pptx

Enter Text in Outline View

Learning Outcomes
• Enter text in Outline view
• Create a new slide

You can enter presentation text by typing directly on the slide in the Slide pane, or, if you need to focus on the text of the presentation, you can enter text in Outline view. Text in Outline view is organized so the headings, or slide titles, appear at the top of the outline. Each subpoint, or each line of bulleted text, appears as one or more indented lines under the title. Each indent in the outline creates another level of bulleted text on the slide. **CASE** ▶ *You switch to Outline view to enter text for two more slides for your presentation.*

STEPS

QUICK TIP
To open a PowerPoint 97-2007 presentation in PowerPoint 2016, open the presentation, click the File tab, click the Convert button, name the file in the Save As dialog box, then click Save.

1. **Start PowerPoint, open the presentation** PMP 2-1.pptx **from the location where you store your Data Files, then save it as** PMP 2-FRClass.pptx
   A presentation with the new name appears in the PowerPoint window.

2. **Click the** Slide 3 thumbnail **in the Slides tab, click the** New Slide button list arrow **in the Slides group, then click** Title and Content
   A new slide, Slide 4, with the Title and Content layout appears as the current slide below Slide 3.

3. **Click the** View tab **on the Ribbon, then click the** Outline View button **in the Presentation Views group**
   The text of the presentation appears in the Outline pane next to the Slide pane. The slide icon and the insertion point for Slide 4 are highlighted, indicating the slide is selected and ready to accept text. Text that you enter next to a slide icon becomes the title for that slide.

4. **Type** Inhaled Poisons, **press [Enter], then press [Tab]**
   When you pressed [Enter] after typing the slide title, you created a new slide. However, because you want to enter bulleted text on Slide 4, you then pressed [Tab] so the text you type will be entered as bullet text on Slide 4. See FIGURE 2-1.

5. **Type** Gases, **press [Enter], press [Tab], type** Carbon monoxide, **press [Enter], type** Carbon dioxide, **press [Enter], type** Chlorine, **then press** [Enter]
   Each time you press [Enter], the insertion point moves down one line.

6. **Press [Shift][Tab] twice**
   Because you are working in Outline view, a new slide with the same layout, Slide 5, is created when you press [Shift][Tab] the second time.

QUICK TIP
Press [Ctrl][Enter] while the insertion point is in the text object to create a new slide with the same layout as the previous slide.

7. **Type** Absorbed Poisons, **press [Ctrl][Enter], type** Poison oak, **press [Enter], type** Poison ivy, **press [Enter], type** Poison sumac, **press [Enter], then type** Fertilizers and pesticides
   Pressing [Ctrl][Enter] while the insertion point is in the title text object moves the insertion point into the content placeholder.

8. **Position the pointer on the** Slide 5 icon ▢ **in the Outline pane**
   The pointer changes to ✥. The Absorbed Poisons slide, Slide 5, is out of order.

9. **Drag** ▢ **up until a horizontal indicator line appears above the Slide 4 icon, then release the mouse button**
   The fifth slide moves up and switches places with the fourth slide, as shown in FIGURE 2-2.

10. **Click the** Normal button ▣ **on the status bar, then save your work**
    The Outline pane closes, and the Slides tab is now visible in the window.

FIGURE 2-1: Outline view showing new slide

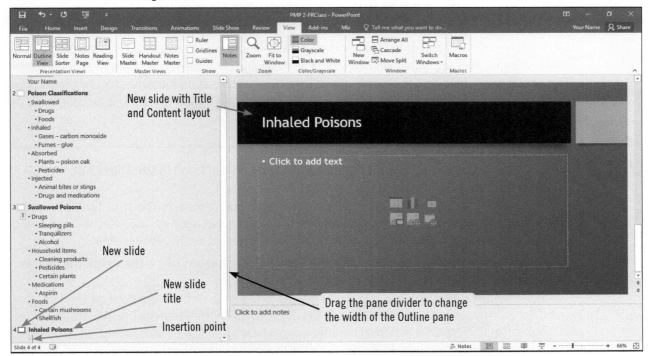

FIGURE 2-2: Outline view showing moved slide

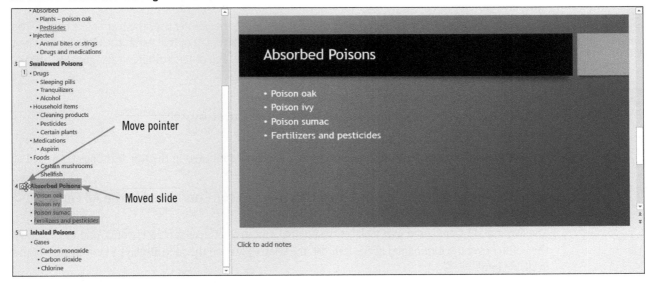

Using proofing tools for other languages

If you have a presentation in another language, how would you check the spelling and grammar of that presentation? Every version of PowerPoint contains a language pack with a primary language, such as English, Italian, or Arabic. Each language pack includes additional languages other than the primary language. For example, the English language pack also includes French and Spanish. So, let's say you have an English version of PowerPoint and you want to check the spelling of a presentation that is written in French. To check the spelling of a French presentation, click a text object on a slide, click the Review tab on the Ribbon, click the Language button in the Language group, then click Set Proofing Language to open the Language dialog box. Click one of the French options from the list, then click OK. Only languages in the list with a spelling symbol are available to use for checking spelling and grammar. Now when you check the spelling, PowerPoint will do so in French. If your version of PowerPoint does not have the language you want to use, you can purchase additional language packs from Microsoft.

Format Text

Learning Outcome
• Modify text characteristics

Once you have entered and edited the text in your presentation, you can modify the way the text looks to emphasize your message. Important text should be highlighted in some way to distinguish it from other text or objects on the slide. For example, if you have two text objects on the same slide, you could draw attention to one text object by changing its color, font, or size. **CASE** ➤ *You decide to format the text on Slide 5 of the presentation.*

STEPS

QUICK TIP
To show or hide the Mini toolbar, click the File tab on the Ribbon, click Options, then click the Show Mini Toolbar on selection check box.

1. **Click the Home tab on the Ribbon, click the Slide 5 thumbnail in the Slides tab, then double-click Inhaled in the title text object**

   The word "Inhaled" is selected, and a Mini toolbar appears above the text. The **Mini toolbar** contains basic text-formatting commands, such as bold and italic, and appears when you select text using the mouse. This toolbar makes it quick and easy to format text, especially when the Home tab is closed.

2. **Move** ⬚ **over the Mini toolbar, click the Font Color list arrow** 🅰️▾**, then click the Yellow color box in the Standard Colors row**

   The text changes color to yellow, as shown in FIGURE 2-3. When you click the Font Color list arrow, the Font Color gallery appears showing the Theme Colors and Standard Colors. ScreenTips help identify font colors. Notice that the Font Color button on the Mini toolbar and the Font Color button in the Font group on the Home tab change color to reflect the new color choice, which is now the active color.

QUICK TIP
To select an unselected text object, press [Shift], click the text object, then release [Shift].

3. **Move the pointer over the title text object border until the pointer changes to** ⬚**, then click the border**

   The border changes from a dashed to a solid line as you move the pointer over the text object border. The entire title text object is selected, and changes you make now affect all of the text in the text object. When the whole text object is selected, you can change its size, shape, and other attributes. Changing the color of the text helps emphasize it.

QUICK TIP
For more text formatting options, right-click a text object, then click Format Text Effects to open the Format Shape - Text Options pane.

4. **Click the Font Color button** 🅰️▾ **in the Font group**

   All of the text in the title text object changes to the current active color, yellow.

5. **Click the Font list arrow in the Font group**

   A list of available fonts opens with Trebuchet MS, the current font used in the title text object, selected at the top of the list in the Theme Fonts section.

6. **Scroll down the alphabetical list, then click Bernard MT Condensed in the All Fonts section**

   The Bernard MT Condensed font replaces the original font in the title text object. Notice that as you move the pointer over the font names in the font list, the selected text on the slide displays a Live Preview of the available fonts.

7. **Click the Underline button** 🆄 **in the Font group, then click the Increase Font Size button** 🅰️ **in the Font group**

   All of the text now displays an underline and increases in size to 40.

8. **Click the Character Spacing button** ᴬᵛ▾ **in the Font group, then click Loose**

   The spacing between the letters in the title increases. Compare your screen with FIGURE 2-4.

9. **Click a blank area of the slide outside the text object to deselect it, then save your work**

   Clicking a blank area of the slide deselects all objects that are selected.

FIGURE 2-3: Selected word with Mini toolbar open

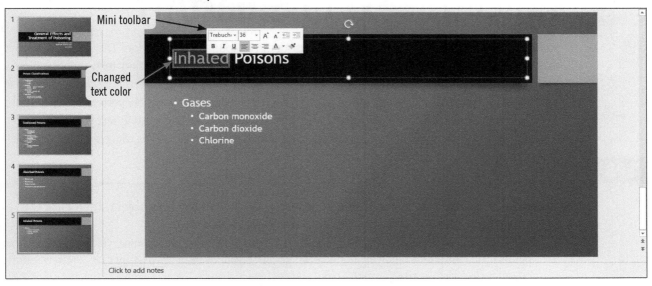

FIGURE 2-4: Formatted text

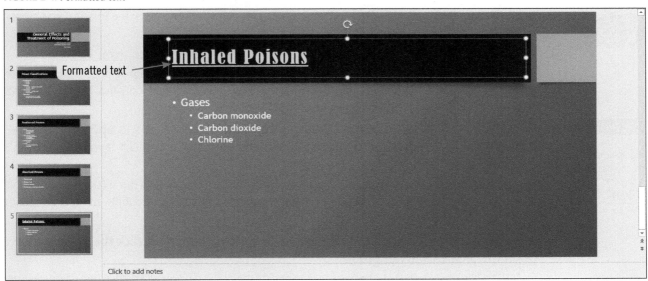

Replacing text and fonts

As you review your presentation, you may decide to replace certain text or fonts throughout the entire presentation using the Replace command. Text can be a word, phrase, or sentence. To replace specific text, click the Home tab on the Ribbon, then click the Replace button in the Editing group. In the Replace dialog box, enter the text you want to replace, then enter the text you want to use as its replacement. You can also use the Replace command to replace one font for another. Simply click the Replace button list arrow in the Editing group, then click Replace Fonts to open the Replace Font dialog box.

Convert Text to SmartArt

Learning Outcomes
• Create a SmartArt graphic
• Modify the SmartArt design

Sometimes when you are working with text it just doesn't capture your attention. The ability to convert text to a SmartArt graphic provides a creative way to convey a message using text and graphics. A **SmartArt** graphic is a professional-quality diagram that graphically illustrates text. For example, you can show steps in a process or timeline, show proportional relationships, or show how parts relate to a whole. You can create a SmartArt graphic from scratch or create one by converting existing text you have entered on a slide. **CASE** *You want the presentation to appear visually dynamic, so you convert the text on Slide 4 to a SmartArt graphic.*

STEPS

1. **Click the Slide 4 thumbnail in the Slides tab, click oak in the text object, then click the Convert to SmartArt Graphic button in the Paragraph group**

   A gallery of SmartArt graphic layouts opens. As with many features in PowerPoint, you can preview how your text will look prior to applying the SmartArt graphic layout by using PowerPoint's Live Preview feature. You can review each SmartArt graphic layout and see how it changes the appearance of the text.

2. **Move ⌖ over the SmartArt graphic layouts in the gallery**

   Notice how the text becomes part of the graphic and the color and font changes each time you move the pointer over a different graphic layout. SmartArt graphic names appear in ScreenTips.

3. **Click the Vertical Bullet List layout in the SmartArt graphics gallery**

   A SmartArt graphic appears on the slide in place of the text object, and the SmartArt Tools Design tab opens on the Ribbon, as shown in FIGURE 2-5. A SmartArt graphic consists of two parts: the SmartArt graphic and a Text pane where you type and edit text.

4. **Click each bullet point in the Text pane, then click the Text pane control ⟩**

   Notice that each time you select a bullet point in the text pane, a selection box appears around the text objects in the SmartArt graphic. The Text pane control opens and closes the Text pane. You can also open and close the Text pane using the Text Pane button in the Create Graphic group.

5. **Click the More button ⩒ in the Layouts group, click More Layouts to open the Choose a SmartArt Graphic dialog box, click List, click the Vertical Curved List layout icon, then click OK**

   The SmartArt graphic changes to the new graphic layout. You can change how the SmartArt graphic looks by applying a SmartArt Style. A **SmartArt Style** is a preset combination of simple and 3-D formatting options that follows the presentation theme.

6. **Move ⌖ slowly over the styles in the SmartArt Styles group, then click the More button ⩒ in the SmartArt Styles group**

   A Live Preview of each style is displayed on the SmartArt graphic. The SmartArt styles are organized into sections; the top group offers suggestions for the best match for the document, and the bottom group shows you all of the possible 3-D styles that are available.

7. **Move ⌖ over the styles in the gallery, click Subtle Effect in the Best Match for Document section, then click in a blank area of the slide outside the SmartArt graphic**

   Notice how this new style changes the fill color and text color of each object to achieve a different effect. Compare your screen with FIGURE 2-6.

8. **Click the Slide 5 thumbnail in the Slides tab, then save your work**

   Slide 5 appears in the Slide pane.

FIGURE 2-5: Text converted to a SmartArt graphic

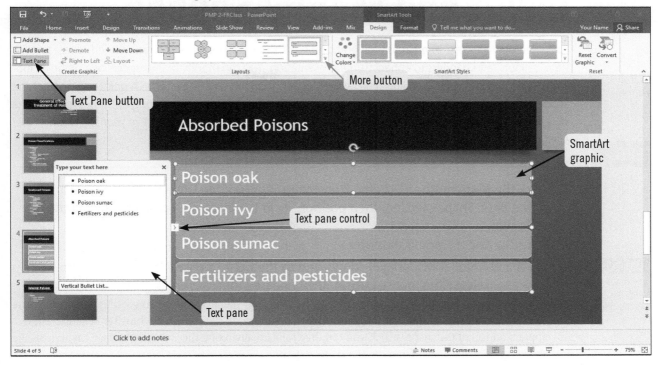

FIGURE 2-6: Final SmartArt graphic

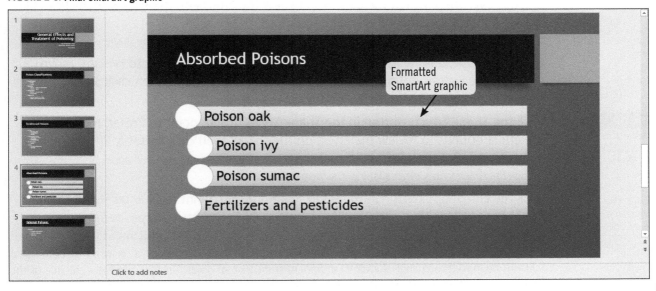

Choosing SmartArt graphics

When choosing a SmartArt graphic to use on your slide, remember that you want the SmartArt graphic to communicate the message of the text effectively; not every SmartArt graphic layout achieves that goal. You must consider the type of text you want to illustrate. For example, does the text show steps in a process, does it show a continual process, or does it show nonsequential information? The answer to this question will dictate the type of SmartArt graphic layout you should choose. Also, the amount of text you want to illustrate will have an effect on the SmartArt graphic layout you choose. Most of the time key points will be the text you use in a SmartArt graphic. Finally, some SmartArt graphic layouts are limited by the number of shapes they can accommodate, so be sure to choose a graphic layout that can illustrate your text appropriately. Experiment with the SmartArt graphic layouts until you find the right one, and have fun in the process!

Insert and Modify Shapes

Learning
Outcomes
• Create a shape
• Modify a shape's
  style

In PowerPoint you can insert many different types of shapes including lines, geometric figures, arrows, stars, callouts, and banners to enhance your presentation. You can modify many aspects of a shape including its fill color, line color, and line style, as well as add shadows and 3-D effects. A quick way to alter the appearance of a shape is to apply a Quick Style. A **Quick Style** is a set of formatting options, including line style, fill color, and effects. **CASE** *You decide to draw some shapes on Slide 5 of your presentation that identify general symptoms of someone having been poisoned.*

STEPS

1. **Click the More button ▾ in the Drawing group, click the Isosceles Triangle button △ in the Basic Shapes section, then position ╋ in the blank area of Slide 5 below the slide title**

   ScreenTips help you identify the shapes.

2. **Press and hold [Shift], drag ╋ down and to the right to create the shape, as shown in FIGURE 2-7, release the mouse button, then release [Shift]**

   A triangle shape appears on the slide, filled with the default theme color. Pressing [Shift] while you create the object maintains the object proportions as you change its size. A **rotate handle**—circular arrow—appears on top of the shape, which you can drag to manually rotate the shape. To change the style of the shape, apply a Quick Style from the Shape Styles group.

3. **Click the Drawing Tools Format tab on the Ribbon, click ▾ in the Shape Styles group, move ⬚ over the styles in the gallery to review the effects on the shape, then click Light 1 Outline, Colored Fill - Green, Accent 3**

   A green Quick Style with coordinated fill, line, and shadow color is applied to the shape.

4. **Click the Shape Outline list arrow in the Shape Styles group, point to Weight, move ⬚ over the line weight options to review the effect on the shape, then click 3 pt**

   The outline weight (or width) increases and is easier to see now.

5. **Click the Shape Effects button in the Shape Styles group, point to Preset, move ⬚ over the effect options to review the effect on the shape, then click Preset 5**

   Lighting and shadow effects are added to the shape to give it a three-dimensional appearance. It is easy to change the shape to any other shape in the Shapes gallery.

6. **Click the Edit Shape button in the Insert Shapes group, point to Change Shape to open the Shapes gallery, then click the Chord button ◠ in the Basic Shapes section**

   The triangle shape changes to a chord shape and two yellow circles—called **adjustment handles**—appear at the top and bottom of the shape. Some shapes have an adjustment handle or two as with the chord shape that can be moved to change the most prominent feature of an object, in this case the right side of the shape. You can rotate the shape to make the shape look different.

7. **Click the Rotate button in the Arrange group, move ⬚ over the rotation options to review the effect on the shape, then click Flip Horizontal**

   Notice that the adjustment handles are now on the left side of the shape, indicating that the shape has flipped horizontally, or rotated 180 degrees, as shown in FIGURE 2-8. You prefer the triangle shape, and you decide the shape looks better rotated back the way it was before.

8. **Click the Undo button list arrow ↶ ▾ in the Quick Access Toolbar, click Change Shape, click a blank area of the slide, then save your work**

   The last two commands you performed are undone, and the shape changes back to a triangle and is flipped back to its original position. Clicking a blank area of the slide deselects all selected objects.

FIGURE 2-7: Triangle shape added to slide

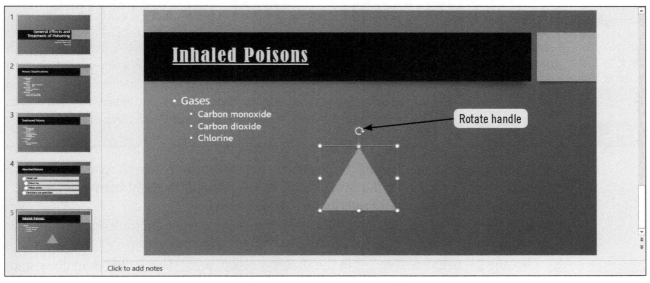

FIGURE 2-8: Rotated chord shape

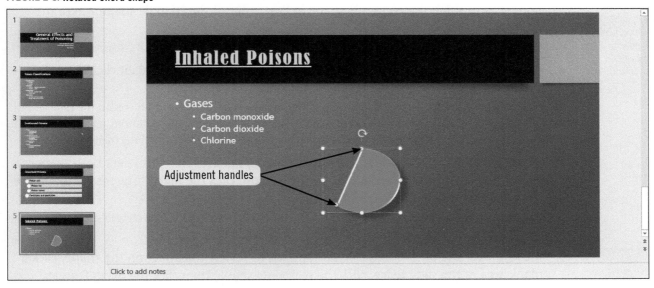

Using the Eyedropper to match colors

As you develop your presentation and work with different shapes and pictures, sometimes from other sources, there may be a certain color that is not in the theme colors of the presentation that you want to capture and apply to objects in your presentation. To capture a color on a specific slide, select any object on the slide, click any button list arrow with a color feature, such as the Shape Fill button or the Shape Outline button on the Drawing Tools Format tab, then click Eyedropper. Move the 🖋 over the color you want to capture and pause, or hover. As you hover over a color, a Live Preview of the color appears and the RGB (Red Green Blue) values, called coordinates, appear in a ScreenTip. Click when you see the color you want to capture. The new color now appears in any color gallery under Recent Colors. If you decide not to capture a new color, press [Esc] to close the Eyedropper without making any change.

Rearrange and Merge Shapes

Every object on a slide is placed, or stacked, on the slide in the order it was created, like a deck of cards placed one on top of another. Each object on a slide can be moved up or down in the stack depending on how you want the objects to look on the slide. **Merging** shapes, which combines multiple shapes together, provides you the potential to create unique geometric shapes not available in the Shapes gallery. **CASE** ➤ *You create a rectangle shape on Slide 5 and then merge it with the triangle shape.*

STEPS

1. **Click monoxide in the text object, position ⬚ over the right-middle sizing handle until ⬚ changes to ⬌, then drag the sizing handle to the left until the right border of the text object is under the word Poisons in the title text object**

   The width of the text object decreases. When you position ⬚ over a sizing handle, it changes to ⬌. This pointer points in different directions depending on which sizing handle it is over.

2. **Click the Rectangle button ▭ in the Drawing group, press [Shift], then drag down and to the right to create the shape**

   Compare your screen with FIGURE 2-9. A rectangle shape appears on the slide, filled with the default theme color. You can move shapes by dragging them on the slide.

TROUBLE
If Smart Guides do not appear, right-click a blank area of the slide, point to Grid and Guides, then click Smart Guides.

3. **Drag the rectangle shape over the triangle shape, then use the Smart Guides that appear to position the rectangle shape in the center of the triangle shape where the guides intersect**

   Smart Guides help you position objects relative to each other and determine equal distances between objects.

4. **Click the Select button in the Editing group, click Selection Pane, then click the Send Backward button ▼ in the Selection pane once**

   The Selection pane opens on the right side of the window showing the four objects on the slide and the order they are stacked on the slide. The Send Backward and Bring Forward buttons let you change the stacking order. The rectangle shape moves back one position in the stack behind the triangle shape.

5. **Press [Shift], click the triangle shape on the slide, release [Shift] to select both shapes, click the Drawing Tools Format tab on the Ribbon, click the Merge Shapes button in the Insert Shapes group, then point to Union**

   The two shapes appear to merge, or combine, together to form one shape. The merged shape assumes the theme and formatting style of the rectangle shape because it was selected first.

QUICK TIP
To move an object to the top of the stack, click the Bring Forward arrow, then click Bring to Front. To move an object to the bottom of the stack, click the Send Backward arrow, then click Send to Back.

6. **Move ⬚ over the other merge shapes options to review the effect on the shape, click a blank area of the slide twice, click the rectangle shape, then click the Bring Forward button in the Arrange group on the Drawing Tools Format tab once**

   Each merge option produces a different result. The rectangle shape moves back to the top of the stack. Now, you want to see what happens when you select the triangle shape first before you merge the two shapes together.

7. **Click the triangle shape, press [Shift], click the rectangle shape, release [Shift], click the Merge Shapes button in the Insert Shapes group, then point to Union**

   The merged shape adopts the theme and formatting style of the triangle shape.

8. **Point to each of the merge shapes options, then click Subtract**

   The two shapes merge into one shape. This merge option deletes the area of all shapes from the first shape you selected, so in this case the area of the rectangle shape is deleted from the triangle shape. The merged shape is identified as Freeform 7 in the Selection pane. See FIGURE 2-10.

9. **Click the Selection Pane button in the Arrange group, click a blank area of the slide, then save your work**

FIGURE 2-9: Rectangle shape added to slide

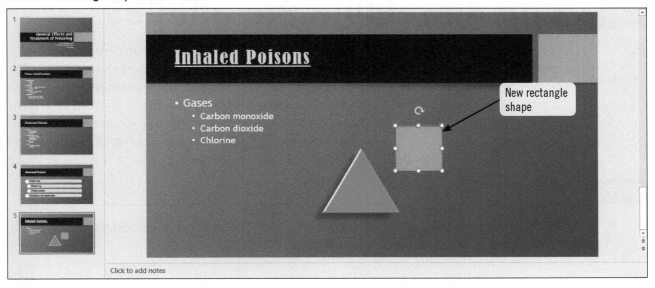

FIGURE 2-10: New merged shape

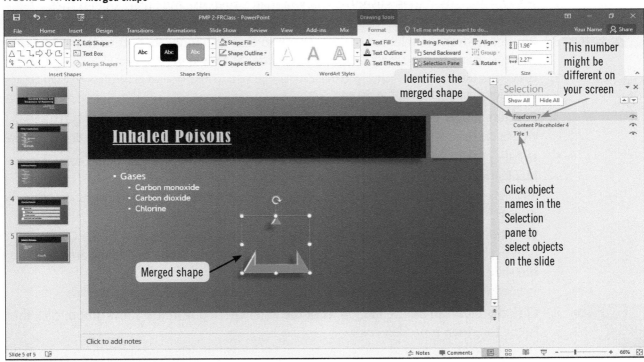

Changing the size and position of shapes

Usually when you resize a shape you can simply drag one of the sizing handles around the outside of the shape, but sometimes you may need to resize a shape more precisely. When you select a shape, the Drawing Tools Format tab appears on the Ribbon, offering you many different formatting options including some sizing commands located in the Size group. The Width and Height commands in the Size group allow you to change the width and height of a shape. You also have the option to open the Format Shape pane, which allows you to change the size of a shape, as well as the rotation, scale, and position of a shape on the slide.

Edit and Duplicate Shapes

Once you have created a shape you still have the ability to refine its basic characteristics, which helps change the size and appearance of the shape. For example, if you create a shape and it is too large, you can reduce its size by dragging any of its sizing handles. Most PowerPoint shapes can have text attached to them. All shapes can be moved and copied. To help you resize and move shapes and other objects precisely, PowerPoint has rulers you can add to the Slide pane. Rulers display the measurement system your computer uses, either inches or metric measurements. **CASE** *You want three identical triangle shapes on Slide 5. You first add the ruler to the slide to help you change the size of the triangle shape you've already created, and then you make copies of it.*

STEPS

1. **Right-click a blank area of Slide 5, click Ruler on the shortcut menu, then click the bottom part of the triangle shape to select it**

   Rulers appear on the left and top of the Slide pane. Unless the ruler has been changed to metric measurements, it is divided into inches with half-inch and eighth-inch marks. Notice the current location of the ⬚ is identified on both rulers by a small dotted red line in the ruler.

2. **Drag the middle left sizing handle on the triangle shape to the left approximately ½", then release the mouse button**

   The triangle shape is now slightly wider.

   > **QUICK TIP**
   > To display or hide gridlines, click the Gridlines check box in the Show group on the View tab.

3. **Position ⬚ over the selected triangle shape so that it changes to ✛, then drag the triangle shape to the Smart Guides on the slide, as shown in FIGURE 2-11**

   PowerPoint uses a series of evenly spaced horizontal and vertical lines—called **gridlines**—to align objects, which force objects to "snap" to the grid.

4. **Position ✛ over the bottom part of the triangle shape, then press and hold [Ctrl]**

   The pointer changes to ⬚, indicating that PowerPoint makes a copy of the shape when you drag the mouse.

5. **Holding [Ctrl], drag the triangle shape to the right until the triangle shape copy is in a blank area of the slide, release the mouse button, then release [Ctrl]**

   An identical copy of the triangle shape appears on the slide and Smart Guides appear above and below the shape as you drag the new shape to the right, which helps you align shapes.

6. **With the second triangle shape still selected, click the Copy list arrow in the Clipboard group, click Duplicate, then move the duplicated triangle shape to a blank area of the slide**

   You have duplicated the triangle shape twice and now have three identical shapes on the slide.

   > **QUICK TIP**
   > Press and hold [Alt] to temporarily turn the snap-to-grid feature off while dragging objects on the slide or dragging a sizing handle to make precise adjustments.

7. **Click the View tab on the Ribbon, click the Ruler check box in the Show group, click the Home tab, then type Skin color**

   The ruler closes, and the text you type appears in the selected triangle shape and becomes a part of the shape. Now if you move or rotate the shape, the text moves with it. Compare your screen with FIGURE 2-12.

8. **Click the middle triangle shape, type Headache, click the left triangle shape, type Seizure, click in a blank area of the slide, then save your work**

   All three triangle shapes include text.

FIGURE 2-11: **Merged shape moved on slide**

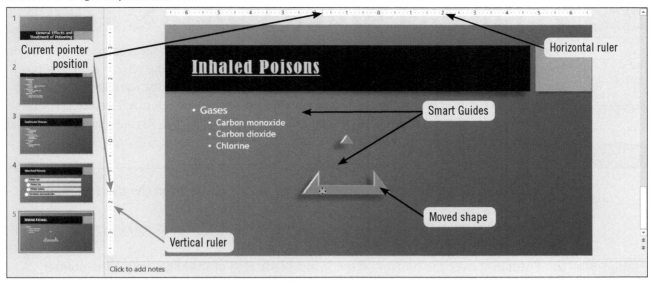

FIGURE 2-12: **Duplicated shapes**

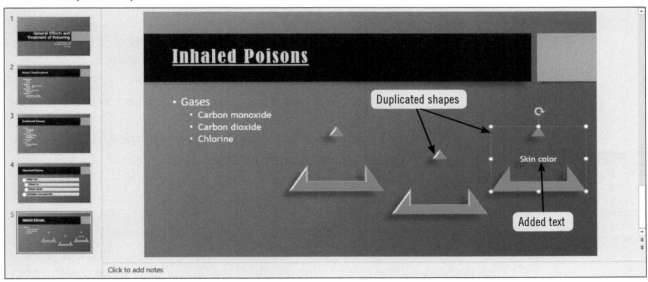

Editing points of a shape

If you want to customize the form (or outline) of any shape in the Shapes gallery, you can modify its edit points. To display a shape's edit points, select the shape you want to modify, click the Drawing Tools Format tab on the Ribbon, click the Edit Shape button in the Insert Shapes group, then click Edit Points. Black edit points appear on the shape. To change the form of a shape, drag a black edit point. When you click a black edit point, white square edit points appear on either side of the black edit point, which allow you to change the curvature of a line between two black edit points. When you are finished with your custom shape, you can save it as picture and reuse it in other presentations or other files. To save the shape as a picture, right-click the shape, then click Save as Picture.

Align and Group Objects

Learning Outcomes
- Move shapes using guides
- Align and group shapes

After you are finished creating and modifying your objects, you can position them accurately on the slide to achieve the look you want. Using the Align commands in the Arrange group, you can align objects relative to each other by snapping them to the gridlines on a slide or to guides that you manually position on the slide. The Group command groups two or more objects into one object, which secures their relative position to each other and makes it easy to edit and move them. **CASE** ▶ *You are ready to position and group the triangle shapes on Slide 5 to finish the slide.*

STEPS

1. **Right-click a blank area of the slide, point to Grid and Guides on the shortcut menu, then click Guides**

   The guides appear as dotted lines on the slide and usually intersect at the center of the slide. Guides help you position objects precisely on the slide.

   QUICK TIP
   To quickly add a new guide to the slide, press [Ctrl], then drag an existing guide. The original guide remains in place. Drag a guide off the slide to delete it.

2. **Position ☝ over the horizontal guide in a blank area of the slide, notice the pointer change to ✛, press and hold the mouse button until the pointer changes to a measurement guide box, then drag the guide up until the guide position box reads 1.13**

3. **Drag the vertical guide to the left until the guide position box reads 2.50, then drag the Seizure shape so that the top and left edges of the shape touch the guides, as shown in FIGURE 2-13**

   The Seizure shape attaches or "snaps" to the guides.

4. **Drag the Skin color shape to the right until it almost touches the edge of the slide, press and hold [Shift], click the other two triangle shapes, then release [Shift]**

   All three shapes are now selected.

5. **Click the Drawing Tools Format tab on the Ribbon, click the Align button in the Arrange group, then click Align Top**

   The lower triangle shapes move up and align with the top shape along their top edges.

   QUICK TIP
   To set the formatting of a shape as the default, right-click the shape, then click Set as Default Shape on the Shortcut menu.

6. **Click the Align button in the Arrange group, click Distribute Horizontally, click the Group button in the Arrange group, then click Group**

   The shapes are now distributed equally among themselves and grouped together to form one object without losing their individual attributes as shown in FIGURE 2-14. Notice that the sizing handles and rotate handle now appear on the outer edge of the grouped object, not around each individual object.

7. **Drag the horizontal guide to the middle of the slide until its guide position box reads 0.00, then drag the vertical guide to the middle of the slide until its guide position box reads 0.00**

8. **Click the View tab on the Ribbon, click the Guides check box in the Show group, click a blank area of the slide, then save your work**

   The guides are no longer displayed on the slide.

FIGURE 2-13: Repositioned shape

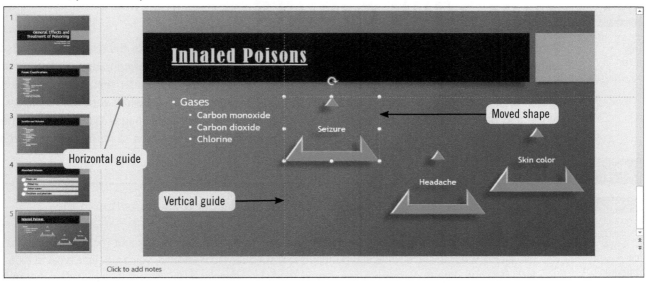

FIGURE 2-14: Repositioned shapes

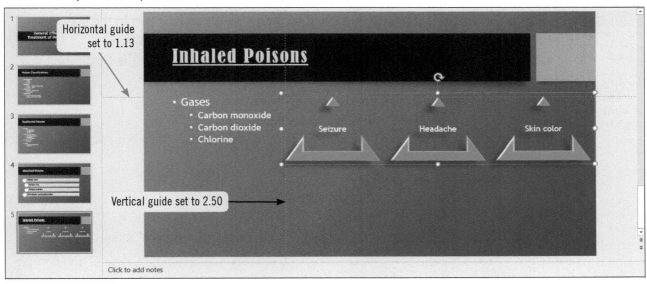

Distributing objects

There are two ways to distribute objects in PowerPoint: relative to each other and relative to the slide edge. If you choose to distribute objects relative to each other, PowerPoint evenly divides the empty space between all of the selected objects. When distributing objects in relation to the slide, PowerPoint evenly splits the empty space from slide edge to slide edge between the selected objects. To distribute objects relative to each other, click the Align button in the Arrange group on the Drawing Tools Format tab, then click Align Selected Objects. To distribute objects relative to the slide, click the Align button in the Arrange group on the Drawing Tools Format tab, then click Align to Slide.

Add Slide Footers

Footer text, such as a company, school, or product name, the slide number, or the date, can give your slides a professional look and make it easier for your audience to follow your presentation. Slides do not have headers. However, notes or handouts can include both header and footer text. You can review footer information that you apply to the slides in the PowerPoint views and when you print the slides. Notes and handouts header and footer text is visible when you print notes pages, handouts, and the outline. **CASE** *You add footer text to the slides of the training presentation to make it easier for the audience to follow.*

STEPS

QUICK TIP
The placement of the footer text objects on the slide is dependent on the presentation theme.

1. **Click the Insert tab on the Ribbon, then click the Header & Footer button in the Text group**

   The Header and Footer dialog box opens, as shown in FIGURE 2-15. The Header and Footer dialog box has two tabs: a Slide tab and a Notes and Handouts tab. The Slide tab is selected. There are three types of footer text, Date and time, Slide number, and Footer. The bold rectangles in the Preview box identify the default position of the three types of footer text placeholders on the slides.

2. **Click the Date and time check box to select it**

   The date and time options are now available to select. The Update automatically date and time option button is selected by default. This option updates the date and time to the date and time set by your computer every time you open or print the file.

QUICK TIP
If you want a specific date to appear every time you view or print the presentation, click the Fixed date option button, then type the date in the Fixed text box.

3. **Click the Update automatically list arrow, then click the fifth option in the list**

   The month is abbreviated in this option and is displayed between the day and the year.

4. **Click the Slide number check box, click the Footer check box, click the Footer text box, then type your name**

   The Preview box now shows all three footer placeholders are selected.

5. **Click the Don't show on title slide check box**

   Selecting this check box prevents the footer information you entered in the Header and Footer dialog box from appearing on the title slide.

6. **Click Apply to All**

   The dialog box closes, and the footer information is applied to all of the slides in your presentation except the title slide. Compare your screen with FIGURE 2-16.

7. **Click the Slide 1 thumbnail in the Slides tab, then click the Header & Footer button in the Text group**

   The Header and Footer dialog box opens again.

8. **Click the Don't show on title slide check box to deselect it, click the Footer check box, then select the text in the Footer text box**

TROUBLE
If you click Apply to All in Step 9, click the Undo button on the Quick Access toolbar and repeat Steps 7, 8, and 9.

9. **Type RMC Medical Training Series, click Apply, then save your work**

   Only the text in the Footer text box appears on the title slide. Clicking Apply applies this footer information to just the current slide.

FIGURE 2-15: **Header and Footer dialog box**

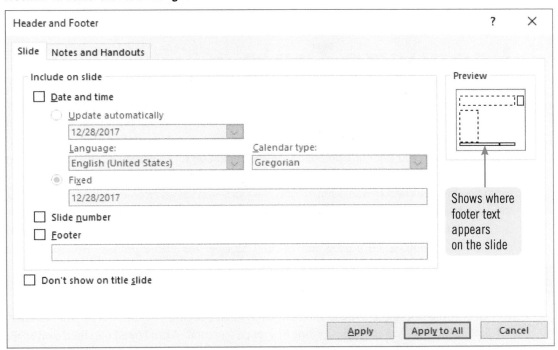

FIGURE 2-16: **Footer information added to presentation**

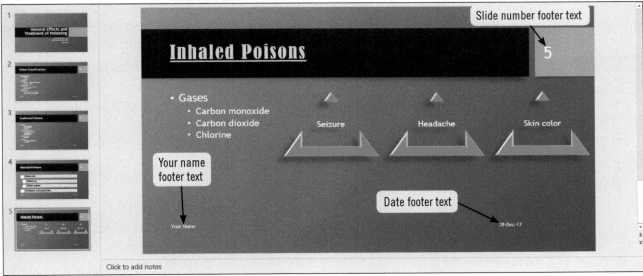

Creating superscript and subscript text

Superscript or subscript text is a number, figure, symbol, or letter that appears smaller than other text and is positioned above or below the normal line of text. A common superscript in the English language is the sign indicator next to a number, such as 1st or 3rd. Other examples of superscripts are the trademark symbol^{TM} and the copyright symbol$^{©}$. To create superscript text in PowerPoint, select the text, number, or symbol, then press [Ctrl] [Shift] [+] at the same time. Probably the most familiar subscript text are the numerals in chemical compounds and formulas, for example, H_2O and CO_2. To create subscript text, select the text, number, or symbol, then press [Ctrl] [=] at the same time. To change superscript or subscript text back to normal text, select the text, then press [Ctrl] [Spacebar].

Use Proofing and Language Tools

Learning
Outcomes
• Spell check a
  presentation
• Translate slide text

As your work on the presentation file nears completion, you need to review and proofread your slides thoroughly for errors. You can use the Spell Checker feature in PowerPoint to check for and correct spelling errors. This feature compares the spelling of all the words in your presentation against the words contained in the dictionary. You still must proofread your presentation for punctuation, grammar, and word-usage errors because the Spell Checker recognizes only misspelled and unknown words, not misused words. For example, the spell checker would not identify the word "last" as an error, even if you had intended to type the word "past." PowerPoint also includes language tools that translate words or phrases from your default language into another language using the Microsoft Translator. **CASE** ▷ *You're finished working on the presentation for now, so it's a good time to check spelling. You then experiment with language translation because the final presentation will be translated into different languages.*

STEPS

1. **Click the Review tab on the Ribbon, then click the Spelling button in the Proofing group**
   PowerPoint begins to check the spelling in your presentation. When PowerPoint finds a misspelled word or a word that is not in its dictionary, the Spelling pane opens, as shown in FIGURE 2-17. In this case, the Spell Checker identifies the clinic name on Slide 1 and suggests a replacement word.

2. **Click Ignore All then click Change to correct a misspelled word on Slide 2**
   PowerPoint ignores the first word, which is spelled correctly, and then corrects a misspelled word. If PowerPoint finds any other words it does not recognize, either change or ignore them. When the Spell Checker finishes checking your presentation, the Spelling pane closes, and an alert box opens.

   QUICK TIP
   The Spell Checker does not check the text in inserted pictures or objects.

3. **Click OK in the Alert box, then click the Slide 3 thumbnail in the Slides tab**
   The alert box closes. Now you experiment with the language translation feature.

4. **Click the Translate button in the Language group, then click Choose Translation Language**
   The Translation Language Options dialog box opens.

5. **Click the Translate to list arrow, click Czech, then click OK**
   The Translation Language Options dialog box closes.

6. **Click the Translate button in the Language group, click Mini Translator [Czech], click Yes in the alert box, then select the words Household items in the text object**
   The Microsoft Translator begins to analyze the selected text, and a semitransparent Microsoft Translator box appears below the text. The Mini toolbar may also appear above the text.

   QUICK TIP
   To copy the translated text to a slide, click the Copy button at the bottom of the Microsoft Translator box, right-click the slide, then click a Paste option.

7. **Move the pointer over the Microsoft Translator box**
   A Czech translation of the text appears as shown in FIGURE 2-18. The translation language setting remains in effect until you reset it.

8. **Click the Translate button in the Language group, click Choose Translation Language, click the Translate to list arrow, click English (United States), click OK, click the Translate button again, then click Mini Translator [English (United States)]**
   The Mini Translator is turned off, and the translation language is restored to the default setting.

9. **Submit your presentation to your instructor, then exit PowerPoint**

FIGURE 2-17: Spelling pane

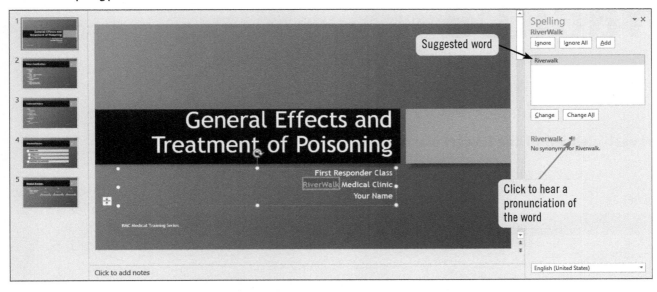

FIGURE 2-18: Translated text in the Microsoft Translator box

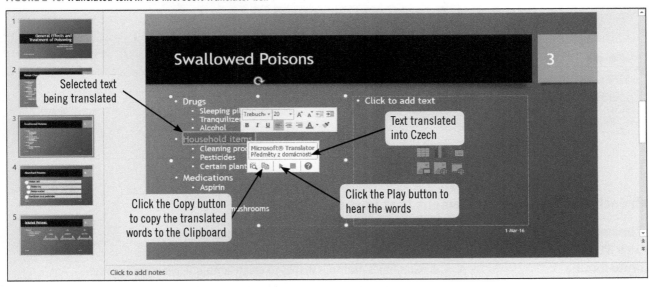

Checking spelling as you type

By default, PowerPoint checks your spelling as you type. If you type a word that is not in the dictionary, a wavy red line appears under it. To correct an error, right-click the misspelled word, then review the suggestions, which appear in the shortcut menu. You can select a suggestion, add the word you typed to your custom dictionary, or ignore it. To turn off automatic spell checking, click the File tab, then click Options to open the PowerPoint Options dialog box. Click Proofing in the left column, then click the Check spelling as you type check box to deselect it. To temporarily hide the wavy red lines, click the Hide spelling and grammar errors check box to select it. Contextual spelling in PowerPoint identifies common grammatically misused words, for example, if you type the word "their" and the correct word is "there," PowerPoint will identify the mistake and place a wavy red line under the word. To turn contextual spelling on or off, click Proofing in the PowerPoint Options dialog box, then click the Check grammar with spelling check box.

Practice

Concepts Review

Label each element of the PowerPoint window shown in FIGURE 2-19.

FIGURE 2-19

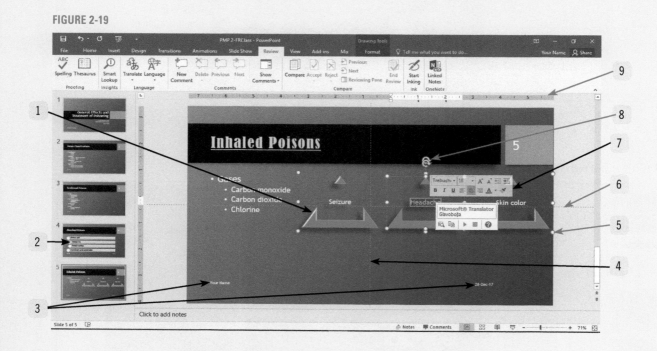

Match each term with the statement that best describes it.

10. **Adjustment handle**
11. **Quick Style**
12. **Rotate handle**
13. **Gridlines**
14. **Merge**
15. **Smart Guides**

a. Evenly spaced horizontal and vertical lines
b. A set of formatting options you apply to an object
c. Combines multiple shapes to create a unique geometric shape
d. Changes the most prominent feature of an object
e. Helps you determine equal distances between objects
f. Drag to turn an object

Select the best answer from the list of choices.

16. What is *not* true about grouped objects?
  a. Grouped objects have one rotate handle.
  b. Grouped objects act as one object but maintain their individual attributes.
  c. Sizing handles appear around the grouped object.
  d. Each object is distributed relative to the slide edges.

17. A professional-quality diagram that visually illustrates text best describes which of the following?
  a. A SmartArt Style   **c.** A subscript
  b. A merged shape   **d.** A SmartArt graphic

18. Which of the following statements is *not* true about Outline view?
  a. Pressing [Enter] moves the insertion point down one line.
  b. Text you enter next to the slide icon becomes a bullet point for that slide.
  c. Headings are the same as slide titles.
  d. Added slides use the same layout as the previous slide.

19. What do you have to drag to customize the form or outline of a shape?
  a. Anchor points   **c.** Slide edges
  b. Edit points   **d.** Shape area

20. Which of the following statements about merged shapes is *not* true?
  a. Merged shapes can be added to the Shapes gallery.
  b. A merged shape assumes the theme of the shape that is selected first.
  c. The stacking order of shapes changes the way a merged shape looks.
  d. A merged shape is a combination of multiple shapes.

Skills Review

1. Enter text in Outline view.
  a. Open the presentation PMP 2-2.pptx from the location where you store your Data Files, then save it as **PMP 2-ERP**. The completed presentation is shown in FIGURE 2-20.
  b. Create a new slide after Slide 2 with the Title and Content layout.
  c. Open Outline view, then type **ERP Guidelines**.
  d. Press [Enter], press [Tab], type **Equipment identification**, press [Enter], type **Define staff procedures**, press [Enter], then type **Identify proper response**.
  e. Move Slide 3 above Slide 2, then switch back to Normal view.
  f. Click the Home tab, then save your changes.

FIGURE 2-20

2. Format text.
  a. Go to Slide 1, select the name University Medical Center, then move the pointer over the Mini Toolbar.
  b. Click the Font Color list arrow, then click Orange under Standard Colors.
  c. Select the text object, then change all of the text to the color Orange.
  d. Click the Font Size list arrow, click 20, then click the Underline button.
  e. Click the Character Spacing button, click Tight, then save your changes.

Skills Review (continued)

3. Convert text to SmartArt.

  a. Click the text object on Slide 4.

  b. Click the Convert to SmartArt Graphic button, then apply the Pyramid List graphic layout to the text object.

  c. Click the More button in the Layouts group, click More Layouts, click Cycle in the Choose a SmartArt Graphic dialog box, click Continuous Cycle, then click OK.

  d. Click the More button in the SmartArt Styles group, then apply the Polished style from the 3-D group to the graphic.

  e. Close the text pane if necessary, then click outside the SmartArt graphic in a blank part of the slide.

  f. Save your changes.

4. Insert and modify shapes.

  a. Go to Slide 3, then add rulers and guides to the Slide pane.

  b. Click the More button in the Drawing group to open the Shapes gallery, click the Diamond button in the Basic Shapes section, press [Shift], then draw a 1 1/2-inch shape in a blank area of the slide.

  c. Select the rectangle shape on the slide, click the Drawing Tools Format tab, click the More button in the Shape Styles group, then click Colored Fill – Aqua, Accent 2.

  d. Click the Shape Effects button, point to Reflection, then click Half Reflection, touching.

5. Rearrange and merge shapes.

  a. Drag the diamond shape over top of the rectangle shape and center it, then send the diamond shape backward one level.

  b. Click the rectangle shape, press [Shift], click the diamond shape, then click the Merge Shapes button in the Insert Shapes group on the Drawing Tools Format tab.

  c. Point to each of the merge shapes options, click Combine, then save your work.

6. Edit and duplicate shapes.

  a. Using [Ctrl] make two copies of the shape.

  b. Type **CPR** in the right shape, type **Airway Kit** in the middle shape, then type **Code Cart** in the left shape.

7. Align and group objects.

  a. Move the vertical guide to the right until 5.25 appears, drag the right shape so its right edge touches the vertical guide, then select all three shapes.

FIGURE 2-21

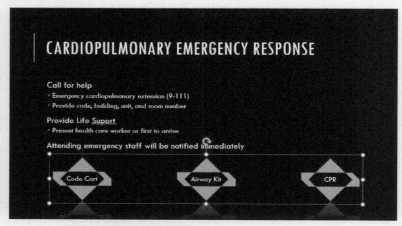

  b. Click the Align button in the Arrange group, click Align Middle, click the Align button, then click Distribute Horizontally.

  c. Click the Group button in the Arrange group, then click Group.

  d. Set the guide back to 0.00, remove the guides and rulers from your screen, save your work, then compare your screen with FIGURE 2-21.

8. Add slide footers.

  a. Open the Header and Footer dialog box.

  b. On the Slide tab, click the Date and time check box to select it, then click the Fixed option button.

  c. Add the slide number to the footer, then type your name in the Footer text box.

  d. Apply the footer to all of the slides except the title slide.

Skills Review (continued)

9. **Use proofing and language tools.**

a. Check the spelling of the presentation and change any misspelled words. There is at least one misspelled word in the presentation.

b. Set the Mini Translator to Bosnian, then view the translation of words on Slide 3.

c. Set the default language back to English, turn off the Mini translator, submit your presentation to your instructor, close the presentation, then exit PowerPoint.

Independent Challenge 1

You work in the Department of Emergency Services in New York. You are a trained first responder and have been asked to update the department's procedures for radiological transportation accidents. You will present the information at a conference later in the year. You need to continue working on the presentation you started already.

a. Start PowerPoint, open the presentation PMP 2-3.pptx from the location where you store your Data Files, and save it as **PMP 2-First Responder**.

b. Use Outline view to enter the following as bulleted text on the Responsibilities slide:
Initiate response
Evaluate scene
Relay information to assisting agencies
Maintain scene control

c. Apply the Parcel design theme to the presentation.

d. Change the font color of the title text object on Slide 5 to Red.

e. Change the bulleted text on Slide 4 to the Trapezoid List SmartArt Graphic, then apply the Inset SmartArt style.

f. Check the presentation spelling (there is at least one spelling error), add your name and slide number as a footer on the slides, then save your changes.

g. Submit your presentation to your instructor, close your presentation, then exit PowerPoint.

Independent Challenge 2

You work for MedFlight, an air ambulance service in Spokane, WA. You have been asked to develop a presentation outlining the company's membership program and medical services.

a. Start PowerPoint, open the presentation PMP 2-4.pptx from the location where you store your Data Files, and save it as **PMP 2-MedFlight**.

b. Choose a design theme for the presentation, then apply a variant.

c. On Slide 2, select the three coverage shapes, then use the Align command to distribute them vertically and align them to their left edges.

d. Select the three shapes, Family Coverage, Application Process, and MedFlight Member, then using the Align command distribute them horizontally and align them to their bottom edges.

e. Select all of the shapes, then from the Shape Styles group apply a Moderate Effect.

f. Create a diamond shape larger than the MedFlight Member shape, then merge it with the MedFlight Member shape using the Union merge option.

g. Select the text in the MedFlight Member shape, then change and format the text to: bold, italic, 20-pt, Georgia font.

h. Group all the shapes, add the slide number and your name as a footer on the slides, then save your changes.

i. Submit your presentation to your instructor, close your presentation, then exit PowerPoint.

Independent Challenge 3: Explore

One of your assignments this semester in your nursing course is to create a presentation on tissue damage. You chose frostbite as your presentation topic. Continue working on your presentation that you have already started.

a. Start PowerPoint, open the presentation PMP 2-5.pptx from the location where you store your Data Files, and save it as **PMP 2-Frostbite**.

b. Add a new slide after the General Description slide with the same layout, type **Symptoms** in the title text placeholder, then enter the following as bulleted text in Outline view:
Loss of sensitivity to touch
Progressive numbness
Pain fades as condition worsens
Skin changes color - white to purple
Affected area feels wooden
Ultimately death of tissue

c. Apply the Banded design theme to the presentation, then change the variant.

d. Select the title text object on Slide 4 (*Hint*: Press [Shift] to select the whole object), then change the text color to Light Blue.

e. Change the font of the title text object to Elephant, increase the font size to 48, then change the character spacing to Very Loose.

f. Change the text on Slide 4 to a SmartArt graphic. Use an appropriate diagram type for a list.

g. Change the style of the SmartArt diagram using one of the SmartArt Styles, then view the presentation in Slide Show view.

h. Add the slide number and your name as a footer on the slides, check the presentation spelling, fix any errors, then save your changes.

i. Submit your presentation to your instructor, close your presentation, then exit PowerPoint.

Visual Workshop

Create the presentation shown in FIGURE 2-22. Add today's date as the date on the title slide. Save the presentation as **PMP 2-Heat** to the location where you store your Data Files. (*Hint*: The SmartArt style used for the SmartArt is a 3D style.) Review your slides in Slide Show view, then add the slide number and your name as a footer to the slides. Submit your presentation to your instructor, save your changes, close the presentation, then exit PowerPoint.

FIGURE 2-22

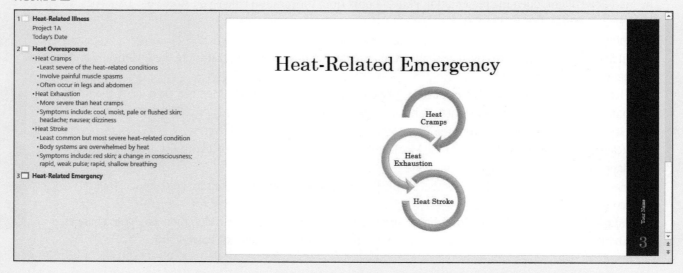

Finalizing a Presentation

CASE In this module, you continue working on the presentation by inserting text from Microsoft Word and slides from another presentation. You also add visual elements into the presentation including a photograph, and a table. You modify the background of the presentation and then set slide transitions and timings. Finally, you animate objects and create an Office Mix.

Module Objectives

After completing this module, you will be able to:

- Insert text from Microsoft Word
- Insert and style a picture
- Insert a table
- Insert slides from other presentations
- Customize the background and theme

- Use slide show commands
- Set slide transitions and timings
- Animate objects
- Create an Office Mix

Files You Will Need

PMP 3-1.pptx	PMP 3-8.pptx
PMP 3-2.docx	PMP 3-9.pptx
PMP 3-3.jpg	PMP 3-10.pptx
PMP 3-4.pptx	PMP 3-11.pptx
PMP 3-5.pptx	PMP 3-12.docx
PMP 3-6.docx	PMP 3-13.jpg
PMP 3-7.jpg	

Insert Text from Microsoft Word

Learning
Outcomes
• Create slides using
  Outline view
• Move and delete
  slides

It is easy to insert documents saved in Microsoft Word format (.docx), Rich Text Format (.rtf), plain text format (.txt), and HTML format (.htm) into a PowerPoint presentation. If you have an outline saved in a document file, you can import it into PowerPoint to create a new presentation or create additional slides in an existing presentation. When you import a document into a presentation, PowerPoint creates an outline structure based on the styles in the document. For example, a Heading 1 style in the Word document becomes a slide title and a Heading 2 style becomes the first level of text in a bulleted list. If you insert a plain text format document into a presentation, PowerPoint creates an outline based on the tabs at the beginning of the document's paragraphs. Paragraphs without tabs become slide titles, and paragraphs with one tab indent become first-level text in bulleted lists. **CASE** *You have a Microsoft Word document with information about injected poisons that you want to insert into your presentation.*

STEPS

1. **Start PowerPoint, open the presentation** PMP 3-1.pptx **from the location where you store your Data Files, save it as** PMP 3-FRClass, **click the** View tab **on the Ribbon, then click the** Outline View button **in the Presentation Views group**

2. **Click the** Slide 5 icon ☐ **in the Outline pane, click the** Home tab **on the Ribbon, click the** New Slide button list arrow **in the Slides group, then click** Slides from Outline

   Slide 5 appears in the Slide pane. The Insert Outline dialog box opens. Before you insert an outline into a presentation, you need to determine where you want the new slides to be placed. You want the text from the Word document inserted as new slides after Slide 5.

3. **Navigate to the location where you store your Data Files, click the Word document file** PMP 3-2.docx, **then click** Insert

   Three new slides (6, 7, and 8) are added to the presentation, and the new Slide 6 appears in the Slide pane. See FIGURE 3-1.

4. **Click the** down scroll arrow ▾ **in the Outline pane and read the text for all the new slides, then click the** Normal button ▣ **on the status bar**

   The information on Slide 8 refers to information not needed for this presentation.

5. **Click the** Slide 8 thumbnail **in the Slides tab, then click the** Cut button **in the Clipboard group**

   Slide 8 is deleted, and the next slide up (Injected Poisons) appears in the Slide pane.

6. **Drag the** Slide 7 thumbnail **in the Slides tab above Slide 6**

   Slide 7 becomes Slide 6. The inserted slides have a different slide layout and font style than the other slides. You want the text of the inserted outline to adopt the theme fonts of the presentation.

7. **Press [Shift], click the** Slide 7 thumbnail, **release [Shift], click the** Reset button **in the Slides group, click the** Layout button **in the Slides group, then click the** Title and Content slide layout

   The new slides now follow the presentation design and font themes. Compare your screen to FIGURE 3-2.

8. **Click the** Save button ▣ **on the Quick Access toolbar**

FIGURE 3-1: Outline pane showing imported text

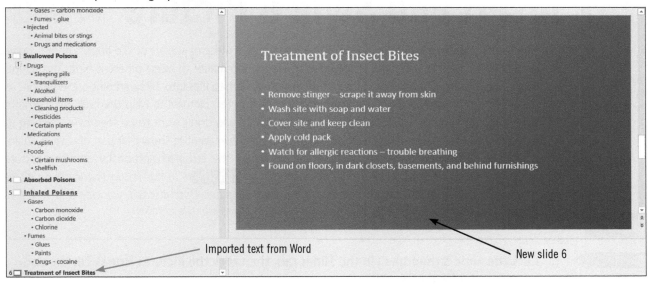

Imported text from Word

New slide 6

FIGURE 3-2: Slides reset to Berlin theme default settings

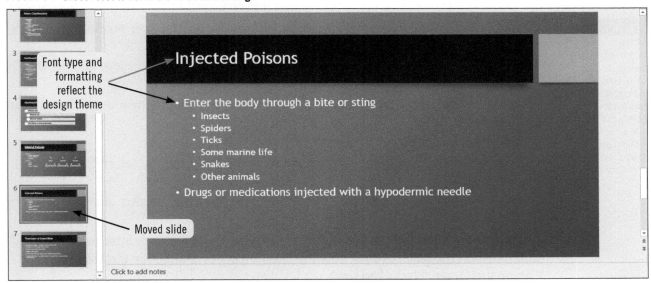

Font type and formatting reflect the design theme

Moved slide

Sending a presentation using email

You can send a copy of a presentation over the Internet to a reviewer to edit and add comments. You can use Microsoft Outlook to send your presentation. Although your email program allows you to attach files, you can send a presentation using Outlook from within PowerPoint. Click the File tab, click Share, click Email in the center pane, then click Send as Attachment. Outlook opens and automatically creates an email with a copy of the presentation attached to it. You can also attach and send a PDF copy or an XPS copy of the presentation using your email program. Both of these file formats preserve document formatting, enable file sharing, and can be viewed online and printed.

Insert and Style a Picture

Learning Outcomes
• Insert and format a picture
• Resize and move a picture

In PowerPoint, a **picture** is defined as a digital photograph, a piece of line art or clip art, or other artwork that is created in another program. PowerPoint gives you the ability to insert different types of pictures including JPEG File Interchange Format and BMP Windows Bitmap files into a PowerPoint presentation. As with all objects in PowerPoint, you can format and style inserted pictures to help them fit the theme of your presentation. You can also hide a portion of the picture you don't want to be seen by **cropping** it. The cropped portion of a picture is still available to you if you ever want to show that part of picture again. To reduce the size of the file, you can permanently delete the cropped portion by applying picture compression settings in the Compress Pictures dialog box. **CASE** *In this lesson you insert a JPG file picture taken by a clinic staff member that is saved on your computer. Once inserted, you crop and style it to best fit the slide.*

STEPS

1. **Click the** Slide 3 thumbnail **in the Slides tab, then click the** Pictures icon 🖼 **in the content placeholder on the slide**

   The Insert Picture dialog box opens displaying the pictures available in the default Pictures folder.

2. **Navigate to the location where you store your Data Files, select the picture file** PMP 3-3.jpg, **then click** Insert

   The picture fills the content placeholder on the slide, and the Picture Tools Format tab opens on the Ribbon. The picture would look better if you cropped some of the image.

3. **Click the** Crop button **in the Size group, then place the pointer over the** bottom-middle cropping handle **on the picture**

   The pointer changes to ┳. When the Crop button is active, cropping handles appear next to the sizing handles on the selected object.

4. **Drag the** bottom of the picture **up as shown in** FIGURE 3-3, **release the mouse button, then press** [Esc]

   The picture would look better on the slide if it were larger.

5. **Click the** number (5.14) **in the Width text box in the Size group to select it, type** 6, **then press** [Enter]

   The picture height and width increase proportionally. PowerPoint has a number of picture formatting options, and you decide to experiment with some of them.

6. **Click the** More button ▼ **in the Picture Styles group, move your pointer over the** style thumbnails **in the gallery to see how the different styles change the picture, then click** Compound Frame, Black **(2nd row)**

   The picture now has a compound black frame around it.

7. **Click the** Corrections button **in the Adjust group, move your pointer over the** thumbnails **to see how the picture changes, then click** Sharpen: 50% **in the Sharpen/Soften section**

   The picture clarity is better.

8. **Click the** Artistic Effects button **in the Adjust group, move your pointer over the** thumbnails **to see how the picture changes, then click a blank area of the slide**

   The artistic effects are all interesting, but none of them will work well for this picture.

9. **Drag the** picture **to the center of the blank area of the slide to the right of the text object, click a blank area on the slide, then save your changes**

   Compare your screen to FIGURE 3-4.

FIGURE 3-3: Using the cropping pointer to crop a picture

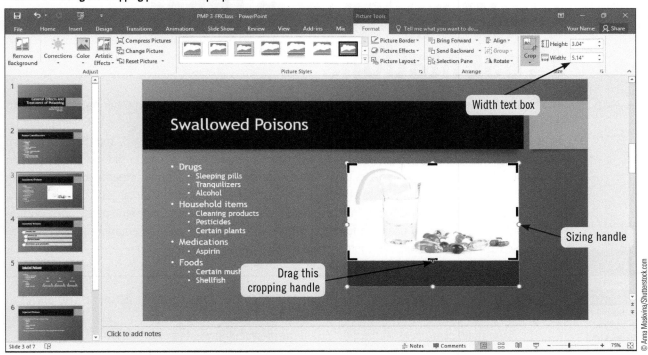

FIGURE 3-4: Cropped and styled picture

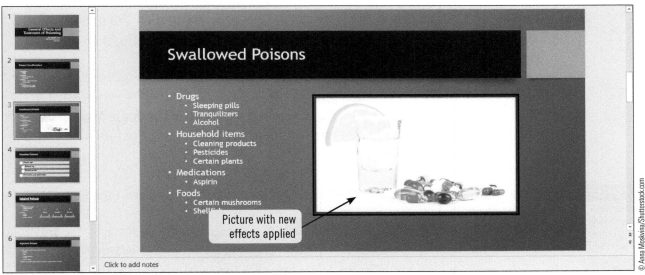

Inserting a screen recording

Using the Screen Recording button in the Media group on the Insert tab, you can record your computer screen with audio and insert the recording to a slide. For example, if you want to make a recording of an Internet video, locate and display the video on your computer screen. In PowerPoint on the slide where you want to insert the recording, click the Screen Recording button.

On the toolbar, click the Select Area button, drag a selection box around the video, click the Audio button if necessary, then click the Record button on the toolbar. Click the video play button. When finished recording, click Windows Logo+[Shift]+Q to stop recording. PowerPoint opens and the recording appears on your slide. Click the Play button to review your recording.

PowerPoint 2016

Insert Slides from Other Presentations

To save time and energy, you can insert one or more slides you already created in other presentations into an existing presentation or one you are currently working on. One way to share slides between presentations is to open an existing presentation, copy the slides you want to the Clipboard, and then paste them into your open presentation. However, PowerPoint offers a simpler way to transfer slides directly between presentations. By using the Reuse Slides pane, you can insert slides from another presentation or a network location called a Slide Library. A **Slide Library** is a folder that you and others can access to open, modify, and review presentation slides. Newly inserted slides automatically take on the theme of the open presentation, unless you decide to use slide formatting from the original source presentation. **CASE** *You decide to insert slides you created for another presentation into your presentation.*

STEPS

1. **Click the** Slide 6 thumbnail **in the Slides tab, click the** New Slide list arrow **in the Slides group, then click** Reuse Slides

   The Reuse Slides pane opens on the right side of the presentation window.

2. **Click the** Browse button **in the Reuse Slides pane, click** Browse File, **navigate to the location where you store your Data Files, select the presentation file** PMP 3-4.pptx, **then click** Open

   Three slide thumbnails are displayed in the pane with the first slide thumbnail selected as shown in FIGURE 3-5. The slide thumbnails identify the slides in the **source presentation**, PMP 3-4.pptx.

3. **Point to each slide in the Reuse Slides pane list to display a ScreenTip, then click the** Scene Evaluation for Poisoning slide

   The new slide appears in the Slides tab and Slide pane as the new Slide 7. Notice the new slide assumes the design style and formatting of your presentation, which is called the **destination presentation**.

4. **Click the** Keep source formatting check box **at the bottom of the Reuse Slides pane, click the** Care & Treatment for Poisoning slide, **then click the** Keep source formatting check box

   This new slide keeps the design style and formatting of the source presentation.

5. **Click the** Slide 7 thumbnail **in the Slides tab, then click the last slide in the Reuse Slides pane**

   One more slide is inserted into the presentation with the design style and formatting of the destination presentation. The design theme of Slide 9 should match the rest of the slides in the presentation.

6. **Click the** Slide 9 thumbnail **in the Slides tab, click the** Layout button **in the Slides group, then click the** Section Header slide layout **in the Berlin section**

   Slide 9 is changed to the Berlin design theme.

7. **Drag the Slide 9 thumbnail in the Slides tab above Slide 7, then click the** Reuse Slides pane Close button ☒

   The Reuse Slides pane closes.

8. **Click a blank area of the slide, scroll to the bottom of the Slides tab, then save the presentation**

   Compare your screen to FIGURE 3-6.

FIGURE 3-5: Presentation window with Reuse Slides pane open

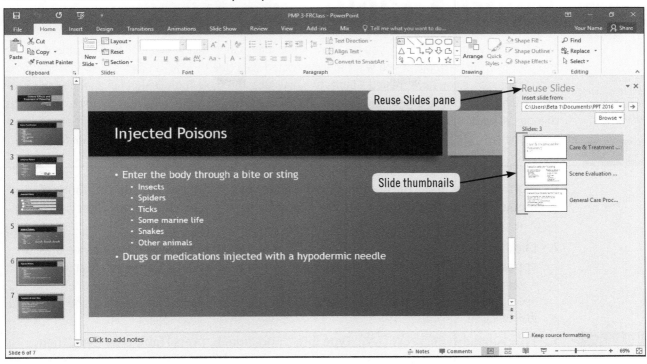

FIGURE 3-6: New slides added to presentation

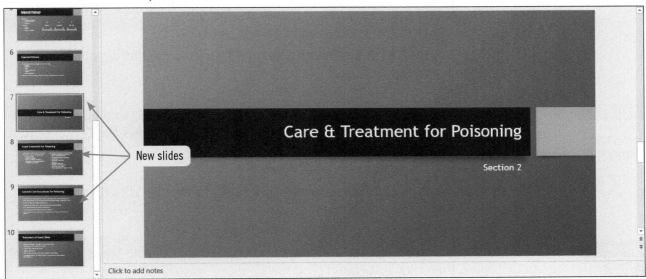

Working with multiple windows

Another way to work with information in multiple presentations is to arrange the presentation windows on your monitor so you see each window side by side. Open each presentation, click the View tab on the Ribbon in any presentation window, then click the Arrange All button in the Window group. Each presentation you have open is placed next to each other so you can easily drag, or transfer, information between the presentations.

If you are working with more than two open presentations, you can overlap the presentation windows on top of one another. Open all the presentations you want, then click the Cascade button in the Window group. Now you can easily jump from one presentation to another by clicking the presentation title bar or any part of the presentation window.

PowerPoint 2016

Insert a Table

Learning
Outcomes
• Insert a table
• Add text to a table
• Change table size
  and layout

As you create your presentation, you may have some information that would look best organized in rows and columns. For example, if you want to view related data side by side, a table is ideal for this type of information. Once you have created a table, two new tabs, the Table Tools Design tab and the Table Tools Layout tab, appear on the Ribbon. You can use the commands on the table tabs to apply color styles, change cell borders, add cell effects, add rows and columns to your table, adjust the size of cells, and align text in the cells. **CASE** *You decide a table best illustrates information for caring for bites and stings.*

STEPS

1. **Right-click the Slide 10 thumbnail in the Slides tab, click New Slide on the shortcut menu, click the title placeholder, then type Emergency Care for Animal Bites and Stings**
   A new slide with the Title and Content layout appears.

2. **Click the Insert Table icon ▦, click the Number of columns down arrow twice until 3 appears, click the Number of rows up arrow three times until 5 appears, then click OK**
   A formatted table with three columns and five rows appears on the slide, and the Table Tools Design tab opens on the Ribbon. The table has 15 cells. The insertion point is in the first cell of the table and is ready to accept text.

   QUICK TIP
   Press [Tab] when the insertion point is in the last cell of a table to create a new row.

3. **Type Animal Type, press [Tab], type Bite/Sting Signals, press [Tab], type Care, then press [Tab]**
   The text you typed appears in the top three cells of the table. Pressing [Tab] moves the insertion point to the next cell; pressing [Enter] moves the insertion point to the next line in the same cell.

4. **Enter the rest of the table information shown in FIGURE 3-7**
   The table would look better if it were formatted differently.

5. **Click the More button ▼ in the Table Styles group, scroll to the bottom of the gallery, then click Medium Style 3 - Accent 5**
   The background and text color change to reflect the table style you applied.

   QUICK TIP
   Change the height or width of any table cell by dragging its borders.

6. **Click the Animal Type cell in the table, click the Table Tools Layout tab on the Ribbon, click the Select button in the Table group, click Select Row, then click the Center button ▤ in the Alignment group**
   The text in the top row is centered horizontally in each cell.

7. **Click the Select button in the Table group, click Select Table, then click the Center Vertically button ▤ in the Alignment group**
   The text in the entire table is aligned in the center of each cell.

   QUICK TIP
   To change the cell color behind text, click the Shading list arrow in the Table Styles group, then choose a color.

8. **Click the Table Tools Design tab, click the Effects button in the Table Styles group, point to Cell Bevel, then click Soft Round (2nd row)**
   The 3D effect makes the cells of the table stand out. The table would look better in a different place on the slide.

9. **Place the pointer ⬚ over the top edge of the table, drag the table down so it is placed as shown in FIGURE 3-8, click a blank area of the slide, then save the presentation**
   The slide looks better with more space between the table and the slide title.

FIGURE 3-7: **Inserted table with data**

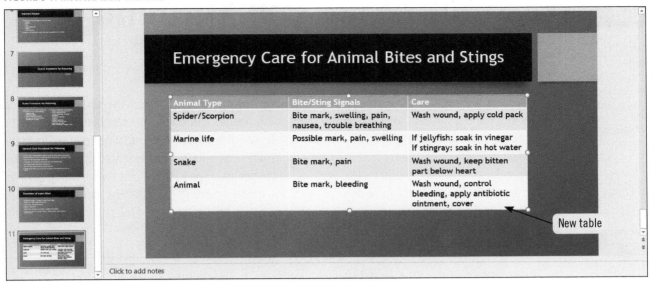

FIGURE 3-8: **Formatted table**

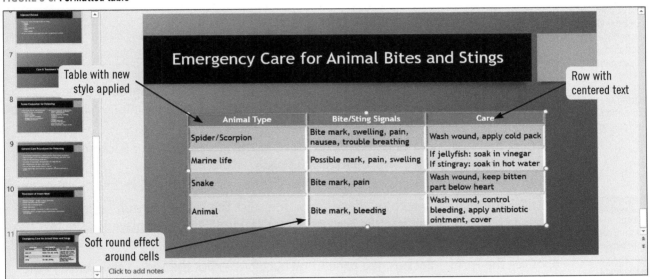

Saving a presentation as a video

You can save your PowerPoint presentation as a full-fidelity video, which incorporates all slide timings, transitions, animations, and narrations. The video can be distributed using a disc, the web, or email. Depending on how you want to display your video, you have three resolution settings from which to choose: Presentation Quality, Internet Quality, and Low Quality. The Large setting, Presentation Quality (1920 X 1080), is used for viewing on a computer monitor, projector, or other high-definition displays. The Medium setting, Internet Quality (1280 X 720), is used for uploading to the web or copying to a standard DVD. The Small setting, Low Quality (852 X 480), is used on portable media players. To save your presentation as a video, click the File tab, click Export, click Create a Video, choose your settings, then click the Create Video button.

Customize the Background and Theme

Learning Outcomes
- Apply a slide background and change the style
- Modify presentation theme

Every slide in a PowerPoint presentation has a **background**, the area behind the text and graphics. You modify the background to enhance the slides using images and color. You can quickly change the background appearance by applying a background style, which is a set of color variations derived from the theme colors. Theme colors determine the colors for all slide elements in your presentation, including slide background, text and lines, shadows, fills, accents, and hyperlinks. Every PowerPoint theme has its own set of theme colors. See TABLE 3-1 for a description of the theme colors. **CASE** ▶ *The presentation can be improved with some design enhancements. You decide to modify the background of the slides by changing the theme colors and fonts.*

STEPS

1. **Click Slide 1 in the Slides tab, click the Design tab on the Ribbon, then click the Format Background button in the Customize group**
   The Format Background pane opens displaying the Fill options. The Gradient fill option button is selected indicating the slide has a gradient background.

QUICK TIP

To create a custom theme, click the View tab, click the Slide Master button in the Master Views group, then click the Colors button, the Fonts button, or the Effects button in the Background group.

2. **Click the Solid fill option button, review the slide, click the Pattern fill option button, then click the Dotted diamond pattern (seventh row)**
   FIGURE 3-9 shows the new background on Slide 1 of the presentation. The new background style covers the slide behind the text and background graphics. **Background graphics** are objects placed on the slide master.

3. **Click the Hide background graphics check box in the Format Background pane**
   All of the background objects, which include the colored shapes behind the title text object, are hidden from view, and only the text objects remain visible.

4. **Click the Hide background graphics check box, then click the Reset Background button at the bottom of the Format Background pane**
   All of the background objects and the gradient fill slide background appear again as specified by the theme.

QUICK TIP

To add artistic effects, picture corrections, or picture color changes to a slide background, click the Effects or Picture icons in the Format Background pane, then click one of the options.

5. **Click the Picture or texture fill option button, click the Texture button 🔲, click Woven mat (top row), then drag the Transparency slider until 40% is displayed in the text box**
   The new texture fills the slide background behind the background items.

6. **Click the Format Background pane Close button ✖, click the Slide 3 thumbnail in the Slides tab, then point to the green theme variant in the Variants group**
   The new theme variant changes the color of the shapes on the slide and the background texture. A **variant** is a custom variation of the applied theme, in this case the Berlin theme. Theme variants are similar to the original theme, but they are made up of different complementary colors, slide backgrounds, such as textures and patterns, and background elements, such as shapes and pictures.

7. **Point to the other variants in the Variants group, click the blue variant, then save your work**
   The new variant is applied to the slide master and to all the slides in the presentation. Compare your screen to FIGURE 3-10.

FIGURE 3-9: New background style applied

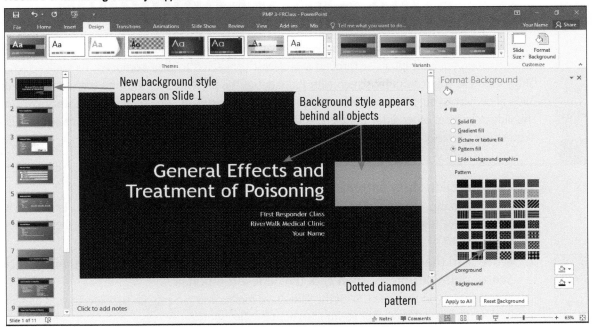

FIGURE 3-10: New theme variant

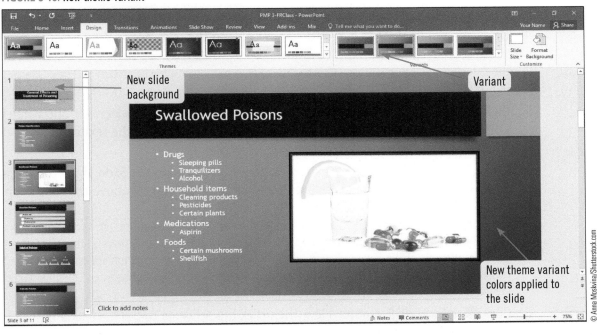

TABLE 3-1: Theme colors

color element	description
Text/Background colors	Contrasting colors for typed characters and the slide background
Accent colors	There are six accent colors used for shapes, drawn lines, and text; the shadow color for text and objects and the fill and outline color for shapes are all accent colors; all of these colors contrast appropriately with background and text colors
Hyperlink color	Colors used for hyperlinks you insert
Followed Hyperlink color	Color used for hyperlinks after they have been clicked

© Anna Moskvina/Shutterstock.com

PowerPoint 2016

Use Slide Show Commands

Learning Outcomes
- Preview a slide show
- Navigate a slide show
- Use slide show tools

With PowerPoint, Slide Show view is used primarily to deliver a presentation to an audience, either over the Internet using your computer or through a projector connected to your computer. As you've seen, Slide Show view fills your computer screen with the slides of the presentation, showing them one at a time. In Slide Show view, you can draw freehand pen or highlighter strokes, also known as **ink annotations**, on the slide or jump to other slides in the presentation. **CASE** *You run the slide show of the presentation and practice using some of the custom slide show options.*

STEPS

1. **Click the Slide Show button** 🖵 **on the status bar, then press [Spacebar]**

   Slide 3 filled the screen first, and then Slide 4 appears. Pressing [Spacebar] or clicking the left mouse button is an easy way to move through a slide show. See TABLE 3-2 for other basic slide show keyboard commands. You can easily navigate to other slides in the presentation during the slide show.

2. **Move** ⬚ **to the lower-left corner of the screen to display the Slide Show toolbar, click the See all slides button** ⊕**, then click the Slide 2 thumbnail**

   Slide 2 appears on the screen. With the Slide Show toolbar you can emphasize points in your presentation by drawing highlighter strokes on the slide during a slide show.

3. **Click the Pen and laser pointer tools button** ⊘ **on the Slide Show toolbar, then click Highlighter**

   The pointer changes to the highlighter pointer ▌. You can use the highlighter anywhere on the slide.

4. **Drag** ▌ **to highlight Pesticides and Fumes - glue in the text object, then press [Esc]**

   Two lines of text are highlighted as shown in FIGURE 3-11. While the ▌ is visible, mouse clicks do not advance the slide show; however, you can still move to the next slide by pressing [Spacebar] or [Enter]. Pressing [Esc] or [Ctrl][A] while drawing with the highlighter or pen switches the pointer back to ⬚.

5. **Right-click anywhere on the screen, point to Pointer Options, click Eraser, and when the pointer changes to** ✎, **click the lower highlight annotation in the text object**

   The highlight annotation on the "Fumes - glue" text is erased.

6. **Press [Esc], click the More slide show options button** ◯ **on the Slide Show toolbar, click Show Presenter View, then click the Pause the timer button** ⏸ **above the slide as shown in FIGURE 3-12**

   Presenter view is a view that you can use when showing a presentation through two monitors; one that you see as the presenter and one that your audience sees. The current slide appears on the left of your screen (which is the only object your audience sees), the next slide in the presentation appears in the upper-right corner of the screen. Speaker notes, if you have any, appear in the lower-right corner. The timer you paused identifies how long the slide has been viewed by the audience.

7. **Click** ●, **click Hide Presenter View, then click the Advance to the next slide button** ⊙ **on the Slide Show toolbar**

   Slide 3 appears.

8. **Press [Enter] to advance through the entire slide show until you see a black slide, then press [Spacebar]**

   If there are ink annotations on your slides, you have the option of saving them when you quit the slide show. Saved ink annotations appear as drawn objects in Normal view.

9. **Click Discard, then save the presentation**

   The highlight ink annotation is deleted on Slide 2, and Slide 3 appears in Normal view.

FIGURE 3-11: **Slide 2 in Slide Show view with highlighter drawings**

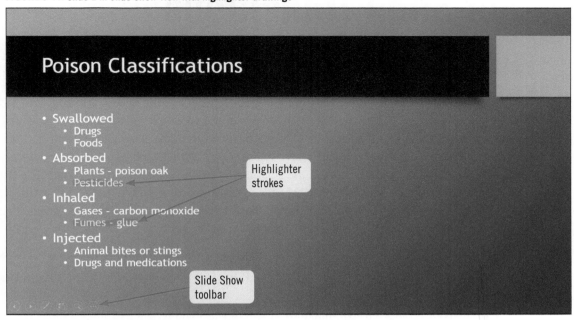

FIGURE 3-12: **Slide 2 in Presenter view**

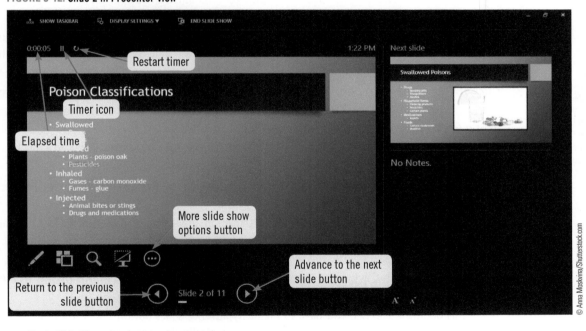

TABLE 3-2: **Basic Slide Show view keyboard commands**

keyboard commands	description
[Enter], [Spacebar], [PgDn], [N], [down arrow], or [right arrow]	Advances to the next slide
[E]	Erases the ink annotation drawing
[Home], [End]	Moves to the first or last slide in the slide show
[up arrow], [PgUp], or [left arrow]	Returns to the previous slide
[S]	Pauses the slide show when using automatic timings; press again to continue
[B]	Changes the screen to black; press again to return
[Esc]	Stops the slide show

Learning
Outcomes
• Apply and modify
a transition
• Modify slide
timings

Set Slide Transitions and Timings

In a slide show, you can determine how each slide advances in and out of view and how long each slide appears on the screen. **Slide transitions** are the visual and audio effects you apply to a slide that determine how each slide moves on and off the screen during the slide show. **Slide timing** refers to the amount of time a slide is visible on the screen. Typically, you set slide timings only if you want the presentation to automatically progress through the slides during a slide show. Setting the correct slide timing, in this case, is important because it determines how much time your audience has to view each slide. Each slide can have a different slide transition and different slide timing. **CASE** *You decide to set slide transitions and 7-second slide timings for all the slides.*

STEPS

1. **Click the Slide 1 thumbnail in the Slides tab, then click the Transitions tab on the Ribbon**

   Transitions are organized by type into three groups: Subtle, Exciting, and Dynamic Content.

2. **Click the More button ⬇ in the Transition to This Slide group, then click Drape in the Exciting section**

   The new slide transition plays on the slide, and a transition icon ⭐ appears next to the slide thumbnail in the Slides tab as shown in FIGURE 3-13. You can customize the slide transition by changing its direction and speed.

QUICK TIP
You can add a sound that plays with the transition from the Sound list arrow in the Timing group.

3. **Click the Effect Options button in the Transition to This Slide group, click Right, click the Duration up arrow in the Timing group until 3.00 appears, then click the Preview button in the Preview group**

   The Drape slide transition now plays from the right on the slide for 3.00 seconds. You can apply this transition with the custom settings to all of the slides in the presentation.

4. **Click the Apply To All button in the Timing group, then click the Slide Sorter button ⊞ on the status bar**

   All of the slides now have the customized Drape transition applied to them as identified by the transition icons located below each slide. You also have the ability to determine how slides progress during a slide show—either manually by mouse click or automatically by slide timing.

5. **Click the On Mouse Click check box under Advance Slide in the Timing group to clear the check mark**

   When this option is selected, you have to manually advance slides during a slide show. Now, with this option disabled, you can set the slides to advance automatically after a specified amount of time.

QUICK TIP
Click the transition icon under any slide in Slide Sorter view to see its transition play.

6. **Click the After up arrow in the Timing group, until 00:07.00 appears in the text box, then click the Apply To All button**

   The timing between slides is 7 seconds as indicated by the time under each slide thumbnail in FIGURE 3-14. When you run the slide show, each slide will remain on the screen for 7 seconds. You can override a slide's timing and speed up the slide show by using any of the manual advance slide commands.

7. **Click the Slide Show button 🖵 on the status bar**

   The slide show advances automatically. A new slide appears every 7 seconds using the Drape transition.

8. **When you see the black slide, press [Spacebar], then save your changes**

   The slide show ends and returns to Slide Sorter view with Slide 1 selected.

FIGURE 3-13: Applied slide transition

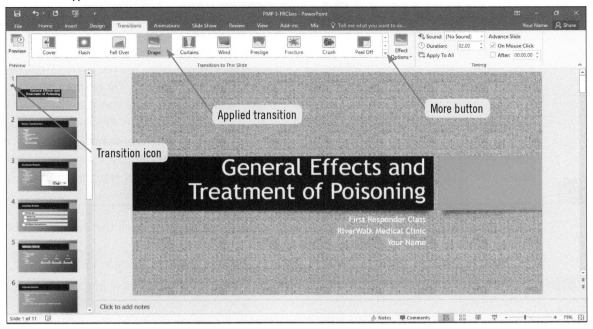

FIGURE 3-14: Slide sorter view showing applied transition and timing

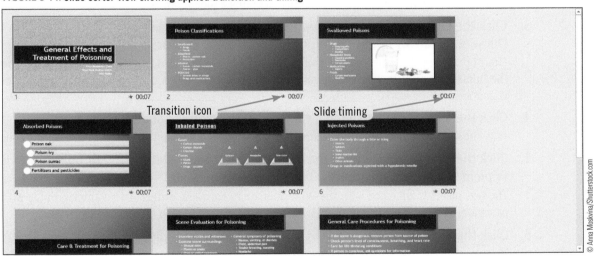

© Anna Moskvina/Shutterstock.com

Rehearsing slide show timings

You can set different slide timings for each slide; for example, the title slide can appear for 20 seconds and the second slide for 1 minute. To set timings click the Rehearse Timings button in the Set Up group on the Slide Show tab. Slide Show view opens and the Recording toolbar shown in **FIGURE 3-15** opens. It contains buttons to pause between slides and to advance to the next slide. After opening the Recording toolbar, you can practice giving your presentation by manually advancing each slide in the presentation. When you are finished, PowerPoint displays the total recorded time for the presentation and you have the option to save the recorded timings. The next time you run the slide show, you can use the timings you rehearsed.

FIGURE 3-15: Recording toolbar

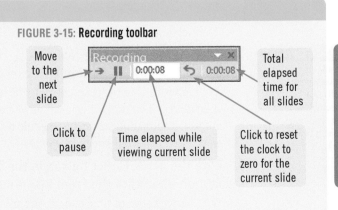

Animate Objects

Learning Outcomes
• Animate objects
• Modify animation effects

Animations let you control how objects and text appear and move on the screen during a slide show and allow you to manage the flow of information and emphasize specific facts. You can animate text, pictures, sounds, hyperlinks, SmartArt diagrams, charts, and individual chart elements. For example, you can apply a Fade animation to bulleted text so each paragraph enters the slide separately from the others. Animations are organized into four categories, Entrance, Emphasis, Exit, and Motion Paths. The Entrance and Exit animations cause an object to enter or exit the slide with an effect. An Emphasis animation causes an object visible on the slide to have an effect and a Motion Path animation causes an object to move on a specified path on the slide. **CASE** > *You animate the text and graphics of several slides in the presentation.*

STEPS

1. **Double-click the** Slide 4 thumbnail **to return to Normal view, click the** Animations tab **on the Ribbon, then click the** SmartArt object

   Text as well as other objects, such as a shape or picture, can be animated during a slide show.

   QUICK TIP
   There are additional animation options for each animation category located at the bottom of the animations gallery.

2. **Click the** More button ⏷ **in the Animation group, then click** Swivel **in the Entrance section**

   Animations can be serious and business-like, or humorous, so be sure to choose appropriate effects for your presentation. A small numeral 1, called an animation tag ①, appears near the object. **Animation tags** identify the order in which objects are animated during a slide show.

3. **Click the** Effect Options button **in the Animation group, click** All at Once, **then click the** Duration up arrow **in the Timing group until** 03.00 **appears**

   Effect options are different for every animation, and some animations don't have effect options. Changing the animation timing increases the duration of the animation and gives it a more dramatic effect. Compare your screen to FIGURE 3-16.

4. **Click the** Slide Show button 🖵, **view slides until you see Slide 5, then press** [Esc]

   After the slide transition finishes, the SmartArt object on Slide 4 spins twice for a total of three seconds.

5. **Click the** Slide 2 thumbnail **in the Slides tab, click the** bulleted list text object, **then click** Wipe **in the Animation group**

   The text object is animated with the Wipe animation. Each line of text has an animation tag with each paragraph displaying a different number. Accordingly, each paragraph is animated separately.

6. **Click the** Effect Options button **in the Animation group, click** All at Once, **click the** Duration up arrow **in the Timing group until** 02.00 **appears, then click the** Preview button **in the Preview group**

   Notice the animation tags for each line of text in the text object now have the same numeral (1), indicating that each line of text animates at the same time.

   QUICK TIP
   If you want to individually animate the parts of a grouped object, then you must ungroup the objects before you animate them.

7. **Click** Poison **in the title text object, click** ⏷ **in the Animation group, scroll down, then click** Shapes **in the Motion Paths section**

   A motion path object appears over the title text object and identifies the direction and shape, or path, of the animation. When needed, you can move, resize, and change the direction of the motion path. Notice the numeral 2 animation tag next to the title text object indicating that it is animated *after* the bulleted list text object. Compare your screen to FIGURE 3-17.

8. **Click the** Move Earlier button **in the Timing group, click the** Slide Show tab **on the Ribbon, then click the** From Beginning button **in the Start Slide Show group**

   The slide show begins from Slide 1. The animations make the presentation more interesting to view.

9. **When you see the black slide, press** [Enter], **then save your changes**

FIGURE 3-16: Animation applied to SmartArt object

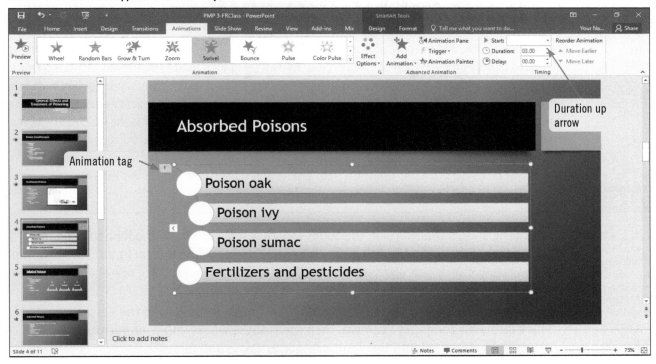

FIGURE 3-17: Motion path applied to title text object

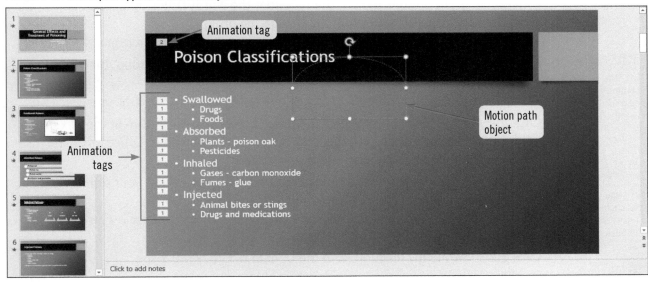

Attaching a sound to an animation

Text or objects that have animation applied can be customized further by attaching a sound for extra emphasis. First, select the animated object, then on the Animations tab, click the Animation Pane button in the Advanced Animation group. In the Animation Pane, click the animation you want to apply the sound to, click the Animation list arrow, then click Effect Options to open the animation effect's dialog box. In the Enhancements section, click the Sound list arrow, then choose a sound. Click OK when you are finished. Now, when you run the slide show, the sound you applied will play with the animation.

Create an Office Mix

Learning Outcomes
• Create and insert an Office Mix
• Publish an Office Mix

Office Mix is a free add-in application developed by Microsoft which, once downloaded from the web, is integrated directly on the PowerPoint Ribbon with its own set of tools located on the Mix tab. Using Office Mix, you create and then insert interactive content onto the slides of your presentation. Content such as a video recording of you giving a presentation, video clips from the web, and interactive quizzes or polls are easy to create. Once you are finished creating your Office Mix, you can publish it to the Office Mix website or the cloud to be shared with others. **CASE** ▶ *You decide to create a short recording introducing poison classifications and swallowed poisons. You then publish the Mix to the Office Mix website. (Note: The Office Mix add-in must be installed from the Office Mix website prior to performing the steps of this lesson.)*

STEPS

TROUBLE
If you want to record audio and video in this lesson, make sure your microphone, speakers, and camera equipment are connected and working properly.

1. **Click the** Slide 5 thumbnail **in the Slides tab, click the** Mix tab **on the Ribbon, look over the commands on the Mix tab, then click the** Slide Recording button **in the Record group**
   The Screen Recording view opens as shown in FIGURE 3-18. The Screen Recording view displays the current slide with navigation, recording, and inking tools.

2. **When you are ready to begin recording, click the** Record button **in the Record group, look into your computer's camera, then speak these words into your microphone:** "Inhaled poisons fall into two basic categories: gases and fumes"
   Your Office Mix recording begins as soon as you click the Record button. If a slide has animations, each animation must be advanced manually during the recording in order to see the animation.

3. **Click the** Next Slide button ➡ **in the Navigation group, continue speaking** "Drugs are common injected poisons today", **drag** ✐ **under the words** Drugs or medications **on the slide, then click the** Stop button **in the Navigation group**
   A small speaker appears in the upper-right corner of the slide indicating there is a recording on the slide.

QUICK TIP
Click the Edit Slide Recording button in the Recording Tools group to delete slide recordings.

4. **Click the** Preview Slide Recording **button in the Recording Tools group, then listen and watch your recording**
   You can move to any slide and preview its recording using the buttons in the Navigation group.

5. **Click the window** Close button, **click the** Upload to Office Mix button **in the Mix group, read the information, then click the** Next button **in the Upload to Office Mix pane**
   The Upload to Office Mix pane displays sign in account methods.

TROUBLE
If you are not sure which account login option to use, check with your instructor.

6. **Click your** account button **in the Upload to Office Mix pane, enter your sign in information, click the** Sign in **button, then click the** Next button
   The new Office Mix is uploaded and published to the Office Mix website. There is a percentage counter showing you the upload and processing progress.

7. **Click the** Show me my mix button **in the Upload to Office Mix pane**
   The Office Mix webpage appears with the new Office Mix you just created as shown in FIGURE 3-19. On this page you can provide a content description, a category, or a tag, as well as set permissions.

8. **Click** My Mixes **at the top of the window, click the** PMP 3-FRClass Play button, **then follow the directions on the screen to watch the Office Mix**
   Each slide in the presentation, including the Office Mix recordings you made on Slide 5 and 6, appears.

9. **Click** Your Name **at the top of the window, click** Sign out, **click your** web browser Close button, **click the** Close button **in the Upload to Office Mix pane, save your changes, submit your presentation to your instructor, then exit PowerPoint**

FIGURE 3-18: Office Mix Screen Recording view

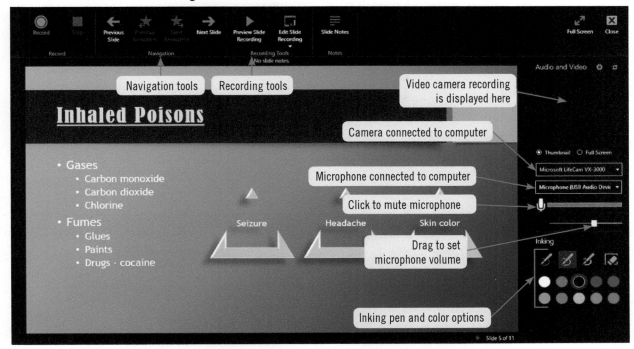

FIGURE 3-19: Office Mix webpage

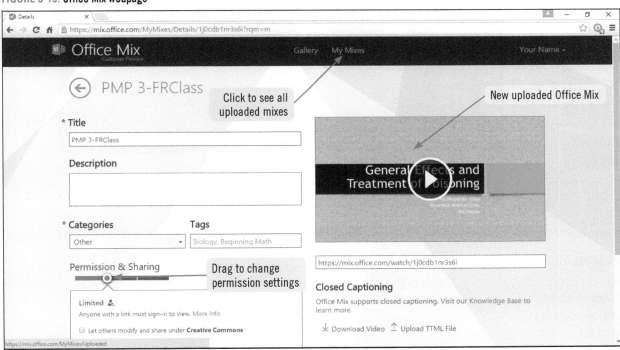

Inserting a multiple choice interactive quiz

Using the Mix tab, you can create a custom interactive quiz that can be presented in Slide Show view or uploaded to the Office Mix website to share with others. On the Mix tab, click the Quizzes Videos Apps button in the Insert group. In the Lab Office Add-ins dialog box, click Multiple Choice Quiz, then click Trust It. A multiple choice quiz object appears on your slide with blank text boxes that you fill out with a quiz question and answers. Be sure to enter the correct answer in the light green answer text box, then add as many other possible answers as you like. You can customize your question by shuffling the answer every time the question is opened, limiting the number of answer attempts, and allowing more than one right answer.

Practice

Concepts Review

Label each element of the PowerPoint window shown in FIGURE 3-20.

FIGURE 3-20

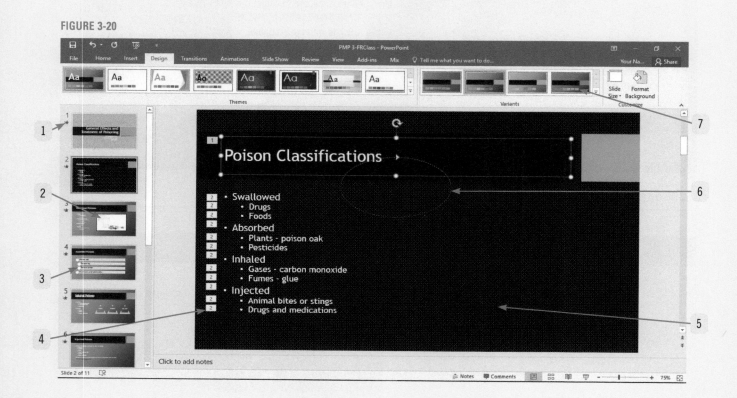

Match each term with the statement that best describes it.

8. **Background**
9. **Crop**
10. **Presenter view**
11. **Ink annotations**
12. **Office Mix**
13. **Variant**
14. **Slide timing**

a. A custom theme similar to an original theme
b. Drawings on a slide created during slide show
c. Add-in application you use to create interactive content
d. Determines how long a slide is visible on screen
e. Hide a portion of a picture
f. A special view you use when showing a presentation on two monitors
g. The area behind the text and graphics

Select the best answer from the list of choices.

15. Use a(n) _____ object to best illustrate information you want to compare side by side.
    a. WordArt
    b. Table
    c. SmartArt
    d. Equation

16. Freehand pen and highlighter strokes are also known as _____.
    a. markings
    b. scribbles
    c. pictures
    d. ink annotations

17. Animation _____ identify the order in which objects are animated during a slide show.
    a. tags
    b. paths
    c. thumbnails
    d. schemes

18. The slide thumbnails in the Reuse Slides pane identify the slides of the _____ presentation.
    a. destination
    b. default
    c. source
    d. open

Skills Review

1. **Insert text from Microsoft Word.**
   a. Open PMP 3-5.pptx from the location where you store your Data Files, then save it as **PMP 3-Jefferson**. You will work to create the completed presentation as shown in FIGURE 3-21.
   b. Click Slide 3 in the Slides tab, then use the Slides from Outline command to insert the file PMP 3-6.docx from the location where you store your Data Files.
   c. In the Slides tab, drag Slide 6 above Slide 4, then delete Slide 7.
   d. Select Slides 4, 5, and 6 in the Slides tab, then reset the slides to the default theme settings.
   e. Change the slide layout to Title and Content for the selected slides, then save your work.

FIGURE 3-21

© Monkey Business Images/Shutterstock.com

2. **Insert and style a picture.**
   a. Select Slide 7 in the Slides tab, then change the slide layout to Two Content.
   b. Insert the picture PMP 3-7.jpg from the location where you store your Data Files in the right placeholder, then crop the white space at the bottom of the picture.
   c. Increase the size of the picture so it is 4" high, then center the picture in the blank area of the slide.
   d. Click the Color button, change the color tone to Temperature: 4700 K, then save your changes.

3. **Insert slides from other presentations.**
   a. On Slide 7 open the Reuse Slides pane.
   b. Open PMP 3-8.pptx from the location where you store your Data Files.

Skills Review (continued)

c. Insert the third slide thumbnail, insert the second slide thumbnail, then insert the fourth slide thumbnail.

d. Close the Reuse Slides pane, then save your work.

4. Insert a table.

a. On Slide 2, insert a table with three columns and four rows.

b. Enter the information shown in TABLE 3-3, then change the table style to Light Style 2 – Accent 6.

TABLE 3-3

Hydraulic Tool System	Lift and Crib Tools	Forcible Entry Tools
Dedicated spreader and dedicated cutter	2-step chocks	Glass master windshield saw
Short and medium rams	Assorted 2 × 4 and 4 × 4 cribbing	Cordless saws
Simultaneous operating power plant	High pressure bags	Hand tools - halligan/flathead axe

c. In the Table Tools Layout tab, center the text in the top row.

d. Open the Table Tools Design tab, click the Effects button, point to Cell Bevel, then apply the Convex effect.

e. Move the table to the center of the blank area of the slide, then save your changes.

5. Customize the background and theme.

a. Go to Slide 5, click the Design tab, then click the green variant.

b. Open the Format Background pane, click the Color button, then click Light Green, Accent 3.

c. Set the Transparency to 50%, close the Format Background pane, then save your changes.

6. Use slide show commands.

a. Begin the slide show on Slide 1, then proceed to Slide 5.

b. Use the Pen ink annotation tool to circle the slide title then use the Highlighter to highlight four points in the bulleted text on the slide.

c. Erase two highlight annotations on the bulleted text, press [Esc], open Presenter view, then stop the timer.

d. Advance the slides to Slide 7, then click the Zoom into the slide button (now called the Zoom out button) on the Slide Show toolbar, then click in the center of the picture.

e. Click the Zoom into the slide button, click the See all slides button, click Slide 1, then hide Presenter view.

f. Advance through all the slides, save ink and highlight annotations, then save your work.

7. Set slide transitions and timings.

a. Go to Slide Sorter view, click the Slide 1 thumbnail, then apply the Fall Over transition to the slide.

b. Change the effect option to Right, change the duration to 2.50, then apply to all the slides.

c. Apply a 5-second slide timing to all slides, switch to Normal view, view the slide show, then save your work.

8. Animate objects.

a. Go to Slide 3, click the Animations tab, click the left text object, then apply the Wipe effect.

b. Select the right text object, apply the Wipe effect, then change the effect option to From Top.

c. Add the slide number and your name as the footer to all the slides, then save your changes.

9. Create an Office Mix.

a. Go to Slide 2, open the Mix tab, then click the Slide Recording button.

b. Click the Record button, speak these words into your microphone, "The equipment in this list is the minimum required," use your pen to underline the slide title, then click the Stop button.

c. Preview your slide recording, close the window, click the Upload to Mix button, then upload your new mix to the Office Mix website.

d. Watch the Office Mix, close the webpage window, close the Upload to Office Mix pane, then save your work.

e. Submit your presentation to your instructor, close your presentation, then exit PowerPoint.

Independent Challenge 1

You work at Memorial General Hospital and one of your jobs is to train emergency staff. You have recently started a presentation on patients under the influence. You continue work on the presentation by inserting objects and changing the slide background.

a. Open PMP 3-9.pptx from the location where you store your Data Files, then save it as **PMP 3-MG Training**.

b. Add your name and the slide number as the footer on all of the slides, apply the Basis Design Theme, then apply the black and white variant.

c. Create a 3-column by 7-row table on Slide 5, then enter the data in TABLE 3-4 into the table.

d. Apply the Medium Style 3 - Accent 4 style to the table, then go to Slide 4.

e. Open the Reuse Slides pane, open PMP 3-10.pptx from the location where you store your Data Files, then insert Slides 2, 3, and 4.

f. Close the Reuse Slides pane, then move Slide 6 above Slide 5.

g. Go to Slide Sorter view, apply the Doors transition, change the Effect Option to Horizontal, change the Duration to 2.00, then apply the transition to all slides.

TABLE 3-4

Substance	Appearance	Administered
Methamphetamines	White powder, pills, paraffin-like rocks	Injected, inhaled, oral
Cocaine	White crystalline powder	Inhaled, injected
Crack cocaine	White crystalline rocks	Smoked
Marijuana	Parsley with stems or seeds	Smoked, eaten
Heroin (opiates)	White to dark brown powder or tar substance	Injected, smoked, inhaled
PCP	Liquid, white crystalline powder, pills or capsules	Injected, smoked, oral

h. Go to Slide 8, apply an animation to the table, change the animation effect option, then increase the animation duration by a half second.

i. View the presentation slide show, use the highlighter annotation tool to highlight text on at least one slide, then save the annotations.

j. Check the spelling of the presentation, submit the presentation to your instructor, then close the presentation, and exit PowerPoint.

Independent Challenge 2

You work for FEMA in Dallas, Texas, and one of your jobs is to train emergency service departments how to make their EMS systems more efficient and functional. You work on completing a presentation by inserting a picture, an outline, and then you apply animations, transitions, and timings. You also create an Office Mix of your presentation to share with others.

a. Start PowerPoint, open PMP 3-11.pptx from the location where you store your Data Files, and save it as **PMP 3-FEMA**.

b. Add your name and today's date to Slide 1 in the Subtitle text box.

c. Insert the Word outline PMP 3-12.docx after Slide 1, then select Slides 2 and 3.

d. Reset the slides to their default settings, then change their slide layout to Title and Content.

e. Apply the green/blue design theme variant to the presentation, go to Slide 5, then open the Format Background pane.

f. Format the slide background, change the slide background transparency, then close the Format Background pane.

g. Insert and format an appropriate picture on a slide of your choosing.

h. Apply a slide transition, change the effect option of the transition, then apply a 5-second slide timing to all the slides.

i. Animate at least two objects, then change the effect option of at least one animation.

j. Create and upload an Office Mix with at least one voice recording and two inking annotations.

k. Add your name as the footer text on the slides, spell check the presentation (there is at least one error), then save the presentation.

l. Submit the presentation to your instructor, close the file, and exit PowerPoint.

Independent Challenge 3: Explore

You work at the Central Miami Health Clinic and you have been asked to create a short presentation on poisonous coral snakes. The presentation will be used to educate children in the public school system. Your presentation should include general facts about coral snakes and how to treat a snakebite. Use the Internet to research relevant information. *(NOTE: To complete steps below, your computer must be connected to the Internet.)*

a. Start PowerPoint, create a new blank presentation, and save it as **PMP 3-Coral Snakes** to the location where you store your Data Files.

b. Create slides to accommodate the information you find, apply a design theme, then change the design theme variant.

c. Locate and insert at least one relevant picture into the presentation, then format the picture using the Picture Tools Format tab.

d. Create at least two objects from the Shapes gallery, enter text in the shapes, then format the shapes.

e. Animate at least three objects, then format the animations as necessary.

f. Check the spelling, then view the presentation in Slide Show view and use Slide Show commands.

g. Add a slide number and your class name as footer text to all of the slides, save your work, then submit your presentation to your instructor.

h. Close the file, and exit PowerPoint.

Visual Workshop

Create a one-slide presentation that looks like FIGURE 3-22. The slide layout used is a specific layout designed for pictures. Insert the picture file PMP 3-13.jpg to complete this presentation. Save the presentation as **PMP 3-Flightcare** to the location where you store your Data Files, then submit your presentation to your instructor.

FIGURE 3-22

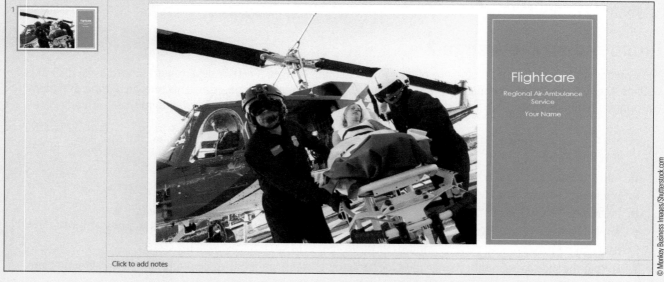

© Monkey Business Images/Shutterstock.com

Index

multiple, applying to single presentation, PPT 12

theme colors, PPT 12, PPT 59

theme effects, PPT 12

theme fonts, PPT 12

Thesaurus pane, WD 36, WD 37

3-D charts, EX 87

tick marks, EX 80, EX 81

tiles, WIN 4

title bar, OFF 6, WD 4, WD 5, WIN 10

title placeholders, PPT 8, PPT 9

To Do Tags, PA 2

toggle buttons, forms, ACC 54

Toggle Filter button, ACC 36

tool palettes, groups, WIN 10

toolbars, WIN 10, WIN 28. *See also specific toolbars*

touch screen(s), WIN 2
Office 2016 apps, OFF 4
PowerPoint using, PPT 3

touch-screen devices, selecting and moving items, WIN 7

U

UIs (user interfaces), OFF 6, WIN 4

unbound controls, ACC 54

underlining text, WD 53

Undo button, EX 10, WD 10

Undo command, WD 15

unfreezing fields in datasheets, ACC 30

unhiding. *See also* displaying
columns and rows, EX 60
fields in datasheets, ACC 30

universal apps, WIN 8

Universal Serial Bus (USB) drives, ACC 69, WIN 28

Universal Serial Bus (USB) ports, WIN 28

Up to button, Save As dialog box, WD 9

update(s), installing when you exit Windows, WIN 19

Update Labels command, WD 141

USB (Universal Serial Bus) drives, ACC 69, WIN 28

USB (Universal Serial Bus) ports, WIN 28

user interfaces (UIs), OFF 6, WIN 4

V

value(s), EX 8, EX 9
columns too narrow to display, EX 58
formatting, EX 52–53
rounding, EX 40–41
sequential, fill handle, EX 39

value axis, EX 80, EX 81

variants, PPT 58

vertical axis, EX 80, EX 81

vertical ruler, WD 4, WD 5

vertical scroll bars, WD 4, WD 5

video clips, capturing, PA 11

view(s), OFF 12, OFF 13, PPT 6, WD 17. *See also specific views*
files and folders, changing, WIN 32–33
presentations, PPT 14–15
of specific areas, enlarging, EX 16
worksheets, EX 14–15

View Shortcuts buttons, PPT 6, PPT 7

viewing. *See also* displaying; unhiding
presentations in gray scale or black and white, PPT 7

virtual assistant, Edge, PA 14–15

web browsers. *See* Microsoft Edge

Web Layout view, WD 17

Web Note tools, PA 15

webpages
annotating, PA 15
live, inserting in slides, PA 12

what-if analysis, EX 2

widows, WD 106

wildcards, ACC 36

window(s), WIN 10–11
active, WIN 12
borders, WIN 12
components, EX 4–5
elements, WIN 10, WIN 11
inactive, WIN 12
multiple, managing, WIN 12–13
multiple, working with, PPT 55

Window control buttons, WIN 10, WIN 11

Windows accessories, WIN 8

Windows Action Center, WIN 32

Windows Clipboard, EX 32

Windows Search, WIN 40–41

Windows Store, WIN 8

Windows 10
shutting down (exiting), WIN 18–19
starting, WIN 2–3

Windows 10 desktop. *See* desktop(s)

Windows 10 UI, WIN 4

Word. *See* Microsoft Word 2016

word(s), selecting, WD 11

Word Count dialog box, WD 36, WD 37

word processing programs, WD 2–3. *See also* Microsoft Word 2016

Word program window, WD 4–5

WordArt, WD 60
applying to text objects, EX 90